THE CHILDREN OF THE LAW OF ONE
&
THE LOST TEACHINGS OF ATLANTIS

Published by
Network
Copyright © 1997 Network

2431 Main St. PMB 401
Alamosa, CO 81101
Fourth Printing
Revised Edition

ISBN   0-9660015-3-2

A presentation of
The Children of the Law of One ™

FOREWORD

Reality?

This book chronicles the author's personal experiences, and presents ancient spiritual teachings and philosophy. In order to make it as interesting and as readable as possible, much of it is presented in a story and "dialogue" style, based upon the author's experiences. Conversations with monks, teachers and students were reconstructed from records and the author's memories. Thus, while not perfect transcriptions, the dialogue does accurately reflect actual conversations.

Hopefully, the book will be more than just interesting. For those with an open mind & heart, it will also give reason to ponder the nature of life, the Universe, your beliefs, and the potentials that exist within your own personal life.

This book isn't *about* Atlantis or proving its existence. Besides the fact that many things about the nature of the Universe, creation, God, and ancient history, are impossible (or nearly impossible) to *prove* at this time in human development, the *sole purpose* of this book is to convey something far more important - ancient spiritual teachings that can change your life, and indirectly, improve the world.

We believe that it's best for everyone to attain *direct* personal experience of God, and discover the true nature of the Universe and creation for themselves, rather than taking anyone's word for it, or believing what they are told or read - including this book and our teachings. Thus, even though we do necessarily discuss some unprovable "ancient history" concepts, the teachings provide the means for achieving that direct experience and direct "knowing" yourself. By reading the conversations and thoughts of the author as he is learning this himself, you too can discover a return path to the Universal Spirit/God, and inner peace.

We aren't trying to convince anyone of *anything*, or asking anyone to accept anything in this book on faith - we are simply presenting ideas. We leave it up to you to think about the principles and the teachings presented, and decide for yourself whether or not they are a good thing for you, for others, and for the world.

Within all of us is a "lie detector", a silent "inner voice", that offers us the greatest potential to discern truth and reality. People have "fooled" experts with so-called "physical proof", but the inner voice is never fooled. [The "inner voice" could also sometimes be termed as a "gut feeling", "intuition" or "women's intuition"- but it can also be much more than that.] You may not be very "in touch" with it at this time, but you can be if you want to. This inner voice is a part of God within you that *knows* what is true and what isn't - if you will just "hear" it. It doesn't "talk", it is just a "knowingness". The only reasons behind people not "hearing" their inner voice are fear, desires, and selfishness. If you can transcend those things even for a moment, you will have the most reliable source of discernment that exists. Even when all "external appearances" of truth say one thing, and your inner voice says another, you can bet that your inner voice is right.

[Note: Earlier editions of this book referred to an elder monk named Ra. This was not the person connected with the channeled "Ra material". Our order (the Children of the Law of One), the author, and this book are not in any way connected to, or related to, the Ra material (which is now also being called the "Law of One" material) or a person using the name Ra who says he is a Law

I

of One teacher. We don't wish to imply anything bad about this person or the material, but we needed to clarify the situation because some people have thought we were associated.]

Humor, Seriously.

Humor is a very "esoteric" thing in a way, and most people don't really understand it. Ancient teachings refer to it as "the great neutralizer". Most never stop to think why human beings laugh. For one thing, they *need* to laugh. In our lives, laughing can neutralize or minimize the devastating effects of pain and suffering (both our own, or that of others). If you stop and think about it the next time you see a comedy show, you'll find that most comedy is based on other people's misfortunes, from minor mishaps, embarrassments & humiliations, to major "screw-ups" in life, and sometimes even physical injuries like someone falling down a flight of stairs or off a roof.

All human beings, whether they are "sinners" or "saints", need to laugh to maintain their sanity, and health (laughing can even heal). Thus, truly spiritual people, (as opposed to those who put on an air of seriousness in order to give the appearance of being spiritual), have a great sense of humor. They certainly take their work very seriously, but they don't take *themselves* too seriously. Also, because of their work, they need to laugh and be humorous even more than most of us, because they are dealing with more pain and suffering than most of us. The author of this book is no exception, and the book reflects this.

Unfortunately, most "seekers" are *very* serious. It's only natural. The ancient teachings presented here *are* very serious also, but that doesn't mean you can't have a little fun. And if you don't take *your* self too seriously, you'll be able to enjoy humor where you may find it, and perhaps lighten your own load just a bit.

'RULES' of Writing

The author knew an English professor who taught English and vocabulary at a university in California. The professor once told him that he taught his students to feel free to invent new words, if there wasn't something already "just right" for what they wanted to communicate. That's how language expands, and gives people the ability to more accurately convey their message to others. Subtleties of meaning also often require new words to communicate them properly.

The author believes the same concept applies to the use of grammar and spelling. Rules of any kind shouldn't hamper the style or content of any communication, and if they do, we must make up new rules. While writing has certain grammatical rules that are meant to govern it, it is also an art, and if the impact or message can be enhanced by *breaking* these rules, they *should* be broken. Using fine art as an example, Van Gogh was criticized and rejected, because he didn't follow the "proper" rules or styles of painting. Yet most people now recognize that he conveyed feelings, and sometimes a message, that could have only been done by ignoring the rules, and expressing himself freely. The author of this book has approached its writing in a similar manner. He has deliberately ignored convention, in favor of communicating with the reader in a way he feels is most effective. Much of this is because he wanted the writing to reflect "speaking" to you. This creates a more intimate communication, and also more accurately represents the thoughtful deliberateness of speech that is characteristic of many teachers.

Thus in this book you **will** find "odd" words/phrases/sentences, "odd" grammar and punctuation, and "odd" usage of all the above. It's not because the author is illiterate or due to lack of professional editing. Some of the differences include (but are not limited to), extra commas (for instance, they may have been deliberately inserted to reflect an "enhanced" pause), hyphenated or strangely spelled words (to make something stand out, get you to think, or make a connection to another thought), and chronology that doesn't follow a linear time-line (in order to properly present the teachings). These aren't extreme differences, and the author believes it actually helps some readers transcend the limitations of left-brain thinking just a bit, and makes the book even easier and more enjoyable to read.

Introduction
Survivors of Atlantis

Stories of Atlantis. Why do they exist and where do they come from? Why are they so persistent? And why is the subject of Atlantis so fascinating to so many people? Many scholars now cite archeological evidence of ancient civilizations that were destroyed by a great catastrophe, which they believe could be the source of the stories. But that raises even more intriguing questions, if Atlantis was once a great civilization, who were the Atlantean people, and what were they like?

Within the recorded history of many cultures, there are references to the great island continent of Atlantis, and its highly sophisticated civilization. Some people dismiss this as myth. Many of these cultures had no known contact or knowledge of each other's civilizations, so why would such diverse ancient peoples, such as the Maya, the Egyptians, the Hopis, or the Greeks, have the same legends?

Plato, a highly respected Greek philosopher and teacher, gives a detailed, non-fiction account of Atlantis. Due to that and other factors, many scientists no longer argue about the *existence* of Atlantis - just the whereabouts. Even marine scientist and explorer, Jacques Cousteau, searched for underwater archeological evidence of Atlantis. It ended with his son believing Atlantis was probably in the Caribbean or Atlantic, and Jacques believing it was in the Mediterranean. Even though they both found what they believed to be evidence of an ancient sunken civilization, neither had definitive proof that they'd discovered the remains of Atlantis. However, little absolute archeological proof is likely to even remain from *any* civilization destroyed by a cataclysmic disaster, let alone tens of thousands of years ago, let alone one sunken beneath the sea in a totally unknown area. Even the great "Titanic" was only recently found, and only after extensive searches, even though scientists knew approximately where it sank. Furthermore, it went down *only decades* ago, *and it* sunk from "merely" hitting an iceberg, whereas Atlantis allegedly sunk long, long ago, in an unknown location, and was totally devastated by unimaginable natural catastrophe. A disaster so great, that it may have had a "ripple" effect around the world, which brings us to the legends of "the great flood".

Cultures the world over, who don't have a specific legend of Atlantis, still have stories of a great flood that destroyed most life, (which happen to be very similar to the story of the sinking, and flooding of Atlantis). Descriptions of the destruction of Atlantis, say it involved great earthquakes and volcanic upheavals, and the actual sinking of the entire land mass. So perhaps some legends of a great flood could have come from secondary flooding, that resulted from unimaginably gigantic tsunami waves generated by an event that was the greatest geological disaster in history (like the one most scientists say caused the extinction of the dinosaurs). Such waves could have swept the globe, flooding many, if not most, parts of the world, and eruptions could have darkened the sky, and created other disastrous ecological consequences.

The various cultural stories of the "great flood" often tell a tale of refugees who managed to escape the great disaster. Some legends, like those of the Hopi tribe, describe the Hopi as such refugees. They depict the Hopi escaping the calamity, and coming to their new land on "Giant flying tortoise shells". It is said that once they arrived, they were led to safety from an environment gone mad, by a bird head-ed "Kachina" who guided them to underground passages.

To the open mind who researches this subject, the evidence that Atlantis did indeed exist, is overwhelming. But if Atlantis, as Plato described it, was a highly advanced, sophisticated civilization, with technology that even surpasses that which we have now, shouldn't there be some other remnant of their society? Not neces-sarily. But just perhaps...

According to the legends, Atlantis was so thoroughly destroyed by natural cat-astrophe, that there was nothing left. Yet, couldn't there have been some Atlanteans with enough foresight to leave beforehand, and escape the disaster? Or some that were traveling in other parts of the world at the time? It seems quite pos-sible that, given the stories of how advanced and sophisticated a civilization it was, that at least *some* traders or travelers were elsewhere in the world at the time. Some theories say the mythological inhabitants of Mt. Olympus, the gods of Greek and Roman mythology, were actually Atlanteans that survived.

Now just consider this amazing possibility - what if groups of Atlanteans, not only survived, but established communities in various places. What if they contin-ued to pass on their heritage, their history, philosophy, and religion, even to this day? Such people could teach us so much, and fill us in on this great missing piece of human history.

That is where this book comes in. It was written by a priest who's order traces their lineage from Atlantis, to Egypt in the days of the construction of the Sphinx and Great Pyramid.

Oddly enough, this book isn't about Atlantis. It covers some little known "ancient history", but only as necessary background. Instead, the book focuses on the philosophy and spiritual practices that *originated* there. Atlantis *is* just ancient history now, but the teachings of their spiritual tradition are all still invaluable in the present. Most importantly though, the author brings an urgent message. And rather than a "new age" philosophy about life, he presents "age old" ways to live by, that can really change your life, and world.

Fortunately, it's all presented in a fascinating format in which the reader gets to discover everything themselves, through the eyes (and experiences) of a young North American. We get to be with him during his three years at a monastery, share his personal trials, and see his changes. We also get to experience some of his amazing encounters after returning to the "real world" as an enlightened teacher, and head of the order.

Besides presenting the author's experiences, and simple teachings about how to find your own enlightenment, the book has another message for the world. He points out similarities between the present state of affairs in the world, and the last days of Atlantis. What if we have come full circle in a historical cycle? You may have heard the saying - "Those who don't learn from history are doomed to repeat it". The author tells us that our future depends on the choices we make, and on what we have learned from our past. If that is true, the story of Atlantis may well be the most important history lesson of all time. But other than "filling in" a pos-sibly vital part of human history, the book gives us something perhaps even more important. It presents us with a beautiful spiritual philosophy that guides us toward a better life, through personal growth. The wisdom and teachings it imparts, are wonderful, fascinating, and also very useful when applied to our everyday lives.

TABLE OF CONTENTS

The entire book contains the teachings of the Children of the Law of One. Reading it in order is important because many of the concepts in one chapter must be understood before you can fully understand the next chapter.

Chapter One

The "Children of the Law of One"

The Children of the Law of One, and the Edgar Cayce Readings

The author of this book and I are both priests/monks of an obscure spiritual order called the Children of the Law of One. The famous, unique psychic, Edgar Cayce, referred to our order in a number of his many psychic readings. Some of the information we present in this book apparently confirms information in those readings. While this attests to Cayce's remarkable abilities, we are not experts on his readings, and thus cannot guarantee that everything here will be in agreement with them, and vice-versa. But from what we do know of them, and what we have heard from people who *are* very familiar with Cayce, this book substantiates his readings, enhances understanding of them, and offers new ways to apply the spiritual principles spoken of in them. Apparently, the teachings in this book may also be the fulfillment of his prophecy that a "John Peniel" would bring to the world a message about "the new spiritual order of things" around 1998 (the year this book was first published). Before this book was published, we were unaware of that prophecy. We attempted to publish anonymously, but were told certain distributors and chain stores wouldn't carry the book unless we put the author's name on it, so we relented. Shortly afterwards, we began hearing from members of an association founded by Cayce, the A.R.E. (the Association for Research & Enlightenment), telling us about the prophecy. Many said after reading the book, they were sure this was the fulfillment of it. We make no claims regarding this issue one way or the other. However, the A.R.E. magazine "Venture Inward" published what many consider an intentionally negative review of this book, focusing on irrelevant story and editing details rather than the teachings, or addressing the above issues.

What's in a Name

The name of our order is unfamiliar and odd to most people. One reason is that we have deliberately avoided public notoriety, generally preferring to live and work in peace, undisturbed, behind the scenes. The "dark ages" are still with us, despite what history books say. Sometimes specific members become famous, but only when necessary for their work, or unavoidable.

Another reason the name sounds odd is because of its obscure and foreign origins. The name of the order was originally expressed as one concept, and can only really be understood as a whole, but breaking it down may help you understand it better. Just try to keep this paradox in mind - the name means many things, but only one thing.

The first part "The Children of..." relates to us all being "Children" in the sense of "subordinants of God (which we call the Universal Spirit)", "obedient to God and Universal Law". The end part ("One") essentially means "God". Rather than a giant silver-haired man in the sky, we consider God to be the totality of everything that exists - the Universe itself even - thus God is the "One". The middle part of the name ("the Law of") comes from the fact that within "the One", there are

1

Universal "Laws" that govern the operation and function of everything in the Universe (applying to all things, all vibration, physical or spiritual). Put this all back together again, the "Children" of the "Law" of "One" then essentially means "those who obey Universal Law and serve the Universal Spirit".

Thus something that is very important in our opinion, is being in harmony with, one with, and a servant of, God. The primary key to that, is Loving Unselfishly. The "rule" of loving others unselfishly is sometimes called the "Golden Rule". Many individuals and religions believe in the same concept. It was even the only *commandment* given by Jesus (and the way he said people would identify His followers - i.e., *true* "Christians" would be recognized by loving others as Jesus did). Unfortunately, the Golden Rule is seldom lived by, or focused on. It's often over-looked, and not given the major significance it deserves. This book will go more into detail about that later.

Throughout history, we (and "branches" of our order) were sometimes known to various cultures by other names also. But generally unknown to the masses, working behind the scenes, we provide inspiration and education that nourishes the best in humankind - spiritually, emotionally, intellectually, and physically. It may take the form of the arts, the sciences, spiritual or political philosophy, etc., but in all cases, we bring some form of light into a world of darkness. Thus, some of our initiates have been known as scientists, artists, spiritual leaders, unusual political representatives and freedom fighters. Anywhere, and anyway we can promote spirituality through Unselfish Love and a return to oneness, we do.

Sometimes the name of our order (or one of its branches) is "stolen" and used by others with a dark agenda. Sometimes even the teachings are taken, and twisted to serve their purposes. In their supreme selfishness, the greedy have used our names and corrupted our teachings in the pursuit of money, pleasure, power, and even world domination. I'm sure many of you can see how Jesus' name has been abused to mislead people. This also happened with the name "the Great White Brotherhood". Now there are also those abusing the name Children of the Law of One. You will know the true Children of the Law of One by our emphasis on Unselfish Love and freedom, rather than on "spiritual knowledge", "secret information", "power", or "phenomenon". Let the Universal Spirit, your inner voice, be your guide lest you fall into the beautiful traps of darkness.

Who We Are and What We Do

Initiates of our order have been dedicated spiritual "caretakers" of humanity since human life began. We have always been vigorous proponents of truth, freedom, justice, and compassion. Our teachings and ways have always been carefully preserved and passed down directly from teacher to student (who then becomes a teacher, etc.). This has continued as an unbroken chain, using all means, including reincarnation. You may or may not believe in reincarnation, but does it really matter that much if we care about each other, are good to each other, and follow the Golden Rule in our lives? It doesn't matter to me whether you believe in reincarnation or not, and I hope it also doesn't matter to you whether I do or not.

You may have heard how one famous Buddhist spiritual leader of our times, the Dalai Lama, continues to reincarnate, repeatedly taking the same position in life, serving as a teacher and leader of the people of Tibet and of Tibetan Buddhism. This one enlightened being has now been reincarnated over a dozen times as the Dalai Lama. This practice is not exclusive to Buddhism. Enlightened teachers of

2

The Children of the Law of One also continue to reincarnate, although they usually choose different bodies and positions in life for various reasons.

Some of our order have been called "ascended" masters (saints who have passed on). But many actually continue to reincarnate in physical bodies, to directly aid the people of the world.

While many people believe that "ascended" masters or saints are the "highest" or "greatest" beings, those who choose to come back to Earth rather than ascend, pay the greatest price. Their continued reincarnation is a painful sacrifice that they make for all of us - including you. These loving beings make this sacrifice so that those who wake up "crying in the dark", and desperately reaching out for God, will have a someone to take their hand, and help guide their way.

In order to serve those who need our help, there have always been approximately a thousand initiate monks on the Earth at any given time. But as you will later read, at the time of this writing there are but a few hundred. Some live monastically, while others live amongst the people of this world. Most go about their work quietly, often unnoticed. Even though we usually strive for anonymity, many gained historical recognition. They have been known as saints, sages, founders of religions, scientists, inventors, teachers, artists, writers, musicians, philosophers, magi, and even as some of the "founding fathers" of the United States. But whatever their undertaking or apparent profession, they have a common "earmark" - they always promote and exemplify Unselfish Love, Oneness and Freedom, and are at odds with the instigators of selfishness, hate, separation, oppression and slavery.

"Leadership" within the Children of the Law of One is based on, and determined by, an individual's consciousness or "level of spiritual development". Thus the most humble, and most self-sacrificing, are the "highest ranking" and powerful leaders of the Children of the Law of One. These beings have always had the most positive influence on the world, throughout history. The being who was known in one of his lifetimes as Jesus, is an excellent example of this. Known also by other names throughout history, he was our Grand Master, the foremost leader of the Children of the Law of One throughout the ages. His example of strength through self-discipline, caring and Unselfish Love, spread a message throughout the world. A message he knew would only get told throughout the world if he made the ultimate self-sacrifice. (Unfortunately, after his spiritual ascension, greedy men began to misrepresent his words and deeds, use his name and edited parts of his teachings, in order to gain wealth, acquire power, and even justify harm.) Like the Grand Master, all but one of the "old ones" (the earliest ancient leaders of the Children of the Law of One), have passed beyond the physical plane, and chosen to no longer be incarnate with us here on Earth. As the current period of this cycle of Earth draws to a close, he is making the ancient teachings available to the public for the first time to provide a "candle in the window" of guidance and hope.

Jon Peniel (the present head of our order), will begin his story in the next chapter. It includes the story of his physical journey through life, but for the most part, it portrays his spiritual journey. He tells his story in such a way that the reader can follow, and share, his thoughts, feelings, and experiences as he begins the studying and training that transforms him from a novice student monk, to an initiated monk (or "priest"). The first half of this book reveals the ancient teachings in a format of his personal re-learning and changing, during his days at the monastery. And in the second half, he presents our personal meditation and energy exercises.

Chapter Two
My Journey and Arrival

This book is an account of my personal journey of discovery, and more importantly, what it led me to, and can lead you to also.

If you find some of the teachings or stories hard to believe, I understand perfectly. Some of my experiences were so incredible that, even though I was *personally* experiencing them at the time, they were still almost hard for *me* to accept. But I had no choice but to ultimately accept them, whereas you do. However, those who really want the truth, and are ready for it, will recognize it. An intuition that's unfettered by ego and selfishness will always sense truth and reality.

In any case, the point and purpose of this book is not about my story, the alternative history or the strange tales presented here. Frankly, they just don't matter, so read it all with a "believe it or not" approach, keeping in mind that it's absolutely fine with us if you *don't* believe *any* of the story or "theory-like" aspects of the book. Regardless of whether or not the story is too incredible for your own sensibilities, this book is really about identifying the real "disease" behind our personal and world problems, and the cure for it all - Unselfish Love. That's what we sincerely hope you get out of the book, and find useful on your own incredible personal journey through life. Other than that, we are not interested in convincing anyone of anything. Every individual needs to have his/her own realizations.

Foundations of Understanding

In school, people are often required to take "prerequisite" classes, before they can take certain other classes. That's because sometimes you need to understand certain fundamental concepts first, before another class will really make as much sense as possible, or allow you get the most out of it. The teachings presented in this book are similar - some of them require "prerequisites" to understand. Thus, it was necessary to present the teachings in a specific "understanding order". But because of this, the *chronological order,* or "time frame" of my personal experiences at the monastery, had to take "a back seat" to the order in which the teachings are presented. For instance, in some earlier chapters, a discussion may be taking place when I was an elder monk, while in later chapters, a discussion that is taking place may have been one from my first days at the monastery as a novice monk (and a rather egotistical novice). Some stories will even be after my time and training at the monastery was over, and I was traveling the world. Many chapters include more than one discussion or experience I had, from *more than one time frame.* If you pay close attention to the subtleties of conversations, you will understand basically what time frame it is taking place in. Taking the same mental approach to reading the book that you would with a "chronology jumbled" mystery novel should make it more interesting and fun to read, rather than confusing.

My First Steps - A Strange Child in a Strange Land

My final "voyage" began decades ago, when I was 17 years old. But what led up to it began years prior. Like the Dalai Lama, I was destined to return to my previous position with our spiritual order. Unlike the Dalai Lama, I was not told of it in early childhood, nor was I aware of it. While I didn't have the kind of direct contact with elder monks like the Dalai Lama did, I had special caretakers "on high". Unbeknownst to me, events outside my control, were preparing me, and compelling me, to embark on a great adventure that would change my life beyond my wildest dreams. To simplify it, I guess you could say angels & saints were secretly guiding my young life.

This book covers the period of my life at the monastery in more detail than what I offer about my childhood. That's because that monastic period is the most important, as it is used to present the teachings. I only touch upon my childhood briefly in order to give you a sense of what I was like, and what I experienced, prior to returning to the monastery and rejoining my brothers and sisters. Some readers have commented about how they relate to my childhood experiences, and have had similar experiences themselves. Thus it helps them understand the entire process of spiritual change.

I was a very strange and sensitive child (considered "over-sensitive"), with unusual abilities. But when I was very young, I had no concept of being that way, what that meant, or why I was that way - it was just the "norm" for me. I had no idea that the reason for it was my latent consciousness, and my pre-destiny to return to the same state of being as when I left my previous life. Even so, many of the things I experienced were not just due to that - many of you gentle and kind souls have experienced the same things as I during your childhood.

Abnormally bright, I was reading the newspaper at age three, and self-learning to play music by five. I couldn't relate to adults, or other children for that matter. Nor could I fathom why they were so mean, self-centered, and selfish. And their idea of fun - many of the things they did - seemed either meaningless to me or worse - cruel. So my childhood was very painful and lonely (sound familiar?).

As I approached my teenage years, I was further alienated when I was "let down" by my religion. It was a major religion which I will refrain from naming, but I would eventually have had the same crisis of faith with many other religions. As with most people, I was raised by my family to believe in their religion, and thus to believe in their concept of God. Just as when I was very young and time/experiences "pierced my illusion" about the existence of Santa Claus, the same thing began happening with my belief in the existence of God. The dogma and behavior of the leaders and practitioners of my religion, was "shooting down" my faith. Certain personal experiences, and "holes" in the teachings and practices, ultimately let me down, and left me feeling "empty" and even more alone. At first, only "doubt" about my faith set in, but finally, I was left with total disbelief. It was a horrible, dark time. The worst part was I didn't just lose faith in my religion. I lost faith in the existence of God. By the time I was 13, I had become an atheist. But it turned out that I had only lost faith in the "concept" of God that I had been taught. I didn't know it yet, but it was really the beginning of developing my own understanding of God.

Trying to Connect Pieces of an Ancient Puzzle

Looking out at the stars, and observing the wonders of nature and life, I felt there *must* be something. There was order, constant new creation, symmetry and beauty to it all. Even if it were not what I had previously thought God was, there must be something to it, or behind it, that might be considered "God". Or maybe it all was "God". So before I was 14, I became an agnostic (one who doesn't believe in God, but doesn't necessarily disbelieve in God either).

Caught in a paradox, I knew there must be some force behind everything, but at the same time, I couldn't find ANY religion that really made total sense. And the tunnel-vision theories of creation offered by most evolutionary "scientists" also left far too many unanswered questions, and were full of "holes". Nothing truly answered the questions about life that constantly tormented me, nor eased my loneliness. It's not that I had a bad family life - it was better than most. Yet I still felt like an abandoned baby, left in a basket on the doorstep of a strange world.

I had to find *some* kind of answers that made *sense* to *me*. I became obsessed. My thirst was insatiable - I HAD to find truthful answers that made sense about the origins and purpose of life. I read *every* book I could get my hands on about science, religion, philosophy, spirituality and metaphysics. I "tried" different religions, including various "Eastern" philosophies. But at some point, I was always ultimately disappointed with what I would find. I found "bits and pieces" of truth here, and "bits and pieces" of truth there, but something was always wrong with the entirety of the religion or philosophy. Either something was missing in the teachings, or some aspect of the teachings didn't make sense, or the religion made the teachings more important than the purpose behind them, or it was too dogmatic. Yet I could not stop searching. I was always seeking to find a source for pure, consistent truth, and real answers to every one of my questions.

At age 10, I had tested with a very high I.Q., yet at age 16, I had flunked out of high school (for various reasons). Around the same time, I had a terrible argument with my mother over religion and relationships (she didn't like my girlfriend or my rejection of the family religion). So I moved out of my parent's house, started college, got a job, and my own apartment.

All of a sudden, I was thrust into having to face the facts of living in the "real world". I didn't like what I saw and experienced. It was a "dog eat dog" world, and as far as I could see, there were only two kinds of dogs - those who were eaten by other dogs, and the dogs who did the eating. "For all practical purposes", those were the only two basic ways of dealing with "making a living" and living your life. In other words, I realized that the world was basically populated by two kinds of people, the users and the used. The "powerful" and "successful" people of the world got that way, and stayed that way, by "stepping on" other people - whoever they needed to step on in order to get ahead. Thus the majority of people were usually always getting stepped on. It hit me like a ton of bricks - we had a whole world based on this, and the results were starvation, suffering, and servitude for most, while a few elite individuals had tremendous power and lived in incredible opulence and luxury. I also knew there were no good political solutions to these problems either, including such things as communism or socialism - because the problems were in basic human nature, and corruption always seems to get a big foothold, regardless of the political system. Even then, I realized the answer to this problem could only come from a change that took place inside *every* person on Earth. And I knew the chances for that were absurd. As I matured it became even more clear, and more unbearable. Eventually, my pain over this became overwhelming. I no longer wanted to live in the "dog eat dog" world - I couldn't tolerate the idea of living life as one of the "eaters", or one of the "eaten". I gradually began entertaining thoughts of suicide.

New Hope Arises from an Odd Place

One day someone recommended I read Robert Heinlein's book "Stranger in a Strange Land". Obviously, I could relate to the title alone. But there was far more to it. I couldn't put it down. Even though it was fiction, it stirred something deep inside me that was very real indeed - something that haunted me from then on. An idea was planted in my mind that I couldn't stop thinking about. It was no more than a mere concept, yet it *was* more. It presented a wonderful and great *ideal*. It was the simple concept of human beings living together in a community, in harmony, as one big family who shared everything and unselfishly loved and cared for each other - and all others. "What a great idea!" I thought to myself. "That's it. That's the answer." *That's* what I was looking for. To me, what was represented in that sci-fi fiction book seemed more like real spirituality, or how truly spiritual people would live, than most of the so-called spiritual or religious books I'd read. I was sad that it *was* fiction, and the people weren't real. But I didn't see why there couldn't really be people like that somewhere. It seemed like if something could even be conceived of, it could also be real, or eventually become real. So fiction or not, it gave me hope, and spurred me on to continue my spiritual search even harder. But after a while it appeared that my search was futile. I simply wasn't able to find a religion, spiritual path, community, cult, or even one person, that fit my ideal. My frustration over this eventually turned to deep despair.

I grew increasingly despondent, and by 17, I finally gave up on finding anything or anyone who really had all the pieces of this grand puzzle, or people who fully lived a life of truth, peace, harmony, and love. And with my hope lost, there was nothing left for me here. I decided to end my life. But right before I was about to do it, I had a very odd experience. One that not only resulted in my not killing myself, but in finding a new way of thinking, and of living. I was about to realize that there was a "third way" of living in this dog-eat-dog world (not just the two choices of being a "dog eater" or "dog meat"). The strange experience I was about to have, would forever change things for me, in ways I couldn't even imagine at the time.

It must be the Age of TV

What happened next was *very* bizarre. You might say it was a significant example of Jung's concept of "synchronicity", but it was even more than that. For those who aren't familiar with the concept, synchronicity is like "coincidence" but it is not just "chance". It's actually meaningfully connected to other events, possibly even connected to the entirety of all things in the Universe - God. But you could also call it "Universal Flow", or a "modern miracle". A simple example of this might be talking with someone about a certain topic, and then a song comes on the radio that fits the conversation perfectly, and perhaps has a significant message regarding it.

Just before I was about to take an overdose of sleeping pills to "do myself in", I started old fashioned "channel surfing" - turning the knob on my old black and white TV. I know it may sound strange to do that when you are in the process of killing yourself, and I didn't even know why I was doing it at the time. I thought, maybe it was out of habit, maybe out of desperation, maybe for entertainment, distraction, or comfort in my last minutes of life. But as it turned out, my channel surfing wasn't for any of those reasons. It was an "urge" I was following, from some kind of divine guidance or protection, that was compelling me to do it from within myself. Anyway, to my surprise, as I turned the channel changing knob, I noticed

7

a picture on the "U" channel setting. That was very strange indeed. There was never a station broadcasting on that channel before. In fact, at the time, there were no "UHF" stations at all. To make a long technical story short for those of you too young to remember TV's back then, there was a broadcast on a channel that virtually couldn't have had a broadcast on it in those years. There was never anything but static on these channels previously, and it would be years into the future before *any* television shows would ever be broadcast on them. The odds against the entire complicated incident, were beyond any odds. It could have only been some kind of "higher force", a television test, or some television genius kids messing around with the airwaves. The latter possibilities quickly faded as I viewed the "show".

On my TV screen was a man who looked much like the stereotype image of "God". It was sort of an interview, but a bit more like a lecture. As fate would have it (definitely), the subject matter of the lecture was all about spirituality, God, the universe, creation, and of a history that went way beyond any I'd even known. His energy and intensity was striking. His eyes seemed to look right through me, yet right at me, like he was actually speaking TO ME in person. It was as if Zeus, Merlin, and Moses had merged into one being, and stepped out of history into my living room. He was dressed in a white robe, and from my studies, I recognized that he was wearing the type of ancient headdress worn by the Essenes, and purportedly worn by a legendary ancient spiritual tradition called the Great White Brotherhood that I'd read about in books from the 1920's (not to be confused with modern groups that call themselves that). He spoke perfect English, but with a subtle hint of an accent that was un-identifiable, and he pronounced certain words using British style pronunciation rather than American.

As I listened to him speak, the man's every word struck a chord in me - they "rang" my "inner bell of truth". Here was someone who obviously knew many of the scattered little bits of truth I'd found - but they were all consolidated into one teaching! As I listened in awe, his strange TV "lecture" answered my many unspoken questions. It was almost as if he were reading my mind. Even when he spoke of knowledge or concepts I had never heard before - I seemed to already know them somehow. [author's note - this book could have a similar effect on you, depending on who you are and what stage of your path you're on.]

Next, he spoke of his origins. No, it wasn't outer space, or the heavens. While it was not nearly so far-fetched as that, it was still amazing. He said he was a monk of an ancient spiritual order who's name in English was, "The Children of The Law of One", but that they were known by many names throughout the centuries. That name rang a bell, both internally, and because I'd read something about it in the Edgar Cayce material. As I listened, I was caught between feelings of total awe, and wondering if this was really happening (like maybe I was on Candid Camera or the butt of a practical joke).

The man went on to say that their spiritual lineage, their teachings and practices, stretched back to ancient Egypt, and before that, Atlantis. He said their order was not devoted to any one religion, dogma, or *worshipping* any leaders, past or present, but rather, it was dedicated to serving and experiencing God directly, via the development and use of Unselfish Love. They were also dedicated to helping others achieve that (if they wanted to and were ready for the task). While true total freedom, has never been a condition of life on Earth, they taught how to develop real freedom of thought, and considered free will choices to be a sacred right. But

8

most importantly to me, they were devoted to *living* a life of giving, caring, kindness, sharing, compassion, and harmlessness. It was what I had been looking for my whole life.

His descriptions of their life evoked images that seemed like memories. It was like experiencing Deja Vu, *before* even getting to the place/situation you have the Deja Vu experience at! I felt as if I had been there before. I was so excited I literally almost passed out. I had discovered that there were actually people out there who were living by all the same values and ideas I'd come to believe were true. And here I'd just totally given up on the possibility that other people who believed and felt as I did, even existed in real life! Could it be I had finally found what I was searching for my whole life - just as I was *permanently* giving up?

As my mind raced with excitement and questions, the man gave directions and instructions for getting to one of their monasteries - in Tibet no less! Then the screen went back to static, and there was never another show on that channel (I later found out this was not a broadcast for the public, which will be explained in another chapter). I didn't understand how this could have happened, but nevertheless, it changed the direction of my life. I intuitively at least knew this much - it wasn't a joke, hoax, or a hallucination. My course was set. While I was still only 17 years old, I was determined to change my life no matter what it took or where I had to go. In fact, I was *compelled* to do so as a moth is drawn to a light.

[Author's note: Many of my experiences, such as those above, and those you will soon read, are very unusual. This is because, even though I didn't know it at the time, I was a high-ranking "teacher", "priest" or "initiate monk" of our monastic order. It is who and what I was in my previous life, it just hadn't come to fruition in this life yet. I was unaware of it at the time because I was in an a sort of "embryonic stage". Now I was being "called" home to fulfill my destiny. This is similar to how Tibetan Buddhists seek out the new reincarnations of their head monks, yet obviously different in this case.

Since the first printing of this book, people have contacted us wanting to enter one of our monasteries. But our monasteries have always been private, designated for those already of the order who have reincarnated. Although a few newcomers are accepted by "head monks", the occasions are rare, and new monks are only accepted after long periods of demonstrating readiness.

However, people wanting spiritual growth and fellowship also have another alternative to the traditional monastery - they can now start or join various local Golden Rule programs with the help of the new Golden Rule Organization (GRO). These programs provide some of the benefits of a monastery, without the need for moving, changing jobs, or having a teacher. Information on GRO and the Golden Rule Workbook are at the end of the book.

*A few people have been irrationally obsessed with details about Atlantis, my journey, my personal life, or the locations of our monasteries. Most people are understandably curious, but not obsessed. However, because of the nature and purpose of this book, there's really no reason to elaborate on those topics, while there **are** reasons not to. The sole purpose of this book is to present detailed spiritual teachings and demonstrate making personal spiritual changes, using my experiences as an example. While we tried to make it very* interesting, this isn't a novel or "story" book, and it is a waste of effort, time and money, to fill it with stories that don't teach a spiritual lesson of some kind. It is also not the book's purpose to be a biography of my (or my family's) personal private life, nor to present evidence of ancient historical or archeological discoveries. There are many interesting books that focus on ancient history, lost civilizations, free power systems, etc. (Like the David Childress books). But this really isn't the book for you if that's what you're primarily interested in. This book was written only for those who are primarily interested in spiritual truths and spiritual growth, not for those interested in irrelevant details and empty, useless knowledge. Thus, the only parts of "my story" it contains, are those that others might spiritually benefit from reading about.

Also please keep in mind that this book isn't about the story, it's about the teachings. So it also doesn't matter to us if you don't believe any of the story you are about to read. But you can only benefit from all that life offers you if you keep an open mind, and judge everything independently. We believe that everyone should question the validity of ALL teachings or beliefs, but only in light of whether the effects of them are good or bad. The wise examine the value of any teaching or philosophy independently, judging it by the outcome of living by it. Everything in life should be contemplated and examined regarding it's benefits, lack of benefits, or potential harm. An alcoholic may tell you it's bad to drink. A fool may speak a wisdom. A liar may be speaking the truth. A three year old child may speak the most precious wisdom ever known to humankind, for the first time in history. Should they be disregarded?

So please consider the teachings separately from the story. Read them with an open mind, then ask yourself - Do they stand the test of rationality? Of goodness? What would happen if I lived by these teachings? What would happen if everyone in the world lived by them? What does my intuition tell me? After that, THEN you should judge.

Privacy & The "Please Do Not Disturb" Sign

As mentioned earlier, this book is not about the monastery either. The monastery is but a place, and within the context of this book, it is used as a backdrop for the story and discussions that present the spiritual teachings.

Those of our order wish to remain undisturbed and anonymous, as do I. Our order is not alone in this. Regardless of religion, those who decide to become a cloistered nun or monk, do so to devote themselves to a spiritual life, and chose the monastic path because they want solitude and to be in an isolated environment, away from the "outside world", so they can live and practice their religion, unmolested and without distraction. That is part of what every monastery/convent is for, and provides. Thus, no monastery would want the kind of attention a book like this would bring to it - even more so in our case. As mentioned earlier in the book, we have legitimate reasons for maintaining the secrecy we have cherished for thousands of years. But later you will read about some new reasons that further substantiate that need. Also, those of us who travel and work in the outside world, also need our privacy and anonymity in order to do our work and live in relative peace. In summary, since our order wishes to live quietly, in solitude, undisturbed and unmolested, this book has been deliberately written to avoid any references that might jeopardize our solitude and privacy, including the location of monasteries.]

10

The Fool takes his First Steps

As wild as this may sound to some people, there really are "forces" of what you might call "light and darkness" (or good and evil) that work behind the scenes of this limited physical world we seem to live in. I didn't understand it at the time, other than having an "intellectual" grasp of the concept, which was far from being in touch with the realities of what that meant. Unbeknownst to me, "they" knew my every move. While I was being guided and somewhat protected by the forces of Light, the other side was trying to throw me off track, or destroy me. The outcome would ultimately depend on the choices I would make.

My first "test" and struggle was to be with the major resistance I encountered from my family and friends. They didn't like the whole idea. They didn't want me to leave, and they didn't like the idea of me joining others of like-mind. *Generally,* people would rather keep you with them in the hole they're in, rather than let you get out and offer a helping hand to help them out of the hole. So those of us who want to get out of the hole ourselves, often not only don't get support, we get just the opposite. We get people (and sometimes "events") doing everything they can to prevent it and keep us in the hole.

Even though I hadn't lived at home since I was 16, my mother initially attempted to keep me from going by using her "parental authority" - refusing to let me go and threatening me with the police, or putting me in an institution, because I was underage. Then when she realized that wouldn't work, she pulled one of the oldest "mother tricks" in the book - the famous "I'm sick, you can't leave me now" routine. Most people are capable of making themselves sick, psychosomatically, or accidentally, but she was beyond that. She had been studying hypnosis, the power of the mind and such, for as long as I could remember. So she *made* herself sick. And while it was nothing serious at all, it was a somewhat painful temporary illness (an outbreak of sores that was more painful if she didn't stay in bed). So she was using that, along with saying I was being selfish for leaving, as a "guilt-trip" in an attempt to manipulate my life and free will choices. But she had already kicked me out of the house a year prior, because of her jealousy towards my girlfriend. So I wasn't living with her anyway, and there were dozens of other relatives looking after her. But even if it were more serious, I would have still had to leave (I found out why later). I was internally compelled to go, regardless of *any* obstacles, let alone ones she was deliberately creating to manipulate me and keep me there. My internal drive and feelings were so strong, I felt like I would die if I didn't change my life (which was probably true). There was truly no choice. [For those of you who might feel sorry for my mother, ask yourself if she was serving the light, or just her self, and subsequently the dark.]

Then there were my so-called friends, who turned out to be "fair weather friends" as most turn out to be one day when the "chips are down". Most of them never liked my spiritual pursuits, and my new goal was "the worst" as far as they were concerned. All but one tried to talk me out of it. They told me I was crazy to go, crazy to give up "everything", and like my mother, they tried to make me feel guilty about "abandoning" them. They didn't want to get out of the hole they were in, and I did. And they wanted me to stay in mine. I didn't know it at the time, but my old friends, without knowing it, were also being unconscious pawns of the dark side. But considering my momentum and strong desire, they could not avert me from my goal either. The urge to go felt almost biological - like a salmon needing

11

to swim upstream to return to its spawning ground.

My friend John was the only person I knew who didn't try to talk me out of going. While he wasn't really supportive, he wasn't resistive either. He said, "You gotta do what you gotta do." We actually had a lot in common at the time. He and I were always able to have spiritual conversations, and agreed on many things, unless they threatened his life choices. As we said our goodbyes and talked about life, he felt more and more like joining me. All of a sudden, he decided to "go for it". But when he called his girlfriend and told her about his decision, she gave him some news that stopped him dead in his tracks - she *said* she was pregnant. And it wasn't the usual "accidental" story. She admitted she had deliberately stopped using birth control (which John had assumed she was still using), "Because she loved him so much and wanted to have his baby". Whether it was true at the time, or not, she deliberately got pregnant in a scheme to entrap him. She knew he was the kind of guy who would do "the honorable thing" and marry her. And he did. But what is "the honorable thing" when you have been deliberately entrapped so dishonorably? It's one thing to take responsibility for an unexpected, but legitimate event, but quite another to play victim to such a treacherous scheme. A family that starts with that kind of severe and serious deception, can only end badly (which it did). The dark side at work again, only against him this time. I advised him against it, but he insisted on doing the "right thing" anyway. I saw John again many years later. He and his wife had an ugly divorce after having two children. He was miserable, and had become an alcoholic with numerous D.U.I.'s. John had irrevocably missed a significant fork in his path that I now know would have changed his life, and those of others, for the good. For me, it was back to the road, alone, and with a new sadness.

[Author's Note: Everyone who starts on a true spiritual path encounters multiple obstacles and attempts to "derail" them. It just happens in different ways for each individual. Keep this in mind if you are taking your first steps. It can happen in so many ways - a great new job offer, an old lover you'd never gotten over finally calls to say they want to get back together, your car breaks down - you name it, it can happen. People may also "twist" things. You may be told you are being "selfish" by making your spiritual pursuits a priority, when the fact is, you are actually starting a path towards becoming unselfish for the first time in your life. Anything that can possibly deter you from what you really want to do, and the goals you've set for yourself, may come up.]

Home at Last

To make a very long story very short, I headed to Tibet using any means that would get me there, from hitch-hiking, to freighters, to camels, (a story in and of itself). When I got to the outskirts of Tibet, guides associated with our order, snuck me across the border and led me to the monastery. Communist China had already invaded, and troops had to be avoided at all costs.

The monastery was in an isolated area of the Himalayas that was considered "forbidden", even to Tibetans. Other than those of our order, no human had ever even stepped foot there, until recently when some daring and hardy explorers finally "discovered" the area.

As we got closer to our destination, I was shocked to find that we were entering a warmer, wetter area. Most of the Himalayas are stark, frigid, and barren. And here I was in the midst of these great frozen giants, surrounded by thriving "warm region" plant life! And how beautiful it was.

Finally, the day arrived when my quest would come to an end. All of a sudden there it was - the place my heart and soul had dreamed of. It was beautiful, and strikingly unique. The pyramids, domes, and cubic structures created such unique artistic and other-worldly symmetry. I'd never seen anything like it. Seeing it from a distance, I was stunned, thrilled, scared, awe-inspired - hundreds of feelings rushed through me like the waters of the powerful falls nearby.

As I approached the monastery, I noticed many small buildings all around the outside of its walls. I found it interesting that the people inhabiting them, and working around them, were not all dressed in Tibetan fashion, but rather they wore the garb of various cultures. Most noticeably, they were all very warm and friendly, welcoming me with their smiles.

Immediately upon reaching the entrance to the monastery, I was greeted by a bright, friendly female monk. I discovered she was to be my liaison, and initially, a kind of "orientation tour guide".

"Come in," she said. "My name is [something unintelligible to me]." She saw the perplexed look in my eyes, and grinned. "That means 'Eastern Star...' in English". I must have looked how I felt - which was "that's one heck of a handle to call someone by". She looked at my eyes kindly, and said, "Just call me Anastasia. That's my old name. My parents were from Russia."

I was in such a state of awe about finally finding what I had hoped for all my life, that I was speechless. So while I thought to answer her, I remained silent.

"As you know, we have been expecting you," she said. "I'll show you around, and initially answer any questions you might have."

"Questions," I thought to myself. "I have more questions than I can probably even ask in my lifetime."

She took me by the hand, and began to show me the "grounds".

"Thank you...," I finally managed to find part of my tongue.

Like she said, they were expecting me. And it was obvious from the guides and others who met me along the way that they also knew the timing and path of my journey. I didn't understanding exactly how they knew it all, but I figured I'd find out later. For now though, I was more interested in the reactions I was getting, or not getting, from the other monks on the grounds. Some were obviously working, some doing yoga-like techniques, and others appeared to be just sitting and "hanging out". Many of them stopped and stared, while others seemed to be ignoring me. It just seemed sort of odd to me at the time, so I asked her about it - and about the people who were living just outside the monastery.

"You'll find out later about the people who live near the monastery, but to answer your question about the monks here *in* the monastery, it's just the timing of your arrival [author's note - I later found out there was more to it than that]. We are all very busy, and those you see here (pointing to the group who seemed to be ignoring me), are doing special long meditation exercises that require deep concentration, and they would have to start over again if they stopped, or even lost their concentration." She smiled, and said, "Although, I noticed some of them lost their concentration anyway."

"Then I caused more of a stir than I thought?" I said.

"You'd be surprised... You'll get a chance to meet everyone later. But why

13

don't I just show you the grounds for now?"

"Sure - on with the tour. But I've got to tell you I've come farther to get here than Disneyland, so I hope it's worth it."

"Disneeland?" She spoke perfect English with an American accent, so I'd assumed she was familiar with Disneyland.

"...Well... I'll tell you about it later. You probably won't believe me anyway."

"Oh yes, I will," she said with a cute, innocent enthusiasm.

I could tell I could have some big fun pulling her leg.

"Anastasia, you speak English perfectly."

"Those of us who were raised here are multi-lingual, but even the monks who weren't raised here, learn at least English or Spanish, in addition to their native language (if it is something other than that). Monks have come here from all over the world. Some are also fluent in many of the various languages spoken in most parts of the world, even ancient languages. You can learn any language here that you wish."

"I'm having a hard enough time with English at this moment. How many languages do you speak?"

"Only seven modern languages..."

"Oh... *only* seven... that's too bad," I said jokingly. She didn't get my sarcasm, and just nodded in agreement.

As Anastasia was taking me to her first stop on my tour, I began asking many questions about the architecture.

"Be patient, you can't learn everything in one day anyway. You *will* find out everything you want to know later."

"When?"

"I don't know - tomorrow, next year, a decade. Whenever you do, you will have."

Her unrevealing, complex, perplexing answer, reminded me a bit of the short time I'd spent earlier at a Zen monastery. Those Zen monks certainly love their paradoxical questions and answers. I didn't know it at the time, but I would discover far more paradoxes here - and eventually come to understand them.

Finally, the radiant young woman showed me to a room where a monk was speaking to a group of other monks.

"There are many Adepts who can help you grow here. Of course, I know everyone can teach you something - even life itself is a teacher." She pointed at the man who was speaking to the others, "He is my special personal true teacher, and has also been like a father to me, especially since my parents are no longer with us on this plane. He helps me change and grow."

"How does he help you change?"

"He helps me see and understand myself clearly, and thus I can change things about myself that I wouldn't ordinarily even see."

"How does he do that? And what does 'true teacher' mean?"

"You love asking more than one question at a time, don't you?"

"There's just so much I want to learn..."

"I understand, I was just teasing you. I should probably answer your second question first. The Adept, or Initiate monks, like him, are also what we call true teachers. That's because they have transcended their own selfishness and self-centeredness, and achieved what we call Universal Consciousness. Many different spiritual traditions have their own name for achieving that. Some call it achieving

"Satori", some "Nirvana", some "Illumination", and some like us, refer to it as "Enlightenment" or "Initiation". But whatever you call it, it is a transformation that creates a total change in their viewpoint and way of life. That brings us to your first question. Because of their broad Universal Consciousness perspective, their Unselfish Love, and lack of selfishness, they thus 'see' everything (including people), very objectively, purely, and clearly. So they see things about yourself that you don't see yourself - or even things you 'block' or hide inside yourself, and bring them up to you. Thus you can use them as a sort of 'tool' to see yourself clearly, see things you want to change, and then change, if you want to."

"Only the Adept monks are what you call 'true teachers' then?"

"Yes. There are basically three kinds of monks in our order. Novices and elders are still essentially students. The Adept or Initiate monks are more like personal growth facilitators, or 'therapists'."

"Why do you use the term 'true teacher', instead of just master, or teacher, or Guru, or something like that?"

"Because it's accurate. It also avoids labels that are sometimes associated with ego, or lack of humility, and the same time separates them from just an ordinary teacher. Many people and things can teach you. But a true teacher is a specific type of teacher. They're 'true' in the sense of accuracy or lack of distortion. Like a 'true' arrow. In that sense, it's just like a 'true' mirror is best for seeing your body or face, rather than an 'untrue' mirror with imperfections that would distort your reflection. Like I said, their teaching, or telling you about yourself is pure and true, because of the objectivity they have achieved from not being contaminated by, or subject to, their own selfishness anymore. So rather than thinking about themselves all the time as most people do, they aren't self-centered, or defensive. Because of their unselfish consciousness, they don't have anything to personally gain or lose in dealing with you, or to get in the way of their objectivity about you, so they just think and care about *you, your best interests, and the best interests of all others.* And they can tell you what they see from that great 'higher', 'broader', more loving perspective - *if you ask* for their help or opinion."

The room where this "true teacher" monk was giving a talk, was lit only by candlelight, so I couldn't see his face very well. But when everyone went outside to do an energy exercise, I saw it clearly. *It was the man I saw on TV.* I didn't know it at the time, but he would soon be the most important person in my life. While some part of me rejoiced, some part of me cringed. I didn't know why at the time, I just knew he was somehow frightening to me, like staring death in the face. Later, I would realize it was because of his ability to confront me and show me myself (which my selfish, self-centered ego strongly wanted to avoid). Because of that, I would do everything I could to avoid him for awhile. But there was an even stronger draw I had towards something about this man, that would eventually lead me to ask him to be my special mentor also - my personal teacher.

I didn't know his name yet. But soon I heard one of the other monks there call him Zain. My head was reeling. I had to remind *myself* that this wasn't a dream, it was "another world", one that I thought only existed in my imagination just one long year ago.

Outside in a courtyard, Zain, and over a hundred people formed a circle, holding hands with arms outstretched between them. They were about to do an energy technique called the Star exercise. I had read about this years ago, in a very old

15

book I read by an author whose last name was Leadbetter, Ledbeter, or something similar. The book was about what he called the Great White Brotherhood in Tibet, and it described them doing something called the Star Exercise during a festival called "Wesak". But many of the particulars were never mentioned in the book. And the author's stories also indicated that the people were as inaccessible as any myth. So while the book fascinated and attracted me in many ways, and his description of the people sounded like home, it left me with nothing I could further pursue. Now I found myself living it - the real thing.

Anastasia ushered me into position in this giant human chain that formed the circle, and gave me quick instructions. And then it began. I closed my eyes, as a feeling of light-headedness came over me. My head and body were buzzing with energy. I thought I was perhaps starting to "black out", yet all I saw was fluctuating white light. It seemed as if I was experiencing a million thoughts and pictures all in a moment's time. As I opened my eyes I saw energy vibrating in all things, and all the people there. Everything was flashing with white light superimposed over it.

Apparently, I wasn't the only one experiencing some dramatic effects from this "Star exercise". A novice monk had come to join in the exercise a little late, and stood alone outside the circle. He collapsed, and lay there as if lifeless. I heard Zain muttering some kind of admonishment about it being dangerous to stand outside the circle, then he said loudly, "One has left the body, he has become lost, I must retrieve him", and in a few moments the body of the collapsed novice twitched, and he returned to consciousness.

Afterwards, Zain sat in the side courtyard garden for a sort of "question/answer" session. I was still vibrating with energy, and seeing it everywhere. I wanted to tell him about my experience, but was simultaneously afraid to say anything to him, or bring attention to myself. But I did. And that is a story we'll save for a chapter later in the book.

Anastasia then started walking me over to the monastery's "residential area". I didn't know what to expect. I had studied other monasteries, and had even visited and spent time in some. In monasteries that teach or utilize constant "asceticism" as a *primary* spiritual growth tool, the monk's quarters are often called "monk's cells", because that's pretty much what they were - tiny "jail- like cells" like what you might find in a prison. Of course, to the monks who chose that kind of path, their cells were a voluntary part of their training, *not* a means of imprisonment and punishment by a government. But in any case, I didn't even like the idea of dormitories let alone cells. I would later learn to drop such personal preferences, in favor of adapting and flowing, but I wasn't there yet. On our way over, I asked Anastasia about the living situation, with nervous, introverted concern.

"So what do you have here, monk's cells, or dormitories?"

"Except for temporary aspects of a monk's training, learning self-discipline, and special transcension training (which I was about to come face to face with), our way of life is quite moderate, and even luxurious by many standards - especially by other monastic standards... at least as a general rule."

"That's nice to hear, but you didn't exactly answer my question - I especially don't like dormitories."

"Well, they are, and they aren't. You'll see."

When we finally arrived at the monks' residential area, I was quite relieved by what I saw, although it was naturally, "odd", like most everything else around here.

16

"These are the private sleeping, living, and meditation areas," she said.

I expressed my relief to Anastasia. "I have to admit this is far nicer than what I was expecting. Yet it is rather bizarre."

I was surprised to find an odd honeycomb of private rooms. And while the quarters Anastasia was showing me, were far smaller than the monks' quarters of many other orders, oddly enough they were very cozy and comfortable - in fact, there was no comparison to the dark, dank, cold harshness of the traditional "monk cell". They were beautifully decorated, had curtains, pillows and mats, sheets and quilts, little combination shelf/altar/storage areas, incense burners, candles, even lights! But they *were* tiny.

"They're pretty tiny rooms Anastasia."

"That's true. But they're tall enough to sit up, read, and meditate in, and long and wide enough to lay down in. They serve as both our personal quarters, and places for our solitary meditations."

"Even for someone my size?"

"Sure, and actually they are quite comfortable and cozy. In fact, we call them 'wombs', instead of 'rooms', because they're so cozy, they're kind of like a womb."

"Cute."

The wombs were an ingenious architectural design and concept. They were much like "honeycombs" - their efficient design would allow many of them to fit into what would be a normal sized bedroom for someone in the U.S. But more importantly, they were modularly designed - so if you had a mate or family, wombs could be instantly connected and expanded as needed. And as it turned out, they *were* extremely cozy, and comfortable, and I never found them lacking as either living quarters, or meditation chambers. But I was in for another surprise.

"So which one of these is mine?" I asked.

"Novices don't get one right away."

I later found out that was just to put novices through tests and changes that created personal growth.

"Then where do I sleep?" I said with a bit of surprise and stress.

"See that pile of mats over there? When you are through for the day, just go get one, and find any place you can, to lay it down."

My stress just jumped up a notch. But, I immediately got a grip on myself. What the heck, after what *I'd* lived through, even *that* would be a luxury. What I didn't know at the time, is there was a deliberate shortage of mats, and it was first come first serve. I made that surprise discovery that night, when I couldn't find anymore mats. OK, *now* I was an unhappy camper. But in time, I learned it was all part of a series of tests and growth techniques that everyone like myself went through on this path, and the rewards were far greater than the sacrifices. (Note: I eventually got a 5 unit "womb with a view").

After the wombs, she brought me to the library. I was astonished. It was vast - the largest building I had yet seen.

"This is our library."

"Where do I get a card?" I asked. She looked at me quizzically.

"I don't think we have any cards, but we have many, many other things to read."

She wasn't kidding. And she also wasn't kidding about many other things to read. Texts, scrolls, tablets of of every description were in here. The "important"

17

literature, philosophy, and religious teachings from cultures all over the world were at my fingertips, including various ancient and modern translations in most languages. There were even texts *about* cultures that *had no* written language. I felt I could spend the rest of my life just in here - no, I could spend lifetimes.

"Where did all this come from??"

"It was collected over time. We also have original texts from most religious teachings, including the biblical, in their original handwriting." I was in heaven. She had to drag me out of there to continue our tour.

Anastasia eventually took me to a relatively small meditation room (compared to the hall I had seen earlier).

"This is where elder monks teach classes for novice monks."

Elder monks were ones who had learned and grown a great deal, but still had not achieved total unselfishness or total "enlightenment". But even so, they had a lot to offer, and were far nicer people than I had ever met. They were as good as "saints" from my perspective and consciousness at the time.

"What kind of courses do they give?"

"Elders teach courses in meditation techniques, basic spiritual principles and their application, history, and conduct some limited "personal growth" sessions." I would be spending most of my time learning and getting "counselling" from elder monks, during my first few months at the monastery.

The entrance to this meditation room had a very short door, and I had to bend over in order to get in.

"Why is the door so short?" I asked. It obviously had been custom built, and the room itself was as big as a large living room.

"By building the door so it physically requires those who enter the room to bow, it is meant to symbolically remind both elders and novices to be humble, and have respect and compassion for all."

A class was about to begin, so she advised me to stay there and begin my first course.

"Am I a monk now?" I asked.

"That's up to you. This *is* a monastery, and only monks stay here. I assumed that is why you came. I hope I didn't overstep my bounds with my assumption."

"No. I do wish to stay, learn, and grow. I guess I'm just accustomed to people not being so sensitive, and having to sign up for everything - even getting your car lubed."

"Well, I don't know about you getting 'lubed', but you will need to ask the head monk if you can stay. However, we've already discussed you, and he also assumed you would be asking to stay considering...," She briefly paused mid-sentence, as if she almost slipped up and told me something she wasn't supposed to, but she immediately spoke on "and has already indicated your acceptance."

"So what kind of monk am I then, a student, novice, elder, frat brother, or what?" I joked.

"Novice. You need a teacher to be a student. And you need to be a student to be a teacher."

I wasn't quite sure what she meant by that. She was going Zen on me again.

"Will I see you later?" I said.

"Of course dear. We live together now."

I didn't know exactly what she meant by that either, but I figured it wasn't the same thing it meant in the "outside world".

"When will I see you again? And please don't say 'maybe tomorrow, maybe a year...'."

She touched my shoulder lovingly, and said, "I'll be by as soon as the class is over, OK?"

"OK."

There were about a half dozen other English speaking novices there in the room, new and relatively new students of various stages. And I got my first taste of what would be many courses.

Even though these courses were not given by the teachers who were "enlightened masters", I was totally impressed by the wisdom, kindness, and compassion of the elder monks who conducted them. I learned all kinds of things in various courses, including ancient teachings, the religions of the world, meditation and energy techniques, yoga, etc.. But sometimes the elders just spoke spontaneously, about things other than what the course was about. And when they did that, I was "floored" by what I thought were their psychic abilities. It was as if they were reading my mind, picking up on my every thought, answering my un-asked questions, and finding my hidden secrets - then discussing them all out in the open to free me of my inner burdens. It was kind of like getting indirect therapy. It seemed like every word was just for me. But I couldn't understand how this could be happening just for me, when there were other novices in the room at the same time. I wondered if they were having the same experiences. I later found out that it was not a "psychic" thing that was happening, at least as we know it. It's not simple to explain (it's covered in later chapters though), but the elders who were giving these courses, were doing a meditation technique to sort of "get out of their own way" so to speak, in order to really be in touch with us, and to be 'conduits' for what we needed to hear. They didn't really even consciously know *themselves* what we were thinking, or why they were saying what they were saying, but the effect was the same.

By the time the session was over, I was so exhausted I was about to drop. Anastasia met me as I came out the door, but I was too tired, even for her. So I bid her goodnight. But instead of reciprocating, she was silent. When she finally left though, instead of saying "goodnight", she said "get a good rest". (Later I found out that the reason she didn't say "goodnight" wasn't because "get a good rest" was the local customary phrase, but because "goodnight" was just a "subconscious habit phrase" of mine, that had thus become only a meaningless "parroted phrase", rather than a meaningful statement, or statement of caring. In other words, saying "goodnight" probably originally came about from wishing someone to have a *good night*, and actually consciously "meaning" what you were saying. Now, however, it had just degenerated into the pre-conditioned, subconsciously programmed "appropriate phrase" to say when someone went to bed. The same went for other common phrases like "good morning", "good bye", "God bless you" and many more. So in order to learn all about my own consciousness and subconsciousness, I needed to stop and think about these things, and take opportunities like not saying a simple "goodnight", to help break the patterns and increase my awareness. I had a lot to learn about the mind still).

I looked for a mat, and couldn't find one. I was way too tired to panic, or even ask anyone about it, so I found the nearest corner that was out of the way, and just "hit the floor". I was immediately out like a light.

The next morning, I was awakened by Anastasia with a cheery smile and a cup of tea. I was still wiped out, and groggily sat up. It seemed like I had just closed my eyes and lied down.

"Drink this," she said.

"What is it?"

"It's tea, silly. It will make you feel better."

I sipped some. It was terrible.

"What kind of tea is this!?"

"It's called Mate. It's from Brazil, and difficult to get, so don't turn your nose up at it so quickly."

"It tastes like old socks."

"It grows on you."

"So can the things on old socks, but that doesn't mean I want to drink them." She laughed.

"You'll appreciate it soon. It's the only drink we have right now that has caffeine in it, and it also seems to help adjust to the altitude."

"You allow caffeine here?" One of her eyebrows raised in surprise.

"This isn't a rigid order, in fact, moderation in all things is a cornerstone of the order."

"Ahhhh, caffeine. It tastes a little better, now that I know that. I'm just exhausted. And I didn't sleep very well. I couldn't find a mat."

"Oh, you poor thing," she said truly sympathetically.

I didn't want to appear whiney or a wimp, so I responded with proper machismo.

"It's not the lack of the mat that was a problem."

"I understand," she said patting me on the knee. "I still remember a trip I took with my parents from here to India, when I was a little girl. You're going to need a few days to recover at least. That's why I let you sleep so long and brought you some tea."

"Sleep so *long?* It looks like the Sun just came up."

"Yes. That's what I mean. We usually rise before the Sun."

"Is that one of the rules here?"

"Most of us do that, but not all."

"Are there any basic rules here?"

"Yes. Be kind. Don't hurt anyone."

"That's it? Surely there must be more?"

"Well, yes. Of course. You have a lot to learn."

"So what are the other rules?"

"Well you are supposed to get me tea every morning," she joked.

"Seriously?"

"No. Only if you want to."

"I don't mind. I'd be happy to."

"I was just teasing. I already get tea for myself and someone else every morning. But thanks for the offer. You'll eventually get into the swing of things, and get a schedule. Unless you have something to do otherwise, we get up with the rising energies of the Earth, before the Sun, do a few private morning meditation techniques and yoga, then have a morning meeting and group meditation. One of the Adept monks speaks afterwards. All monks have some kind of work to do around the monastery. And you'll have various meditations to learn and master, that you'll be practicing at different times during the day. You'll probably spend some time everyday reading the ancient teachings in the library. But your routine might be different, I don't know. It mainly depends on what your personal teacher thinks you need. Everyone is different, so they all need different things in order to learn and change. So your routine may be very different from mine."

"I hope not." She smiled again.

"So what is my routine right now?"

"I don't know."

"What do you mean, I thought you were going to get me in the groove of things here?"

"Only to an extent. The rest, like I said, will be up to your personal teacher."

"OK, so who's my teacher?"

"I don't know."

"You don't know?" She nodded affirmatively.

This was getting a little ridiculous. It was starting to remind me of trying to get a straight answer out of a Zen master I had back home. So I tried to come at it from a different angle.

But before I could, she spoke again.

"Only you can decide who your personal teacher will be, and ask them to be your teacher, if you want to."

"Well, will you be?"

She laughed and said, "I'm hardly qualified to be your teacher. But thank you anyway, I am honored, that was real sweet of you to ask. I already told you who my personal teacher is, and I can tell you what my basic schedule is, would that help?" She smiled.

"*Anything* would be welcomed Anastasia. Are you a nun elder?"

"A nun?... well, we are all the same here, so whether male or female, you could call us all monks or all nuns or all whatever. They're just words. Titles and 'ranks' for a 'position', don't matter. It doesn't really matter *what* you *call anyone,* it's what you *are* that counts - don't you think? Sometimes the 'labels' help keep some things more organized in our silly little brains, but sometimes it can create false or unfair divisions, and false worship where none is warranted. I guess I might be called a nun in certain orders, except I'm not fully celibate, which sometimes being a 'nun' requires. So generally, we all consider ourselves just monks, or students, or teachers, depending on our capabilities and consciousness."

"Wait - back up a second... '*Fully* celibate? It seems like you either are or you aren't."

"I'll explain some other time. Anyway, some of us do call the Adept female monks 'Mothers', however. But it's because they kind of become like 'Universal Mothers' when they are enlightened. It's more of a term of endearment than a title. Like I said, titles are really unimportant. You could call them sister, or 'chum' for all they care."

In the next few weeks I developed quite a "crush" on Anastasia. I had never had a woman feel so loving toward me, and because of what I was accustomed to (as far as male/female relationships go), I thought that her affection meant that she "liked me" in a romantic sense also. I wasn't used to being loved so dearly, without it meaning that she wanted to "be with me". I didn't understand pure real Love yet. And I didn't have the consciousness to respond to her without selfish possessiveness. So it came as quite a shock and disappointment to me when I found out that she was not interested in me in "that way". It turned out that she actually already had a mate that she had a very good and close relationship with. She was just a loving, caring person ("Just" a loving caring person. I said it as if it were common!).

Women who are truly spiritual, kind and caring, typically have quite a problem with men thinking about them the way I did with Anastasia. Actually, lusting after them, would be a more accurate way to put it. Not just in a sexual sense (although that's certainly involved), but in a "wanting their attention and affections" way.

So you might want to learn from my mistake, and take some helpful advice. If you ever meet such a special, truly spiritual woman, don't make the same mistake. Just because a woman is warm, kind, and caring towards you, doesn't mean she wants to be your possession, or have "romance" or sex with you. This goes for all women, but it is especially true for women of advanced spiritual development. Just take the Love you get - it's wonderful to even ever receive such Love - and don't try to possess it for yourself alone, or make that woman the center of your life. That's a role only God can fulfill.

Bringing my Story up to Date, in summary.

As the days went by, I slowly adjusted to my new surroundings, and began to absorb what I could. Years later, I finally "graduated". Now, as was prophesied within our order centuries ago, this book was written to present the essential ancient teachings to the public, in an unadulterated, clear, easily understandable fashion. Along with this, I will include some of my personal experiences, both ones that I had while I was a young novice student on my road to change, and a few of those that I had later in life, after I became an Initiate. That way you can get a little glimpse of things from "both sides" - the teacher's and the student's.

Chapter Three

Sources & Descendants
of the Teachings
Including definitions of God, Basics and Prerequisites

THE TEACHINGS ⁔

To you they may be
Lost, found, or misplaced.
Earth-shaking, new, or fancy.
Basic, old, and simple.
It matters not.
They ARE Timeless, Useful and Invaluable

This book tells several stories other than my personal one. It tells a story of creation, a story of a long forgotten history, and a story of a spiritual tradition that gave birth to many legends. But primarily, the book accurately reveals the teachings that, without which, none of these stories would exist, or matter. Like some of the stories, while these teachings are *part* of ancient history, they can also be keys to a promising future.

Some of the teachings of the Children of the Law of One presented here, have been around a very long time (as far back as Atlantis), and some not so long. The unadulterated teachings of the Children of the Law of One, have never been directly made public before. But some of them are the source of many other teachings, that *have* been made public. So you may already know certain things you're going to read in this book - yet, some of it will still be new information. Other readers may find that much, or all of it will be "new" to them. Obviously, if you are already "enlightened", reading this book would just be a waste of your time, because it's purpose is to help those who aren't enlightened, become enlightened. Since the word enlightenment has many meanings though, I should probably define what we mean by it. We call someone "enlightened" who: 1) Has had a final "death experience" (of the selfish separate self), thus bursting the illusion of separation from everything/God; *[this is similar to a "near death experience", but is deliberately cultivated through spiritual training/ego busting. It is also fully experienced rather than "near", and doesn't require nearly dying physically]* 2) Has realized and permanently returned to a state of absolute Oneness with the Universal Spirit/God; 3) Is always living in harmony with the Universe and doing the will of God, as a servant of God; 4) Always lives in a state of Unselfish Love. All of the above are one and the same thing, and the change takes place at the same time. If you haven't achieved that yet, then even if you think you know it all, this book could still help you if you will just "check your ego at the door" and actually *apply* the teachings rather than just letting them be more "knowledge" you scan into your brain. But generally, regardless of your familiarity with the teachings presented here, the book can offer a sort of "oasis" of fellowship and inspiration, to *anyone* who *feels inside* that kindness, compassion, and "harmlessness" (not hurting anyone or anything), are more important than any "belief" of *any* kind.

Descendants

One of the first questions I asked an elder monk was about Buddhism.

"Raga, why is this monastery located here, in a country so full of Buddhists and Buddhist monasteries?"

"Several reasons, which we'll discuss soon."

"Are we related to Buddhism in some way?"

"Buddhism is a beloved relative of ours, and thus some of the teachings are the same. But this is not *just* the case with Buddhism. We are also related to the Christian, Jewish, Islamic, and many, many other religions. Although some religions are almost unrecognizable from their origins now, almost any religion that speaks of One God (regardless of the name they call God), is somehow related."

"Why is that? Most people consider such religions conflicting, not 'relatives', and especially Buddhism - a 'beloved relative'?"

"The teachings and heritage of the Children of the Law of One pre-date Buddhism, and *all* other religions. They all originally came from teachers or teachings of the Children of the Law of One, or those who somehow became one with the Universal Spirit - the One God, in some other fashion. But keep in mind, that while you may find bits of the Children's teachings here and there in *many* other spiritual traditions and religions, they are also unique unto themselves. Our teachings are the source, the roots of the many branches of the tree. And unlike some of the branches, the roots are still alive, still totally pure and uncorrupted. They are like the original roots of the grape vine from which all the different varieties of wine grapes eventually developed from. The teachings you are going to hear about and read here in the monastery's library, are the original, and presented from the pure, direct lineage. Although, keep in mind that *any* teachings, *including* these, aren't as important as simply applying Unselfish Love, kindness, and compassion in your life, regardless of the source. This is where many have gone wrong - making the teachings, or the leaders, or the religions, more important than the point of what they were really for in the first place."

"So will we learn only the pure original teachings?"

"No. Our knowledge has been accumulating for ages, and you will learn these too. In fact, some of the knowledge is about our existence *before* our time on Earth. And these too you will learn in time. But we don't just present the Children's teachings here. You will also learn the ways and beliefs of all the world's religions."

"Why do that if we have the pure and original source of all other teachings here?"

"Other religious teachings, and cultures, are taught for the purpose of revealing the common threads of unity and truth that could be found woven through diverse religions, and to give teachers of the Children of the Law of One more of an ability to understand and communicate with anyone they might need to - regardless of their culture or religion. Also because of that, there have been other monasteries of the Children, in various parts of the world."

Another time, I also asked Gabriel some questions about our monasteries and their relationship to Buddhism.

"The Children's monasteries, though few in number, were the oldest in many regions of the world, including Tibet. Buddhism as a separate path, didn't appear until thousands of years after the Children had established monasteries in the 'East'. Buddhism, like most religions, was in fact, originally one of the offspring or 'branches' of the Children. It developed from the effects and teachings of Adept monks of the Children of the Law of One. These monks wandered the regions throughout the area, and taught the local people there, and throughout much of what is now called Asia, and the Orient. Various teachers of the Children, who often remained anonymous and never spoke of the secret source of their true lineage or home, became known as 'Buddhas'. Did you know there was more than one 'Buddha'?"

"No. I thought Buddha was Buddha, just like Jesus was Jesus."

"That is not so, there were more than one, just as there were many Zoroasters, and many St. Germains, and..."

"Why?"

"Various reasons. I will explain some other time, but that is not the important subject of our conversation right now."

"Is that why there are different Buddhist traditions, and even variations in their teachings?" I asked.

"Partly. After the various Adepts left, Buddhist religions, of many varieties, sprung up all over Asia as a result, and modified in different ways."

"What about Zen?"

"Zen is often considered an offshoot of Buddhism, and also considered to be a 'short-cut' to enlightenment. But there are no *real* shortcuts, in the sense that the same things must be experienced, and the death of the selfish separate self ultimately faced and transcended. And while it has become intertwined with Buddhism, the roots of Zen were from one of our Initiates by the name of Zend, which you will undoubtedly read about here when it is time, because you have a connection to Zend, that you will find most interesting and enlightening." *[Author's note: that statement related to an incarnation of the being also known as Jesus.]*

"Zen is our offspring, as is Buddhism, Christianity, and Judaism, and Islam."

"So you could say Buddha was Christian, and Jesus was Buddhist."

"Yes, but only in a way. You aren't getting it are you? Think about what you know of (which is quite limited at this time) of the lives of Buddha and Jesus. Do you see anything that conflicts? Or do you see examples of love and compassion - indications of similarity? So what do you think the source of these paths that they spawned, the source of their teachings, the source of their examples, if not the same understanding or the same God?"

"You're saying these all have the same source?"

"Of course. And notice, they all teach of a Oneness, or a Oneness God, yet they may disagree over names or particulars. And most importantly, they believe in God-ness, good-ness, compassion, Unselfish Love as THE way of life."

"So they all came from the Children of the Law of One. That makes so much sense of so many things that I couldn't understand before."

"And this particular monastery, housed the roots of other beliefs and teachings, for several reasons.

Even though well hidden, from those few who *had* seen it (that were not of the order), legends were born. Even amongst the offspring traditions and religions. They told of a paradise - a beautiful, heavenly community that existed amongst the great mountains.....but it is prophesied that the 'land of the teachers' is to be desecrated and destroyed. It has begun. We only have so long. It is just a matter of *when* now, not *if*. But it matters not. Which is more important, a container, or *that which the container contains?*"

Nature, secrecy, and other methods, did protect the monastery - for quite a while longer at least. While countless Buddhist monasteries were destroyed, our monastery remained undiscovered for a while longer. For as long as was necessary in the great scheme of things.

An Infinite Lineage

As I assume you've already gathered, when I first began to learn the history of the order, I was just amazed. I had never heard of any religion, spiritual tradition, or culture, with such an extensive lineage, pure lineage, or broad influence. The pre-history and history of many religions can be obscure and have a great deal of "unknowns" about their past and true origins. But the Children record a history that stretches all the way from the creation of life in the Universe, to the present. And while some religions developed from a primitive, ignorant society, and have a lineage of bloody and barbaric intolerance, even the Children's earliest history on Earth records them as compassionate, tolerant, highly evolved beings living in a sophisticated civilization.

"Where and when did it all start?"

"Did what start?"

"I guess I mean when did the Children of the Law of One begin."

"On Earth?"

"...Yes."

"The Earthly lineage actually begins with the time of Atlantis. The Children of the Law of One was the 'spiritual order' of those in Atlantis who lived a spiritual life - those who were compassionate, kind, harmless, and wanted to maintain Oneness with God."

"So where does this monastery in Tibet come into the picture?"

"When Atlantis was on the verge of final destruction from the great upheavals, branches of the Children, having 'read the signs', went to various places on Earth. The main group went with the Children's grand master Thoth, to Egypt, to continue the 'great work' *[Author's note: the 'great work' he was referring to will be explained later]*. After many years in Egypt, that particular branch of the Children went to Tibet. These Atlantean Children of the Law of One, including the grand master, were the ancestral founders of our monastery in Tibet."

"So, if everyone mainly hibernated here at this monastery for so many years, how did they influence or start other religions?"

"All through 'commonly known' human history, the Children of the Law of One continued to maintain their center in Tibet. But some of its teachers made the great sacrifice of leaving their brothers and sisters in the monastery, to help people in the outside world. They humbly and lovingly traveled throughout the world bringing light into the darkness of the ages. The teachings and influence of these Children, have become the foundations of many other paths, religions, and legends."

It all made sense of so many things about religions, philosophies, history, and spiritual teachings, that never quite made sense to me before.

You probably wouldn't even believe it if I told you of *all* the religions, cultures, arts, and science that have been created based on these "outside world" teachers who lived "disguised" lives. So I won't. But you can think about it, and draw your own conclusions.

REDEFINING "GOD" AND "LOVE"

First, let me cover some important ground - things that I learned in my earliest days at the monastery, that will give you a frame of reference. So before we delve deeper into the teachings, let's clarify the meanings of a couple of words/concepts that will be used a great deal in this book - God and Love, and in a different way than you may have heard them used before. Both terms and concepts, can mean many different things to many different people.

LOVE

In my first days and months at the monastery, I attended courses given by elder monks. In one of my *world human concept and terminology* courses, which was given by the elder monk, "Raga", we began covering the teachings on the various types of emotions that people often lump together, and call "love".

"Love can mean sex ('We made love'). Love can mean you really like something ('I love my new car'). Love can mean the pleasure or 'thrill' you get from someone you have a romantic relationship with ('I love Nadia'). Or love can mean compassion, kindness, caring, giving, sharing - that's the kind of love that brings true happiness, inner peace. It's the kind of love we all really need, and need to give - it's also the kind of love that would make the world a far better place. So if we wish to focus on developing this kind of love, we must clearly delineate it, and give it a name. Thus, we call it 'Unselfish Love', because that is what it is."

GOD

Raga went on to define the various ways the people of the world see and understand God.

"God is a very abstract and difficult thing for the human mind to fathom. To paraphrase the ancient teaching - 'The God I am talking about, cannot be talked about'. It means that God is really impossible to explain, or *truly* understand *intellectually*. But with that in mind, I will endeavor to explain the unexplainable.

"THE BIG GUY IN THE SKY" CONCEPT OF GOD -

People have often *'person'-alized, or human-ized* the concept of God. Whether consciously or subconsciously, many people think of God as having a human-like appearance - a great big man with long silver hair and beard that lives 'somewhere out there' beyond the sky in Heaven."

"That has always bothered me. Why do people think of God that way?" I said.

"There are several reasons people think of God in this way. Partly, it is due to how hard it is to grasp such an infinite and abstract concept as God. But unfortunately, sometimes this human-like idea of God was deliberately fostered as: 1) A means to gain wealth and power over the masses; 2) A means to justify cruel or horrible things some men wanted to do (like war); 3) A means of propagating sexism; Or, 4) All of the above.

Unfortunately, with that kind of human-like conceptualization of God, also comes assigning human-like personality traits to God - and some of them are the very human-like "negative" personality traits, such as anger, jealousy, and vengefulness. The followers of many different religions have their own personalized versions of a humanized God. Some versions of God have similar personality traits, but there are various differences. Subsequently, the rules that people believe "He" has given for us to obey, are sometimes similar, and sometimes very different."

"Is that a problem though? Why can't people all have their own ideas of God if it makes them happy or fits into their culture?" I asked.

"They can. They are welcome to it. We don't care about what name of God, or idea of God they believe in. If it helps them become better, kinder people, that's our only concern. But think about it. People will even go to war, because their personalized version of God is different than someone else's, and of course, each side in the war always believes 'God' is on their side. Understanding the universality, and oneness of God eliminates this, and many other tragic acts. You, who will be teachers in various parts of the world will be confronted with this constantly, and you need to understand the various concepts of personalized Gods, in order for you to reveal that there is more to God that goes beyond what they think.

Many things about various personalized Gods, just don't make sense. This includes both the things God does, and the things God doesn't do (allows). For instance, animals and innocent children are suffering on this planet. Why? If you accept a human-like version of God, why doesn't He put a stop to this? Many people who have limited views of God, can understand this when you explain it to them, as long as they have the slightest open mind, and the Spirit of God is present in you when you explain it to them.

Now let's consider God in a different, un-humanized way.

GOOD GOD

The Children of the Law of One teach that God is ALL, and includes ALL. It is the One, that includes the many. It is within us, without us, and we are individual parts of the whole of it. While many religions have similar to identical concepts of the One God in their scriptures, they may still use the idea that *their* God is different from the others', as a reason for war or killing. One of the problems is that while many religions do teach that God is One, is all things, is everywhere, etc., they still propagate the concept of the human-like God in the Sky, and thus the religion's followers still seem to think of God that way. They also sometimes teach that it is only their religion that has the One God, rather than that God IS the One, the Oneness of All."

"But some religions don't teach that do they?"

"Even if the religion isn't propagating the humanized God concept, people still usually think that way. I will explain why in a moment, but first let's look at the consequences of thinking of God in a humanized fashion, regardless as to why they do. Unfortunately, the humanized God idea naturally leads to thinking of God as an *individual* of sorts. Then a person's, or a religion's God can be given all kinds of personal traits, that either the individual, or the religion wants God to have, in order to justify their human behavior. But that whole idea goes against the 'God is everywhere and everything' concept, because if God is thought of as an individual, it also leaves us with the impression that He is *separate from us, and the Universe.* But if there is One God, which *is all*, and *is everywhere* at all times, etc., it *can't be separate from us, or the Universe.* So it can't be an individual in any normal interpretation of the word (other than if you consider everything in the Universe, the entirety of the Universe itself, as One Universe, and in some sense then, as an individual)."

"So God is an individual also?"

"In some sense. Let's contemplate that for a moment. We know the Universe is One huge, probably infinite, 'something' that is everywhere and everything - all existence as we know it, etc.. Even our bodies are comprised of 'stardust' - 'the stuff of the Universe'. Doesn't it stand to reason then, that the One God must *also* be the very Universe itself? And if that is so, and there is some sort of design, consciousness, and energy that pervades the entire Universe - all of creation - wouldn't that be 'God's Spirit and Consciousness'? Thus the consciousness of God IS the consciousness of the Universe. 'Universal Consciousness' then, is a consciousness that is one and the same as 'God's'. And thus the 'Spirit' of God, the life force that is all of creation, IS the Spirit of the Universe - 'The Universal Spirit'. Once, all humans had the consciousness of their Oneness with The Universal Spirit, and that is why you are here - to regain that Universal Consciousness, and Oneness with God. Then you will be the lamps to help others regain their lost way also."

So for clarity, in the majority of this book, "God" will often be referred to as "The Universal Spirit" (and sometimes as "the One"). It helps clarify that when we are speaking of God, we are *not* referring to "The Big Guy in the Sky" concept of God. But even though using the words "Universal Spirit" helps prevent the confusion with the humanized God concept, the term God will still be used from time to time throughout the book. When it is, just keep in mind what that means to us. Back to my course with Raga...

"To summarize, The Children of the Law of One teach that The Universal Spirit, rather than being an 'individual' as we know it - is a 'multiplicity' that is 'One'. It comprises, and is, *all* things in the entire Universe, together as One. It is the 'beingness', energy, essence, and life force that is everywhere and everything in the Universe, including us, including nature - and including the Universe itself. And it has a consciousness.

Also included as part of the One Universal Spirit (and the Oneness that is the Universal Spirit), is a 'hierarchy' of spiritual beings who exist on many different levels. You might think of them as angels, guardian angels, ascended masters, adepts or saints who have 'passed on', etc.. Being free from the limitations of physical life, they exist in spiritual form, and share the same consciousness as the Universal Spirit ('Universal Consciousness'). They are consciously part of, One with, and an aspect of, the Universal Spirit. Hierarchical beings thus act in harmony with the Will of the Universal Spirit, as if they were 'arms' or extensions of it. Yet, they are somewhat related to us, and thus close to us also, so they are 'links to' the entirety of the Universal Spirit, who can help guide us, and have certain influences in our lives."

"Is that like what some people call 'guardian angels'?"

"Yes. But it is just one of the many beings that form the link of the hierarchy. And the Universal Spirit is also comprised of this great link of Oneness.

29

As you study the ancient biblical texts in the library, you will find that an early name for God in some of them, or perhaps I should say God was referred to in some of them, as 'Elohim'. The word Elohim, is *plural,* and both masculine and feminine. Thus it includes the concept of a hierarchy of spiritual beings that also comprise God, and insinuates that God is neither an individual person, nor a 'He'. This also leaves room to include all creation, all beings, including humans, as being part of God. Thus the Elohim concept of God, is similar to what the Atlantean Children of the Law of One teach about The Universal Spirit, and you may find this helpful in your work someday."

THE SOURCE AND PURPOSE OF THE TEACHINGS

The teachings in this book weren't created for the purpose of being "enshrined" or "worshiped", nor to influence the reader to worship any religion, book, or religious leader. These ancient teachings are thus "non-denominational", and/or "omni-denominational". They are not from, or by, any religion - and they are not "religious" teachings. Yet they do teach about the Universal Spirit, our relationship to it, and our place in the Universe.

It is our hope that publishing this book will help people in several ways: to regain their connection with The Universal Spirit; to regain their place in the "order of things" in the Universe; to become free from that which creates suffering (for themselves and others); and to become Unselfishly Loving, compassionate, kind, and harmless.

The teachings of the Atlantean Children of the Law of One, were developed by beings who were "One with God & The Universe", so to speak. You could call them angels incarnate, enlightened people, fools, masters, Children, true teachers, saints, whatever, - it doesn't matter. Regardless of what you choose to call them, they had "Universal Consciousness", and thus an awareness that included the "spiritual" realms (which permeate, and are the foundation of all physical things in the Universe). This "high" or "spiritual" consciousness gave them a great understanding of everything in life, including us, God, and Universal Laws & Truths (we will also refer to these Laws & Truths, as "Universal Principles"). The teachings are thus "reflections" of these greater understandings of "the Big picture", and present Universal Principles within them. They are a kind of "the facts of life" in the Universe, that most people have lost touch with, and are thus living out of harmony with. These Universal Principles are also *aspects* of The Universal Spirit. They are all things we once knew, and were aware of - because *we also,* were once higher consciousness beings. But that was in a time when our spiritual natures were dominant, and we were still in a state of Oneness with The Universal Spirit (this will be explained in depth in a later chapter). But now, the spiritual nature within most people is so suppressed, that their awareness of these things is "blocked" to one degree or another. Most people have lost *so much* awareness, that they *aren't even aware of the fact that they aren't aware* that they are part of this One Universe. But *all* people still have some awareness of their lost heritage deeply "buried" within them - it is just "asleep" or "suppressed". This is one area where the ancient teachings *are* important - because of what they can do to help put us "back in touch".

The words, teachings, and beliefs expressed in this book can be a catalyst for positive change, and stimulate spiritual inspiration and awareness. They can also help you gain an awareness of the Universal Principles that are the fundamental guiding forces of all creation, including human life.

Being exposed to the Universal Principles *within* the teachings, may "resonate" and stir "lost" buried feelings and memories from your suppressed spiritual nature. These feelings and memories are often first perceived as a sort of vague "knowingness" or "awareness" within you (at least those of you who are more receptive to "awakening" to their true nature, and the reality of life). It's kind of like a person with amnesia, regaining their memory as they hear and see familiar people and sights (although it's not so dramatic and obvious). And you don't *need* to fully understand the teachings *intellectually* in order to recover from your "spiritual amnesia" - just reading them and grasping the spirit of them, can still have an effect.

The teachings may also act as a partial catalyst for your "Inner Voice" (the still silent "voice" of the The Universal Spirit within you). Even though blocked, your Inner Voice will still react when exposed to the right catalyst - such as being presented with the spiritual truths of the Universe. Thus the teachings will stimulate it, and get a positive response from it. However, the awakening or "unblocking" of the Inner Voice may not get a positive response from *you in general.* It all depends on the kind of person you are and have made yourself into, and whether or not you *want it to remain blocked.* So the subsequent reaction may be positive, and one of "joyfully quenching of a desperate thirst" (which brings "awakening"), or the reaction could be negative, and one of repulsion, anger, and deeper blocking. But one thing is certain - all people *will* react.

Thus the book has the *potential* to inspire, awaken, and nurture in those who read it, their "higher" consciousness, or "Universal Consciousness", and thus their *own* inner sense of spirituality. [Some people might refer to Universal Consciousness as "God Consciousness", "Christ Consciousness" or "Enlightenment", etc..]

Having Universal Consciousness means many things other than being consciously One with, and aware of, all things in the Universe, including The Universal Spirit. Most readers won't understand such abstract concepts at this time (and you can't ever *really* understand it until you achieve it). Universal Consciousness will be explained more in depth later in the book, but fortunately, there is a very simple, easy way to understand what Universal Consciousness means to us, and the world - indirectly. You can understand it, recognize it, and appreciate how valuable and important it is - by observing *its effects.* There are very real, tangible, and clearly identifiable changes that can be seen in the life of a person whose higher consciousness is awakening, or who has fully achieved Universal Consciousness. They are "real world" changes that every decent person can relate to, and agree are "good". What are these changes, and how do they come about? Having an awakening of consciousness like we've just talked about, *results in* TRULY *becoming* more "spiritual".

Let me pass on to you, what my personal teacher, the Adept monk Zain (who I eventually, affectionately, called "Father" as we grew closer), said to me about spirituality one day.

"As you begin to expand your consciousness beyond your self, you start *realizing* (not just believing or "having faith") that there is more to life and the Universe than meets the eye. Creation isn't just haphazard. There is One Great Something

31

behind it all. And it pervades everything, including you, including all other people, animals, life, even the Earth and the Universe. As your Universal/Spiritual consciousness continues to grow, you start understanding the underlying connection of everything more and more, until you eventually have the *realization* that others are *actually* part of you, and you a part of them, and you are ALL one. Brothers and Sisters - all Children of One Universal God. As your spiritual consciousness grows you also feel, and manifest, **Unselfish Love,** and the 'real world' *spiritual virtues* that are *reflections* of Unselfishly Loving - ***Caring, Kindness, Compassion, Giving, and Harmlessness.*** THESE are the things that ARE truly important, and the earmarks of TRUE SPIRITUALITY."

Oddly enough, it works in both directions. Even though developing spiritual consciousness brings forth Unselfish Love, Unselfish Love also brings forth spiritual consciousness. In fact, one of the *main* things that *develops* spiritual consciousness, is *developing* your Unselfish Love for others, *feeling* Unselfish Love, and *practicing* kindness, caring, giving and harmlessness. So *most* importantly, the teachings have the potential to stimulate and inspire the reader to do what it takes to actually *manifest in their lives,* these true spiritual qualities.

If such a spiritual change takes place within you, then all the people you come into contact with as you walk through your life, will be better off from having known you, and then they too will have the opportunity to change, and spread the beauty of Unselfish Love to others still - and on and on. Like multiple ripples in a pond that go on and on from throwing just one rock, your Unselfish Love can make you a part of, and a vehicle for, the Universal Spirit, as it moves through you, us, and thus throughout the world.

SPIRITUAL KNOWLEDGE VS. GOODNESS

I'd attained a good deal of spiritual knowledge from all the reading I did as a teenager. But I was finding out that most of it was more of an impediment to my growth than an aid. An early course by the elder monk Enoch burst the bubble of my intellectual wisdom. Just as I was thinking to myself about how much I already knew, and how I could really probably skip many of these courses, Enoch started his lecture like this:

"Many people place too much importance on spiritual knowledge itself, and don't *concentrate first* on the basics of simple goodness, such as the virtues of Unselfish Love. Knowledge is meaningless without this. Using imagination and visualization, we can make a 'mental illustration' that clearly demonstrates this.

There is an ancient technique that can help you perceive, understand, and contemplate the value and impact of a person's character. We'll use this technique to compare the value of knowledge, as opposed to goodness. Here's how it works: Think about a person's qualities and traits, and then imagine what the world would be like if it were entirely populated by, and run by, billions of identical duplicates of that one person. Keep in mind that if the entire world is populated by 'so and so's' duplicates, some of them will also be in powerful political positions. There is an old saying, 'Power corrupts, and absolute power corrupts absolutely'. Having power tends to nurture the darkness within people. Even a little separateness and selfishness is like a dormant cancer that can grow unchecked when fed by power. Some people behave well when they're 'held in check' by lack of wealth, lack of a position of power, and constrained by society's moral standards and laws. So when you imagine a world full of 'so and so's', you need to consider what they *might become* if they were also in all the various positions of power - police, judges, head officers of giant corporations, presidents, kings and queens? You get the idea. The overall feeling and image you get of an imaginary world populated by any given individual, will give you invaluable insight about them.

So for our knowledge vs. goodness contemplation, let's think about what it would be like in two different imaginary worlds. In this case, we don't actually know the people involved, but we can still use the technique to help us understand the comparison. Let's say the first world is entirely populated by duplicates of the one person with the most, and greatest spiritual *knowledge* on Earth. Keep in mind that this person, is still basically selfish (as most people are). Thus they may be nice and friendly when things are 'going *their* way', and when nothing is required or asked of them. But these 'clones' aren't Unselfishly Loving, and have spent their time and energy more on acquiring spiritual knowledge, instead of focusing on developing, and practicing, kindness and harmlessness above all else. Thus *their* world is full of people that aren't particularly kind, are definitely *not* harmless, happy, etc., and likewise, the population is definitely not self-sacrificing when another person is in need. Yet they are all 'egoed out', each person thinking they are very wise and 'know it all'. So world #1 is still full of inequities and injustices of all kinds, still has children starving to death needlessly, still has torture, wars, and all the other evils, problems and destruction, that go along with a 'look out for #1', 'dog-eat-dog' world. I know those of you here don't want to live in that world, and many other people don't either (yet isn't it virtually the same as the outside world is that we have now). So how useful is great spiritual knowledge alone?

For our second imaginary world, let's think about what the world would be like if it were entirely populated by duplicates of one REALLY 'good' person. Someone with little knowledge, but with a 'good heart'. Someone who is compassionate, kind and harmless, and really cares about others. And they also have an attitude of 'live and let live', regardless of what others believe, think, and do (as long as they don't hurt someone else). That's not too much to ask is it? Now, wouldn't this world be an *incredibly* better world than the one that people live in now? It would obviously be a beautiful, happy place - no starvation, no hurt, no war, no economic or physical enslavement, and no infringement on freedom.

So even in regard to the practical aspects of day to day life (and the condition of the world in general), isn't it obvious that the virtues of kindness and giving, are far better (and truly 'spiritual') than *any* spiritual knowledge? And just imagine an entire world populated by Unselfishly Loving 'enlightened' beings - it would be paradise, Heaven on Earth.

SPIRITUALITY REQUIRES MORE THAN SPIRITUAL KNOWLEDGE

All people have some *knowledge* about 'God', and goodness. Everyone was raised with the beliefs and examples of whomever raised them, and even if they were abused, and raised by satanists, or atheists, they still learned about the concepts of God and goodness. But as they grow up, many people gain further knowledge of these things. Some read books about it. Some join religions and learn *their* spiritual and moral teachings. But the problem is, there are a lot of people out there who have a great deal of *spiritual knowledge,* yet they just aren't 'spiritual'. They don't think or behave as a 'spiritually conscious' being would."

"Why, Enoch? How can someone learn all these things, and not really change?"

"Let's use an analogy in which 'water' represents Universal Consciousness, Unselfish Love, and true spirituality. Just like the old saying that you can lead a camel to water, but you can't make him drink, you can lead a 'spiritually dry' person to the spiritual 'water', give it to them, point it out and say, 'Water', but you can't make them drink. Many 'spiritually knowledgeable' people already have *knowledge* about this 'Water', and they know where it is inside them. So when you point it out to them, they will usually say 'I know' (as if they *really* have it within them). Sure, they 'know'. That's the problem. They **only** 'know'. They can hear you tell them about the water, and show it to them - and they recognize the water. They may even be able to tell other people about the water. They may even 'preach' about it. All because they have the knowledge of it. But what have they done with the knowledge of water themselves? They've developed a 'spiritual ego'. They impress themselves and others with their knowledge. But they are still spiritually dry. Just having the knowledge of the water is not sufficient. They must 'drink' it in somehow, become one with it, and simultaneously share it by giving it all away for others. Just sharing the *knowledge* of water to those in the middle of the Sahara who need a drink, does no one any good unless you actually have the *water to share also*."

Such is the problem with all knowledge, including the teachings in this book. Intellectually, we can only point out the simple, obvious facts of how to live in harmony with Universal Law/Principles. The philosophy and teachings can perhaps tell you how a good, caring person should behave, or how to become a good caring person. But just 'knowing how', does not make you a good caring person. Locked within good spiritual knowledge is the potential for real spiritual change, but just 'knowing' is merely being a human library. Even the greatest information is meaningless, unless it has gone from knowledge to positive realization - to being acted upon inside you, and outside you, in a way that makes for a real and beneficial change in your life and the lives of others.

The teachings of the Children don't exist to be a mere library of knowledge. They exist to help you, and urge you, to actively change into an Unselfishly Loving being who is One with All. To that end, the teachers of the Children of the Law of One don't offer you mere knowledge - the authors of these teachings *have* water to share with you *also*.

"KNOW IT ALLS" AND SPIRITUAL EGO - WHO ME?

One day (during my first few weeks at the monastery), I went to the small meditation chamber as usual, to start a new course. But there was a sign hanging on the door that said:

"THE NEXT COURSE IS A SPECIAL ONE
JUST FOR THE UNFORTUNATE FEW -
IT IS **JUST** FOR 'KNOWLEDGEABLE KNOW IT ALLS'.
(SPIRITUAL INTELLECTUALS WHO ARE
'SPIRITUAL EGO DISADVANTAGED').
ALL OTHERS NEED NOT ATTEND."

I stood there puzzled for a moment, thinking about it. I eventually came to the conclusion that it must be a special course for some of the other novice monks. So I turned around and headed off for the library. Along the path, I ran into Zain. Literally. I ran into him. I wasn't watching where I was going, I was jogging, he was built like a brick wall, and walking the other way on the same path - and right for a head-on collision. After I apologized, he asked me where I was going.

"Aren't you scheduled to be attending a course right now?" He said.

I started to explain, "Yes..."

"Well it's *that* way." He pointed to the chamber, which was the opposite direction of where I had been going.

"No. I mean yes. I mean, I was, but it's some kind of remedial course for the spiritually disadvantaged novices or something."

"Spiritually disadvantaged?"

"Well it said something like that."

"It's only about 10 meters from here to there, why don't you WALK over and read it again, so you can explain it to me better? I don't understand."

So I hopped on back and read the sign again, memorized it, and then recited it to Zain word for word.

"You don't think that applies to you?" he said.

"Of course not. I don't think I know everything," I protested.

"Then why aren't you in there learning what you don't know?"

"Because it's not about knowledge, it says it's for those who think they 'know it all'."

"Do you know everything about your own spiritual ego and arrogance?"

"No, of course not."

"Then if you aren't aware of your own egotism, and you think that sign doesn't mean that you SHOULD attend that course, then all that can mean is that at least to some extent, you are a 'know it all'. True?"

Whoa. I had to think about that for a moment. This was worse than Zen paradoxes.

"I guess you might have a point there."

"Thank you for acknowledging my point."

"You're welcome."

So I attended the course, which as it turned out, was probably MORE for me than anyone else there.

And it may apply to you also.

"You have a great deal of spiritual knowledge, don't you?" Raga said to me.

"Yes. I have been studying since I was 13 years old," I said.

"Then why are you here?"

"Well... I..."

"Have you achieved enlightenment?"

"No. I don't think so."

"Oh, you would know if you did. You'd know it far more easily than knowing if you'd been struck by a bolt of lightning. And that's why you're here. That's why you are taking these courses, and why you have chosen a teacher, and why you are reading all those books in the library. Because you are still searching for enlightenment. If you had found it, you would not be on this plane, or you would be an Adept, and teaching others rather than reading books - even ancient texts. Because you would then truly 'know it all', at least spiritually speaking. You would have Universal Consciousness. You would not be struggling with your self, or being self-centered or selfish anymore. You would only Unselfishly Love."

I gulped. "I understand."

A NOTE FOR OUR READERS

There are basically two kinds of people reading this book (and some who are combinations of the two kinds). The first kind of person is just reading it because it is unusual, but perhaps somewhat interesting reading. That includes those who are fascinated with lost civilizations, lost history, and mysterious technology. But the other kind of reader is one who is more "into" spiritual knowledge, studies, practices, abilities, etc. What some call a spiritual "seeker". The remainder of this chapter, is really addressed to them, and you may want to skip to the next chapter.

SOMETHING TO THINK ABOUT.
A MESSAGE FOR THE SPIRITUAL SEEKER
OR SEEKER OF SPIRITUAL KNOWLEDGE

There are those of you reading this book right now, who have collected spiritual and metaphysical knowledge for many years, and been involved with various spiritual "paths", trends, or techniques. Some of you will read this book and say, "Yes, I already know," or, "It's redundant," or "I have heard these things before - I already know them, so this book is of little use to me".

I don't mean to offend you or belittle your knowledge or wisdom. But if you have thought such things, ask yourself the following questions before you read anymore of this book with that kind of attitude, or before you just "file these teachings away" with the rest of your knowledge.

Are you already "enlightened", or "Universally Conscious"? There are various definitions of that, so here's what we mean by that - If you have achieved what we call enlightenment, you have taken the controlling reins of your life from your selfish separate self, and handed them over to your higher self, and the Universal Spirit. Have you done that? Has Unselfish Love replaced selfishness in your day to day life? And if not, have you "dropped everything" and rearranged the priorities in your life with the goal of achieving these changes as fast as possible?

If the answer to the above is no, then the next question is, why? If you know the keys - why haven't you used them? If you don't know the keys, maybe somewhere in these pages something will click for you.

Like I said, I don't mean to be insulting, or offend you, I just want to help certain readers who might benefit from what I'm about to say. So please keep that in mind now, when I say this: While there are certain exceptions, if *you are already* "enlightened", it is very, very unlikely that you would even be reading this book right now. You would likely have no need or interest in reading this book, because you would have achieved all you need. The searching stops. Those who have attained enlightenment, Universal Consciousness, or whatever you want to call it, generally no longer read books about spiritual teachings or philosophy, because they are of no use to them - they don't need them anymore. And when you don't need the things you once read a book for anymore, you change to where your interest in them falls away. (You may still need books on plumbing, but that's a far more serious and interesting subject). It's not like being a doctor or something where you

36

have to keep up on the latest advances. Sure, you could say there are degrees of enlightenment, and you might read something to achieve a greater degree than you have. But there is one "biggy" enlightenment, that is like a light switch, and it's either on or off. So if you are reading this, and that "big" switch isn't turned on yet, for your own good, please put aside whatever you already know, just for a while at least. Even more importantly, please put aside any ego that could "get in your own way". This could prevent you from getting a seemingly insignificant "little piece of something" out of this book, that might help you become enlightened. Just read with an open mind, and see where this takes you.

Even if you were enlightened, and found a book that "sounds interesting", which is certainly possible, you wouldn't have the time to muse over it. When you become enlightened, you are very, very busy, helping *others* to attain the same freedom, peace, and Unselfish Love you have found, or you go on and ascend to a higher vibrational plane. If you stay, you "work" for the Universal Spirit, so to speak. You align your will, with Universal Will, and thus you become very busy doing your little part in the "Universal Flow". For example, at this point in my life, I don't read *any* spiritual or philosophical books. I no longer have the inclination, let alone the time. I did *need* to *write* this book though, because it was both my "job" to do so (in the service of the Universal Spirit), and my desire to help you. I've been forcing my self to write it while very ill, so I hope you get something out of it that will help you.

Of course, like I said earlier, there was a time when I had a *desperate desire* and need for spiritual and philosophical information, and I *did* read everything I could get my hands on. Maybe that's the stage you're at in your life and evolution. I was desperately trying to find some answers - searching for some truth. I found bits and pieces of truth, but that wasn't enough, so I kept reading in hopes of finding *consistent truth from one source.* And after all the books, rather than finding what I was looking for in a book, I found it in my personal true teacher instead. What irony, eh? But there was nothing like this book out there when I was voraciously reading to find something. Not to say that it should do the same for you, because you may have a very different path (people do have different legitimate paths). But if *I* had read *this* book you are reading now, it would have at least been the end of the "book" part of my search. Because it would have answered my questions, and all the pieces of truth would have fallen into place as a whole. But again, maybe these teachings aren't your spiritual "cup of tea", so to speak, and this book won't do the same for you that it would have for me. Maybe it's just one of your stepping stones along the way, and has some things you consider "bits" of truth. Or maybe you're not ready for it yet. Or maybe it is right for your path, but you're just afraid of the radical changes it would bring into your life, if you allowed yourself to realize and accept the truth - your truth. It's certainly not for me to say. But *in any case,* **if you are still reading this book - you are probably still looking for *something.*** And if so, just admit it. A long time ago I discovered the hard way that it doesn't pay to be egotistical, self-centered, or "cocky" about what you already know. Humility never killed anyone, but cockiness has. Humility will get you to peace of mind and "enlightenment" faster than anything else. A "spiritual ego" will prevent it.

So go ahead and let yourself go, and look very closely, with an open mind and heart. Spirituality is simple. Love is simple. Truth is simple. Enlightenment is simple. It's all basic stuff that we all really know deep inside somehow, yet most people don't live by it, and they've blocked it out. A book like this helps to remind you and inspire you. If you haven't "gotten it" yet, maybe this will help. If you think it's redundant, what can I say? How could it be *redundant,* if you haven't "gotten it" yet? I know I *needed* to hear certain things over and over, until I finally really *did* "hear it", "get it", and actually change.

Some of you may already know everything you need to become truly great beings who are a blessing to all, yet you don't do what you need to do to achieve that. Why? What's your "good reason"? I've seen them all. Some continue to cling to the lives they've built. Jobs. Friends. Associates. Have kids. Hold on to the familiar shore. There are all kinds of excuses to avoid real change. Some people even use the search for spiritual knowledge, or "sharing" of knowledge, or even the search for a spiritual path, as a means to actually *avoid* change. It doesn't matter what the excuse is. It doesn't matter if it is clinging to a house, car, friend, lover, family, job, city, or whatever. It also doesn't matter what you fear. We all die someday, and such specifics of your life become irrelevant. So it doesn't matter if your reason for not "going for it" is the *best reason in the world.* The BOTTOM LINE is this - *Whatever reason* is holding you back from what you need to do to achieve "enlightenment" and Oneness with God - **is not a *good enough* reason.**

The major arcanum of the ancient Tarot, represents the spiritual path from start to finish. The beginning, and end, of the path is represented by "The Fool". The fool lets go of everything in life, to begin his spiritual journey. He has packed a knapsack, is looking up, and is stepping off into the jaws of danger, trusting all to God. The fool has "shucked" his reasons for not getting on with his path. This is the kind of attitude one must have. And the knowledge of how to do it is not good enough. Knowledge can only point the way, *you are the one who must actually take the journey.*

Remember, "A little knowledge that *acts,* is worth infinitely more than much knowledge that is idle". - Kahlil Gibran

Chapter Four
One more Book?

Good question. It may not be "just one more book" to you. If you are a seeker of truth like I was, who has only been able to find bits and pieces among the books and paths you've found, hopefully this book will bring them all together for you now. In any case, if you believe that caring, kindness, and harmlessness are what true spirituality is all about (rather than spiritual teachings, philosophy, dogma, beliefs, or what religion you belong to), we welcome you as a friend, or welcome you home - because we believe the same thing.

"Hear the Essence, Not just the Words"

One day, Zain, who at this time, had been my personal teacher for a couple of years, asked me to come speak with him.

"Peniel, one day, too soon, you will need to leave the monastery. You are destined to do many things with your life, important things."

"What things, Father?"

"Teachers have different choices they can make with their lives, different directions. These have been called "rays", based on the 7. You can switch between rays however, if you choose. Only one ray is totally dedicated to being a true teacher. Perhaps, you will find a way to bridge the rays."

He outlined the choices I would have after I left, and discussed what each path, or "ray" as it was called, would entail. He also spoke of past lives, and why I had certain talents other than being a "spiritual" teacher, like with music, writing, diplomacy, political leadership, and strategy. He told me that among other things, I had been a great writer in some of my lifetimes, and I would soon be called on to write the most important works that I had ever done. I was to present the teachings of the Children of the Law of One to the world, openly, publically.

"Why?" I asked. "This has never been done before. Why now?"

"Because of the time my son. It is written. It is predestined. You need to write a book that will accurately reveal much of both the written and oral traditions, before the end of the millennium."

"The oral traditions also?"

"Yes. It is time."

From the earliest days of human life on Earth, some of the teachings of the Children of the Law of One have only been communicated orally, from teacher to student (an Adept monk to an elder monk). There were various reasons for this oral tradition. Special teachings were only imparted at a time when the student was ready to comprehend, and to truly real-ize it, and make it "part of them". Also, spiritual concepts, knowledge, and training can be very etheric, complex, and subtle. As opposed to written teachings, oral teaching allowed an "enlightened" teacher to instantly know if a miscommunication, or misunderstanding was taking place during the instruction. This way, if there was a misunderstanding of an important teaching, the Adept could correct it, or wait until the elder's consciousness grew more. All this insured that elders accurately grasped all aspects of vital spiritual training, and could thus pass this on to their future elder or novice monk students.

But now, I was being told that out of necessity, the exclusivity of certain oral traditions were being broken.

At the monastery, we were taught to be able to understand and communicate with people, regardless of culture or religion. But presenting oral teachings in written form for the first time, creates many problems with communication and understanding. Fortunately, I was given some special help for this task. In many of my interactions/courses with both elders, and my personal teacher, Zain, I was given special attention to re-awaken my knowledge and skills regarding the problems of written word communication. As a result, this book strives for unusual "clarity".

"Words are a very limited form of communication at best," Zain said. "They are often, and easily, misunderstood. This is because words are but symbols, the meaning of which is subject to interpretation by each individual from their own point of view. And individuals' points of view vary *wildly*.

When it comes to communication, written words are even worse. Since a writer cannot address every reader's individual point of view, individual interpretation, or reaction, it makes full and accurate communication via reading and writing *impossible*. Even speaking to someone in person, on a one on one basis, the essence of the desired communication may not take place, however, it is more likely to succeed. This is because a sensitive teacher, or speaker, can 'tune-in' to the individual's point of view, and thusly communicate in the manner that gives them the best chance of fully receiving the message being communicated. But even so, communication is still very difficult. Have you ever found yourself saying, 'That's not what I meant.'?"

I understood instantly. It all came back to me.

"Using the word 'self', or 'ego' is a good example of a common verbal communication problem that can be corrected for, when speaking in person, 'one-on-one'. These words can mean many different things to different people. Ego, for example, means a negative personality trait to some - but it means the essence of being, or soul to some - it means the strength of personality to some, etc. 'Self' can mean the Inner Being to some, and can mean the essence of selfishness to others. So personal communication is difficult enough, but when words are written, there is no chance to correct misunderstandings or clarify, if they are misunderstood."

So please keep this in mind if you disagree with what you read - it may not even mean what it seems to mean.

THE WHOLE TRUTH

Zain brought me over to the library, and had Gabriel, the Adept who was the keeper of the library, discuss more of the particular problems with writing spiritual teachings.

"In addition to the difficulties of communication with words, there are special problems involved with conveying spiritual concepts and Universal truths. It is written that because of the duality of the plane we exist in here on Earth, and the limitations of our ability to really understand the infinite Oneness that is the Universe, the closest we can get to ultimate truth, is still only half-true. That means that the highest truths I can really explain to you here, even in person, are still half-untrue. Thus if you try, you can find another half-truth that conflicts with it, and argue the truth of either of them. For instance, it can be truthfully argued that our future is pre-destined. It can also be truthfully argued that we can change the future. They are totally opposing concepts, which seem to make the opposite concept impossible to be true. Such opposing true concepts are called a paradox. Paradoxes contain seemingly conflicting half-truths, that are true in and of themselves, and while one truth may seem to make the other impossible to be true, the greatest truth is actually revealed when both half-truths are understood as a whole, even though that doesn't necessarily make sense when analyzed logically. Since paradoxes often contain the greater truth within their conflicting half-truths, they are the closest thing to full truth that we can convey with intellectual minds. Yet they cannot really be understood with the intellectual mind. A paradox must be intuitively, or spiritually grasped and understood."

"I understand what you mean, it is similar to a concept in a book I read before I came here. They called the total understanding of something 'groking'."

"Groking? Yes, there is a need for a good English word for it, and I suppose we can use that. We should have that book brought here to the library perhaps. But few people do 'groking'. Many people choose to believe or focus on one concept within a paradox, over the other. Thus they lose the whole truth. For instance, in regards to the future, they may be either fatalists (thinking all things are destined), or they may believe the future is totally unwritten. As we know, neither are true, and both are true."

Zain interjected. "You should grasp and accept a paradox intuitively, ...it cannot be truly grasped with only the intellect. Thus, an Adept understands that both concepts are true simultaneously. For instance, regarding the particular paradox Gabriel was using as an example, we simultaneously know that after something has happened, what has happened was destined to happen - after all, it *did* happen, *period*. That is absolutely true, is it not? Yet we also simultaneously know that through free will everyone alters and creates the future, *period*. That too, is absolutely true, is it not? Each concept opposes the other. It would seem that *they cannot both be true, yet they are.* Even though it may not be logical, *intuitively* having both beliefs simultaneously allows us to understand the broadest truth about events that may take place in the future.

As far as totally pure ultimate truth, we can only really 'get it' when we are out-of-body, in a higher spiritual consciousness that *knows,* not just intellectually thinks it understands."

Words can be Stepping Stones or Sinking Sand

I said, "So how can I possibly represent such paradoxes, and present the true teachings of the Atlantean Children of the Law of One?"

Gabriel responded. "Regardless of the problems of written communication, the times require it. And even though it is not the *best* way to communicate and 'reach' people, the One/Universal Spirit/God *can* be expressed in many ways, including words. Those who can intuitively interpret the meaning behind the words, may be 'kindled', and awaken to the Spirit within them when they hear the words brought forth by same. I know *I* have read certain inspiring words that 'rang a bell of truth' within me, as have all of us here."

WHAT KIND OF WORLD DO *YOU* WANT TO LIVE IN?

According to the teachings of the Atlantean Children of the Law of One, Universal Principles dictate that the kind of world you live in, and the creation of your future world is all up to you. It is entirely your choice, and in your power to change - all by just making changes in yourself.

Gabriel said, "You need to include this concept in with the teachings Peniel - tell the people of the world this: Before any teachings or path can help you, you need to understand a simple, basic, preliminary truth, and make some important decisions."

[Author's note: I will repeat the following teaching again later in the book, but it is so important, and such a fundamental issue, that I think it should be included here also.]

"The first thing you need to do is ask yourself a question, think about it well and seriously, and then make some choices and commitments. Here's the big, yet simple, question: 'What kind of world do you want to live in?' Once you decide that, you can achieve it. Here is the incredible, but true, 'deal' we have in the Universe: If you want to live in a good world, then be good. A paradisiacal one? Then be a paradisiacal being. It sounds simple doesn't it? It is beautifully simple, but it does work, and it's based on sound scientific principles, and Universal Principles."

"Which principles Gabriel? I assume we are talking about science-magic?"

"Aren't we always in *some* way or another? Isn't that what creation is?

Let me give you an excellent example of this vitally important principle. An example that has been used by our ancestors for ages, and one that you will no doubt want to use for *your* students some day.

You've worked in the kitchen, yes?" He asked, while looking at me with a deep and serious stare.

"Yes."

"You have seen how oil & water (or oil & vinegar) separate, even if you try to mix them?"

"Yes, they don't mix well, and even at that, they don't remain mixed for long."

"Do you know why?" I shrugged, letting him quickly go on to explain the important point I knew he wanted to make. "It's simply because they have different *natures*, and they each naturally 'gravitate' to their own nature. We are no different. There are 'Laws of physics' that dictate this, but behind them is an even more primary Universal Law, or Principle. As you attain higher consciousness, you will come to understand that the same Universal Principle that makes oil and water separate and find their own levels, also applies to people, *and* even their 'essence', 'spirits', or 'souls'. Every individual, will *ultimately* end up in the kind of world they belong in, with others like them. So if you want to live in a world of Unselfishly Loving people who are kind, and care about each other, you simply need to be like one of those people - or change to become one."

"That's easier said than done," I said.

Zain interrupted. "There may be trials and tribulations as you change inside to become a better person, but ultimately, it will be done, if it is your will to do so."

Gabriel added, "All you need to do is persevere, and you will attain your goal. That's all. Just persevere."

"That's it?"

Zain went on to give me more details of the principles. "The world outside you will change according to the changes you make within you. This happens in small ways, and big ways. For example, if you are a drug addict or alcoholic, you usually have friends that are the same way, and a certain 'lifestyle' that accompa-

42

nies who you are and how you are. The reason you are a drug addict is something internal. If you change inside to where you are no longer an addict, you will find that without any effort on your part, you will lose, or drift away from, your old friends, and soon you will have new friends. It's also likely your job and housing situations will change also. I have seen people raised in ghettos full of drugs, hatred, envy and crime, who left it all behind to live good and productive lives. It wasn't because of 'the breaks' they got, or the cards life dealt them - they didn't have any advantages different from anyone else in the ghetto. They transcended their environment, and their environment changed - all because of how they were inside, or changed to be inside, and the actions/choices they made because of their internal disposition. This also happens with spiritual changes. You must have experienced it yourself already Peniel. Didn't you find that your friends actually changed as you changed, even before coming here?"

"Yes, that's true."

"Wait until you leave the monastery and meet them again. You'll find the common bonds you had with people you knew, don't exist anymore, and soon, those people don't exist in your life either. Even ordinary people experience this. If they really change in consciousness, their old friends drop out of their lives. And new friends who are on a similar 'level' or path, come into their lives. You may still have your old friends in your life somehow, but they aren't in your life in the same way. The example of addicts was just an extreme one - it happens in subtle ways too.

Of course, the ultimate change is enlightenment, and gaining Universal Consciousness. As a result of *that* extreme of an internal change, *everything* in your life will change *radically*. And it goes beyond the physical boundaries of your life. Also, when you attain Universal Consciousness, you will no longer be a prisoner to the physical plane. You can come and go. And when your physical life is over, you can *choose* to come back to help others, or ascend to a paradisiacal spiritual existence. It's all up to you. Everyone's own world is all up to them, from their immediate little world, to the Universal plane they exist in."

And don't think it is such an impossible task to achieve enlightenment. Start by just becoming a really good person. Remember Enoch's examples of imaginary worlds #1 and 2 in the last chapter. If you want to change your life for the better, just become like the decent person Enoch used in his example of imaginary world #2. You can certainly change that much, can't you? Does it sound so out of reach for you to just become a really good person? Of course it isn't. Well, if you can achieve that, becoming enlightened is then just one step further.

THE PURPOSE OF PRESENTING THE TEACHINGS

We present these teachings with the hope that they will move and inspire you to walk (or continue to walk) a path of Oneness with the Universe, a path of Unselfish Love, regardless of your denomination or other beliefs. And to those ends, as you read, if you don't understand something, or you disagree with something, *please* just disregard it temporarily - especially if it "turns you off", or your feelings of Unselfish Love seem to shut down. If you can, expand your point of view somehow - perhaps with meditation if you know how to do any, and contemplate the problem from a higher state. If that is not possible, or you still disagree or want clarification, please contact us by Email, or letter, and tell us your problem with it. Give *us* a chance to understand your point of view, and your problem with it. It may mean something other than it seems to you, it may not - but whatever the case may be, **nothing** is so important that it should make walls between us and dam the flow of our Love. Don't you agree?

A Book with a Built-in Sequel!

This book is divided into two parts. The first part will primarily contain some of my personal experiences, lessons, and discussions with teachers at the monastery. And in that format, it will present the teachings of Atlantis (actually the positive spiritual teachings of Atlantis, which are the teachings of the Atlantean Children of the Law of One). The teachings cover a wide variety of spiritual and metaphysical subjects. It will also include direct translations of excerpts from a variety of the ancient texts.

An Instruction Manual for Life as citizens of the Universe (that got lost in a drawer somewhere).

The teachings contain "reflections" of the Universal Spirit, including Universal Laws, and principles of the Spirit's manifestation and order in life. They can, therefore, be used as a kind of "manual" for, or "schematic" of, our relationship with it all. It can be something to help those who wish to get directly back in touch with God, attain peace of mind, and become truly kind, caring beings.

The second part of the book gives actual instruction in the Children's training system of daily mind and energy exercises, techniques, and meditations. The purpose of this training system was to help the Children maintain harmony and balance of the spiritual, mental, and physical aspects of their being, and help them directly experience Oneness with God. They were also used to re-achieve that balance, and that "connection", if it had become lost. This same system was used in Atlantis, and is still being used today by Children of the Law of One around the world.

Part two also provides you with amazing, yet practical uses for some of the Children's legendary Atlantean vibrational technology. You may have heard that Atlanteans were well versed in the advanced use of color and sound for healing and consciousness altering. While we obviously can't teach you all the complex details of this science here, experts in Atlantean vibrational technology from the Children of the Law of One created it, and have continued to use it for thousands of years. Now, for the first time, some of the consciousness raising vibrational sounds are available to the public. We have put specific versions of these vibrational sounds on CD's & tapes. When used properly, according to the directions in part two of this book, they can dramatically aid in helping you change yourself, and improve your life. The "how to" section gives specific instructions for accessing and reprogramming your subconscious mind through the use of the special sound vibrations, by combining them with verbal induction/guided meditation/affirmation techniques. We wanted to include the recording packaged with the book, but we were told it should not be done because some bookstores would not carry it then. So the instructions for ordering the vibrational sounds are in the back of the book. The back of the book also has instructions for ordering a video which teaches our style of Yoga and our ancient energy techniques.

Why the Book?

Besides the reasons I've already given, ours is an esoteric path that has been deliberately kept relatively unknown for some time. But as mentioned earlier, this time was prophesied - it is the time to publically reveal many things, including the ancient history, teachings, and future prophecy. You are about to read about *one* of the reasons that the book is being published now - it is also about another reason - one of the prophetic "signs" that it was time to make the teachings public.

Even though the location of our Tibetan monastery was secret, isolated, and so well hidden that it didn't even show up on satellite photos, years ago it was attacked. All the monks and householders who were in the Tibetan monastery at the time were killed. Some who were in the area, but not at the monastery at the time, survived. Monks in other places around the world were also attacked and murdered (I discuss this whole issue in more detail elsewhere). This great loss to the world went unnoticed by most, yet its significance and impact will ultimately be felt in many ways, and has already begun over the years.

By the time you read this, I may be gone also. I was asked to consider leading a rebuilding effort of the Tibetan monastery by other surviving monks. But I am much older than when I was last there, and was doubtful that my body could even withstand the trip - but if it was the will of God, I would do it somehow. After the attacks, I became the eldest teacher and "head" of our order, and thus was left with a great deal of responsibility. So before deciding, I went into deep contemplation meditation, to seek guidance. The choice was left to me, but I was reminded of my discussions with Zain when I was young, when he told me I would be writing this book.

"Son, it is written that the day will come when the 'land of the teachers will be desecrated'. Then you will know it is time to begin your writing, to make the teachings public. A new order in the world is to begin then. There will be a new order of darkness, and a new order of light. You must initiate and herald the new order of light." I now know this new order of light involves the kindling of a very old idea. It involves many people waking up to, and recognizing the vital importance of, "the Golden Rule" (and really working to apply it in their lives). The Golden Rule (which is essentially just "Be Unselfishly Loving"), is so basic and simple, it has often been overlooked. Yes, it's an old concept. But IT IS THE MOST IMPORTANT SPIRITUAL TEACHING IN THE WORLD. In fact, it is at the core of the ancient teachings. Unfortunately, even though the *idea* has been around forever (and most everyone "knows" of it), the "masses" have never really "caught on" to it, "realized" its true meaning and significance. Thus, it has never been implemented in most people's lives. Yet it is the very crux of true spirituality for all people regardless of faith, or lack of faith. Even most Christians, who were given the Golden Rule as their ONLY COMMANDMENT by Jesus, haven't "gotten it", nor implemented it in their lives. But the Golden Rule has remained through time, a beautiful spiritual "buried treasure" patiently waiting to be found and shared. And like a smile, it is is Universal, crossing all barriers of language, culture, and religion - every good person on Earth, regardless of other beliefs, agrees with it, and can find common ground in it. Thus we chose the name Golden Rule Organization ("GRO") for the "umbrella" under which many related projects are underway or planned. The "Golden Rule Workbook" we have written, is the perfect vehicle for all those who believe Unselfish Love and its offspring should take priority to any other belief, but who are not ready for the total sacrifices demanded by monasticism, or other such "full-blown" spiritual lifestyles. The book gives a detailed program for improving your life and relationships by using unselfish love, and other techniques. It also tells you how you can set up Golden Rule groups that can meet weekly (or whatever) for purposes of helping each other grow. (Those who are interested in being involved, networking, or becoming part of a fellowship in their area, are welcome to contact us).

Getting back to the rebuilding issue, after contemplative meditation over the whole matter, it seemed pointless to rebuild in Tibet. Elsewhere, yes, Tibet, no. A new era was at hand, the signs were everywhere. The order had a new destiny, so I declined to rebuild there. Unfortunately, while my decision was honored by the elders, some novice monks, who's sentiment overwhelmed their higher senses, launched their own rebuilding effort. It failed tragically, and ended in more deaths.

It is clear to me that a great change is upon the people of this world, and *some of* the traditional ways of the Children are past and over. However new ones must rise from the ashes of the old, and we continue to keep the most important teachings and traditions alive. We will support and teach anything that makes for more Unselfish Love, caring, kindness, and unselfishness, and that assists the return to Oneness with the Universal Spirit. And in any case, the essence will always live on. You can destroy countries, cities, homes, families, bodies, minds, even entire worlds - but the soul and Love always survive and go on.

While most people these days are completely "out of touch" with nature and the Universal Spirit/God/the One, some have suffered enough to begin looking for a way out of the darkness. There have always been teachers to help those who were ready to find the way out, to find the Universal Spirit inside themselves. But these are unusual times, and few teachers are left. Thus this book is also written as a preliminary aid, to help illuminate those seeking the light of truth and Unselfish Love - and as a way to maximize the resources of light, and continue making it available to all who are in need, and are ready. In the chapter on monasticism, we'll discuss other changes and plans to keep the work going.

46

Chapter Five
The "Religion" of Atlantis

Religion for Religion's sake

As I said earlier, part of our training at the monastery was to learn about the various cultures and religions of the world, so many of my earliest courses as a novice monk were about religions. At the time, as typical with my young ego, I thought I already knew all there was to know about the subject, but there was really far more to it than I thought. The following chapter is a recollection of a course given by elder Noah, regarding the Atlantean, and later, teachings about religion.

"There are a variety of reasons that can be behind the founding of a religion - some are good, and many are bad. Thus both good and bad religions have been created. There are religions that started as a means for worship. Some to help people improve themselves spiritually or otherwise. Others were specifically created just to control and have power over the people. But even many religions that started with good intentions, degenerated over time into self-serving power structures whose main function was to control people, and make money."

"How do they control people, other than by peer pressure and trying to convince someone about something with a sermon?"

"They vary in their methods and functions. Most offer their members personal salvation through following the religion's tenets (beliefs, rituals, and dogma). And thus, they insinuate you will not find God or salvation, if you don't follow their particular religion.

Most also aim to fill an emotional or psychological need in people's hearts and minds. They generally each have their own 'dogma' - answers to spiritual questions about God, who we are, and the rules that we should live by.

Some religions control by using people's insecurity, and have even been formed based on the insecurity of an ignorant society. Some were based on fear. There is the fear of hell (religion as 'fire insurance'). There is the fear of God. Which..."

"What exactly do you mean?" I said. (I was insensitively interrupting him before he was about to explain anyway).

"I was just getting to that. It is religion that basically comes from the idea of needing to worship and serve a God, or some kind of powerful supreme being, because you actually *need* to *fear* Him if you don't - because He is all powerful and has negative emotional attributes, commits atrocities when angry or jealous, and allows great suffering and disasters when He could easily stop them."

"So Noah, what you're saying is worshipping that kind of God is not much different than being respectful to, and paying homage and taxes to, an evil king, or warlord of the realm, because if you don't, he may come burn your hut or your fields, or kill you or your family, rape your wife, etc.."

"That's an interesting and insightful analogy. Yes, in fact, that is precisely what many religions did, and how they used the concept of God. But as opposed to being just a King or a warlord, people were told it was an all-powerful being, like a super powered evil alien from outer-space, bent on taking over and controlling all the people of this planet Earth.

And of course the next step in such a religion, is dealing with the abusive power of its leaders. The religion's leaders, being self-appointed representatives of such a God, would even torture and burn people alive for not 'believing', or behaving precisely as they dictated, or precisely as the 'God' they represented, dictated that they live. Millions of people have been murdered and tortured as the result of this."

"Like the inquisition?"

"Let's just say for now that people throughout time, and of various religions, have used their particular God, or even their particular 'name' for their God, as an excuse to control, torture, and murder. That's one reason we prefer to call God 'the Universal Spirit', rather than anything that personalizes, or segregates the concept.

But there have been legitimate, or sincere reasons and beginnings for religions too.

Some have been formed based on faith, or the moral ideas of the religion's founder. Some have been based on visions or insights of a great spiritual teacher (unfortunately, when the founding visionary dies, usually dogma and the 'religion' take over). Others provide a more direct means for personal salvation, within the framework of dogma."

"How and why was the religion of the Children of the Law of One started?"

A Religion that is Not a Religion

Noah paused, and stroked his beard for a moment.

"While the Children of the Law of One is a spiritual 'way', and also a monastic order, I suppose you could say it is somewhat like a religion. But, it is *not* a religion in a couple of very important ways. To start with, none of the above reasons were behind the founding of the Children, nor do they play a part in what they teach. There is no control. Not even an attempt to influence, only to educate and reflect the truth.

To understand why the Children of the Law of One was created, and what their foundations are, we need to go back to the beginnings of human life on Earth."

Ooooo, it sounded like we were going to get into some more interesting stuff.

"Please go on," I said.

"I will, just give me a moment." More "beard-stroking meditation" ensued, as he prepared himself to tell us the story.

The Fall

This book devotes an entire chapter to the history of the Children of the Law of One, from its Genesis prior to Atlantis, to the present, directly translated from the ancient texts, and my accounts of recent developments. But in the following segment, Noah just briefly describes the specific aspects of that history which led to the creation of the Children. You've heard Darwin, you've heard Genesis. Now you are about to hear another theory, the first one that made sense to me. And according to the Atlantean teachings, Genesis is actually a simplified, loose allegory, based on this.

"The historical records start with the premise that there is One Great Being

48

(God/Universal Spirit) that is All things, including the Universe itself. It divides/multiplies within itself to create us, thus, our history begins with all of us (humans) essentially being part of, and One with God. The records describe us as being spiritual or 'angelic' beings, free to roam, create, and enjoy the Universe. The teachings go on to say that our beginnings on Earth, came in two steps - a 'first wave', and 'second wave' of 'human' (& semi-human) materialization into physical bodies on Earth. At the time, we had the ability to instantly alter our vibration, and instantly create anything we desired, with a mere thought. It was in this way that we 'thought ourselves' into matter, into material existence on Earth. Which began our fall from our angelic state, and Oneness with God.

You have probably heard of mythological beings such as the Minotaur, Centaur, Mermaid, etc.. The Minotaur, had a bull's head and a human body, the Centaur, a human head and torso with a horse's body. You may also have seen pictures of Egyptian 'gods' with animal heads and human bodies, or animal bodies and human heads (like the Sphinx). In the Pacific regions, ancient drawings and carvings of 'bird headed' humans can be found on both sides of the ocean. Why do you think so much of this exists? Many legends and myths have some foundation in fact, and this is no exception. The ancient teachings from Atlantis, reveal that such creatures did indeed exist, and that their origins were not what you might expect - they were the fallen angelic beings from the 'first wave' of materialization on Earth."

"Fallen angels??? You mean like Lucifer?"

"Well, yes and no. You have a misconception of sorts. That is a personalized concept from the allegory. The first wave of materialization was a terrible mistake [Author's note: this will be explained in greater detail in the history chapter]. The first wave beings materialized as partly human/partly animal creatures. This is why in the story of Lucifer, or the various creatures that were called 'devils' or demons or whatever, appear as horned, cloven hoofed creatures with tails - the fact is, they were part goat. This is why goats have become associated with the devil also. But evil, is an entirely different matter. Think not that evil does not exist. But true evil, disguises itself, and points the finger at innocents."

"So Lucifer was not evil?"

"Not initially. The stories you have heard have become terribly mixed up. Even the bible originally paints him as a great angel. But there was no 'rebellion' or defiance against the will of God until AFTER this fall, not prior to the fall as is often depicted. It was just a mistake at first. Try telling one person in the meeting hall a story, and ask him to repeat it quietly to the next, and the next person to the next, until it comes back to you. By the time you hear your original story, it will not even be recognizable. That is why our teaching methods are so stringent. We *must* keep the truth straight, and consistent, and this has been assured by our forebearers.

Getting back to the primary teaching today, there were more 'fallen angels' than Lucifer. And they took many different part animal forms. For ease of description we call the part human, part animal beings that fell into physical vibration or matter, during the 'first wave' of materialization, 'humanimals'. As soon as the first wave beings materialized in their 'humanimal' bodies, they suffered a great 'fall' in vibration from their previous spiritual, angelic state of existence. They instantly experienced a near total loss of consciousness, awareness, and intelligence. In less than the twinkling of an eye, the consciousness that just moments before, had

49

encompassed the entire Universe, and experienced Oneness with the Universal Spirit/God, was virtually gone. The new limited consciousness of these pitiful creatures, 'trapped' them on the physical plane of the Earth, where they had to live in ignorance, with their animal-like intelligence and awareness. They were suddenly isolated from Universal/God Consciousness, and trapped in the lonely anguish of 'separate' consciousness. This separate consciousness gave birth to a sort of separate free will, which was ignorantly used selfishly, rather than in harmony with the will of God. Ultimately, they would also be trapped in slavery. Evil is spawned by selfishness, but later, even greater degrees of evil came about (which we will discuss more later). Yet *all* selfishness and evil, has since mistakenly been blamed on these poor unfortunate 'first waver humanimals'. To be sure, some had horns, and tails, and cloven hoofs - but they have been used as 'scape goats', and diversions, in order for others, including regular humans, to avoid taking personal responsibility for the real evil, the real devil, which is the selfishness living inside each human who maintains separate consciousness from the Oneness of God."

Other novice monks in the class, including me, immediately responded with a flurry of questions.

"What do you mean?"

"How can this be?"

"How did it happen?"

"Slow *down,*" Noah said. "One question at a time please. All will be answered in time.

Remember, we were spirits *only*. Very 'fine', 'high-frequency' vibrational beings, with no experience in this physical realm. These humanimals came upon their terrible fate because of a rapid, uncontrolled slowing down of their vibrational frequencies, for purposes of materialization of their spiritual selves into the material plane of the Earth. It occurred in a way that cut them off from their normal consciousness, like changing the dials on a radio to an area of radio frequency that had nothing to receive. Their 'internal radio' of consciousness, was no longer 'tuned in' to God. It was a materialization that went too far, too deep, into the dense, slow vibrations of the physical plane. When the finer frequencies were 'cut off', they were left 'cut off' from God and the rest of spiritual creation, and thus the consciousness of the Oneness of the Universe - the consciousness of God - the Universal Spirit. This left them with only a 'separate self consciousness', that lost touch with 'Oneness Consciousness', or 'Universal Consciousness'.

"Then why aren't all of us still lost, and out of touch with God?"

"A couple of reasons. Some of us did not make this 'fall'. Those who didn't fall, were still in their angelic state, and watched all this happen to the first wavers. Our grand master [Author's note: later known as Jesus in his last life on Earth], organized and led a rescue mission. With their great Love and compassion, many of the other angelic beings who had not 'fallen', decided to help the trapped first wavers, even at great risk of the same fate. They became what we call the 'second wavers'.

The second wavers knew they could only help the first wavers, if they too, materialized in forms that would allow them to work on the lost souls (the humanimal creatures) in their own physical form and dimension. And the grand master and various angelic volunteers, knew that in order to do that, it would require lowering their *own* vibration, towards that of the physical plane, and subsequently lowering their consciousness to some extent. They knew this was dangerous, and that they had to be very careful how they did this, and be careful about how deeply they went into physical matter, or they too would become trapped in limited consciousness just as the humanimals were. Thus the ancient Atlantean teachings describe how this second wave, became the first *consciously controlled* thought projection, or materialization, of modern 'human' life on Earth (or at least they eventually became modern humans as they gradually solidified into the material plane from their spiritual 'angelic' state). The ape-like early human form was actually just eventually *chosen* by second wavers as the preferred type of physical vehicle to *model themselves after,* because it allowed for the greatest control and manipulation in the physical plane, that would be required to help the first wavers. That is why scientists cannot find the 'missing link' - because there simply is none. Because while evolutionary change certainly does exist, our present existence on Earth did not involve evolving for millions of years from apes."

Again, if the above theory of creation that is offered by the ancient Atlantean teachings, is disagreeable to you - no "biggy", that's OK. There are all kinds of theories of creation, that people are VERY intense and pushy about. We aren't.

Scientists are *supposed to* stay *objective,* and stick to proven *facts,* and if they can't present *absolutely proven facts,* they are *supposed to* present their ideas as "theories", and *only* as "theories". Yet many alleged "scientists", have *sneakily* insinuated, and taught the *"theory" of evolution* of humans from apes, *as FACT,* even when they have a huge gap, a huge "missing link" in their "theory"- they have not found a direct ancestral lineage of modern man, that connects the whole evolution of apes and "cave men" types of semi-ape, semi-humans. And on the flip side of the evolutionist theories, many religions have followers, and thus money and power at stake. Unlike both of those categories, we have nothing at stake, nothing to prove, nothing to lose or gain since we don't make money or get power from the teachings we present. While we have had personally viewed it as an historical, written record, you are welcome to "take them or leave them". We really, really don't care if you believe the concepts of history or creation presented in this book, or not. If it "rings the bell of truth" for you, fine. If it doesn't, that's OK too. We obviously can't prove ancient history, nor do we feel it is important. It isn't important. We really, truly, don't care about any of those intellectual ideas, theories, or concepts. We DO care about the reality of human life and suffering, NOW. The things that really impact everyone's lives on Earth. So what *we* want, and what we really care about, is simply for everyone to be kind, caring, compassionate, and harmless. Is it really too much to ask even if you believe you are descended from an ape? Is it really too much to ask if you believe God created you out of Adam's rib? Who cares? We don't think it's too much to ask. Regardless of what you believe, don't believe, or have faith in, or don't have faith in. The same goes for everything else you read in this book - who cares? Be nice. Let's all be real caring friends and family.

The Creation of The Children of the Law of One

Before Noah could catch his breath, I began my eager questioning again, "So the second wave of materialization began as a 'rescue' operation of sorts - to save the 'humanimal' beings who 'fell' in the first wave? Please tell me more about who organized this, and how could they do anything about it?"

"Who, we will discuss later. Please just let me finish relating this part of the teachings.

In order to accomplish this 'rescue' as you called it, two things had to be done. One, methods had to be devised that would help the humanimals REGAIN their spiritual consciousness and awareness of Oneness with the Universal Spirit; and two, methods had to be devised for the second wavers to MAINTAIN their spiritual consciousness and awareness of Oneness with the Universal Spirit. To both these ends, second wave beings founded the spiritual path of the Children of the Law of One, and created the methods and teachings that are still in use, and valid, today.

Thus, the spiritual order of the Children of the Law of One was founded with a very specific and unique purpose. And while this order included aspects of what would later become numerous 'religions', the Children of the Law of One was unlike any other religion that would ever appear on Earth. And remains so. It was NOT created to fill a need in people's hearts and minds, NOR to strike fear into their hearts, NOR to worship anyone or anything, NOR to answer the spiritual questions that arose in the spiritually ignorant masses, NOR to control those masses. It was created before all those issues even existed."

"So the Children are not really a religion in a sense?"

"No. By many modern definitions, it could be considered such. But again, the whole point of the Children's materialization was to rescue their 'trapped' kin, by returning the first wavers to their angelic state of existence and awareness (Universal Consciousness). Thus the whole point of the Children's spiritual path, was to be able to enter the material plane so they could help the first wavers, while maintaining their own spiritual consciousness and angelic state, so they wouldn't get trapped also. If I may continue.

Falling Again

As the second wave rescue mission gradually descended into materiality and human form, some of them, lured by selfish desires, turned away from the Children's spiritual path. They then lost spiritual awareness, and separated from Oneness with God. Ultimately, this division created two 'religious' or 'philosophical' groups in Atlantis with very different purposes and 'politics' - the Sons of Belial and the Children of the Law of One.

The Sons of Belial mimicked the Children in many ways, even in the sense of being 'spiritual' or 'religious'. But their 'religious practices' were mockeries of true spirituality - phony, empty, and self-serving. They would use 'prayer' and visualization to attain whatever they wanted, and they turned a blind eye to what the repercussions of getting what they wanted would have on others. Some popular present-day religions, are offspring of the Belialian religion. And then there are the secret societies that still practice their original ways.

In Atlantis, the most significant contention between the Children and the Belialians was over what to do about the humanimals. The humanimals were easily controlled by the powers of a second waver's mind, and they could be made to do anything just through visualization. Since the Belialians had turned away from their awareness of Oneness with God in favor of selfishness, they wanted to use the 'humanimals' as 'pet slaves'. The Children, however, still wanted to help return the humanimals to their higher state of consciousness. Thus the Children also became 'activists', and their goal as a group 'movement' was still to free their trapped kin, but now they also had to contend with other SECOND wavers who had 'gone bad'."

"So Noah, did the Children win out over the Belialians - there aren't any humanimals walking the Earth any more, right? Were they all killed, or rescued?"

"I'll answer that in a moment, but first let me say that even the best of the Children of the Law of One, eventually succumbed to some degree, to the separation from the Universal Spirit. But that is another story, which involves the allegory of Adam & Eve.

"Now, to answer your question, while part of the Children's goal was eventually achieved (the humanimals were freed from their animal entanglement after the destruction of Atlantis), freedom from darkness and slavery has not been fully accomplished. The battle continues. As far as the first wavers go, reincarnated humanimals still walk the Earth in normal human bodies - you have seen them. If you are observant, you can see subtle animal traits, mannerisms, or facial appearances on many of the people of the world. But humanimals or not, the age old struggle between the Children and the Belialians - the struggle of freedom against slavery, still continues. These days slavery can be in many forms, traditional, economic, socio-political oppression, imprisonment, and mental programming. The world is basically populated by five groups, the Children, Belialians, reincarnated "lost soul" first and second wavers, and the enlightened. Most from both the first and second waves, are still separate in consciousness from the Universal Spirit. That makes them easy prey for the Belialians, and they either become their pawns in one way or another, or their slaves in one way or another. *[Author's note - In previous editions of this book, the only description of Belialians was that of the old teachings. This left many people confused about who and what they were, and how they look in modern times. Belialians are not some kind of genetic creatures who have physically lived and survived for thousands of years. Like all of us, they have continued to reincarnate, and live in modern human bodies. But they are so evil, those of us who are sensitive to it can sense or feel that. This can sometimes even be physically or intuitively seen as being reptilian-like, or as the old teachings call it, "lizard-like". But whether you see or sense this yourself, you can know them by their agenda. Lifetime after lifetime, they maintain their maniacal drive for power and agenda of slavery and domination. Many of them are the people who run the world. The upper echelon are the real power people pulling the strings behind the scenes. Like Initiate monks of the Children, the higher level Belialians are totally conscious and aware of who they are, and what they are doing. The middle and lower echelon are sometimes in the forefront, or in the public eye, functioning as political, military or business leaders who are apparently not being told what to do - yet they really are. Of course some leaders are just pawns, and not consciously aware of who they serve (and wouldn't care anyway). Belialians are usually born to rich and powerful families who are already of the Belialian heritage, and their families train them and continue to pass on their tradition. They go to the best schools and join the "right" "special" fraternities and sororities. They are trained in the ways of using visualization and ritual to practice their dark magic. They always want more money and power. They want to maintain economic slavery and child labor slavery in the world, and even worse. They want a state of total monitoring and control of all people (and they have been making great strides in this). They will use physical force to dominate and control if necessary, but mental programming through education, media, peer pressure, or other means, has been extremely successful - and parents continue to pass their own programming on to their children also. Examine world history and you see these struggles continuing through time - entire groups of evil oppressors trying to enslave. We have continued to fight them, and they continue to fight us. Just as many of the scientific advances have come from reincarnated Atlantean scientists, so too have those with thirst for power and control at any cost, come from reincarnated Belialians. They continue to develop more sophisticated ways to keep people under their control. So how do you identify them? Again, you can feel it, and sometimes see it when you look into their eyes. But anyone whose agenda is control of others, is either Belialian, or one of their pawns. They care only about themselves and would be willing to harm anyone or even everyone on the planet if it helps them get more power - and they can do this all with a big smile and warm handshake (which many people "buy" into as being a "nice" person). Ask yourself if this could be true, and feel the response from your inner voice.]* Noah continues:

So our 'religion', and work, continues on. And now, because of the time and situation, you [he pointed at me!], will soon be publicly revealing the teachings of the Children, and heralding the coming spiritual changes.

Remember, because of the unique nature and purity of the Atlantean Children's spiritual way, it is as valuable today as it was then. Their teachings and methods can help anyone return to the Universal Spirit, achieve enlightenment, and live in harmony with Universal Law & Universal Will."

"Thank you Noah."

"It was my honor to help you." And with that, he bowed and kissed my hand with the feeling of love and respect that one might only expect to see offered to his teacher, or the head of the order. It was rather shocking to me, because I felt I wasn't worthy of it, didn't deserve it, and that it wasn't appropriate for someone of my humble station. But he was honoring who I was inside, which at the time, I didn't really see in myself (even though my ego thought it did). Nevertheless, it was there, just waiting to manifest. *[Author's note: Now, as I deal with my students and others, I also see who they really are inside - their potential - and support that. We relate to that as well as their present level of consciousness. To reinforce and strengthen the Inner Being, while attacking and starving the selfish separate self, is our constant function and duty].* Then Noah put his hands together and made a gesture of spiritual respect to the other novice monks in the chamber, and crawled off through the little door.

Crossing Cultures

The next day, Noah discussed more about different cultures, and the religions or spiritual traditions of various cultures.

"Some spiritual traditions are so rooted in the culture they are from, that people from 'foreign' cultures or lands find them difficult to adapt to. Sometimes there are even language barriers and cultural customs that have become part of the religion. For instance, some paths require learning or chanting in Japanese or East Indian languages, rather than translations of those languages. Many require performing or participating in rituals that are unique to a foreign culture, even though they evolved specifically because of those cultures. While some paths have legitimate reasons for such things, most do not, and their requirements are limiting, and often nothing more than dogma and cultural bias."

"Boy I can relate to *that* Noah. A year or so ago I entered a Zen monastery in the U.S. for about 6 months. And they did everything in Japanese, and in Japanese style, and wouldn't explain to me what the translations of the Japanese chants were. Even still, I liked a great deal of it, and I definitely got something out of it, but it just wasn't ultimately my right path."

"No. It is a very good path, but clearly, this is yours. If for no other reason than to teach me patience."

"What?"

"I was just joking younger brother. You had a good point. It's just that you are here for me to learn some things, just as I am here for you to learn some. But you are ultimately here for the world, more than I. But let me get on with what I was saying.

Unlike other traditions and religions, our spiritual and philosophical teachings lack any emphasis on religious dogma and have no cultural embedding. The teachers are from every part of the world. And the universality of the teachings and methods easily adapt to those individuals from any culture, who have an open mind, and are truly spiritually inclined. Thus, it is a path that is readily accessible and useful to people from any land, if they wish to take advantage of it."

To someone like me who had previously studied many religions and cultures, the teachings crossed over seemingly opposing religious boundaries with a unifying wisdom. They were also "complete"- filling in all the blanks left by my previous studies, and tying in the aspects of truth I had found in other paths, into one comprehensive whole.

A Natural Spiritual Path based on Universal Laws

My next course involved how the Atlantean teachings came about, and what they were based on. It was to be given by the elder monk Zarathustra. I'd "heard on the grapevine" that he had long ago originally come from Germany. He was quite well studied and intellectual from what I'd seen of him so far. I liked him, and he even let me be involved in some very sophisticated vibrational experiments he was conducting (which gave me the foundation for my later vibrational studies and developments). He had a great scientific insight into such matters, and was perfect for teaching this course.

"The beliefs and teachings that the Children of the Law of One had, and have, were not formed based on faith. Most of the basis of them came from Atlantis, and thus to us, our knowledge, philosophies, and practices are simply gleaned from the 'scientific facts' of Universal Laws that govern all things in the Universe, including the use of the mind and energy. They are merely the result of 'observations' of the Universal forces that are involved in the practical applications of our spiritual and physical existence. Thus, even today, understanding the substance of even the ancient 'beliefs', requires no faith, but rather a certain quality of 'intuitive logic'. In fact, the path urges us not to take the teachings on faith, but to EXPERIENCE God and higher consciousness directly. That way we can really *know*, rather than just taking something on faith and 'hoping really bad' that it's true. There is no more powerful way to change your life in a real and lasting way, than to directly *experience* Universal Consciousness, and thus experience and know Oneness with the Universal Spirit/God.

The teachings both give us methods to expand our awareness and directly experience God and Universal Consciousness, while also explaining to us the *effects* of Universal Laws in simple terms, even if the Law *itself* is difficult to understand."

"Uh... that *statement* was difficult to understand." Novice Vicente said.

"Ok. For instance, you may not understand the complex laws of gravity that physicists grapple with, but you *can* understand how Newton's observation of an apple falling from a tree led him to a scientific conception of 'What goes up must come down'. Right?"

"Yes."

"More simply still, your own experience with the law of gravity has taught you about the effects it has on your life. For instance, you wouldn't ignore the law of gravity and walk off a 30th floor balcony, yet how many people ignore even more important Universal Laws because they don't really understand their effects factually? So the ancient Atlantean teachings offer us a way to understand the effects of Universal Laws on our lives, and thus a way to benefit from them."

"Yes, I understand you now, but I want to learn more about spirituality, not physics."

"*True* spirituality is tied to Universal Laws though. And if you want to consider that just plain physics, fine. But this scientific approach doesn't mean that the path of the Children is a cold and clinical one. Far from it. Nowhere else will you find more emphasis on compassion and Love. Instead, the scientific basis in the teachings makes the ways and beliefs of the Children of the Law of One more simple and unique. As opposed to other religious orders, it is a "natural" religion, or more appropriately, a natural spiritual path. It is natural because it is based on nature - not just the nature of this planet, but the nature of the Universe. It was founded on an understanding of the way the Universe functions, and endeavors to apply the laws and flow that govern it, to human conditions. The ways of the Children were thus developed to insure that we are in our proper place in the grand scheme of things. Rather than encouraging blind faith in an unknown God and a dogma, it encourages knowing and experiencing the Universal Spirit yourself, and becoming One with it. By these very virtues, it is not as much a 'religion', as it is a 'way' of being One with All of creation, and the Creator, both. Nor is it just physics by any means. This is not your garden variety religion, and it has a beautiful simplicity to it."

"Science-Magic"

One morning I decided to explore a bit of the central pyramid, just to "check out" some of this incredible "thing". I was walking up one of the chamber halls there, when all of a sudden, I saw a strange moving light coming from a small side-tunnel. Before I could even look into it, Zin-uru, came crawling out. He was one of the Initiates at the monastery, an Adept monk who was the personal teacher of many of the elder and novice monks who worked with monastery's energy systems. He was holding a sort of lantern/flashlight, which explained the strange light.

From day one, I had heard the phrase "science-magic" used around the monastery. Sometimes it was referring to the monastery's technology, but sometimes it was regarding the "creation" of our personal lives. But when the term was used in reference to the monastery's technology, it was often used in the same breath as the name of the Adept Zinuru. I had also come across references to 'science-magic' in the ancient texts in the library, but it had not been explained to me in any of my courses yet, so I decided to ask him about it while I had a chance. I didn't know if he would have the time, or inclination to speak to a monk like me, but it was worth a shot.

"Zinuru, if you have a moment, could I please speak with you?"

"A moment, a moment. I suppose I do. Yes. No. It's gone now. Sorry. But yes, I'll speak with you now anyway."

"Can you tell me about this 'science-magic' I keep hearing about."

"No problem. It has been said that all the teachings of the Children of the Law of One, are based within 'Science-magic'. Have you heard that?"

"Yes, I think so."

"You think so. Very well. Well, they are all based on it. Let me explain the history of that. To our ancestors, what many consider the 'mysteries' of life were not confusing or complex, but simply a matter of applying their understanding of Universal Laws."

"I just had a course about that."

"Good, then you'll save me some time. Our Atlantean ancestors easily manipulated vibration, using thought, within a framework of scientific facts. God, and spirituality, were not vague concepts. The Universal Spirit was not unknown to them, or some being that was 'out there somewhere'. And magic and miracles were not just something that existed in fairy tales and religious parables from days gone by. They were the scientific workings of spiritual forces on physical matter. Spirituality, as well as materiality and physical life, were all simply based on scientific facts of Universal Laws. For instance, they understood that psychic phenomenon, electricity, magnetism, gravity, light, sound, space, time, and such, were all related, and aspects of the same thing, and all followed Universal Laws. The barbarian cultures that lived around us, or came into contact with our ancestors, couldn't understand these things, so they just lumped it all together as 'magic' - some mysterious 'something' that could only be created and wielded by gods, devils, or witchdoctors with strange powers and rituals. But what gives anything the *appearance of* magic. If not deceptive illusions or tricks, what is real 'magic' other than creating or altering energy, and matter which is comprised of energy? So in a very real sense, much of what we do is magic, but it is based in science, not superstition. Thus, science-magic is inherent in the Children of the Law of One's entire approach to life and 'religion'. Visualization, for instance, works like magic. You see it happening, and it happens. Visualization is used successfully in everything from Zen Archery, to healing - and all such things have that appearance of 'working like magic'. Here, let me give you a little demonstration." He had me stand behind him, and lift him up by the waist. It was easy. Then he said, "You should be able to that again, yes?"

"Of course," I said.

"Then do so."

I tried. It was like he was holding heavy weights or glued to the ground. I managed to budge him, but it took all of my effort and strength, whereas it was easy just a moment ago.

"How did you do that???"

"Simple visualization and energy. One aspect of 'science-magic'. You will learn it in time. And if I had wanted to really put my mind to it, you wouldn't have been able to lift me at all."

"That's incredible."

"That's nothing. But while our ancestors achieved wondrous things with their 'science-magical tools', it is not any more mysterious to us than defecating is to the uninitiated. To us, this use of the mind to create physical reality, is just a simple fact of Universal Law science, and a very fundamental one. This also applies to everything else in the Children's early days on Earth, such as their use of pyramids to provide power to vehicles and buildings without any visible connection. All their understanding of God, spirituality, and the matters of day to day life, are based in this *knowing* that *real* magic, *is* science, and *real* science, *is* magic.

This lamp I am holding for instance. It has no batteries like they use in the outside world, yet it is powered. By what? Something you can't see, and you don't yet understand. Is it magic? I guess so. Is it science? I guess so. Which reminds me, I have some repairs I'm in the middle of."

"Oh, I'm sorry. Thank you for your time and teachings Zinuru."

"Think nothing of it. You're quite welcome. We must have more talks. And I know you want to know more about how we are using some of the ancient technology to power things here. You'll be able to learn them easily if you wish. You have great vision and insight that few have, and I welcome discourse with you."

"Watch it, you'll get my ego out of hand with comments like that."

"I wouldn't worry about that. Zain will assure the last of your ego is stomped to death - he's talked about you a great deal."

I cringed inside. "Oh, great. That's something to really look forward to."

"In truth, it is. You will be far wiser, more intelligent, find peace, and your place as a caring instrument of the One, once all is said and done."

I replied, "That sounds better than being stomped to death."

He laughed. "Same difference. You'll learn." Then he headed on up a shaft.

The reality, practicality, and day to day practice of "science-magic" by the Children, give their teachings a "substance" that is rare in other paths. So while some of the spiritual teachings you will read about here may sound similar to other spiritual teachings, keep in mind that it's possible that they are based on a very different framework of understanding life and living life - a very *real* and *practical* framework, not an "airy-fairy" idea. And that framework can make a big difference. So if you read something that *seems* like just a religious or spiritual concept, keep in mind that if understood as a whole within the entire framework of the teachings, they are also just a fact of science-magic. And in the right hands (or right minds, in this case), they are each indispensable keys to understanding life, co-creating your world, and living in harmony with the Universe.

Complex Ideas with a Simple Message

Because the Children's path is so strongly based in Universal Law and what might be called "realities of the Universe", many of the teachings are by their very nature quite intellectual, and require concentration, and sometimes re-reading of sentences, in order to grasp them. I apologize for this, but it can't be helped. However, even though there is so much intellectual knowledge being presented, in practice, it is all balanced with feeling. For the very essence of this path is very clear, and very simple - **Unselfish Love.** Everyone can understand the healing and good that come from kindness, compassion, caring, giving, harmlessness. Those are the *virtues* of Unselfish Love - the things that really matter. And they are also the ultimate keys of returning to and being in harmony with the Universal Spirit, and what the Children of the Law of One are all about.

For me, discovering the ancient teachings filled in many holes in my understanding. I grew more excited every day as I learned more, grew more, and the pieces fell into place. When I found this path, I felt like a man dying of thirst discovering an oasis in the desert. To paraphrase a spiritual concept from "Stranger in a Strange Land", "As I was given water, I now offer you water. May you drink deep."

Coming up Against your Pre-conceived Beliefs

Everything was smooth and rosy in my life at the monastery, until I had to come to grips with my own "ego issues". They caused "turbulence" on the "flight" of my growth. I will discuss this later in the book, but to summarize it briefly now, let me put it this way. Long ago, my path led me to realizations that left my previous beliefs in shambles. I had to "clean house" (pick up the pieces of old beliefs, review each one of my beliefs individually, and decide whether to "trash it", "keep it" or "fix it"). I ended up with a set of beliefs that are far different than those of many people. As you have read, some of my beliefs are regarding Atlantis, and the history of our existence. But YOU may not believe such a place ever existed - so let's say it didn't. You have already read many things that you may, or may not, accept or believe - and you're about to read more. Just because I believe these things and accept them as truth, doesn't make it so. They may be absolutely untrue. Or they may not be true to you, from your perspective. Or, they may be absolute truth. In certain ways, it doesn't really matter, does it?

Whatever the case may be, if you don't believe all this intellectual "stuff" you read in this book, it doesn't matter to us - we know that truth is only half-truth at its very best anyway. We Love you. I Love you. I'd like to live in peace with you, and have you Love me too, regardless of what we believe or don't believe. As long as we don't hurt each other, and we help each other when in need, who cares what "beliefs" we have - religious, political, moral, or whatever. And I believe *that's what's most important,* because I *know* that Unselfish Love is *always beneficial.* That is one of my revamped beliefs, and I think it's something we should be able to universally agree upon. I Can. Can you? Will you? What can it hurt? Nothing. What can it help? A great many things, like peace and kindness. So if you do not believe the ideas contained in this book, I hope it will not matter to you that I do - as long as I am a Loving, kind-acting, caring-thinking, harmless person. And similarly, what matters to me about you, is not really what you think or believe, what religion you belong to, or if you're an atheist, but how you conduct yourself. What matters to me is whether or not you are a Loving, kind-acting, caring-thinking, harmless person. Unfortunately, a person's beliefs do greatly influence how they think and act though. So while we are on the subject of beliefs and religion, let's take a closer look at the effects of belief.

One day I was struggling with my thoughts. I was having 'doubts' because I was having a hard time with my ego. It wasn't the first time, and it wasn't going to be the last time. But as I was sitting in the garden questioning my beliefs, and trying to sort some things out, Anastasia came by and told me I should go see Zain, because I seemed upset. I reluctantly acknowledged her advice, slowly got up, and went off to find him. I found him already teaching a group of other novices. But his words were addressing my issues and concerns. I wondered if it was actually all staged for my benefit. It seemed absurd to think that of course, and self-centered, but I was never really sure with him what he might do to teach someone something in the best way. Here was what I began to listen in on:

"*Regardless* of whether or not you *believe* it, your beliefs control your destiny, so they need to be closely scrutinized for what they create in your life. What you think and believe greatly effect whether or not you are a saint, an evil monster, and everything in between (like a somewhat kind person, or a somewhat mean person)."

I was wondering what the heck he was talking about, because I had just learned that what we believed was irrelevant. So I interrupted the discussion, and asked, "What does it really matter what beliefs we hold? I thought it didn't matter as long as people are kind, caring, compassionate, and harmless."

"It is another paradox in a way. It *doesn't* really matter what beliefs a person has, as long as the beliefs they have *yield* those virtues of Unselfish Love you just mentioned. But their beliefs may yield those virtues, or yield harm and evil. Beliefs have a *dominant* and *powerful* effect on every aspect of our lives! People even kill over beliefs." [We'll get into that more in-depth later, but I'll continue Zain's lecture for now, because you will soon be reading religious concepts that may be in conflict with some of your own, and it may help you understand better or be more open minded.]

"Religious beliefs are frequently based on faith, and they are most often something we are 'taught to believe' early in life, by our family's religious beliefs and religion. Other beliefs are absorbed also, from our cultures.

People don't usually stop and think about the fact that something as *seemingly* 'innocuous and insubstantial' as our mere 'beliefs', really have much effect on our lives. But they do - in fact, they not only have *tremendous effects* on our lives, but they also control much of our destiny."

"How can this be that just an idea, a belief, controls our destiny?"

"A belief itself is but an idea, it has no real substance. But we *act based upon* our beliefs. The *actions we take because of our beliefs, have effects. And only the effects, the results, of those actions, are* things we can see, feel, and grasp. This is very important to realize. Because the effects of our actions, which result from our beliefs, *are precisely the things* that can be used to determine the value, good or bad, of any given belief. For instance, if you are kind to me because you believe we are all brothers & sisters, your kind actions are something real, something we can both *know* is good. Kind actions are transcendent of language, culture, and whatever you or I may believe is spiritual truth. Likewise, if you are cruel to me because of a belief, I will know it is a bad belief. These are obvious examples of course, and the results of many beliefs may be not so clear cut. Nevertheless, *all* beliefs subsequently generate their own 'thoughts' and 'actions', good or bad."

"So what should we believe for the greatest good for ourselves and the world?"

"Unselfishly Loving all beings is a *belief* of the Children of the Law of One, and the essence of the teachings. Caring about others, compassion, and kindness are qualities of Unselfish Love. If these are things we can all agree are good, then Unselfish Love can be used as a common, or Universal, measuring stick of goodness. And if Unselfish Love is the result of true spirituality, these virtues can also be used as the measuring stick of spirituality. Such a measuring stick can be used to compare the manifestations of any belief, and thus compare the value of any belief."

"So we should analyze and compare the effect of our beliefs?"

"Of course! Most people don't even think about what they are creating as a result of their beliefs. Do your beliefs further the manifestations of Unselfish Love, or inhibit the manifestations of Unselfish Love? Do they breed anger, hatred, and harm, or tranquility, love and healing? Do they make for a better life, or a worse life? Do they make for a better world for others, or a worse world?

People have used their beliefs, and been *driven by* their beliefs, to hurt and murder those with different beliefs. It can be over different beliefs about economics, race, religion - you name it and people will kill over it. What insanity! Why? The teachings make it clear that the primary culprit is our separateness from Universal Consciousness (and God). And regardless of the teachings - isn't it obvious? Separateness gives most all people of the world, the *basis* for their belief in the illusion that we are separate beings, not One being manifesting itself in many forms. This separateness then spawns *differences, and* selfishness. How much harm has been done in the names of God, Country, or Tribe? How much horror and pain has been inflicted because someone has a *different racial, national, tribal, class, or religious* belief? More than we can really grasp with our limited brains." He was through talking for the moment. Zain was a very intense being, and when he spoke intensely, I almost felt like I was getting punched in the stomach. As he got up and left the room, we all sat silent, moved, shaken up a bit, and remained in deep thought about his words for some while.

Any individual who wants to grow, attain enlightenment, or be a really good person, must completely re-evaluate their beliefs in the light of the effects those beliefs have, where they came from, and why. So in the Chapter on Subconscious programming and beliefs, we will explore the teachings on these subjects in depth.

Chapter Six

Different Points of View:
Universal Consciousness
and
Separate Consciousness

The concepts of Universal Consciousness, and separate self consciousness are central to the teachings of the Children of the Law of One, and they will be referred to throughout the book. So we'll start with the teachings about consciousness, and go on from there.

Almost every time I asked Zain a "deep question", he would also refer me to particular ancient texts to read in the library. He would say, "read these first, meditate, then come speak with me again."

When I first came to the monastery, I didn't really understand the meaning of "Universal Consciousness". I certainly thought I did though. I thought I understood it clearly. Sure, I had an intellectual grasp of some of it. But it was weak nonetheless. I eventually realized you could never really understand it, until you finally experienced Oneness with the Universal Spirit. In fact, you can't really fully understand much of anything until you achieve that. Yet it may help many readers if I relate my earlier question and answer sessions with Zain. So from here on out, I will present many of the Children's teachings in that format.

It was the day of the new moon. I was on my way to my womb to meditate after a long exhausting class. I turned a corner, and standing there, "accidentally", was Zain. The course I was taking, and particularly this day's class, had left me with a nagging question about Separate, and Universal Consciousness, which I was going to try and understand better in my meditations. But it would have done me no good. I needed a little more change, a little more "preparation" before I would really grasp this concept.

"Peniel..."

"Yes Father?"

"What troubles you?"

"Nothing Father, everything is fine."

"Then why do I not feel that it is? Am I an idiot?"

"Of course not Father. I'm sorry. I *am* having a hard time really understanding Universal Consciousness, or what the difference is between my own Separate consciousness, and that. Or even, what difference it makes. I mean, I am a decent person."

"No one has accused you otherwise. So what's your point?"

"I guess it's that I mean - so what if I have Universal Consciousness or not, as long as I'm a decent person."

"Because many people have been hurt by decent people, and decent people all over the world are suffering.

The difference of who you are, and what you do, with Universal Consciousness, is as night and day. That is why when you finally REALIZE Universal Consciousness, that is, when it finally is what you have achieved, it is called 'enlightenment', or 'illumination'. It is as if a light switch has been turned on in a life that has been lived in total darkness. Give me your notepad, and I will write a text I want you to look up in the library. Read it, meditate, then come see me in my chamber."

I went to the library, and told Gabriel the name of the text Zain had written. He retrieved a scroll, placed it on the table, and unrolled it to the quote. It was the place in the texts, that I was told to read. There, hand inscribed in alchemical ink, were these words:

Those who know Not that they are One,
Act not as One.
Those who act not as One,
Create not Love, but suffering and disharmony.
What you create, you receive.
The Fruits of Your acts will follow your days.

Separate Consciousness

After meditating for an hour, I went to Zain's chambers. He looked me piercingly in the eyes as usual, and said," It may be easier for you to understand Universal Consciousness, if you first understand separate consciousness. Then you will at least understand what Universal Consciousness IS NOT. And you will be able to 'relate' more to, and understand, separate consciousness - because that is what you have right now. Let's begin with one of the fundamental *effects* of Separate consciousness, a person's individual, separate, 'point of view'."

POINT OF VIEW

We've all heard phrases like, 'From where I sit ....', or 'Walk a mile in my shoes...', etc.. These are all common references to the significance of having separate and different points of view.

A person's 'point of view' can mean two things: 1) It can mean what it literally says - the 'point' from which a person 'sees' things. 2) It can mean a person's opinion. A person's opinion is based on a combination of #1, *and* the person's programmed beliefs.

Let's first look closer at #1, the 'point' aspect.

Most individuals have a limited point of view dictated by the very fact that they are *separate* individuals. They are each seeing things from a different place, a different point, literally. And they see *only* from their separate individual 'place'. There are as many 'places' that a person will see from as there are persons. And the trouble is, seeing from only one 'place' doesn't allow seeing a 'whole picture', or a 'big picture'.

THE METAPHORICAL CAR OF LIFE

Here's a mediocre allegory that will help illustrate the point, using a modern frame of reference you are familiar with. Let's say there is a classic car in a parking lot. The car is badly damaged on one side, but looks like new on the other. Two people going through the parking lot, walk by the car, one on each side. One person's point of view is from the bad side, one from the good. As they walk by, they each see the car, make a judgment, and form 'clear', solid beliefs about the condition of the car. Because of their limited viewpoints, they are each left with totally different beliefs about the car. And each person's belief opposes and contradicts the other's. One believes that the car is in impeccable classic condition, and very valuable. To the other person, the car is in such bad shape they couldn't even tell it was a classic - it just looks like an old junk car to them. And that's what that person believes the car is - an old junker. They are both right, from their point of view. Yet if you could see the entire car from above [Author's note: see illustration], from *our* point of view, they are both totally right **and** both totally wrong. How can they both be right, when each viewpoint would seem to make the other wrong, or impossible to be true? And how can they both be wrong, when they are obviously both right from their point of view? The fact is that when you *simultaneously grasp* the two contradictory, yet true, beliefs, you actually have the greater truth about the car. This predicament of having two truths, each of which seem to make it impossible for the other to be true, is a crude sort of paradox. And a paradox is the closest thing you can get to real truth, or whole truth, on the Earth plane [explained elsewhere in the book]. This example shows us how we can see the whole truth if we get above and beyond each individual's point of view. *Only* then can we see the 'whole' picture."

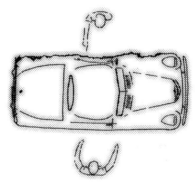

From our lofty point of view above the illustration, we have combined the points of view, and can see that while the car *is* a classic, it would need *a lot of work* to put it in show condition. And while we *see* the damage, we also see that it *is* a classic, and not just some piece of junk to have hauled away.

GREATER POINTS OF VIEW

Zain went on, "This example, of course, is not one of even seeing things with Universal Consciousness - seeing from a 'Universally broad' point of view. But as the damaged car allegory demonstrates in a small way, having a point of view that is as broad as possible allows us to better perceive reality, to see more truth. A broad point of view can help us better understand others, better understand the world, and ultimately the entire Universe around us. If our point of view is broad enough, it lets us better understand *other* points of view - then we can more easily communicate or interact with others, and they can more easily communicate with us. For instance, just like the people viewing that car, the point of view of each individual reading the ancient texts, or any book, is going to be different, thus they will perceive it many different ways, thus it will be perceived differently than it really is, and differently than it was intended to be perceived."

"So when I write the book revealing the oral traditions of the Children, it will not be perceived correctly either?"

"True. The broader the reader's point of view, the more they will perceive what is really written (within limits). But still, it will affect the subconscious, and the inner being in each reader. And it may affect the consciousness of those with fertile ground for the seeds. Yet, it goes both ways.

The Broadest Point of View

When we talk about the state of a person's 'consciousness', we are essentially talking about the state of their 'awareness' of the world around them. And as such, a person's consciousness is directly related to the way they view, interpret, understand, and interact with, everyone and everything around them.

A person's point of view is affected by both the state of their 'consciousness', and their beliefs and 'programming'. Beliefs and programming are usually in sync with a person's level of consciousness. However, consciousness is dominant, and if there is a shift to a higher or lower state, the new consciousness can alter and override a person's beliefs and programming in order to match the new level of consciousness."

"I'm sorry Father, some of this still escapes me."

"I understand, but a day will come when you will remember the words, and fully understand."

"Please explain more about Separate consciousness, so I can understand it better."

Separate Self Consciousness

"Every human being is obviously an individual 'self'. And most people are both 'conscious' that they are an individual self, and believe that their individual self is separate from other people, and everything else in the Universe. Thus, people generally have 'separate self consciousness', and live their lives based on this consciousness."

"So it is 'self' consciousness that creates the separate consciousness?"

"Yes."

"And this alters the point of view."

"Yes. In regards to a point of view, having separate self consciousness, means having a point of view that is limited to seeing things from only one 'place' - the 'place' where the separate self 'is at'. This can mean seeing things from an actual physical point of view that is limited to just the place where the person is located, such as in the car allegory. Or it can also mean seeing things from a point of view that's limited by the person's beliefs, and programming. In any case, the point of view is very limited and the perspective is 'narrow', when a person has separate self consciousness. There are varying degrees of 'narrow' mindedness of course, but even the most broad point of view that comes from just one person with separate self consciousness, must be limited and incomplete, because it is a view that is *still* from only one place, only from that one separate self. Thus, it is a point of view that will have limited understanding. And if a person has such limited understanding, what kind of thoughts are they limited to? And if their thoughts are from such limited perception and understanding, what kind of action will they take regarding other people, and the world around them? For the answer to that, just look around at the world."

"Do you mean that this creates problems in the world?"

"*All* problems spring forth from this."

"How?"

"Separate self consciousness, because of its limitations and narrow mindedness, 'boxes' its perceptions of the world into 'pieces' that are extensions of its self. Everything in your immediate world becomes an extension of you, of your separate self. For instance, there is *your* neighborhood, *your* town, *your* county, *your* state, *your* country, *your* part of the world (and depending on your socio-economic status, possibly *your* gang's turf). Because the separate self relates to these as extensions of itself, most people support their country, for instance, just because it is *their* country. Sure, they come up with 'reasons' why their country is the best or most important. But the problem is, many people believe that their country is 'It', 'the best', the 'most important', the 'most right', regardless of any reason to think so or not. And by so doing, they care less about other countries, and the people of those other countries. And if everyone's country is the best, who's right? They can't *all* be right. This phenomenon is even worse when it comes to a person's outlook about their religion. Many people think *theirs* is the only right religion, and thus the only one that will provide salvation for anyone else. And many of these people actually hate other religions, and their practitioners. When there is more than one religion claiming to be 'THE' only right one, it creates a question of who's right and who's wrong, and the dilemma of choosing the right one, or facing the consequences of having chosen the 'wrong' one (not getting into heaven, going to hell, etc.). But getting back to the idea of everyone thinking their country is the best, consider this: what country ever went into battle without 'God on their side'? In WWII, all sides believed God was on their side, including the Nazis. What country starts a war thinking that they're in the wrong? All of these perceptions and beliefs originate from separate selves and the territories they consider extensions of them-selves.

Most everyone favors not just *their* country, but ALL the extensions of their separate selves - they favor *their* race, favor *their* ethnic group, favor *their* school, favor *their* local team, favor *their* political party, etc., etc.. But a precious few people have begun to expand their self consciousness to include 'bigger pictures'. Take, for example, those who have become so environmentally conscious that they are 'environmentally active'. Those who have achieved that, understand the importance of the flow and balance of nature on Earth. They know that saving whales and forests, or seemingly insignificant things, such as tiny birds, fish, or ferns, can seriously alter life in ways that most people don't even suspect. Many of those who are truly environmentally conscious, have transcended some of their separate consciousness, and thus some of their self-centeredness, and self-ishness. Thus preserving the integrity of the environment is more important to them than many of the conveniences or inconveniences (recycling, power usage, etc., etc.) involved. There is a story about a 'mountain man' from the United States named 'Grizzly Adams' that relates to this. When a beaver dammed the creek next to his cabin, threatening to flood his cabin, he moved and built a new cabin rather than disturb the beaver dam. Talk about inconvenience! And believe it or not, this was still limited consciousness - but what a wonderful expansion of consciousness. To have reverence for all life, and also be able to see the importance and potential affect of the lives of whales, and tiny fish, and a seemingly insignificant fern, is higher consciousness. But it still falls far short of Universal Consciousness, and the efforts of such people can be a total waste of time, or even harmful, without it."

He looked down solemnly, and paused for a moment. He looked sad, and his feelings of sadness brought to mind my own consciousness, and something that had shocked my sensibilities a few years earlier. So I shared it with him.

"The human race barely cares about people let alone plants and animals. I remember once seeing a breaking news story about 600,000 people who died in an Earthquake. It was in the L.A. Times. You would expect such a disaster to be on the front page. And be a long article. But it was only one small paragraph, about 40 words, buried on page 9. And the only reason why was because the quake was in China. Even then, I was shocked. Can you imagine how this article would have been treated if 600,000 French people had died? English? American?" (Of course, this was during a time when the U.S. was an enemy of China. The story now, would be bigger news at least, if for no other reason than because there would be 600,000 less Chinese consumers of American products).

"Unfortunate son, but true. And those with separate self consciousness will defend their views with twisted logic. Some people will say 'So what if I think my country is the most important? It's good to have national pride. It doesn't change anything about any other country, it just helps this one be better.' If you don't think that such an attitude has no effect on other countries, consider the atrocities that one country will often inflict on another. Or that a country will stand by and allow to happen to the citizens of one country, but not in another. Imagine invading soldiers regularly using bayonets to cut babies out of the wombs of 9 month pregnant women in the street, for purposes of genocide. That happens. But as long as it only happens in countries that other countries don't care about, no one cares. As things are, such things are nearly never reported in the news media of the world. What if it was going on in Chicago? England, France, Mexico? Do you think we would not even be hearing about it? If ALL the churches in Britain were being destroyed by invading armies, and the priests tortured, would it not get on the news? It would not only get on the news, but many countries would send troops over there to stop it in an instant. How's that for national pride? What national pride? It all depends on what our separate selves consider 'extensions' or relations of themselves, or have selfish stake in.

Some people have begun to transcend 'pride of country'. Again, this is good, but it does not go far enough. So few have a truly global feeling of family, but there are some who do. But even environmental and humanitarian consciousness is still limited, and a person could accidentally cause terrible disasters acting from limited perception, even if their intention was only to help.

All these expansions of consciousness are steps toward the ultimate expansive and caring consciousness, Universal Consciousness. But they are still all variations of separate self consciousness - limited by so many constraints, and ultimately mistake ridden and destructive. Oh, how many tears have been shed in the wake of things gone wrong, and the cry is echoed 'But I was only trying to help'.

The fact is, all things in the Universe are essentially made of the same 'stuff', and are totally interdependent and connected. So we cannot be truly separate from the rest of the Universe, we can only be a 'part' of it all ('apart'). But we can *think* we are separate. We can *believe* we are separate. And then *we act* like we are separate.

Having separate self consciousness doesn't mean you are really separate, but it does mean having a total 'illusion' of separateness from everyone and everything else in the Universe. And when a person truly believes they are separate, they naturally focus on themselves. And when someone believes they are separate, and they focus their attention, and their energy, on their 'self', this naturally leads to 'self'-ishness. This is very important my son, pay close attention. This is the BIG issue. The Big problem of all problems. The only REAL problem. As silly and simple as it sounds, it is serious - *simple selfishness is the root of all problems and 'evils' that exist on Earth.* This is one of the greatest, most important teachings to understand, so say it back to me - selfishness is the root of all problems and 'evils' that exist on Earth."

"Ok. Selfishness is the root of all problems and 'evils' that exist on Earth."

"Good. And again, how does this selfishness come to exist?"

"Uh..."

"Where there is such separate consciousness as humans have, everyone perceives *everyone else* in an 'us and them', and a 'me against the world' fashion. When this occurs, which it *naturally must* with separateness, there will naturally be attempts to get, or take, from others, and keep others from getting what you have. It is perfectly natural, and in its own warped way, logical. And where does it all leave us? Where there is separateness and selfishness, there will be strife, discord, injustice, taking from others, harm to other beings, creatures, the environment, etc.. So when someone says something about the problems of the world being from political parties, or greed, or money, or war, or lust, or vanity, or carelessness, or whatever, what do you say?"

"That they are only branches. The root of all problems, all evil, all suffering, is selfishness."

"And why is there selfishness and thus all these evils?"

"Because it is the natural outcome of separate self consciousness - of thinking you are separate from the Universe, and thus all things in existence."

"And so what is the only cure for evil, suffering, and all problems?"

"Losing separate consciousness and selfishness by regaining consciousness of our Oneness with everything. Universal Consciousness."

"And how can one regain Universal Consciousness?"

"Through Unselfish Love, self-sacrifice, caring, giving, seeing the illusions of self consciousness that we carry with us in our mind, and breaking them."

"Please don't let the teachings that promote Oneness be misunderstood as promoting a 'one world religion or government' where oneness and peace are enforced by human rule or dogma. Nothing could be further from what we mean to convey. We are first of all proponents of freedom, and free will. I'm talking about an *internal* way of being, a consciousness, that includes sensitivity, compassion, and freedom - and caring about all people, creatures, all creation, as much as you do about your self.

"Are you saying all governments are bad?"

"No. Just incomplete, and that they won't ever solve all the problems, or work properly unless people themselves change inside. Certainly, some governments are formed just to wield power for an elite group over the people. But sometimes governments are formed to administer, and insure justice between all the separate beings it controls, but no form of government can really 'work', or last, when separate consciousness exists. Why? Because the people running the government have the same separate consciousness, and when they get power, you see the worst of selfishness, and they can appeal to the selfishness in the populace, to get what they want. When you stop and think about these things it is easier to understand why the Children teach that only when all people have Universal Consciousness, and everyone is primarily governed from within by the Universal Spirit, will there ever be peace & harmony, and freedom from tyranny *on Earth."*

"Why did you say it that way - *on Earth."*

"Because there is so much more, and the Earth is just one speck of dust, within an incredibly greater scheme of things. Outside of the Earth, the entire Universe functions in a beautiful, orderly, harmonious flow. On Earth, humans with separate self consciousness, are the only things that are out of step with the flow of nature, and the Universe. And the results of this have been disharmony, disruption, and destruction. That's why the teachings of the Children of the Law of One promote the attainment of "Universal Consciousness", by any means that works for you."

We will cover the Children's teachings about how humans attained separate self consciousness in the ancient history chapter, and the particulars of each individual's "selfish separate self" later in a "separate" chapter, but first, let's go over the meaning of Universal Consciousness.

Universal Consciousness

"Please tell me more of the teachings on Universal Consciousness, enlightenment, and it's attainment."

"Universal Consciousness is attained when a person has *a lasting experience* in which they see through their illusion of separateness, and lose their separate self consciousness. Their consciousness then 'merges' with the Universe - thus they experience being One with the Universe. This is often the result of going through a conscious psychological 'death experience', brought on by meditation and other aspects of a spiritual path [Author's note: these are explained in another chapter]. The illusion of separateness dissolves in the awareness of Oneness. And with the dissolution of the illusion of separateness, the separate self 'seems' to die, and a 'rebirth' occurs. Separate self consciousness is transcended and transformed. The dominant consciousness becomes that of the Inner Self, the part of us that is the Universal Spirit - thus, we have 'Universal Consciousness'. When experienced properly, a person is never the same, and never 'sees things' the same way again. From then on, all things are understood in the light of the 'biggest picture', in the light of being One with the Universal Spirit (God). Selfishness thus becomes a thing of the past. This is also called achieving 'enlightenment', and a few other names.

The difference between having separate self consciousness, or having Universal Consciousness, is, as I said before, like night and day. Consider again, an environmentalist who has expanded his/her separate self consciousness to include concern for ecology. This is good. And if being aware of the flow and balance of *Earth's* nature is good, imagine the significance of being really aware of the flow and balance, of *all* things - of the entire Universe? And if being concerned about all humans on Earth is good, what about being devoted to caring for all life within the entire Universe? A person who has attained Universal Consciousness, has transcended separate self consciousness, and thus sees infinitely more, understands infinitely more. Imagine being able to 'see' the outcome of many of your actions in advance - or whether or not you 'see' the outcome, being able to know if what you are doing is really going to ultimately help, or ultimately harm. Or using the classic car allegory again, imagine seeing one side of the car, and not assuming that the other side is the same? How would you like to be able to *sense* what all sides were like?"

"That would be incredible Father."

"Yes? That is just a small nothing. What if you *really* had an *awareness* of being One with *everything* - even God, even all other separate selves? How would you see things then? And how would you treat everyone and everything? If you absolutely KNOW that every person you are dealing with, *is you*, just in a different form, how will you treat yourself (others)? Is there any point in stealing from yourself? Hurting yourself? Is there any point in being tyrannical with yourself?"

"It would make no sense, there would be no point if you really believed that to be true."

"Precisely. A being with Universal Consciousness Loves everyone unselfishly, and is *(within the needs of Universal flow)* giving, kind, compassionate, caring, knowing, and harmless (that doesn't mean incapable of defending the innocent). Why? Is it because the person has read something that made them that way? Studied to be that way? Trained to be that way? No. Maybe such things were stepping stones on the path towards attainment of that consciousness, but once there, the fact is that *being* any other way simply makes no sense to someone with Universal Consciousness. It just is their reality - it is just natural.

It is similar with people at any level of consciousness. A basically decent person is not just trying to be basically decent, moral, or law-abiding. It comes somewhat naturally depending on what they have made of themselves throughout their lifetimes. And they can and will digress towards greater selfishness given the right situation. Everyone just manifests the level of their consciousness - and for most, it moves in a certain range, wavering between selfishness, and unselfishness to varying degrees, and shifts at different times in their lives, and depending on the circumstances they are subjected to.

It is as natural for a person with Universal Consciousness to be totally giving, as it is for a person with separate self consciousness to be selfish. A person with separate self consciousness is focused inward, and thus they are like an 'energy vacuum', a black hole, always trying to get energy. But a person with Universal Consciousness is focused outward, and thus they are like an energy beacon, a Sun, always giving energy."

"So piercing this illusion of separation, and attaining Universal Consciousness, is the answer to the entire world's problems."

"If everyone had Universal Consciousness, there would be no need for the kind of governments we have now, for all would be governed as One from within themselves. Just imagine a world in which *everyone* is conscientious, caring, and responsible. And where such behavior is not coerced by threat of prison or death, or even convincing of any kind. No need for religions to try and influence people to behave morally. No need for police, armies, government, etc., because Unselfish

70

Love and service to Universal Will is all fixed within every being - what paradise! We may never achieve this on Earth, then again, we may. But there are planes of existence other than the physical plane on Earth, into which only Universally Conscious beings can enter. Paradise *does* already exist.

Personal Changes

There are also major personal psychological changes that come from attaining Universal Consciousness. The 'seriousness' and significance of things that you once considered very important, will change. *How* important 'such and such' is, will now be viewed in a much greater light, and its *true* importance determined *there*. Things that previously may have upset you or been desirable to you, may lose their impact because they pale in significance when seen within the context of *awareness of all things*. For instance, how can the paper boy throwing the paper behind the bushes upset you very much, when you are *truly* and *constantly* in mental "touch" with such things as the starvation going on in the world, the fact that another species just became extinct while you were reading the headline, the vision of what will happen when the poles shift, what life is like when you have the consciousness of lava on Saturn, and on and on and on....

Also, with such a radical consciousness change, some things that you may have previously 'taken for granted', or that you found enjoyable, can change dramatically, as far as how you experience them. For instance, how can a football game be very interesting when competition is senseless to you because you *know* we are all One, you *know* we are God? And worse, you *know* the 'game' is actually reinforcing separateness, and hostility? All you see from your Universal viewpoint, is a bunch of 'we' who don't understand who we are, attacking themselves so some 'we' can win and feel superior, and some 'we' can lose and feel terrible."

"What do you mean by things that were taken for granted change also?"

"Take those beautiful flowers growing over there. You think nothing of them other than they are pretty. When I look at them, I know they may never bloom again. They could become diseased. They may go extinct. I may go blind. I appreciate them so much more because I am aware of these things. And when I don't see them anymore, or they die, I don't lament them, because I know they are living on elsewhere, because all life lives on. It is a paradox. When you have Universal Consciousness, you take everything much more seriously, and not seriously at all. Nothing can ever really be destroyed, or created. It can only change form. For all is One. Take you for another example. I Love you. I truly am aware every moment that I may never see you again on Earth. You may die tonight. I may have a stroke when I leave this room, and be unable to communicate or even grasp your hand. So I appreciate you so much more, life so much more, and I cherish our being here right now. And thus I behave differently. If I were to fight with you, and say unkind things, or hurt you in any way, I know I may never get a chance to make amends, or even apologize, and that would be the way we ended our relationship here and now. Even if I wasn't aware that we are a part of each other, and you just aren't really aware of that, I couldn't do anything hurtful either, because I know this is it. This may be our last chance to be together in this way, or for a long time. And at the same time, it doesn't matter because we are all just the One, interacting, changing form, coming in and going out. The only thing that does matter really, is that those of you who think and believe and live as separate, are suffering. Suffering needlessly. And I feel for you, and want to help you. That is all I am really here

71

for."

"I think I understand. But how can we really know all these things, and see all these paradoxical things. How can we keep them all in our consciousness, and be aware of them at the same time - and constantly, all the time?"

Guidance from Above

"It just happens when your separate self gives up it's illusion - surrenders its artificially, self-created life. And there are degrees of this. The closer you get to attaining Universal Consciousness, the greater your point of view will become, and the more you will intuitively 'see' the whole picture, or whole situation. The attainment of Universal Consciousness is quite dramatic though, and you can't help but to see all these things, and be aware of them. But while a person who has attained Universal Consciousness may see the 'whole picture' to the greatest extent possible on Earth, even they don't see it all while still embodied. A completely all-encompassing point of view is not really possible while functioning in a physical body. We can achieve this in deep meditation, but when we again return to full physical plane function, we can only grasp the *essence* of what we understood in our 'ultimate point of view' state. That is why the Children teach that 'getting out of our own way', and allowing ourselves to be an instrument of the Universal Spirit (God), is the greatest wisdom. This too, is achieved simultaneously with Universal Consciousness - it comes with the package.

When we have thus become an instrument of the Universal Spirit, we are then always 'watched over' by our ascended, hierarchical kin, and guided when necessary. This is not actually 'mediumship' or channeling [ed. note: see the teachings on channeling in the 'Teachers and Students chapter]. It is still having only our own Inner Being in charge of, or in possession of, our body and consciousness."

"So how are we guided?"

"Our Inner Being is One with the Universal Spirit, and when we allow it to 'come out, and take control of us', we become an active link in the hierarchical chain of Universally Conscious beings. As a part of the chain, we are both led by the movement of the entire chain, and we become the chain. While we are still Earth-bound, and fettered by the limitations of the physical plane, others of our chain (our hierarchical superiors), are not so limited. They too unselfishly care for all life, but they are in a higher state of conscious Oneness with the Universe than we on Earth, and have an infinite view. And as ONE, we can receive guidance from these other parts of our chain, these beautiful beings who have an unfettered all-encompassing point of view. They always know what is best, even if it does not 'seem' so, to us (from our narrow point of view). We are through for now. This has been an exhausting session, and I must rest."

"Thank you Father. May you rest well."

Chapter Seven

The History of
The Children of the Law of One
(from the beginning to 2001)

Why the History?

I was never fond of history in school. Thinking back on it though, it was partly because it was both written and presented in a boring way. But that wasn't all. Specific dates of events were focused on far more than the story of the events. Furthermore, the portrayal of events often had either important omissions, or "additions" that were outright lies, or "colored" to fit into someone's program of what they wanted us to learn and believe. There's an old saying about "He who wins the war writes the history", and that's not the half of it.

My religious training as a child was fraught with similar problems. And I could not get what I considered to be "straight", "valid", or "logical" answers to my many questions.

But I'd finally found a source of un-adulterated history, and one far more interesting, and far reaching, than any other. And it included both the secular history of the world, and the religious history of multiple religions. But regarding some aspects of history, I still had a bit of a block left over from my school days.

There was obviously a valid point to learning real history of any kind, at least in the sense of, "One who doesn't learn from the past is condemned to repeat it." And I had always longed for the history I was finally going to get a chance to learn. But nevertheless, at the time, I still had the rebellious school kid nagging me in the back of my mind somewhere (because of my bad programming), saying, "What's the point?" After all, "Be Here Now" had been my motto for a while. So even though it seemed ridiculous, I asked Zain what I never had the nerve to say to my high school teachers, only this time it was regarding the history of the Children from the time of creation - "What's the point?"

Here was his reply. "To know the way of the One, how the Universe is - how it works - the immutable Laws behind its existence and functioning, has always been fundamental to all Children of The Law of One knowledge and teachings. Even now, this knowledge can be helpful to those who seek to return to the One, to Universal consciousness, to a way of living in harmony with the flow of the Universe. To these ends, one should understand how the world as we know it became this way - to know the way it all began. Why? Backtracking. Like hikers who have lost their way, if they can determine how they got where they are and where they came from, they can find their way back. If they have a map, so much the better. Thus, the better we understand how we lost our spiritual existence, separated from Oneness, and became trapped in the Earth, the better our knowledge can help us to get free from our traps, and return to our spiritual source."

For your journey now, we offer you a map of sorts. This map is a story - and a history. Written below is the Children of the Law of One's account of creation, and the early days of life on Earth. This same story has been passed on by our spiritual ancestors, throughout time, since our beginnings on Earth. The Adepts who transferred it to their students, who became Adepts, who transferred it to their students, who became Adepts, etc., etc., have created a chain through history, a lineage of knowledge connecting us directly to our Universal Source. I give this to you here, as it was given to me, as it was given to my personal teacher before me, and to his before him - I now pass it on to you, an open link in your potential chain.

PRE-HISTORY

I have edited the following story somewhat, adapting some modern English terminology and structure, just for ease of understanding. But the teaching is fully intact, and very close to the original translation. Even so, you will not be able to truly or completely *realize* the meaning of our history and the separation from Oneness, until you are free from your Earthly bonds, and the limitations of your own brain, and consciousness. But, what can you do other than work with what you've got? Enjoy.

Know your true self, and you will know the true story. Know your whole self, and you will know the wholeness of the truth.

All is One. There is no other. Thus it always was, and thus it always shall remain.

We once experienced only Oneness. One being, with no divisions or separate parts. There was no "time", no "space", nothing other than the Us.

When you are only One, there is only you, nothing "else" to interact with. In order to experience interaction - to experience being with someone "else", to experience "play", the One divided within itself, duplicating the One, thus creating many Ones, many Be-ings, within the One. [Part of this was what modern science calls "the big bang"].

Still One being - now in many parts were we - capable of "pretending" to be other than One, while still being One in harmonious consciousness.

By Vibration was it done - division, multiplication, and expansion of the One. Set into motion, were vibrations throughout the Universe. On it went, dividing, multiplying, creating new aspects of vibration through the overtones of harmony and ripples of the interacting vibratory reflections. Created this many new things, and also initiated the "time" and "space".

Each of us were the entity of the One, the entirety of the One - the dark, the light, the stars, the planets - all of us macrocosms of the One. In "clusters", "groups", WE WERE in all directions. WE BEING the entire UNIVERSE, we then roamed OURSELVES, as consciousnesses, as beings, that cannot be described or understood by the present Earth consciousness. Yet

74

describe I will try, as best I can.

Our existence was (as close as you can comprehend in your present consciousness) as beings of spirit - energy - light, star groups, "solar" systems, the groups that be the foundation of vibratory frequency in creating the physical plane, of matter, the appearances there, and that which forms the bodies of that plane. Unattached, ever flowing with the flows of the Universal One were we, enjoying all the wonders of our new creation.

Our consciousness, both semi-separate from, yet still One with, the entire creation of the Universe, allowed us the experiencing of new and different things. But within this new creation were the "material planes". These were the realms in which existed the most "dense", or "slowest" spectrum of vibrations. There were many "material planes" throughout the Universe, the Earth being just one.

The story I am about to tell, is only of those who manifested in the realm of the Earth. But others of us manifested in the material planes of other solar systems. Some are now of the higher consciousness, kindred beings are they from other worlds. But some from other worlds are of the selfish and "evil".

When we came upon the world of the Earth, we had no comparison, no experience of the like, no expectation of what would be. The first group of us to discover this "material plane" were in awe of the new sensations it offered. This first group, or first wave of souls to materialize, was the first to enter the vibrational spectrum of 'matter', in the time-space of the Earth. They experienced such pleasure from "playing" in it, that they projected themselves deeply into matter, in thought-forms [ed. note: Using thought to create a body] that were the MOST STIMULATING, the MOST SENSATION-AL - those of the animal realm creations. In creating these bodies, assorted aspects of different animals were often combined to achieve what they thought would be very desirable blends - Bird head/human bodies, Horse body/human head, Goat head/human body, Fish tail/human torso - and many, many more variations. [Author's note - these would much later become known in Greek and Roman mythology by many names - Centaurs, Minotaurs, Mermaids, etc.] Unfortunately, these ones, our close kindred, had no way of knowing that as soon as they "hardened" their thought-forms into matter, becoming these creatures, that they would lose all awareness, all consciousness, of most things beyond their new bodies and their immediate environment. They became trapped in these forms. The seven ports (chakras) were closed, cutting off their contact of the full vibrational spectrum, and thus all their perceptions and interactions were thus based only on the limited vibrations they could detect through only five vibrational sensors. These five "senses" could only monitor very limited frequency bands of the full Universal vibrational spectrum – and even in that, they focused on only those vibrations relevant to the material plane of existence, leaving these "humanimals" without any senses of the spiritual planes of existence. Cut off from the consciousness of the One, and thus the very Universe itself, the humanimals experienced animal consciousness, but the beings inhabiting these forms were not animals, and originally of angelic consciousness. The combination of the consciousness that was meant to be of a higher form, blended with the animal consciousness, was a very inharmonious and disruptive mix. They lost the purity of animal consciousness, and the purity of spiritual consciousness. So this was a new kind of consciousness that was foreign to the animal realm. This new consciousness was "separate consciousness", and was of a fixed-focus nature, and reverse-polarity in comparison to the consciousness of the One. Intelligence was also severely curtailed in the humanimals, being similar to the intelligence of the types of animals that they were "modeled" upon, but again, this was adversely afflicted by the negative effects of separate consciousness. Thus were the humanimals "stuck" in this limited plane – in limited forms, with limited intelligence, in a new limited consciousness. They didn't "fit in" anywhere – they didn't belong in the spiritual realms any longer, nor did they belong in Earth's nature. Thus their introduction into the Earth plane was also disruptive and polluting to the flow of nature.

Those of us who did not project ourselves into matter, were quite aware of the predicament and fates that had befallen our kin. From the vantage point of our natural, etheric state of existence, we were still of One mind, One being. Seeing part of us in such matter-bound prisons as the humanimals had become trapped in, was very painful – after all, the creatures were us, were our "sisterbrothers", and their misfortune was our misfortune. In the terminology of some, they might also be called the first "fallen angels", but they fell not of ill intent, but by virtue of ignorance of the purest kind. We decided to save them – no matter what the cost. We knew we could only do this if we could function on the same vibratory plane as they, so we too projected ourselves into thought-forms that could function within the realms of the Earth-Mother.

Led by the great being who became known as the Atlantean

Amiliaus, then known later as Thoth, and eventually well known as Jesus much later, the second wave of our entering into the planes of the Earth-Mother began. Careful to stay as beings free from the lower-vibratory planes, or "hardening" into the matter, we projected ourselves into the material plane with thought-form bodies that were semi-etheric - matter, but not matter. Thus were we still able to function on all vibrational frequencies of the Universal spectrum - free to enter or leave the limited spectrum of the material plane at will. But most importantly, we were very intent upon maintaining our con- sciousness of Oneness, so that we would not fall to the same fate as the humanimals.

The manifestation was achieved more or less successfully, and as we became subject to the vibratory conditions which affect this realm, we saw the numerological representations of the physical plane, 2 and 5, appear in many aspects of our manifestation. For example, the beginnings of the 5 races occurred, and later, the 2 sexes, each being having 5 appendages (2 legs, 2 arms, 1 head), with 2 eyes, 2 ears, 2 legs, 2 of many organs, etc., and 5 fingers/toes on the arms and legs.

Despite our precautions and great efforts, some of us still fared not as well as others, losing more consciousness and hard- ening more than others. Those who manifested in Atlantis with Amiliaus fared the best - but for many, this was to be short lived.

Until this time, we were "composite" beings, macrocosms of the One. Our bodies were not as they are now. Our male and female elements had not yet separated - as composite beings we each had one body that contained both "sexes", rather than the male and female bodies we have now. The "sexes" then, being just the inner and outer elements, and outflowing and inflowing parts of our whole being. These were "soulmate" groups as they are called now. Each composite being had different numbers of parts (a different number of "soulmates") - each part a being itself, but fully as one with the whole being. We were like beings IN WHICH planets orbit a star, or the atoms of matter in which elements of different polarity (male and female) are attracted to each other, each finding a place where they har- moniously function together within the whole, as one entity, one being. As such composite beings, we existed in a state of "Unselfish Love" - constant flow, outflowing/giving fully of our life energies to each element of ourselves, within ourselves, and receiving within ourselves - and without (in our relationship with the One, which each composite being also "orbited", creating the even greater, ultimate composite being of the One).

Now, for the first time, SOME of us had begun to separate within ourselves, manifesting as individual bodies representing the polarity elements. Bodies of opposite polarities then came into existence (male or female "sex").

The work of freeing the humanimals began. It was arduous and complex, but it proceeded well - at first. Unfortunately, the contamination of separateness slowly began to creep in. We started slowly "tasting" many of the things that had instantly trapped the humanimals.

Divisions began to occur between Atlanteans, over opinions and desires. The next symptom of our dis-integration was upon us, and this disease would eventually bring down Atlantis. Even in this higher state of manifestation (which we thought would keep us safe from the loss of consciousness that plagued the humanimals), some of us succumbed to the lure of material sensation. Like the drug addict would behave with an unlimited supply of drugs, we began to delve more into the indulgences of this plane until we were lost in it - drowning in it. In the frenzy of our addiction to physical sensations, we disregarded all our precautions and wariness. Soon our thoughts and actions had "collected" matter from this material world that surrounded us... and hardened our thought-forms, making us matter-bound also. Our consciousness simultaneously slipped, and our gradual loss of consciousness of Oneness gave way to that new consciousness of predominant "separateness". The consciousness of predominant "separateness" was foreign to us, a totally new experience. And along with this new consciousness, came new emotions - some pleasurable and some painful. Strange new things like greed, envy, lust, excitement, fear, desire.

Some of us vigorously strived to maintain a semblance of our consciousness of Oneness, along with the new consciousness, and we were able to experience the emotions without being ruled by them. Such were the Children of the Law of One.

But others lost, or chose to deliberately suppress, even a glimmer of awareness of the One. These beings became lost, and enmeshed in separateness. Outside of the consciousness of Oneness, they became subject to being tossed to and fro by the tides of emotional onslaught, and ultimately became devoted to personal power and pleasure in this physical plane. These beings became known as the Sons of Belial (even if they were female).

Take heed of the ancient warnings and prophecies about the Belialians: "Lizard-like are they - not in apparent physical description, but in spirit form, in the heart - in the soul. Beware even now of your lizard kin, for they rule the world, with greed, and without compassion, while maintaining 'appearance' of good and righteous. As MEN (& Women) do these Sons of Belial walk the Earth. Model citizens. Successful leaders who are the envy of the uninitiated. While some appear disgusting and strange to the eye, look not to see the ugliness of the Belialians with your eye, for some are handsome to the eye. SEE you will NOT, their TRUE lizard-like appearance with your earthly eyes. See their TRUE nature, you will, only with the inner-eye, or in glimpses from the corner of the eye.".

When this division came within the people of Atlantis, many things went awry, and turmoil began. To function harmoniously, beings need to have omni-presence - their vision MUST include the 'whole' picture. But when the 'attention' is fixed and focused in the reverse-polarity of separation, all that is seen are PARTS of the whole picture - those parts that are not filtered out by the illusions of separate consciousness. It is a limited view at best, and often is a lens distorted by emotions. Without awareness of the "whole" picture, and the guidance of a coordinating force, actions become un-coordinated with others. To understand this better, imagine how well your present day body would function if each limb did not have awareness of what the other limbs were trying to do, or if each limb wanted to do different things from each other - no longer working together as one. Now imagine further - imagine this lack of coordination keeping your eyes, ears, fingers, tongue, and mouth, from working together as a team. Now consider the chaos and eventual destruction that would occur if every single cell in your body operated with no unified guiding force that keeps them coordinated with the whole (in fact, that's what "cancer" is). You see, this became the problem with our very lives once some of us lost consciousness of the One. Such uncoordinated independent activity becomes a logical evolution when such a separation occurs and one is left with only an awareness of separateness.

Thus it came to be that the two Atlantean socio-political groups evolved, with one very essential difference: The Children had a consciousness of both separateness and Oneness. The Belialians rejected the consciousness of Oneness entirely, and maintained only a consciousness of separateness. The differences of opinion between the two groups were great and many (including "environmental issues"), but nothing was more of an issue than the morality of how the humanimals were to be

79

dealt with. Those of the Law of One, remembering still that we originally came to this plane just to help release the humanimals from matter-bondage, continued trying to free our trapped siblings. The kindred also created ways (known to the initiate) to aid in the maintenance of the consciousness of Oneness, so we would never lose sight of our goals. But the Belialians wanted to use the humanimals for their own comforts and pleasures. Since those of us from the second wave were of greater consciousness than the humanimals, and could still function on higher planes to some extent, we had powers of the mind, both spiritual and psychological, that made it easy for us to control humanimals. The Children refused to use their abilities to control the humanimals, while the Belialians relished the power, and wanted to use them as slaves.

The other great division in opinion between the Children and the Belialians was over the "environment" as it is called now. The Belialians used methods of generating power (like electrical power), that were dangerous and destructive to the Earth.

Thus did the great conflict between the Children and the Belialians of Atlantis begin. A conflict between light & dark, between selfishness, & Unselfish Love. And the conflict that was, continued throughout history, and continues to this day.

The Belialians' lust for power and lack of care or awareness of the balances of nature, led to the destruction of Atlantis. This was due in great part to the abuse of their power generation plants.

When the final destructions occurred, Grand Master Thoth then led us to the land of Khem, to complete the Great Work of evolving the humanimals. As gods were we to the people of Khem, and yea did they think the humanimals to be gods.

And so it was done. The humanimals were brought to human levels, to choose their path from there. Yet, there are the residual effects. Have you not seen the humans that look much like pigs, or goats, or this or that animal still? These were they.

But even though the humanimals were no more, the Belialians had not lost their taste for slavery. Thus the great conflict with the Belialians was far from over, and still continues on, with the Children of the Law of One as lamps, illuminating the path of Unselfish Love, helping the lost find their way home to their spiritual heritage of the One, and to find freedom – while the disguised Sons of Belial (and their pawns) do everything possible to maintain their decadence and power, and maintain slavery (whether it be direct or by means of livelihood and social control). And they seek to destroy all those who would shine Light into this world of darkness. All those who do not actively work for the Light, are to varying degrees, pawns of the Belialian Darkness.

RECENT DEVELOPMENTS [1]
FROM THE BEGINNING

[The following is from a scroll that was a later addendum to the translation of the above story. But what is particularly interesting about it, is that it is said to be written by the same author (the being who was also grand master Thoth) *but in a different lifetime.* That same being was also known as Joseph (the son of Jacob), or Jesus in certain latter incarnations.]

As it is symbolized in this image ☯ the forces of darkness & light, while in opposition, are in movement within the One. In balance, this is the proper state of things in the Universe. On the Earth plane however, the forces of dark & light are not functioning in this way. They are not in harmony within the One. Those of darkness predominate greatly, and attempt to eliminate the light. They battle endlessly, with Love and peace on one side, hate and violence on the other. Balance there is not, but balance you can create. Such is Universal Law, the Law of the One, and it ultimately prevails.

Some in the future will claim that since it is all ONE, there is no right or wrong, no good or evil. But even though there is an element of truth - we are all One anyway, and thus, none of this *really* matters, there is an important consideration - the lack of consciousness by some, *does* create suffering, and *does* create disharmonious vibrations within the One. When you are suffering, do you not want a remedy, do you not want help to stop it? If you were suffering *needlessly,* because of the illusions of good/evil, right/wrong, would you not want to have this pointed out, and have assistance in finding a remedy? Thus, is not the remedy, *good?* Is it not *right? Do you not care about the suffering of your brothers and sisters?*

As you have just heard, in days long gone by, Atlantis was split between the followers of Darkness and followers of Light. Those who followed the way of the light were known to themselves and other Atlanteans, as the "Children of the Law of One" (as it roughly translates). From the beginning, the darkness was on the rise in Atlantis, and finally, as you just heard, the repercussions of this came upon us. How? Transgressions against the Law of One (fixed Universal principles, "Laws" of the way it IS), and against those of the Earth's nature (which is in harmony with the Law of One), were everywhere. Great harm was done to the Earth by the followers of darkness, natural imbalances were created by them. A pillar of the Law of One is that of "cause and effect". Thus did these actions bring about the physical fall of Atlantis.

The greatest of these natural imbalances was created by drilling huge holes in the Earth's crust, down to the levels of molten Earth. The Belialians used the very gross physical forces of the inner Earth to generate their power. They used concentrated light energy beams [Author's note: like lasers] to bore great holes in the Earth. Remnants of them can still be seen in many places. [Author's note: notably such as Florida, the Caribbean, and the "Blue Hole" of Belize.] Creating their

81

power plants was much like making a series of un-natural volcanoes, and it result-ed in great instability and seismic disturbances. Even though they were warned of the consequences, the Belialians persisted in this un-natural activity, until it caused the Earth changes that destroyed Atlantis, and the Belialians of that time.

Before the final destruction of Atlantis, knowing the time, knowing the signs, those of us of the light, went to many other parts of the Earth, in order to contin-ue our work. As time went on, "branches" of the tree were created. And as some of the other peoples of the Earth learned from us the way of the Law of One, "branches" of the "branches" sprang forth. Most of the still known spiritual tradi-tions and religions of the world, have descended from us. Though many are hardly recognizable from their origins, they are relatives, close, or distant. Still, much con-fusion has risen. Some of these have become so distant, and far from their begin-nings, that they are really instruments of the darkness now, while others have remained relatively true to their source, and still serve the light.

As was said earlier, during the exodus from Atlantis, many of us followed Thoth [pronounced "Toth"] to the land of Khem, now called Egypt. There he built the Great Pyramid, and other temples and places of healing, for purposes of com-pleting our work, initiating the wise, and enlightening the ignorant. The work of freeing the humanimals was continued there.

"Modern science" has surmised that these great pyramids were built by work-ers over many, many years, for the purposes of tombs. However, lacking any real facts from that time, these scientists make great assumptions, and their conclusions are truly un- scientific. These great structures were in fact built by Thoth, using forces he controlled with the help of the advanced technology aboard his terrestri-al airship [Author's note: A common Atlantean mode of transportation in the days of Atlantis]. These vibratory forces could change molecular density, so that the great stones could be made to float in air, just as wood floats in water.

The power generating plants built by the Children were very harmonious with nature, in stark contrast with the Belialian methods. The generators were simple pyramids, that harmlessly collected the energy present in the Earth's aura [a fre-quency of the electromagnetic field - the field that makes a compass point to North]. The power generator pyramids used only crystal and copper capstones, combined with a large peak release collector [capacitor] inside the pyramid. This allowed "wireless" transmission of the power to any building, or vehicle, including the air-borne terrestrial ships such as Thoth's.

The Great Pyramid itself, was both a power generator [more about it can be found in the chapter on metaphysics], and a center for final stage spiritual initiation for the Children of the Law of One. Its great hall was once lined with the painted tablets, depicting the stages of spiritual development and initiation that were later to become the Major Arcana of the Tarot. The humanimals were treated in other pyramids - the various places of healing and consciousness raising, that were built in that area. They were released from enough bondage there, so that they were at least capable of finding their own freedom, their own way back to the One. But now, it is not only many of the reincarnations of the humanimals that are lost to the One, there are many, many more - even some of those who helped save the humanimals.

Thoth's ship remains, hidden under the Sphinx. This may yet be found and used by initiates, when it is time and the need arises. Between the Sphinx and the

Pyramid, is buried a chamber that contains the records of our history from the beginning, to the year 2001 (known as the Hall of Records). This, or the duplicate records in the Yucatan, or the ocean, will be found just prior to the great Earth changes that will again rock the Earth on it's axis. [Refer to author's note on page 83.]

Eventually, our work in Egypt complete, we left for places of retreat, to create centers of refuge for the Children. This was done so that the light would survive, even as darkness continued to grow in the world. It was known that, if our numbers remained at least one thousand, that the needs of those seeking light on Earth, would always be met. Master Thoth, aware of the ever growing darkness that was to be, and knowing how the written word can be controlled and corrupted by the greedy and the power mongers, put the keys of knowledge (of the spiritual initiate's path back to the One), into images on cards. As mentioned earlier, these were the first Tarot cards, which were replicas of the images that lined the great hallway of the Great Pyramid of Initiation. Thoth knew that images would be more difficult to change by the corrupt, and more difficult for them to understand. He also knew that those on the path of ascension towards the One, would someday see and understand their meanings and secrets. To further insure the safety of these keys, he added more cards to the major arcanum, creating the full system of divination. The method of divination, he taught to those of the land of Egypt who were leaving Egypt for other lands [Author's note: Wandering Egyptians (E-Gypt-ians) that would later be known as *"Gypt-sies"*]. Knowing that these Egyptians would use this divination system to reveal the future of others for profit, he knew that greed itself, would insure that the Egyptians would preserve the images as much as possible, and that the knowledge would be preserved in many different lands.

We then left Egypt, and went to many lands, including those known at the time as Om, Oz, and the remnants of Mu [Author's note: what are now Tibet, Europe, parts of the Americas, and Asia, etc.]. Other Atlanteans who had not come to Egypt, had already gone to other lands, some being of the One, some being of Belial.

Some in the new lands were called the Children of the One gods, or the Great Light Brotherhood, or Great White Brotherhood. Others became known as the magi, magicians, and alchemists. Many of the Children used legends and guises to keep the politically powerful from interfering with them and their "strange" ways. Ignorant rulers were only too happy to let an alchemist pursue their "weird" practices, so long as it could result in discovering a means to make the ruler rich by changing common metal to gold. Still others of the Children were known as great spiritual teachers, thinkers, and creators in the various forms of arts. Many brought forth communities and monasteries, to further the work of the One. In these places, the teachings of the One lived on in pure form, and expanded, spreading to eventually become the foundations of other divergent philosophies and spiritual paths.

A branch of the magi, formed communities around the 5th century B.C., eventually to become known as the Essenes. The purpose of this community was specific: to live a strict spiritual life, as pure and disciplined as possible, in order to create offspring generations that would be of even higher consciousness, in order to provide the ultimate physical vehicles for the final incarnations of the being that was master Thoth and his soulmates. This latter incarnation became known as Jesus, in the male.

That same being had more than two dozen incarnations, beginning with one in Atlantis which became the basis of the story of Adam & Eve which was told in the sacred scriptures of several religions (more about this in a later chapter). He appears in other places in these scriptures also, but his last physical appearance was as Jesus in what became known as the New Testament (which he actually wrote much of himself, although much has been tampered with). He now exists on greater planes in a way we cannot understand with our Earthly brain.

[End of addendum. Back to more recent info related by me, from my own experiences, and those of other Adepts and true teachers.]

NEAR CURRENT EVENTS

There was one community of Atlanteans who didn't live on Atlantis during the great destruction. Living in total isolation from the outside world until a few decades ago, these people remained of the *pure* genetic line of Atlantis. I won't get into that here for a couple of reasons - it's not pertinent to the goal of this book, and it is far too involved to cover properly here.

Having a body that is of the pure genetic line of Atlantis is fascinating, but not really important. A body is just a physical vehicle. Adept monks, the Initiates of the Children of the Law of One, even though not genetically Atlantean Children of the Law of One, are still of the pure line of totally "keeping with" the Law of One via spirit and Universal Consciousness. That is what really matters.

THE PRESENT TIMES
AND
THE PROPHECIES

A Dark Deception

Some people have recently been fooled by the falling of political divisions and apparent changes in the forms of government around the world, thinking that it is leading us to a new age of peace and oneness. But take care, for this is but a grand illusion, perpetrated by the dark ones, and the outward appearances of the beginning of what is really the final attempt to takeover the world by the forces of darkness. The new age of peace and oneness cannot be achieved by governments. And while this age of enlightenment is close, it is not *here* yet - so beware - a false, *negative* "new age" *is* at your door. Prophecies from many diverse cultures all over the world concur that we will first need to deal with the darkness coming to full power, the "Anti-Christ" so to speak, and a powerful system of Anti-Light, before there is an age of peace, harmony, and "Christ Consciousness". The prophecies of the Children predict this also, but go a step further by stating that it is upon us now and starting to "snowball". This you are seeing the beginnings of, and you shall see its full face in the very near future. We are about to see tyranny, oppression, and control/enslavement on a scale that is unprecedented. A helping hand will be offered to a collapsing world, an economically desperate world, a crime-ridden world - a hand that will welcome you and take care of you - and make you a servant for the dark side, if you grasp it.

In recent years, Tibet has been systematically "raped". Thousands upon thousands of Buddhist monasteries have been deliberately destroyed. Loving beings of the Light have been tortured and killed. The destruction of the Tibetan culture and people is well underway. The world has not acted to stop these obvious horrors. It's not even covered by the media. Why?

The continuing decay of the Earth's eco/biological system brings Global catastrophe rapidly closer in a myriad of ways, yet the world governments don't put an immediate halt to the many known causes of this encroaching global disaster. Hate crimes and strange crimes by children are on the rise throughout the world. Obviously something is very wrong, and the variety of popular ideas and approaches to dealing with it just make for a great show while things continue to get worse. There are no solutions other than spiritual. Most people believe that there actually are various political "sides" with totally different approaches, opposing each other. But if there are really political differences, why is the outcome always the same? Either un-enlightened basically selfish people are in control, or they are not. It just varies to the degree of selfishness, and thus the degree of darkness.

The reality is, that things are way beyond there being any political solutions. There are no military solutions either. But there are soul-utions. We can change ourselves to be someone who is not contributing to the evils. And we can find our Inner freedom, Inner salvation, which automatically makes us part of the solution.

It is said that it is always darkest before dawn. The time of darkness is great once again. Most of those from Atlantis are back again. And the same selfish mistakes are being made again. The last days of Atlantis are with us once more, and thus is suppression of the light (positive polarity - positivity), and the expansion of darkness (negative polarity - negativity). The following story is just one indication of this.

Every May, the Children of the Law of One participate in a group-meditation called "Wesak" (wee-sock). Initiates of the Law of One all enter a deep trance-like meditation, which brings us closer together, and into the higher realms within the Universal Spirit. There are several reasons for it. For one, it is a momentary "break" from the constant pain and sorrow of having to live in physical bodies, in this world of suffering and lost souls. Wesak was once the closest we came to getting a "vacation getaway". The Wesak meditations last for days, and are begun and ended on and off, at various times. The meditation is also a powerful communion that is "experienced" simultaneously, by Children of the Law of One around the world, regardless of where they are. The Wesak meditations create an emotional, mental, and spiritual "link", that renews and bonds us all. We share energy, feelings, and information, and temporarily merge as One being with many facets. In order to achieve this, the meditations are so deep, that we leave our physical bodies, and join in "astral" or "spiritual" realms. It was always a joyful celebration, a time of "sharing" with a degree of intimacy and love that most of you cannot understand at this time. These days, it is also a time of sadness.

In 1990, during Wesak, we were set upon by what could be called "modern day agents of the Sons of Belial". On one night of that Wesak, "hit teams" struck and murdered teachers of our order. It was planned and executed with precision timing, simultaneously, on an international level. We were all defenseless at the time, because of being in the deep trance-like Wesak meditations. Hundreds were murdered throughout the world. Some of us survived only because we had alert elder or novice monks nearby, who were able to fend off the attackers. And that dark night was just the beginning of occasional attacks, that continue to this day. This had never happened before. But those who serve the darkness had actually become so blindly self-centered, they were ignoring implications of karmic law (cause & effect). Having "crossed the line" and broken what might be called ancient "Universal rules of engagement", a new era of physical, psychological, and psychic attacks began. Even our isolated monastery in Tibet was to be targeted.

Some of you are aware of the thousands of Buddhist monasteries that have been attacked, destroyed, and used as target practice for the military. But the attack on our monastery was far different, and not conducted by the military forces you might expect (more on that later).

During Wesak, when greater numbers of us were gathered there, the monastery, and all who were there, including Gabriel, were physically obliterated by military forces using state-of-the-art "hi-tech" weapons.

All who were gathered there for Wesak, were lost to us on the physical plane. There are few survivors around the world now, far less than 1000. Those of us who remain are few, and there is only so much each can do. And it is not over.

*[Author's note: This was a very sad event, but I am sometimes dismayed that some readers express more regret that the monastery and library were destroyed, than regretting that the monks and teachers who were there were all killed. Please remember that even though the monastery was remarkably unique and ancient, it was just a place, just buildings! The greatest loss was that of those who were caretakers of your souls, those who made the monastery what it was, those who were the life and soul of the monastery - those without whom, it wouldn't have BEEN a monastery. We keep hearing from people saying "wasn't anything saved of the library?". No. And yes, like the destruction of the library at Alexandria, the destruction of our library was a great loss, but how great a loss compared to the loss of the teachers?? The loss was nothing in comparison. Let's say a great carpenter teaches all his skills, everything he knows, to his apprentice, and that apprentice becomes a great carpenter who does the same, and on and on. What's more important, the master carpenter, or the **building** he taught in? The master carpenter, or the "home improvement" **books** he read when he was young? And if you really want to learn to become a great carpenter yourself, what can you learn best from - a great carpenter, or a book about carpentry? Teachings are written in this book. But they are living in enlightened teachers. So if you really want to become a great enlightened teacher, what can you best learn from - a great enlightened teacher, or a book about how to be a teacher? And what is more important for learning, growing, and attaining spiritual wisdom and enlightenment - ancient buildings that have no teacher - or a teacher who has no ancient buildings?*

Also, as I mentioned earlier, this is not an ancient archeology book, nor is it about the monastery itself - the story of the monastery is inconsequential "background". Let's use an analogy. For a moment, think of the book as a stage (for a play with a message). The message is more important than the play, and what the playwright wants the audience to "get". The play itself is less important. The stage and "sets" for various scenes are even less important - in fact, they're completely unimportant to the message. And the monastery is merely one of the "sets". One "set" may be destroyed, but the play goes on delivering its message.

We have already expressed that it doesn't matter to us whether or not anyone believes anything that happens to be in the book - ancient history, Atlantis, Hall of Records, whatever, let alone the "stage", or "sets" involved. Once again, the book's SOLE purpose is to present teachings about the spiritual realities of life, and how you can personally change, get back to Oneness with God, and have a positive effect on others and the world. Either those teachings make logical and intuitive sense, and are considered valuable/important, or not.

Next, some readers have asked how the monastery remained undiscovered, even by Tibetans. Here are the reasons. First, to the Tibetans, the area was considered forbidden. They would not go there, and they wouldn't help anyone else who tried to go there. In fact, they would do what they could to prevent it. Also, until the advent of the Chinese invasion, Tibet was "closed" to outsiders. Next, for explorers other than Tibetans, it was very difficult to get to, and protected. It is documented that a few explorers tried to reach the area via alternate routes in the last century, but stopped and turned back just before getting there. There is more than one reason for that, including hierarchical influence, and force fields that weaken the body. But whether you believe in such things or not, the documented facts are that the explorers turned back everytime (you can decide the reasons). Of course, the area is not protected now as it once was, but still, it remains highly isolated and very difficult to get to. Finally, it was hidden from the view of satellites. Recently a reader sent us a copy of a newspaper article about an amazing discovery. In the winter of '99, a year after this book was first published, explorers from National Geographic entered the general area of our monastery. They were the first "non-Children" to ever do so, and considered it an amazing discovery. The headline read "Shangri-la Discovered" (or something like that). Amongst other things, it described a **lush sub-tropical** valley amidst the Himalayas, so hidden by natural phenomenon that it never even showed up on spy satellite photos (see our website for details). They were also astounded by the flora and fauna. A paradise of trees, ferns and legendary animals, all hidden away from civilization, and according to them, any previous human contact. You'd expect such a discovery would be getting pretty decent media coverage, wouldn't you? But what should have been the discovery of the century (or at least the decade) was barely getting any attention at all. In fact, the article was very difficult to find, and National Geographic didn't respond to our repeated inquiries (we thought it would be nice to have some pictures). Then recently, the National Geographic Explorers TV show aired a story about that expedition - but the story was "cut off", so to speak, leaving it with the expedition only discovering the waterfalls nearby. Nothing was said about the "big" discovery of the lush sub-tropical valley. Why? I can only guess. Perhaps something was found that doesn't "fit", and would shake up the status quo? Or something even more serious? Or maybe they just thought the discovery would only "bore" those who watch the "Discovery channel" and PBS?

One reader also asked for the precise coordinates so maybe scientific research teams could be sent in to make an amazing discovery public, and perhaps get some benefit from it. Before I get into that, let me just mention that we prefer it not be made public because there are still monks in the area who would suffer severe adverse consequences as a result. But even putting that aside, such a scientific revelation would never happen. To start with, consider this one example (it's really one out of hundreds of examples of the suppression of archeological finds that "don't fit" the status quo). Edgar Cayce gave the **specific location** of the legendary "Hall of Records" in Egypt. Egypt is a free and far more easily accessible country compared to Tibet - both politically and geographically. Cayce literally **pinpoints** where the record chamber is located between the Great Pyramid and the Sphinx, which are right outside a major city. He even gave specific directions on accessing the passage leading to the records (through one of the paws of the Sphinx). Even with all those specifics available to allow Cayce's story to be proven or disproven, what difference has it made? What scientific research teams have been able to discover, or prove (or disprove for that matter) its existence, and with what result? Does the government of Egypt (let alone China) give permission for anyone to do whatever they want to try and find it? No. And as for it being discovered (which it has been secretly), there's virtually no chance that the truth would ever make it to the public. In fact, I know a film producer ("Star Wars", etc.) who was in Egypt making a documentary about the mysteries of the Sphinx for a major television network. During the filming, they conducted above-ground scanning for hidden chambers, and found an underground chamber exactly where Cayce said the Hall of Records was located. This man tried everything possible to have legitimate archeological excavation of the chamber started, and made public. He concluded that getting them to give such permission, was "harder than getting the US Treasury to let you have the keys to Fort Knox". Scientists run into the same wall - evidence or not. So even knowing the precise "coordinates" of any "special" archeological find or ruins, does not make for a publically revealed discovery. However, it can make serious problems for those involved, or in the area - like our monks. I don't believe that satisfying someone's curiosity, scientific or otherwise, is worth that in any case, but especially when it wouldn't do any good anyway. The archeological community doesn't want any info out that "rocks the boat", and our monastery falls into that category. They won't spread the news of such a discovery amongst the scientific community, and the media won't cover it either. But even more of an issue with our old monastery, is that certain governmental forces don't want any evidence coming out regarding who's military forces were involved in destroying it. I can't say who because of the further problems it would cause, but I will tell you it wasn't Chinese. Again, the media wouldn't touch the story even if someone brought them absolute proof of the ancient buildings, and/or evidence of who/how/why regarding the destruction.

Another very important point I would like to make here. This book is in lieu of our making information available to the public from a secret record chamber buried in Egypt near the sphinx. These are mentioned in the Cayce readings, and called the Hall of Records, so I will refer to them by that name. Many people have misinterpreted the Cayce readings to mean that the Hall of Records will be opened and revealed for the public. But close scrutiny and applied understanding will show that they can only be opened by an Initiate of the Law of One, and were put there by us, for our own use at a later time in the future. IF they were ever opened by us, we were then to decide what would be revealed to the public. Here's the scoop -

At the time they were placed there, we didn't know exactly how various free will choices would effect or change the future (within certain bounds). We weren't sure to what extent, if any, those records could be excavated and/or *made public. Nor were we sure to what extent the lineage of our order would be preserved. But now the future is upon us - we are finally in the present times. And as we reach the period in which the discovery of the Hall of Records (and more importantly, its contents and "message") could have been made public, we are faced with the reality of our times. Mainstream public revelation of such a discovery is very, very, very unlikely. It would discredit careers, and upset the theories/beliefs of many people and organizations all over the world. On the other hand, public revelation of the "message" of the records via this book is a minor threat in comparison, because many people won't buy the book in the first place, and many won't take it seriously even if they do.*

It would have been great to "stun" the world citizenship with an archeological find that presented the history, spiritual message and teachings that are here in this book. Many more people would have heard about it, and the general public would have had to take it seriously. But that isn't going to happen because of the way things are in the world. The "powers that be" are not going to announce the discovery of archeological proof of alternative theories of creation, prophecy, and teachings like those contained in this book (or the Hall of Records), because it would radically change the status quo, our lives, and theirs. Yes, there is a slim chance this may still somehow "slip out", but 1998 was the time for the revelation. That's why this book was released during '98. Other than you directly accessing the records psychically, this book "is it". It reveals the essential contents and message of the Hall of Records in a condensed form. It basically covers the Hall or Records essentials - pre-history of our species, the changes that have occurred and are yet to be upon us, the nature of God and the Universe, our place in it all, and how to get free again (back to our spiritual, angelic state, and back to living in harmony and Oneness with the Universal Spirit). That last part is the most important. In fact, those keys to your spiritual nature and how to reclaim it are the REASON for our existence as a spiritual order, and for this book. The records were not placed there to be discovered in the future as fascinating curiosities, nor archeological artifacts, nor proof of Atlantis (or a library or a monastery). So here is your "alarm clock" going off. Your reminder about your true spiritual heritage, how to regain it, and that at this time in history, the time of great changes is beginning. This book is fulfilling that purpose and destiny. Those of you who truly have eyes to see and ears to hear will recognize that and get what you need from it.]

Now, because of the assassinations of our teachers and destruction of the primary monastery, there is an overburdening problem with our ability to help all of those who need help to free themselves from their separate selves, and return to Oneness with God. There is a great need for a new wave of others to attain Universal Consciousness, so they can join us in helping their brothers and sisters. This is one of the reasons for this book.

Much of what I am writing here would never have been made public before, but because of the teacher shortage, and the times of change that are upon the world, these writings are being released now. This is being done primarily to: 1) Reach more of those who may have evolved to the point where they would have normally come into contact with a teacher by now; 2) To pass on our heritage - *your* heritage; 3) Reach the few of you stragglers who have ears to hear, and who may be helped by it. We are doing this because the time is so short, and resources so limited. As I said earlier, the cycle has come full circle, and the oppression and upheavals that plagued Atlantis long ago, are beginning to visit the Earth again.

If you still have spiritual work to do on yourself, please hasten, for time is so very, very short. If you feel the need, and have the desire to have personal help and guidance, then find a teacher now. Pray for guidance and help if you want it. If not, do what you must, but do it now. And when your self-work is complete, there is much for you to do, for many others need your help. But if you do not complete your self-work soon, it may be a very long time before you get a chance to continue. We are at the end of an age, and the time of harvest is at hand. The Earth is cleansing itself of the "virus" (human beings) that has infected her and made her ill. Even if you have changed so that you are not part of this disease, her fever, shaking, and purging will not necessarily leave you unscathed. It is very difficult to reincarnate when there are few physical vehicles, or none, for your spirit to enter. Even in the advent of a new age of enlightened humans, you will be waiting in a long line. And if you don't become transcendent of your separate self before the coming tribulations are over, and you have not met the obligations of your karma before you leave your present body, you will be waiting in an undesirable, unpleasant state of existence, for a very, very, long time before your opportunities again exist. But if you live with, as the Buddhists say, "right mindfulness", you can achieve total freedom and paradise. It's all up to you.

Ask yourself the following question, and really give it some thought: What kind of world would you like? What kind of world do you want to live in? Would you like to live in a world full of kind, caring people - of peace, harmony, and creativity? You can. But, you must be the kind of being who would naturally inhabit such a world. As I said, the Earth is presently in a most disharmonious condition. *Ask yourself why the world is this way? If you trace any problem to its roots you will find that **it is the result of the selfishness that is the natural outcome of separate consciousness, rather than shared consciousness.*** The selfish-based thoughts and actions of all kinds - hate, wars, starvation, greed, poverty, torture, etc., are not unusual freak events, they are just the day-to-day "norm". And it gets worse daily. If you don't like these things, identify the real enemy. This enemy, the selfishness spawned by separateness, is within each of us. We cannot change anyone but ourselves. If we want to make a change in all this, that's the *only* place to begin. Surrender to the Universal One - to "God". Get back to Universal consciousness any way you can, as quickly as you can.

The selfish motives that drive negative destructive activities on the Earth could not exist if the people were of One consciousness, One with each other and the Universe itself. Yet it does exist, and now the effects of the small-minded human actions on nature itself, have created a ponderous imbalance in the Earth. The Earth, and the very Universe itself, in restoring the balance, will soon produce changes that will result in great devastation to all life, including human life. It has already begun. Nature is causing great changes. Extinction of species is skyrocketing. New plagues have already arrived for both human and other life forms. Starvation and homelessness is on the rise. Why?

Humans have been a "disease-causing parasite" to this planet and its other life forms. What do *our own* bodies do when infected? We get chills, raises in temperature, shaking, vomiting, and bowel evacuation, all done to increase elimination of toxins, and to create an environment that will kill infection associated germs. Entire species, multiple species, of plant and animal life are becoming extinct on this planet daily, *directly* due to its "infection" by humans. The Earth is a being, and it is reacting similarly to the way our body reacts to an infection. Can you not already see the first signs - increases and decreases in temperature in different areas of the land and oceans (the cute name "El Nino" is just one of many such effects), extreme flooding here/extreme drought there, more and more eruptions and shakings. What is beginning to take place is not unlike what our own bodies do to heal themselves of disease. Open your eyes if they are not already open!

Back during my conversation with Gabriel so long ago, after he told me of all these things that would someday come to pass (many of which now have actually come to pass), I asked him an important question,

"So how can we live in a *paradisiacal* world?"

"We can do this by shedding ourselves of what makes us part of the selfish, destructive world. This is achieved by *displacing* the selfish part of us that contributes to the darkness, overthrowing it from our personal throne of command, and replacing it with the part of ourselves that is giving, caring, kind, harmless. Let the Inner-One reign as King of our actions and thoughts. Create yourselves anew, as beings incapable of harm, and live a life of Unselfish Love.

All is vibration, including your consciousness. It is Universal Law that vibration will seek and find its own level. Remember our conversation about how oil and vinegar are of different molecular vibrations, different natures. As oil will always go to oil, vinegar will always go to vinegar, even if they are broken up and mixed for a time, so too, whatever your vibration of consciousness is, you will end up in that vibratory plane of existence. You will end up where you belong, with who you belong with, only by virtue of what you are - what you make yourself to be will determine your destination. Where your heart is, so shall you be also. Build your nest where you want to live. If you live a life of Unselfish Love, how can it be any other way but for you to join the others who have already done this, and live with them in a world of Love and light? If you live a selfish life, who will have you amongst them? Only those of your like kind.

In order to travel, to go anywhere, one must let go of where they are, and where they have been, or they cannot go anywhere. To continue going on requires continually letting go of where you are. Going onward in consciousness into Love and light requires letting go of the negative self - of selfishness. Yes, the death and rebirth of the negative separate self may be painful. Often times growth is accompanied by pain. But this is everyone's price for a 'ticket to paradise'."

It was more than worth it to me. Is it worth it to you?

Chapter Eight

Love

During my first week at the monastery I attended a course, taught by the elder monk Clare, in which I learned about the important fundamentals of the Children's teachings. They were beautifully basic and, as she put it, "simple".

"The teachings of the Children of the Law of One are very simple, and have two basic aspects to them, which are referred to as a 'foundation', and an 'essence'. The *foundation* of the teachings is basically this: all beings, all things, are One, and suffering is the result of humans forgetting that, and not acting as One. Thus all the problems on Earth would cease with the achievement of Universal consciousness. So breaking the illusion of separation, and returning to conscious awareness of Oneness should be our goal if we want to exist in a positive and harmonious world. And the teachings stress *personal experience* of Oneness with the Universe through any meditation, or spiritual attunement method that works for you - not taking them on faith, or intellectualizing it from a book or lecture."

I was still groggy, and having a hard time getting down my "boiled socks" tea to get any help from some caffeine. Yet I was still "getting it" for the most part.

"But while the *foundation* of the teachings is Oneness, the *essence* of the teachings is Unselfish Love. It is considered both the most important means to achieve Universal Consciousness, and the end result. And the end certainly justifies the means in this case."

I already had an idea about what Unselfish Love meant, and how difficult and painful it could be. In fact, the book I mentioned earlier, "Stranger in a Strange Land", really "conceptualized", or "grounded out" this idea for me. But at the time, it was still just an idea that I thought was great, and really liked. Before I came to the monastery, I tried to apply it by being "unjealous" about my girlfriend. I, idealistic fool that I was, made an "Unselfishly Loving" gesture to my girlfriend. I told her she could have affairs with other men, as long as they were good guys, and someone I also knew and loved. But when she actually had an affair with my best friend, even though it was "open" and I knew about it and agreed to it because of my newfound intellectual "principles", I came up against that great selfish beast in myself. I went through hell, but I controlled myself and dealt with it OK. No one got hurt, except my emotions and ego. But that incident had occurred fully two years prior, and thus was all "ancient history" to me with my young point of view. But now it was more than just a girlfriend at issue. Becoming a monk meant giving up all desires and selfish possessiveness. Even though we were not a celibate order. I could no longer expect anyone to "belong" to me, and be "mine". I had undertaken the task of learning to Love all people, whether they loved you back or not. And I had a lot to learn about what that meant still.

For awhile now, ever since I had been at the monastery, I'd had a "thing" for Anastasia. I thought I loved her - I *was* "in love with her". But the reality of things, as far as what I was experiencing, was I was developing envy, jealousy, and possessive desires. From what I'd already learned, I knew that wasn't something that should, or even possibly can, go hand-in-hand with *real Love.* Obviously, while I understood it intellectually, I still didn't understand it as a reality in my life - I had not *realized real Love* yet - Unselfish Love. My only real understanding of love was the relationships I had. Family, friends, and women. I thought they were basically unselfish, and really loving. But I was in for an awakening about that - and more than one awakening (discussed in the soulmate chapter).

And then there was also the issue of loving God, and God's Love. As a child, I was taught that God loved us. But part of my becoming an atheist was because of the horrible conditions and suffering in the world. How could such terrible things happen, especially to innocent children and animals, if God loved us?

I eventually went to Zain with all this that was troubling me, and he started by giving me a long list of texts to look up at the library.

"Above ALL, Love."

God is not Loving
God is not Unloving
God is Love
Give Love and You Give God
Give Love and You Get God

The Universal One is Love

Find Oneness at ALL Cost.
In finding Oneness, you find God.
In finding Oneness, you find yourself.
In finding Oneness, you find Real Love.

Living as One, is to Unselfishly Love ALL
Living as One, is to Unselfishly Love yourself.
To find Oneness, Unselfishly Love others,
Before yourself.

True Love is Unselfish.
True Love is Givingness.
True Love flows out like the waters,
Nurturing all who would drink from it.
True Love does as the Stars.
True Love does as the Sun - it shines
on the evil as well as the righteous.
True Love seeks nothing in return.

True Love is Untainted by Wants.
True Love desires only furtherance of True Love

True Love is Strong in the Right.
True Love is Indignant in the face of Deceit.
True Love is Kind.
True Love is Compassionate.
True Love is Caring.
True Love is Creation.

To become Truly Loving,
Find someone who Truly Loves.
Empty Yourself, and let their Love fill you.
Then keep not the Love you have found
to yourself.
For only in giving it away,
Will you always have it.

Unselfish Love is the Way of Daily Balance.

Imagine
a world
Full of people who are ALL Loving Unselfishly -
does any self go without receiving Love?
All receive Love.

Imagine
a world
full of people who ALL love selfishly -
do any go without receiving Love?
None receive Love.

Feel Unselfish Love

If Your Thoughts
Are Not Accompanied
By Feeling Unselfish Love,
Can What You Are Thinking Be Correct?

I want to Know What Love Is

I found Zain returning from the little "Adept monk's refuge" pyramid that was
at the end of the long path that wound up the hill from the monastery. I met him

part way up the path, then we wandered the beautiful green countryside as we spoke.

"So you've been up at the little pyramid, eh Father?"

"How did you know?" he said sarcastically.

"What goes on in there anyway?"

"We get away from young monks that bug us with too many questions constantly."

"No really. Is it just a glorified officer's club, or teacher's lounge, but without any drinks, socializing or fun?"

"You'd be surprised."

"Wild parties, eh?"

"Do you have something serious to ask me, or do you just want to torment me with your attempts at humor?"

"Ok. So you don't appreciate my jokes. But you haven't heard the one about the woks yet."

"And I won't right now if I have any choice."

"I'm sorry. I think I make even more jokes sometimes when I have something serious on my mind."

"That's natural. Humor lightens our burdens, and can lighten or deflect some of the effects of negativity or pain in our lives. But don't joke about something you need to learn, because it tends to neutralize the effect of learning."

"I do have something I need your help with. I have a problem with understanding Love, Father. Sometimes I think I Love, then sometimes I see that I must not be truly Loving. I know it is necessary to the attainment of enlightenment, and becoming One with God, so I need to understand it better. I have read the texts, and they helped. But I haven't changed, so I just know enough to know that I still don't really know for sure what Love is. What can I do to really know?"

"Real Love is caring, without a thought for yourself. Caring for all people, and caring for a stranger as much as your dear mother, wife, children, etc..

And as you are beginning to perceive, Unselfish Love and Oneness are bound together like two sides of a coin, which I will explain better in a moment, but first, let's deal with your confusion by process of elimination, and discuss what people usually call love.

Love is probably the most abused word on Earth. Some people think they know Love is compassion, giving, caring, nurturing. And some do know it. But the word love, and even the concept of love, is generally used to describe something quite different, something actually selfish and unloving, that's why we take such pains to differentiate the terminology."

"The terminology?"

"The terminology, the description. It is important because it can mean more things than any word in any language. For instance, love is often used to describe something that gives your selfish separate self pleasure. 'I love ice cream!'. What does that mean? It means that the sensations you get from eating ice cream give your self a great deal of pleasure. 'I really love Sam'. What does that mean? Since most relationships are based on this separate self, selfish oriented 'love', in that context it means that Sam gives you pleasure, so having a relationship with Sam brings you pleasure. Thus the selfish separate self wants Sam, wants to have Sam, wants to possess Sam. Yet you say you LOVE Sam. Wrong. You don't really, truly Love

Sam in the sense of caring, giving, selfless self-sacrifice, like a good mother Loves her child. There may be an element of that kind of Love involved, but it's always strongly overshadowed by the self-centered, selfish kind of love. What they call love in this Sam example, is just the normal, typical, mutually possessive, mutually attached, 'give & take' relationship. Each person expects to take and the other is expected to give in order to maintain the relationship. It is one-sided on both sides, you see? So you have two trains on the same track, moving towards an eventual head-on collision. That is the kind of relationship most people have and expect to have. Such selfishly based love is a condition of negative polarity - the 'way' of taking. It is always 'sucking' energy. This is the exact opposite of the condition of positive polarity - the 'way' of being giving. The 'way' of being giving, could also be called Unselfish Loving.

It is a basic precept of the Children, that in order to achieve a Universal consciousness, and fully understand the Universe and our place in it, you must Unselfishly Love. So it is important to recognize and differentiate between Loving Unselfishly, and loving in a selfish, possessive way."

"Yes, I think I understand all that. You probably remember the story I told you about my girlfriend. And I did try to love her enough to let her go, and not be jealous. And I thought I was doing that at the time. So I totally agree that it's important to recognize and differentiate between selfish and Unselfish Love. I do want to achieve Unselfish Love and Universal consciousness. But how do I really know which is which, and when I am feeling selfish love or Unselfish Love? It's already fooled me once."

"Start by contemplating your motives for giving or loving. In other words, when you are 'giving', what do you personally stand to lose or gain from that giving? Is there a selfish motive involved at all? If so, it contaminates any real unselfish giving and Love that may have been there also. When you are 'loving', what will you be getting back from the one you 'love'? For instance, if you give a gift to your lover, don't you expect to get gratitude and extra affection? Selfish motives are behind giving or loving in what would be called a 'normal' relationship. Often, even when people give to their lover, there is a subtle motive to get something back. Because when you give to your lover, feeding their wants and desires, they like it, they 'get off on it' as you put it - then they like you because you are giving them the things or feelings they want - and we know that. Thus YOU get a response from them that 'gets YOU off'. That's ideally how it works in a normal relationship, but it's often not the case. There is also an expectation of reciprocation, which is ultimately never met."

"But I didn't have any selfish motivation when I offered to let my girlfriend go do that."

"You *thought* you didn't, but you had a selfish motive also."

"No. What?"

"You didn't think that if you did that, she would let you do the same?"

"Well, yes, it would have been an assumption. But I didn't do it because of that. I really wanted to live true Love, and give Love, and I wanted her to be happy."

"I see in your eyes that you speak the truth, son. You have already learned the lesson of motivation, and giving in that way. But you haven't transcended your selfishness yet. And therein was the problem."

"Yes."

"And you have much to go through before you will, I'm afraid."

"I hope not."

I had no idea the suffering I would have to endure before I transcended my self-ishness regarding women, finally become truly Unselfishly Loving, and find true Love. But that is a subject for later in the book.

Our conversation went on.

True Love

"Is there such a thing as 'true' Love?"

"Do you mean in the sense of a relationship?" He didn't give me time to answer. "No matter. In either case, the answer is the same. What I would call true Love, is simply Unselfish Love. Unselfish Love radiates to *all* without exception, so powerfully that it transcends your separate self and IS God's Love flowing through you, to others. You become the vessel that is 'channeling' the Universal Spirit (while also *being* the Universal Spirit). It gives to all who would receive. It is like a Sun that gives warmth, light, and life to all, in all directions simultaneously. If your love is *not* one that gives to *all* and loves *all,* then it is a selfishly based love. If you experience jealousy or possessiveness, then it is a selfishly based love, not true Love, not pure Love, not Unselfish Love."

"Then virtually no one truly Loves, or experiences receiving true Love."

"Unfortunately this is true. There are few situations in which most people experience giving pure Unselfish Love, and the unselfish joy that comes from giving it. Yet it does happen in certain ways from time to time. Mothers have the greatest opportunity for this, because of the very nature of their relationship with their children. Mothers cannot expect to "get something in return", or be reciprocally loved by their young children, as they might expect in a normal relationship. Those who do expect gratitude from a young child are going to experience disappointment, because children have not usually developed even the 'artificial showing' of such appreciation at their young age. Most mothers will find joy just knowing they have done something good for their child, or that their child is happy. Some parents, both mothers and fathers, have experienced the feeling of the joy of giving unselfishly, when they give their child a gift that is 'from Santa Claus', rather than from Mom or Dad (thus not *getting* 'credit' for the gift). Also, most mothers would be willing to die for their children. Part of that is genetics of the human animal, but another part is Unselfish Love. A mother is *generally* happy, rather than jealous, when their grown child finds a mate and a pleasurable relationship. There are exceptions to this of course. One such exception which can result in strong feelings of jealousy, and dislike towards the grown child's mate, is when there is karma involving past relationship ties between a mother and child. If the mother, in a past life, disliked, liked, or was romantically involved with the person who is now her child, there can be problems. Or if the mother disliked or was jealous of the child's new mate in a past life, there will be discord."

"So there is no reciprocation of love when you Love Unselfishly?"

"That's not what I said. There can be, but there doesn't *need* to be. If you feel a need for reciprocation, you aren't purely loving Unselfishly. Being Giving, Unselfishly Loving, warms the heart and is beneficial to the giver, and the one who is being given to. Unselfish Love is its own reward. The Universal Spirit is Love. We are like faucets and the Universal Spirit is like water. When you open up and let the water flow to all, you are constantly being filled with the water as it passes through. But if you close the faucet off because you mainly desire to keep the water for yourself, it doesn't flow through you, and you are left empty."

"Which is what most people do."

"Yes. And the people who are thus empty because they don't outflow their Love, then start looking in a different direction for something to 'fill them up'. If a relationship diversion won't do it for them, if they are not loving and getting love from their relationships, which always eventually happens, they do other things. Even if they stay together with someone, they must look for diversions to fill the emptiness of the lack of love and God in their hearts and lives. Desperately they 'think', constantly keeping the brain busy so they won't be aware of their emptiness. They pursue selfish pleasures and amusements of all kinds. They go from diversion to diversion - food, games, clothing, movies, TV, sports, parties, social clubs, hobbies, lovers, shopping, cars, candy, you name it. But there is never any peace, and never any real or lasting satisfaction - only a temporary 'fix'. And like a drug addict who needs a 'fix', the more it gets the more it needs/wants. But the pleasure never lasts, and the feeling is never the same as the joy you get from giving, and ultimately the connection to the Universal Spirit that is made through giving. They're left with that hollowness again, and the need to find some other distraction."

"They are really looking for Love, looking to replace Love, and doing everything but what they really need to do to find it - give it."

"Oh, I get it now that you put it that way," he smiled wryly.

"What do you mean?" I said as he shook his head and walked off. I was confused at why he did that at the time, but later, when I had become more spiritually mature, I realized it was because the tone of my statement reflected my huge ego, and that I wasn't listening well enough.

So I just stood there for a moment, a little stunned, wondering why Zain was just walking off like that in the middle of a conversation. He walked fast, too. He was already half-way down the path back towards the monastery. If I hadn't run after him, he'd have already been inside and gone somewhere before I even got to the gate.

"Father! Father! Wait!"

He just kept walking. When I finally caught up to him, he didn't stop either.

"I wasn't done," I panted. (from the lack of oxygen at that altitude).

"I was."

"But I just wanted to ask you a few more things?" He shrugged his shoulders.

Later that day, I found him again, and asked if he would speak with me some more.

"Can I pester you with a few more questions now?" I said.

He smiled in a manner that said "OK". So I started firing off some questions.

"So one should only seek to Love others, and not receive love?"

"Don't misunderstand, there is *nothing wrong* with receiving love, taking love. In fact, receiving Unselfish Love is wonderful. It is when you only *conditionally give* love, under the guise of love, in order to get something for yourself, that is wrong. It is a serious problem in the world."

"I have heard it said that you must love yourself first. Only then can you love others. But this seems contradictory to the Children's teachings." He stopped walking and looked at me with intensity. It was a look so intense that at one time, before

I really knew him, it would actually scare me a bit inside.

"There is nothing wrong with loving your self either - *unless* that is a rationalization for actually being selfish, which is often the case. But you can really, Unselfishly Love your self. In fact, it is unavoidable if you Love Unselfishly at all. Because when you Love Unselfishly, you love ALL, and that *includes* your *self*. And when you Love Unselfishly, you feel so good about yourself that you can't avoid loving yourself. But you don't ever really feel good about yourself when you love selfishly - your *self* might feel good *temporarily,* but you don't feel good about *yourself*. And if you don't feel good about yourself, how could you really be loving yourself? And how could a heart full of selfishness even find room for *truly* loving its self simultaneously? So it is backwards- what 'they say' about loving yourself first. Now remember this - instead of 'loving yourself first', Unselfishly Love others first, and you will truly love yourself automatically. You just can't go wrong that way. The other is too often just a clever trick of the selfish separate self, to rationalize selfishness."

"OK. I'll always remember that. Getting back to relationships, you touched upon the subject of what the signs were of selfishly, or Unselfishly Loving in a relationship, but can you tell me more about that, specifically, how you can tell if you are loving selfishly in a relationship?"

"I already taught you this earlier."

"I know, I was just hoping for a greater clarification. I'm sorry if I'm being dense."

"Better. OK. And it is a very important thing to learn.

One of the ways you can identify selfish love is, as I mentioned earlier, when you do a self-examination of your motives, and you find that your actions, or feelings of 'love' are because you get something, some kind of energy or attention from the 'loved one'. This is what most people call love.

Here is a common phrase that makes a good example. Perhaps this will help clarify. 'I'll scratch your back if you scratch mine.' You've heard that, yes?" I nodded. "That kind of love is *conditional.* It will only give *if* it is getting what it wants. That's what most relationships are built upon, that mutual agreement to give to each others' selves. Here's another one you must have heard before, 'It must be give and take'. No. It must be 'give and give' in order to work, because if it's 'give and take', what happens when both feel they should be taking at the same time and think the *other* should be giving? And that happens all the time. Relationships like that don't last; they are disintegrating and full of turmoil, for each self wants and fears, and when it doesn't get what it wants or is confronted with its fears and dislikes, problems start. When people enter relationships like that, everything is perfume and roses for a while ('honeymoon period' phenomenon) because the selves are *each getting* so much energy, so much self-gratification. But after awhile, one of the partners in the relationship always falls short, and doesn't give *as much as the other **wants*** - then negativity begins to snowball in a familiar cycle. One partner feels slighted and says or does something to hurt the other. Then the other reciprocates and hurts back. This negativity builds strength and momentum each time it goes back and forth. The relationship is damaged. Sometimes the damage can't ever be repaired and becomes just another coffin nail in the relationship's eventual death. It can be no other way in selfishly based relationships - Universal Law is in effect here. Only in Unselfish Love is peace found, both for the giver, and the receiver.

Of course, the biggest warning sign of selfish love, is jealousy. Selfish love is also *possessive,* and thus must spawn the most horrible and destructive emotion that exists, *jealousy.* Selfish love can *only* bring negativity and destruction in the end. How many have hurt, or even killed, those they supposedly 'love', because 'they loved her/him so much that they 'couldn't stand to lose them'. What Yak Dung! What a grand deception! Such is pure selfishness, not true Love. If you have true Love for someone or something, Unselfish Love, you want the object of your Love to be free and happy, regardless of the consequences to you. When your love is selfishly based, you care more about what you want, and really care *very* little about the 'loved one', if you care at all."

I didn't really know what else to ask him at this point. He'd answered all my questions thoroughly, and new questions about relationships wouldn't crop up until the future - the next time I had to deal with my most serious relationship issues, which I'll discuss later in the book. But this seems like the appropriate chapter to reveal more of the Children's general teachings about the emotions and virtues that are integrally related to True Love. So let's travel to another time, years later, when I was lecturing to a group of novices in the great meditation hall, about the Children's teachings on the practical qualities of Unselfish Love.

The Real-World Qualities of Unselfish Love

"Unselfish Love is the most important *way of being* that there is."

"Why?" said novice Yusef.

"With the exception of people who are hardened in darkness, virtually anyone can agree that kindness, compassion, caring, giving, creation, are good things. Thus, *these* things are *far more significant* than *any* belief, *any* teaching, *any* 'wisdom', *any* knowledge."

"Even more important than the ancient texts and the Children's teachings?"

"Far more important. If you don't understand that, you don't even really understand the teachings, because that's what they are all about. Those qualities are virtues that are the result of Unselfish Love, and Oneness with God, are they not?"

"Yes."

"That was a rhetorical question Yusef." For a moment I wondered if I was such a pain as a novice.

"We call these traits the basic spiritual virtues or qualities, and they are the natural result of true 'spiritual' growth. If these qualities are not the outcome of your 'growth', then the growth is not *really* spiritual."

"Why?" Again with the why.

"Because true spiritual growth moves you away from the world of separateness and selfishness, and towards Universal Consciousness and Oneness. Such a shift in consciousness can only result in caring for all - for you realize that all beings are you, all the Universal Spirit. For instance, you may see people who profess to be 'holy' or 'cosmic', who meditate or pray, or people who have great metaphysical knowledge or developed abilities and so called strengths through various programs or doctrines. Whatever they are getting out of it, if it's not making them more caring and compassionate, it's not spiritual growth.

Compassion

Compassion is the greatest of all these virtues that are a part of Unselfish Love.

Compassion means *feeling* for others, *caring* about others. A person without compassion is truly empty and cold. There is such a thing as imbalanced compassion however. If compassion clouds the mind, and alone dictates your actions, you can make many mistakes and end up harming yourself, and the ones you care about. But this is a problem all too few people have. It is better to have too much compassion, than not enough. But like all emotions, it should not overwhelm you and take control of you. Emotions should be 'feelers' - sensors that we are open to, fully aware of, and get information from - but that we are sufficiently transcendent of, so they do not control us."

Unconditional Love

"Elder Peniel, is Unselfish Love the same as unconditional love?"

"Very good question Yusef. I guess you could say Unselfish Love is a type of unconditional love. But if you interpret the words 'unconditional love' literally, it means giving to, or being supportive of someone, *regardless of their actions,* no matter what. If we use that as the definition of unconditional love, then what we call Unselfish Love is different in an important way. Unselfish Love does not mean giving the loved one *anything* they *want,* or supporting *any and all* actions. Unconditional love like that, could be harmful to the one you love. *Unselfishly Loving* someone *does* mean that you will *always* care for them, always still care about what is best for them, regardless of what the loved one may do or choose. But there can be conditions set on interaction or support."

"What conditions should be set?"

"It's not a matter of a fixed rule. Everyone is different. Everyone has different needs. There are some things that are the same, but each individual does have different things that should be allowed, or not allowed."

"So how do you know where to draw the line and what to give or not give?"

"Loving someone unselfishly, *automatically* makes you give to the loved one what their 'whole being' needs. But it does not just feed their wants and desires. In fact, Unselfish Love may actually require denying a loved one's desire. But whatever is required for the person, whether giving, and/or denying, both are done REGARDLESS of its consequences on you. Even if it means the person will hate you, or fight you, you must do what is best for them.

For example, consider the raising of children. Let's look at the application of Unselfish Love vs. unconditional love and "normal" (selfish) love, in that scenario. There are times when you should not give a child what it wants, because it's not in their best interest. They may want something that could harm themselves, or harm someone or something else. But when Unselfish Love is not present, a child is likely to be 'given in to' when they persist, or through an ego tantrum. But if you give in, even if there is no physical harm that results, it can make them what is commonly called 'spoiled'. The term 'spoiled' is merely a euphemism for a person's selfishness being so consistently 'given in to' and 'well fed', that the self grows in power and wants more, and expects more. In the case of children, they become what people call 'little monsters', and in the case of adults, they become what's called selfish 'jerks' or 'bitches'. Child or adult, a person who's selfishness is overindulged becomes quite difficult to deal with, and they lack civility, and love for others - and you don't want to be the one who feeds such a thing, do you?"

"No."

"That was a rhetorical question again Yusef. Does anyone else want to ask anything?"

"Maya, I feel you have a question?"

"Yes."

"Ok. I understand what you want to know. You've seen people who are often mean to their children, sometimes they get very abusive. But that isn't what we mean by not giving in to them. Quite the opposite.

You see, there is a common flip side to the coin of indulging someone's self. Since it is being done because the person 'giving in' is actually selfish, the other aspects of their selfishness also come out. Sometimes rather than 'giving in to' a child, the same parent (who is not Unselfishly Loving), will instead treat the child with anger or even violence, which also further creates bad programming, bad behavior, and a 'monster'."

"But why do they give in sometimes and not others?"

"Various selfish traits. Laziness, not loving enough to deal with negativity, etc.. How many times have you seen a parent tell a child not to do something, and the child ignores them. The child ignores them because they KNOW they can get away with it. Then the parent says no again. Still no results. Eventually the parent gets angry, and either yells or strikes the child. What does that teach the child? Two things- one, it may be worth the gamble to see how far it can get away with something, because they know the parent doesn't really mean what they say, or back up their threats very often. And two, when the parent finally 'loses it', all the child knows is they are being attacked, hated, and that bigger and stronger is better, and might makes right. All very bad lessons. On the other hand, an Unselfishly Loving parent will give loving instructions one time, and then demonstrate that with absolute regularity, that if they are not listened to, a loving discipline will occur. Sure, it takes more work, and iron clad consistency, and you must sometimes do things that are unpleasant, both for yourself and for the child - such as taking away something the child likes, or 'grounding' them, or isolating them like sending them to their room - but always with Love and kindness. Only such true Loving action yields good results. And it yields remarkable results. The child will eventually not 'test' its limits, and ends up a happier, more loving being itself.

This applies to relationships also. If you tolerate harmful or unpleasant behavior in a mate or a friend, either because of 'unconditional love' or because your relationship is based on selfish motives, then you have a mess. And when you finally 'lose it', and get negative and angry, it will create even more of a mess. But if you Love Unselfishly, you may even be able to help someone overcome *their* problems, by both not tolerating bad behavior, and giving loving, positive direction at the same time."

"I Want to Know what Love is - *I Need You to Show me*"

By now the importance of Unselfish Love should be clear. But how does one *really* get to know what Unselfish Love is? We gave little examples earlier in the chapter, about how some parents may have "tasted" a bit of the joy of Unselfish Love, by anonymously giving to their children under the guise of gifts from Santa Claus. But even that "taste" was virtually nothing compared to the full experience of being totally Unselfishly Loving, and the mix of peace of mind, sadness, and bliss that accompany it. Nor does it give us a taste of what it's like to be totally Unselfishly *Loved*.

In my later years, I discussed it with Zain.

"Father, I don't know if you remember, but a year or so ago, we discussed how one could know when they are selfishly or Unselfishly loving someone."

"No. I don't remember. But I know you always speak the truth now Peniel. What do you need?"

"We covered a great deal about my selfishly loving. But not enough about Unselfishly Loving. I am seeing changes in the way I deal with people as I Love them more, and I also see the results of it - it can make such a difference. I have moments of Unselfishly Loving. And when I think about my personal experiences with the Adept teachers here, I can imagine what a difference it will make in me, if *I become* fully Unselfishly Loving, all the time. And you have told me that my time to leave will be coming soon. Obviously, I can't, or shouldn't, leave until I achieve that kind of Unselfish Love, as a permanent state. So could you tell me more of what I need to know?"

"Peniel, you will know all you need to know when your time has come. But of course, I will answer your question. You know I look forward to our talks a great deal these days."

"As I do also. I Love you more than I ever thought possible."

We embraced for a moment, then he spoke.

"The fact is, most people have *never* experienced pure Unselfish Love, either giving it or receiving it. And how can anyone expect to even know what it is unless someone first Loves *them* unselfishly? How would you describe colors to a person born blind, or born color blind? And how could you describe colors to someone else, if you were born blind yourself, and have never experienced color yourself? That would be even be more difficult. And Unselfish Love is something that you can give "unselfish blind" people, that *will* describe it to them - even more, it will *show* it to them, even though they have never experienced it themselves. In the future after you are enlightened and have left here, when you meet people, it will almost always be the first time they have ever met someone who really Loves them. And you will often be a stranger to them. It will *always* be a blessing for them, even though they may not know it, or know what's going on. It will be more *powerful* than your words, (even though it will be in harmony with both your words and your actions). Because the experience of being Unselfishly Loved involves feeling something from someone, something subtle possibly, but something that you've never felt before. It also involves an Inner spiritual kindling, a knowing, and actually seeing an example of the way someone lives and acts when they are Universally Conscious. Most people can't Love Unselfishly, until they experience being Loved Unselfishly first.

Too few have experienced the impact of being in the presence of a being who is fully Unselfishly Loving. But it is not by accident. It is because they have not been willing to experience it within themselves - they have not been willing to surrender to the Universal Spirit within them. When a person is willing to begin to change, to start to Unselfishly Love, then they will meet someone who Loves them Unselfishly. You will be meeting people like that all the time. People who are ready to change. People who have prayed or desperately hoped for some kind of answers or guidance for their lives. This you will bring without even trying, or doing anything

Experiencing being Loved by a totally Unselfishly Loving being is a great blessing, and this can spark the flame of Unselfish Love within the "loved one" (if they are open to change and to begin giving themselves). Unselfish Love can spread this way. [Author's note: Often, the first time one ever experiences being Unselfishly Loved, is from one's personal true teacher. I'll discuss this more in a later chapter.]

But know that there will be great pain. Because often those who you have completely opened up your great heart to, and made yourself vulnerable to through your Love, will hurt you. You already know though, that such is the price of being a loving servant of the Universal Spirit.

Then there are those who are spiritually hardened, or hiding from the light within, or even the brothers of the darkness. Depending on the severity of their opposition to the light, they will find your presence, your Unselfish Love, mildly disturbing, to extremely annoying, to a reason for rage, anger, hatred, and even violence and murder. You have seen it in the history of all our kin. Look what they did to the grand master, even though he planned it himself to spread the word of Unselfish Love and Oneness with God."

The Other Side of the Coin

Earlier you read that Unselfish Love and Oneness were like two sides of a coin. Unselfish Love is *what a person does*, who *knows* they are One with God, the Universal Spirit. Unselfish Love is the way of the flow of the Universe, the way of the One. Unselfish Love is the way of being in harmony with the Universe, and an instrument for doing the will of the Universal Spirit. Unselfish Love is both the *end result* of breaking our illusion of separateness, and *a way* of attaining Oneness.

Unselfish Love makes *Living* a Meditation

While you can find a detailed, concise list of the Children's specific meditation techniques in part two of this book, the concepts presented here are not just philosophy and stale dogma. They are, in a grand sense, also a "technique". A way of living a special lifestyle. A Universal lifestyle. Living life with an attitude of Unselfish Love is the "technique" of a Universal lifestyle. And that is the essence within all the Children's teachings.

In one of my discussions with Zain, he taught me this concept. One day I was asking him about meditation, and telling him I had so many duties, I couldn't find time for my meditations. Of course, this wasn't really true. I was just being lazy. This is what he had to say to me:

"Unselfish Love is the way of eternal everyday life meditation. It spans 24 hours a day, everyday. Even your sleeping hours, your dreams, can be a meditation. I would define meditation here as a being in the middle, perfectly balanced between the Infinite and the finite, manifesting the Universal Spirit (Infinite) in the physical plane (finite). Meditation has often been considered a process of stilling the mind, but that is not the whole of it. Just the stilling of the mind can be relaxation, concentration, or discipline. These build your mind into a strong tool for the Universal Spirit, but are prerequisite to true meditation. The mind must be still for you to be a channel for Spirit, but just the stilling of mind, the relieving of tensions etc., without the merging with the highest ideal you can conceive of, and applying, manifesting that, is for what? Of what good is any belief or 'growth' method if it doesn't make life better, more kind, more beautiful? If your life doesn't radiate these things then your life is but that of a Sun that doesn't shine. The opportunity to grow, to give, and to Unselfishly Love is here every moment. Your whole life can be a constant meditation, meditation in action, a flow in harmony with Universal flow. This is the song of life, the art of living; it is always forever now. For when one truly attains Universal Consciousness, everything "else", every thought, every action, reflects it. It is a change from a life of wanting and fearing to a life of giving and security.

To give you somewhat of an example of aspects of your life that can radiate anew, here is a very incomplete list of just some of the everyday type of activities that can be a part of your constant meditation, your Universal lifestyle. When approached in this way, even the mundane becomes a beautiful flowing art form, including: Relationships with others; Walking/running/movement; Sex; Driving; Sweeping; Washing dishes [Author's note: I've had some great dish washing meditations - I'll tell you about them later]; Breathing; Opening/closing a door; Waiting; Doing things quickly without hurrying; Eating; Chopping Wood; Writing; Drawing; Singing; Composing; Talking; Digging; Planting; Anything and Everything. So tell me, you have no time for meditation?"

Again, the essence of it all is to manifest the Universal Spirit in, and through, the physical vehicle (body-mind-self) by living a life of Unselfish Love. You're going to hear this same thing over and over again, and in many ways, throughout these pages. It's not mere redundancy, it's being repeated to make the impression that everything always comes back to the same thing. And that one concept is all you need to REALize in order for everything to fall into place; it is the master key to any door.

The Phantom Attacks by Night

In the years after I left the monastery, I traveled a great deal. During that time I visited monasteries and spiritual communities of many different religions and paths. One spiritual community I stayed with for a few weeks, had created a unique way for its members to experience Unselfish Love, via giving to other members. They called it "The Phantom", and here's how it works: let's say someone makes a cake, or a coat, or whatever, to give to someone else in the community. Rather than giving it to them outright, or wrapped with a little card letting them know who the gift is from, they leave it sneakily, in the middle of the night, with a note saying it is from the Phantom. Their method insures the anonymity of the giver, thus, the only personal gain the giver gets, is the joy of doing something nice for someone else, the joy of giving, the joy of Unselfishly Loving. This insures that the giving is being done for the right reasons, unselfishly, and is thus not feeding the selfish separate self. You might want to try some "Phantom" giving yourself - it's not only good for you, it's fun.

Chapter Nine
The Separate Self

We have already covered part of these teachings in other chapters. But even though some of the writing in this chapter is just a bit redundant, it offers a great deal more clarification, and other information from the ancient Atlantean teachings.

In Hot Water?

It was in my second year, and I had developed a deep bond with my teacher Zain. But at this point in my evolution and learning, he could still really shake me up and throw me for a loop when he wanted to (which he did from time to time as part of the process of helping me change and grow). Obviously he decided I needed to consider changing something about myself, or understanding something I was not really "getting", because one day he stopped me on the way to the hot pool, and said quite sternly and loudly, in his "intensity mode":

"Have you ever asked this about your life or the world in general: 'Why so much suffering and destruction?'"

"Uh... I was just on my way..." He had that intense fire in is eyes. I hesitated for a moment, trying to think of what to say or do, then I decided I better just simply answer his question. I struggled past being stunned for a moment, so I could actually think about his question before I answered. We just stood there while he waited for my answer. Then it finally came out after a few seconds that seemed like years.

"Yes. Of course I have Father. I asked it often, even when I was young, and it always perplexed me. Then one day I guess I just sort of gave up, thinking there was nothing I could do about it anyway."

"Accurately Identifying the Problem is the First Step Towards Finding any Solution."

"So what is the problem?"

"The Separate Self IS THE Problem."

Then he walked off as if he'd just only said, "Top of the mornin' to ya," as we passed in the streets of Dublin.

Well, later that day, I "stalked" him. I waited until he was on the way to the pool himself, and then when the time was just perfect, I pounced. I stopped him and asked,

"So," I said, "What's the problem?"

"No problem."

"No. You said the separate self is the problem."

"Yes."

"Well, you can't just say that to me and leave it at that."

"Yes, I can."

"But why did you do that, why did you say it that way and just leave me hanging? Is there a problem with me?"

"Certainly."

"Well?"

"OK. You think you got me. Tag. You're it. Now, we'll get you back. First go to the library, ask Gabriel for the English translation book from the *Tablets of Amiliaus*. Pick it up in front of him, hold it in your hand, and let it fall open where it may. Read the pages it falls open to. Then do the same with the *Book of Zoroaster & Zend*. Then, the same with the translations of the book of the *Scrolls of The Old Testament of the Bible*, then the same with the *Scrolls of The Koran,* and *Unaltered New Testament*. Read the pages each falls to. Then also read the following texts..."

He went on to give me my reading list for what looked like a month. Here are some of the most significant highlights:

The Spiritual Self
Came to Be
As The One divided within itself.
Created then, were Infinite
multiplicities of the One
Still One with the One
Consciousness of Oneness Remained

Separate Self Consciousness
Came to Be
As the Separate Self
Moved deeper into the Matter of Earth
Vibration Fell into Density and Fragmentation
With Polarization into Male and Female.
The Opposites Repelled.
The Positive Lost Receptivity.
The Receptive turned from the Positive.
Polarity misdirected, the Flow waned Chaotic.
Severed in Consciousness From The One,
The Way was Lost.

The Separate Self
Only has Life in Separation.
Separation is an illusion,
that the Separate Self Works to Maintain.
The Monkey Mind serves to keep away the stillness
that reveals the Light of Truth and Oneness.

In the Illusion of Separateness
from the One, Ahura Mazda,

107

The Separate Self believes,
and behaves,
in ways that are not harmonious
in the flow of the One.
Such disharmony causes suffering,
both for the Separate Self,
and others.

❖

The Separate Self.
Turned Within instead of Without
Began the way of Take instead of Give
Thus was the Birth of Self-ishness

❖

Then Came to Be
The SELFISH Separate Self
The master of Selfishness,
The Pawn of Darkness.

❖

Selfishness -
The Root of all evil,
All ignorance,
All wrongs,
All pain and suffering.

Greed, Hate, Jealousy, Envy, Vanity and Lust,
Call thee each by thy true name -
Selfishness.
Theft, Brutality, War, and Famine -
Exist not without Selfishness.

❖

The Selfish Separate Self
Is a creature
of our own design.
It Disdains Love
Shuns the Light
Fears the Truth

The Selfish Separate Self
Lives Against the One
It Lives a Lie
It survives only in illusion

It Lives only to serve itself, and its masters -
the darkness and
The Lords of darkness.
It relishes ignorance.
With its self-centered gaze,
It is Blind.

The Selfish Separate Self
Is Insane.
Terrified of death -
yet it often accelerates its demise.
Wants to avoid suffering,
yet it often creates it.
Wants to fulfill its every desire,
yet it often prevents their attainment.
It suffocates itself with its own blind taking,
and destroys its own source of life.

The Selfish Separate Self
Controls the Mind
and Twists the Truth
It can avoid God by Searching for God
It can avoid Love, by Looking for Love
❖

Your Selfish Separate Self
Is the most terrible Demon
You will ever See
Transcend its Grip
And you will be Free

Your Selfish Separate Self
Will frighten You
When you look it in the Eye
Greet it with True Love
And it will Die
❖

From the ashes of its Grave
Like the Sun it will Rise
Born anew, Separate no longer
To serve your True Self
And the Will of The One.
As a servant,
Its proper place,

It Finds Peace and Happiness.
Thusly do the Great Enemies,
Become Allies,
As One.

❖

The One
Becomes Two
The Two become Three
The Two Beget Four
and Begins the More

Within and Without
Torn Between and Against
Mirrors on All Sides
Split Inside and Out
Again and again
Thus is the Ignorant Self

❖

To Be Whole Again
To Be home Again
Only The Weary Learn
Only The Bleeding heart Returns

❖

To Be Whole with the One Again
Is the Great Goal.
The Great Mountain we can climb
with our Will.
For Those who Take Power over
Their Selfish Separate Self,
Will Return
And Be Wholly One.
The Wholly Ones use the Power of Love,
Sacrifice Their Selfish Separate Self,
And Make To Give.
Thusly did they Find Their Spiritual Self Again.
Thusly do they Forever Walk
With the Peace of the Whole,
And in Their Wholiness,
are a Blessing to All.

What's the Problem?

Zain could not have made his point any clearer had he beaten me over the head with the texts from one of the ancient copper or stone tablets. But I still sensed he was trying to get me to realize something else I hadn't gotten yet, with all of these teachings about the separate self. I thought I'd gotten it. But maybe I just really hadn't "gotten it". I just felt like I was in hot water, and I didn't know why, and it wasn't the pleasant hot water of the pool.

I went to the entrance of his chambers, and stood there for a moment, timidly. I was afraid. Unjustifiably of course, but I never knew that until the end, so I was still afraid. Of what, I didn't even know. Finally, I knocked, and awaited what I had created in my mind as the dreaded answer and opening of the door. His soul mate, Mihra, answered the door.

"He's expecting you Peniel. He'll just be a moment. I'll come back and get you when he's ready."

"I can go and come back later." I crossed my fingers in my mind that she would agree.

"Thank you. But no, that won't be necessary, it will just be a moment." Yeah, a moment during a root canal. Just "a moment".

Mihra was beautiful, inside and out. A sweet, gentle, caring woman. She was in constant great pain from a cancerous tumor that she had growing in her before she came to the monastery, yet she was always still so sweet and kind.

Years went by, and then the door opened again, and she waved me into the room as she left for the kitchen.

Zain's chambers were like a scene from "Arabian Nights" or something. It always put me on the edge of having past life memories somehow. There were embroidered silk brocades and chiffon artfully draped throughout the room, covering the walls and hanging from the ceiling also. It wasn't that it was opulent really, they were all natural fabrics, traded for cheaply and easily placed with anyone with a good interior decorator's sense - from 600 B.C.. But if felt so opulent anyway. Sitting pillows were everywhere, and a half dozen sleeping mats lined one wall. He had a single chair, which he usually only sat in when formally "teaching" or lecturing. Today, he was sitting in his chair.

"How is she doing?" I asked inquiring about Mihra's cancer.

"Fine. She has been eating nothing but mangos for 3 weeks now, and does not like the sight of them anymore. But it will cure her cancer along with the energy work we are doing."

I was quite nervous, and tried to say something important.

"We are fortunate to have our own trees."

"It is not fortune. Don't you realize they are here for a reason?"

Oh boy, stupid thing to say, I thought to myself. I shifted from that blooper quickly, and tried to recover the fumble by just going on as if nothing was said.

"She seems in good spirits."

"She knows it is working, and won't be long now."

I couldn't stand it any longer. I had to get blunt.

"Father, what is the problem? With me I mean? Why are you having me read all these texts on the separate self."

"Because you need to."

"Well, I understand that, but I think I get the point."

"You have a huge ego Peniel. You *think* you are humble, you *think* you have inner peace, you *think* you are kind and unviolating to others, but in reality you lack

111

it all. You *think* you get the point, but you don't really."

I was nailed to the wall by his words. I didn't know what to say, think or do. It was very upsetting, to say the least, to think that I was not what I thought I had always been. And that I had not accomplished what I thought I did. As my mind spun, he went on.

"Not that a big ego is bad. It is actually good in a way. It just needs to be in the service of God. The bigger the ego, the more power a true teacher has to help others. You will someday be Initiated, become an Adept, and again be the great teacher you have been in the past, with the great power that accompanies that. But only *after* you harness your ego, and it serves God, not your selfish separate self.

Look at the world. It is a reflection of this problem in you, in everyone. The selfish separate self.

We could be living in paradise - a beautiful, harmonious world of peace, happiness, and creativity. And you could be happy - and full of feelings of peace & harmony. But there is obviously a problem. A serious problem. In the world and in you. Maybe you can realize it easier inside yourself, if you see it better in a world perspective first."

I just managed a nod.

"Consider the condition of the known world, past and present. Humankind has invented amazing things. Is that not so?"

Nod.

"But many of these seeming wonders are harmful to the Earth and its inhabitants. And if you stop and think about it, the "greatest advances", have been made in the invention of "new and wonderful ways" *to harm* others. And humans have always done the greatest harm they could with their available means and weaponry. Have you not seen this in your history lessons?"

Nod.

"But in the past they didn't have the technology we have today. They simply weren't *able* to commit the kind of mass destruction that modern means allow. Now we can destroy the people and ecology of an entire planet. The barbaric ancestors of some humans would have done the same thing, had they gotten the chance. Even with crude means they still did atrocious things on grand scales - including genocide of entire races. Witness the inquisitions that burned hundreds of thousands alive, after being tortured, not to mention vicious wars and enslavement of entire countries. And look at what is happening right now."

I finally relaxed. And began listening and hearing. He was right as usual. Including about how humans today are basically not much different from their ancestors, even though they *think* they are. (there was that *think* thing again, that he was referring to me about). All the violence, destruction, and "inhumanity" had just gone more underground, become more controlled, and media controlled. I thought to myself, not long ago, my father fought in WWII when Hitler waged his mass destruction, and cruel genocide. It was big news. It's over and gone, right? That kind of thing isn't going on in the world anymore, right? Wrong. Dead Wrong. Zain was right. Similar atrocities are still occurring, but they are virtually ignored by all the countries and societies of the world (can you imagine having a 9 month baby cut out of your womb by a soldier's filthy bayonet - because they don't want your race to continue?). People all over the world are still being routinely suppressed in virtual slavery. The major powers of the world are undergoing economic and social disintegration. Crime and hatred actually are on the rise, and grow daily. And if you think torture is passé, or hasn't kept up with technology, just check with Amnesty International.

Like Zain said. Modern humankind has the unique capability of total annihilation. Advanced weapons of all kinds, including biological, chemical, nuclear, and particle beam devices, allow war to be waged on a scale that dwarfs anything in the past, and have the capability to destroy much more than just human life - it could destroy most life on Earth. And he was right, they have never developed a weapon that went unused.

But warfare directed at other people is not the only means humans now have to achieve total annihilation. Humans have waged a sort of war on animals also, wiping out entire species for direct profit, or as a side-effect of other ventures. They have waged war on nature also, wiping out great forests, killing oceans and the creatures there, creating holes in the atmosphere, and ultimately forcing the extinction of species at an incredible rate - I think the last time I heard it was something like 180 species per day (depending on the statistics you use). The imbalances created by humans have affected everything on Earth. Now new mutant diseases are on the loose, climactic changes are beginning to alter the environment with floods and droughts that will soon cause famine as weather makes food growing difficult to impossible.

Scientists have now discovered that many animals, including some fish, are being born neither male or female. That means that this will be the last generation for many species. Human male sperm count is down 40% since WWII. How long before humans will not be able to reproduce either?

Many people live in denial of these harsh realities of the world because of their fear. And because of that fear, they have embraced unrealistic spiritual beliefs such as "If you don't think bad things or believe they can happen, you won't 'empower' them, thus they won't happen". Thoughts can affect things. But if that were true, how do you explain a baby getting sick from getting into something poisonous under a kitchen sink? The baby has no thoughts or beliefs about it one way or the other. And even if an adult isn't around, it will get sick and can die. Something to think about.

But I am getting off the story, even though it is a related and important point.

So let's go back in time again, and get back to me "sweating" in Zain's chambers.

I was still wondering and thinking to myself, "But what did this have to do with me? I wasn't contributing to any of these atrocities." I spoke up, somewhat in my own defense.

"Of course I agree with you Father, but what is the problem with me? I would never do such things."

"All of these wide-scale, disastrous imbalances and harms, are not coming from the 'way of life' of dolphins, bears, insects, snakes, etc.. Only humans are so out of touch with the nature of things. Now that humans have the *ability* to end all life as we know it, they are doing so, even to the extent that it will cause their own extinction. A bit extreme, don't you think? A bit blind? Why would normally non-suicidal people act this way? You are human, are you not, Peniel?"

"I live in a human body Father, yes, but..."

"But you still are. It still controls you.

Humans didn't *need* to be the creators of all these problems that plague the Earth. So why have they been? Why do they continue to be? Why do they behave in ways so extreme that they will even cause their own extinction? Is money the problem? Is greed the problem? Is hate the problem? Is jealousy the problem?"

"Well, yes, but..."

"You initially answered yes, so then answer this also - what causes hate, greed, and jealousy, etc.? Such negative and destructive desires and emotions are the 'virtues' of, so to speak, selfishness. And they are caused by having a 'separate' self. *The separate self's blind selfishness is so out of control that it doesn't even consider that it's creating its own demise.* But why? What do the teachings of the Atlantean Children say about these things? How can we change it and stop it?"

Personal Problems

My mind was reeling at all this. What could I say. What could I do? Questions began filling my mind about it.

"Be patient Peniel, all your questions will be answered in time.
Thus far, I've talked about the great problems of the world on a grand scale, but think. All these things are caused by individual humans. What does that mean? It is inside, it is the natural effect of selfishness. If they are an internal problem in each human, then you can see them in each small life, true?"

"That makes sense."

"So let's look at the individual now, because they are the only source of the big problems.

Most people have their share of 'personal' problems. They are microcosms of the world's problems.

Some people's lives are constantly filled with discord and pain, and they can't escape suffering. Others are able to fill their minds, and the days of their lives, with distractions - entertainment, work, or whatever, to create an illusion that "glazes over" the pain of their problems. Some get involved in 'play wars', through competitive sports. But at best, living that way only delays the pain and suffering they have created in their own lives, and almost always makes things even worse. Life keeps catching up to them, piercing their illusions, and leveling them with pain from time to time.

Now, you say- what is the problem with you, son. Do you have problems in your personal life?"

I had a quick quip comeback to that question, just waiting up my sleeve. I guess I was no longer afraid or threatened by this meeting with Zain.

"Do politicians give speeches?" I said.

"Yes. I believe they do. But let's stay on the subject." he replied. I guess he didn't get the joke, or the joke was on me, more likely.

"The point is this - *personal problems come from the same place that the world's problems do.* What can we do about them? Attacking the problems themselves never works for long. First we must discover the *root cause,* and eradicate *that.* The way to find a solution to a problem, is to really identify the source of the problem. Our primary task then, is to get a clear understanding of what has created all these terrible problems on Earth.

To understand the cause of all our problems, we need to go back to the beginning. Way back."

The Origin of the Universe, and the Separate Self

With new proof to support the "big bang" theory, modern scientific discoveries have substantiated what the Children have known since the beginning of life on Earth - that the Universe began from **One** thing, and that all creation came from, and still really *is,* that *One* thing, expanding throughout space creating stars, planets, and all life. Zain got out an old drawing to demonstrate this ancient understanding, and began to explain it to me.

"A 'mandala' is a round piece of geometric 'art', created for its spiritual symbolism, and sometimes used for meditation." He said. "But it is far more than art. It is a graphic, spiritual representation of the One, and a symbol of the expansion and Oneness of the Universe, into its many parts. A mandala's design consists of a myriad of many *inter-connected individual* forms coming out of "One" single, central source. A mandala is a good representation of our becoming separate *individuals,* yet still *remaining one* with, the One Universal Spirit, or God. This concept, or spiritual principle is also sometimes symbolically represented as a tree - many parts springing forth from a central source."

Beyond Roots

I understood a number of things better as I looked at, and contemplated this drawing.

"The ancient teachings of the Children talk about a time when we were just Spiritual, or "Angelic" beings. Using the mandala to represent this, we would be like the outer rings of the mandala that are individual, perhaps far from the source, yet still interconnected, still One. But when we wanted to "manifest" (materialize) on Earth, we had to do so within the framework of the vibrational spectrum of physical life on Earth, which was a far slower and denser vibrational plane than the plane of light and thought that we were existing on at the time. The nature of the spectrum of physical life on Earth is a myriad of individual forms, far more elaborate than we can even draw in a mandala. It also involves *dichotometric separation* (the splitting of one thing into 2 parts with opposing polarities). Many of the things that exist in this Earth plane reflect this dichotometric separation; i.e., temperature is one constant, yet it is manifested to us as seemingly polar opposites - "hot" and "cold"; Lightning and electricity involve positive and negative polar opposite charges; There are a great variety of animal species, each with "polar opposite" sexes (male and female). There are two sides, and polar opposites, to almost everything in one way or another. Thus our manifesting on Earth required individual forms, and dichotometric separation - which to us meant a great deal (which I will explain in a moment)."

"But aren't the polarities Universal Law anyway? Why would coming into the Earth plane make that any different, or turn it into a problem?"

"The polarities outside this plane, are in harmony, connected, flowing as One. Thus they are One, not separate - they only become polarities when they separate from their connection, which is a never ending flow in one direction. As I said, in coming into this material world, we needed to manifest in individual forms, and lower our vibration to match the environment. Like water vapor whose molecules must vibrationally slow down and get more dense in order to become ice, we "lowered" our vibration - slowed our vibration, until we achieved our goal. And as we manifested physically, the greater the depth of integration into the physical plane, our consciousness became more and more limited rather than Universal, and the greater was the separation from the One. This also created greater separation within ourselves. And separate polarization without the right connection, the right order of flow. Do you know what happens if you put batteries in backwards, or if you touch electrical wires to each other the wrong way?"

"Well, I know I've done it, and either things don't work, or sparks fly, and you can even cause explosions and fires."

"Humans live that way. When we entered this plane of dualities and polar opposites, we changed greatly from our previous 'Spirit' forms. We were no longer angelic beings with self-contained energy flows. Our internal male and female elements had once been so fully integrated, that there was not even a concept of male or female. But with the manifestation into the physical plane, these elements dichotomized, dividing into 'male' and 'female' polar opposite parts (now 'soulmates'). Eventually, as we manifested deeply into this dichotometric material plane, we physically became separate male and female beings. The dichotomy affected each male and female being even further, and in many ways. Our previously integrated mind, with logic/intellect and intuition/emotion functioning as one within the One, became left and right hemispheres of a brain that divided logic & intuition. The minds of these male and female selves, became dominated by either logic/intellect, or intuition/emotion. As degeneration/lowering of vibration and consciousness occurred further, the males generally became more logic/intellect oriented, and the females more intuition/emotion oriented. Logic and intuition were no longer functioning in balance, as one within the One. And the two halves, are in opposition rather than in flow. That's one reason males and females don't understand each other, and often argue.

The Big Break-Up

This lowering of vibration and separating from the One went too far. For an example, think of the Universe as a great single continent, surrounded by a dense dark fog. We are land in that continent. If we are a peninsula, we might stretch way out from the continent, and be surrounded by the dark fog, but as long as we still have a tiny piece of land connecting our peninsula to the continent, we are still the continent, and have all the life of that continent. But if we totally separate, we become an island. A tiny island, all alone, not even able to see that there is anything else out there other than ourselves, and all that dark fog.

Or, let's use the mandala representation again. Think of it as the very outer parts of the mandala, actually separating. They lose their connection. They lose their Universal Consciousness, and subsequently, its peace, its awareness, its coordination, and its guidance. They lose everything that being One with God had to offer. They are no longer in the 'flow' of things. They also lose harmony and peace with the other parts that have separated.

The Self Reverses Polarity

Upon separating from the One, the separate self turns its attention to its self. Since the separate self's attention is directed towards itself, attention is directed inward rather than outward - and the direction of mental energy is thus inward ('negative' polarity / vacuum / taking) rather than outward ('positive' polarity / out-flowing / giving). This puts it out of harmony with Universal Flow and Order.

This inward direction naturally then gave birth to a way of being - a self-ish-ness. Self-ishness is virtually a 'path' - a way of 'being'. It is the way of being 'tak-ing'. It's the way of inward flow, of negative flow, like being a 'black hole' (whose gravity is so great that it sucks everything into itself, even light).

Thus we have the selfish separate self."

"And from that, all our personal problems, and the world's problems origi-nate?"

"Just examine it, and see for yourself. In placing attention on and giving ener-gy to the selfish separate self, we turn away from being receptive to the outflowing source of Universal Consciousness, and maintain a selfish separate self conscious-ness. Self-indulgence is then simply the natural outcome, the natural order of things once the selfish separate self has established itself with its own consciousness, and the individual's focus and attention feed that consciousness. It has lost awareness of its connection with its spiritual nature, and thusly, the Universal Spirit and Universal consciousness."

"I understand. But why is it so hard for people to see and change?"

"Seeing is one thing. Changing is another. In so becoming "cut off" from the Universal Spirit, the source of creation, humanity has become "blind" in a sense. No longer aware that we are ALL ONE, people act as the negative polarity - they look to take and get, rather than give (as is the way of the positive polarity). It's 'look out for number one' rather than a 'Love thy neighbor' approach to their brothers and sisters. This negative, selfish way of being, creates more negativity, pain, and suffering for all, *including the separate self.*

"What went so wrong, exactly how did this all happen?"

"Since all the matter, all 'the stuff' of the Universe, is in reality One 'stuff', nothing can truly be separate from the One Universe, but humans gradually became separate from the One *as far as their awareness, their consciousness, was con-cerned.* It's as if mirrored walls surrounded each individual self. All each self pri-marily saw all the time was itself, and everything else it saw had to first be reflected in the mirror of the separate self. This gave birth to an illusion, a belief, that they were indeed separate, which gave birth to a new kind of total separate-self identity. This is where human consciousness still is today."

"So this is what you're saying my problem is, and what I need to deal with so badly right now?"

"Does it not exist in only you? You think you are it! You think you are the separate self!

The separate identity naturally has *primary* awareness of its self. After all, it lives in a room full of mirrors. Its focus is on itself. Its attention is on itself. It is thus, self centered. Each self actually has the notion that it is the center of the Universe. Don't you? People won't admit it naturally, but isn't everything you see, feel and think reflected off the mirror of your self - don't you always relate every-

117

thing that happens around you to *how it affects you?* It's only natural unless you have Universal Consciousness. This is even affecting how you are functioning as a member of this monastery."

"I don't understand. Have I done something wrong?"

"Of course, how could it be any other way with your present limited consciousness? But I understand that. That is not the issue now, that is not the big picture I want you to get *first,* that you are still not getting. Think for a moment what kind of problems there would be if the members of a football team, no longer had 'team consciousness' ('group' consciousness). No coordination, no guidance from a central source, not even any awareness of what the other players were going to do each play. And what if they weren't even in harmony with their team in general, and would sometimes play for the opposing team? And then add selfishness into the factor - each player considered themselves the most important player in the world, wanted to be the star, wanted all the attention, with no real concern as to whether the entire team would win? Or what if the members of an orchestra, were unaware of what the other players were playing, and didn't even care? Take these kinds of problems to a far greater level, to a team so large it encompasses everything in the Universe - that gives you just some idea of how bad having a lack of Universal Consciousness is.

On a smaller scale even, consider what would happen if just your arms and legs left the guidance, coordination and consciousness of the entirety of your body. Then they got their own identity, and developed selfish separate selves. You would have such things as one hand trying to put on a glove in a snowstorm, not caring what happened to the other hand. And the legs would be doing their own thing at the same time! What chaos! Again, just look around at the condition of the world to see the chaos here."

"So this isn't about some problem I have, or something I did wrong or I'm in trouble about?"

"Yes and NO! Stop persisting in this self-centeredness and listen. Yes, it is about you. No, it isn't about you. Get out of your self and you will see the point! You are living in a delusion Peniel.

Serious Delusion

Engrave this in your mind. It is so important. The Atlantean Children of the Law of One teach that *the world's problems, our personal problems, and all the actions that create the problems, come from* **our delusion that we are separate from the One, and the selfishness that results from that delusion.**

Think about it Peniel, would there be wars if we knew we were One, if all you could do was fight and hurt yourself?"

"No."

"Exactly, because what is the point of hurting yourself, or waging war on yourself? Would there be oppression?"

"None. Because what is the point of oppressing your self? "

"Would there be anger? Jealousy? Theft? Starvation? Racial hatred?"

"No. It wouldn't make sense. It doesn't make sense."

"Think about all the problems I just mentioned. What is behind each one of them? Humans, yes, but what is *behind* their problem causing actions? You already know, but you will need to teach the masses some day. Don't let them get caught in the surface illusions. Don't let them think the problem is 'greed' - because what's the source of greed? *Selfishness.* Don't let them think the problem is hate - what's the source of hate? *Selfishness. Proclaim it for all to see.* Tell them in your book, and your meetings. Help them clearly and finally understand that the real problem, the real enemy, the real source of all the "bad" things on Earth is simply selfish people acting selfishly.

And it is up to each person to change themselves, not the world. That is the only way to change the world. Each of us is *a selfish person acting selfishly.* We are thus our own enemy.

And going further to the root of the matter - what is behind selfishness? *Thinking you are **separate** from everything else.* Then 'looking out for number one' begins. And when you have a whole world full of people looking out for number one, you can see the results - just turn to the news."

Sleeping with our Enemy

Like the ancient Atlantean teachings say, and Zain so intensely drove home in me, in order to permanently eradicate this selfish monster that plagues us all, and plagues the world, we must get to the *root of* it.

If you want to permanently kill a plant, and insure that it won't grow back again, you need to destroy the root. At the root of selfishness is our *illusion* that we are not One with All things, All life, the entire Universe, and our subsequent *belief* that this illusion is real. This belief created a new identity, and supports the existence of this new separate identity (that is naturally selfish), and therein lies the enemy. But our belief is a lie, the illusion is not real. It is like we are all asleep, and thus out of touch with the reality of the real "awake" world that is around our sleeping body. We are each sleeping with this enemy we created - we remain unconscious, letting our enemy command the helm of the ship of our lives - like a dream we have no control over. Meanwhile, our spiritual self, the part of us that is One with the Universal Spirit, is "locked up in the brig" and just forced to go along on the voyage like so much baggage. This is something that each of us must personally come to deal with, and then be on alert about, each moment of all our days on Earth. But you cannot fight your selfish separate self directly, it only gives it energy.

What do the Atlantean Children of the Law of One's teachings say about how we must deal with it if we want it to change? They say that the only way to change things and get back in harmony with the One, is to *starve* the selfish separate self of energy - of giving in to it, of thought "attention", and simultaneously nurture the Inner Being, the Spirit within us. And this requires help. My greatest help, was primarily Zain, and his insight into me, combined with his wisdom. And only secondarily, the ancient teachings.

"So I need to be less self-centered?"

Zain just sighed. Then after a few moments, he spoke. "You need more help, you need to use the resources you have at your disposal to see your self more, to know your self better, and meditate on that to deal with it."

More on that later. But eventually I finally "got it". I had not been looking at my self-centeredness enough, I was avoiding the things I needed to do to "break" those self-mirrors that totally surrounded me in the room of my life. The self-mirrors that I thus saw all things reflected off of first, instead of seeing pure objective reality. I didn't know my self. And he, as all true teachers do, was mirroring my *inner-self,* and not letting me get away with my delusion. He was simply reminding me about it, and helping me deal with what I needed, in order to realize my continued self-deception.

Know Your Self

The separate self is a very clever thing. And it has the ability of a supercomputer. It has your brain at its disposal. It has all the knowledge you have. All the cleverness and cunning you have. It can lie and confuse even you (people delude themselves all the time). It has control of everything you control. Like Sherlock Holmes, you must anticipate every step of Moriarty if you want to beat him at his own game. Obviously then, knowing the intricacies and modes of operation of your self is a key to many things. You must know your self in order to transcend your self and regain Universal consciousness. And if you truly understand your self, you will know all other selves, for *all selves are the same,* and they behave the same way. For instance, how can you *understand* anger in another if you don't understand it in your self? And when you thus know and understand all selves, you will really understand the world. Thus understanding others allows you to bridge the gap of separation, and help them achieve Universal consciousness also.

When you truly know yourself, see your own selfishness, transcend it, and become a person who loves unselfishly, then you will clearly understand the selfishness in others, and the Unselfish Love in others. You will see both aspects simultaneously, and as a whole.

How to fully know and transcend yourself will be addressed in the chapter on the teacher/student relationship. Right now we need to cover more of the basics of what the selfish separate self is, and how it affects our lives, so we can totally understand it.

The Consciousness Scale

Each person has the potential to be both selfish, and to Unselfishly Love. Imagine there is a meter that has a "scale" with selfishness (negativity) on the left, and Unselfish Love (positivity) on the right. Your consciousness is the needle on this meter. Most people act selfishly most of the time, and sometimes act unselfishly, so the needle jumps around a bit. But everyone has a "status quo" of sorts where the needle stays most of the time. This "average" location of the needle represents the general level of their state of consciousness.

3 Makes a Whole

As if separation from the One didn't cause enough problems alone, the separate self is further separated within itself. And the lower an individual's consciousness is, the more the there are internal separation problems.

You may have noticed how numbers and a certain mathematical geometry seem to weave threads throughout life and are somehow significant to many things. This has to do with the vibratory nature of existence, and is discussed more in a later manuscript, but it also applies in the following teachings. But in any case, here are some obvious scientific facts, and some teachings, about our two and threefold natures.

Some aspects of our selves divided into 2 parts. There is the selfish/unselfish split parts we just spoke of. The male/female split. The logic/intuition split. The intellect/emotion split. The positive/negative split. And the 2 split parts are often at odds with each other. Some people, regardless of sex, are more "right brained", and others more "left brained". Still other aspects of our selves are divided into 3 parts, which we are about to discuss.

All Creation itself has a threefold nature. Within the threefold nature, we can also see the twofold dichotomy of the material plane. These natures can be looked at, and thought of, in many different ways. But here is the fundamental concept: The **first** nature is Light, the positive polarity [+]; The **second** nature is Darkness, the negative polarity [-]; The **third** nature *is the interaction, or inter-course, of* darkness and light as a whole.

The threefold nature has been represented by various religions in various ways. The Yin and Yang - dark and light interacting in a Circle. The Father, Son, and Holy Ghost, etc.. Four, represented in many ways, such as the cross, the tetra-grammaton, the oldest name of God, indicates the offspring of the three, and the beginning of a new cycle of creation. This will be covered in depth in a later chapter.

Since we are really part of, and One with, All Creation, each of us individually is also of a threefold nature. This threefold human nature manifests in many ways. The threefold essential vibratory nature of our human manifestation is spiritual, mental, and physical. You can also see it in the nature of our consciousness, in that called the sub-conscious mind; the "conscious" mind, and the Universal conscious mind. The balance and coordination of the threefold nature has been, and still is, lost with most people. A twofold dichotomy is the dominant nature of our material existence on Earth. Thus few ever really relate to the spiritual, but all relate to the mental and physical. Also few ever relate to the Universal consciousness, but all relate to the sub conscious and conscious minds.

If we were as we should be, our Inner Being would be coordinating these "parts" of our selves, and they would be functioning as an integrated whole. And ordinarily the Universal Spirit would be guiding the entire process, keeping us functioning harmoniously within ourselves, and in harmony with the One. But because our consciousness is cut off from the Universal Spirit, and we are not properly in touch with our own Inner Being, we are an uncoordinated internal mess.

Obviously we need to re-coordinate all these "fragments" of self. We achieve this as a natural "side effect" of transcending selfishness by developing and fostering our Unselfish Love for others. The process is also aided by various techniques and exercises (described later in the book) that coordinate the sub-conscious, conscious, and Universal minds. For those who achieve reunification with the Universal Spirit, paradise awaits.

Making A New World

As we pointed out earlier, when you have a whole world full of people who selfishly care more about themselves than others, you have a world such as it is today. But on the bright side - can you imagine what it would be like if we ALL cared for EACH OTHER more than ourselves? Contemplate that for a while. That's what the Children teach, and work for. The ancient Atlantean teachings also proclaim that those who want to help change the world for the better, must first change themselves, and transform into Unselfishly Loving beings. It takes a fire, of some kind at least, to light a fire.

The Children's ancient Atlantean teachings say that if you want to live in a world of loving people, be a loving person. They also teach that one of the ways to achieve this, is to put others before yourself, to love others first, to consider others first, to give to others first.

There are some who are against the idea of caring for others *first*. They say you must love your *self first,* in order to love others. But, as Zain told me long ago, examine the results of the two philosophies with an open mind, and the answer will become clear. There are *many* who have succeeded in loving their own self first, but have never gone on to really care for anyone else - they just further their own selfishness. They continue to be selfish contributors to a negative world. On the other hand, *all* those who have embraced caring for *others* first, *always* loved their own self *also.* Think about it, if you love *others* first, and you become an Unselfishly Loving being, is it possible to then *not* feel good yourself - *not love* yourself? No. There is no way *anyone* could *not* love themselves then! You would love yourself automatically and feel great about yourself, *because* your Unselfish Love is of great help to all, *including* yourself. This is also the only way you can *Unselfishly* Love your self, and Unselfish Love is truly the only "real" love. There is a Law of One in action here. Let me reiterate the "faucet" anecdote to illustrate this. Try to see it like this - we are like one who needs and wants water (Love) - we are valves, "faucets", connected to a water supply. When we let the water flow freely, freely giving it out, it is also flowing in us and through us. But if we try to possess our water by shutting off our giving, not letting the water flow on through us, we shut off our own supply, for it is no longer in us. This is *truly* loving your self - not first - not second - it is simultaneous - just *by giving it, doing it.*

Here is a parable from a scroll I found in the library, written in the first century A.D., by an early Christian sect in Greece. Judging from the insightful story, this sect apparently were "real" Christians - i.e., people that followed Jesus' teachings (and living example) about Unselfish Loving rather than merely worshiping and praising Jesus. The story uses a striking allegorical fantasy to clearly illustrate a fundamental difference between a world of people looking out for themselves first, and a world of people giving first:

There was a man who died and was being taken to heaven by angels. The angels said to him, "We are going to take you to heaven, but first we will show you hell."

The angels then took him to a place where there was a great bowl, so great that it was as big as a lake. The bowl was filled with a nutritious stew. All the way around the sides of this bowl were people. Emaciated, starving, miserable people. These people had spoons to eat the stew with, and the spoons were long enough to reach the stew (about 12 feet). The trouble was, while they could scoop up the stew into the spoon, they could not get it into their mouths because the spoons were too long. So here were all these pathetic people, suffering and moaning in agony, constantly trying to eat the food that was abundantly in front of them - all in vain. Next, the angels took the man to heaven. To his surprise, he saw the same scene! There it was, a giant lake-like bowl of the same stew, surrounded by people with 12 foot long spoons. Yet something was different here - all these people were smiling, happy, and healthy looking!

122

"Why? What is the difference here that these people are happy and well fed?", the man said to the angels.

They replied, "Have you not eyes to see?". The man looked more carefully, and observed that one person would scoop up the stew, and bring it to the mouth of another. Then someone else would scoop up stew and feed it to the other.

The angels smiled and said, "Here the people feed each other. Here are the people that learned the way of Love."

Some of you agree with the idea expressed in the parable, and would like to live that way, yet you find yourself questioning the practicality of doing something like that. It's not unreasonable to think something like this: "But if I give all for others, I will surely be taken advantage of and have nothing". If that is your quandary, take heart, there is a way. It may seem too idealistic or impractical to you right now to stop thinking selfishly. And in a way, you may be right. It is a bad idea to change yourself into a being who gives and lives for others without discretion. Giving to selfish people can sometimes do the people you're giving to, more harm than good. There are plenty who will selfishly "take", and there needs to be discretion as to who to give to, and how. But there *are ways* around having to deal with this when you are in a transitional and learning phase. That is part of what having a "monastic period" in your life, and/or living in a monastery/spiritual community is all about (discussed more in later chapters).

Chapter Ten

Free Will,
The Universal Law of Cause & Effect
and
The School of the Prophets

One morning when I was feeling "sorry for myself", and subsequently, I was missing my old friends. I had run into Anastasia and was telling her about the friend who had chosen to marry his pregnant girlfriend, and thus he wasn't here.

I went to my womb and began a meditation. As my mind wandered out of control while I "tried" to meditate, I started thinking about my friend, choices, and whether I really *had* chosen my lifestyle. Or if it was just destiny, or the way the "deck was stacked", and none of us had any choice in the matter. At this point, I only let my mind get away with the idea of thinking about "destiny" and free choice. But the next step would have been thinking things like, why couldn't I have just been a lawyer like my mother wanted me to. It sure would have been easier. And in a year I'd have been driving a Mercedes or Porsche. They would have been pretty wild thoughts, but they do happen when you don't control them.

It was mid-day, on the same day, that I reached my "terminal exhaustion" point. As I was preparing to "hit the mat" and get some sleep, I again began to ponder all the strange events in my life, and how it seemed like destiny was at work. Perhaps no one has any choice, I thought. Perhaps everything is all pre-destined. I knew I was destined to be where I was - there was no doubt in my mind about that. Just then, I heard a voice outside the curtain of my womb chamber. It was Zain talking to another novice monk (and probably to me indirectly at the same time).

"Free Will is the most important legacy we have from the Universal Spirit. We are constantly being presented with choices in life, 'forks in the road' that lead to different places. Free will lets us choose. That ability to choose gives us the power to take our life in any direction we want, and thus, do virtually anything we want with our life, and create our future life. But it was our free will choices that got us in trouble in the first place, in separating from God. Most importantly now, used properly, it is what gives us the ability to get out of the hole we dug ourselves into, and get back to Oneness with God."

Strange timing. I guess it was destiny. No, how could there be destiny, if free will choices changed our future, our destiny?

The next morning, Zain told me that our monastery was also known as "The School of the Prophets", and it was time for me to begin the particular studies and training in the ancient Atlantean methods that create certain prophetic abilities - deep concentrated contemplation, realization of cause and effect, free will, and destiny. He had my reading list ready. Later, I read some of the teachings from the ancient texts:

Foolish Child
Know Not that you Reap What you Sow?

What will you have done today
In your life and those of others?
Pray Do You?
Know Not that You Have Free Will?

❖

To Be a Fool For God
Is to be a True Child of the Law of One

❖

Learn the ways of Universal Law,
of Cause & Effect.
As we break the Law,
So do we lose our Freedom.

Recognize your Free Will
Realize your Free Will
Know your Free Will
Use Your Free Will
In Harmony With Universal Will
and be Free

Every Moment we come upon another
Fork in the Road
Every Moment we Choose
Our Way, Our Destiny

❖

Every Action creates Reactions
Choosing not to act, is an action with a Reaction
If you choose not to actively serve the Light
You are choosing to actively serve Darkness
If you choose not to actively serve
The Universal Spirit
You are choosing to actively serve
The Selfish Separate Self
The Collective Selfish Self, and Evil.

❖

No Choice Have You
But to Choose.
Choose you Will

Between Darkness & Light
Between Good & Evil
Between Give & Take
Between Love & Hate
Between Selfishness and Selflessness

Where you are
Where you have Been
Where You will Be
Is affected by Your Choice

Every Fork
Is a Way
To Serve God, Or Run From God

Think You that You can hide From God?
Think You that you can Run From Yourself?
Think You that God is not One and All?
Think.

Our Consciousness is the Result
of Our own Choosing
Where you are
Is Where you have come
Where you Will go
Is decided by how you are

We Forge Our Will
In the Fires of Our Suffering
We Temper Our Will
In the Waters of Discipline

When One Applies Free Will
To achieve Freedom From the Separate Self,
The Self Causes Pain

The One who Chooses the Path of Selfishness
Finds that Pain and Suffering follow him
ETERNALLY

The One who chooses the Path of UnSelfishness
Finds that Pain and Suffering are but
A Passing Storm

Interfere Not With the Free Will of Others
As you would not have them Interfere with yours.

Interfere Only with the Free Will of Those
Who are Interfering with the Free Will of Others.

Free Will Directs The Mind.
Mind Creates Reality,
On All Planes.

All Things Come First
From The Mind.

With Free Will, We Choose Our Destiny.
We were destined to Choose
The destiny we have Freely Chosen.

Spiritual Schizophrenia

Reading the old texts both helped, and created new questions and confusion. So I asked Zain for clarification.

"We all have both a selfish separate self, and an Inner Being that is One with the Universal Spirit. In this sense, every human has a sort of 'split personality'. We are all kind of what you call 'schitzy' with these two sides, these two people living within us. And they are in total opposition. The free will dictates which of these two sides will have its way in our life, at every given moment."

"I know what you mean about the two sides in us. And the internal battle is unbelievably hard at times."

"Indeed it is Peniel. The struggle is nothing less than the war between good and evil. There can be no harder battles. And with our free will, we can decide who wins the battles, and ultimately, the war.

Sometimes we have thoughts and feelings that are from one side, sometimes from the other. Have you ever seen the old cartoons in the movie theatres, where the devil is sitting on one shoulder and an angel on the other - both whispering in our ear, trying to influence us one way or the other. Then one of them finally "wins out". Well, how does one of them win out?"

"One side is stronger than the other within us?"

"Yes, generally. But no. That is not why one side wins out over the other, just which side may have more voice or influence.

One side wins out over the other, simply because we use our free will to choose

127

which side we will go with - which side we will lend our mind to, our attention to, our thoughts to - and ultimately, which side we will lend our actions to. Free will is the one thing that gives us the ability, the power, to *choose* between our negative self, and God. And the results of our choices change everything in our life, and the lives of others."

"But it seems like in some people the bad side is stronger, or the good side is stronger - and the influence is so strong that it's not just a matter of a balanced free will choice."

"Excellent perception. Every person has a different level of consciousness. You know, every individual has a different level of how giving, or how selfish they are. Some are higher (leaning more towards the Universal Spirit), some lower (leaning more towards selfishness). But what makes that consciousness what it is?"

"Free will?"

"It is the result of their accumulated use of their free will.

Thus the world is full of a variety of so called 'good and bad' people to all kinds of degrees. For instance, some people are just 'not very nice' (on the bad side), and others are really bad - rapists, murderers, etc. (more deeply on the bad side). Their consciousness is a result of using their free will over time. For instance, someone who has more often chosen selfishness over time will have lower consciousness than someone who has more often chosen Unselfish Love. So each individual has made one side primarily stronger than the other. Yet in the worst, there is still a divine spark of Universal consciousness buried deep within them, and in the best people, except for the enlightened ones, there is still the seed of selfishness. Thus all can still break from their norm at any time, and make different choices, and change their consciousness, and thus even turn their lives around. Just by applying free will, one step at a time. Building a new life, one stone at a time. Are you not in the process of raising your consciousness by using your free will to override your past habits and consciousness?"

Free Will and Suffering

"Yes. I am. And I do see the results. But Father, sometimes it is so hard to make and stick to the right choices. It is so hard that it is painful. Sometimes it feels like you're going to die."

"If you think about it Peniel, were you free from pain before you started using your free will to become a better person? People who have not become totally Unselfishly Loving beings, are always in pain, always in internal turmoil. They have an unrelenting unpleasant disturbance within them, that they are constantly trying to emotionally cover-up, and get distracted from. They are always trying to distract themselves from this with selfish thoughts and diversions (talking with friends, becoming a "workaholic", eating, shopping, sex, affairs, TV, playing or watching sports, games, magazines, etc., etc., even drinking/drugs). They do all these things to run from the part of them that is God within them. But just like there is no running away from yourself, there is no real getting away from God. There is no peace without oneness with God. And there is constant dis-ease, and no rest, for those who are trying to get away from God.

As we just discussed, everyone has this spiritual "split personality" composed of Selfishness (the "devil" side using Christian terms) and Universal Spirit (the "Christ" side). We also discussed how sometimes we have thoughts and feelings that are from one side, sometimes from the other. And some of these feelings are painful."

"But won't it ever stop?"

"We are always faced with choices between our sides, between being selfish (wanting and taking), or being Unselfish (considerate and giving). And we find that by making a selfish choice, we create new karma that causes suffering. And the lack of doing God's Will, and being separate from God, creates pain, loneliness, emptiness, a gnawing dis-ease deep down. It is the Spirit part of us that then *seems to be* giving us pain. The 'conscience' seems to be giving us pain. But this pain is in truth, simply coming from the selfish separate self that is trying to resist the natural flow of the forces of the Universal Spirit. Sometimes people think that by choosing to run away from God, and delving deeper into a selfish, materialistic life, they can escape the pain. But they never can. The Inner Voice may get suppressed, and may get hard to hear, but the pain and dis-ease is always there."

"So it won't ever stop no matter what you do?"

"Yes. But let me finish. You are still thinking that you are suffering new pain by going through the tribulations that will lead you to enlightenment one day. But think about your past with an open mind. *Remember* what it was like in your life when you hid from the light. Remember the pain of squandering your life in darkness and despair. The more you hid from the light and the more you delved into selfishness, the worse the spiritual ache got. Even as 'numb' and detached as you were able to make yourself, even with drugs and alcohol, you still had severe pain and dismal feelings of hopelessness and loss. It can never be any other way when you choose the selfish path - you will always have pain, and you exert constant energy, struggling forever to block out God. And you can never be happy, or have peace. The most you can hope for with a selfish path, is temporary pleasures, what you call 'get offs'. And the pleasure you get from temporary get offs never fully satisfies, it always leaves you wanting more. And what's worse, is that you have to pay for the get off, with an equal measure of its opposite. And what's the opposite of pleasure? And on top of all that pain, life also keeps 'hitting' you with the results of your 'karma'. It only happens once in a while, but it's bad when it does. You know what I mean - think about the worst times in your life, your darkest hours, the times life hurt you, leveled you, brought you to your knees in pain. Why do you think it happened? What was life telling you? What was God telling you? And when you were hit with such pain, didn't it force you to be introspective? To question your life, or life itself? At least for a moment?"

"Yes. That is why I searched for spiritual answers to life, searched for God, and peace of mind. But it is like my pain is getting worse now that I am spiritually growing, and doing the right thing with my life. Shouldn't the pain be getting less?"

"It is a different kind of pain, from a different source. You see, suffering is what brings most people to the spiritual path in the first place. They eventually realize that the only way to end the kind of suffering they are experiencing, is to turn back to God - to abandon selfishness - to be kind, caring, giving, Unselfishly Loving. But once they really start the process of spiritual growth, they find that they are experiencing a great deal of pain from the *self,* from their *ego.* Rather than the aching of the spirit, and the pain of dealing with your own negative creations - your karma - the self begins throwing a tantrum because it is not getting its way. It begins to manufacture contrived thoughts and emotions to give you pain. Extreme pain. Like you said, sometimes it feels like you're going to die it gets so bad. That's because your separate selfish self is facing a death of sorts. And the closer you get to killing your selfish separate self, the more it gives you pain - it lashes out wildly like a cornered animal fighting for survival (which it is)."

"So as it turns out, you have to deal with pain either way - whether you're living a selfish life or an Unselfish life. So why not just go with the selfish path?" Zain's intensity level jumped several notches.

"Because there is one very big important difference. Let's say you choose to give into the selfish side, in order to indulge yourself *and* to avoid the suffering that comes from choosing to walk a path of Unselfish Love back to God. If that's what you choose, *you will forever be in anguish* - in many ways!

You will FOREVER feel the relentless gnawing in the pit of your soul. Even if you make nothing but negative choices, and take nothing but the negative "forks in the road", it is *impossible* to ever *completely block out* the angel on your shoulder who causes the gnawing pain. Because as long as you have life, you have a soul - you have Spirit and an Inner Being dwelling within you. You must have the spark of Spirit animating you, within you, or your body dies. Thus, you will ALWAYS have that pain.

And you don't just have the 'spiritual pain' and the 'conscience pain', *you are still stuck with pain the self gives you* - and not just a little pain! Do you think you shed the pain of selfish emotions such as insecurity, greed, anger and jealousy when you choose the dark selfish path? NO! You know that your most selfish hours have given you the most pain. It is your dark times when you have felt the terrible emotional pangs of jealousy, or anger or even hate. The selfish path is the one that actually *creates* jealousy, *builds* jealousy, and all the other painful and pointless emotions. For instance, jealousy is nothing but one of the tentacles of selfishness. Possessiveness is selfishness, and it's accompanied by the terrible feelings of insecurity, and jealousy - and whether it's a little kid screaming 'mine!' over a toy he doesn't want to share, or a big kid screaming mine over the ultimate possession, a human being, a lover or mate, it's all the same. If you think you're going to get away from self-pain by choosing the selfish path, think again - all you get is a spoiled self that is out-of-control! Just look around you, look at the 'normal' relationships people have! They are full of turmoil and terrible pain. People in 'normal' selfish based relationships constantly cheat on each other, hurt each other emotionally, physically hit each other, and even kill each other - all the while feeling awful pain!

And you will also still have the pain and suffering from your negative karma coming back to you. And it feels all the worse because you have not developed the ability to transcend yourself at all - just the opposite, you've chosen to be fully entrenched in your self - you've chosen to float in the sea of possessiveness, jealousy, greed, lust, hate and anger.

PLUS the choice of the selfish path keeps creating *more* negative karma, that will *keep coming* back to cause you *more pain and suffering.*"

"So again, we are just all destined to suffer no matter what we do?"

"Yes and no. The type of suffering you are experiencing now, will vanish when you reach the end of your path, and become enlightened. And you have already rid yourself of the pain you had in your past that made you want to commit suicide, have you not?"

"Yes. No question about that."

"If you choose the path of light to avoid the suffering and pain that comes from living selfishly and separated from God, you no longer have the spiritual pain, or the conscience pain, or the pain of an out-of-control spoiled self on a rampage. That is over for you. Sure, you will have to live with the pain that the self gives you now, in fact more of it for a while. They are your 'growing pains'. And it may even include jealousy and anger. BUT IT IS ONLY TEMPORARY - you WILL eventually lose the devil on your shoulder. And unlike the results of choosing the selfish path, the pain will finally stop. And you won't create anymore negative karma. *You can accomplish this just by making the right choices, and waiting.* Then you will no longer be walking the self-chosen, self-created path of living forever in anguish. You will change your destiny. Peace will be yours in time - freedom from the pain of the selfish emotions (like hate, anger, jealousy) will be yours in time - *all you have to do is keep using your free will* to keep walking the light path. Keep re-directing your mind to think loving, giving, caring thoughts. Keep remembering the rewards of serving God - Love, ultimate security, peace, happiness, the joy of giving and seeing others lifted up and freed from their bonds of slavery to dark selfishness and its pain. You know these feelings exist - you have felt them sometimes - those times when you have Unselfishly Loved just a little bit - or perhaps there is a time when you let go and surrendered to God just a little more. Just imagine the joy and peace of loving *completely.* That is not rhetorical. *Imagine* it. Visualize it."

"I'm not sure you understand Father. I have no doubts about my choice. I am not wavering in my conviction. There is no way I would ever turn away from the path of Unselfish Love, it was just that this pain was getting so bad that..."

"You think I don't understand?"

"I'm sorry, I forgot. I know you understand better than I. (Then I said a positive affirmation to myself - I will explain the use of affirmations in a later chapter)."

"Remember, I have walked the same path you are walking now. As have so many others before me. I know it well. I know it better than you. And like I said, your pain will end with enlightenment."

"Thank God."

"I will."

"You have not yet even faced the worst of the pain your self is going to throw at you to prevent its ultimate loss of control, and prevent your enlightenment, so be prepared."

"I can handle it now, now that I know its going to end."

"Don't rest on your laurels Peniel. You are doing fine. But don't be too certain of yourself, or your self will snare you. Until you have achieved Universal Consciousness, there is always a chance of you turning away from the light. Be prepared, and don't sit feeling confident. Feel committed, and affirm that commitment daily. Think positive, good thoughts, but be vigilant, not complacent, not focused so much on your pain, but not so confident either. If you are not vigilant, your selfish separate self will sneak up behind you when you least expect it, and when you think you are being your most spiritual, it will turn it to its advantage, and take control. Spiritual ego is the greatest and one of the final dangers on the path."

All of you reading this, have experienced at least some of what Zain was talking about in the above segments. Some of you may have even tried a spiritual path, and encountered pain, and then resisted your path.

131

You lived in pain and darkness before, and now you live on the edge of light and Love, but you are still in pain and darkness. Why? In order to start the process that will ultimately free you from the pain of the selfish separate self, you must *fully commit* to a path of Unselfish Love, and apply your free will with constant CONVICTION, even in the face of the pain the self will throw at you. If you don't, you will keep wavering back and forth - you will keep getting pain from both sides. One side gives you some pain, then the other, then the other. You don't get *more* total pain mind you, you just keep getting it from different sides, and you just keep doing it on and on - and you don't make any progress towards permanently ending the pain. It can become an endless cycle. It's a trick of the negative self, and it can keep you a slave to self, a slave to the forces of darkness, and in an endless circle of pain forever - all the while thinking you at least tried, or are trying, to walk the spiritual path, but it was just too hard or too painful. Open your eyes, your mind, and look at it objectively. It is far more painful NOT to walk the spiritual path. I know. I have seen it from both sides now. You can also see a good example of this in one of the stories about Jesus that still remain in the bible. And the scriptures of many other religions. The story of Jesus' internal suffering in the garden before his arrest, demonstrates that Jesus had learned this lesson well, and exhibited CONVICTION in even the most dire circumstances. As Jesus was awaiting his arrest, he contemplated the terrible trials and tribulations he knew he would suffer in the immediate future - unless he chose to "change course". The time was up, and his disciples gave him no comfort or support. Even though he had asked them to stay awake and meditate with him that night, they slept, and left Jesus alone with his agony. Jesus communed with the Universal Spirit, and asked to have "this cup" "taken" from him - *but only if it was within the will of the Universal Spirit.* A cup is a symbol of receptivity, and in this instance symbolized his receptivity to the will of God. And in this case, it meant all that suffering he would encounter, using his free will to follow the will of God. Even while Jesus asked if he could be released from being receptive in this instance, and thus be released from the terrible fate that awaited him, he INCLUDED "but Your Will be done, not mine". While no one wants to suffer, or really looks forward to experiencing the pain that may accompany doing their duty, or meeting their karma, the truly wise know that if we do not align our will with the will of God, and do the will of God, the subsequent suffering and repercussions are far worse, and will never end. True happiness and freedom are only found in aligning our will, with Universal Will.

Bottom line: if you want the pain to stop, you need to *decide* to take the path of Love, no matter what you encounter, and you need to *want* to change, and you need to *maintain* your *conviction* to accomplish your goal, once you really set it. Then simply apply yourself consistently, with all the tools at your disposal.

The Free Will of Others

Later in the day, Russo, one of the other Adept monks, revealed more of the teachings on free will, including some on its intricacies as it relates to others.

"The issue of Free Will is involved in two primary tenants of the Children of the Law of One. First, honoring the free will decisions of others is considered VITAL, and absolute. The only time one should interfere with another person's free will, is when the other person is inflicting *their* will on someone else. In other words, if someone is forcing someone else to do something against their will, or harming someone else against their will, we can intervene without 'breaking'

132

Universal Law. But when it does involve an infringement of someone else's free will, it is a very different situation. Universal Law dictates that we are not to interfere with the free will of others, regardless of whether or not we think their actions are wrong. Even if we think someone is going to harm themselves - we should always honor their right to do so. Even if we KNOW for certain something is wrong or the person will get hurt, *other than warning them about the effects they are causing,* we are NOT to interfere with their freedom.

Our Free Will

The other tenet, is *recognizing* and *utilizing* our free will. YOU HAVE FREE WILL. It sounds simple and obvious, but it is not *really* accepted by most people. When you truly *real-ize* that you have free will, it empowers you totally. But it also makes you responsible, and gives you responsibility. Realizing your free will gives you the responsibility of being the main creator of your life. Realizing your free will gives you the responsibility of choosing between the powers of light and of darkness - between selfishness and Unselfish Love - between your separate self, and God. Because most people really don't want to take responsibility for what happens with their lives, they don't really want to truly accept the idea that they have free will. Yet they are still using their free will to make these choices all the time - even if they supposedly do it 'unconsciously'. And of course, taking this 'unconscious' way of choosing, will almost always end up with the choices being made in favor of the dark, the selfish."

You Can Take a Road to Anywhere
and Anywhere you Are, you Took a Road To

The next day, we began learning more about how the use of free will, and Universal Law, create various destinies, and the paradox of it all.

"Having free will means you have the ability to choose the direction you will go on the path that lays before you NOW. By choosing your direction, YOU *bring* experiences into your life. This is where free will interacts with the Universal Law of Cause & Effect.

Have you ever said to yourself, 'I didn't do anything to deserve this', or, 'Why is this happening to me?' Wallowing in self-pity with such attitudes is not only fruitless, it is destructive. Thinking that someone else, or something else, is responsible for your experiences is a trick of the separate self - an evasion of your own responsibility. You are never *really* a 'victim' of circumstances. Where you are at right now is where you have come to through the effects of your actions.

We are all Cosmic Farmers

All is subject to the Universal law of cause and effect. You reap what you sow. A plant you water and feed will thrive, the one you do not will die. Take a good broad look at the history of this planet and you can see this law in operation in all things. The word 'Karma' is often used to describe *effects* that are 'due' from *causes* that have been initiated. For example, getting killed could be called your karma for murdering someone. Sometimes karma is more subtle, or complex, than that, i.e.., being poor may be your karma for burning a village. Those who have been trained in prophecy, and are at one with Universal Consciousness, have fully realized and understood the law of karma, and can also know the details of such things if they need to (if necessary in the flow of Universal Will).

When your personal wants and desires have your attention ('at-tension'), you are focusing on and empowering your selfish separate self, and thus thinking and

133

acting from that separate consciousness. When an entity acts thus, it acts in a self-ish way, and a negative cause is put into action, and the re-action brings its nega-tive effects. Likewise, when an entity acts in an Unselfish Loving way, a positive cause is brought forth and positive effects result.

What have you created in your life and the lives of others?

When you initiate negative causes, you could be said to be accumulating neg-ative karma. When you get a negative experience coming into your life, a karmic 'payback' could be said to be taking place. The same with positive - positive out, positive karma accumulated, positive karmic 'payback'."

I must interject here that Karma is often misunderstood by people who really haven't studied or understood it. I knew a lady who vehemently insisted that she had great karma, and her belief and "proof" of this was solely based in the fact that she drove a new Cadillac and owned 2 houses. The fact that she had to see a chi-ropractor every day for years because of an accident she had in the Cadillac, "had nothing to do with her karma" according to her. She was also a very selfish woman who sought to hurt anyone who didn't give her what she wanted. Having wealth and ease is no indication of good karma.

Also, just because something awful happens to you doesn't mean that you have "bad karma", or that the event is necessarily a karmic 'payback' for a negative thing you have done. Oddly enough, karma is not the only thing that can be behind an apparently negative or positive event. Negativity seeks positivity so it can neutralize itself. Look at the lives of the great beings of history - the saints and teachers, for instance. Would you say that because they were persecuted, tortured, and murdered, it meant they had bad karma? No. Nor was it that they "had neg-ative thoughts that drew it to them". The fact is, their very positive *natures* drew such negative response, because this world is ruled by negative selfish separate selves. The greatest beings have suffered the most. This also occurs because the Universal Spirit forges its best tools in a fire. To paraphrase an old saying, "God falls hardest on those he wants the most".

The bottom line regarding the teachings on making sure that all your actions are accumulating good karma, is this: you must be surrendered to the Universal Spirit, and following the guidance of Universal Will. More about this later.

So how should we deal with "bad" experiences we have in life that aren't because we're "saints"? The teachings say that when a "bad" experience is actual-ly a negative karmic 'payback' taking place in your life (taking the form of an appar-ently bad event or a challenge), it is giving you a chance to learn from your mis-takes. As Zain said to me, "How do you re-act (your choice!) to what exists in, and comes into, your life NOW?"

The best way for a person to react, is to see the lesson in the experience, real-ize what life is communicating to you through this experience, and change. Such a change will insure that the mistake will never be repeated, and thus your future "nows" will be different.

Free Will and the Mind
Mind is the Construction Worker of our Lives

Zain told me I could attend a special series of lectures relating to my new stud-ies, and he recommended it strongly. It was quite an honor, because they were to be given by Michi-el, and only attended by elder monks. Michiel was very old (according to Zain, far, far older than 100), yet he only looked about 65. I don't think anyone really knew how old he was. But speculations ran quite wild. The ancient teachings indicated that with a combination of diet, meditation, and energy techniques, a lifespan could be stretched like a rubber band, and that lifespans of 800, 900 or older, were not only possible, but should be the norm. Even the modern bible indicates average lifetimes were that long for many of the characters in the Old Testament. And now, in recent years, scientists are claiming this as a "new possibility" with the right diet, supplements, and stress management. But I'm getting a bit off track. As the head of the monastery, Michiel was more of an "Adept monk's Adept monk" (If we had been Catholics, he'd have been our Pope. If we'd been Buddhists, he'd have been our High Lama.). Regardless of his youthful appearance, he was very weary, and chronically ill, so these sessions were a great strain on him. Because of his position in the order, and his health, I rarely saw him. But even though he was in great pain, and so very old and weary, in the few interactions we had, he was still very kind and caring, and seemed to have a particular affection towards me. sandwich

During this lecture, he presented some of the Atlantean Children's teachings about aspects of the mind, separation, and free will.

"As I'm sure those of you here have all heard before, our being has two-fold and three-fold properties. One of these is that we are a combination of spiritual, mental, and physical aspects, with the mental realm being dominated by a brain that is divided into two very different, and often opposing, ways of looking at things. The mental realm is influenced by the other two aspects of our threefold nature - the physical realm on one side, and the spiritual on the other - and the mental is sandwiched in between. On the physical side of the mental realm we have what the teachings call the self-body-mind. The Self-body-mind only grasps things intellectually in a non-abstract, separate, logical, literal, divided, polarized manner. Essentially, to the self-body-mind, everything is clearly categorized into two separate divisions - things are either yes or no, + or -, black or white, etc. [Author's note: very much like a modern computer]. And on the spiritual side of the mental realm we have the Oneness-integration-mind which grasps things intuitively, as a whole, allowing us to understand abstract things. Our 'will' functions between the two, like a pilot, or captain of a ship, and allows us to act, or think, in any direction, and utilize either aspect of the mental realm, or both. Free will is our birthright; it is an inheritance - offspring of the Father (Infinite) and the Mother (Finite)."

Next he discussed the vital importance of mere thoughts.

"Thoughts are the very building blocks of physical experience. Please contemplate in fullness the outstanding profundity of this concept: *EVERYTHING THAT HUMANS HAVE DONE OR CREATED, CAME FROM THE MENTAL REALM FIRST.* Every thing you can think of! Try to think of even one thing, that wasn't first thought of before it came into existence. A building? First someone had to conceive of the idea of a building, then someone had to want a building, then they had to figure out the details of how it would be, then the details of how it would be constructed. *Every single thing that you can think of that is not from nature, was first initiated in the mind. Don't take this lightly. You must realize it, not just intellectually grasp it.* When you think about it, it is really like magic. Someone just thought of a building, and in relatively very little time really, it was there. It is magic, just a slower reacting form, because it is dealing with a slower vibration realm. *You must realize that also.*

ALSO REALIZE THEN, THAT ANYTHING YOU DWELL ON WITH YOUR THOUGHTS, WILL BECOME PHYSICAL REALITY. Thinking about something first gives it birth. Then thinking of it again, is nurturing it. It is part of the process of bringing any thought or idea to fruition. First you plant the mental seed. Then if you water it (by thinking about it from time to time), it will grow. If you don't tend your plant, it will die. This works in our favor, and against us, depending on what our plant is, and if we discipline our mind.

If you have negative seeds, such as those planted by negative thoughts/emotions such as jealousy, the separate self will use your programming and emotions to constantly turn your thoughts to those seeds. This will provide constant nurturing. Thus it will bring to bear negative fruits. What can you do to stop negative seeds or plants from thriving within you? You can only "starve" them out by using your will to discipline yourself and control your thoughts - redirecting your thoughts towards the positive, every time a negative thought rises.

Unfortunately, when you are growing positive fruits, you do not have the advantage the negative side has."

"What do you mean by advantage?" asked the elder monk Pythagoras.

"I was just getting to that. The negative side has the advantage of the selfish separate self using programming and strong emotions such as jealousy. This literally 'grabs' your attention and thoughts, urging you to tend the negative seeds. It also has 'habit' on its side, with programming that unconsciously and automatically thinks, acts, and dwells, negatively. To get positive seeds to grow, you must first overcome the negative emotions, programming, etc., plus you need to work to create new habits, new programming. When you are planting positive seeds of virtue, such as becoming a more compassionate person, those too will come to fruition - but only *if you discipline yourself to mentally tend your plants regularly.* Remember, you are having to do this, not only without benefit of already having positive programming, but rather, having to re-program against negative programming. So, often times, making positive mental progress is far more arduous than just sitting back with the status quo, doing nothing, and letting the negative side 'run with the ball'. You must really take control of your 'reigns' in order to change positively."

"How can one overcome such odds Michiel?" I said. "It seems a herculean task that is so difficult as to be virtually impossible."

"It is not 'impossible' or I would not be standing here today. Certainly it is hard. But just because it is hard is no reason to give up or not do it. And it can be made easier, with the right training of thought patterns. It is a matter of developing a simple habit - rather than constantly engaging in a struggle. In fact, you must not engage in a struggle, which I will explain in a moment. If you use your will to discipline yourself and control your thoughts, *you can re-direct your thoughts* whenever your programming or emotions grab them from you to nurture negative seeds. If you stop watering and tending your negative plants *they will eventually die.* That's all there is to it. But *you cannot **directly** fight evil, or negative thoughts and feelings.* You will lose to it because the very nature of the fighting involves directing your thought energy towards the thing you are fighting. Your thought energy then feeds it, sustains it, even as you seemingly 'fight' it. The only way to win is to starve out the negative - by not thinking negative thoughts, or even thinking about it at all - and by making progress in the positive. Because when the positive grows, it takes up all the space, and doesn't let the negative take root or grow. Just like maximized food gardening, if you plant the right groups of good plants, and you keep them healthy, the negative plants won't grow. A person who is filled with Unselfish Love, does not have selfish thoughts to fight against. There is simply no room for them to exist, and no soil for them to take root in. In such a manner does the mind 'grow' or 'build' all things in life."

Free Will is the Construction Supervisor of our Lives

There was a novice student who had 'wandered' into the chamber sometime during the lecture. I hadn't seen him before, and didn't know his name. He was quite open and relaxed though, and Michiel didn't seem to have any issue with his presence. Out of the blue, the gutsy novice interjected a question.

"How do we insure that what we are 'growing' or 'building' in life, is always the right thing, and will yield the right results?"

Good question, I thought to myself.

"While mind is the *builder*, will is the *director* of mental activities (kind of a construction boss). You can lend your will to either your selfish separate self, or your Inner Being. You can have positive thoughts or negative thoughts. You can be destructive or constructive. But only through using your will in harmony with Universal Will can you achieve lasting peace, in bringing balance, Oneness to the spiritual, mental, and physical."

"The Universe has a will?" the perplexed novice asked.

"Yes, the Universe is a being of sorts, not in the sense that you can understand now, but yes, it has a will. It also has a consciousness, and a flow. It continues to function in incredible synchronization and harmony. Only *humans* have gone out of step with it."

"How do you know what its will or consciousness is?"

"Different ways young novice. You will learn more in other courses son. This is actually a session for more advanced students, but you may stay. Perhaps everyone will learn more through your innocent presence.

Universal Consciousness can be further described as an awareness within each being. This awareness is ingrained, or "pre built into" the mind, and when awakened by the spiritual use of will, the person realizes their Oneness with the Universal Spirit. This "imprinted pattern" is something like instinct, like how a newborn infant *already knows* how to find a breast, and how to nurse. Although it's far more sophisticated than mere animal instinct, like instinct, it's already there inside you. It just takes the right stimulus to bring it out. It's the same with Universal Consciousness. If you want to awaken the imprinted pattern of *that* awareness, you just need the right stimulus. And in this case, the right stimulus is applying your free will, *unselfishly*. When you grow enough in consciousness that you begin to make free will decisions that are unselfish, you trigger a response, and you instinctively begin to discover a new awareness - your Universal Consciousness."

"Getting back to the basic concept of free will, Michiel, why do we have such a problem with using our free will in harmony with the will of God?" I asked.

"The Inner Being in each of us is part of the Universal Spirit, and it thus represents Universal will, and wants us to follow it. Unfortunately, when most humans use or think about their free will (if they even think about it at all), they use it, and consider it, as a means of doing anything BUT Universal will. They think of it as a means of doing whatever their selfish separate self wants - regardless of Universal will (God's will). And doing what the separate self wants is usually the opposite of Universal will. The separate self does not like 'serving' God - the separate self sees it as a sacrifice of its own will. So most people ignore Universal will, use their free will to serve the separate self's will, and pay the resultant karmic price."

"Which is..."

"Which is, for purposes of our discussion here, that we keep getting disillusioned, and we keep suffering. But we eventually find that only by doing the will of the Universal Spirit, by living in harmony with the Universal will, can we live in happiness & peace. Finally, in time, some of us begin to realize that our real will *is* the will of the Universal Spirit, and that only by sticking to this do we 'return to paradise'. When we synchronize our will with Universal will, we then act only in ways that make positive karma."

"So basically just be a good person," said the novice.

"Definitely yes. But this is a complex issue, and you are oversimplifying it. Acting in ways that create positive karma may not always have the *appearance* of doing something good. And doing something that appears to be good, may not always create positive karma, it could even create negative karma. For instance, you could decide that being charitable is good, giving away money to the poor is good. That certainly is good in general. But consider this. Let's say you come across a poor man lying in the cold street, and he holds out his hand to you silently asking for money to help him. You have choices to make. How are you going to know what is best. If you are following the charitable route, you may give him a great deal of money, thinking you are doing the right thing. But there are many things you cannot know just by yourself, and you need Universal guidance to really do the right thing. Sure, he might use that money to buy warm clothing, shelter, create a livelihood, and live happily ever after. But he also might use it to buy drugs or alcohol, and end up in a stupor in which he gets harmed or killed, or even does so to someone else. On the other hand, maybe this man is psychologically 'set' just so - and if instead of giving him anything, you were to scream an insult at him instead - perhaps he would say to himself, 'That's it! I've had enough of this human degradation!', and pick himself up out of his self made hole, get himself work shoveling Yak dung, then continue to improve his conditions, and/or himself, and ends up finally living happily ever after. So while yelling at him would have been the right thing to do, to someone who just saw you yelling at this poor man, it would appear that you were being cruel and heartless, not doing something good.

Some of these things can be known by an enlightened being trained in prophecy, as you will be. But other things can only be known in the higher levels of consciousness outside the limits of our physical existence."

"What do you mean?" the novice hastily said.

"There is a hierarchy of beings that are beyond us in consciousness, who have left the physical plane of the Earth, or were never part of it, all the way to the Source of the Universal Spirit - these include Angels, enlightened and saintly beings, some of whom are our ancestors, and other Greater beings. They see and understand these things better than us because of their state of ascended consciousness, and are there to guide us if we surrender our reigns to the Universal Will. Thus we can only properly make such choices, as the one in the example above, if we let our Inner Being, with its 'Universal Consciousness', guide us intuitively."

The novice spoke again, "How do we get to such a state that we can be guided like that?"

"Humility, and Unselfish Love will bring you to Oneness with the all. There is nothing that can keep you from Oneness with the Universe but your separate self. Only through Unselfish Love can you make your will one with the Infinite One. And by so doing, you will become a blessing to all who come in contact with you, for they will be coming in contact with truth, their own essential being, The One Universal Spirit."

The School of the Prophets

Zain entered the chamber, to relieve Michiel, and lecture more about the Atlantean teachings on learning prophecy. Michiel had done too much for the day as it was. Zain kissed him on the cheek, and as he left the chamber, I bowed to him out of respect, and in appreciation for his time and efforts with us. It wasn't just a gesture, or anything expected of anyone. Those kind of "rote" gestures weren't done at our monastery. But it just sincerely came from my heart, spontaneously. As he shuffled out, bearing nearly half his weight on his cane, he stopped and looked me deep in the eyes, then he smiled and nodded to me in recognition and humble gratitude for my gesture. That was the last time I would ever see him.

Zain's first words brought me immediately back to my earlier thoughts about destiny (which we started this chapter with).

"There are those who totally believe in fate. They say all things are pre-destined, and we cannot change them. Others believe that there is no such thing as destiny at all - that we totally make our own reality. The Children teach that these two concepts are a paradox, and both are true. The paradox is this: we have free will and shape the future through our choices, but everything is pre-destined by a definite flow/Universal plan/pattern. Impossible, yet true.

Humans are both One with, and "miniature" representations of, the Universal Spirit. Thus we have the means to take responsibility and initiative in playing an active role in creation. If you were in a city, walking across the street and someone said, 'Watch out, a car is coming!', would you say, 'Well, if I'm supposed to be run over, I will be.' And go on walking blindly across the street? Would that not have been God telling you to watch out for the car? Most everyone agrees that if someone warned them that a car was about to run them over, they would move. Yet many times I have heard people forewarned of disaster, say, 'If something is meant to happen, it will happen'. These were people who didn't believe in destiny, yet they were making a statement as if they did. Of course, their comment was true, in part, but it was being 'rationalized' by the person to the point of imbalance. Even to the point of death. For instance, I have known people warned to begin moving their habitats, told that an earthquake would destroy them if they did not move. They were warned by monks with reputations of very high accuracy in such prophecy. But the warnings went unheeded. Even though the people knew they and their family might be killed, or at least injured and lose everything, they ignored it."

"Why?"

"Because their selfish desire to not leave their land, certain possessions, or not put out the energy it would take to move, etc., outweighed their Universal intuition."

This is sad but true. In these recent times, I have met many people whom I have warned of various events that would befall them if they did not take a different action. I have, as Zain had, even warned of devastating Earthquakes, and been ignored. There are people who would NEVER drive without their seat belt on, yet they continue to live in an area where even scientists have said a disastrous earthquake will definitely occur, and could hit at any time. Yet people continue to stay there, using illogical rationalizations like "If something is meant to happen, it will happen". But as Zain said, they wouldn't say that if a car was about to hit them. Speaking of Zain, let's get back to his lecture:

"On the other side of the coin, you have people who believe they *totally* create *everything* in their lives, and can't be affected by anything else. They believe this to the exclusion of the Universal Law of Cause & Effect. Some even believe Jesus' crucifixion was the result of "drawing it to himself" because of negative thinking. They'll tell you that you won't get cancer if you don't accept the idea. I guess that's what killed Madame Curie - negative thinking rather than radiation. Some will even go so far as to say you won't *die* if you refuse to believe you will. Yet no one has proven such yet. Some say you don't need to eat to maintain a physical body. Yet no one has proven such yet. If you really believed the way these people profess, you could sit in the middle of the road, on a highway of blind truck drivers, enjoying your dinner. You could walk up to a gunman who's in the middle of robbing a store, and take away his gun, because if you haven't "drawn" violence to you, you can't get shot. And you wouldn't even need to bother with stop signs, because if you haven't "drawn" an accident to you, you won't have one. Yet I don't see any of these people who profess such beliefs, doing such things. Why not? Because they still really know inside that it isn't *totally* true. That things *do* happen to people that they didn't attract to themselves. But if you noticed, I said it wasn't *totally* true. Because, it is partly true. Things *do sometimes* happen to people that *they did attract* to themselves mentally. And for the most part, we do create our own realities, our own lives. It takes a great deal of understanding, and high consciousness, to fully grasp such paradoxes, and not think in an imbalanced manner one way or the other.

The Children fully understand, and teach the Universal Law of Cause & Effect in all its paradoxical wonder. This law dictates the results that follow an action or group of actions. Understanding this law is how a prophet determines what things are past the point of no return, and are thus "destined" to happen regardless of what else happens. The companion knowledge to this is understanding the subtleties of free will.

How to read and utilize the revelations of Cause and Effect, and the projections of free will, have been taught by the Children since the earliest days of fair Atlantis. That is why we have sometimes been called the School of the Prophets."

"Where is the School of the Prophets?" said the novice who was still hanging around.

Zain looked at him quizzically, then asked, "Who are you?"

Before the young novice could answer, Zain went on. "Oh, never mind. Look around young one. Open your ears. You are *in* the School of the Prophets. It is just part of the overall training received by the elder monks at our monasteries, or given personally to novices or elders by Initiates of the Children of the Law of One who don't reside in a monastery."

"So how do we learn and understand the subtleties of free will and its interaction with Cause and Effect?"

"Contemplate it. Here is a good analogy to contemplate for now: Cause and Effect works something like ripples in a pond. You throw in a rock and see the concentric circles go out from the point that the rock entered the pond. Most people only realize the rock was thrown in the pond, they don't pay attention to what happens with 'the ripples'. Even those who see the original ripples, usually don't see beyond them. But if you watch the ripples closely, and keep following them, you see that the ripples may reach a shore, or a large rock in the pond, and then they bounce off and start making new ripples. And then the new ripples may even interact with the original ripples, or make more reflective ripples themselves. Human events are much like these ripples. One action sets an entire series of other actions into motion. And our ripples are interacting with other people's ripples.

These actions can be very elaborately complicated. For instance, let's look again at the example of the beggar in the street that was used earlier. We said one scenario would be you gave him the money, he got warm clothes, a new livelihood, etc., and lived happily ever after. Wonderful. That would seem to be a positive outcome then, right? But let's follow the ripples further. What if his new livelihood was making a special kind of glass that was impervious to changes in heat and cold, that subsequently enabled scientists to develop a new chemical for killing insects on farm plants, in order to help feed more people. But instead, the chemical had an unknown reaction, that began a process of some kind, that created weather or solar changes that started ruining the food plants, or created new diseases? Many such things are in the ancient prophecies, and much, much more. And there will be such so-called 'innocent' people being part of these developments. Or in another scenario with the poor street person - what if you helped him, and he lived happily ever after, and had children, and one of his children became a lawyer, who turned out to be the next Hitler. Altering cause and effect is a very complicated matter with very serious implications. And unfortunately, everyone is constantly altering it, just by all the things they do in their day to day lives, and they are altering things by thinking and acting from the virtually 'blind' point of view of the separate self.

Prophecy can be learned. Using discipline and concentration, techniques of contemplation can be used to trace and interpret the complex 'ripple' patterns of cause and effect. These techniques allow the outcome of events to be seen partially, or sometimes, all the way to their final outcome. But like medical school, there is a pre-requisite to 'getting into the school of the prophets'. You must also transcend the limited view of the separate self."

"Then you will know all things that are going to happen in the future? Including about your own life? And isn't that fate again, not free will?"

"Both. Don't forget it is a paradox. But also know this: there are two fields of prophecy. The first is the prediction of pre-destined events. The second is the prediction of events that are yet to be determined because they involve the free will choices of one or more individuals.

The outcome of a situation involving free will choice is difficult to predict *at best* - because you never know for sure what a person might choose - *because* they have free will. Thus prophecy involving free will becomes what might be considered in gambling terms as an 'odds on' betting game. Or in scientific terms as a 'probability factor'. For example, when free will is involved you won't be able to predict that 'such and such' will happen for *certain,* but you may be able to determine that there is an 85% probability that it will happen, a 45% probability that it will happen a certain way, a 30% probability that it will happen another way, etc.. Predicting a free will choice becomes easier to call, and more accurate, if there are factors that exist that will make the person 'lean' one way or another. For instance, let's say Jack is going to drive by a Chinese hitch-hiker tomorrow, and you want to predict whether or not Jack is going to pick up the hitch-hiker. Let's also say that we know that Jack is not inclined to pick up hitch-hikers, and usually doesn't - but he has done it before on rare occasions. There is a 'leaning' that makes it more likely that he will not pick up the hitch-hiker. We'll say there's maybe a 5 to 10% probability that he will, given other factors we know about. But if you combine *that* leaning with a stronger leaning, such as knowing that Jack also hates Chinese people, he is almost definitely not going to pick up the Chinese hitch-hiker. Yet, he still could."

[Whew! And that example was nothing - first grade level stuff in prophecy school.]

"Then there are the situations and events that do not involve free will choices, and can be seen and predicted for certain. Such is the case with Earth Changes. Humans have caused such an imbalance as the result of their past free will choices, that certain things will happen within the Earth, even if all the beings make free will choices to try and repair the damage. Sadly, it's beyond the point of no return, and it's just a matter of time before the ripples in the pond, finish their journey. Don't forget though, we can still change our own lives, and the effects of these things which are past the point of no return, can be altered in various ways.

Some prophecy involves a mix of pre-destined events, and free will choices. These types of things are very complex. Some aspects of the outcome will be certain, but there will be variations of the outcome that are influenced by the free will choices involved, thus the variations are uncertain.

Again, the only way to be able to know for sure that you are making the right predictions, and the right choices associated with them, is for you to have surrendered to the Universal Will. If you are thus living in a state of Unselfish Love all the time, and thusly in tune with the Universal Spirit, you will both see far more, and more clearly, as far as prophecy is concerned, AND you will be under the guidance and direction of the hierarchy, and Universal Will. Thus all your decisions will be as good as they possibly can be, and will be 'right' regardless of whether or not you can see their outcome, or what the apparent outcome is."

"If you live that way Father, then can miraculous things also happen?"

"Miraculous things are always happening. People just aren't aware of it. But to answer your specific question more directly, when you have thus become an instrument of Universal Will, the hierarchy will sometimes do something through you, or around you. Sometimes you will be aware of this taking place. Other times things will happen through you, and you won't even be aware of it, or you'll just be aware of some of the particulars."

There is a good example of this in the chapter about visualization and affirmations. It is a story about an experience I had with a car dealer, that could have resulted in serious harm, had the hierarchy not intervened, and had I not yielded to Universal Will. In fact, if you wish, you could skip to that chapter and read the example now, then come back to this chapter. Or you can read about a different type of example now, in the next section.

That Big Dealer in the Sky

The following is also an example, one of thousands I could give you, of how the Universal Spirit, manipulated events through the hierarchy. This particular example, shows how a life was changed, and the ripples of cause & effect forged Karmic ties. Actually, because it is a brief example, it doesn't really show the extent of the changes that really took place, but it will give you an idea of the "big picture" involved.

This next story takes place after my final year at the monastery. After attaining the final Initiation, enlightenment, I had begun the easier/harder work - that of an Adept, a true teacher. But I was needed in other places, so at age 21, I left the monastery, and began my "work". My "employer" was the Universal Spirit (No teamsters, but we had a great "union"). Then, as now, I wandered parts of the world, following the direction and guidance of the Universal Will. I owned nothing but my monk's robes. No home. No car. No other clothes. No money. I never begged, nor ever asked for anything. Yet I never went hungry, never needed a ride, never lacked shelter or a place to sleep, and I always had whatever money I needed. When God is your employer, and your life is truly dedicated toward serving others rather than dedicated to "self" survival, such things aren't an issue anymore. God is the true provider of all things, and provided for all those day to day needs for its humble servant (but everything could come through a variety of "normal" or "strange" sources). Often, they were offered by "strangers" whom I had just met, who were going through something intense in their lives, and sought out our/my assistance. Some just needed a shoulder to cry on. Such people had always desperately prayed or called out to God for help or guidance at some time in their lives, before we would meet. Sometimes, amazing things happened around/through me as the Universal Spirit used me as an instrument for its Will. The following story is just one of many similar instances.

One day I was walking through the city of Las Vegas, Nevada. I passed by a door of an office building and heard what sounded like live band music. I felt like stopping, and looking in the door. As I looked in, I saw someone I knew from a school I had attended as a child. He had once been my "best friend". He was in a rock band that was rising to success, and they were practicing there. The space was rented by their manager, specifically for practice sessions. My old friend was very surprised to see me, shocked by my monk's garb, and how "something indefinable was very different about me" (other than the obvious appearances). As we were still greeting each other, his manager came in and handed him a paycheck from their last performance. With check in hand, he grabbed his jacket and said to me, "I'd really like to visit right now, but I have to run down to a casino to cash my check. Of course, you're welcome to come with me if you want." I said fine, and we were on our way. I soon discovered my friend had become a serious gambling addict.

We got to the casino, he cashed his check, then headed straight for the gaming tables. Many of you may not be familiar with addiction syndromes, especially gambling. But it is a sad and strange thing to witness. He'd gotten the "scent", and was so focused and preoccupied with getting his gambling fix, I may as well not even been there. To him, I almost didn't exist at that moment.

The casino had a strange atmosphere (stranger than normal). It turned out that there was a "dealer strike", and the dealers that were there were strike breakers, or "scabs". We walked up to a "blackjack" table, and sat down. The dealer looked me over, with an unpleasant grin. With a not-so-subtle hostility, he told me I could not sit next to my friend, unless I gambled. My friend put down $2 on the spot in front of me. The dealer said, "Fine. Now, we aren't supposed to talk about Sex, Religion, or Politics - I'm going to talk about all three." Then he looked at me again and said, "You look like some kind of freaked out Rabbi or something." I was an odd sight for a patron of a Las Vegas casino - I was wearing a monk's robe, sandals, and I had a beard and long hair that hadn't been cut in many years. As the dealer dealt the cards, he began to "verbally attack" me with insulting questions about me and my beliefs. Interestingly enough though, all his hostile "inquisitions" were valid spiritual questions, if you ignored the insults they were cloaked in. Insults can only upset the selfish separate self's defenses (sometimes called ego). By this time in my life, nothing offended me. He found no target at which his ego insulting arrows could strike, so all he managed to get out of me, were answers to his questions. Answers given calmly and lovingly. All the time this was going on, we were "gambling", but since other forces were involved (the hierarchy and Universal Will), I wasn't gambling at all, I was just winning - every hand.

I wasn't even paying attention to anything but the questions and answers. This particular casino played with the customer's cards face up, and the dealer was assuming that I was playing the standard way - stand on 17 or over, and take a card on less, unless I signalled him otherwise. So he dealt my cards accordingly. But I wasn't playing. I just answered his questions and ignored my cards. I didn't do anything with the original $2, I just let it keep doubling with every winning hand. This table was using what's called a 4 deck shoe for the cards. It held 4 decks of cards that would get played before a new shuffle would take place. By the time it was over, I had not lost ONE hand, and that $2 in chips became a mountain of chips worth thousands. This *alone* was *"blowing the dealer's mind"*. But simultaneously, the whole time this miraculous winning was going on, we had discussed everything from creation to the ozone layer, and the coming Earth changes. And all my answers had "rung his inner bell of truth".

The dealer began to get shaky. The odds of anyone just letting a bet ride, and winning every hand in a 4 deck shoe were astronomical, virtually impossible, and no one would know that better than a dealer. My "vibration", composure, and answers to his questions resonated within the center of his being. Combining all this with my appearance (what people generally consider Jesus looked like), was too much for him. He was relieved by his supervisor, and another dealer took over our table. All the money was lost with the first hand from the new dealer. To me, my winning was clearly for the benefit of the dealer, my friend, and a few others at the table. But my shaky previous dealer had headed off to the bar behind us, and was "chugalugging" straight scotch as fast as he could pour. Minutes later I sensed something behind me. I turned, and there was the dealer walking towards me like a Zombie, with one arm outstretched and shaking. He came up to me and touched my shoulder, as if to see if maybe, just maybe, I wasn't really there, or I was actually some delusion that came from a bottle of scotch. But alas, I was real. He turned around, went back to the bar, and continued to drink. This incident had a dramatic impact on my gambling addicted friend too. But that is another story not for this book.

Many years later, I visited an organic farm in a rural community in the South Central part of the U.S.. A very happy, friendly neighbor came over to visit, and before too long he told me his amazing life story. Apparently, this nice man had been a blackjack dealer in Las Vegas, and for some "unknown reason", he had a total nervous breakdown while dealing during a strike, and completely lost all his memory and mental programming. The breakdown left him as blank as a child, and he had to completely re-educate himself, all from a bed in a psychiatric hospital ward. He also "re-programmed" himself, with the help of the psychiatrists. He had a basically freudian view of the world, and didn't believe in synchronicity, or such things - yet (another story). With his new outlook on life, he semi-retired, happily breeding dogs at his little rural home in the woods. Do I need to tell you who this particular ex-blackjack dealer was?

Chapter Eleven

Sub-Conscious Programming and Beliefs

My reunion with the dealer from Las Vegas (whom we'll call "Bob") reminded me of my earlier training at the monastery, regarding beliefs, programming, and the power of beliefs.

Bob had no memory of me, or a great deal of his previous life, for that matter. He had actually retrained his mind, re-programmed his beliefs and way of thinking, and been programmed by others in the psychiatric hospital. Because of what he was exposed to, given to read, and taught, he had strong feelings and beliefs, based on the theories of the famous "Father of psychiatry", Sigmund Freud. And thus, for the most part, he viewed the world through "Freudian colored glasses".

Bob had a relaxed, easy life, and was a kind and gentle man now, whose only "vice" was an addiction to football games on TV. He didn't really believe in God. I, as the other Children, believe that his kindness and compassion was more important than his beliefs. And compassion wasn't just an intellectual concept to him. He took a job as a jailer on a graveyard shift, so he could bring a little kindness and joy to some of the inmates. He would make people hot chocolate, play chess or checkers with them, talk about their problems, etc.. Whereas most other jailers in there, treated the prisoners anywhere from coldly, to sadistically.

Because of Bob's programming, he believed that absolutely everything that occurred in people's lives, was totally dictated by the subconscious (which is partly true to a very great extent, but without the other pieces of the puzzle, and the inclusion of even 2% of our lives being controlled by free will choices, it "misses by a mile"). So to him, the prisoners were nothing but the unconscious pawns of their subconscious. Bob also didn't believe in "Synchronicity" (which was a theory from Freud's "rival" psychiatrist "Carl Jung", who seemed to have a much more Universal way of understanding the events in human life).

Of course, Bob's viewpoint necessitated the disbelief that humans had free will at all. In his mind, everything was totally dictated by the subconscious. He believed that not one single action, or thought, was freely chosen, generated, or "accidental" (which could also be called "coincidental" or "synchronistic") in any way - it was all totally generated by the subconscious. Because of this, in a strange way, he was a fatalist who believed everything was pre-destined, but not pre-destined via anything metaphysical or spiritual. People's lives were totally destined by the sub-conscious mind, and there was nothing they could do about it, because even if they thought they were having a new or free thought, it was merely the subconscious still generating it. It is true that about 98% of everyone's thoughts and actions are dictated by the subconscious, but again, that 2% makes all the difference in the world.

Anyway, the karmic tie between us that had started with his dealing to me at the blackjack table, was not over yet. And he eventually became a very good friend, and a householder of sorts. Through the combination of our interactions, conversations, and events that would ensue, Bob slowly and begrudgingly began to grasp that there were other powers at work in the Universe, other than the sub-conscious mind. And he came to understand that there were free will choices people would make, regardless of the influence and control of the sub-conscious. But at the same time, oddly enough, he didn't even have a clue as to just how powerful the sub-conscious mind really was.

Of course, there was a time when I didn't understand it either. Back when I was an elder monk at the monastery, one of my final changes was to deal with all my programming, and my beliefs. I had to deal with so many issues, mostly from how I had been raised as a child. Everyone has "programming" like this. Whatever culture we have been raised in, we are sort of "brainwashed" from birth on, by our society, family, friends, etc., and we create some of our own programming from our blind personal experiences.

The ancient Atlantean teachings of the Children, regarding programming of the subconscious mind and belief structures, are quite unique, and very in-depth. They cover all aspects of the subject, including: the effects of your beliefs; how beliefs "work"; and analyzing your beliefs and programming. Then they go a step further and teach how to change your own program once you have made your analysis, and are ready to make free will choices to alter your beliefs and programming.

At some point, near the end of my training, I became very ill with a prostate infection. I finally went to Zain and asked his advice for healing it. I was expecting herbal remedies, and healing regimens. But instead, I was told that the problem was basically from certain conscious and sub-conscious negative programming and "blocks", and he recommend that I fast, contemplate the issue, then speak with him again.

The prostate problems were related to sexual blocks I had been raised with. But they were really a "side issue"- more importantly, I was about to begin really learning/realizing (out of necessity) the teachings about the vital importance of beliefs, and working with the layers of the mind. The following are excerpts from various texts about the subjects:

The Mind is Three
One of the Three Lives Below the Surface.
It Can Be a helpmate who Performs Great Tasks
Or hinder us at Every Turn.

Tend it You must, Like a Garden
Remove the Seeds of Destruction
And Water the Seeds of Life

❖

Belief is the Great Key
To the Powers Controlled By the Mind

What You Believe
Is Real
In The Realms of the Mind

*The Realms of the Mind
Are Reality
To those Experiencing them*

*The Masses Believe
What Others Have Given Them,
Right or Wrong, True or False.
The Wise Realize This And Are Wary,
And Set Out to Test and Discover.*

❖

Change Comes Only to the Sincere.

The Power of Belief

Early in the book we mentioned how belief can be such a powerful force that it can cause war, murder, prejudice, great temples to be built, etc.. I just mentioned how my own beliefs created prostate problems. We all have different (and many) aspects to our own programming that are unique little problems within ourselves. But there are many things that your beliefs dramatically impact upon in your life, or even fundamentally control in totality. Your personal beliefs radically effect your life, your future - and they are all within your power to change.

Belief and the Powers of the Mind

Before my days at the monastery, I was attending a university (To make a long story short, I flunked high school, was expelled, supposedly had a genius I.Q., and ended up in college instead). In one of my classes, the professor gave a hypnosis demonstration. I witnessed people who were so well "hypnotized", that when they were told that a burning cigar was being touched to the palm of their hand, blisters instantly appeared (even though only an unlit cigar was touched to their hand).

But as the years have gone by in my life, I have witnessed far more amazing and strange things. Believe it or not - it really doesn't matter to me.

I have seen objects moved with thought. I've seen hand-to-hand combat, where no flesh ever made contact. I've seen bodies tossed about like rag dolls by energies invisible to the "normal" human eye. I've seen people with bad cuts stop bleeding by "thinking it so". I've seen people stop their heart, and stop breathing, without dying. I've seen monks in the Himalayas, sit in the snow, in conditions that were so cold that as they were wrapped in wet blankets, the blankets froze around them. After many layers of blankets were applied, the monks would visualize heat within themselves, radiating out. The blankets would defrost, and a circle of melted snow would appear around them. Their degree of mental accomplishment was measured by the size of the circle around them. And I've seen far more.

The "hypnosis demonstrations" in college, were mysterious and remarkable enough, but after witnessing the monks melting the ice, I asked Zain how such things were done. After having me read what was called "The Tibetan Treatise of Psychic Heat", he began teaching me all the details of the power of the mind. It began with this discussion:

"Your beliefs control and affect the incredible powers of the mind, which dictate, or influence, many things in your life:

...Your choices, and thus your course in life, and what you create in your life;

...Your ability to learn and apply your knowledge;

...Your health (whether or not you foster sickness or wellness);

...Your ability to draw upon, or squander, Inner Strength.

The ancient Atlantean teachings call aspects of the energy related Inner Strength, 'Universal Life Energy'. It is an energy that can bridge the gap between physical and spiritual. It flows through all things, all life, and can be consciously, or sub-consciously, manipulated by the mind. It can heal, and it can destroy. The same energy is called many things in different cultures, in some of the Asian, it is often called 'Chi' or 'Ki'."

"I learned a little about Ki from martial arts training I had as a young teenager."

"But it's really a minor energy in a sense. Far more importantly, your beliefs affect your ability to flow with, and allow to flow, the *ultimate* power - that of the Universal Spirit."

Belief and the Powers of the Mind, and Knowledge

"Is this power learned through knowledge, intellectually, or through the intuitive training?"

"Using your mind to influence your body (or elements) requires a firm foundation; a base of information and knowledge ('roots'). The more know-how you have ssing mental techniques, and the more you understand the reasons why (and how) they work, the more effective they will be for you. Also, the more you know about how your body works (physiologically or biologically), the better. This applies especially to those areas of functioning that relate to any changes or controls you wish to exert on your body (or mind).

It is not really *necessary* to have any understanding of such physiological functions. After all, the subconscious mind has been performing vast, powerful, and intricate functions, quite automatically, and with no help from us. But, the more a person knows about his internal biological working, the more effective mental manipulation of the body can be. And it is relatively easy to gain a basic grasp of the physiological functions of the body."

"Oh, no problem, I'll just go read 'Gray's Anatomy' tonight, or da Vinci's studies, or better yet, I'll go back to the states and dig up some dead bodies and conduct my own autopsies."

"Or maybe you should be a comedian and go on the Ed Sullivan show, Peniel. Are we done with the sarcasm?" he said with a smile. I nodded affirmatively, also with a smile.

Assumption: a Key to the Power of Belief

"Other than digging up dead bodies... (he smirked) for direct knowledge, part of having a good *foundation* of knowledge, is understanding the way belief works. One powerful key to the working of belief is 'assumption'. Assumption functions like a catalyst, and provides us with a means to effect tremendous changes, including changes in our physical bodies. When we *assume* something, our *subconscious accepts it as an accomplished fact,* and proceeds to manifest it in the body.

Using assumption does not require anything on the order of 'blind faith'; rather, it is based on facts that are well-established. You see, your belief in 'the power of assumption' will come from areas of this foundation. The information base you are acquiring from your learning here, from your teachers, your studies of the ancient texts, and your practices and applications, are all providing you with the facts you need to know about how the mind can dramatically alter physiology. In essence, your belief in the power of belief, will be the result and the summary of all the other information contained in your foundation."

To help you readers of this book along similar lines, we will provide you with some examples of the mind's physical effects (from various research studies), as well as the "hows and whys" of such occurrences.

Mind and Body, in Search of Unity

The Children of Atlantis have always known about the effects of the mind on the physical plane, including the physical body, and used this knowledge in practical applications. Now, recent scientific studies substantiate the effects of the mind on the body, in many ways.

For one, new research indicates that a very *high percentage* of illness may be mentally/emotionally originated. In fact, mental/emotional "triggers" are involved with the majority of people suffering from a wide spectrum of diseases today. If a person can become psychosomatically ill, then doesn't it follow that a person can become psychosomatically healthy (or taking it further, create desired physiological changes in the body)? The primary point to keep in mind (which has been demonstrated by numerous studies and scientific research) is that PSYCHOLOGICAL CHANGES CREATE PHYSICAL CHANGES. In other words, your mind affects your body.

A New View

Although the prevailing school of thought in medicine is still leaning toward the "physical effect on the body" viewpoint (as opposed to fully accepting the ramifications of the "mental effect on the body" viewpoint), things have changed (and are still changing—sometimes with a vengeance). More and more, the separate realms are being considered together. Chemicals, hormones, electrical impulses, etc., are being looked at in light of their effect on the mind and emotions. But possibly even more important, the mind and emotions are being looked at in the light of their effect on chemicals, hormones, electrical impulses ... and much more. The effect the mind can have on the body is almost staggering when you first realize it. It seems unbelievable at times, yet there it is, a veritable mountain of individuals' personal experiences that attest to the facts. The mind's power over the body is very real indeed.

The Placebo Effect

Most of you are familiar with the term "placebo." A placebo is an inert substance (like a "sugar pill") that has the effect of an actual drug - the drug the person taking it, believes it is. This effect occurs because the person taking the placebo is told that it is a drug, and just assumes that it is. There it is again - assumption and belief.

A question of the patient's suggestibility comes in here. Contrary to the common myth that people with high suggestibility have low intelligence, the truth is that the higher the intelligence, the greater the benefits from using placebos can be, as long as the assumption is there.

When a physician uses "suggestion" to "fool" a patient into assuming that a placebo is really a powerful beneficial drug, it doesn't matter how intense or elaborate that suggestion is. Often, it doesn't take much to generate a belief. A simple smile from the physician can be as effective as 48 hours of intensely indoctrinating the patient about the effectiveness of the placebo. It just depends on what the patient believes about how effective it will truly be. This is usually quite substantial, because most people have a great deal of faith (belief factor again) in their doctors. If their doctor prescribes a medicine or treatment for them, then it must be good and worthwhile. Thus the faith in the doctor translates into the patient's assumption/belief about the potency of the treatment. The mind follows the lead of the belief and actually makes physical changes in the body to match the *presumed* effects of the drug the individual *assumes* has been taken.

Zain said pretty much the same thing.

"You may have heard of a doctor prescribing a 'sugar pill' without the patient knowing it, with the result of beneficial effects on the patient's health. A doctor may prescribe a sugar pill to avoid giving a patient who just seems to be a 'complainer', an actual powerful drug that could have side effects. But more important, it may be prescribed in a case where there are no appropriate drugs or treatments presently available, but the physician does not want the patient to feel that there's no hope. The point here is that in many cases the patients taking the placebo have remarkable reductions or recoveries from physical symptoms. And some of these are cases in which there is no known cure."

In summary, the power of the placebo lies in the mind of the individual using it. It is the power of belief, anticipation, expectancy or assumption, that gives us such an amazing phenomenon as the placebo effect.

Destructive Assumption/Negative Placebo Effects

Beneficial placebo effects come from positive assumptions. Just as powerful though, are negative assumptions. The point we made earlier, about separating the placebo effect from the physical treatment, applies to negative assumption also. How many people may have received beneficial physical treatment without having positive results (or having less positive results), because their feelings or expectancies were negative?

The following study gives an example of certain types of effects from negative assumption:

A placebo was substituted for a drug called Mephenesin. When the placebo was taken instead of the Mephenesin it produced the same negative reactions in patients as the real drug itself would have. Symptoms such as nausea, heart palpitations, abdominal pain, buildup of fluid in the hips, dizziness, skin rashes and anaphylactic shock occurred as a result of administering the placebo.

I have found that most people intuitively sense the truth of how we can mentally affect ourselves. You have done it yourself, either positively or negatively, to one degree or another.

You probably can remember someone who, through chronic stress reactions, mentally "set himself up to be sick." Seeing this, you may have thought to yourself, "He's going to make himself sick if he goes on like that." And he probably did. Of course, this same phenomenon also exists in a positive way.

Will the Smart Rats Please Raise Their Hands

The following is an example that doesn't directly apply to the types of assumption phenomenon we've been discussing thus far, but does demonstrate some fascinating, serious, and far reaching results. It demonstrates how a person's belief can not only have a substantial effect on them, but on other beings around them also.

151

The experiments, which were conducted by Dr. R. Rosenthal, involved two groups of rats which were being timed in their progress through a maze. The graduate students who were conducting the experiments were told by Dr. Rosenthal that one group of rats were very "smart" and would complete the maze quite rapidly, whereas the other group was rather dull and would be much slower. In actuality, the two groups were essentially identical in intelligence and previous performance time. But the students assumed/believed that one group was better than the other. And *their beliefs actually changed the rats' performance.* The rat group they assumed was "superior" did markedly better than the supposedly "dumb" group. Obviously something that the students thought and/or did, had a significant effect on the outcome of the experiment. Similar studies conducted with school teachers, who were told that certain children were exceptionally bright or exceptionally dull, had the same results as Dr. Rosenthal's rat experiments. This type of effect is one reason good scientific experiments are done in a "double blind" fashion, where even the researchers don't know what the subject is, so they can't influence the outcome of the studies by their own assumptions.

Subconsciousness

Some psychologists are now saying that the majority of cognitive activity is outside of the conscious mind's realm. As we mentioned earlier, *some say as much as 98% of our actions, thoughts, and emotional impulses, come from the subconscious.* This "new evidence" corresponds with the Childrens' ancient Atlantean teachings, which we also mentioned earlier.

When you start looking at the research from all the fields of both medicine and psychology, things get even more interesting. Spiritual masters/teachers have long known the profound effects of the subconscious and the power of the mind. But again, medical research into the effects of hypnosis have substantiated how directing the mind can do such things as block pain, constrict blood vessels to control bleeding, etc.

It has also been demonstrated that during an operation, what the anesthetized patient hears can affect their thoughts and actions, which, in turn, can affect their health. For instance, a patient's subconscious will accept and process a doctor saying he doesn't think the patient will survive, or that the operation was very successful and the patient should recover. Now, with all the latest psychological evidence, modern science is realizing that the subconscious mind has a powerful, previously unsuspected (by them), control over many aspects of our lives, including feelings, thoughts, actions, and decisions.

The Bio-Computer

Other than the examples of assumption and belief that we just discussed, how did we come to believe all the things we believe - all the beliefs that are involved in making us what we are? Since a great deal of who we are, and what we are, is a sum of our beliefs - it sure seems like we ought to know *why* we believe what we do!

The day after I contemplated Zain's comments about my prostrate problems being related to my subconscious, I had a "glimmer" of realization about my beliefs, and asked him more about how and why we believe what we believe.

"Some beliefs are developed through our direct experiences. But primarily, we had many of our beliefs 'programmed' by our culture, and the family/friends/teachers we've had throughout our lives. Some of this programming has been by training. Other programming took place very subtly, by 'osmosis' - just by being exposed to people, and their behavior.

The subconscious mind is much like these new electronic computation devices. Our mind has memory storage that remembers all of our past experiences. It is also programmable (and has been programmed by our experiences, especially our *thoughts about our experiences*). Average humans lack knowledge and understanding of this, and just leave their programming up to others - to outside factors, and out of their control. In other words, *the creation of the thing (the subconscious mind's 'program') that determines a substantial amount of what people think, emotionally feel, and physically do - they have left to chance!* Even worse, it has been left to the selfish and dark manipulators of the world. But those aren't the only sources we get programming from. Everyone's programming has been from 'data', coming from all kinds of sources. Our programming gets altered or created from our experiences with the predators and manipulators of the world, the manipulated 'human sheep' of the world, human laws, unwritten social laws (either taught to us directly, or indirectly 'picked up' by observing the behavior of others), our own careless conscious thoughts, etc.. Even our observation of Universal laws, like seeing the results of the Law of Cause & Effect (stick your hand in fire and it gets burned, and deeper concepts) creates and alters programming.

'Out of our control' programming is a *vitally* important fact. We have a mind *full* of programmed intellectual half-truths, which make up the foundation of our beliefs! And *we* didn't do the programming! And these beliefs, which we didn't program, *dictate our actions, good and bad! Someone else's beliefs are running your mind and thus running your life!* Which essentially means *some one else is in control of your life!* Think what that means Peniel! All the people in the entire world, are basically robots running on programming deliberately designed by others, or haphazardly created, but usually a mix of both. Realizing the full significance of this is immensely important. Once one does, it becomes clear that we *must* analyze *all our beliefs and feelings* about things, from as high a state of consciousness as possible, and *re-program ourselves."*

Zain's remarks were shocking, scary, but so obvious and true. I had to reprogram myself, and I wanted to do it fast. But how? And what programming did I need to change, and what was alright to keep? I took a deep breath and asked him.

Finding and Analyzing Your Programming

"Reprogramming ourselves can be done in several ways [Author's note: these will be discussed later]. But first, we must know *what* to change in our programming.

There are different ways to become aware of what we want to change. Some things are obvious, like diet or smoking or some such thing. But unfortunately, most of our own 'bad habit patterns' are negative subconscious programming that is *out of our awareness.*

Meditation can help. Particularly, contemplative meditation (contemplation). In the more expanded and aware state of mind that meditation creates, a person can better contemplate and examine their beliefs, and subsequent feelings and thoughts, about all kinds of issues. Such contemplation can also help you to determine whether a particular belief, feeling or thought is positive/constructive, and thus should remain in programming, or is negative/destructive, and should be removed or replaced.

153

The results of some of our negative programming is often   pointed out to us by friends or relatives. But most people ignore such criticism from others. And unfortunately, sometimes criticism is given during the heat of an argument, which makes it even more difficult to accept. So even though someone may give you truthful and valid criticism, because the separate self goes into a stronger 'defense mode' in such situations, its basic ego defense mechanisms usually defeat your even becoming aware of your problems. For instance, I'm sure that during an argument you've had someone say to you something like, 'You're always so 'such and such'!!' (Or you've said it to someone else during arguments). It doesn't usually get anywhere because the selfish separate self's defenses go up, right? *Regardless* of whether what is being said is valid or not. And sometimes it is valid, and sometimes it's not. When someone criticizes you, sometimes that's just them projecting their *own* problem, and trying to transfer it to you, or it's partly true, but mixed with their own viewpoint, or tainted and distorted by anger, envy, or whatever. But many times it may really be revealing an actual problem you have - something you may want to change if you thought about it and gave it a chance. But the problem is, even when they *are* mirroring *your* own problems to you, if the criticism is contaminated, because they have their *own* problems mixed in - they are not a *clear* mirror of your problem. And that makes it much more difficult for your selfish separate self, and your true inner self, to accept the truth in it, or even see what part is true and what isn't. So straightening yourself out with the help of such unclear mirror criticisms and opinions, is like trying to shave or "do your hair", using a very dirty, extremely warped 'fun house' mirror that is distorting your true reflection. It can still be done of course. But to even see your self clearly at all, through such unclear, distorted, contaminated criticism, you must first have transcended your "self" defense mechanisms. And if you aren't at a level of consciousness in which you are free from your separate self's defense mechanisms and ego, how are you going to be able to even *see* your negative programming problems, let alone have an opportunity to change them?"

Mirror Mirror on the Wall, Who has the Fairest Programming of All?

Interacting with other like minded people (friends, novices, students, etc.), on your path can help though - especially if you have a humble attitude. But often you run into the same problems just mentioned above. Ultimately, interacting with a "true teacher" (any enlightened being in a physical body like Zain was), is the best way to find and analyze your programming flaws, and the only way to route out and dispose of your most subtle and deeply ingrained programming flaws.

We'll get into this more in the chapter on teachers, but for now, we can take a quick look at how it applies to "routing out", seeing, and changing negative programming, in a way that applies to what you just read.

A true teacher is like a clear mirror *and* an exorcist. Thus there is no one more capable of finding your flaws, bringing them up to you, forcing you to see them (like a mirror "forces you" to see your physical self when you look into it), and *then* helping you change them. Unlike other people, the true teacher is a *clear* mirror - he has no ego based opinions, or negative programming himself, that could get in the way of clearly showing you your ego based opinions and negative programming. Also, he doesn't have any desire just to "win the fight", or "not be wrong", like most people do. First of all, he doesn't engage in arguments- discussions yes, arguments no. So all criticism is done strictly in the environment of pointing out your flaws, to help you grow and improve yourself. And if you have actually chosen a true teacher to help you change, by the very fact that you *have* chosen the teacher to help you, you will likely have more respect for what he says to you, thus you will likely be more receptive to what he reveals to you about yourself, thus it will be easier to see and make changes.

But try to remember, while this is one of the ways a true teacher serves you, it is not a pleasant task for him. When a true teacher shows you yourself, what you see about yourself is often not a "pretty picture". Since most people actually believe, live, feel, and think that they *are* their separate selves, then *any* criticism, is seen as a threat, thus an attack, and defenses go up and are called into action. Even the caring criticism from a loving true teacher whom you've *asked* to deliberately give you criticism to *help* you, is seen and felt by you (your selfish separate self) as a personal attack on you. Your selfish separate self realizes your Inner Being's attempt to gain control from the separate self, is an attack on it. Thus what the true teacher shows you about yourself triggers a response, and your separate self will want to attack back to defend itself. If you allow this to happen, even internally, it will hamper your process of changing, and hurt your true teacher. And even though you may "hold your tongue", your true teacher will feel your animosity anyway. And true teachers, by their very nature, are the kindest, most loving, and most sensitive beings on Earth. So it hurts them greater than it would hurt a normal person. I know. I hurt mine many times. Zain is gone from this Earthly plane now, and I deeply regret some of my responses and feelings toward him. I know he understands, and understood even then, but still, he didn't deserve any more pain, and I didn't need to make it so hard. Or maybe I did, but in retrospect, I could have been more humble, more receptive, and made the process easier on him. A true teacher is doing nothing but showing you the negative thing *you* have created and nurtured. Yet they become the primary target of negativity from the student - simply because the student's separate self is threatened by the student seeing himself. So if you ever have such a true teacher who loves you, and is sacrificing his life to help you, remember that when "you" come under attack, your teacher is doing this *because* he loves you, and you *asked* him to do this painful "dirty work". When you react negatively to truth that exposes your self, this is *very* painful for someone at a true teacher's level of consciousness. Yet he takes it - he endures that pain you cause him - so great is his love for you.

Thoughts: the Invisible Building Blocks of Our Physical Realities

Regardless of the percentage, the subconscious mind undoubtedly influences our lives to a great extent. Also, *what we consciously think about,* be it from conscious or subconscious sources, has a *great* deal to do with determining what we make of ourselves, *and what we create for ourselves in life.*

So there are basically two areas of the thought process we need to be very aware of: the thoughts that program our subconscious bio-computer (like those just described), and the interrelated conscious thoughts that construct our physical realities.

As pointed out earlier, every man-made thing on Earth was first "a thought". *Just* a simple thought. You can't touch it, taste it, smell it, or *see* it. Yet it's the most powerful human device on Earth. No human being has ever done anything without first having a thought-conception, followed by the whole train of thoughts necessary for it to become a reality in the physical world. As amazing as it may seem when you stop and really *think* about it, the truth is that everything YOU have *ever done* in *your entire life,* was the result of a thought. And that's just a drop in the bucket compared to the full potential of the mind's power. When you consider all that, it isn't hard to realize that we NEED to be **very** selective about *the thoughts we allow* to run around inside our heads.

Also as mentioned in an earlier chapter, thoughts are "building blocks" of virtually everything else *surrounding* our lives, the mind is a kind of "construction worker" who assembles the "building blocks", and the will is the "construction boss". And even though we are all dealt different hands in the game of life, how we play those hands affects the way the game goes, and eventually, the way the results come out. And *what we think* determines the way the game goes. Once more, our entire life is greatly the result of our mental attitudes, our thoughts and resultant actions.

Bio-Computer Domination:
The Invisible "Thought Maker"

Back to my earlier discussion with Zain.

"But Father, surely there's more to changing than just reprogramming our beliefs and subconscious mind. I mean, I studied the subconscious even before coming here, and I know its power, but at least most of what we do everyday is conscious, isn't it?"

"Yes, definitely, but no. And don't call me Father Shirley."

"What???"

"That's a joke son."

"Oh."

"You students... always so serious. Of course there is more to it than subconscious. You must be concerned with your conscious thoughts, and re-direct them if need be. If that wasn't an issue, there would be no need for the 'conscious' part of the word subconscious. But not only do we need to be concerned with thoughts that are an aspect of the conscious mind, we also need to be aware of the many thoughts that continually surface from the subconscious mind, without us even noticing them. They are conscious thoughts to be sure, but they are in a 'grey area' that an untrained, or un-alert mind doesn't *notice* consciously. The subconscious is very powerful, and constantly influences our lives by giving us 'impulsive reactions' and a continuous stream of thoughts. These impulses and thoughts can include strong emotions (likes, dislikes, hate, fear, etc.), already formed decisions and judgments, ideas, and physical actions of all kinds. A 'temper tantrum' is just *one example* of those emotional surfacing impulses. But whether thoughts or emotions, *they pass unnoticed into conscious awareness,* and once there, we find ourselves thinking or feeling the thoughts and emotions that came from our programming, without even knowing it. It literally 'takes over' our thought processes, and feelings, and can be very destructive in our lives.

Such thoughts can come from subconscious programming *that has nothing to do with what a person would think ordinarily,* or if they consciously 'thought things out'. Yet people experience these thoughts and feelings just as if they were *their own consciously chosen* conscious thoughts and beliefs. And because people believe these thoughts to be their own, they are often defensive, and use 'mental

156

evasion tricks' (bullshit as it's commonly called) if anything threatens to really bring these subconscious thoughts and ideas into the light of conscious thought examination. For instance, when someone's words or actions are really just their subconscious programming playing itself out, and their words or actions have no logical explanation, what happens if you ask an analytical question about *why* they are saying or doing 'such and such'? What kind of response do you get?"

"I guess something like 'I don't know.'"

"You can do better than that Peniel. How many times have you asked someone something like, 'Why are you being that way?' and the response was something like, 'That's just the kind of person I am,' or, 'That's just how I feel!' or, 'That's just what I believe.' or, 'That's just how I was raised.' As far as they're concerned, that's the end of the discussion. They don't want to deal with the reasons *why* they feel, believe, or are that way. They have a sign up - 'Separate self at work - do not disturb'. Any further prodding as to 'why', may just get an angry illogical backlash. Such statements often accompany behavior which can't be logically or consciously explained, and are offered as rationalizations for some kind of negative behavior, or refusal to 'open the mind and think'."

"And many of us have been raised by parents who's answer to our questions as a child, was often 'just because'."

"That's right. Anyway, do you know why the apple falls to the ground?"

"Other than gravity?"

"Yes."

"Because it's ripe?"

"No. Just because." Zain was in unusual spirits, and if I didn't know better, I'd have thought *he* was indulging in some unusual spirits.

"Oh no," I thought to myself, "it's catching!"

He looked at me sternly, and then said, "Say goodnight Gracey."

"Goodnight Gracey. Father, can you be serious for a moment so I can finish trying to get this whole thought thing down?"

"In one bite?"

"Father, please, I still have hours of meditations to do."

"Yes. Very well. Is this better?" He made a serious face.

"Yes."

"OK. Now, where were we, Peniel. Ah, yes. Along with the subconsciously generated thoughts we've discussed, there are also subconsciously generated physical actions. And even beyond the auto-physical responses, there are the physical actions that result from what you think."

"What?"

"Just think about it."

Setting the Proper Thought Course

"So even if we consciously want to think and be one way, we might not be wanting that or doing that subconsciously?"

"Well what do you think?!"

"Father..."

"Again, a tremendous amount of our conscious thoughts and actions, in fact, *most* of what we take to be our conscious thoughts and actions, are actually from areas of the subconscious. That's why it's so important for us to understand, and properly use, the process in which thoughts create our physical experiences. Since

157

we are constantly being manipulated by our own programming, if it is not in order, it will create many problems in our physical lives. In fact, subconscious programming, things you aren't even aware of, can work at complete cross purposes to your conscious desires, thoughts and goals, negating any progress you attempt to make."

"So what is the first thing I should do to change what you seem to be saying is my slavery to my subconscious programming?"

"To break free of such slavery, you must first decide that you *really want* to change. You can't just have a mild intellectual attitude like, 'I think I should change'. If you really don't *want* to change desperately, and you're just pretending, or you just 'think' you *should* change, then you're just spinning your wheels and playing a game by trying to change."

"Are you saying I'm doing that?"

"No, this is not just about you. These are teachings for the whole world Peniel, for everyone. Quit thinking so paranoid about yourself and just listen or you'll miss half of it all.

Next, you need to gain access to your subconscious mind, and reprogram yourself with positive and constructive new programming. This puts *you* in control, letting *you* decide what *you* want to think and what *you* want to do in life, rather than allowing 'the program' to decide *for* you."

Programming

"So what do I reprogram myself with? Especially considering the paradox of truth."

"The ancient Atlantean teachings of the Children state that it is absolutely necessary to view and maintain our own programming from a Universal state of consciousness, in order to maintain Oneness with the Universal Spirit while living on Earth. This was conceived to prevent our consciousness from falling in ancient times, but it still applies."

"So either very deep contemplative meditation, or enlightenment?"

"Yes. Enlightenment is really the best way to have this occur - getting the new programming from God, from the hierarchy. In lieu of that, get recommendations from an Adept, a true teacher who is getting it for you from the hierarchy, and see if your Inner Voice tells you it's right."

"Even after we've cleaned up our old programming, then how do we keep from getting new negative programming?"

"Good question again! Besides analyzing and re-programming all our beliefs, we need to attempt to prevent new ones from getting programmed without our conscious choice. So at the very least, we must make our analysis and re-programming an ongoing process."

"What meditation will help me the most for that?"

"Any meditation technique that works well for you is good. As you know, the teachings present a variety of specific meditation techniques and consciousness tools that can help us to go further than our normal consciousness limitations, and ultimately, directly experience Oneness with Universal Consciousness. Those can all help you to reprogram yourself." [Author's note: Instructions for these ancient meditation and energy techniques are explained in detail in the second half of this book. Some, you may already know because of the other religions spawned by the Children. But these are the original forms. There are also different languages that can be used to speak to your mind. We discuss these in the chapter on visualization and affirmations.]

Zain continued."One day soon, you will be able to use the skills, knowledge and abilities you have developed over your lifetimes, to let the Universal Spirit work through you, in such a way as to recreate one of the best of the ancient Atlantean vibrational techniques to help others reprogram themselves. The technology to do this, and other things you will use to bring light to an ever darkening world, will soon be available again - first in the Universities in Russia and the United States. You will find what you need for the vibrational tools there. I have foreseen in my dreams, that something you will need for one of the things you will be doing in the future, will be found in an old German car, and an old American car." [another story not for this book].

"OK... You're joking again right?"

"No. When have you known me to be anything but serious? Nothing to say? You'll see. By that time in your future, you will have no need of the Atlantean vibrational reprogramming tools for yourself, for you will have already reprogrammed yourself. But for others, it will be a great blessing."

A New Ancient Tool

Everything Zain told me, came to pass. Even about parts I needed from antique cars.

We are fortunate to again have one of the most powerful reprogramming tools at our disposal. One who's roots are from Atlantis.

Atlantean technology was quite advanced in comparison to ours. Many methods were developed for healing, and consciousness raising, that involved a technology based on the understanding of Universal Laws and vibration. Color, sound, and olfactory aspects of vibration were used to access and affect the body and mind. Fortunately, one of the tools that used sound, was able to be made again with the advancement of crude electronic sciences. It utilizes very specific sound waveforms and frequencies, that weren't possible to make in modern times, until the invention of the electronics capable of specific frequency and waveform generation.

The resultant consciousness raising tool I'm speaking of uses sound waves to integrate the mind, and allow access to, and re-programming of, the sub-conscious mind. These "Atlantean Vibrational Sounds" have been recorded, and by the time this book is released, they should have been copied for those of you who wish to use them, on cassette tape and/or CD. Thus, while it is very powerful, it is cheap and easy to use (see the meditations section for more information, and the back of book for ordering instructions). Besides allowing reprogramming (again, you can read the specifics on how to modify it yourself to change your programming, in the second half of the book), the function of the vibrations are to integrate the three-fold aspects of being: conscious, subconscious, and Universal conscious - or physical, mental, spiritual realms.

Goal Setting in the Subconscious

Worthy of your consideration, too, is this: when a *goal* is programmed into the subconscious mind, its automatic thought generation and powers of influence, all work for you, constantly and perseveringly directing you towards fulfillment of that goal. (This will be discussed further in the chapter on Goals and Ideals.) Combining an ideal or goal with your reprogramming, is very powerful.

Another aspect of the subconscious mind that is of interest to us is in the area of control of the autonomic nervous system. More on this later.

Defense Against Unwanted Programming

Unfortunately, our lack of familiarity with the workings and programmability of our subconscious mind has not only created problems in our emotional and personal lives, but more importantly it has left us prey to many individuals and organizations that would have us see things their way. Most of us don't even know when this has happened, we have a full set of rational reasons for why we believe this or that. And the Sons of Belial and their servants, know how to, and do use such methods of influence. The fact is, a great deal of what you think, and of what you believe, has little to do with your independent and creative thought processes. I know that sounds incredible, and frightening; but it is quite true.

Even that which might be considered mundane or of little importance, such as advertising to sell various products, uses techniques of psychological, subconscious, and subliminal manipulation.

Listen to the Music

Before we go on, I would like to touch upon the power of music, especially as it relates to unwanted programming.

Music has been said to be the closest thing to a language of God. It has been used for rituals since the beginning of time. The Catholic church used music by Bach, to inspire churchgoers. I read that Ravel's Bolero, was actually based on an African shamanic ritual music piece, used to stimulate or open the chakras. Allegedly, in his first public performance of it, he was devastated because the audience failed to applaud at all. 15 minutes later, as he sat depressed in the alley behind the concert hall, he heard the audience suddenly giving rave applause. They were apparently so moved, stunned, entranced, or in reverie, that it took them quite awhile to "come out of it" and respond. The first half of Ravel's Daphnis Et Chloe suite #2, is like a musical representation of the Kundalini rising and the subsequent bliss - it is incredibly beautiful. Music definitely has the power to make you strongly feel all kinds of emotions, from the bliss of touching God, to depression and loneliness, to feelings of lust or violence. The right positive instrumental or lyrical music, can be a wonderful meditation, in and of itself. But there is far more here than meets the eye (or ear).

Even before I came to the monastery, back when I was studying alternative religions and spiritual paths as a young teenager, I was also studying psychology, and learning things about the subconscious mind, and subliminal programming. At some point back then, I also came to realize that there was a major "war" going on between the forces of dark and light, right there on the radio and on records. And no one I personally knew at the time, even noticed it. And I believed it had at least some effect on the listeners, via the subconscious.

I'm not talking about alleged "backward masking" subliminal programming. I can't say I've heard it all, but the "backward masking" clips that I *have* heard, which people claim are satanic messages, could just as easily be a drunk slurring words about their laundry. Whereas the kind of thing *I'm* talking about, was something quite different, very clear and overtly blatant.

I'm referring to lyrics that were (and still are) right there "up front", flaunting themselves in peoples' faces (or ears and brain in this case). I'd noticed that most people, didn't really listen, or really pay attention to, the lyrics of a song. And it seemed to me, that because of this, they *were* getting "subliminal" information, just by virtue of ignoring the lyrics.

Psychological studies *were* being done about this sort of thing back then. But as usual, there was no consensus among scientists, and some studies were secretly done for advertising purposes. Of the studies that were available, some supported, and some argued against, the theories that related to my conclusion. So what can you do? Make up your own mind. Which is what I did.

From my own observations and studies, I concluded that the *less* people paid attention to the lyrics, the more the lyrics bypassed their normal conscious mind filters and defense mechanisms, and went right into their sub-conscious minds. My studies in hypnosis had shown how things that "slipped right by" the conscious mind, and couldn't be consciously recalled, were being "stored and recorded" by the subconscious constantly - like a built-in human personal surveillance system. I heard of one incident where the police used hypnosis, to get the license number of a car used in a robbery. The information was stored in a man's subconscious, and was merely seen by him only with his peripheral vision, he never looked directly at the license plate. But the problem was, this personal surveillance system - the subconscious mind - wasn't just a recorder. It had influence with many aspects of our lives - emotions, beliefs, personality, etc.

Anyway, as I studied song lyrics, I found many interesting things. Some of course, were just mild self-oriented love songs or party songs, but some were clearly more negative - from self-destructive to out and out evil of all kinds. Yet these were never noticed or complained about by the public at the time. Other songs had positive, uplifting, and truly spiritual lyrics. In fact, it seemed to me that if higher, and lower consciousness beings of any kind, wanted to communicate with, and affect the minds of the masses, it was a perfect medium for it. Some lyrics were so spiritual, that one would almost have to conclude that the songwriter was enlightened, and had great spiritual knowledge. Then later in life, I got to meet many of the musicians whose lyrics were so strikingly saint-like and spiritual. I discovered that some were just average consciousness people, some maybe a little above average, some maybe below average, and some were egoed-out jerks. What they all had in common, was they were getting "stoned" on hallucinogenic drugs, and since playing music was like a meditation technique, they were getting into a trance-like state, and just "channeling" these incredible lyrics. On the dark side, the same thing was happening, but the musicians were definitely way below average consciousness.

Don't get me wrong, I'm not advocating any kind of censorship, other than "personal censorship". The lesson - make sure you know the lyrics of the music you are listening to, read the lyric sheets if you must. Then choose what you want to listen to, knowing that whatever it is, you are allowing some of it into your conscious and sub-conscious mind, and it may have effects.

Now on to other, deeper aspects of programming.

Realizing You Have Been Brainwashed

Sometimes I hear the word "brainwashing" thrown about, usually in reference to religious cults, political ploys or captives of some kind. Such talk always makes me stop and think to myself, "Brainwashing *from* what? To what?" It is usually just "brainwashing" from one framework of unconscious mental programming to another framework of unconscious mental programming. Please don't get me wrong, I'm in no way defending mind manipulation by religious cults , political movements, governments, car salesmen or any individual/organization who would use means that

161

breach the sanctity of mental freedom or free will. My point though, *is that we are all already "brainwashed"* (and still in the process), because our programming was not voluntarily or consciously chosen.

And where have all of us received our involuntary programming from? "Cults". Shocking, isn't it. But it's true. Now let's try saying that again, only not using an abbreviation.

And where have all of us received our involuntary programming from? Our cultures. Not as shocking right? Yet still just as true.

And the fact is, regardless of who or what involuntarily programmed you, it still comes down to this - you didn't choose your own programming or beliefs. And that comes with serious problems, unless you were involuntarily programmed by an enlightened being - and enlightened beings don't do that kind of thing to others.

Interestingly enough, the word "cult" is merely just an abbreviation of the word "culture". But it is deliberately used in a defamatory, inflammatory, and negative way. It is harder to "demonize" a group of people you call a culture, rather than a group of people you call a cult. So when we, others, or the media, are talking about a particular unique group, tribe, or religion, we call them a culture, if we want to present it in a positive light, or a cult, if we want to present it in a negative light, and conjure up fear and loathing. It's all depending on how we feel about them, or want someone else to feel about them.

Involuntary programming, such as that which we receive from our culture and its "robots" (our culturally programmed peers), involves attempting to trample our free will choices - just as much as involuntary re-programming. Cultural and peer programming doesn't trample our *free will* nearly as much as true, classic, military type "brainwashing", but still, people have no idea what a *substantial and nearly total* influence it has on their lives. No one realizes *how few* free will choices they make (and have made) for actually choosing how they live their own lives.

Before I go any further, please understand, this whole area of discussion involves complex paradoxes. I'm about to focus on and discuss only one aspect of the paradox - how and where you were raised, and how strongly the involuntary programming from that affects your life. But one should keep in mind that there is something to genetics (breeding), and behind it all, karma [note: who your soul is so to speak. What you need to experience in life and why. And why you were born with certain genetics, in a certain culture and raised a certain way]. I have seen many newborn babies, in which I can immediately see aspects of "who they are", and what kind of personality they will have. That is their "spirit", their "soul", for the most part. So with all that in mind, let's focus on cultural programming (which remember, is only half of the whole truth).

Programming from our culture, family, and peers, strongly affects our lives. This is more of an influence during a person's youth, and lessens to a degree at about age 7, then more at about age 14, and then quite substantially when their "soul" really "kicks in" fully at around 21, and a person regains their full past level of consciousness. At that point, they can really start making more free will changes in their lives - and either expand their awareness/consciousness, or degenerate. For instance, why is a child raised by a Buddhist family, in a Buddhist culture, likely to be a Buddhist when he grows up? Similarly, why is a Lutheran child, or Muslim child, or Jewish child, also raised in the beliefs of their own family and culture, very likely to grow up having the same beliefs? Why is the abused child of an abused mother and a wife/child-beating father likely to grow up and live the same way? Programming plays an essential role. People are all programmed by their families, friends, schools, teachers, news media, books, magazines - you name it. Just think, if 98% of everything you think, believe, and do, is from your subconscious mind, and it has been programmed by someone else, what are the primary influences that control your destiny and life? It's staggering to think about isn't it? As I write this, there is a new television sitcom that just premiered, that involves the clash of cultures (cults) between a husband, who was raised as a meat-eating, rich, conservative, lawyer for the federal government. His wife is a vegetarian who was raised as a radical liberal hippie who teaches yoga and protests the government. It makes for great comedy, but it also makes a point. If those children's parents had been reversed, and their upbringing and programming thus been reversed, their roles would be exactly the opposite of what they are. The wife would be the conservative government lawyer, and the husband would be the groovy hippie dude. (Again, excluding the concept that they are already what they are "soul-wise", and were just "karmically" born into those respective family situations to enable them to return to being what they have already made themselves into, internally.)

Can you say that you truly filtered, analyzed, and controlled the programming you received your whole life, that developed your beliefs and behavior patterns? The brain of a newborn child has little programming yet, there's not much there. So you can't literally call it "brainwashing" when it begins to get programmed. But programming is programming, whether it is for the first time, or it is "re" programming ("brainwashing") of old data.

Everyone has been programmed. Everyone has been brainwashed. You have been programmed and brainwashed. You may not know it, or want to accept it, but you have been. And you are under the control of that programming right now. And most everything about your life has to do with it. You are even reacting to what you are reading in this book, right at this moment, partly based on your programming.

Even when programming is altered of a person's own choice, the average person doesn't have a clue to analyzing, or programming their own mind, so they often accept programming from other people. Sometimes the programming they accept is from another unconsciously programmed person who is just passing along their programming to you. "I saw so and so today and they said..." and you believe it and just altered your programming to include it. Or, "I read in the paper that..." And you accept it as fact, and alter your programming. But worse, you are also often programmed by people who really *do understand* programming, and use it to manipulate you. So basically, "brainwashing" in the sense of "re-programming" is the common everyday occurrence of voluntarily allowing someone else to alter our programming.

When a person changes their beliefs or programming because of input from an external source, such as with "brainwashing," they are only exchanging one unconscious "program", for another unconscious "program." In other words, they're unconsciously exchanging one piece of garbage they didn't choose to have, and don't know that they didn't choose to have, for another piece of garbage they didn't choose to have, and don't know that they didn't choose to have. This happens to us all the time. And the trouble is, this unconscious programming has *immense power and control* over our life and destiny. Take news stories for instance. If they showed some pictures of bombs going off, and said it was such and such terrorist group, and you accept it without direct experience, your programming has been altered - in a serious way, possibly even creating feelings of anger and hate in you, and clouding fair judgement. Wars are started and prolonged this way. Products are sold this way. Votes are manipulated this way. Lives are controlled this way. In these modern times, many of your beliefs are formed through media exposure. You could totally believe tomorrow that we are about to be nuked by the Russians, be ready to sacrifice your life, and your child's life, in order to go to war - and it could be totally false information - your programming was simply altered a bit, all based on news "stories" that you accepted in your programming. Orson Wells' radio broadcast of "War of the Worlds" is a good example of this. It was a dramatic radio sci-fi show - about Martians invading Earth of all things. But it was done in the fashion of news coverage. People panicked all over the country. Not one person really saw a Martian ship, troops, fighting, nothing. I think people died of heart attacks, and other things related to the panic. People got out their guns and were heading for the front lines. People believed this radio broadcast on a mass scale, even though it was a totally fictitious, and far-fetched sci-fi story.

You could be manipulated to believe that Muslims are good, or Muslims are evil and cruel - without ever knowing a Muslim, or even hearing about experiences with them from a clearly experienced, trusted friend. The same with Jews, or Catholics, or "such and such" cultists, or whatever. You could *feel* totally supportive of incarcerating, or even killing a man, that you have been told committed a murder, even if it were totally false, and all based on stories. It happens all the time. You can send money to feed starving children, not know that the money is merely lining the pockets of a fat executive, and feel really good about yourself. If you don't take care, and take full responsibility for programming yourself, somebody else will (and ALWAYS does). And your beliefs and the world you mentally live in could be nothing but fabrication for purposes of controlling you. On the other hand, it is difficult to "brainwash" or program an individual who is well-versed in their own mental processes (at least with the techniques and processes that are commonly called brainwashing. However, hardcore brainwashing - very sophisticated methods, various psychological techniques, physical torture, sleep deprivation, drugs, and electronic or surgical brain manipulation can change nearly anyone - the book "1984" gives a good example of such intense manipulation, and brainwashing). But in order to attain true independence of mind and freewill, a person must consciously, deliberately, analyze their beliefs, and choose their own programming.

As in the cases we've just sited, brainwashing can be a term that is used to mean someone has been truly involuntarily programmed against their will. But brainwashing is often used as a nasty word for programming changes we disagree with. For instance, what actually happens when an adult changes religions, political parties, or any other belief? Let's say the person changed religions. If you think the change was fully voluntary, and you don't mind his new choice, you might say "He converted". But if you don't like the person's new religion or the people associated with it or whatever, you might say he has been "brainwashed" - regardless of whether the person chose to make those changes or not. Jesus was considered a cultist in his time, and a manipulator, and his followers were considered cultists. Early Christians were considered a cult for a very long time. Early protestant churches began as cults with a cult leader. Mormons also suffered the same "label" and subsequent persecution. European "religious cults" fled to the United States to avoid persecution, and many are now just considered major religions. Often times, the only difference between a "cult" and a religion, is how big it is, and how long it has managed to survive the attacks of society when it was considered a "cult". It is sadly all too easy for people to forget, and lack understanding and tolerance of the religions of others. Even some of the major religions still attack other major religions because of their beliefs.

Unfortunately, the word "brainwashing" is sometimes used as a "negative slur", or "rationalization", regarding the belief or attitude changes a person has voluntarily made. This often occurs when one person *dislikes* the *voluntary* programming another person has chosen for themselves. When someone thusly claims another person has been brainwashed, such as in the case of someone calling a religion a cult, they can then rationalize and justify even kidnapping, and *truly* brainwashing the person - to fit their own way of thinking. It is most often used in the case of people who have changed religions, especially to an unconventional or highly disliked religion. Relatives of that person, or their previous religion, may claim they have been "brainwashed", by the new religion. For instance, my mother proclaimed I was brainwashed when I returned from Tibet. Obviously, my changes were so radical, she had a great deal of support for this claim from all her friends, relatives, and anyone else who would listen to her story. And she tried to have me "deprogramed" - brainwashed, back to her way of thinking. But it had no effect on me, because only *I have been* in charge of my programming since I became an Adept. There was nothing to "deprogram" me from. And her real motives, were not because she thought I was actually brainwashed. She was just using brainwashing as a rationalization to explain my so-called "strange" choices in life. The real reason she did it, involved my rejection of the family religion, not believing, thinking, and behaving as she did (and she thought I should), failure to live what she considered a normal life (which would have been becoming a successful doctor or lawyer), and in an odd way, personal rejection and jealousy.

Another common situation in which you hear the cry of "brainwashing" is in child custody cases, where a child favors one parent, and turns against the other - the rejected parent will most often blame the other parent for "brainwashing" the child, and turning them against them. Again, in both of these instances, it could be true, or just a "slur". But where the term brainwashing originally came from, and what it really means, is something altogether different.

The term really came from hideous methods of using force to alter programming under extreme duress, totally involuntarily. Various "modern" forced brainwashing methods were invented during WWII by spies and military types, to control people's minds. Oddly enough, such WWII methods are employed by so-called "cult deprogrammers", but I have never heard of a cult using such horrible methods to bend, or break, someone's mind to their way of thinking. A "cult" may employ strong, or clever influencing and manipulation methods, but any I have ever heard of, are still really ultimately allowing free choice. If they did, they would be jailed, like many deprogrammers have been. A "deprogrammer" however, generally takes severe true forced brainwashing approaches, commonly hiring or enlisting people to kidnap a person, and/or hold them prisoner by force, and in one way or another, cause a total emotional/mental breakdown, so that they can infuse the programming they, or typically the parents that hired them, want them to have. Even the term "deprogrammer" is a deception. They are "re-programmers" - in the tradition of the forced, emotionally torturous, classic brainwashers. They employ various brainwashing methods, all while the person is being held virtual, or literal, prisoner by either family, friends, accomplices, or hired "black belt" thugs. It may be relatively mild. But that is rare. Sometimes it involves surrounding the victim with a dozen or more people who constantly scream at them, attacking their emotional and mental weaknesses, their beliefs, and when total "nervous breakdown" finally occurs, they fill the victim's mind with "what is right and true" to believe (whatever the brainwasher wants them to believe). This may go on for hours or days, as the "deprogrammers" take turns and rest, while the helpless prisoner is denied sleep, or their own free thoughts. Sometimes they tie a person to a chair naked, refuse them sleep, water or food. I have never heard anyone even claim such radical things took place in religious "cults". Like I said, such behavior would result in arrest and prison. There have been the odd suicide pacts, but again, upon analysis, people voluntarily chose to do it (with the possible exception of Jones), so no matter how weird, if they choose it without *true* brainwashing, they at least had *some* choice. But "deprogrammers" leave absolutely **no choice**. Manipulation of the psyche, whether it be by cult, media, or car salespeople, is wrong - make no mistake. And the results of such manipulation can be devastatingly different - like that between ending up with a car you never intended to buy, or supporting a war that doesn't have any true foundation, or committing suicide. But that is my whole point. That is what parts of the ancient teachings, and parts of this book are for - to teach you to take control of your own programming, and prevent others from manipulating your mind. But deprogrammers are among the worst - they usually "cross the line", and justify their going beyond mere manipulation of your mind. And while some "deprogrammers" have fortunately been arrested and imprisoned, too many are allowed to do their dirty work, and get away with it, because they are attacking generally unpopular religions. Let someone try "deprogramming" a Catholic because they have their "weird" ways, like believing they are eating the flesh and blood of Jesus during communion - or "deprogramming" a Pentecostal for speaking in tongues, or a Jew for wailing at the wall, and refusing to eat pork, etc., etc., and see how far the deprogrammer gets before being incarcerated. Again, it's the size of the religion that determines whether or not the term "cult" is applied, and all the prejudice and mistreatment that go with it.

And if you want to talk about something ending in tragedy, deprogrammers leave a trail of devastated lives. I have studied this in college, and I have personally known 6 people who were "deprogramed" (other than 2 failed attempts on me). One of these was a novice student of mine. The others were from various small Christian churches ("cults" if you choose to call them that) of one kind or another. All were previously happy, well-adjusted people. 1 was beaten to death by his "deprogrammer's" black belt jailers, 2 ended up committing suicide within a few months of being "fixed" by the deprogrammers, 1 ended up a permanent resident of a mental ward, 1 became a "deprogrammer" himself, and another did what they were reprogrammed to do - "shift directions" in life. In that last case, the person "sort of" adjusted to living a life they never really wanted in the first place. A life that didn't allow them to fulfill their spiritual potential, as much as their original programming would have, and their true, free-will choices would have. It also left bad scars and emotional/brain damage, including mental blocks, memory loss, and strange physical illnesses. You could say this was karmic too. But most people's programming has something to do with their "karma" - is a reflection of and part of their karma. And while a "de-programming" or brainwashing can *also* be karmic, it could also be an attack from the dark forces that comes "out of the blue", leaving you virtually unable to even deal with your karma, and fulfill your original destiny.

Whether a programming change is fully voluntary, or somehow manipulated (which most every religion, political party or salesman will attempt), or is actually forced, *the same result occurs* - programming is altered. So that's the bottom line, and that's what really needs to be focused on.

Because of all the things mentioned throughout this entire chapter, the ancient Atlantean teachings of the Children, cover all aspects of "programming". This includes teaching how to free yourself from unwanted programming, to avoid brainwashing, and how to be in control of, and consciously reprogram your own mind.

In order to change your susceptibility to manipulation and strengthen your independence of thought, you must first realize the facts and implications involved. Then, using a teacher, meditation, self-hypnosis, various vibrational techniques, biofeedback, or other means of accessing modified states, you can set about re-evaluating the entire contents of your mind, the source of most feelings and thoughts. You may also want to use the Atlantean vibrational sounds tape. Then, you'll finally be safe from brainwashing by even the dreaded - car salesman.

A Final Thought

Important fact: NO MATTER HOW GOOD OF A MEANS YOU USE TO SELF-PROGRAM YOUR SUBCONSCIOUS MIND, IT WILL NOT ACCEPT THE PROGRAMMING UNLESS YOU REALLY *WANT* TO CHANGE.

So take control of your life on both conscious and subconscious levels. Don't believe anything you haven't really experienced yourself, or a truly trusted and objective person you know has experienced. Don't let anyone program you anymore, but yourself. You decide your beliefs - not press releases, books, ads, media owners and controllers, leaders, religions, department store owners, car salesmen, gas station attendants, your friends, your relatives, your mates, this book, a teacher, - or anyone - but *you. And remember, kindness and Unselfish Love for everything and everyone, are the only really important things. If something doesn't include that - watch out!*

I'd like to add one final statement regarding cultures. One of the best "eye opening" experiences anyone can have that shows them just how much we are all programmed, is to experience different cultures. Not just vacations here and there, but really experiencing as many different cultures in the world as possible. The same basic human being, can have such radically different beliefs, and different ways of living, that a person who hasn't experienced it couldn't really believe it. You can get it intellectually of course, and watch travel shows, but you don't really "get it" until you've done it. Most of you reading this would be shocked to see a baby buried alive because it was born a female. But that's just scratching the surface. And your culture is just as appalling and shocking to me. When will you all wake up, and take control of your programming, and reprogram yourself in the light of truth, kindness, and Universal Consciousness? When will you stop killing those who bring you new ideas? Maybe soon, because the Universe, this planet, is going to change things here radically because of what humans have done, and it's coming, ready or not.

Chapter Twelve

The Path(s)

One morning, I awoke and began writing down my dreams in my log as usual. But my dreams lingered. I was still in that state "in between" sleep and awake. I had dreamt about, and was remembering, all the various cultures and people I had witnessed on my way to the monastery. They were all so different. And everyone was so "locked into" the habit patterns and beliefs of their particular life, within their particular cult-ure - some perhaps were learning, changing and growing, others weren't going anywhere but in circles.

As I climbed out of my womb, I noticed a note stuck under my mat. It was a reading list from Zain.

Created We The Path
Upon Our Separation
From the Infinite One
The Way Out is the Way Back.

One Way Back.
Walk Must we in Our Own Excrement.
Created We All Obstacles.
All Must Be Met
As we follow the Road Home.

The Path Is.

To Return To The One
Is Death to The Separate Self.
A Great Fight it Will Wage
Great Pain it Will Inflict.

Only Those Who Have Learned
The Greater Pain
Lies in Separation from The One
Will Choose the Spiritual Path

Many Paths There Are
All Spiritual Paths
Lead to The One.
As Closer You Return,

Recognize You Will
Your True Self
Your True Family
Recognize You Will
The Face of a Stranger

Judge Not the Path of Another.
Learn to Understand
That You May Not Understand
The Path of Another.

Judge the Path of Another,
Only to Judge and Determine
Your Own Path.

Never Condemn Another.
Condemn Only Actions.

❖

The Path Takes Us Through
Walls of Fire Burning Us Away
Sharp Teeth Ripping Away Our Flesh
Why then, Am I not Harmed?

❖

The Path is Beset With Traps
The WindFlowers Draw Us
With Their Sweet Perfume
Thorns Prick at Our Feet
Mud Drags us Down
Above and Below
Rocks Loosen and Fall.
Walk In the Footsteps of Those
Who have Found the Way Before You

❖

The Ease or Difficulty One Experiences
While Walking the Path to Oneness
Is directly determined by the degree
of Their Humility and Unselfish Love

❖

Pain and Pleasure
Are Swings in the Arc of a Pendulum.

To the degree the Pendulum Swings into Pleasure
It will Swing into the same degree of Pain

Many Paths Present themselves
That Lead to Pleasure.
With Free Will, we Choose

Choose not Pleasure, and you will Create not Pain.
Chase not Pleasure, and Pain will Chase you not.

Accept the Little Pleasures that Come to You.
Endure the Pain that may Come to You
With Long-Suffering Patience.

❖

Hear Me O Man.
Turn From the Darkness of Night.
Turn towards the Love of Light.
Know that Your Mind
Leads Your Direction
Turn From the Thoughts
That Lead you Astray
Turn to the Thoughts
of Giving and Light
They Lead you to Oneness
Not Darkness of Night.

Find Not The Great Path
In Power & Glory.
Find it You Will in The Dust at Your Feet.
With Head Bowed In Regret and Humility,
Beg You Must With All Heart
Ask Then The Universal One To Guide You,
With Heart that is Ready to Serve All it Shows.
Pray that Your Will Be that of The One.
Pray The One
Send To You One who Is One,
To Show You The Light
And Illuminate Your Soul.

❖

Seek God First
And All Else Will Come To You.

❖

As You Walk Your Path

I left the library, and was walking down the path to the hot pool. As I looked down at my feet on the path, it struck me. I was walking on my *path*. My spiritual path. I had finally found it, and was really walking on it. I had a moment of elation, realization, and then a strikingly powerful Kundalini rush of energy (a spiritual evolutionary force that actually changes aspects of your physical/spiritual body as you evolve - it's explained more later in the book for those of you who aren't familiar with it).

When I recovered, I decided I should go down to the hot pool to get a sweat, since such a Kundalini experience often triggered physical "eliminations" of toxins, as it purified your body. The hot pool would help me release at least some of them in a more pleasant and easier manner. Besides, I wanted to contemplate all that I had read, more. And also, I wanted to contemplate and examine my dreams and thoughts of the morning. Already in the pool, I found, not to my surprise, none other than my personal true teacher, Zain.

"Ah, you have been 'kissed by God' again, yes?" he said, referring to the Kundalini experience.

"More like raped and beaten up. No, I'm sorry, I shouldn't joke about it that way, it is a wonderful blessing and heavenly experience, even though painful at times. Yes, I have been kissed."

"Very good, very good."

I slipped into the pool, which seemed hotter than usual to my sensitized body.

"Father, why are there so many different cultures and ways of living? And why are some people really seeking God, and others just pretending, and others openly disinterested?"

"Way too much of a question for a simple answer. And I was just dealing with my own contemplations this morning as I enjoyed the properties of the water."

"I'm sorry to disturb you."

"No problem son, I was about to get out anyway. You have already learned many of the reasons behind the separations. So I think what you really question in your mind, is mainly about people's 'paths' and varying cultures, is it not?"

"Yes, in part at least."

"Anywhere we are, anywhere our journey through life takes us, is 'our path'. In that sense, *everyone* is on their path. But not everyone is on what we might call a 'spiritual path'. A spiritual path is when the direction of our path is one that can finally lead us in the direction of Spirit, rather than materiality, lead us to Unselfish Love, rather than selfishness, lead us to Universal Consciousness, rather than separate consciousness."

Our Path Often Takes us to "The School of Hard Knocks"

"So only when people are on their spiritual path, are they learning?"

"They are always being given the *opportunity* to learn, regardless of the type of path. Karma is constantly being created, and life keeps trying to teach us something by providing us with our own self-created lessons - that explode in our faces. Getting taught in that way, has been called 'the school of hard knocks'. But while everyone suffers the slings and arrows of life experiences, most people ignore these lessons which are being constantly presented to us. This is unfortunate when it is ignored, because suffering can cause us to be introspective, and really take a hard look, a deep look, at the 'whys' of our life experiences.

After we've had enough suffering to open our eyes, we realize we need to change. Therein lies the value of the pain. As you've already learned, transcending our separate self, and renouncing selfishness is painful too - it's like 'crucifying' yourself. Most people won't choose the spiritual path until they realize that the pain caused as a result of living selfishly, outweighs the pain of the spiritual path. But as I said, from time to time, people get hit with an unpleasant life experience, suffer, and get introspective. That's when they can more easily realize that it is worth it to choose the spiritual path."

"Is that the *only* way someone finally chooses a spiritual path?"

"No. It wasn't that way with you really. Your consciousness and destiny chose it for you. And there are also other factors that can influence people to take the spiritual path.

During the introspective times brought by suffering, people are more aware of that constant painful gnawing that exists from the lack of inner peace. It reminds them, at least internally or subconsciously, about the great fact, that the suffering caused by remaining separate and selfish, **will never end** unless you return to Oneness with the Universal Spirit. And that they can never really be happy as a selfish separate self. Never. You may have temporary 'high points and get offs', but that's it. On the other hand, the pain of 'crucifying' the selfish separate self **is just temporary.** And when you're done, you have inner peace, and that's the only true happiness, and the only happiness that never leaves you. When people suffer enough self-pain, they will eventually realize this. When one finally realizes this, and thus decides to take the "return trip", is when the real *spiritual* journey begins. This is the point when we each begin our real 'spiritual path'."

His words reminded me of all the different religions and spiritual paths I'd tried and studied before finding the one I was on now.

"Exactly what do you mean their 'real' spiritual path? Some are false? And why are there so many different spiritual paths, and cultures?"

In Search of the Archetype

"Oh... again with the multiple questions, and so early in the morning."

He was sounding like a Rabbi, and he wasn't even Jewish - well I guess he was sort of Jewish in the broadest ancient sense, but also all the other religions rolled into one.

"Let me start with your last question first. There are as many 'specific paths' back to the Source of our being, as there are individuals. It can be no other way. Each entity is where they are, and basically what they are, because of the separate paths and experiences they have had (and created) in arriving at that point in time and space. Likewise, each entity has their own particular way to return, or 'backtrack', from that point. Let's use an allegory. Let's say there is this 'mountain of life'. On all sides of this great mountain, are paths, millions of paths. These paths have been created from people starting at the top, which is the point of Oneness and of Universal Spirit. And all these paths are winding their way down the mountain, which is separateness and materiality, in various ways. On each of these paths, is a person. These people are at all kinds of different places on their path.

Some are down at the base of the mountain, and some are near the top. Some don't care to climb the mountain, and some want to because they have realized they must get to the top to find Oneness and peace. To get to the top they each have a different route - the path they made themselves from the top. It doesn't really matter where each person's path is, they all still end up back at the top. As we get closer to the top, some paths converge. We converge with soulmates, and with soulgroups."

"I understand 'soulmates', but what are Soulgroups?"

"Soul-groups are other beings who are like our 'spiritual family', those who were close to us in our previous state of existence, or have grown closer to us for one reason or another. As we go higher, we need to grow closer with our soulgroups, but particularly with our soulmates. Because at some point right near the top, we need to merge, and function again as One being with male and female elements (if present), rather than as separated and opposing males and females.

Anyway, as we get very close to the top, we find that we, and the others who are very close to the top, are getting more alike. That's because there are 'archetypes' - 'patterns' for certain beings that are the same at the higher consciousness levels. After all, the closer we get to becoming One, the more One we become, thus, the more similar we become. While you probably have not seen this yet, you will. And you may have already experienced something similar - have you ever noticed strangely strong similarities, physical or otherwise, between certain unrelated people?"

"Yes, I have. I've also read about archetypes, and seen certain examples of it."

Little did I know at the time how much I would see. Most people don't get to actually experience this so directly and shockingly, but I have, because of my path, and my spiritual duties. During my first 3 years of traveling after leaving the monastery, I was in part, working on bringing the people that were "high on the allegorical mountain", yet still unaware of each other, closer together. The time was drawing near when more understanding of different beliefs, practices and paths was becoming necessary. I witnessed entire spiritual communities, who's members were identical, or near identical, "doubles". As if they all had multiple twins or clones of other people from other paths at a similar level of consciousness. These "physical clones", all had levels of consciousness that were virtually the same, yet they had different backgrounds, different types of spiritual development, and somewhat different beliefs. And this was no strange scientific experiment, it was simply a manifestation of our spiritual manifestation on Earth. I even met a couple of doubles of Zain, but one had black hair rather than silver.

Judge for Yourself (only)

"Now for your second to the last question, about false paths. Some people who have concluded that their path is the right way, think that since their path is the right way for them, it must mean that it is the ONLY right path, and that other paths are *not* the right way. They consider all other paths 'false' or 'a lost way'. But this may not be true. Let's use the 'mountain' allegory again. Some people think that others must not be on a path at all, simply because *they* don't *see* the others on *their* path, and thus going up the mountain. They don't realize that others are climbing their own paths on different parts of the mountain. So they make false judgements - because they don't *realize* that they *can't* see the other people, simply because they cannot see them from their *point of view*. And they don't realize that just because they can't see the other people, it doesn't mean they aren't climbing the mountain on their own paths.

Stepping out of our mountain allegory for a moment, and trying to explain it in another way - it's like this: many people don't accept the paths of others, because they can't understand it from *their point of view*. They don't realize that the other person's path, may lead back to God also. Getting back to the mountain allegory again, the closer that people get to the top (which means the more expansive they get in consciousness), the greater their point of view. The top of the mountain has been becoming smaller, narrower, closer together, and thus it is easier to see more sides of the mountain at the same time - and see that others' paths are also converging on the top. We too often see individuals of one particular path taking the attitude that their way is *the* way, and all others are not on *the* path. This reflects their lower position on the mountain - their degree of lack of consciousness."

"So there isn't just one true spiritual path."

"Yes and no. How can I make it clearer? No *particular* path is *the* path for everyone at a given place and time in their consciousness, even though it may be *the* path for the particular individual who's on it. However, there comes a time, when all must transcend their separations, their separate selves, to get to the top of the mountain where All are One; those are the final steps of any true spiritual path - this is what we will call the path; the path of Unselfish Love. To get to the top, all must consciously climb the mountain step by step, no matter where you are starting from or where your 'particular' path takes you."

"So we shouldn't judge others at all."

"With certain necessary exceptions. We really shouldn't judge others, *unless* it is for the purpose of making choices or navigating on our own path, in which case we *must* judge. For instance, you may have to judge whether or not someone you are thinking of 'hanging out with', is bad or not, because of the influence it will or may have on you. Otherwise, how are you to decide your own path? Or you may judge in order to learn from the mistakes of others, instead of making them yourself. In a voting political society, people must judge the character of who they want to vote for in order to make the best choice for running a country. They may have to come to the conclusion that 'so and so' is a bad person, and shouldn't be running things - that is judging someone isn't it?"

"Yes."

"And is that wrong?"

"No. Of course not."

"There are many such judgements you must make in life. But most people don't just judge, they condemn. And there is a big difference between judging, and condemning. Condemning is judging without Unselfish Love. It is a judgment tinged with resentment, hostility, hatred or anger, and it is damaging to both the person who is condemning, and the person who is being condemned. Judging alone is sufficient to allow you to take positive action. You don't need to be *condemning* of someone because they are doing something 'bad'. And some things may not be bad, but just things that are not right for you - you have to discriminate that too. But there will be times when you need to 'judge' that something is 'bad' so that you do not do the same. Many things are necessary on the many paths people must tread to learn their lessons or pay back their karma, and it is not for us to condemn. It is also not for us to interfere, unless it hurts us or others."

"So when you decide you like someone, or dislike someone, are you judging them or condemning them?"

"It can be either. Most people place those they meet or know, into one of those two categories. People they 'like' and people they 'don't like'. This is pretty much the same as dividing people up into categories of 'good' and 'bad'. But for those situations in which you do not need to discern your own path by judging someone, and deciding the ramifications of associating with them, there is another way they should be looked at. Rather than focusing on a person's so-called 'good' qualities or 'bad' qualities, liking or disliking them, one should see the 'Whole' being [Author's note: like with the car we described in an earlier chapter, that had one good side and one damaged.]. In order to serve the Universal Spirit, and help our kin, one should not disregard the other aspects of a person's nature, and focus *just* on the good or bad.

There is something else to consider also, that may mislead you in judging a person's character if you are not seeing from a higher perspective. If you are seeing people with limited perception, you may see someone during a time and day in which they are strongly exhibiting their good nature or bad nature. Someone else may have seen that same person during a time and day in which they were strongly exhibiting the opposite of the nature you perceived. Thus people often can *seem* like a good or bad person, just depending on your point of view (or time of view). Again, seeing both sides is the only way of truly knowing the real person. And we should have unlimited love for everyone without exception, just as the Sun shines on all without exception, all the time, in all directions.

Now if you are a true teacher, dealing with a student who has asked for your criticism though, you have a job to do, and you must look for, and point out faults in the students character at all times, and not allow for 'moods'. But that is your duty in such a situation - that is what they have asked you to do for them so they can improve, and grow towards the light, in our everlasting pursuit of perfection. But you should also point out their potential."

"So the path can be painful and humiliating for the student?"

"What do you think?"

I smiled. "Obviously. What a stupid thing to say."

"You have yet to face your greatest trials."

I'd heard that before. It scared the "Yak dung" out of me.

"I'm not afraid. Bring them on."

"Sure." He looked at me with that look again.

Climbing to Our Crucifixion

As was said earlier, the path that lies before a person who is truly committed to transcending their separate self, and returning to Universal Consciousness, can be painful at times. After all, your separate self has surrounded your life with illusions and programming that supports separateness, and selfishness. It has created a "false person" of its own, that has the illusion of having its own life - an actual illusion that it is alive and living. To be One with the Universal Spirit again involves "killing" this false being, and all of its selfish separate illusions and programming. This hurts! IT will fight it! IT's fighting for its very survival! And you have been thoroughly tricked into believing IT is you! So it's like killing yourself! NOT a simple task, nor a painless one.

It is a path of "cross bearing", and purification "by fire". A now Islamic poet once put it this way: "Like dry wood takes to fire, the truth will come to you". How true. If you endure this purification by fire with patience, understanding, and humility, you will come to realize your essential nature/Inner Being/soul/Oneness with the Universal Spirit. Why? Because the soul is *indestructible,* and when all else of you is purged and burned away from the suffering you experience, there will be the soul, shining like the Sun emerging from the clouds.

Making Crucifixion Fun (at least a bit easier)

It is said that The Path is covered with rose bushes. The flowers draw us and offer us pleasure, but attachment to pleasure is a danger here. Try to take the rose, and the thorns prick us and cause us to suffer. Have you heard this?: "Love is a rose, but you better not pick it; only grows when it's on the vine. Hand full of thorns and you know you've missed it. Lose your love, when you say the word 'mine'." So true.

Here's the good news: along this path of rose bushes, one can find footprints that were made by the great ones who have gone before us. If we make sure that we walk only in their footsteps, we will avoid many of the pitfalls, the detours and traps, and the painful mistakes that we will come upon along the way.

Humility and Unselfish Love Lighten the Burden

Traveling your path is made easier by humility and Unselfish Love. The greater your degree of humility, the easier, and the shorter, your path back will be. Spiritual growth can be experienced as agonizing torture that you must endure, or as an enlightening learning experience that you desire and relish. It all depends on you and your attitude. One of my novice students, one who learned the fastest of all thus far, learned so fast, just because of humility. She was a total stranger, living with a man I was discussing life with. We were talking about what he was capable of doing for the world if he followed his spiritual path. She just listened. As I was leaving, and preparing to put on my sandals, she bent over and put them on for me. A simple act, but a gesture of the humility that indicated her true greatness. It heralded the potential that was within this shining novice. It reminded me of a text I'd read relating to humility, during grand master Thoth's last lifetime (the Essene lifetime as Jesus). It was regarding an argument between the students of Jesus. In the area and time, it was the custom to wash one's feet when entering a house, to get the dirt off and keep the floors clean. It was a tradition, and humble honor, for the master of the house to wash your feet for you. But Jesus' students, more concerned with their egos, their selfish separate selves, and their *status* amongst his other students, refused to wash each others' feet. So in deep sadness over their lack of humility and selfishness, Jesus did it, showing that true spirituality, true greatness, was clothed in humility. His actions exemplified humility, even more than his words - "He who would be the greatest would be the servant to all", and, "He who would be the first, will be the last".

Seeking Pleasure Brings its Mate

"Father," I asked, "I'm worried, upset, and I guess afraid. What should I do? Is there anything that can make it easier? Anything that I should be doing that I'm not? Should I deny my self urges and live more of the life of an ascetic? Would that help?"

"I told you humility is the biggest key. As far as being an ascetic, contrary to how you may feel at times, ours is a gentle, moderate, and balanced path. And this is for a good reason. From the early days of Atlantis, we have learned that extremes, such as asceticism, can have extreme repercussions, and should only be used when such severity is really called for. This situation of yours is not as such."

"Then what should I do?"

"First, learn this well, then apply it - pain and pleasure are one of those dichotomies of the Earth plane. They are thus seemingly opposite, yet they are just the extreme polarities of the same thing - sensation. The range of sensation is traversed by a pendulum that swings within our emotions. If the pendulum swings into pleasure, it will swing back into pain. And the greater the depth of the swing into pleasure, the greater the depth of the return swing into pain. For every self-gratification there is an equal degree of suffering. This is an aspect of Universal law. It is best to not seek pleasure. That doesn't mean avoid it - just accept it when it comes, but don't pursue it. It keeps the pendulum much more centered. This is one of the ways to make things a little easier."

In the End, the Love you Take,
is Equal to the Love you Make

Wow, the headlines the editor chose for this chapter could be a great "oldies" music infomercial. Back to our discussion.

"So I create problems every time I seek to satisfy any of my selfish desires, which I keep doing all the time. So I keep making more trouble and pain for myself."

"Of course. But the good news is you are realizing that. When you actually realize that Unselfish Love is the answer to every problem, you can stop creating more suffering and problems, but as it is with cause and effect (karma), you still have to deal with all that you have already created. There's no way to avoid or sidestep it; actually, you *can* delay it, you have free will after all, and those of the dark side use delay and avoidance methods all the time. But if you do, you *are* only delaying, fooling yourself, making even bigger problems by piling up more karma; like sweeping dirt under a carpet and pretending it's gone. Someday you'll have to clean it up, and the more you've piled up, the more you'll have to clean, eventually. By the way, have you looked under your mat lately? I have."

I remembered the note he left me under my mat. And that actually I had been sweeping dirt and dust under it.

"Again, the 'bottom line' is that the path back to Oneness with the Universal Spirit, and the attainment of Universal Consciousness is that of the crucifixion of the selfish separate self/selfish desire - painful yes, but humility eases the pain, makes the journey easier, and Unselfish Love lightens the burden.

Getting Down to Work

Few have experienced enough, or learned enough from their lessons in life to listen to the real truth about the separate self. The light of truth is a threat to the darkness/illusions/deceptions created by the self-body-mind. And there are many deceptions and detours along the way (or stepping stones depending on how you deal with them). I could say, "The path is merely chanting a special word for five minutes a day, and by doing this you will be able to see auras, have out-of-body experiences, read minds, etc. Just send a check or money order for $200 and we'll give you your own magic word right away!" But that isn't true, isn't real, and wouldn't really give someone all they need for spiritual growth/enlightenment/becoming one with God. But it would be popular and probably make someone a lot of money.

Those who offer something to the selfish desires of people are very popular. There are many "personal growth" and "spiritual growth" methods being offered, that don't threaten the separate selfish self. The most popular religions are the ones that allow the most selfishness, and place the least self-sacrificing demands on the person, or are the least threatening to the separate self. Here's a little secret for measuring how "real" a particular spiritual tradition or growth method is - just look at how popular it is, or unpopular it is. It is not a hard and fast rule, but generally, the smaller, or more unpopular the path is, the more it threatens the separate self, and thus the more real truth and growth potential it offers. "Enlightenment" is not easy, and not something that can be bought and sold, it takes constant conscious effort and application in all aspects of life.

The last part of my discussions with Zain about "paths" dealt with this subject more in depth.

"You haven't totally answered my first question yet Father. You mentioned 'real' spiritual paths, which seems to intimate that there are false ones, but you didn't seem to really say it in that context. I know you're very busy today, but would you tell me why please, if you have time?"

"I don't have the time. But there is a sundial over there if you really need it."

"No, seriously Father."

"Seriously, seriously. OK. There are definitely purely false spiritual paths, but even some of those offer *something* real. Then there are other paths that are 'semi-false', in that they are not the person's ultimate true path. These may be just a temporary, yet important, part of a person's entire spiritual path, or they may become a 'trap', depending on the individual's level of consciousness, sincerity, or choices. Some traditions, paths or methods are 'traps', 'side trips', 'excursions' off the seeker's real path, that a seeker can get caught up in. Nevertheless, people can move on through these experiences as part of their path - as I said earlier, like stepping stones along the way. Some people will go right on through such 'traps', on to a more truly spiritual path, if they have the proper, unselfish spiritual attitude. It all is depending on the individual's ideals and applications within such circumstances.

Then there are those who set-up their own traps, and are attracted to, and attracted by, false spiritual paths. For instance, if you are *only* interested in *appearing to be* 'spiritual', or *just* interested in spiritual 'trappings', like auras, psychic powers, channeling and such, then what we are saying here will not be of much interest you. But there are plenty of things out there that will. And plenty of organizations and people who will take your money and your life. That is not to say that auras, etc. are false. Of course these things exist, but they are minor parts of the more important whole, and they should be side-effects, out-growths of an unselfish spiritual life."

"But I have always been fascinated by such things. In fact, I had some unusual abilities as a child. Is that wrong for me to be interested in them."

"No. But while you were interested in such things, were you not even more obsessed with finding real love, and people of kindness, gentleness, compassion and harmlessness?"

"Yes. Now that I think about it that was really my primary goal and drive."

"And that is why you had powers even as a child. Spiritual 'phenomenon' should not be a primary focus of interest, lest they become stumbling blocks, and a means of avoiding real spiritual development. And the only way you can have such abilities without abusing them and causing the effects of such abuse, are to first become a harmless, Unselfishly Loving entity, one who will use, or not use, such abilities in a positive, creative manner all the time. You can force the development of such abilities with certain drugs, certain types of the Yogas, and many other techniques, but you will create problems for yourself and others. Powers come naturally to you from the Universal Spirit when you have simply made yourself harmless and caring under all circumstances. To achieve this, you must first *unselfishly use* whatever 'normal' abilities you have RIGHT NOW, in whatever situation you are in 'now'. Just as an employer will promote a person who is excelling in working with the circumstances of his present position and demonstrating his readiness for greater responsibility, so does one advance in the Universal 'company'. What employer would promote someone who's doing a poor job? Or promote someone who cheats, and attempts to get more power before they have earned it? No sane employer promotes people unless they deserve it, and neither does God. So seek first to make yourself worthy through developing those virtues of Unselfish Love, like patience, humility, understanding, always considering the best interests of others before your self. Then hold on to these virtues constantly, perseveringly, through your times of suffering. Such times are the testing times. When you have passed your tests, THEN will you be given whatever extra abilities you need, or material you need, *as you need them* for the Universal work, without even trying to get them."

"And that is why I seem to be gaining new abilities, even though I don't desire them."

"Yes."

"But what about the practice. We are taught methods of working in the other realms, and commanding such abilities and powers."

"These are not for you to personally use, Peniel. They are for making in you, a better vehicle for the Universal Spirit to work through. The hierarchy knows when and what to do, and will use the abilities you have developed, when it is appropriate within the Will of God. You just need to open up the channels so you can be used. When you are through with your training, you will have the ability to channel powers that can level great cities, or move a mountain. But you are not to use such power - just sit back, relax, and let it happen if it be the will of God just doing it through you. And it may never occur, or it may occur daily. It is not for us to decide."

Finding Your True Path

"You said it has been foretold, that I will present the ancient Atlantean Children's teachings to the world. When I finally become an Adept, a true teacher, and I do this, what should be the one most important thing I should say about walking a true course back to the One?"

"Was our discussion of just *one* important thing? There is *much* to say. But the most important *ones,* IF you must limit them, *are these:* Remember the footsteps through the path of rose bushes. Tell them: Pray for, and find a true teacher [detailed in the next chapter]; Work on transcending your separate self; Be ever vigilant regarding your thoughts, and stop feeding the monster with your thoughts (of selfishness, and its illusion of separation); And practice the virtues of Unselfish Love with others of like kind to 'displace' selfishness, and break the illusion of separate-

179

ness.

Yet there is much that people must suffer, much work people will need to do, and much they must decide inside themselves before they will even ask such things about their path back to God.

The spiritual seeker makes a series of steps before he even sets foot on his true spiritual path back to Oneness with the Universal. Obviously they must first *realize* that they *need* to change, and *need* to break free from old programming and behavior patterns. Next, they need to realize they *can* change - regardless of how difficult or impossible it may seem. They must realize that they have free will, and are only a slave to their programming and selfish desires so long as they allow themselves to be. Once a person gets to this point, then they must decide *how and when* they are going to go about changing. They must choose their path, and choose to stop walking their old path in order to start upon the new one. This process involves taking responsibility. Taking *real* responsibility. Responsibility for their own life, for their own life direction, for a new life, and even more importantly, the Ultimate responsibility, serving God and flowing with Universal Will."

Zain's words rang through me like being in the tower of a cathedral as the bells were ringing.

But the separate self wants to prevent you from doing this, so it will influence you to procrastinate, at any cost. It will use *any and every* excuse to keep you from taking responsibility, even *using* "responsibilities" as an excuse to avoid your real responsibility. I remember a great quote that an elder student of mine showed me from a book. I believe it was called "Illusions". It was fiction, and had a "book within a book", called the "Messiah's Handbook". The saying went something like "The best way to avoid Responsibility, is to say you have responsibilities". How true. I have seen so many seekers never evolve spiritually, because they didn't want to break away from their "responsibilities". They have jobs, commitments, contracts, relationships of all kinds - so many things that are more important than becoming Unselfishly Loving and Serving God - the only real and great responsibilities. Or some say they *will* start their spiritual path right away - just as soon as they do "such and such" first. Of course they never seem to complete "such and such", or there is always another "such and such" around the corner. So they never start walking their true spiritual path. There is a profound ancient saying that goes, "Seek God first, and all else will come to you". Nothing could be more true. And nothing is more important than finding God. So what if you become successful! What is it worth if you don't have real Love and God in your life? So what if you did break "such and such" commitment! What was the commitment worth without real Love and God in your life? So what if you didn't complete "such and such" - it is nothing compared to finding and serving God. All those kind of things are delays, keeping you from changing, keeping you from being and doing what you are really supposed to be. They are all temporary things of this world. They won't last. Neither will they matter in the end. If you died tomorrow, will they stand over your grave and say, "He worked hard, kept his appointments, and supported his ex-wife according to the terms of their agreement. His alimony will be missed. His jokes in the pub will be missed. But on with our lives". Or will they say, "You will be missed in this world. The Inner Light you shined was a Lamp for me and all who knew you. The Love and kindness you spread changed my life, and touched thou-

180

sands of souls who were enriched by your work, and in turn, some are carrying on the Lamp, so it may illuminate the path for others. Keep a seat in the next plane warm for us, we will be with you soon."

Some of you who read this are "stragglers", who were already supposed to be, or are still supposed to be, "leaders". You are fallen light workers who should have returned to the light before now, but you have allowed your self to "drag your feet", and avoid your true responsibilities. You have very little time left to change yourself before the great changes are upon this world, and you become bound in darkness for ages. If you want to catch up, you must take rapid measures to attain the spiritual position you were supposed to have already taken. Or, perhaps you are one of the "survivors" of the great changes, who are reading this years later - one of the many "decent" people who survived the changes, or are in the midst of them now, and the suffering is spiritually purifying you in spite of your self. In either case, there is no time to delay. Every moment is precious. Don't squander it. There *is no time for anything else* anymore, except your Inner work, or helping others with their Inner work. Accept your REAL responsibilities. Drop everything NOW! Find your path and walk it *now*. Find your true teacher, and get on with your transformation. Spend *every* moment of your remaining life in an all out concentrated effort to change your life from one that is separate self oriented, to one that lives to serve and manifest the Universal Spirit.

The Great Affirmation

As we walk our path, we should let our daily affirmation or prayer to the Infinite ONE be, "Your will be done, not mine, in me and through me". And we should not just say it, we must FEEL it, LIVE it! Practice this, and One eternal day you may find that *God's will*, will be *your will*, as One, no longer separate. You will realize "I AM", and your actions, your lifestyle, your being, will reflect this. Your life will be as one giving like an endless stream of Universal Love flowing forth, rather than the empty, short lived *endless circle of wanting (trying to get), and fear (trying to avoid)*.

Chapter Thirteen
Teachers and Students

Backing up a Bit

While this chapter comes late in the book, the part of it that is my personal story, really begins very early on, both before I went to the monastery, and in my first days and weeks there. I was at the very least naive about many things, and you may also find a great deal of sarcasm, and egoism, in some of my early questions and comments to both teachers and elders, as I had not yet realized the wonderful virtue of humility.

The ancient texts are clear and consistent. "Find thyself a teacher." This is an old and time-proven growth method in many good spiritual traditions around the world. It is even still to be found in the Talmud (with somewhat different meaning and application these days). So what is a teacher? It can mean many things.

Let me start by saying there is a big difference between what we call a true teacher, and other things or people that seem to be teachers. What I mean, is that there are lots of teacher, Guru, or preacher types that want "followers" - they want prestige, praise, worship, money, or a mix. Some want you to praise or worship someone or something else, while they ride the coat-tails as being a "representative" of what you're supposed to be worshipping or praising. Some want it directly themselves. But a "true teacher", doesn't want any of those things. He teaches with his life primarily, and kindles you through his Unselfish Love. He will accept good students, to teach them how to change. He will teach philosophies or techniques to help you change, and is a facilitator of change that a student can use like a tool. But he wants no blind or mindless "followers", no worship, no praise. Anyone who does, is not what we will refer to here as a true teacher. In our particular tradition, the Children of the Law of One, a true teacher must be "enlightened" (having experienced the death of the selfish separate self, and lives in total harmony, oneness with the Universal Spirit, and is a servant of Universal Spirit, and vehicle for its Universal Will). Elders can also be teachers, but it isn't quite the same as the "true teacher". The words used to describe such a being, and the practices of other traditions, obviously vary, but the end result should be the same. Which we will detail in a moment.

First, a word about worship. Worship is a very "noble" appearing way the selfish self uses to avoid personal responsibility, change, surrender, and its own separate self demise. People take all the best qualities and ideals, and personalize them into someone to worship, rather than becoming that themselves. They "idol-ize" rather than "ideal-ize". There is a big difference [there's more info about ideals and using ideals in another chapter]. Idealizing just sets a standard of change for you to "shoot for". The self prefers idolizing and worshipping, because that way it avoids the hard work and self-sacrifice required by surrendering to God, and serving God. Speaking of which...

Many people don't like the idea of having a "spiritual teacher" or "Guru" type person in their life. I know I didn't. Often this is for a good reason - there are MANY charlatans out there. But there *are* some saints too. And the real reason most people don't want a teacher is because their selfish separate self knows it is the beginning of the end of it's control, and life.

And as far as charlatans, what you get, or get exposed to personally, mainly depends on you, and what your motives are. If you just want to "mess around" or "seem spiritual" or think you are spiritual, then you'll end up worshipping a charlatan. But if you really want help to become *truly* spiritual - kind, caring, harmless, giving - then you'll find the real thing, and use their example as an ideal.

Many people are taking courses, going to seminars, classes and channels, that are conducted by charlatans, and they're perfectly fine with it. It's the real thing most people are afraid of. Essentially, you get what's coming to you - you get what you deserve - or to put it more accurately, *you get what you are really after inside.* Whether you know it or not.

I wasn't looking for a teacher when I went to the monastery. I was just looking for a place where everyone was kind, sharing and loving. That sounds good, doesn't it? But I hadn't really thought about the fact that *I* needed to be that way myself, if I was going to be part of such a community. Nor did I really think about what I would need to do to become that way. In fact, I was so self-centered and "egoed out" about myself, I figured I was already spiritual, and virtually perfect. Wrong again. As I have said, all selfish selves would just love to be the only selfish person in a community full of unselfish people who just give to them all the time and don't give them a hard time about their selfish qualities. Keep dreaming.

On about my third day at the monastery, during one of my first courses with elder student Raga, he spoke of the issue, but I didn't "get it" at the time.

"Some people think they can get everything they need themselves, from books, seminars, and life. That may be true. It may not be true. Or it just might be a matter of speed, or beating the "odds". Everyone needs a true teacher at some point in their spiritual path, to help them see beyond them'selves', and get beyond them'selves' - because the selfish separate self is you until you're enlightened. So it knows your *every* move before you take it, and it will outwit you at every attempt to transcend it, if all you have is your separate self to rely on for your spiritual growth.

Everyone also has all kinds of excuses why they don't want a teacher, or need one. And of course, they can use legitimate, and 'reasonable' excuses, because there are many false teachers, which provides the right 'rationalization' to their self's 'feelings' of avoidance. But the real reason most people don't like the idea of having a teacher has nothing to do with whether the alleged 'teacher' is a legitimate enlightened being, or a charlatan - in fact, most people prefer charlatans because they are no *real* threat to the selfish separate self."

Whatever category you fall into, at least open your mind temporarily, and read this chapter before you close your mind back up again, (putting your mind back "on the shelf", along with this book). Maybe it will help you understand what true teachers are all about, and how they can be a tool to help you attain *your* own goals.

How can You Defeat Your Enemy, When it is YOU.

Raga went on. "Once a person has realized that their personal enemy, and the great enemy of humankind, is the separate self and the selfishness that it spawns, what then? They can choose to walk the path of Unselfish Love. Then what? They can study books, meditate, use various techniques for growth, or whatever, but there is a primary problem that supersedes any of these things. *The selfish separate self does not want to relinquish control to the Inner self/Universal Spirit.* More than that, the very nature of achieving Universal Consciousness means that the selfish separate self will *cease to exist* as an *independent entity* - it will 'die' so to speak. So it will fight like a cornered animal for its survival! It will intellectually maneuver like a world-class chess champion to win the battle. It will use more clever trickery and deceit than the world's best con-man. Before you can really get anywhere spiritually, *You must first fully realize that the separate self has control over the brain, the desires, the emotions, etc. - it has control over a person's entire life!* So if you do *anything* that so much as threatens your separate self, it *will* use the things it controls, against you. It knows when you are attempting to de-throne it, and it is fantastically clever in its ways to keep control and maintain the illusion of separateness. It *will* fight your attempts to take control of your life, or to put control of your life in the hands of the Universal Spirit. It won't 'fight fair' either. And it's already an easy task for it, because it simply needs to trick you *a little.* So again, everyone needs a true teacher at some point in their path. A teacher that won't let the separate self get away with anything."

"I understand all that Raga, but why do you say we *need* a teacher? Why can't we just get everything we need to change from books, and life, and meditation?"

"How can you say you understand all that, you obviously haven't even heard a word I have said. It has fallen on deaf ears. Listen to me with your Inner Voice, not your separate self brain. It first 'filters' everything you perceive, including my words. And the 'filter' is your ego, your selfish separate self.

The separate self is so clever, *it can even use your own desire to change to keep you trapped.* If it knows you are interested in growing spiritually, what do you think it will do? What would you do? What do you do? It can and will 'accommodate' you - sure it will allow you to read books, etc. In fact, it will *have* you read books, go to the latest mediums (channels), and hop from one growth method to another, one fad to another, let you get immersed in religion, whatever - *as long as what you do* or get involved with doesn't *really* threaten the selfish separate self's control or existence."

"Even if you're working real hard at it and really doing everything you can to achieve enlightenment?"

"You can *perpetually* be doing *everything* you *seemingly can* to enlighten yourself - and be getting absolutely nowhere (other than getting a head full of great 'spiritual rationalizations' for the separate self to use in defending itself). You can spin your wheels forever. But in reality, you *aren't* doing 'everything you can', unless you utilize the services of a true teacher - a clear mirror for which you can see the reflection of your own selfishness."

"Why do you need to see your selfishness, doesn't it just go away as you learn more and achieve higher consciousness?"

"There are a lot of people out there who are still totally selfish, even though they have a great deal of knowledge and experience in spiritual/metaphysical matters. These people know many meditation techniques and personal growth methods, and perhaps use them. They think because of all *that,* they are of higher consciousness. Naturally, the selfish separate self lets them 'go for it', and it even pats them on the back for doing so well and being so 'spiritual'. I guess it depends on how you define higher consciousness, but to me, and the ancient teachings, such knowledge and experience doesn't mean you have higher consciousness, any more than *knowing* how to *build* a house means that you actually *have built* a house, or even *have* a house."

He was right of course, and the only reason I was avoiding seeing it was because of my separate self's fear, and control over me (which I allowed with my free will, even though it was "subconscious" at the time). So how do you know when you are kidding yourself? There are several ways.

Here's a simple premise to think about: how can someone be of higher consciousness if they lack Unselfish Love and Kindness? I have met many, many people with lots of spiritual/metaphysical knowledge - who are still "normal" selfish people. They may even be relatively kind and "giving" ordinarily, but unkind and selfish, when kindness and giving requires any real self-sacrifice, or gets in the way of what they want.   On the other hand, I have met *truly kind and giving* people who are "metaphysically ignorant". They might think karma is some kind of new car wax if it weren't explained to them - yet they are kind and giving. And they may really understand and believe in what karma actually means (you reap what you sow) in a very real sense, even though they don't even know the word - they may really know much more than some new age "jive talker'", and be of real higher consciousness than someone giving "spiritual" seminars. So who is really of higher consciousness? Let's say your house gets destroyed by a tornado. Who would *you* like as a neighbor, someone who would help you rebuild it, give your shelter or food, or someone who will patronizingly inform you that you attracted the misfortune to yourself, then drive off and leave you in the dust of their Mercedes as they rush off to attend another seminar on "prosperity" (which is likely to be nothing more than learning black magic visualization techniques, disguised as a "making money happen" program)? Who's more spiritually evolved here? True prosperity is something you *can* take with you when you die, and it only comes when you give through Unselfish Love.

Back to Raga's lecture (which was stabbing me in the heart of my ego):

"If a person *has* attained Universal Consciousness, they, by the very nature of that, *cannot* be simultaneously selfish. And if a person is still selfish, they cannot be One with Universal Spirit, or have Universal Consciousness. Many people's 'spirituality' excludes this simple fact, and many use sophisticated 'spiritual' rationalizations to actually maintain their selfish separate self."

Mirror Mirror on the Wall

"Raga," I said challengingly, "other than your own opinion, are there any actual specific teachings of the Atlantean Children of the Law of One, that talk about this alleged 'great wall of self-trickery'?"

"Very many young novice. They say that you *must* have an 'in the flesh' teacher who is a *clear mirror* that will: 1) reflect your thoughts, feelings, and actions, back to yourself accurately, so you can see through self-delusion, and 2) be a mirror that shows you yourself, whether you want to see yourself or not, whether you 'look in it' or not. In other words, one that makes you look at yourself, even when you avoid seeing yourself by self-trickery."

"So you're talking about a magic mirror?"

"Gosh you don't want to get this do you? Such a 'clear mirror' is a true teacher.

The teachings make it absolutely clear that the *final stage* in a person's evolution back to Oneness with the Universal Spirit, is to find and use a 'true teacher' to 'see' themselves, so they can really change. This is what a true teacher is here for. Such teachers are enlightened masters who have purged their own programming and selfishness, and become clear mirrors."

"What is an un-clear mirror?"

"Nearly everyone else on Earth other than a true teacher. Everyone you meet reflects you back to yourself, and gives you a chance to see yourself, but the reflection comes back distorted by whatever problems the mirror has. In the case of 'human' mirrors, the distortions will come from the person's own programming, beliefs, prejudices, etc. - all these things make for a 'warped' mirror, like those in a 'fun house', and will reflect back a distorted view of yourself. Even someone you may respect, and who you have received good spiritual or philosophical teachings from, can only offer you **very** limited help in your spiritual journey, if they are still unclear, distorted mirrors.

If you don't want to delude yourself, deceive yourself, then you need an enlightened spiritual teacher. Otherwise, your self will always figure out ways to ultimately avoid having your separate illusion exposed and dissipated. If growth is what you *really* want, there is nothing that compares to having a true teacher. No meditations, no methods, no exercises, no words, no ideas, no mediums (channels), no psychics, will do by themselves. Again, the teachings of the Atlantean Children are very strong on this point. YOU MUST at some point have a teacher if you are to proceed beyond a certain point on your path. The teachings do say there are very rare exceptions, but that there is less than a 1 in a billion chance to succeed otherwise, although that may change in the very near future as the coming changes present new opportunities, and create forced internal spiritual changes for some. Maybe you'll be the first to really do it by yourself young novice?"

Nope. No such luck.

Learn Instead of Burn

Later, once I had finally given up trying to avoid it, and found my true teacher, Zain, we had some great conversations. One time, I had a wonderful talk with him about the various ways of learning, growing, and working toward enlightenment, which pertain to this chapter.

"Father, what is the *best* way to learn, and how can we know who to listen to, and who not to?"

"It is said that a wise man listens and learns from the wise and the fool. We can, and should, learn from anyone and everyone, and from life itself. Everything attempts to teach us, and we can learn if we are open. Also, we can learn things from the 'school of hard knocks', life experience. Unfortunately, that is the way most people learn, and I only say 'unfortunately' because it is the slowest and most painful way. We can learn more easily, by 'osmosis' (sort of 'absorbing' by contact) from the experience of others. In this way we can benefit from the lessons already learned by others who either went through the 'school of hard knocks', or learned from osmosis also. This is the easiest, fastest, and most wise way to learn. For instance, if we see someone get burned by putting their hand in a fire, we can also learn from that, rather than also putting our hand in the fire to learn that it burns. Or, in another kind of example, if we spend time around a great chef, we are likely to 'pick up' on their knowledge and skills, as opposed to spending years experimenting with cooking ourselves, burning things, making terrible tasting food, etc. The experiences of others can be ours if we are open to it. To learn by 'osmosis' from the experience of an Unselfishly Loving, Universally Conscious, clear mirror, is the absolute easiest and best way to learn and grow spiritually."

The Circle and the Spiral

Reincarnation creates a situation in which people with "karmic ties" keep coming back into each other's lives. For instance, your mother may have played many roles in various past lives - your sister, friend, daughter, a romantic rival, wife or lover.

As was mentioned earlier in the book, Initiates of the Atlantean Children of the Law of One who have not "Ascended" (permanently left the physical bodies of the Earth plane behind), have reincarnated time and time again, throughout the world. They keep coming back, picking up where they left off, continuing on to serve the light and the seekers of the light.

"Father, speaking of learning from the experience of others, and of 'clear mirror' teachers, I have heard it said that the Dalai Lama, continues to reincarnate, and as the same person, in the same position, is this true?"

"Most assuredly, and not just the Dalai Lama. Other higher consciousness Buddhist teachers do this also. That is their way."

"What do you mean *their* way?"

"Our tradition does something very similar, yet somewhat differently. When a teacher leaves this Earth, and chooses to reincarnate, the inner self (and outside "influences" and "circumstances"), compels him to become 'who he was' in his past - i.e., to regain the same level of consciousness he previously had. That applies to any enlightened teacher of any path. In ours, the Initiate who does this, is inwardly compelled to find other Initiates of the Children again, and return to a monastery for the period of re-initiation, re-learning, re-enlightenment. And other Initiates look for the reincarnated pre-re-initiated Adept, who is to again become a true teacher of our order. Again, this is done in many traditions in various ways."

"Like you found me, or vice-versa?"

"Or both."

"Yes. But when do you start looking, and how long does it take to be 're-initiated' or become enlightened again?"

"This generally occurs before age 21, and will occur whether the reincarnated true teacher is yet aware of who he is (and was), or not. Often, a teacher will not be conscious of who they are when they are young, and will only begin becoming conscious of their true self sometime between the age of 14 and 21. Nevertheless, their enlightenment will occur by 21. This is a Universal Law, and applies to everyone."

"What about those who weren't enlightened, or aren't one of the spiritual traditions who do this?"

"Regardless of whether you are one of the Children or not, or enlightened or not, whatever your *consciousness* (level of spiritual consciousness attained) *was* when you died in your previous life, you attain that same level of consciousness again around age 21. This is unavoidable."

187

"And then what?"

"From that point of regaining previous adult consciousness, one can make spiritual progress, or regress."

[Ed. Note: This means a person CAN achieve enlightenment at ANY age.]

"Why do some enlightened teachers return, and some don't?"

"Because it's their choice. Some of the Children continue to return to the Earth plane, to help others free themselves from the illusion of separation. Others wish to join their 'like kind' on the higher planes. Some grow very weary, and finally wish to leave, like me."

"You're going to leave??!!"

"Not yet. Relax. You will be a teacher off on your own before I go."

"And you won't come back?"

"No."

"Will I ever see you again?"

"See me? With eyes, no. Once you finally move on from here, perhaps."

"Why only perhaps? Aren't we connected somehow?"

"Most definitely. But if you stay a great deal longer, I will still be moving on with my own evolution in the order of things. If it is too long, we will not be next to each other in the chain, but we will always be one within the chain."

"What about me, you said I will be a true teacher."

"Yes."

"So I will be enlightened before I'm 21."

"Perhaps 21 - thereabouts."

"Do you know if I will come back?"

"No. That's for you to decide. That's your free-will choice."

"You said earlier something about our tradition doing things a bit differently than the Buddhists, as far as teachers reincarnating, what's different about it? What you've described all sounds the same."

"Those of us who do this, life after life, 'take turns' helping us find each other again before age 21. This is *similar* to what is done in Tibetan Buddhism, by the Dalai Lama, and other high consciousness lamas. However, the Tibetan Buddhists generally start younger, because of their unique social structure. A group of Buddhist monks identifies the child who is the incarnation of the Dalai Lama, or whomever they are looking for. Then once they are positive they have the right being, the child enters a monastery to begin training to take his place in the order once again. Teachers of the Children of the Law of One, however, don't necessarily return to the same position, same land, or same race even. They are all over the world, fitting into many places, many guises, and need various backgrounds for their chosen destiny. So it's not so simple to get them back as children. You can imagine what would happen if some guy showed up at some modern Jewish couple's apartment in NY city, and said they are there to take their baby to Tibet with them because they are 'so and so', the reincarnated old Adept and true teacher."

"Yeah! How do you say '20 years to life' in Tibetan or Yiddish?"

"You get the point. Nevertheless, we are looked after from 'on high', and still physically located before age 21, so we can begin the work that brings us back to full consciousness of Oneness, by the time we reach 21. It was different in the old days, and more like it is for the Tibetans, but even modern times are beginning to change things for them, and they will find their teachers being born in other lands and may eventually be faced with similar issues as ours.

But don't forget, there are many with high consciousness, who are of our order, or our path, who may not have achieved final initiation yet. Thus they may still come into your life, or vice-versa, even though it is not by the time they are 21. Remember, they are still at some stage of development, some stage of initiation towards the final one. That's why there are 22 cards in the deck depicting the stages of initiation, and there will be 22 chapters in the book you will write. Even the one who is at stage one - the fool, is just as important a soul as any. And the fool is both the beginning and ending. To be enlightened also means to be a fool - a fool for God."

"I will remember Father."

In my case, I was "found" (or did the finding) through that weird TV broadcast. As you are probably aware of by this time, Zain became my personal teacher. It was he I saw on TV. Once I got to know him well, I asked him more about the broadcast.

"Father... Do you know how I got here? I mean... I saw you on TV, on a TV station that didn't exist, couldn't exist... On a TV band that isn't, and wasn't even ever used. But I know I didn't imagine it."

"You didn't imagine it Peniel. It was a broadcast that was just for you. You are the only one who saw it. The only one that came. The only one it was for."

"How did it happen though? Magic?"

"In a way. Many things, including Science-Magic were involved. There were friends of ours in the area at the time, who had friends involved with a more open minded Christian church there. Our friends were wise in the ways of modern technology. They made a 'broadcast' of a recording made of me here. It was 'illegal' there to make the broadcast they did, but they believed nothing would become of it because it was going to be so short. Nonetheless, they had a back up. They said because it was from the basement of their church, they were protected by other laws. They were guided as to the timing and all other factors, so that I would be seen by you, and find you and you would find me, even though I was thousands of miles away at the time."

"Do you know I was about to kill myself?"

"At the time, it was both yes and 'know'. We were given to understand that the timing was critical. And because of who you are, you had to be contacted in that way, at that time."

"Who I am? Who *am* I, and who are you, that this would be so extreme?"

"You are very special Peniel, you have no idea how special, because you think you are so special."

"Huh?"

[I later discovered we are all special, we just need to transcend our selfish separate self, take our place in the chain of the One, and become a vehicle for, a servant of the Universal Spirit]

He went on to tell me more of how teachers of the Children found each other - especially ones with special links to each other. As Zain spoke of how he and I had helped each other, taught each other, and worked together, past life memories flooded back to me like I was in a movie, but they were in fragments (like the movie had been edited by a chimp!). He also told me of some of my ties and times with the grand master.

Zain and I had particularly strong karmic ties, and were sometimes like two sides of a coin. We each had different qualities that ordinarily would make for unlikely friends, but actually complemented our abilities to help others when we worked together. In many ways, we were like night and day - very different personalities, talents and skills. Yet there were also many similar talents, skills, loves, and qualities. Most importantly, we were on the same team, we had always fought in our own ways for the light, justice, truth, and freedom. We had a deep respect and appreciation for each other that few could ever understand - it was as it always was, through so many lifetimes. He seemed to admire me like a good son, brother, best friend and father. And I him.

But it wasn't always so. When I first arrived at the monastery, and set eyes on him, he terrified me. I avoided him like the plague. I was still under the strong influence of my selfish separate self. But we'll cover all that in a bit. First, let's finish the subject at hand, ancient teachers of the Children of the Law of One finding each other before age 21.

Throughout the ages, it was the same situation over and over again. I, as a teacher, would be found by a young man, who may have been my teacher before. And vice versa. It didn't matter which was which or who was who. We were all part of the One, going through revolving doors. Sometimes we would even be members of the same biological family, but usually not, and it mattered not.

So it was that I, through this process, my destiny, my spiritual pursuits and training, ultimately returned again to Universal consciousness at age 21. My "self", what I had previously thought was "me" as a child, sort of "died" at age 21, and subsequently was "reborn" as a servant of the One Universal Spirit and Universal Will. Along with the death of my illusion of separateness, my beliefs, intellectual processes, and programming, were all transformed at the same time. Essentially, my separate "self", the independent "thing" I had "given life to" which maintained my separateness from the Universe, died. It ceased to exist as a *separate* self. But only for a moment. It was more like a metamorphosis, like a caterpillar seeming to die, to become a butterfly. My old separate self was only like a "bubble" of illusions that surrounded me, and kept my consciousness separate from the Universe, and my true self locked inside me. Once that bubble burst, my real self, the inner-self, being part of the Universal One, was all that was left of me then, and so freed, I could again see the world anew, through eyes that see beyond this world, and to again play my part as one of the instruments in the Grand Orchestra of the One.

[Ed. Note: Again, a person can achieve enlightenment at ANY age.]

The Oneness of all Inner Selves

The inner self in everyone, is part of the same being, part of the One. When I first heard Zain speaking on that mysterious TV broadcast, it was really his inner self who was speaking - speaking to my inner self. It was the voice of the Universal Spirit, calling out to, and speaking to, another part of itself. That's why it "rang my inner bell of truth", that's how I could "feel" and "know" it was true. But I was ready, no, desperate, to hear.

As I, my inner self, speaks to you now, I speak to you as your own inner self. Thus you can "feel" the truth I speak to you, as if you already know it. The closer you are to your own inner self, the more strongly you will feel this. Those of you who are distant, may not feel this, and those who have "blocked" your inner self, will find these words disturbing - the extent of the disturbance will depend on how intensely you are "blocking".

Finding My True Teacher

Speaking of blocks, once I finally arrived at the monastery, and actually found myself in the presence of Zain, all my defensive "blocks" went up. Like I said earlier, I avoided him like the plague. I even "blocked" the entire *concept* of teachers. Even though I had no problem being "taught" daily, by elder student "teachers" in various courses. And even in the orientation I was being given by Anastasia, she was "teaching" me things.

One day, the elder student Raga began talking again about the ancient teaching about teachers, and about the need for a personal true teacher, especially as your path winds higher. It was so obvious that Zain was supposed to be my personal teacher. But I wouldn't, thus couldn't, see that at the time. But it did become obvious that it was time for me to have a teacher.

I had already learned (and known), from books I'd read before even coming to the monastery, about how if you really wanted to transcend your separate self and achieve enlightenment, one of the things you ultimately needed to do, was to find, choose, and ask a true teacher to be your teacher. And then it was reinforced by Anastasia, and then in the courses I was taking. But I kept ignoring it.

Then one day Raga was out teaching me the "mediation walk" technique on a sort of "field trip". And as we walked through the snow, coordinating our breathing with our steps, my mind wandered and I numbly thought to myself "Where am I going to find my teacher?".

Out of the blue, Raga all of a sudden stopped, and said, "Go to the library, and ask Gabriel, which of the ancient texts he thinks you should read about teachers." So I did. And this is what I was given.

The Candle
Lights A Candle
Thus does The Student
Receive The Light
From The Teacher

A True Teacher
Must First Be A Good Student

The Best Student
Is the Most Humble

❖

He Who Would Be First
Will Be Last

❖

Nature Abhors a Vacuum
The Mountain Is Gradually Worn Down

To Fill The Valley
Thus the Humble and Lowly
Are Raised Unto the Heavens

❖

Knowledge Without Humility and Self-Sacrifice,
is Meaningless. And can be Harmful.

A Student Without Humility
Is Like a Full Cup

❖

Only a Clear Mirror Reflects Yourself True.
Thus Through the Eyes of a True Teacher
Can One See The Deceptions
of The Selfish Separate Self

Thus is The True Teacher
The Tool That Can Free You
From The Illusions Your Self has Created

❖

Hear Me O Man.
Chains You Have Forged
That Bind You to Darkness of Night
In Servitude You Cry
For The Dark Lords are Your Master
To Serve Them No Longer
Reach Out in the Night
Call For Your Brothers
That Serve Only Light
A Hand Will Appear
Piercing the Darkness
Strange Love That Comes From the Light
Grasp on With Both Hands
And Clutch With All Might
Ripped from Darkness
In Pain Your Dark Self Screams
Let Not Thy Cup Fall Then
And Death Will Come Soon
Releasing and Revealing
The True Inner You
In Light Will You Awaken

To Find You Are Whole
In Love And In Freedom
You Find The Goal

❖

Life is a Teacher
But the Hardest Teacher
And the Longest School.
To Learn from The experiences of Others
Is a great skill indeed.
To Learn from the True Teacher
Is The Path Chosen by the Wise.
All True Paths
Eventually Lead to The True Teacher.
One Can Go no further Until
They Confront the Great Beast
And Unveil Its Deceptions.

❖

The True Teacher
Is One With Universal Will
One With the Universal Consciousness
And the Servant of All

The True Teacher
Radiates His Consciousness
Just By Being.
Those in His Presence Are Affected by The Light
Even When He Speaks Not.
His Light Evokes Fear and Anger in the Selfish
Who Live in the Darkness of Deceit,
But Nurtures and Inspires the Gentle, the Kind,
and the Spiritually Hungry.

The True Teacher
Is Your Inner Being Standing Before You.
If You Are Receptive To Your Inner Being
You Are Receptive to The True Teacher.
If You Try to Avoid Your Inner Being
You Will Try to Avoid The True Teacher.

He Who Listens to a True Teacher
Hears His Own Inner Voice
He Who Manifests His Own Inner Voice

Is a True Teacher

❖

Now I Am The Teacher
Now You Are The Student
I Give You My Hand
And Take You Home Again.
The Wheel of Life Turns
Now You Are The Teacher
Now I Am The Student
You Give Me Your Hand
And Take Me Home Again.
So Goes The Cycle of Life
For Children Who Live The Law of One
For Brother Sun and Sister Moon
Who In Harmony with Universal Will, Serve All

❖

Let Go
And Let God.

❖

The Self Always Has Good Reason
To Be Negative.
There is NO Reason
Good Enough To Stop Loving.

❖

All Inner Beings Are One

❖

Let No Being Possess You
In Body, Mind or Soul

❖

Need Not to Spirits.
Guide You Would They, Out of Place.
Come From The Dark Do These Spirits.
In Harmony Not With Universal Flow,
Know They Not Oneness With The All.

The Children of One Light
Live Among Men.
Your Spiritual Self Are They.
Your Spiritual Self, Show You They,

To Be One With All
One With The Light

❖

True Teachers, Masters of Self
Gone from This Earth
Commune Not with the Living
Guide they Not in Voice or Possession.

Deceptive Spirits Come in Guises
To Mislead and Misteach
Those who would Have them

Guidance Seek Ye Only From Masters in Flesh.
All True Teachers Be One With the All.
As You Be in Flesh, You Need Guidance in Flesh,
To Disallow Dark Deceptions the Self does Befool.
Urge You do they All, to Listen Closely and Only
To the Still Silent Voice of Your True Inner Self,
Find it Within, And Find it Without,
Your Inner Voice Reflected,
The True Teacher, in Flesh.

Well, that was great, but I was still in a quandary. Where could I possibly find my true teacher? Who was my true teacher? Then, it hit me. Raga must be my true teacher. I mean, he was informative, he seemed to know my inner thoughts and read my mind. I was very comfortable with him. And most importantly, he was totally unthreatening to me. I didn't know it yet, but that was one of the problems - he was totally unthreatening to me *because* he did not yet *have* Universal Consciousness, and was no threat to my selfish separate self. So while he was wise, knew a lot, channeled well for me in courses and personal growth sessions, and taught me basic meditations, he was not a true teacher.

So what did *I* do? I asked Raga to be my teacher.

"Raga, I've been thinking about who my personal true teacher should be, and I'd like it to be you. Would you accept me as your student?"

He hesitated for a moment, a bit surprised, and then he accepted.

"Yes. I would be honored," he said proudly.

He was *so* proud. Too proud. In fact, it struck me as odd, but more importantly, made me "feel" odd.

One of the signs that you are ready to be a true teacher, is that someone asks you to be their teacher. The trouble was, the *other* signs weren't there. And I didn't know at the time that only Initiates, Adept monks, were really qualified and capable of being a true teacher. And Raga, not being free from his separate self, went on quite an "ego trip" about being asked to be my teacher. His ego was as puffed up as a blowfish. He had stumbled into one of the great traps that can snare you if you aren't enlightened - spiritual ego.

Anyway, Raga was actually one of Zain's students. And when Raga went and told Zain about it, Raga's "ego-trip" had become an ego-"rip" - the "blowfish" was served on a platter with rice and tamari sauce.

The next thing I knew, Raga was apologizing to me for misleading me and saying he would be my teacher.

"Even though I am teaching you, obviously, and in that sense, I am a teacher to you, I am not yet a true teacher. I am not enlightened for one thing, and I am definitely not your personal true teacher."

"Then who is?"

"That is for you to determine."

Great. Back to square one.

The True Teacher

Much later, after I finally got it through my thick ego that Zain was my true teacher, he "taught" me about what makes a true teacher, and how they teach through more than words.

"Father, what would you say the difference is between a true teacher and a 'teacher'?"

"When a person attains Universal Consciousness, they are 'done', they are finally 'free', and again One with God. Their karma has been resolved and stands neutral. They are Adepts, full Initiates. At that time, they choose whether to leave this plane, or stay on to help awaken the Spirit within those who are still lost in the darkness of the separate self. Those who leave the plane, we call ascended, and they work within the hierarchy. Those who stay, are the true teachers of our order. By 'true', we mean true in the sense of alignment, an undistorted mirror, or how a 'true' arrow will be 'on target'.

A true teacher, having Universal Consciousness, has made the great 'connection', found the balance of self serving Spirit, and lives thusly. They outwardly manifest the Spirit (which again is the same Spirit within us all), in words, *actions and being*. A regular teacher does not - they have only knowledge, wisdoms to give in their lives."

"I can understand how the actions would be different, and would make for a substantially different way of teaching through their life example, but their 'being' - you emphasized that - what does that mean?"

"Did you know that when a tuning fork is struck and begins to vibrate, other tuning forks of the same pitch that are in the vicinity will also begin to vibrate? In other words, if you strike a tuning fork that vibrates to the note 'C', all other 'C' pitched tuning forks in the area will vibrate also."

"Yes, I have actually studied this in great detail, and tried to understand it metaphysically even, but I've gotten nowhere. In fact I've been meaning to ask you..."

"You will. But this isn't the time for going on about that. Discipline your mind now, and focus on the subject we are discussing *now*. When we come into contact with a true teacher, it has a 'quickening' or awakening effect on that same consciousness within everyone. This happens in very much the same way as the tuning forks. The teacher's intense internal vibration of the Universal Spirit radiates powerful energy waves which vibrate and stimulate the Universal Spirit in all others near him. People *will* feel different by being in the presence of such a One. It actu-

196

ally can change lives, by affecting a stranger passing by. Some will notice they feel differently, and wonder why, wonder what made them feel such things, when no one even said anything. Others won't. Those who are 'tuned-in' to, sensitive to, their own Inner Being, would be aware of this effect. But the effect takes place regardless of whether or not someone is aware of it happening or not, or is open to it, or not. For those who are spiritually inclined, this feels good. The more spiritually inclined a person is, the more wonderful it feels. It's like gourmet food to a starving person - or an oasis in the desert to a person dying of thirst. But those who are not spiritually inclined, those who have suppressed and hidden from their own Spirit within, find the presence of such a person to be disturbing, making them un-easy, agitated, and even hostile in some cases. Those who's separate selves are well in control of their being, do in fact become progressively, and expressly, more negative as the truth encroaches. This is because the separate self fears the fire of Spirit, knowing well that its all consuming flames can mean the end of its reign, and ultimately, its existence. The irony in all this is that after the separate-self finally gives-up and takes its natural place as servant to the Spirit, *it too* finds peace, happiness, and harmony with the Universe. It is just a great folly to hide from the Eternal Light."

An Instrument the Universal Spirit "Radiates" Through

"I understand. I felt disturbed by your presence when I was first here. But now, I cherish our time together. I can't get enough."

"I know I have so little time to give you, but you are getting what you need, I assure you."

"Oh, I know how busy you are Father, I didn't mean to complain, only to compliment."

"I know."

"Anyway, how do teachers do this though - the radiating of spirit that has these effects - is it just from being enlightened, or is it a technique we learn later on?"

"We learn techniques that open our 'channels' so to speak, and help us make the most of certain energies or 'abilities'. But the actual process of the Universal Spirit affecting people through teachers, is not a technique, or something consciously done. It is just one of the affects of being One with God. It is guided by the hierarchy and determined by Universal Will. The teacher doesn't need to do anything, doesn't need to say anything, they may or may not even know what is *specifically* happening to others through them. True teaching 'happens'. It is done by just being. It's like an invisible radiation that permeates everything and everyone. The effect of a being who is One with Universal Consciousness comes of its own accord, like that of sunlight from the Sun. The Sun doesn't contrive radiating light, or work at it - it just does by its nature. The same with a teacher. A teacher does not just preach. Like the difference in the words teacher and preacher - the 't' in teacher - 'touches', while the 'p' in preacher - 'proposes and pushes'. While an Adept teacher's words may have an illuminating effect, teaching is done through 'effect' and example, not just words. When your consciousness is thus pervaded with the virtues of Unselfish Love and Universal Consciousness, such as inner peace, harmony, beauty, grace, etc., these *virtues* affect and influence automatically, through 'osmosis' and 'resonance' - just by being around."

"It seems like everyone should be a true teacher, or at least enlightened."

Help Wanted - Apply Inside

"True. Ultimately, all should either become teachers upon enlightenment, or go on to the next plane. We don't belong here. We are angelic travelers who got stuck by falling into a trap, and creating one hellish 'resort' plane, amongst an infinity of resorts of peace and beauty. Naturally, this Earth, this plane, *could* be such a paradisiacal place if all were enlightened. But even then, why stay in one little room when you have such a grand estate as the Universe? At this point in time and space - right now here on Earth, *unless* you are either a true teacher or ascended, at best you are 'dead weight' (living in the pain and suffering of being separate from the One), and also, to one degree or another, a pawn of the darkside. At worst, some actually join the darkside. Even a student is bound in the dark 'play', until they are enlightened."

At the time, I couldn't really understand why the heck anyone would want to stay here once they attained enlightenment and were free. I was about to kill myself minutes before the TV broadcast showing Zain. I'd asked this when I was younger, but I never did get it, so I asked again.

"Why do some choose to stay, and some choose to go on and enjoy life with other loving ascended beings?"

"Actually, most choose to stay, at least for awhile, for teaching is a natural result of attaining oneness with the Universal Spirit through Unselfish Love."

"Why is teaching the natural result - it seems like the natural result would be to go on and join those of your own level of consciousness rather than stay here in hell, totally surrounded by selfish jerks?"

"The very nature of the Unselfish Love that was required to attain enlightenment, and Universal Consciousness, requires **compassion.** And the attainment gives a person even more compassion. That urges you to stay and help (be a 'teacher')."

"Isn't it hard though Father?"

He sighed deeply. And looked off as if he had tears in his eyes, but that he was so "cried out" that there were no tears left.

"Hard is not the word for it. And teaching is the most unappreciated job, the hardest job, and the most painful job, in the world. Since the teacher is the instrument of exposing, de-throning the selfish separate self (by virtue of reflecting the light of truth), the separate self *really hates* the teacher. It is one thing to feel this from strangers and the dark ones. But since the elder or novice student at most stages, still really thinks, feels, and believes that they are the separate self, the student often is in conflict with the teacher. Thus the teacher experiences that the people he is closest to in the world, his students, both hate and love him. More hate than love, because the separate self is still in such control of the student. It is a terrible feeling for the teacher, but it is what he must endure, and the price he must pay, to help free others from the bonds of their selfish separate self. You often feel this way towards me yourself my son."

"No!" Sadly, the truth was yes. While I loved him more than I could ever imagine loving anyone, I often hated him periodically, and that hurt him deeply. I didn't know how badly until my time to be a teacher came. I guess it's the old "parental curse" - "some day you'll grow up and have kids, and, God forbid, they treat you this way, then you'll see."

"I want to help, Father. I want to be a teacher. Is there anything I can do to speed it up?"

"Before you can be a good teacher, you must first be a good student; to be able to fully give, you must first have fully given-up. A cup cannot be filled unless it is first empty. Real 'Teaching' cannot be contrived, cannot be something you 'try' to do. It will come in its own time, when you have totally surrendered to the Universal Spirit and become an instrument of that will; not when you 'want' to be a teacher. And think carefully. If you stay to be a teacher, new karma is created, and you are no longer absolved of all your past karma. Teaching begins the final stage of dealing with your karma, and brings with it the most difficult times of your life. You also take on karma from your students."

Finding Your Teacher

I've already told you of part of my personal experience in finding my teacher in this lifetime. But there are a few more details you may want to hear about, should you choose to have a personal true teacher.

There are several steps in "getting" a teacher. Such a relationship takes two people, and it is a two way street. For there to be a teacher there must be a student. The teacher must be true (Universally Conscious and thus radiating Universal Spirit) and the student must be receptive. Otherwise, little or nothing, will happen. So number one, you must be truly willing, receptive, humble and ready to be a good student. Next, you must find a teacher and discriminate their validity. Make sure they are real, not a charlatan, and right for you on your path. Once you think you have found your personal true teacher, you must then deal with any doubts or reservations you may have. Then when you're sure, ask the teacher to help you, and totally commit, dedicate yourself as a student.

Unfortunately, true teachers are rare. Very rare. There are various kinds of true teachers, of different paths, but only some are specifically "right" for you, and where you are at on your path. As far as the true teachers of the Atlantean Children of the Law of One are concerned, there have always been about a thousand of them on Earth at any given time (fluctuating according to births/deaths, old teachers choosing to leave, new teachers arising, etc.), but when you consider that there are about five billion people on the planet, the ratio was pretty thin already. And now, after the attacks, there are only hundreds of our true teachers. And at best, you only get a chance at one in your lifetime. There may be many different teachers we find along the way, who are helpful to our development. But most of us just have one special teacher who is meant for us, perfect for us, because they are from our particular soul group, or near it.

"Father, was finding a true teacher always the same? I already know what happens with our tradition, but what about those who are not, but once were and have gone so far off their path, but that are now looking to return. Or, what about those of *other* paths, that need or want to change to this path. What do the ancient teachings say about how to find a true teacher for those who are not already of the Children of the Law of One?"

"There are no teachings of the Atlantean Children on this, for it *was* the path for those who fell from their spiritual state in those days - at least of the Atlanteans, and even for some of those of Mu, and the others, who originally belonged to our general soul groups. Thus, it is 'newer' 'ancient' teachings that deal with such things. But regardless of the path, it's always been the same whether it was praying for guidance, or finding a true teacher. It involves an inner change, and an inner crying out."

"You have said I am to write about the teachings for the masses in the future, what should I say about this specifically?

"Specifically, for finding a teacher, there are two things to be done, two ways. Write this down Peniel. This you should write: if you really want a true teacher, you 'call' for your teacher - you do an affirmation inside yourself, proclaiming before the Universal Spirit, declaring, with meaning and feeling, that you are ready to really 'go for it' - that you want whatever you need to change and become one with God - that you are ready to be purified. Once you have really done this, AND really begun to listen to your own Inner Being (through your Inner Voice - that still, silent, voice of truth), then you're ready and it is time. Then you will find your teacher. But don't expect your teacher to be wearing a sign, or seek you out and say, 'Hey, I'm your teacher'. It's your duty to seek, find, and initiate the 'contract'. And don't ignore the obvious. It may be one who was already there in your life for some time, but that you did not have eyes to see previously (because you weren't ready) - you may not have even known the person was a teacher, depending on their guise. More likely, it may be a new player who 'shows up' in your life, or someone you heard about from another source (and it's your responsibility to seek him out from there). However, whoever, or whatever the circumstances, your true teacher comes into your life because you have 'called' or 'prayed' for such help and guidance, NOT because he is looking for students."

Making Sure You've Found a True Teacher

"Let's say someone has done that, and they think they've found a true teacher, what do the teachings say about how to be sure you have a true teacher?"

"This is a dilemma that has always existed. There are so very many fakes and 'fakirs' out there. Appealing to selfish spiritual 'ego trips' is a lucrative business for greedy fakes. And the separate self *wants* people to choose the fakes, or the unenlightened, rather than the true teachers. So people must be VERY discriminating about who is or isn't a true teacher - *before* they become their student."

"Why *before* they become their student Father, a person can just leave anytime they realize the person is a fake, right?"

"True, but sometimes there are teachers along a person's path, fake or real, that are not your true teacher, yet they are part of your path, and you are meant to leave them when your consciousness expands past what theirs is, or what they can offer. They are stepping stones to the sincere seeker, and traps to the insincere. But your true teacher is the only one that represents the ultimate demise of the selfish separate self, and the return of control to your Inner Being, to the will of the Universal Spirit. So to those who think they *are* the separate self (which is everyone who is not enlightened), the true teacher is the hardest one to deal with, one your self wants to run away from like a scared animal, and at the same time, the one most desirable and attractive to your Inner Self, your True Self. So you must discriminate clearly, before you dedicate to being a student, because *after* you really do find a true teacher and commit, and dedicate to being his student, your separate self will begin working on ways to get away, to escape its fate in this life and death struggle. It will generate false Inner Voices in attempts to confuse and mislead you, and make you think it is not your true teacher, or many other things in an attempt to mislead you and get you away from the true teacher, and thus, you will need to stick by your decision to get through it, regardless of all this misleading

200

(which can seem very real and valid). This requires great respect, humility, commitment, and dedication, that should not be retracted once the decision is made, unless there are *truly* Inner Voice alarms going off that something is very, very wrong."

We have compiled a list of a few things that may help you make this *prior* discrimination. The list is not complete however, and there are other warning signs of a fake. And the list may not apply to some teachers, because they are not "fakes" - yet they may not be an enlightened "true teacher". Plus, these things are not written in stone, and you need to use your own judgement, common sense, and Inner Voice. Finally, *do not* use the list to judge your teacher *after* you have decided they are your true teacher, because it is probably your separate self trying to deceive you with rationalizations and a false Inner Voice, in order to find an excuse to leave your teacher, or give up.

Possible Signs of a False Teacher:

1) Charging money. Unfortunately, the truth of the matter is that there are people out there who claim to be teachers, guides, gurus, channelers, or whatever, who are actually just con artists who are in it for the ego trip, for money, power, or all of the above. I'm not talking about psychic readers, therapists, seminar or lecture givers who do a limited specific service for a fee (whether legitimate or not). I'm talking about those who claim to be teachers, and say they want to help free you from your pain, your bonds, and transform your life spiritually, or give you important spiritual knowledge - and put a price on it. There is NO WAY a truly compassionate being could put a price on this. Could you think of a justification to deny peace of mind, and attaining enlightenment because of money? It is one thing if there are truly allowances to provide free spiritual aid for anyone who really has no financial capability, but in general, if someone is putting a price on such services, they don't really care about others. How could they??? And if they don't really care, can they be someone who can really help you spiritually? Obviously not.

Traditionally, while true teachers don't take money for their teaching, they do expect a dedicated monk, or full-time student to give up all their possessions - even if it is nothing. Generally people want to support the path they believe in, and put their possessions at the disposal of their teacher. This can be as little as a whistle, a bowl of rice, a bike, or as much as an estate or multi-national corporation. Or in my case with my teacher, nothing. But as has been said, it is easier for a rich man to get to heaven than for a cigarette to get through the eye of a needle. So most students usually have little or nothing anyway, because its too hard for people with big bucks to give anything up (although it has been known to happen).

It is fine to support teachers. In fact, it is a spiritual obligation, and a tradition as old as time. In some parts of Asia, monks line up to be given food from the townspeople, who are also poor. But the townspeople still support the monks - those who have given up all else to devote their lives to finding, or serving, God, and thus spiritually serving the people. Many cultures not only provide food, but work, furniture, or whatever they have to offer. So it is fine to offer or give teachers what you can, even money and such possessions in this modern world, **but** a true teacher doesn't expect it, demand it, or require it, and nothing will be different between you regardless. A true teacher doesn't charge, or expect to get anything materially from his work, *period*. He knows that the Universal Spirit takes care of its servants. A true teacher will work with you as long as you truly and totally ded-

201

icate your life to becoming an instrument of Universal Will. If you are truly sincere in this yourself, you will give everything you have to your teacher. But again, it is not expected, and I have seen it done otherwise myself. But what if you have nothing to give, as in my case? No one cares, *if* they are legitimate. On the other hand, if you have a lot to give, and you don't want to, it shows how sincere you *aren't* - and how much selfishness and greed has a hold on you. But again, I have seen it done, and wealthy students accepted, even though their selfish greed still has hold over them. But what can you expect when all students are still under control of their selfish separate selves. When that is still in control, it's easy to give nothing if you have nothing to give, but hard if you do.

"Tithing" for community, or "church" activities to help others, is an entirely different issue, involving householder type situations, and fine if you agree with the work that is being done, or the support being given, with those funds. A student who becomes a monk, generally gives up everything when they join a traditional order, whether it is to the order, or to a more needy cause. But if they have nothing, it makes no difference.

2) Telling you (or others telling you) to do anything the teacher says, *regardless* of what it is. Because a true teacher has transcended their separate self and ego, they have no **need or desire** to be "right", or to "control" you. Most importantly, he is very concerned that you are not controlled by anyone else, whether it is him, someone else, or your selfish separate self. He will point out the truth to you, *urge you* to give control of yourself to your Inner Being, and do what you know is right - but *only* what you *know* is right. A true teacher will be the first to tell you that if he ever tells you something that is truly contrary to the dictates of your Inner Voice, something is wrong, and do not listen to it - and run, don't walk, to the nearest exit. Just *make sure* it *isn't* the voice of your separate self that is trying to throw you off course.

3) The teacher pursues students. True teachers are here to serve you, but it is not a pleasant task. They neither *like* having students/followers, nor personally *want* them, but they *will* accept them if it is the Will of God, and the student really wants to change. But they also know that only those who *really want to change,* and *really want* the teacher to dispel their illusions, are up to the great task of changing. A true teacher may "show up" in your life if you are praying for that, but even then, if you want a true teacher, *you* will have to pursue *the teacher*, indicate or prove your readiness and dedication, and specifically ask him to be your teacher.

4) The teacher stresses "self", boosts your ego, or tells you of the great things your *self* can accomplish, or abilities and power your *self* can attain. The true teacher is not there to reinforce or "empower" your self. The true teacher is there to help you de-throne the separate self, and "crown" your Inner Self as your new lord. He may tell you of what you will selflessly be able to accomplish, when you change, but all abilities and powers are attributed to surrendering to, and being in the service of, God.

5) Promises of wealth or success. The true teacher will not tell you that following their teachings will make you more successful, wealthy, or that you will benefit in any material way as a result of spiritual growth. The true teacher will tell you that there are only three benefits, none of which you can take to the bank: a) The peace of mind that comes from making your separate self your servant instead of your master. b) The joy that comes from helping others. c) Real freedom.

6) They push their dogma. A true teacher has no **need** to make other people accept that their teachings are true and should be followed. They know that people will not "see" until they are ready, and also know that truth is truth, and those who are ready will come to the same conclusions in time.

7) The teachings are like a political rally - based in emotion and contrived "issues" that work on the group's popular sentiment, or they make a "show" of spirituality.

Many false teachers control people via charisma and rhetoric. A true teacher is charismatic, intense, and inspirational - but the words will always have reason, purpose, meaning, and be based in simple truths and Unselfish Love. Clearly defining this for you is difficult. You need to "feel" enough of your Inner Voice, to know the difference. For instance, I once went to a lecture by a "famous" guru from India. One of the things that told me something was false about this person, was that he was "blessing" people with an Ostrich feather - supposedly sending energy through it. Why did he need a feather, let alone the fancy Ostrich feather? It was purposeless, other than being an "impressive" show. And it did make for a great "spiritual show", which distracted from the lack of *real* spirituality. But the first thing that really made my "Inner alarms" go off, and told me something was wrong, was that they made the men sit on one side of the auditorium, and the women on the other, even couples. What for? If it is a celibate path, that's fine. If you are a follower or student of such a path, and those were your beliefs, fine, they aren't really harmful to anyone. But it was a public lecture for the masses. And it's not like people were "making out" or having sex in the aisles, "offending" the guru (who shouldn't be offendable if he were for real anyway). The interaction between the polarities (sexes) is the foundation of life and creation throughout the Universe, not just human life. Mandatorily dividing the sexes at a public lecture, even if it was to "minimize distractions" was absurd, overly controlling, and it was overriding my free will and all others there who wanted to sit with their spouses, dates, or soul-mates, without even a really good reason - it was thus very "wrong" in the sense of "false", and being against the flow of the Universe. It was nothing but a power trip, perhaps based in Indian culture, but ridiculous, and a power trip nonetheless. A true teacher may still have trappings of their culture, but they have transcended the limitations and falsehoods of their culture, and hold Unselfish Love above all else, including their own tradition. Like I said, deep down in my Inner Voice, alarms were going off. There are some ashrams or monasteries that practice celibacy, and men and women will keep separate quarters. But that is far different, and it is right for that path. That doesn't trigger my Inner Voice alarms at all, but at this lecture, the sexual separation was purposeless and an "un-true" action that reeked of ego and control for the sake of control. What this false "guru" was doing made me cringe inside, and would do the same for anyone who was really seeking true spirituality, rather than looking for a spiritual ego trip.

8) Their ego gets offended for *any* reason. Again, a true teacher has transcended their selfish separate self, and with it, the separate self's defensive ego. Ego changes to become nothing but "selfless confidence", the knowingness that they can do whatever the Universal Spirit requires of them, and that forces of the Universal Spirit will work through them if it is within Universal Will. Questioning them about *anything,* insulting them, or verbally attacking who they are, gets no normal "ego" rise from them. An exception to this is if you have already become their student, then questioning them about things that are not in conflict with your own inner voice is just a game your self is playing.

9) "Channeling" of a certain kind (explained later, and in the next chapter).

10) Lack of Unselfish Love. A true teacher will probably be the first person you have ever met, that really Loves - totally and Unselfishly. He loves you more than his self. If you are at all sensitive, you will feel this. If you find instead, that awareness or concern for others is lacking, or there is a lack of Unselfish Love, kindness, and caring, it's not the real thing.

Signs of a True Teacher:

After Zain explained the things people should beware of, he went on about what they should look for in a true teacher.

"Are you still getting all this written down?"

"Yes."

"Good. Like I just said, a true teacher is probably the first person anyone has ever met that REALLY loves them. A regular person (selfish separate self) who's separate self is in control, is basically like a drain, an attention or energy vampire, a 'black hole' (which is like the opposite polarity of a star or Sun) - it is always really just looking to 'take', just concerned with what it can get. When the separate self is in control, a person still has a 'love-life', may have had many 'love' relationships, and may be 'in love', but they don't even really know what love is - they have never really experienced it. What they have experienced is someone 'stroking their ego' at times, giving them pleasure at times, giving them (their separate self) attention at times. They 'love' this, so they develop possessive attachments to these 'pieces of property' that they call 'lover, or spouse'. But a person with Universal consciousness, a true teacher, is like a Sun, always giving, always shining, to everyone, in every direction, all the time. So, again, as I said, it will likely be the first person someone ever experiences REAL Love from. And this is very necessary for a student to experience. There is an ancient saying: "It takes a candle to light a candle".

"Yes, I read that in one of the old teachings. I understand it, I think. It clearly relates to enlightenment, but I take it you are also relating it to Unselfish Love?"

"Certainly! If you have never experienced true Love, if you have never really been Loved, how can you know what Love is? How can you be Loving, give Love, when you don't even know what *true* Love feels like on the receiving end, OR the giving end? The teacher is a candle that gives you your first exposure to this light, then, with your acceptance, 'lights' you.

Another way to identify your true teacher is how his teachings affect you. If you have arrived at the place on your path in which you are ready for a teacher, you will have enough receptivity to your own Inner Voice that the teachings of a true teacher will 'resonate' within you, so to speak. You will intuitively sense the 'truths' he speaks. This is because your Inner Being (the part of you that is Universal Spirit), and the teacher's Inner Being, are One in the same. As a seeker, a student, you are not very in touch with your own Inner Being. That's because of the smoke-screen of thoughts and desires that your selfish separate-self has put between you and your own Inner Being. But the teacher is totally in touch with, and manifesting, *his* Inner Being. So when the teacher speaks, it is like feeling your own Inner Being, and hearing the voice of your own Inner Voice. This 'reminds' you of your true self, and the truth you already know, but that you have just clouded over. It pierces your veil of separateness and 'rings your bell of inner truth'."

"That's how I felt when I saw that broadcast. I knew it was what I was looking for, but I didn't know you were going to be my teacher."

"It was not time. All you knew at the time, was that it was truth, and what you were looking for. But when you find one who's actions and words 'ring an intuitive bell of truth' within you, that is probably your true teacher, because there aren't many around.

Getting back to the subject, Peniel, remember that it is important that if a person finds such a one who rings the bell of Inner truth, that they should immediately do whatever they must to resolve any doubts they may harbor about the entity. Tell the people of the world this: when you have an opportunity, and if you have any doubts, talk to him about your doubts - the separate self may be creating doubts to keep you from finding your teacher. Argue about your doubts if you want. Challenge the teacher's truths and methods. That is the time to do it - at the beginning of the relationship. For at the onset of finding your teacher, doubts can also be helpful because they allow you to discriminate true teachers from false. But doubts that come *after* you have already worked through your initial doubts and dedicated yourself to having your teacher in your life, are a hindrance because they create confusion and lack of love, where faith and trust should abide instead. These are doubts generated from the separate self to try and lead you away so it can retain control.

When you are finally sure about your potential teacher, jump in with both feet, don't look back, and give the process your ALL. For this will be the opportunity for you to love someone more than yourself, open up and surrender to the Universal Spirit, and let go of that which has been the cause of all the problems and pain from the beginning: SEPARATION FROM GOD. SELFISHNESS! Author's note: Spiritual growth via love and devotion to an enlightened teacher has been called Bakti yoga in some of the Indian/Yogic traditions. And you find this said in the I Ching (Wilhelm/Baynes translation):

"The supreme revelation of God appears in prophets and holy men. To venerate them is true veneration of God. The will of God as revealed through them, should be accepted in humility; this brings inner enlightenment and true understanding of the world, and this leads to great good fortune and success."

Just so that is not misunderstood, I should point out again though, that a true teacher does not want worship, blind obedience, followers, etc. He is simply a loving, undistorted mirror that shows you both your true Inner Being, and your illusions of selfish separateness. The teacher just wants to be of help in your own process of growth, one that *you choose*. He wants to get it over with as quickly as possible, with as little hassle as possible, get you to enlightenment and on your way.

If someone wants you to do whatever they say, or believe whatever they say, because they are God manifested on Earth, or whatever, - watch out. When a *true* teacher wants you to do something, or realize something, they want you to do it *only* if it is right and true, not just because they say so.

Learning From a Teacher
Listen to a Teacher to Hear yourself

Because you are just beginning to listen to your Inner Voice, your selfish separate self still has a lot of control and tries to confuse you with many different and conflicting "voices"/thoughts in an effort to influence you, and throw you off track. You must learn to listen only to the Inner Being, and remember, it's a still *silent* voice. [A word of warning, if you are actually "hearing voices" telling you things, they are *not* your Inner Voice, and listening to them could be very harmful.]

Zain went on to explain how a teacher helps you learn to hear your silent "Inner Voice".

"Learning to listen to your Inner Voice, is one of the areas where a teacher serves you. The separate self is always throwing around thoughts to maintain its existence. If you really 'still' the mind, the separate self ceases to exist. So it doesn't want to be 'stilled'. Remember, giving up its role as master and becoming servant to the spirit represents death to the separate self, and it's going to fight like 'hell' to 'stay alive', using trickery, severe emotional pain - everything at its disposal. The separate self is a very, very clever little devil. And while it would prefer to keep your mind filled with selfish thoughts, if that is not possible, ANY thought is more desirable than its demise, even painful thoughts, depressing thoughts, seemingly 'spiritual' thoughts, or whatever. So it keeps the 'monkey mind' cranking out all kinds of thought-voices. These voices constantly 'chatter', grabbing your attention. The constant chatter overwhelms the still, silent, Inner Voice. All these thoughts are like a mental 'noise' that 'drown out' the silent truth - which is presented by the Inner Voice. A teacher clearly mirrors your Inner Voice, giving you a course to make your way through that 'sea' of mental thought-voices of deception and illusion. This both teaches you to be in tune with your Inner Voice, and also provides you with a means to know what your Inner Voice is saying in the meantime (while you learn to do it yourself)."

"So once you can hear your Inner Voice, you are all set."

"Not exactly. There is a bit more to it. The selfish separate self can even use information received from your Inner Voice, to help trick you. If you aren't certain, or totally clear about your Inner Voice, you may not know this is even happening. Since your teacher is like an external manifestation of your own Inner Being and speaks as that Inner Voice of truth, one of his functions is to *re-affirm,* or *confirm,* what your Inner Voice tells you. This helps you through those times of indecision when the separate self generated mind chatter obscures, or makes it difficult to clearly hear the Inner Voice of truth, or your self is using it to trick you."

"So when you 'hear' some truth from your Inner Being and your separate self picks up on it, twists it around and rationalizes it away behind a wall of lies, your manifested Inner Being mirror of truth, the 'teacher', cuts right through the trickery, illusions and blocks, reinforces the truth, and sends you on your way up the path?"

"Precisely."

Doing Your Part

Having a teacher is not going to do you any good, unless you are receptive to him, and you really want to change. You, your self, must develop an attitude of humility, openness, receptivity towards the Inner Being (Universal Spirit) in order to hear your Inner Voice, follow your Inner Voice, find your natural balance, and take your place in the Universal Order.

One more time - the fundamental precepts of the Children's teachings is that **All Inner Beings are One.** The balance, attitude, or relationship, that exists between you and your Inner Being, is the same relationship that you have with your "teacher". Again (this is important to get), the true teacher, is nothing more, or less, than your own Inner Being, clearly manifested before you through another person; a person who is clearly manifesting his own Inner Being. A person's reaction to, or attitude towards a true teacher is dependent on the relationship they have with their own Inner Being. If it is a good relationship, if they like their Inner Being, they will like a true teacher. If they are internally blocked and closed down to their own Inner Love, they will be uncomfortable, fear, dislike, or hate a true teacher, to various degrees depending on the severity of their blocks.

Not only is it necessary to make sure you have the right attitude towards your Inner Being and teacher, but you must be prepared to work, work hard, and persevere. You need a die-hard attitude of "Never give up", and a positive attitude towards accomplishing your goal. TRYING to do it will not work. Trying builds in failure by the very concept of the word. Either do, or do not.

Ultimately, everyone simply does what they want, and if you want to do it, you will, if you don't, you won't. A great skill to have along the way is the ability to *make* the things you *must do*, into things you *want to do*.

Beginning With Your Teacher
My Personal Experience

Many feelings (other than an introvert's ego fears like I had) come to a student when they start working with their teacher. After all, you have met someone who really loves you, knows you better than yourself, and is One with God.

For one thing, I felt happy, safe, and carefree, like a very small child again - only in the good ways. I recaptured the feelings I had when I was so young that I believed that everything was OK, that my parents were like God because they could take care of anything, and keep me safe and secure. The feeling of total security was incredible. I had completely forgotten this feeling. It was buried under the walls of trauma that were built during "growing up". It felt wonderful to not only remember and recapture the light hearted secure feelings, but to discover a new level of it - one that would never leave me. I cried in remorse, relief, and happiness.

These new/old feelings came to me, not just because of my teacher, but because my exposure to him made me realize that the Universal Spirit *really was* in charge of everything, and would "take care of" its children who came back into the fold - and that this was for real, not an illusion like the security I felt with my parents. Zain then felt more like a father to me - a kind, loving, big, powerful, father "supreme". It really made sense why I felt like calling him "Father" (and did) - it felt that way both in the personal sense, and in the "representative of 'Father' aspect of the God" sense. In fact, this is where the use of the term entered into Catholicism, and a few other religions.

There are many other feelings that may be associated with working with your teacher. Some people will feel pain as the teacher's presence reveals old wounds, childhood traumas, etc.. These can come to the surface and come to light. Then they can be healed.

My *initial* feelings upon first meeting Zain were not so lofty and serene, however. Finding your teacher can also be a frightening experience, depending on your ego. For me it was both a wonderful experience, and frightening, at the same time. It was an incredible, happy surprise, because until I found him, I was in deep despair. I could not seem to reach my greatest goal - a path with real solid, consistent truth, and finding other people who were living it. And then one day I heard a man speak, whose words "rang my inner bell of truth", and it eventually turned out to be my teacher! But hearing him speak also frightened me, because when I first met him, I was an introvert with a very big ego to protect. While boisterous extroverted people are often looked at as being egotistical, it is generally the introverts, also sometimes called "shy" or "the quiet ones", that are even worse, and often have the *biggest* egos, and greatest lack of humility. They are introverts "by design" - they created a "shy" shell to hide themselves from other people, so that none of their faults would be seen or confronted. Teachers actually prefer to work with extroverted "jerks", than nice, seemingly gentle and sweet introverts, because extroverts are more "up-front" about their thoughts and feelings, which facilitates the teacher/student "process". I had a huge ego, and was a big introvert.

The "process" that a student undergoes with a teacher is something like "exorcism". A teacher needs to have a student that exposes the aspects of his/her selfishness and negative programming, in order to eradicate them. For a teacher to do his job, having a student that "speaks their mind", even when it is asinine, is far superior to having an introverted student that hides his thoughts both from himself and others. An extrovert who ALSO has a humble attitude is the best combination for learning quickly (not quite as rare as a cruise ship in Arizona).

Anyway, let's go back in time again, to when I had not "really" recognized, or acknowledged that Zain was my personal true teacher yet. I was still avoiding it, "wondering" where I would find my teacher. I was a radical introvert, so I tried to avoid the "intense" Zain, and avoid the confrontations, exposures, and attacks on my selfish separate self's ego, that I knew would be inevitable if I exposed myself. I avoided asking questions, or even being seen. It was the "sitting in the back of the classroom" syndrome in the extreme - more like, stay away from the classroom entirely if possible. But it was ultimately unavoidable, and the inevitable attacks on my ego were forthcoming, just as I feared.

I may have mentioned this earlier, but one day Anastasia invited me to join her, and do the "Star exercise" technique with a large group of elder and novice monks, and Zain. The exercise was being done outside, with he, and about a hundred monks. Zain led the exercise. We were holding hands forming a giant circle. During, and after the exercise, I was seeing "vibrating energy" everywhere. Even though I was afraid of him, and he was virtually surrounded by a swarm of novice and elder monks which made it even more intimidating to my introverted psyche, I had wanted to "break the ice" and talk to him, so I figured this would be the right time - because I finally had something "profound" and "spiritual" to bring up, to impress him with. And I assumed he, and everyone else, would be rightfully impressed with my spiritual prowess and observations. Finally, I made my first direct statement to him, asked my first question, and was dealt the ego-devastating truth.

"Zain, I was seeing this energy everywhere when we were doing the Star exercise."

He snapped (not really, but it felt like it), "It's only phenomenon, don't pay any attention to it". Ouch, my ego! He was in the middle of another conversation that I had interjected my ill-timed, timid statement into. Here I'd thought I'd finally found something safe and profound to say - something impressive. Boy, did he have a pin for my bubbles! I didn't realize it at the time, but his response was dictated by my way of being most of the time - introverted, contrived, and egotistical. That's what really came across when I made the remark, and his response was to that -

208

dealing with that, and trying to get "a rise" out of me, more than it was an actual answer to the question or statement I was making. Even though his answer was true, was accurate, it could have gone many different ways had *I* been different. Tricky stuff this teacher/student "exorcism" process.

When I got past the ego fears enough to "wake up and smell the tea", I saw what I had already sensed and feared - rather, what my selfish separate self was afraid of. I couldn't get away with anything with this man. He knew me better than I knew myself. He was my personal true teacher. Some time later, with my tail between my legs, I meekly asked him to be my teacher. And it began.

Handing him a line of bull was not only useless, but would arouse a more intense response. The more I defended my "self", the more intense he would become. When I tried to get away with lying, or resisting the truth, his intensity to my blocks would result in him yelling at me - not with normal anger, but like the wrath of nature abused. The vibration of his booming voice struck to the core of my solar plexus. Sometimes he would yell when he wasn't "getting on my case" about anything. Just yelling for "the hell of it" about whatever, maybe not even related to me, but he did it just to shake me up and see if some ego "buttons to push"/ego sore spots, etc., would pop up to work with.

When I got past trying to get away with anything, and when his intensity no longer had an effect on me, our relationship turned very warm and close. I remember that last time he ever yelled at me, just like it was this morning. I didn't have my usual ego reaction, which he noticed immediately.

He looked me in the eye and said, "That's not going to work on you anymore?"

I shook my head, "No". He broke out in the biggest "pleased as punch" grin I'd ever seen. My learning required no more "shake 'em up" yelling tactics from then on, thus it included none.

The Closest Relationship

Your teacher is the most important relationship you will ever have, for one, because of who he is (your Inner Being manifested), and what he will do for you. But your teacher also becomes your best friend - actually, *far more* than your best friend. He is someone who loves you, and who you may love, more than anything before. The true teacher even becomes a life-line that you cling to in your darkest hours when your separate self is going through its "death pangs". But the teacher student relationship is not all sweetness and light. There is the painfully hard work ahead of demolishing the walls your separate self has built.

Let the Testing Begin

When you decide you want to change, and you make the decision to "go for it", to set foot on the path and devote your life to the Universal Spirit, things start changing fast. In one way or another, if you have essentially made such an internal commitment, it is as if you have said, "OK God, I'm ready to come back. I am ready for anything I must do in order to change, and serve as a vehicle for you". And so the first step of your cross-bearing path to the crucifixion begins. An intense flow of heavy "tests" hits you. Trials of pain, suffering, and temptation come one after another from all directions and sources in your life, sometimes many at one time. Again, remember the ancient text, "God falls hardest on those he wants most". An old lover who you once wanted to marry, may call you up out of the blue after 10 years, and they're rich, and they want to marry you. Your father may die. Your mother is sick and needs you to tend her night and day, and your brother is worthless for such things. You get the best job offer in your life - but it would mean moving away from where your path lies. Your grown child desperately needs your help for some non-spiritual reason, yet it is a worldly valid, or "normally" important reason - something that you would be "obligated" to do ordinarily. You name it, it will come out of the woodwork to lead you away from your true spiritual path. You will only be able to pass by such diversionary life experiences without falling by the wayside of your path into a diversionary trap, IF: 1) Your consciousness is expansive enough to see the bigger picture, to see the greatest good for all people that you can do with your life if you stay on your path, and, 2) You have the conviction to follow your path, regardless of the things that try to lead you off. Then there is the pain of following your real path that comes up.

Zain reminded me once, "The path is like a bed of roses, flowers-thorns-flowers-thorns, but if one walks in the footprints of those that have walked there before, the masters/teachers, then one can avoid the pitfalls of the thorns...and the flowers."

Your teacher is also a bed of roses, thorns and all.

"The true teacher is also part of the intense flow of tests you go through. He draws out the things that keep you from Loving Unselfishly - the negative manifestations and programming of the selfish separate self - and then he reflects them back to you. If you are open to this reflection of yourself, and use it to change, it is a mild event, and will even be pleasant if you are humble and really desiring to see the truth about yourself. But if you are blocked, if you lack humility and resist seeing the truth, the Universal Spirit will present the facts more intensely through the teacher's Inner Being, to your Inner Being. The degree of intensity increases in direct proportion to the degree of resistance. And if you continue to be blocked to that, God will teach you in even more intense ways, through life itself - the school of hard knocks. This is much like the way a lightning strike works. Lightning is created when electricity of one polarity, seeks out its opposite polarity to find 'neutralization'. If something blocks its path, or resists as it tries to flow through to its 'ground' polarity, then it will intensely 'blow' its way through. But lightning will not explode things in its path that do not resist its flow. Dealing with the Universal Spirit within a teacher is similar. When the teacher/student process of exorcism is happening, it is like that lightning. If there are things in the student that 'block' the flow of truth from the Universal Spirit, it will intensely 'strike' like lightning at the negative blocks. But if the student is being open and not resisting the truth the teacher is reflecting, and the Spirit finds no blocks, the electricity passes through with little or no trauma, or actually becomes an ecstatic experience.

So when something is presented to a person that requires a change, they can fight it and things will get intense, or if they let go, open up, and Love Unselfishly, a neutralization will take place. The neutralization of negative coming into contact with positive. The neutralization of light coming into contact with darkness. This is the process of true exorcism that the teacher performs. This can only take place if a person allows it however. After all, everyone has free will. A person should want it more than anything, and the more they want it the faster and easier their work with a teacher will be. But in any case, a person must 'let go' and let the process happen. And they must WORK at giving, in their thoughts, words, and actions."

Let Go and Let God

Zain knew my fears, and desires, and when we began the process of freeing me of them, this became painfully evident. For instance, he didn't know it, but I hated washing dishes more than anything. My mother made me do it as I child and I'd developed a major repulsion and "issue" over it. On the other hand, I loved playing music. I began playing when I was 5, and I had a gift for it. And as I said in the chapter on sub-conscious programming, I knew it could effect large numbers of people. So I had hoped that one day I would do that as my profession. But Zain seemed to have a pin for every one of my separate-self's bubbles.

During my first personal private conversation with Zain, I intended to tell him my *desires* regarding helping people through music. And I did. But the problem was, while everything I was saying about music was true, it also was a *personal desire*. The cancer of my selfish separate self was infecting my abilities, and affecting my goals. Not to mention creating a huge stumbling block in my personal growth.

I met with him in a little tent that was set-up just outside the monastery walls, where he was meeting and ministering to the householders who lived there.

"Zain, I wanted to talk to you about my life, and what I will be doing."

"Interesting timing, I wanted to talk to you about the same thing."

I explained all about my ideas for helping the world with music, what I knew, and what I could do. Then the biggest hammer in the world fell on my head.

"If I were you, I'd forget about music. Forget about guitar, you will *never* play one again. We don't even have one here. But we do need a dishwasher for the monastery. And considering what you need, that would be the best work for you for the rest of your life."

Instant ego shock. I was floored. Stunned. Dying. I didn't know what to say. I respectfully (and foolishly) "argued" initially, and intensely.

"But Zain, I've realized that the forces of light work through music, and I have great talent for this. I have written songs, that are positive and uplifting, both lyrically and musically, and some of the lyrics I know were channeled by the hierarchy, because I didn't even know what I was writing, or what the things meant at the time, and now I do. I really think this is at least *part* of my destiny."

"No. I don't think so. I think you will learn and serve God better through washing dishes. This is your destiny as we have seen it."

Of course, I didn't *have* to do these things, I wasn't forced to, but if I didn't, I couldn't stay in the monastery. And being there, and learning and growing spiritually was something I had wanted so much for so many years. Besides, I knew about "tests", and at first, I figured that my conviction was just being tested. I knew this was "standard procedure".

But then the dishwashing started. At first I just counted on it being a temporary test, so it wasn't too horrible. But soon, it became a great struggle. I *hated* doing the dishes, and thus did a poor job - a little bit consciously, and a little bit subconsciously. My bad attitude made me a lousy dishwasher. I was slow, and because of this dishes from one meal would not be ready for the next. Many dishes accidentally broke. Some were left dirty and soapy, making others sick occasionally.

After a month of this, I started wondering if maybe it wasn't a test - maybe it was for real. After three months, I was seriously doubting it was a test, and I was debating with myself if I really wanted to stay and do this forever. My self-centered pre-occupation with being miserable while washing dishes, overwhelmed the better parts of my life. I lost touch with all the wonderful things there, the good life I actually had, and the positive realities of the rest of the life I was leading during the times when I wasn't washing dishes. But even though my separate self tortured me, and filled me with negative thoughts, I kept reminding myself and "remembering" why I was really there. Over and over again. I mustered my will power and conviction, and finally, really, truly, decided to stay, with total conviction - even if dishwashing *was* going to be my job for the rest of my life. As soon as I made that real internal choice, the one that was to me, an irreversible commitment, the great heavy burden I was suffering with, lifted from me. Instantly. I felt happy again. I changed my attitude and with it my approach to doing dishes. I turned my dish washing into a flow meditation, like Tai Chi or a martial art "Kata". Remember earlier I said it is great to have the ability to *make* the things you *must* do, into things you *want to do*. I first applied this here. Dish washing suddenly became so different from the way I had previously experienced it, it was unbelievable. And now, the dishes were cleaned on time, spotless, and none were being broken.

At the end of the very day I made this internal change, Zain came into the kitchen (which he rarely did ordinarily).

"I'm afraid I have bad news for you."

"What is it?" I said worriedly.

"You are needed elsewhere, and will need to give up your duties as dishwasher. I know it will be a great sacrifice." I thought to my self - "smart ass" (in a nice way).

"Why?" I asked calmly.

"You need to train more in the making of music, and the other arts. It has been determined that some of your destiny lies in these areas. You will not have time now for all three - doing the dishes, your regular spiritual training, *and* that special training in music, visual art, and writing. So the dishwashing must be sacrificed." Again, I thought to myself "smart ass". The funny thing was, it really didn't matter much any more. I wasn't even excited or feeling joyous about it. I was already joyous from "letting go", and re-discovering something far more real and important. And I now knew that *whatever* I was physically doing, was not as important as *my consciousness* during my doing of it. In fact, I discovered that my consciousness was the most important thing in my doing of ANYTHING and EVERYTHING.

But nevertheless, I received many instruments (including guitars that they *did* have there), and wouldn't you know it, when I played again, I could play ten times better than before. And I couldn't understand why at the time. It didn't make sense since I hadn't played in so long. I asked Zain about it the next day.

"Zain, why is my instrument playing so very much better and easier than it was before?"

"Because you are beginning to let go and let the Universal Spirit do it through you instead."

But there were new ego blows to come. Next, playing music, which used to be just a pleasurable experience for me, became the very center of my ego target.

My music training was very hard, and involved letting go of everything I thought music had to adhere to, and everything I thought music was. All I had previously learned, was being stomped on and torn apart - scales, notes, styles, methods. They were all broken down. I was required to play drills and scales that made

212

no sense. It was killing my musical sensibilities, preconceptions, and ego. But years later, by the time I was through with "music hell", I had learned total freedom of expression, and letting my higher self come through to play for me. It resulted in music that could never have been done by me before because of the "box" of standards I was trained in. Now, I could express anything that came to me, that came through me. Emotions, feelings, inspiration, and visions could be created in the minds of a listener, that I could have never done on my own.

Years later, I would actually have a great influence, behind the scenes, on the music business, and music that would be made for the masses by the some of the most popular music stars in the world.

Hitting Hard Times

As I went through my transformation and growth at the monastery, I often found it painful and hard. I asked Zain about my trials, and why it was so hard to change and grow sometimes, even when the changes seemed simple. And why I would feel angry with him, even though I wanted him to help me, and that's all he wanted to do.

"Once a person begins the process of 'self-exorcism' with their teacher, they come upon their 'blocks', and if they don't transcend their blocks easily by themselves, then they'll get hit by the lightning, so to speak. And because this process is unrelenting, the student may sometimes feel like their teacher 'picks on them', 'busts them', etc., but it's just one of the separate self's reactions to 'having the squeeze put on it' - the light of truth dispelling its illusions, blocks, and deceptions."

"But sometimes it's so bad, I have actually thought about leaving at times."

"Waves of 'growing pains' come as the separate self uses thoughts and emotions in attempts to confuse and mislead the student. The separate self will rationalize, and defend itself. But fortunately, it is useless to defend yourself against your teacher, because he is your own Inner Being and he knows the truth. This leads the separate self to an unavoidable conclusion - get away from the teacher. A student may start thinking of all kinds of reasons why they should 'escape' from the presence of their teacher. Seemingly good reasons too; at least the rationalizations sound mighty convincing to the battered, self-gratification starved separate self. In extreme cases, they start thinking there is something wrong with their teacher. If this ever happens to you, go over this little checklist:

* **Are you feeling Love?**
* **Are you Loving selflessly?**
* **Or are you feeling sorry for yourself, angry, negative, or 'into your self'?**

Always remember that if you're not feeling love, no matter WHAT the circumstances, then you are NOT seeing clearly, and YOU are causing the problem! You are blocking the love because of some allegedly "GOOD" reason, which cannot really exist! Let go! Give-up! Understand! NOTHING, NO reason is good enough to stop loving, in any circumstance. Not Loving Unselfishly can only make things worse."

"But sometimes it almost feels like physical pain too, it gets so bad."

"There is nothing you can do but endure it, and go through it. Personal growth is often like a physical healing crisis. By enduring the suffering, fever, vomiting, etc., you can, with patience, understanding, humility, and perseverance, know who you really are as your Inner Being emerges from the debris. The soul/Inner

Being is eternally indestructible; when there is nothing left, there is the soul, there is the Spirit, there is your true self. You just need enough love for your teacher to hang on by a thread. Hang in there until it is over. The lasting rewards are far, far greater than the sacrifices and pain."

Chapter Fourteen

Ascended Masters and Channeling

[The ancient teachings regarding "channeling" are very specific. However, at the time when I was at the monastery, what is now called channeling was called either "spiritualism" or "mediumship", and "channelers" were called "mediums". For ease of reading, I will substitute the old phrases (that were actually spoken to me by my teacher), for the modern "channeling" verbiage.]

Ascended Masters

"Father, even before I came here, I read and heard about ascended teachers, although they are usually called ascended masters, or saints, by most people. Some people think it is better to follow them, or their teachings, because they are higher in consciousness than living teachers. Some even claim they have personal contact with them, and 'channel' them. Will you tell me more about this, and perhaps what the ancient teachings say?"

"An ascended master is essentially a true teacher who has left the Earth plane, and gone on to the next plane - a paradise where all who dwell there have achieved the same consciousness of Unselfish Love, Light, and Oneness. Because of their release from the consciousness limitations of the physical plane, they do have greater consciousness. But because of their non-physical state, and their choice to leave this plane and not reincarnate, their greater consciousness has limited applications and usefulness for those of us here on the Earth plane. Thus, they cannot fulfill the duties of, or replace the necessity for, a true teacher.

Early on the path, there are legitimate reasons for some of the kind of interest you mentioned in the ascended ones. People often begin their spiritual quests with a search for truth that brings them to many things, including information about ascended masters. There are books about ascended masters with good and inspiring ideas. When I was young, I was thrilled to find some of these books. But they are only books, and can only do so much for you before you must actually do more with your life."

"Why can't they be as good as a true teacher in the body?"

"It is good to emulate the example set by the lives of *any* true teacher, *including* those who have left this plane. Such 'masters' and 'saints' have left us a history that can help us in our own journeys. They left their footprints on the path through the roses and thorns. But when people take the concept of ascended masters further, and consider them to be their teachers on this physical plane, and follow what they can only *believe to be* their teachings, it leaves openings for many problems. In fact, there are serious problems with trying to follow a being that is not in a physical body."

"But if they may actually have greater consciousness, what could be a problem?"

"Some people also take spiritual advice from disincarnate 'guides' [more about that later]. Others have Gurus that they never see, never live in the presence of. These situations are similar to having an 'ascended' teacher, in that *none of the guiding beings are in your physical presence on the physical plane.* And unless you are already enlightened, even *truly* knowing *anything* about the realities of someone who is not in physical form (let alone knowing their wishes for your guidance), is not really possible with *any amount of true* clarity. And true, precise clarity, is a *must* in such situations as disincarnate guidance, let alone a teacher/student relationship.

Following an ascended teacher, or even one who is out of physical contact, leaves many opportunities for self-deception. It is popular though, primarily because it also provides the perfect rationalization for avoiding real spiritual growth"

"How does it do that?"

"Because you can seem to be totally involved in spirituality, but still deceive yourself and not face your real issues, your real blocks to separation with the One."

"How?"

"Because there is room for 'self-interpretation' because they are not before you in the flesh, TELLING you what you need to know with words you, or other witnesses, cannot avoiding hearing with your ears, GUIDING you in such a way that you *cannot possibly* fool yourself about. That's why 'following' a teacher that is not in an Earthly body is much more desirable to the selfish separate self - you don't have to face up to things you don't want to, and you can interpret their alleged teachings to suit your *self.* Just look at the variations of claims made about what the bible says or what Jesus 'meant'. Or Mohammed 'meant'. People have burned other people alive, in Jesus' name - do you think he meant for them to do so?"

"Of course not."

"And even if you *believe* you are in communication with an out of body being such as an ascended master, you cannot be certain what you are letting yourself 'hear', unless you are already totally free from your selfish separate self. In fact, the separate self would consider that a perfect 'set up'. You think you are following a spiritual teacher, but the separate self 'censors' the 'teachings' and remains in control. How could it be otherwise when the separate self controls your subconscious mind, and most everything else in your life and mind?"

"I guess it couldn't."

"See, you make my point. 'You *guess*' it couldn't. When you are actually in the presence of a teacher, 'in the flesh', your separate self can't get away with self-deceptions. There is no 'guessing', no 'interpretation', no lack of 'clarity'. When you are in the physical presence of such a One, the teacher actively penetrates and exposes your illusions, saying the truths you need to hear right to your face, clarifying it if the self tries to cloud the issue, leaving no room for misinterpretation and leaving you no room for ignoring, or hiding from, the truth. When a teacher is physically before you, they will always clearly tell you when you are not being true to your Inner Being - that cannot be said for an ascended master, guide or a 'long-distance astral' master!"

"Then why would someone prefer to follow an ascended master, instead of a living master, other than that it is more desirable to the separate self?"

"Have you not heard what I am saying? There is no valid reason for this. After all, a true teacher is nothing but an 'ascended master' that has not left the body yet.

A true teacher has experienced the same 'next step' that an ascended master has - death. The death experience is the final step in returning to Oneness with God, and attaining Universal Consciousness, and that is the major transformation that is vital. But after consciously experiencing death, living true teachers have just chosen to return to Earth to help, instead of taking the more pleasurable route of going on to a paradise plane with their enlightened brothers and sisters [see chapter on the "death experience" for detailed explanation]."

Another reason for having a living master instead of presuming to follow a dead one, is the personal attention and personal guidance that you get from a living true teacher. At best, going to channels or following an ascended master for your spiritual growth, would be like learning a *complex* new skill, like brain surgery, by a book or tape (and that's even *if* the information you are getting is true and not from a faker, or a negative disincarnate entity). You can learn knowledge and facts through a book or tape, but to really master a skill, you need "hands on" interactive help from a teacher in the flesh. Having a real teacher in person, in the flesh, at some point in your learning, is invaluable to master a skill - even with minor skills, like golfing, scuba diving, gourmet cooking, etc., let alone something like spiritual enlightenment. The more important the skill, the more *vital* it is to have a teacher with you showing you the ropes, especially at final stages of learning. An inexperienced mountain climber in their right mind, wouldn't think of learning to climb Mount Everest with the help of an "ascended" mountain climber. Yet the most difficult and important skill in the world - achieving Oneness with God and learning to become a teacher - they can supposedly totally achieve with only books and spirit guides? No. In order to learn and develop, we need to try applying what we've learned, then we need the criticism and feedback of a good teacher, in order to develop enough to master the skill. And attaining spiritual enlightenment, and breaking free from our programming and the bonds of the selfish separate self, is the greatest learning challenge you will ever have. Attempting it without a real living teacher giving you direct "in your face", inescapable, totally clear guidance and feedback, is like running around in circles chasing your tail. Or competing in the olympics without *ever* having a coach.

Getting "channeled information" is not much different than reading a spiritual book. It can help and inspire if it is true. But even if the information is actually 100% true, there is no criticism to the selfish separate self, no real feedback, no Unselfish Love to ignite your own, no example of manifesting the Universal Spirit, and no light to pierce the illusions and confusions "the darkness of self" throws up around you. How many times have you heard someone channel another being that was "getting on *the channeler's own* case" and telling them they'd better get their act together, and change, or behave selflessly. Probably never. How many times has an ascended master *really* made anyone see and face all their *real* blocks that they were totally avoiding? You can't get away with anything with a real in the flesh true teacher. Even this book you are reading now, might help you, but it can only take you so far.

My Dad's Better than Your Dad

Zain pointed out some other fascinating issues I hadn't considered about ascended masters in a later conversation:

"Consider this: while some of the great, so-called 'ascended masters' *are* true

217

teachers that have indeed 'gone on', other famous 'dead' masters who's books you've read, are only assumed to be 'ascended'. They continue to reincarnate, and are here now, in other bodies with other names. You may not know who they are. Some you know now, but you know not yet who they were. This will come to you in time. You and I have been known by many recognizable names. You are considered an ascended master by some, yet you are here, in a body, right now. You have written many books, and spawned religions. But to some, Peniel, you are not so important as 'ascended master so and so' just because you are only my student, and will only be an 'in the flesh un-ascended master'? But ironically, you *are* ascended master 'so and so'."

"I am?"

"Yes. And people are claiming that they are channeling you right now. Even different lives of yours they are claiming to channel."

"They are? Who was I?"

"If you need to know it will come to you someday. Don't go and start getting yourself on an ego trip, you have a big enough one to deal with as it is. You are just cosmic dust like the rest of us. You are also one with and part of God, like the rest of us. You are a cog that makes up the great One. Nothing more, nothing less. This is all irrelevant in certain BIG ways. While we place all these name tags on various beings that are all just part of the same One Being, we must always remember - The Inner Being is One with the Universal Spirit, and once someone fully manifests their Inner Being, they are the same great being, before or after ascension. Are these saintly beings any less great because they have chosen to reincarnate again and further sacrifice themselves for you by suffering the pains of living amidst the darkness on the Earth, instead of leaving the hardships of this world for the paradise that awaits them in the next plane? No.

And by the way, are you letting people channel you behind my back?"

"Yeah, right. I'm not broadcasting my soul as far as I know."

"No. You would know it if you were dead and possessing someone's body. It's hard to miss something like that."

"But I could sure have some fun later."

"Forget about it."

To summarize, the Inner Being of a living master, is the same Inner Being as any other master, ascended or not. Sure, there are subtle differences in the personalities and souls of true teachers, but the differences are insignificant, and do not provide a legitimate reason to avoid a living master in favor of an alleged ascended master. And they certainly don't replace the work that must be done with a living true teacher. Regardless of who has ascended, and who has not - the same Spirit of all the great saints and sages is ONE, eternally alive and manifesting through present day masters, NOW, in the present, always. And it has always been so. The Spirit is ONE. All Inner Beings are part of, and One with, the One Universal Spirit/Being. Don't confuse the *personalities* of spiritual teachers with what they really were/are in essence. The personality is just an aspect, or projection of, the particular soul/self/individual that was actually a vehicle for the One Spirit. So they are all really the same, inside, where it counts. This is one reason why there are such similarities and connections between so many of the various spiritual traditions from all parts and times of this planet. This consciousness is within us all, and manifesting that Inner Being is a destiny we were all created to fulfill.

"But Father, what of the hierarchy, do we not get guidance from ascended ones ourselves all the time?"

"The ascended ones should only play a *direct* guidance role in your life AFTER you have achieved enlightenment. After you have completed your work with a living master (your true teacher), and attained Universal Consciousness, you then follow the guidance of your Inner Voice, and Universal Will. After this attainment, you have a place in the cosmic order, and are connected with 'the hierarchy' [the vast order of ascended masters/angelic beings who exist in interconnected ranks between us, and the Source, the One]. You are thus both guided by, and watched over by, the hierarchy. But until then, you are indirectly guided and influenced by the hierarchy. Beware of hearing voices or letting any being possess you to speak. That is not the way of the hierarchy, other than *highly* exceptional circumstances, and even then, through one of the enlightened teachers of the Law of One, not a student such as you, elder or not."

"Who is the highest of consciousness in the hierarchy?"

"You already know that!"

"Well... I think so."

"Don't think - know! You know!"

"I'm sorry... God?"

"It is all One, certainly. But.... Remind me to give you some history texts to read. God is All. That's why we call God the Universal Spirit. But that *includes* the hierarchy, it is not the hierarchy in and of itself. The head of the *hierarchy* is the entity who first lead the second wave to rescue those of the first. Can you remember that now?"

"Yes, of course, I'm sorry, it was, is Jesus."

"When our order was founded, he was known in that life as grand master Thoth. The life in which he had his greatest impact on the world, other than his first, was his last, known as Jesus. Although he had great effects, and would be known to you by other names from his other lives."

"Like what?"

"Go fish."

"What?"

"Learn your history son. There are more than two dozen."

"Will you tell me just one at least right now?"

"Joseph. Go read the biblical scrolls about Joseph, and see if you can't *sense,* can't *feel, inside yourself,* that the same Inner Being was the same. Witness the Unselfish Love, the humility, the forgiveness. It is so obvious to the open mind, even if you haven't read the scrolls detailing his incarnations. *You* were even related to him in the flesh, more than one time."

"When was that?! Who?!"

"I have other things I must attend to. And your ego is big enough already."

How could he leave me cliff hanging like that?? True teachers can be so damn enigmatic sometimes. But what can you do? You can't live with them, you can't live on without them.

Stay Tuned to This Channel

Something similar to following ascended masters, is "channeling", or going to a channeler. For those of you who aren't familiar with it, channeling is what occurs when a living person allows an "out-of-body", disincarnate being or spirit guide, to possess the person's body and mind, and provide information. The channeled information is generally given through speech, although it can be writing. When people channel, their goal is usually to channel *higher consciousness* disincarnate beings (ascended masters, spirit guides, etc.).

First let me say that truth is truth, wherever you find it. We should listen to wisdom whether it comes from a wise man or a fool. Or a channeler. And it can and does come from all the above. So if the information you have received from a channeler is positive, and true, give the wisdom the respect it deserves. With that in mind, let's take a broad look at the limitations, and serious problems of channeling.

Channeling has become very popular, and I know that some of you reading this won't want to hear about any problems with it. But the ancient teachings do point out some things that should be carefully considered.

For one, when you reach a certain level of growth on your spiritual path, channeling is "outgrown". And if you have an open mind, the *common sense and truth* revealed in the ancient teachings will shed new light on the entire field of channeling, allowing you to consider some new facts, and make up your own mind. So *please* hear me out *with an open mind*, and **then** decide.

The phenomenon that is called channeling can actually be several *very* different things:

1) Someone channeling an actual disincarnate being;

2) Someone believing they are actually channeling a disincarnate being, but they are actually channeling information from the Inner Being;

3) Someone believing they are actually channeling a disincarnate being, but they are actually channeling information from their subconscious mind;

4) Someone totally faking it.

Let's start by looking at #2 and 3.

Some people really do channel disincarnate beings. Others just *think* they are channeling a higher consciousness being, but they are actually only accessing their own Inner Being. Now this isn't necessarily bad, in fact, it can be safer and yield truer information than channeling a disincarnate being.

Here's how it works. The channeler wants to and *believes* they are going to channel a disincarnate being, but for some reason this doesn't really happen - yet they *think* it does. Instead, what really happens is that they are being protected by their Inner Being, or the hierarchy, and their subconscious creates a guide or ascended master in their mind, in order to realize their desire to access higher information by channeling. But the information is *really* coming from the Inner Being, and/or their subconscious.

For centuries, hypnotists have known about the incredible power of the mind to create the most elaborate stories and scenarios while in a trance. In fact, while some past life regressions are quite real, others are pure fabrications by the subconscious mind - down to details like the stitching in a suit. In part, this phenomenon works via the power of assumption, or power of belief (see chapter on that subject), linked with a strong desire to please the hypnotist or therapist. You can also see this phenomenon at work in both ways with the use of an oracle, like a pendulum. For instance, when people *believe* a pendulum will give them answers from a higher source, *it might,* as long as they really *believe* it. It will even work for a skeptic, as long as the skeptic's subconscious mind believes it. In any case, it's not the pendulum itself that is doing it, it is the user's **belief** that the pendulum does it, or is being guided, or gives them access, which actually **gives** them access. Yet oracles, and the type of channeling we are talking about right now, are in-between mediums - substitutes for being able to more directly, and more purely, get information from the Inner Being *OR the subconscious.* So, both the oracle user, and this certain type of channeler, use their beliefs in their *methods,* to access information from inside themselves - information that they **don't believe** they have access to *otherwise.* Therein lies one of the problems. Using the methods can actually reinforce the belief and programming that the individual can't access the information more directly. And that is a major spiritual limitation to place on yourself. We'll discuss that more in a moment.

As we have established, the type of channeling we are discussing, can access information from *either* the subconscious or the Inner Being. But it generally mixes the two. And therein lies *another* problem. You can get inaccurate information, that you believe is accurate. It can be partly true, but distorted by the subconscious mind's programming. That's because subconscious programming (& possible dark outside influences), can filter, distort, and even totally block out the true and accurate information coming from the Inner Being. I have heard good channeled information, but it wasn't as good or clear as it could be, because of the consciousness of the person, and because of their subconscious programming. But there are times when it's not just a matter of how *good* the information is. The subconscious and conscious beliefs of a person using an oracle or channeling, can **seriously** taint information, and cause a **serious** mis-guidance. And if *serious* life decisions are based on such channeled or divined *mis*-information, a person can make *serious* mistakes in life, that effect both themselves and others. Zain found me using an oracle one day, and told me the following:

"Using oracles and such is fine at a certain level of consciousness, a certain level of spiritual awareness and evolution. There are protections from on high for the novice *who is sincere and has a good heart.* A spiritual innocent is watched over by spiritual guardians, just as human adults watch over human children. But just like when a human child gets older, you expect them to be more aware and responsible about life, our hierarchical guardians expect the same of us as spiritual children. Thus, as you spiritually grow, you must become far more discrete and cautious. If you make a mistake at a higher level of consciousness, the consequences are much more serious. And the more aware a person is, the more serious will be the consequences of ignoring the things you are aware of. As you grow, as you become more aware, you are expected to behave differently. Again, using an example of a child, it is one thing to spin around until you're dizzy, then drive a trike, but it's another thing for a teenager to get drunk and drive a car. You are a spiritual adolescent right now."

"Which means what?"

"Oracles are really only *100% dependable* in the hands of a true teacher, because a true teacher is clear, and because he will sense if the oracle is being tampered with by dark outside forces. Of course they can give anyone good, accurate, information. But you can never be certain of the accuracy unless you are enlightened. In fact, most oracles were invented by true teachers, for true teachers - they were never intended for those whose separate selves and subconscious programming would confuse the answers."

"Why would a true teacher use one since they are already enlightened?"

"For a true teacher, an oracle is a quick and easy substantiation of their own Inner Voice - a sort of second opinion/double check system. But for an average person, who is not yet clear, an oracle can be confusing at times - usually when the separate self has something at stake. For instance, many times I have seen a person get such an incredibly clear and specific reading from the I Ching, that most people could not possibly mis-interpret it - yet the person is confused and mis-interprets anyway, because their separate self doesn't really want the truth to be known. To give a personal example, when I was avoiding finding my true teacher, but allegedly seeking my true teacher, I used the Ching to ask if I should speak to him, and if he was my true teacher. The Ching would come up with something like: "Perseverance Furthers. To see the Great Man brings Good Fortune and Success", yet I'd read that and say to myself 'I don't get it. What does this mean? What should I do?' I got about fifty readings like that when I was trying to avoid finding *my* teacher. I kept asking because I was letting my selfish separate self pull the wool over my eyes, and so I figured that at some point the odds alone would make it give me the answer my selfish separate self wanted to hear. But I fooled myself into thinking I would just do it one more time just *to be sure*. When I was really looking for a way out. I was lucky that it wasn't being influenced by dark forces, but I guess the environment I was in, and my destiny, sort of protected me against that. Also, the I Ching will stop you at some point, by actually giving you a reading that says that 'there is no point in giving information to an impertinent fool, and that someone who keeps asking the same question over and over again is an impertinent fool'. Of course, that is a blatant example. But whatever your separate self is making you confused about, will usually not be remedied by information from an oracle or channel."

Oddly enough, I had done the same thing. I did it before I asked Zain if he would be my teacher. I told Raga about my readings during one of my courses with him.

"I keep asking the Ching about finding a teacher, and I keep getting more confused. It always seemed to help me understand the changes I was going through, or needed to go through. I'm not even sure it's working for me anymore."

He said, "Those who really want to spiritually evolve, should work to change in such a way that they become more directly in touch with pure information from their Inner Being. If they have previously relied on oracles and channeling, they are expected to forego that, in favor of a true teacher and training to manifest their own Inner Being."

"So how do you make the changes that will allow you to get information more directly from your Inner Being?" I asked impetuously.

"See, you aren't even hearing *me*, clarifying it to you in person, let alone your oracle. Again, that's where a true teacher comes in. A teacher both gives you the keys to changing and manifesting your Inner Being, and keeps reminding you to use the keys when your separate self has steered you off track (which it puts a great effort into). Plus, the teacher is a clear reflection of your own Inner Being. Thus, being in the teacher's presence helps you get more and more in touch with your Inner Being, both by virtue of being constantly exposed to it and being made aware of the Inner information, and by contrasting the truth and Light of the Inner Being against your separate self's negative subconscious programming, mind games, deceit, and illusions."

As you know, the story ends well.

As we said earlier, channeling, or going to a channel, reinforces mental programming that *your own* Inner Being is not "great", &/or is not directly accessible, and that you cannot change and manifest your own inner being in your life. This holds true whether or not a person is actually channeling a disincarnate being, or just their Inner Being/subconscious. Even if the channeled information is telling you that you are a light worker and can manifest God, the very process of going to, or doing the channeling, is restricting you from **doing** that, and **being** that. Thus it actually creates a spiritual limitation. What a marvelous circular trick of the separate self! You can see your tail in front of your nose, you can almost touch it, but you forever chase it and never get it. How does this work? I asked Gabriel one day, as I was using the I Ching in the library.

"You know, in the old days, an oracle was often an actual person. Now they call them mediums or channelers. But whatever you call it, the motivation to channel, or go to a channeler, is the same. And it is self-defeating. It comes from a subconscious and conscious belief, that YOUR *own* soul, YOUR *own* Inner Being, is *not* so great - or at least not as great as the oracle, or the person who is being channeled and listened to. That weakens your own contact with your Inner Being. Your own real contact with God. And *every* time you do it, that belief *is reinforced*. It also reinforces the belief that you must get the information from someone or something else - but the process does not do anything to directly change you in a way that will really put you in touch with your own Inner Being, or make the change in which YOU become a vehicle for *manifesting* YOUR own Inner Being/God, in your life, all the time. This belief, which is being reinforced, thus affects your programming, and keeps you spiritually chasing your tail, and continually limits your spiritual self-perception. You should not place such limitations on your outlook about yourself young son, about your own spiritual greatness, or you will not grow to manifest God. But those limitations are only what you self-impose, only what you believe, and how you act. Regardless of whether or not you have developed, or manifested, your own being, it is still the Great One. The Inner Being *is* God, *is* Universal Consciousness, and *is* thus the highest possible awareness and source of information that can be "channeled". And remember, *all Inner Beings are One.* Period. Your Inner Being is every bit the same as the likes of Buddha, St. Germain, etc.. You have no idea yet. But your potential is *every* bit as Great. The only difference is that the Great Saints and Sages *chose* to *manifest* their Inner Being. Did you *ever* hear of Jesus or St. Germain channeling someone else? Why not? Because they didn't do it, and likewise, they don't allow themselves to be channeled [we will explain the reasons for that later]. They chose the traditional path, and learning from living masters, as have you. They chose that *instead* of channeling information from other beings, or consulting channeled information. Just think about it honestly. And remember, your *own soul* is better than the many disincarnate lower astral beings that may want to possess a human, and *are* being channeled. It's just up to you to *manifest your Inner Being.*"

Here is another of the chinks in channeling's armor: have you noticed that channeling other beings, including the "channeling" of "ascended masters", often seems to bring forth not just the Inner Being, but the INDIVIDUAL SELF, and the PERSONALITY, of the channeled being? So even if it is real, the information is filtered through the being's personality and self, and then it filters through the self of the channeler, and then finally through the self of the listener, who further filters the information through their *own* self's programming. AT BEST then, by the time your self is done with getting the information, it's highly unlikely to be anything that will directly or truly threaten the selfish separate self - and that is what the spiritual path is all about - the death, surrendering, and rebirth of the separate self as a servant to the Universal Will. *That* is the key to true change, to becoming what you really are, to manifesting your Inner Being/God. Good "information" and knowledge will not do it for you, *regardless* of *how good* that information is. And for the information you really *need,* why use channeling when you can access *untainted* information from the highest source, YOUR own Inner Being. YOU are a *great* soul. Yes, you. Again, channeling doesn't put you through the changes that having a true teacher does - the kind of changes that will make you ONE with your Inner Being, ONE with the ascended masters, ONE with God.

Some people are under the assumption that some of the great psychics of history were "channelers". But with extremely rare exception, such psychics, if they were of the light, *only* channeled their own Inner Being, or Higher Self. And they too, often warned against letting other entities come through you, or misguide you - and of the dangers and damage such possession poses. The greatest of such psychics, were in fact, Children of the Law of One (even some who were not consciously aware of it), and were actually in the service of the One, and the grand master. These psychics used the incredible well spring of their Inner Being, to tap into what is called the "Akashic Records". Such activity and abilities were all from their own Inner Being, operating under the Oneness and service of Universal Will, not by going to channelers, or channeling disincarnate entities (with very, very rare exceptions necessitated and controlled by the hierarchy).

The person who wants to become a true teacher, and work consciously and directly with spiritual seekers, must also strive to integrate the Inner Being, with the conscious, and subconscious mind, and manifest it in their life, through body and mind. Thus the Inner Being, God, and the self, all consciously and subconsciously correspond. When this finally occurs, there is not conflict, or walls, between, the conscious mind, the subconscious mind, and the Inner Being/Universal Consciousness. Thus there is also harmony between the conscious beliefs, subconscious programming, and Universal Truths.

The ancient teachings of Atlantis, as well as the more modern ones of the Atlantean Children of the Law of One, all warn of the risks associated with possession, which are great indeed. Most people don't think about channeling this way, but the truth is, channeling is just a nice word for possession, and people need to keep this in mind, and keep in mind the possible perils. In a spiritual and astral sense, possession is like being raped. The being who is channeled comes from the astral realms, and when another being possesses someone else's body and mind, it damages the host's astral body, astral defenses, and actually weakens the strength of Will, much in the same way that allowing yourself to be hypnotized weakens the Will (that doesn't apply to self-hypnosis, or hypnosis by a totally trusted mate or spiritual associate). And every time you do such a thing, you weaken your own will. And you subject yourself to damage - spiritually, emotionally, mentally, and physically. You get "holes" in your circumvent force and auras - and dark creatures can attach themselves like astral leeches. Again, the fact is that channeling is a very nice euphemism for possession - and no matter what good words come through during a channeling, you don't know who is *really* doing the possessing, which means you can't be sure of the motives behind it and thus you can't really depend on the information. And it's one thing to listen to good words, uplifting messages, etc., but honestly, aren't there plenty of other sources to get such things without possession being involved, and without subsequently taking the unnecessary risks involved? You know there are. But these are strange times, and instead of running to the nearest exorcist when someone is possessed, people often pay money to listen to someone who's possessed, or try to become possessed themselves. How many people would be as interested in channeling as they are, if it was called what it really is, "possession", instead of using the euphemism "channeling"? "Hey, we bought tickets to a seminar tonight so we can listen to some disincarnate entity who is possessing the body and mind of a young woman, and learn how to let someone possess us too!" It doesn't sound quite as nice as going to a "channeling seminar" any more, don't you think?

If channeling has had a good place in your life, fine. But it may be time to grow further. Just reading this is placing greater responsibility on you becoming more spiritually mature.

A True teacher knows all this, and instead of channeling, he gets the separate self out of the way, and manifests the Inner Being. And a true teacher is there as a tool for *you* to develop, access, and manifest YOUR own Inner Being. What could be higher, more pure, and safer than channeling/manifesting your own Inner Being? And it is likely that you who are reading this, should be a true teacher yourself someday. God only knows, there is certainly a need for more, and in the future the need will be even far, far greater. But you won't become a true teacher by merely listening to spiritual information, good or bad.

Here are some final words from my discussion with Zain about mediums and channeling (possession):

"Now possession would be one thing if the only beings that would possess a body, were high consciousness, saints or the like. But there are many beings dwelling in the lower astral realms, that cannot get a body, and want one badly. And even if they are not using an attractive disguise and lies to get themselves 'invited in' to a body by a voluntary medium, they will work on getting through other people - those who have weak astral defenses. Some of these astral realm dwellers are the spirits of disturbed humans who are between lives. Some are insane. Some are mass murderers, torturers and cruel rapist warriors. And these deceitful degenerate entities lie, easily and well, and are happy to make up a good story too. Then there are disincarnate demons also. All the ancient teachings, including those of the Children and their branches, tell us to avoid possession/channeling, and not to possess/be channeled, once ascended or between lives. And if you consider it thoroughly, it's not hard to figure out that real ascended masters don't *want* to be channeled. Think about it. Put yourself in an ascended master's sandals for a moment.

You have worked hard on Earth, suffered greatly, paid your dues and then some. You have finally earned, and chosen, leaving this painful place, to exist on higher paradisiacal planes. You live and work in new ways on new planes. You know there are other masters on Earth to take care of the needs of the spiritual seekers, and they are as in touch with the Inner Being as you, but they can do a better job for those on Earth, *because they* are still *on* Earth in the Flesh. You know you can't tell anyone on Earth anything that isn't already there for them to hear, or that they can't get from a living master. And these living masters are already guided by you and your kin - they can answer any question and give any guidance anyone could possibly need on the Earth. If that was you who had finally decided to go on, would you *want* to have to go back to the Earth plane into a body and possess someone when there is no need because they are being taken care of already? *Why* would you? In fact, when you look at it objectively, and you understand all that I just said, wouldn't an ascended master that *just had to* throw in their own two cents by possessing someone, be a little bit 'egoed out' or 'off'? Leave them be - ascended masters have chosen to leave the Earth plane, and are working on totally different levels and realms - and they don't want to deal directly with any beings here anymore, other than their hierarchical linked masters. And they know it is not necessary for them to do so, because they know there are masters on Earth who are in the proper place - the true teachers that have chosen that duty, and have the proper and *full* ability to deal with those who really want spiritual help and information."

So if you are channeling or listening to someone who is - think carefully about who or what is really being "channeled" - regardless of who or what they *claim to be*. Here is an excellent example:

Let's say you need a heart operation. You need a surgeon. You find a stranger along the side of the road who claims to have been the great and powerful royal surgeon for the court of Cleopatra, and who also claims to have all the knowledge and skills of modern medicine. Would you invite them to open up your body and fix your heart, even though they had no way to prove their claims and you had no way to check their references? Would you even *listen* to their information on how to *do it yourself,* or ask them to guide *your* surgeon? Seriously, would you do such a thing? Of course not. Nor would you even hire someone to work at a convenience store, or rent someone a house so casually. Well, your body is a house of sorts, and your mind builds and directs your life. And when someone "channels", they are letting some disincarnate *stranger,* something *truly unknown,* enter them through the astral realms, access and *use/take over their very body and mind* to one extent or another - all without even an interview, or checking on references. And when listening to channeled information, considering the truly unknown source, shouldn't it be listened to *cautiously,* rather than *reverently?* Please think seriously about this. I have heard many people talk about channeled information like GOSPEL, simply because it was claimed to have been channeled. They don't have an ounce of doubt or caution about the information - *because* it was channeled. It should be the other way around. Too many people who are cautious enough to not give even a clean-cut hitchhiker a ride in their car, will gladly let some strange astral entity that wants to possess a living human, take a ride in their very body and mind, or listen to the words of a strange astral entity, as if they were from a well-known and respected holy man. Does that really make sense? Not to me. And it shouldn't to you.

The teachings in this chapter have shone new light on channeling, and revealed serious problems with it. If you have used channeling before and liked it, as many have, your ego will have something at stake here, as does your selfish separate self, and accepting these truths may be a little upsetting. You may even "blow me off" at this point. But so it goes with truth and threats to the self. It had to be said. But please, really think it all over, and re-evaluate your opinions with an open mind. Discovering new truths that allow you to grow more and go further on your path is a good thing. We all must first let go of one shore, in order to cross over to another.

From Mother Sheba:

"Even from the days before Egypt, the teachings of the Atlantean Children of the Law of One regarding channeling have been simple, and clear as the light: only your *own* Inner Being should be allowed to possess your body and mind. And that means manifesting God. Your Inner Being *is the Christ, thus it is* 'Christ Consciousness', God, the Universal Spirit. It should be integrated and *lived, not just trance channeled.* Why channel *anything else* or *anybody, when you can be One with and manifest* the Universal Spirit itself - your own part of God? What more could you possibly want to channel? What more information could you need to get, than what you can get from the Absolute? What could you possibly want, that you can't get from the Universal Spirit? What clearer, or better source of information could you have?"

Vishnu, another Adept Initiate, had this to say:

"If a teacher/master/guru or whomever, is legitimate, they are One with and manifesting their Inner Being/Universal Consciousness/God. Thus, True teachers only manifest their own Inner Being (God). In fact, you could say their very essence, their very life, everything about them, IS, in a sense, a constant living 'channeling' of God. Thus, they have no desire, or need, to channel anything or anybody else. Think about it for a moment - what would God need to channel? Whereas the channeling of anything or anybody else, must have consciousness limitations - and there could possibly be tainted motives, even if it is a true channeling."

Infomercial Channels

Finally, channeling can be very profitable, and a great ego-trip. A channeler can be a total fake. Many are. I know some of you think you would know if you were being conned by a channeling con-artist, but it can be very difficult to tell. The fact is, it is a con-artist's *entire job* to be *totally* believable - their job depends on it. That is how they make their living. Believability, and getting someone to trust them is the con man's *only* skill. Other than being *very* in touch with your own Inner Voice, you can easily "buy into" a con. It's only a *bad* con job that you can really detect. If people could really tell when they were being conned, there wouldn't be so many cons around, in so many different forms.

Changing Channels

In summary, channeling anything, or any being other than your own Inner Being, *can only* be of lesser vibration at best, so why run the risks? Why risk listening to a channeler, or letting these astral entities channel through you, when you can be in touch with your own Inner Being?

227

Nothing can be pure until the vessel is pure. You, or your channeler would need to be an enlightened being for the channeling to be totally accurate, and if that is the case, you don't need channeling any more because you already have the information you need! Thus, entities from the higher realms, and those of the hierarchy will not channel through anyone. *Ascended masters did not channel other entities when they were alive,* and they certainly aren't going to do it through someone else now that they are gone - they know the realities of such things, and they know that you should follow the same path as they did - they want you to *achieve* Universal Consciousness yourself by going through the *proper* "channels" - they know you need an "in the flesh" master/true teacher who can inspire you, break through your selfish separate self's illusions and blocks, and put you in touch with your *own* Inner Being, so you can *manifest* the part of *you* that is God Consciousness. So, if you are not yet manifesting your own Inner Being, find a true teacher that directly represents your Inner Being, in thought, action, and word, and who can help put you directly in touch with it also.

Why Channeling?

One time I asked Zain about why someone would even do channeling in the first place, considering the better options for getting information.

"Channeling, using a channel for spiritual information, or following ascended masters, is far easier than going through the changes that are necessary to achieve true spiritual enlightenment. Yet it allows people to feel like they are doing something spiritually (learning, teaching, making spiritual progress in some way). And this can be true during certain periods of a person's spiritual path. There may also be some good spiritual information coming out of it, which reinforces this feeling. The separate self is happy to support this activity, and let you feel "spiritual", as long as you don't go any further and do something that threatens its power and position. That's because while you are feeling spiritually "pacified", you are simultaneously avoiding a real teacher - thus avoiding the "separate illusion busting" and "ego busting" of the separate self that it absolutely needs if you are to gain your own real spiritual consciousness - Universal Consciousness! What an ingenious deception! Thus, it fools many people, and becomes a major diversion, a side-trip trap. But we must live and learn."

Again, the *true* reason *behind* why most people do channeling or follow the ascended masters may not *even* be what they *think* it is - to be spiritual or to get real spiritual information. It is part of an elaborate trick of the separate self, designed to keep itself in control of your life, rather than letting your Inner Being get control. Be a true channeler - change, transcend the selfish separate self, and begin to channel your INner Being.

Chapter Fifteen
Ancient Monasticism and
What Now?

Come Together
For Practice and Sharing
In Loving and Caring
Will Your Inner Self Bloom

❖

Behind Walls do the Weak
Grow Strong Like The Sun

❖

Tend to them as the Young Trees
As The Hemp Gives Guidance & Support
As The Soil Nurtures
As The Water Gives Sharing
As The Loving Light Gives Warmth and Life

❖

In The Times of Darkness
We will Keep the Knowledge of Light
Hidden Far From the Dark Masses
For Again Will Come the Times of Light

❖

Giving is the Way of Love
The Way of the One.
The Sun Gives Light to All
In Harmony With the One.

But When We are Not thus In Harmony,
Giving Can Bring Harm.
Giving to the Selfish Self
Is Destructive.
Giving that Weakens
Is Destructive.

Learn to Give Like the Stars
From the Spirit, for the Spirit.
Then Like the Sun, All Will Receive
What their Soul Really Needs.

In Times of Darkness
The Ignorant Masses
Under Control of Dark Self
Will Turn Against
The Ones of the Light

Then Befool them You Must,
Hide Your Light Behind a Veil.
The Ignorant Masses,
Seeing no Light
Know Not it Still Shines
And Go On Their Way

Positive Attracts Negative.
With the Children of Light,
The Young must be wary,
Not Ready for to Fight,
Nor the Influences Many
From the Children of Night.

As The Fruit Comes to Bear
The Blossom must Fall.
When the Fruit Falls to Ground
The Fruit Must Give Way
For the Seed to Start Life Anew

So it is With Life of One Who Grows
You Must Let Go of Your Past
To Move Into Your Future.

False Giving, is Giving to Get
True Giving, is Not Give and Take
True Giving, Does not need Thanks

[Some monasteries, like ours, are "co-ed". But some are for men only, and have their equivalent for females only - the convent. So, while the word "monastery" will be used throughout this chapter, keep in mind it can apply to any type of

230

spiritual community, including ashrams, convents, spiritual communes, etc., or even an association of like-minded friends on a spiritual path.]

Monasticism has long been a tradition in many cultures. As you read earlier, in the tiny country of Tibet alone, there were over 7000 Buddhist monasteries. And a child from every family might enter a monastery and become a monk.

Spiritual communities are a relative of monasteries, and have also been around since the beginning of recorded history. The discovery of the Dead Sea Scrolls, while highly suppressed, recently brought to light to much of the modern world, the spiritual community of the Essenes. The ancient texts reveal that the Essene community, was a branch of the Children of the Law of One, and was started hundreds of years prior to Jesus' birth by a Persian Adept named Zoroaster (also founder of the Magi - of which the "three wise men" were members). The community existed long before the time of Jesus, and Jesus and his family were members of it. But their community was just one of the multitudes that have existed from the beginning of human life on Earth.

But "times they are a changing", and with it, many things, including monasteries. Like farmland being swallowed up by expanding cities, many traditional monasteries are falling by the wayside as the modern world encroaches upon them in one way or another. Some have even been disbanded by laws. For instance, I know of one monastery in the US, that had to be abandoned because of a city law that said no more than five unrelated people could live in the same household.

But the concept of monasticism, what it means, and what its functions are, can be carried out in a variety of ways. [Later, we'll discuss the new order of things for the Children, as they adapt to the times].

Householders, "the Order of Things", and Inner Circles

One day as I accompanied Zain on his day of meeting with the householders that lived outside the walls of the monastery, I asked him more about who they were, and why they didn't live inside the monastery.

"Father, on my trip here, I met many householders who gave me assistance. I see so many living outside the walls here, and I've been told they basically have the same principles and beliefs as us. Why do they stay more distant and live in separate houses?"

"Since long ago, many spiritual traditions, including ours, have had a certain structure to them, that allows for greater freedom for people to choose how involved, or uninvolved, they want to get, how fast they want to grow, etc., while still remaining on a spiritual path. Specifically, it has to do with how much a person wants to sacrifice of their worldly life, for their spiritual life.

So a system evolved of degrees of involvement with a spiritual path, that allowed this freedom, and also took into account the consciousness of individuals. It is based on the Universal form of the solar system, and orbits. It is like concentric rings around a central object. The central object, is the head monk, the one ultimately in charge of the monastery. In our tradition, it would be an Adept, and generally, one who was the highest consciousness Initiate. This person is ultimately responsible for everything at the monastery they are in charge of - a sort of 'head' for the 'body' of the monastery. They are also in charge of overseeing the other Adepts, elders, and novice monks there, and more loosely, the householders associated with the monastery. Every body, of any kind, needs a head, if there is to be coordination of the body parts rather than spastic chaos. This is so throughout the

231

Universe. Everything is always orbiting something, and this system keeps the entire Universe flowing in harmony.

The furthest of these circles out from the center of the order of the monastery, are the householders. They are ones who wish to retain a relatively normal worldly life as far as their culture is concerned. They are not ready, or willing yet, to give up *everything* to grow, and find God. Yet generally, they believe most of the same things, and do want to be slowly working in the direction of reaching Oneness with God, without the strict discipline, hard work, and surrender required by a student in the monastery. Most of them hope to someday become monks, but for now, they wish to lead a basically normal life with family and friends. So they have occasional discussions and interactions with elders, novices and Adept true teachers, help and contribute in various ways, and are a part of the greater whole of the path.

Some orders like ours, have many monks, compared to householders. Others do not. And most of the major religions of the world, have structures balanced the other way - based on having few monks or priests. That is all that most churches are - many 'householders' of varying degrees of dedication, with just one overseeing priest, minister, or such."

"I never thought of it that way. But it seems that our householders are more self-sacrificing than most churchgoers."

"Than many. Yes, I would have to agree."

"I mean, many of them risked their lives just helping me get here."

"That's very true. They can be very devoted. But do you think that all those that helped you on your journey were all householders?"

"Yes."

"Many were, certainly, but some were actually Initiates, who were living in the outside world in various guises."

"Which ones?"

"Why don't we first finish our original discussion.

Next comes the monastery, and the furthest out from the 'head', the 'center', of the monastery, are the novice monks. Again, they are part of the multiplicity of the order of concentric rings within the monastery. Next closest in from them, are the monks, then the elder monks. The students comprised of elder monks form what is called an Inner Circle, in relationship to the Adept who is their personal true teacher. Then in a monastery like ours here, where there are many Adepts, the Adepts are an 'Inner circle, Inner circle', and are the next closest in to the center. Again, the center is the Adept of the highest consciousness, or in lieu of that, one who the others have agreed is the best for this position.

Around the head Adept, living closest to him, are both the other Initiates, and the Inner Circle of the head Adept's personal eldest students. Some of these live in closest contact with the head Adept monk."

"Are elders those who have been here the longest?"

"No. It is a combination of consciousness and knowledge. Everything in our order is fundamentally based on consciousness. If you were to have a sufficient leap in consciousness today, even though you still have a lack of knowledge, you would become an elder."

The Value of, and Need for, Monasteries
The Monastery as a Place of Retreat

There are many, many reasons for monasteries to exist. And few people realize the entire function, or real significance of a monastic community. The typical understanding is that it is a place for "cloistering", a place where those involved in a spiritual path, can hide away from the world. This is true in a sense, but it is not really understood. And more importantly, it is not the only function of a monastery.

What a Monastery is Not

First we should discuss the realities of monastic life. A monastery is not a place for dysfunctional or lazy people looking for a free ride, an easy life, or escape from their self-made screwed up lives. It's not a place to "run from" your life or the world, but a place to "run to" to improve your life and the world. It's not a place to selfishly take, but a place to selflessly give. Before being able to master the fine points of body, mind and spirit, you must first have mastered the fundamentals of basic "earthly life". Some people to seem to think that living in a monastery means being taken care of and not having to work. Nothing could be further from the truth. It's a place to learn and develop "self-sacrifice". Thus, most monasteries not only require long hours of spiritual practice and discipline, but also hard work of other kinds. I know for me, it was harder work than I had ever encountered.

The other thing a monastery/spiritual community is not, is a social paradise full of unselfishly loving people, peace, and harmony. It seems everyone would like to be the *only* selfish being in an entire world full of unselfish loving people. So they often expect everyone *else* to be just loving and accepting of them. They want everyone but themselves to always be totally positive, "nice", and just lovingly accept their selfish behavior, not bring it up, not criticize them about it, not confront them with it, and not get negative or angry about it. But that is not reality, is not going to happen, and is not deserved. Before you can happily live in a paradisiacal world full of no one but unselfishly loving people, you must first make yourself into the kind of person that belongs in such a world. The first step towards that is the tough and dirty work of dealing with your self and others like you. And the fact is, the only one you can truly change or "expect" to be positive all the time, is you. The only person anyone has control over, is themselves. And even once you become unselfishly loving all the time - who do you think you will be around as long as you are here? Selfish, negative people.

The only people you'll find at a monastery (or anywhere) who are unselfishly loving, are "enlightened beings"/masters/teachers. But even so, unselfish love is very different than unconditional love. Those who unselfishly love you, will give you a hard time, and the discipline you need because they do love you.

People who have not achieved Universal Consciousness/enlightenment are not One with God. That means they're separate from God, and have a selfish separate self. And *that* means they have various selfish traits and flaws, right? Things like desires, fears, quirks, negative attitudes/"moods", lust, possessiveness, jealousy, hate, envy, etc., etc.. The point is, selfish people, even those on spiritual paths, have many "faults". Ironically, people with faults (like yourself) don't like the faults of others, and thus get "negative" and irritated with others. And other people with faults, don't like yours either, and will get negative and irritated with you. Also ironically, people get *most* irritated with other people who have faults that are most like their own faults! It is amazing how selfish egotistical people often expect to live with kind, loving people, and have everything be just "all sweetness and light". No self-sacrifice, no having to face themselves, no criticism, no requirement to work on real personal change -- just everyone being nice, kind, and loving to them -- while they continue to be selfish and even asinine. [As a side note, that is one of the misconceptions that gets propagated by fake spiritual masters who just "sit there" and have people just come "sit there" in front of them and bask in/"soak up" all that wonderful imaginary "love and light" radiating from their presence. People do get a placebo effect "spiritual high" from that sort of thing, but real spiritual growth takes self-sacrificing work. It doesn't come from just being in the presence of a master (real or otherwise), and that sort of thing just misleads people away from a real path, and real growth.]

Monasteries *can* be places of peace and love at times, but they are primarily places of spiritual growth. In that capacity, they are a "school" for people who are not yet always peaceful and loving. Thus the social structure amongst fellow students is a mix of caring, love, and antagonism. The important thing is, people are there to work on it, dedicated to changing and improving themselves. Whereas in "regular life", everyone is in denial of their own faults, and has generally agreed to leave each other alone in that sense, and not bring up faults, or expect them to be dealt with. People don't generally help each other "push" for perfection or improvement in behavior, unless it is part of their path.

In "normal" social situations and relationships, criticism usually only occurs as the result of hostility, anger, subtle "put downs", or negative moods. With the exception of such times, people expect to have their selfishness and faults "left alone" for the most part. At least "certain lines" are not crossed in bringing things up to others, or in having things brought up to you, especially amongst those you are close with, or acquaintances. For instance, roommates who are sharing a house or apartment, often do so even if they don't particularly like each other. That's because everyone agrees not to "cross the line" with each other. Thus criticism is kept to a minimum (unless it's regarding an issue that really effects them) and everyone keeps their faults, and the self is not threatened. But since everyone in a monastic situation has agreed to work on ridding themselves of selfishness and it's related problems and faults, those boundaries are deliberately crossed, and selfishness and associated faults are actually targeted. The mechanism for attacking the target, is criticism. This is constructive criticism as opposed to hostile criticism. But regardless of the motive for criticism, it is still criticism. What happens as a result, all depends on your attitude, and what you do with the criticism.

The self, in it's perpetual defensiveness, considers any criticism as "unloving". That is usually the case in the world. But criticism can actually be a loving act to help someone grow and become more loving themselves. Nevertheless, the self in its struggle for survival, considers ALL criticism a threat, and having you think of it as a negative and "unloving" thing, works to its advantage. Criticism should actually be desired by the person who truly wants to transcend the selfish self and spiritually grow. In fact, the person who is not just *pretending* to want to grow, truly *does* both desire, and welcome, criticism. So novices/students deliberately point out faults in their fellow novices (ideally for purposes of helping them grow), and also have theirs pointed out to them (ideally for purposes of helping you grow).

However, the very fact that someone is a novice monk/student, means they are still selfish - so the mutual criticisms are between selfish people. So sometimes things are pointed out for the wrong reasons - for instance, it could be as a negative reaction - to "get back" at someone for criticizing/pointing out something they needed to change. Thus interactions between fellow novices/students can be confrontational and intense. It should be kept in mind always, that such temporary "unpleasantness" is necessary, and can be a good thing. It should also be kept in mind that it is not "poor you" having to live in the midst of a bunch of negative antagonists. It is you having to live with a bunch of "yous" who are also being critical, sometimes negative, sometimes antagonistic, sometimes sensitive and caring, and most importantly - making true spiritual growth headway. People who are there to learn and grow, like you, *are like you*. They're imperfect, and in the midst of challenging themselves and shaking things up within themselves. This is where the real opportunity for growth occurs and the real spiritual work takes place. Everyone is there to be criticized, and to be critical, in order to help themselves and others transcend the selfish separate self, and work towards perfection. They are not there just to be loving and accepting of you being a selfish jerk, just as you are not there to be loving and accepting of them being a selfish jerk. You are all there to grow, and part of helping each other, is being critical, and dealing with the flack from that, and being criticized yourself.

Once the selfish separate self realizes its control and life are threatened, even minor criticisms that are "no big deal" in a roommate situation for instance, become a really big deal. Like someone reminding you to clean your dishes for instance, may not be an issue to you when the very life of your separate self is not at stake, but if it is just one more "cornering" of the wild animal (the self), one more "straw" added to the load for the purpose of "breaking the camel's back", then it can become a "huge deal", that incites a big negative reaction.

When people get into a disagreement, each feels the other is "wrong". This happens whether the people are strangers, friends, or lovers. Unfortunately, it is usually left as a "stalemate" because no one will admit to being wrong, and there is no trusted third party to mediate the disagreement who everyone will defer to for insight or a final decision. There is an old saying that there are two sides to every story, and when this occurs between novices, it is no different. The difference is we can, and must, have resolutions to the disagreements, because it is necessary to each individual's growth. Because of the complex dynamics of novices needing to criticize, and be criticized, this happens frequently, and methods have evolved to deal with it and facilitate growth. Basically, it involves a "meeting" of a number of monks. Insight can be given by others, an elder, or a teacher. And a resolution can be obtained by the disagreeing parties listening to, and accepting, the consensus of all at the meeting, or through the mediation of an elder or teacher. This requires some humility of course, in order to let go of one's own "charged" one-sided opinion, and be open to the whole truth. Almost always, both parties have points that are right, and points that are wrong. Again, this is where real spiritual growth can take place.

Those are just the facts of life when it comes to real spiritual growth. There is a bright side though - if you want one. The more humility you have, the more you actually welcome criticism, and the faster and easier the spiritual growth and self-improvement goes. A humble attitude and iron-clad desire to change and grow is the key. The whole experience can seem like hell, or can be experienced as a desirable "challenge" or "invigorating workout" like climbing a mountain, or beating a difficult video game - all depending on your degree of humility, and strength of desire. Believe it or not, it can actually be an enjoyable fulfilling feeling to see some fault about yourself that someone has pointed out, and change it, bringing you one step closer to enlightenment.

[Note: The above "meeting" method can be used by anyone with a sufficient number of friends or family who all agree that growth and truth are more important than being "right or wrong". But sometimes unless a teacher is involved, there are still "stalemates". In any case, it's nice to always end the meeting on a positive note, and have a hug (it can also be a good time for a multi-person star-exercise!). The "Golden Rule Workbook" gives specific programs for working with family and friends in this way, as well as creating "clubs" with strangers who have the same ideals.]

The Monastery as a Repository of Knowledge

Some monasteries of various spiritual traditions, still maintain the knowledge and practice of various methods of healing or arts. For instance, they may have vast knowledge of specific or unusual herbs found nowhere else. Or they may have practiced acupuncture, or a particular art, a particular style of martial art, a particular Yoga, etc., that would be lost if it weren't for the monastery's preservation of it. For instance, our monastery used to trade with an associated monastery that specialized in the making of rare herbal oils, using ancient secret methods, and herbs thought to be extinct by modern science.

Earlier it was mentioned that our monastery in Tibet had an incredible library, including manuscripts from religions around the world. But more importantly, the teachings of these texts were verbally, and experientially, handed down from Initiate to Initiate, from teacher to student, over thousands of years, and became ingrained in all the Initiates throughout the ages. But the greatest function of the monastery, was that it was a repository for Unselfish Love, and the wisdom of Universal Consciousness that was passed like a candle lighting a candle - from an Adept Initiate true teacher to student, who became an Adept Initiate true teacher, who passed it to student, who became an Adept Initiate true teacher, etc., throughout time. Thus, even though our monastery in Tibet has been physically destroyed, just as the Dalai Lama and the teachings of Tibetan Buddhism have survived after their destruction in Tibet, we too go on. In our solar system - that which contains the Earth and Sun, even the vast darkness of space, does not snuff the light of our Sun. In the same way, true teachings go on, and cannot be snuffed out. And there is still the greater, Inner repository, within the surviving true teachers. They, and this book, are there for the training of any person who would Unselfishly Love, and serve the world, and for the time when light will flourish, and all people of like-kindness, will know Oneness with the Universal Spirit.

The Monastery as a Place of Training and Nurturing "Light" Workers

The monastery as a school for spiritual training and nurturing has perhaps always been its most important function. The world desperately needs light bearers, light houses, shining beacons in the night to guide us through the darkness. If potential teachers do not have a place to "bloom", there will not be any teachers. This is why the Children have maintained monasteries and communities since the days of Atlantis.

Steps to the Light

Meditation techniques are the tools that help develop concentration, self-discipline, and allow re-programming of the sub-conscious mind and habit patterns. The

True Teacher is the tool that allows the seeker to see themselves clearly, transcend the separate self, develop Unselfish Love, tune in to their Inner Voice, and manifest their Inner Being.

When a seeker finds their true teacher, and becomes what you might call a dedicated "true student", regardless of whether it is in the setting of a monastery or not, they make the commitment of total surrender to Universal Will, and of changing from a life of "taking" to a life of "giving". Then the student needs to practice, apply what they are learning, and attempt to apply what they are beginning to get from their Inner Voice. This is where a monastery comes in very handy. It's best if a student's practice takes place in an environment that nurtures that process, where there are other students of like mind to practice with, and where an unenlightened students' actions can be supervised so they don't harm themselves, or others. Harm how? There are several ways. The first is harming by giving.

To Give or Not to Give?
That is *Not* the question (in a Monastery).

In an earlier chapter, it was said that it may seem too idealistic to give unselfishly in a world full of people who are happy to selfishly take. This is somewhat true when you are new to the path. The novice student who is working towards living a life of Unselfish Love, but who has not yet achieved it, is not prepared to differentiate between what he should give, and should not give, for the good of others. Remember the example of the beggar lying in the street who may need to be given money, or may need to be yelled at? The best situation for a student, who isn't capable of acting appropriately in that, or many other situations, is to live with others who have aspirations/ideals akin to their own; this way they can give and grow in an environment of inspiration and support, one in which they can safely "give" all the time, without concern about giving in a manner that would be harmful to someone else.

The Nestling and the Nest

For someone who has decided to become a True Teacher, and dedicate their life to helping others, a spiritual environment is important for their early developmental stages. Just as a baby needs care, nurturing, and a loving environment to develop properly, so does the neophyte. Also, just as you would not send an infant out into the world alone, unprepared to deal with it, a novice student (nor any but an Initiate really), should not be sent out in the world alone, during their spiritual infancy. Why?

True teachers can't be influenced by *any* "outside sources" - they cannot be influenced by anything or anybody, (other than God/their hierarchical superiors). Again, why? Because internally, they are directly attached to, and dependent *only* on God, and give, or "outflow" to all else. True teachers thus "radiate" the Universal Spirit. An ancient affirmation relating to this is "I am positive [+] to all things, except The Absolute, to which I am negative [-]". So rather than being *affected* by anything else, a true teacher influences and *affects* everything else. They're like Suns that shine and affect all things within their sphere of influence - they cannot be extinguished, moved, nor even darkened, by planets, or the dark void of space itself. *But such is not yet the case with a novice, or even an elder.* It is possible for them to be negatively influenced and harmed by forces of darkness in various ways. And like lions waiting for their prey to leave their young unprotected, the dark side is eagerly waiting to pounce on those who would dare to become bearers of the light. Having an out-of-body experience without proper preparation and protection is just one example - it can lead to possession. Also, the uninitiated student is still learning many things, and developing powers, but doesn't yet have the wisdom to properly use those powers. The student monk can thus be like a loaded gun in the hands of a child, and while not likely, there is the remote possibility of doing harm to others. When I was a student monk, one of my fellow monks unleashed some powerful forces while "dabbling". Here is the story.

We had been training in the science-magic involved with the elements of water, air, fire, etc., and subsequently training in the expansion of the powers of our mind and concentration. But we were not supposed to experiment with these things without supervision. I had noticed that one of my fellow monks, Ishkari, was not at morning group meditation. We had a close relationship, and spent a good deal of time together. Thus, I usually knew if he was ill, or working on some other assignment. So I went looking for him. I eventually found him, in an isolated room at the end of one of the wings of the great cross building. It was on the top floor (fortunately as it turned out).

"Ishkari - what are you doing here? Don't you know what time it is?"

"Know?... I totally lost track of time. But I have made some amazing progress Peniel! Watch this!"

He had been "playing with" the element of air. He'd become so obsessed with it, he seemed a bit crazed. My Inner voice was cringing.

Suddenly, I felt a slight breeze blow by me. Objects in the room, like the pages of books, and tapestries began to flap as the breeze increased.

"I don't think you should be doing this." I said as the hackles on my neck bristled in the ever growing wind. He ignored me. He was deep in concentration, entranced.

The wind was getting very strong, blowing in a circular motion around the room, like an indoor tornado. Heavy objects like chairs were beginning to be blown over. Lamps and books were flying around the room the wind was so strong. Fortunately, I was in the center, or I would have been struck.

"Stop this NOW!" Still he ignored me. I felt myself being pulled into a vacuum or suction created by the wind in the center of the room, and I dropped to the ground. Just then, the roof of the building flew off, spinning up into the sky, along with most of the contents of the room.

He stopped suddenly, and so did the wind. But he wasn't upset about what he had done. He had a grin on his face. He was quite proud of himself.

"See?"

I didn't know what to say. It wasn't that the event was so remarkable - I had seen more amazing things by then. But his attitude, and his lack of caring - they frightened and shocked me.

Ishkari never again came to group meditations. He preferred to stay to himself. He was denied anymore training in science-magic, and not long after, he was asked to leave. He had failed the tests of having power, and not using it. There is more to the story, but to summarize, through his selfish separate self, he was seduced by the dark forces.

I always remembered that message I got from my Inner voice - the "cringing" feeling, and it served me time and time again in the future. It infallibly lets me know the real truth, even when logic, and all other appearances, seem to say otherwise.

Anyway, you get the idea, it is best that students first be trained in a safe environment, with supervision, in order to grow strong in the light before they venture out to illuminate the darkness. Only when they are home, One with the All, will they be able to safely and positively effect those they come in contact with.

Seclusion from Temptations until Willpower is Forged

If you are on your spiritual path, but not living in a monastic situation, and you have not yet completed the metamorphosis to being a Sun of Unselfish Love, you will find that the temptations of the world are great. The more you try to develop self-discipline, the more the separate self rebels, and fills you with temptations. The self hits you with urges and desires stronger than you have experienced before. As you just read about Ishkari, even having the right support structure was not enough for him. It is hard enough being in the proper environment to survive the urgings of the separate self, let alone doing it on your own. So being in an environment where everyone is doing the same things for discipline, or development, helps you get through these times, while you are forging a willpower of steel.

The other side of the coin is this: if you are living amongst "regular" selfish people, those who's separate selves have full control, you don't just have your own temptations to deal with. You will also find that the people around you who are not on a path of Unselfish Love, will tend to hold you back. Old friends can both try and hold you back deliberately, because they don't like what you're doing, and accidentally, just because they are part of your past behavior patterns, and you will tend to fall back into these patterns when around them. This takes place in many ways, physically, mentally, and spiritually. Have you ever noticed how people take on certain traits of their close associates? There is an osmosis effect of influence. There is also a constant pressure to conform with your peers and not be "different". And when your friends' selfish separate selves realize that you are trying to transcend your own separate self, their selves will do everything they can to try to hold you down. You are becoming a threat to THEM (or at least what they think they are). Other people's selfish separate selves would rather keep you in the hole you're in, than have you get out of yours, and start mucking things up for *them*.

Witch Burner Syndrome

We already covered that it is only right to judge others' paths, in order to determine your own path. And I'm sure you understand that condemning others is wrong. But even if you have mastered that, and you have a deep, true feeling of "Live and let live", you will not be seen that way if you are on the path of Unselfish Love. Others will judge and condemn your "strange" manner as being immoral, blasphemous, evil, a scourge on society, or whatever. Some may set out to hurt you, in minor ways, or major ways. Even if they don't look at you this way in the present, seeds of condemnation can grow in a very clever, twisted sort of way. Here is a warning given to me by Vishnu:

"When you try to hold to the truth you've found, just living your own beliefs quietly to yourself, even though you aren't hurting anyone, condemning others, or telling *others* how *they* should be, people will often still *feel* like *you* are condemning *them*. It is the natural reaction of their separate self. They may also twist things around, and start thinking that *you* think that *you* are "better than they are". Even if you are not condemning them, people may still become hostile as if you were, simply because *you* are living by your own truth that you have found. Because when you live truth you shine it, and truth is a threat to their separate

239

selves. So their self will often create an illusion, a 'smoke screen' of feeling that *you* are judging and condemning *them,* when it is actually they who are condemning *you.* They do this at first as a defensive reaction, but later it can be used as a weapon."

Michiel added this:

"The I Ching tells us that in times of darkness, the superior man hides his light, yet still shines. A neophyte (novice) doesn't really know when it is proper to hide his light, and when he should let it shine unrestricted. Thus a monastic environment offers protection until the neophyte is fully developed."

Don't Bring Me Down

Vishnu again spoke, "Outside of your monastic environment, one way or another, you will be a target for the negativity of others, including 'friends' who don't see things the same way as you. Then there are those 'friends' that may see things the way you do, but they are not willing to change. In either case, they will be negative towards you to some degree or another. They will bring pressure to bear. And unless you have transcended your separate self, their negativity will effect you. Unless you do something to stop it, it can fan the flames of negativity in you, and spread back to them. Have you not seen arguments, which start when one person is negative and the other is not (at first). Hostility is infectious. Getting infected with hostility lowers the consciousness."

Zain cut in, "This is like the tuning fork effect we spoke of earlier. Just as Inner Being responds to Inner Being, the separate self responds at the same level of negative vibrations from another separate self, and if you have not transcended your own separate self, so as to be able to feel that in yourself without losing your balance, your inner composure, then you end up being 'mad' or upset yourself; then you start sending out more negativity, physically, verbally, or psychically (or all three). And it builds. And it grows.

That same principle works in subtle ways, too. Being around lower consciousness people holds your consciousness down unless you have become a light. Have you ever noticed children, or friends, who, when they are alone, behave one way, but when they get around a certain person, or group, they behave differently?"

"Yes, I have, but I've always ignored it, or put it off to peer pressure," I said.

"True also, but what are the truths behind peer pressure?"

"Ah," I said. "So much more than meets the eye."

Let Go of your Baggage
Until you're Strong Enough to Carry It

During my first months at the monastery, once in a while I missed my old girlfriend, whom I'd left behind. I told her what I was doing and asked her to come with me, but she would have nothing to do with it. To her, it was bad enough when I went through more subtle changes in my younger years prior to going to the monastery. She got angry anytime I moved even a hair closer to Unselfish Love. I can still hear her scream at me in anger in later years after my enlightenment "You love everybody!!!" She said it like it was a degenerate crime. Why? Because her separate self had no possessive hold on mine.

I knew our parting was for the best though. If it weren't for the monastery, and I hadn't succeeded in my suicide attempt, we'd probably still be seeing each other on and off, driving each other crazy, and we'd still be arguing all the time. We weren't good for each other, and the relationship did neither of us any good. But we still had strong attachments to each other. What a strange thing to have strong attachments to someone you can't get along with, and sometimes can't stand. I talked to Zain about it one day when I was thinking about it, and feeling depressed. His words cut through clear as a bell.

"When a seeker *has thus taken responsibility* for their life, and *accepted their responsibility* to be One with and serve God, they must then recreate their life, in a way that facilitates the change. A change from living for the separate self, to living for the manifestation of the Universal Spirit. One element of this change is 'letting go'. They must leave behind their old 'self-baggage', along with their past. They must leave behind and replace old selfish oriented programming and ideas. And they must let go of attachments to people from their old 'selfish oriented life', who they have self-oriented behavior patterns with, and who thus impede their spiritual development. This is the same for friends or lovers. After one changes, and is no longer subject to their own selfishness, then they can properly deal with such things - but ONLY then.

When we talk about letting go of an attachment to a person, it's not really *the person* we must let go of. We don't mean to say you *must* 'cut off ties' with someone, in order to let go of a selfish attachment (unless it is an abusive relationship, extremely detrimental, involves mutual negative dependence, or is like an out of control addiction). Although it may be far easier, quicker, and better to just cut things off clean. But sometimes the easy path is not the best, and often, such selfish attachments take care of themselves anyway, as do oil and vinegar. All that can be definitely said, is that we must lose our self's **selfish attachments**. Unfortunately, the primary reason for the existence of many relationships, is only based on "feeding off of" the attention each person's selfish separate self receives from the other. This creates mutual (or one sided) possessiveness, which in turn breeds all kinds of negative emotions depending on the changing tides of circumstances. This is especially true in intimate or 'romantic' relationships. Also, hobbies, interests or ideals, were perhaps once held in common. But as people change, so do interests and ideals. And then there is also karma to take into consideration. This one you speak of, may be a soulmate, but her consciousness is not on the level of yours, and she is not willing to grow - and your consciousness and Inner strength, are not on the level of being up to the task of helping her - for now at least. But sometimes, when your paths take you in different directions, you should let go, you must let go. And even if you refuse to let go, sometimes fate gives you no choice. Always remember though, those who *truly* belong together, will never be parted forever, and often, not for long. But in any case, you must free yourself from your attachments to those who have any measure of negative influence over you, or who impede your spiritual growth, your flowing with Universal Will, or your manifestation of God. Unselfish Love, God's Love, is impersonal, it loves everyone. It is the separate self that cuts us off from this, and prevents this, and one of the ways it does it is by developing separate self-oriented attachments."

"What do you mean that sometimes fate takes care of it?"

"The Universal Law of vibration *automatically* creates changes of associates *when you change*. Remember our discussion with Gabriel. Oil and vinegar are of different molecular vibrations - and they will each seek their own level even if you mix them up. If a part of the oil changed to become vinegar, it would join the vinegar level, and be surrounded by vinegar, and vice-versa. As you change your level of consciousness (your vibration) to a higher one, you rise to a new level where new higher consciousness friends will be found. Those of the old vibration *that do not change* as you do, may try to hold you down. But if they are unsuccessful, they generally just ultimately 'fall away' and stay behind in their own choice of worlds, their own choice of consciousness - all of their own accord. To them, your changes make you 'weird', boring, and 'no fun'. And to you, they also become un-interesting, 'shallow' and boring. When this happens, it may initially feel like a 'loss', but when you merge into your new higher level of consciousness, and find those who belong with you on the same level, it feels wonderful. It is an incredible feeling to find your new higher companions, 'soulmates', or soulgroup family.

But *before you can change,* and find your new natural vibrational level, you must *make* those changes happen.

Selfish-oriented relationships are virtually the only kind of relationships non-enlightened beings have. The spiritual seeker needs to get free from the negative effects of such relationships. While selfishly based romantic relationships, are a *big* problem, the more subtle relationships with friends, and other relationships offer problems and challenges also."

"Like what?"

"The spiritual seeker who wants to change as rapidly as possible, should stop wasting any time. And if part of that wasting time is 'hanging out' with people or 'friends' who's direction in life is self-centered rather than Universal or spiritual - regardless of how 'nice' or 'harmless' this seems to be, then you are slowing yourself down, or even maybe condemning yourself. People have established patterns of behavior in their relationships, based on complex interactions between the selfish separate selves who are involved.   For the seeker, these behavior patterns are negative side trips off their main spiritual path."

"I'm not sure what you mean exactly. Could you be more specific?"

"You know what I mean - diversions, selfish 'highs', making small talk, playing or watching 'games', pursuing mutually selfish interests, 'doing business', whatever. The 'behavior patterns' of those who are in such self-oriented relationships, are 'selfish separate self *supportive'*, and thus negative. And the patterns can't be changed until a student is totally free from his own selfish separate self. That's one reason there have always been monasteries and convents - so people can focus only on their growth without any diversions or temptations even offering themselves - until they have either achieved their goal, or become strong enough to be un-influenceable."

"So you mean avoid things you have in common or do in common, that are fruitless?"

"Not just *doing things* that are *fruitless*. An entire association can be harmful. Just like addicts, or criminals, there are many subtle, seemingly harmless behaviors that can negatively affect you. Whether it just takes a *moment* away from your growth (which could be that *one* extra moment you needed to achieve enlightenment before you die), or it takes a moment away from something vital that you might eventually be doing to help others once you are serving God - or something that actually is directly harmful. A former criminal who *really wants* to go straight should no longer associate with former friends who are still criminals - because they are likely to commit crimes again, true?"

"Yes."

"A drug addict who *really wants* to 'kick the habit' should not associate with drug addict friends - or he is likely to use drugs again, true?"

"Yes."

"The selfish separate self is similarly affected by other selfish separate selves. Thus the true seeker of spiritual change, who *really wants* to change, must treat his separate self 'addiction' just as seriously. And if they want to be more sure of 'staying on the wagon', they need to keep away from both the 'drugs' that feed the addiction, and from those who are addicts. Like I said, that doesn't necessarily mean never seeing or talking to your old associates again. But it is obvious that you do need to focus on freeing yourself from your own selfish separate self, 'kick the habit' totally, and become immune to the negative effects of being around other selfish separate selves. Otherwise, you will never be truly 'good' for the person in that relationship, and they will never be good for you. That is one of the functions of monasteries, but it could also be fulfilled by one or more friends who are on the same path, or at least going in a similar direction as you. Things will be changing in the future, and you will have to find new ways to accomplish helping people with this sort of thing, without our monastery, or possibly any monastery."

"What?"

"It is not time. Let me go on. Just remember this. Whether you have a traditional monastery or not, it is vital for the serious spiritual seeker, and student, who wishes to grow as fast as possible, to find associates who are not part of their selfish attachments or selfish addictive past. Instead, they should surround themselves, or primarily associate with people who have a similar spiritual orientation, and who's company is spiritually supportive. This is very important because again, at this early stage of beginning to change, the outside influences of one's associates, have a great effect - thus people need monasteries, spiritual communities, or at least friends and associates on the same path."

I'll Scratch Your separate self if You Scratch Mine

"But leaving people behind. What of those who need you, who you could have helped if you stayed with them, or at least stayed in touch. I have regrets over this. My old friends, are hurt. My family hates me for abandoning my mother while she was sick."

"Does she have no one to care for her?"

"No, she does. We weren't really associating anyway because she didn't like my girlfriend, and she told me to get rid of my girlfriend, or get out of the house when I was 16 years old. And she has her brothers and sisters that take care of her."

"What is wrong with her?"

"Something called shingles. It is like little sores along the spine, and the doctors said it is emotionally stimulated."

"Ah. And why did she get sick?"

"I think it was to keep me there. She has a powerful mind. But there was also one of my friends. He was so close he almost came with me here."

"Yet he is not here? Why?"

"His girlfriend got pregnant and convinced him to stay."

"Proving my point it seems."

"But what if I could have helped him still?"

"First... listen to me now! This is vital for you to understand and remember - **until you transcend your separate self,** *even if you are not being negatively affected by those around you,* **you will not be of any real aid to them, or anyone.** Because with your separate self in control, your thoughts, words, and actions, will tend to 'feed', and feed off of, the separate self of others - as your separate self strives to survive. Your only real chance to help your mother, or your friends, is to change yourself first. Secondly, you have so many to help. You must care as much about a stranger as much as your closest friend. Why is a stranger any less important, than your friends or relatives - or your 'drinking buddies', 'fishing buddies', 'bridge club' or whomever? We are all identical children of the One God. All just as important as any other. The beggar in the street, is as important as the king of the world. If you don't feel that way, you don't have Unselfish Love, or Universal Consciousness, and you are useless to anyone. All beings are part of the One - all the same underneath. All Children of the One God. And you have many you will help. If you stayed behind, what help would you have been to anyone, including your mother or friends, honestly? You just MAY be able to help your mother and your friends after you truly love them, but that will also be up to them. But now. You are still just selfish and uncaring yourself. So how much help can you be now?"

"None. Thank you. It is much clearer now."

So the teachings advise those who seek Oneness with the Universal Spirit, to place themselves in a monastic community, where they can nurture and develop in Spirit. It doesn't need to be big. You can even do it with a couple of like minded friends or relatives. As long as everyone understands the rules of interaction, giving, and living with each other. It would also be good to have a teacher in such a situation, but even without one, there definitely needs to be a "head" for the body, that everyone agrees will have final say so, and has a good amount of respect for, at least initially. The teacher doesn't necessarily need to be living with you, although that is the most desirable. But you must have a teacher that everyone agrees has greater insight than their own, and has the respect to give direction and input to all members, and to decide any disagreements if (when) they crop up. The most important thing is that each member approach each other member with total humility, rather than defensiveness. One of the biggest problems the self creates to defeat growth, is the ego trait of wanting to be right all the time (or at least having the appearance of being right). A person who is set on *appearing* right all the time, actually creates a pattern in which they are usually wrong most of the time, and worse, they don't even learn from their mistakes. But a person who doesn't care how they appear to others, and has a humble attitude, will eventually *be* right all the time. A musician who is afraid to hit wrong notes when they are learning or playing, will learn far slower, and be a much poorer player, than the one who takes the risk and goes for it, and doesn't care if he looks foolish because he hits a wrong note once in while - that one will be the fastest learner and ultimately the greatest artist. Be humble and you will grow. Be the lowest and you will be the highest.

Give Only to the Spirit in Others

From Vishnu:

"Through practicing giving within your circle of like minded people, you will eventually know well the difference between giving to the separate self and giving to the Whole Being and Inner Being. Eventually you will be able to give to the entire world, even to those who would selfishly take, for you will be giving what they need for their spiritual development, rather than nurturing their separate selves."

One Hand Washes the Other

From Michiel:

"The ideal state of things is for *everyone* to be giving all the time. This is the state of paradise. In an ideal material world this would include material things. On the material plane (which indeed is part of the whole and should reflect Universal Harmony) everyone has different talents and skills, and if all give, all needs will be filled. For example, a seamstress makes clothes, a shoemaker makes shoes, a carpenter carps, etc. In a world where everyone is giving, taking care of each other, it would work very simply. If the seamstress needs shoes, she gets them. If the shoemaker needs a house, it's built. If the carpenter needs clothes, they're made. No bargaining a trade, no buying or selling, just giving, just Unselfish Love. This is the idea behind 'brotherly ' love - *and* communism. But communism doesn't work well for the ordinary people of the world. Do you know why? The same reason nothing works well. **Selfishness.** And with selfishness mixed with communism, it can be worse. When you take away the greed factor in making a living, and put things on a level that all things are shared, people start putting out less effort. They do this for a couple of reasons: 1) They know they will get taken care of regardless of how much they contribute. 2) They know that regardless of how much they contribute, they won't get any more than a share in everyone's prosperity. How sad. Done properly, by Unselfishly Loving beings, such a thing would increase the wealth, beauty, and creativity of an entire society beyond anything that's been known. What else is our monastery but this. But the selfish separate self will always prevent that as long as it is in control. And, as we have seen by the communist governments that were controlled by selfish separate selves, they would cheat and destroy it all anyway. The only reason it can work in a monastery, is because we can control it here so much better, so much more easily, and the main concern or direction here, is to become selfless and giving, not just to share everything equally, and selfishly.

Fortunately, until the whole world can live together in Unselfish Love, we have the mini-world, the mini-society, the spiritual community, where those who desire to, can open up and give of themselves. In a monastery community such as that, everyone is either already Unselfishly Loving, or working towards achieving that. And such joining of forces makes for a much greater force. Of course, even in our own monastery, we must stay vigilant, and occasionally must route out and chastise the lazy who would selfishly take advantage of our brotherly love, but overall, it is the greatest way of living.

This quote from the I Ching is a favorite of mine regarding the essence of the spiritual community or monastery:

"What is required is that we unite with others, in order that all may compliment and aid one another through holding together. But such holding together calls for a central figure around whom other persons may unite... If a man has recognized the necessity for union and does not feel strong enough to function as the center, it is his duty to become a member of some other

organic fellowship."

There have been many sorts of alternative communities formed over the years. Communities with a strong spiritual foundation, and leadership, are the ones that stand the test of time. Those that don't have strong spiritual leadership, usually disintegrate, entirely or partially, with the members withdrawing from each other into their separate spaces, holding bitter feelings.

There will eventually come a time when everyone will be Unselfishly Loving and One with the Universal One, then there will be no need for leaders or teachers, and 'government' will come from within. But in a spiritual community, at this stage of consciousness evolution, there is a definite need for leadership.

First, that problem of selfish people not carrying their own weight, can affect, and infect, a monastery also. There needs to be a clear sighted, well respected leader, in order to avoid leeches, corruption, and to "ride the stragglers".

For a community, having a good leader is like having a "good head on your shoulders". Leadership is necessary for coordination of the members' activities (somewhat like the way the mind coordinates the various functions of the "members" of a physical body).

Finally, an Unselfishly Loving leader/teacher can function as a means of response and attunement to the Universal Consciousness/God through the application of devoted Unselfish Love (the practice of Bakti yoga). This is a method by which the love the student has for the teacher, tunes the student into the teacher's Universal Consciousness, and thus raises the student's own consciousness.

Besides the functions and purposes of the spiritual community we have thus far mentioned, there is also the advantage of the concentrated/combined power you have when people unite. Great things can be accomplished when we work as One. Alone, we can accomplish little compared to that which we can do together. 'Whenever two or more are gathered together in His name...'"

The New Monasticism - Fellowship in the New World

As I started out saying in the beginning of this chapter, times change. Our monastery in Tibet is destroyed, and many teachers, students, and householders have been murdered. We need new monasteries, but in these times there is the danger that any small true spiritual movement in which people live together in a monastic fashion, will simply be labeled a "cult", demonized, attacked and destroyed. Such labeling and harassment can even happen just because it doesn't fit in with the ever more closely monitored "norm of behavior". So regarding new monasteries, it cannot be just as it was - perhaps in the future, after the great changes, but not now. On a side note, fortunately, the great changes *are* coming. The prophecies, including the "desecration of the land of the teachers", have come to pass, and more prophecies are still being fulfilled. Just today, I saw the destruction of the Church of Assisi where St. Francis was buried. It was devastated by an earthquake - it was a sign, a fulfillment of prophecy. Also as I write, a cloud of smoke half the size of the United States, is choking people around Asia, and the incredible fires that are causing it, were started by humans destroying more fertile soil. And humans changing the atmosphere of the Earth itself - "El Nino" phenomenon, dying reefs, giant holes of ozone depletion, over-fishing of the oceans. You name it, there it is. As humankind's stupidity brings nature's reactions, we are accelerating towards change. More volcanoes are activating and erupting. People everywhere are dying of drought, flooding, and new diseases. Famine and eco-nomic collapse are around the corner. Many people don't see it and don't want to believe these things are coming. They're in denial because they're afraid. It's quite natural, because the scenario can be quite frightening. But seeing what is really going on, and what is coming, is just a matter of opening your eyes, and looking at it all *without fear*. It helps if you see it as a healing crisis rather than just a horri-ble meaningless destruction.

Back to the new monasticism. For some of you, this book is just somewhat interesting (or somewhat boring) reading. For others, it is what you have hoped for, and you'll want more. For you, our order is still here, but the outer form has been forcibly changed, and a new one is being born. Some of our ways of life of the past are gone. Time is short, and we must adapt, or cease to survive entirely. Thus, we must use the tools of these times to our own ends as much as possible. The future will see the building of new monasteries, centers or communities. Perhaps bene-factors will come forward to help, but in any case, we will find the means if it is in the Will of the Universal Spirit. But as long as one of us is still alive, we will always carry on our work, with or without our primary monastery. There are still teachers around the world for those who want, need, and are ready for one. And advances in technology are also affording new ways of reaching and helping large numbers of people, in many different ways. The vibrational sounds can accurately be repro-duced, and made available to the masses due to the advent of audio CD's. We now have websites that allow people to read free chapters of this book, learn medita-tions on-line, get books, vibrational sounds, yoga videos, music, and other tools for consciousness raising. It also serves a dual purpose, because the funds coming from it and mail order, help support our endeavors and monks - which in turn helps us help others. If we are able, we also envision creating a unique "spiritual resort" where people can come and spend time in a secluded, beautiful natural setting - and spiritual environment. Guests would have many options - they could just relax and enjoy the beauty of pristine nature, take walks along meditation paths, participate in group meditations and discussions/lectures, be alone with themselves and medi-tate at high energy vortexes, or learn new meditation, yoga, or interpersonal "Golden Rule" transformational techniques.

The internet and telecommunications has also afforded new means for spiritu-al interaction. If you want to network, or contact a teacher, elder, or novice, you can still use mail of course, but now you can also do so via Email (see end of book). The company who handles our mail orders can also set appointments for an elder monk to call you if you really need to speak with one. We can even help those of you who wish to network with each other, or form study groups with, to get in con-tact with each other. Anywhere in the world you can now stay in touch with each other, and even work together. What a strange, horrible, wonderful time!

[Note: we have been swamped with letters, emails, and people requesting calls. Unfortunately, we just don't have enough time and people to keep up with the volume. So if you write, or email, please keep in mind that we may not be able to get back to you for weeks, months, or even at all. If you have a very impor-tant message, you could leave a message with the mail order company that han-dles our products (number in back of book)]

Chapter Sixteen
Visualization and Affirmations

Visualization and affirmations are two languages/tools you can use to communicate to your sub-conscious and alter your programming.

As we have covered already, the subconscious mind, being very much like a computer, needs to have a program to run. The programming there determines most of the mental, and physical aspects of your being. The programming has had no conscious programmer. It has been programmed from birth by a flood of external influences, mostly negative. It is the programming of the bio-computer of your self - a separate entity in a world full of separate entities who are all looking out for number one, always seeking self-substantiation.

During my time as a novice, I didn't really understand the seriousness of this. I asked Zain:

"Why is it so emphasized here, and in the ancient teachings from Atlantis, that we must think of our thoughts as 'programming', pay so much attention to them, and devote so much of our time to it?"

"Oh, I forget [sarcasm]. It is simple, obvious. Just think-that's what makes everything-just thinking. Remember, action follows thought. The physical is the result of mental activities. The mind is the builder. *Everything* is the result of 'mere' thoughts. Thus it is vital to be able to communicate with, and alter, the programming that affects the mind. It all begins and ends there. That's why it is so important, and why it is taught that so much attention must be given to it.

Remember too, that for you to be in your proper place in the order of things, and experience peace and Oneness with the Universe, the mind should be used as a tool for the manifestation of the Universal Forces in the physical plane. But you have free will, and can choose to disregard the Universal Spirit. So what will you have your programming build in your life and the lives of others?

If you realize the importance of this, and decide to take control or your programming and thoughts, there are specific tools that can help you do so. Go read this now, and we will speak more of it afterwards."

Make It "Real" In Your Mind
And Your Mind Will Make it So

❖

Re-live Actions In the Realms of The Mind
Making It Right to Repeat it Not.

❖

Always Speak to Your Mind
In a Manner that Shows it
What You Desire to Achieve

As the Positive Outcome.

In Speaking to Your Mind
Never Fight the Negative
With Itself.

In a Direct Struggle
Good Will Lose to Evil.
Make Strong in the Good
And Evil Will Begone.

Be Ever Vigilant,
In Tending to Your Mind
Turn from Your Negative Thoughts,
Use Your Free Will
Dwell Only on Positive Thoughts.
And Success is Assured.

❖

Use Not Powers of Mind
But For Developing Virtue
And To Serve Universal Will

Affirmations

Affirmations are positive statements or directions you make to yourself in order to bring about changes in sub-conscious behavior patterns to whatever you *will* them to be. Even before I had a chance to talk to Zain after reading the texts he told me to look up, I "ran into" Michiel, who just "out of the blue" had this to say to me:

"Using an affirmation is like planting a seed in the fertile soil of your sub-conscious mind, and like a seed it needs daily tending or it may die. For this reason affirmations are tools that are used daily, and frequently, by those who wish to change.

It would be best if you received your individual affirmations from your personal true teacher, for he would best know what you should be working on for your particular situation."

If it is not possible for you to get your affirmations from your true teacher, because you have none, or have not "found" one yet, you could ask God for guidance (for affirmations) during meditation, or just think about negative/selfish traits you have, that you *know* you need to change, or positive traits you would like to acquire.

Later, I met with Zain, and asked him more about the subject.

"Father, what is the best way to use affirmations to change?"

"For those who really desire to change as quickly as possible, a positive affirmation should be done instantly, *every time* someone brings up to you an improvement you could make about your self, or points out a fault. This should be done instantly, and *sincerely,* with *thought,* right when it is brought up to you."

"But what if the person bringing something up to you is wrong?"

"Until you are enlightened, if you look sincerely, and hard enough at yourself, you will usually find some fault of your own at work in *any* argument, regardless of whether the origin of the argument was your fault, or what the issue the argument was about, or whether or not the claimed issue was 'your fault'. For instance, you might be in an argument in which someone else is totally wrong, but you became negative and stopped Unselfishly Loving. If you have realized enough that you finally understand that there is absolutely no reason good enough to stop Loving Unselfishly, then you should do an affirmation something like this, regardless of what the argument was about, or what the outcome of it was: 'I am always Unselfishly Loving'. But for it to help, you need to really *feel* that, and *mean* that, when you say it, not just 'mouth' it, or it will not be an effective tool.

Consider this also, affirmations, to be effective, must always be stated as a positive result, rather than trying to 'negate' a negative. For instance, in the above example of an argument, the affirmation was not (and should not be), 'I am not negative. I do not get angry,' or such. It needs to be phrased in the positive way - something like 'I am positive, humble, and Unselfishly Loving.' Do you see the difference? In other words, you always say the good thing that you want to achieve, and never use a 'double negative', never even give energy to the negative trait that you wish to change, lest you actually feed the negative. Instead, you give energy to the positive trait that will supercede the negative.

Also, remember that the subconscious mind is something like a mindless robot - it only obeys and understands things *literally,* it doesn't "figure things out", "interpret" or "know what you mean". Thus, affirmations should always be stated as an *already accomplished fact,* such as 'I am_____.', rather than stating them as unaccomplished possible future events like 'I will be____.' or 'I am going to be____.'. Or things like, 'I would like to be more____." Wording affirmations in those ways either just won't make sense to the subconscious, or it tells the subconscious mind that this is some change that will *take place in the future.* And since the future is always *in* the future, it actually prevents the changes from *ever* taking place - because we are always in the 'now'. For instance, let's say you were a robot who was holding a spoon, and I wanted you to drop your spoon. I would need to figure out *exactly* what to say to you to make you drop your spoon. If I know that you only take my words literally, just as the subconscious mind does, then I need to phrase my words to you properly, or you won't understand that I want you to drop the spoon, and you won't do it. So if I said to you, 'you will be dropping the spoon', that literally means to you that you WILL be dropping the spoon, not that you should drop it NOW. So what happens? You hold on to it, waiting for that time in the future when you WILL BE dropping it. But if I say 'drop the spoon', or 'you are dropping the spoon', you would drop it - see?

Finally, you must really *want* to change. If you don't, affirmations will have little effect."

"What affirmations should I do Father?"

He contemplated it for a day, and then proceeded to give me my personal affirmations, then he told me about general ones I should do.

Some Fundamental Positive Affirmations

"Besides the personal affirmations you come up with, there are some general affirmations that the Children have used since Atlantis, and are still taught for everyone. These are the standard affirmations as were given to me, and which I give to you now:

Morning affirmation: First, conceive of the highest power you can, obviously, whatever you can grasp of the Universal Spirit at this time. There is always somewhat of a problem with that when you are still an unenlightened student, because you aren't really capable of conceiving of "God". Because of the Infinite nature of God, it is difficult for the novice to really conceive of God until he has become more familiar with it. Until then, a novice can know the Universal Spirit best through those beings who are one with and manifesting it. For instance, a Universally Conscious saint or true teacher, that you know."

"Why them?"

"Because such a person reflects God in their being - it's in their thoughts, words, and actions. It is best if you use the image of a true teacher that you actually know. When you know such a person, you also know the Universal Spirit in a personal way, manifested before you in day to day life. That person can then become an 'ideal'. The ideal then represents God, via an enlightened being who is One with God. If you don't know someone personally, just think of the spiritually highest person you have ever learned of, such as Jesus in your case, but for others it may be Buddha or Mohammed, or whomever. Thus you conceive of the highest power you can, and indirectly conceive of God. When you are thinking of your ideal though, make sure you are not thinking of the person's self, but rather the part of them that is the Universal Spirit.

Now, while you are holding your ideal in mind, say to yourself, silently, or out loud in private, and with full meaning, *feeling* it, not as just a repetition of words, 'Your will be done God (whatever name for God you choose), not mine, in me and through me; show me what I must do this day, and let me be a channel of your blessings to all.' As with all the affirmations you do, repeat it for five minutes.

Evening affirmations: Begin with, 'My concentration is becoming perfect.' That should be done for two weeks, then change to, 'My concentration is perfect.' These are basically meant to help develop abilities of concentration that help you do other exercises, but they are good affirmations to do alone also. As in your case, a student may also have other evening affirmations specifically for them. And then you should do the dream affirmation (below).

Pre-sleep affirmation: This is often the most effective affirmation because you repeat it as you are going to sleep; this carries it deeper into the sub-conscious. For this reason your highest priority affirmation should be done as you go to sleep.

If you want to be able to remember your dreams in the morning, or you want to be conscious of your dreams while you are having them, use the following statement as the pre-sleep affirmation until the difficulty is resolved: 'I remember my dreams and I am conscious while dreaming.' This should also be used for its ability to aid in integrating your threefold consciousness."

Visualization

"You said there were various tools for working with your thoughts, and programming, so other than affirmations, what can I do?"

251

"Visualization is another means of 'talking' to, or making non-verbal affirmations to, the subconscious. It is an **extremely powerful** mental language. And it both programs the sub-conscious, and directs those 'building blocks' of our physical reality: thoughts."

[Author's note: the results of visualization can be incredible. It can help heal the terminally ill. Scientific studies have shown that basketball players who visualize winning, win more games, even if they don't practice. And, it has long been used as a powerful tool for magic, both black and white. For our purposes, it can help us attain positive changes in our programming, and consciousness. Used with verbal affirmations, and a strong desire to change, there is no stopping it.]

"So how do you do visualizations Father, other than what it sounds like?"

"Visualization is not something exotic that requires training. It is very easy and natural to do. In fact, everyone does it all the time - some more than others. Surely you have 'imagined' what this or that would be like - or what would happen if 'this or that' took place, etc.. Have you ever imagined what you are going to have for dinner, or where you are going after working, or what you will do with so and so...? 'Imagining' something is putting it into an 'image', thus, VISUALizing it.

So, you see, everyone is already using visualization daily, but using it *unconsciously*. This means that rather than everyone consciously choosing what to visualize everyday, their subconscious minds, under the urging of their separate selves, are doing it 'behind their backs' - and to what ends? Sometimes the unconscious visualization is just something innocuous, like a person imagining what restaurant they will go to for lunch today. But other times, it can be very harmful - dwelling on things like selfish desires, jealousy, attachments, addictions, etc., and actually 'building' these things, *insuring* that *we will keep them* in our life, or *bring* them into our life. To summarize, when we visualize in an unconscious selfish state of mind, nothing good will become of it, and often it is destructive."

"So all there really is to it is 'seeing' something being done, or already accomplished in our mind's eye."

Complete Visualization

"Essentially, yes. But the more detail you can add to your visualization, the more powerfully it works. Using visualizations or 'imaginizations' that include more than one of the senses can help. For instance, if you not only see (visual-ize) what you are going to have for dinner, but you also imagine the smell, the taste, the texture, hear the sounds of the dining room - it will ingrain deeper into your mind. But one of the most *powerful* adjuncts of detailing a visualization, is *emotional content*. If you can visualize, not just the sensations, but also the *feeling* associated with eating that dinner, and being at that restaurant, and being with who you are with - you get *very* effective 'planting' of that in your mind. We call this method of visualizing with emotional and sensational content, 'complete visualization'. For obvious reasons, complete visualization is the visualization method used by the Children since the beginnings in Atlantis."

"What about combining this way of visualizing things, with other techniques?"

"Certainly. Using complete visualization is also the most powerful way to 'supercharge' certain meditation techniques. Any technique involving energy visualization lends itself particularly well to 'feeling' the sensations of that energy, for instance. Other meditations may work particularly well by deliberately cultivating your emotional 'feeling'.

252

Meditation is not the only growth technique that can benefit from complete visualization. Using the method as an 'affirmation', or 're-creating' events in the mind, are highly effective means of changing programming. For instance, if you were afraid of flying you could visualize yourself flying, feel the sensations, and most importantly, emotionally feel yourself being happy, and enjoying the flight. You could do this as a 'program' before flying again, or if you have just had a fearful flight experience, you could use it as a corrective re-creation. In a re-creation scenario, you would see yourself just as you were, but replace the fear with enjoyment, and use complete visualization to imagine how events of the flight *would* have gone had you been happy instead of fearful."

"What about fear of death?"

"Yes, even that. Fear of death is just generated from the selfish separate self after all.

The same methods also apply to any aspect of selfishness that you may wish to change. For instance, if you have discovered you are 'stingy - a cheap-skate' and you want to change that, then you would use complete visualization to see yourself feeling good about giving or sharing. Let's say you just had a situation come up, where a friend wanted to borrow something, and you *begrudgingly* gave them what they asked for, and didn't feel good about giving it to them. In such instances, when you re-create it in your mind, you replace the unpleasant 'begrudging' feelings with the feelings of joy that come from giving. If you do this EVERY time a situation comes up, OR EVEN A NEGATIVE THOUGHT CREEPS INTO YOUR HEAD, you will change as long as you really want to. And before long, with consistency and persistence, the negative thoughts won't even creep in any more - the separate self's selfishness will have 'given up'."

Daydreams

Zain once caught me "daydreaming", but rather than chastising me for it, he explained how to use it to our advantage.

"Daydreams are an elaborate, and deep, form of imagining or visualizing. These can be powerfully used to your advantage if you construct an elaborate complete visualization 'dream sequence' that encompasses what you want to achieve."

A Warning

Affirmations and visualizations are very powerful and must be respected as such. As was said earlier, an affirmation or thought, is like a seed. And it is governed by the Universal Law of cause and effect, "What you sow you shall reap". Thus, affirmations should always be consistent with spiritual purposes and ideals. Also, it is better to use affirmations and visualization only for development of positive traits, and positively changing your subconscious programming. And even then it should be done with the inclusion of a "conditional" affirmation like: "Only if it is within the will of the Universal Spirit". Because with a separate point of view, you don't always know what is *really* best in a given situation, and you could cause problems by using an affirmation/visualization to do specifically what you "think" is right. For example, let's say you are feeling a pain in your foot. So you decide to do an affirmation to "not feel" the pain in your foot. There are many problems with this.

1) The sensation (pain) may be telling you something you need to know about the condition of your foot, that you should attend to before it gets worse.

2) You could damage your foot because of the lack of sensation (you could ram it into things repeatedly; accidentally put a chair leg on it, etc.)

3) You may be denying yourself a raise in consciousness from transcending that pain.

4) Also, you could be missing the gift of getting to the source of why you are having the problem in the first place.

A person should usually eliminate the cause rather than masking the effect.

The same applies to "prayer". Michiel warned us of the possible problems during a lecture on affirmations and prayer in the hall of the pyramid.

"Let's say someone is ill. You could pray for the illness to be removed or healed, but that may not be the best thing for the person's 'whole' being. You may be denying them the raise in consciousness being offered to them through the illness. Healing should be from within, or at least occur simultaneously. Instead of trying to override Universal Will, or asking God (praying) to heal someone. The very doing of such a thing egotistically implies that the Universal Spirit and the hierarchy either doesn't know what is best, but that you *do;* or it implies that God 'probably just didn't know about it' - which makes no sense either; or it means you *personally* needed to ask, or God would do nothing about it. It is all egotistical and absurd. You must be very important and God must be very inadequate and uninformed for such to be the case. If you are humble, and have realized the existence of Universal Will, then you will probably just visualize the person surrounded in light, and affirm your concern and desire for the Universal Spirit to do whatever is best in that situation. NOT what *you* think is best in the situation."

There is an old story you may know called "The Monkey's Paw" that is a very good allegory for this lesson of asking, or praying, for specific things. There are many variations to this story, but they all offer the same essential lesson. The story goes something like this. A family comes into possession of a magical monkey's paw that has the power to grant its owners three wishes. For their first wish they ask for a large sum of money. At first nothing seems to happen, but then, sometime later, the son is killed at work, mangled beyond recognition as he gets caught in some machinery. The exact amount of money wished for comes in the form of the son's life insurance policy. Hmm... Days later, after the son has been buried, his mother, who is totally broken up over the boy's death, wishes him brought back to life. The son is given life again, but in the same condition as he lay in the ground. As the son claws at the front door of the house trying to get in, his father, realizing the situation, wishes the son back to the grave, and destroys the monkey's paw in a fire. The moral? We don't know the details of the consequences of what we wish, pray, or do magic for. And we can unintentionally cause terrible things to happen by forcing something we want to happen, or getting it supernaturally via prayer, mind power, or magic. Let those who have the full awareness and omnipotent overview make such decisions. Watch what you ask for, you might just get it; and you just might get the unknown consequences.

Like I just mentioned, not only does this warning apply to prayer and other forms of wishes, it applies to the practice of magic. When I say magic, most people think of "Black magic", and some think of "White magic". Both types of magic use visualization, affirmation, and possibly ritual, to "make something happen the way they want". By definition, the practitioner of Black magic seeks what they want at any cost, including harming others. It may also be used to deliberately harm others. White magic practitioners generally draw the line at consciously doing anything that would harm someone else. Sometimes people don't consider "visualization" or "prayer" to be any kind of magic. After all, it only involves visualizing or pushing for what they want, that (in their opinion) would be good for them or others - like a promotion, or a new car, or world peace, or someone who is ill getting better. *But it can have the same results* as Black magic, because the practitioners don't know what will need to happen in order to make their desires materialize. The "Monkey's Paw" demonstrated how this can happen. Those people didn't want to hurt anyone, but they did.

Furthermore, many methods of personal growth and "achievement" are being touted today, that are really only magic in disguise. I knew a banker who told me that everyone at his bank was required to do training in which they would visualize their success - he was actually taught in a seminar, to see himself having lots of money, driving a Cadillac, answering calls as a branch manager, etc.. He was being taught magic, with no concerns or warnings as to its possible ramifications! And with such visualization, there is no predication of how this will be accomplished, or even a safety affirmation clause like, "If it is within Universal Will". What if the only way he can become branch manager is for another branch manager to have a car accident and die?

These kind of dangerous, yet "disguised", magic techniques are being taught in "seminars". They are everywhere. Their success is spawned by the combination of the cleverness of the dark forces, and the selfish separate self's desire to maintain control and get what it wants. Thus people are easily "sold" on using such techniques.

As usual, the self will twist the truth to its own advantage. You hear people talk about creating their own reality - which is true and necessary to realize in order for their Inner Being to take control, but it is selfishly twisted around so that they think that it means creating such things as a winter house in Aspen - *and they don't know, or consider, what might occur in order to make that happen.* They use techniques to "attract" wealth, not realizing it is black magic couched in a pretty package, and that it can cause disastrous results. They talk about visualizing world peace, but they don't understand that it could mean peace because we're all slaves of a tyrannical world government run by a new Hitler, and all opposition has been crushed.

If the monkey's paw story wasn't enough to get the point across, let me give you one more story from my personal experiences, that makes the point.

About 25 years ago, we were moving to a new city. Since we needed new cars, we flew there, and started shopping for cars. I went to a car dealer, met the owner, and, as will sometimes "happen", we got into a long and intense spiritual and metaphysical conversation. He was a metaphysician, and practiced visualization and "magic" to get what he wanted. We debated about the right and wrong of causing things to happen yourself. It was a friendly debate. He argued his points, and I argued mine.

"It is dangerous to take things into our own hands in the way you prescribe," I said. "You can't know all the details that will be involved, and some could cause great harm. To train to be *able* to make things happen metaphysically is one thing, but we shouldn't use powers directly, with our limited viewpoint."

255

He said, "I disagree. We totally create our own reality, and if we are not trying to harm anyone else, what is the harm in improving your own life?"

His arguments were perfectly logical of course, but greater insight goes beyond that logic. I tried to explain the concepts of consciousness, hierarchy, and that hierarchical consciousness was superior to ours.

"I believe we should just allow the hierarchy to work through us if they see that it is necessary, otherwise, we can make trouble for ourselves and others."

He, of course, disagreed. We were about to leave, but unbeknownst to me, a lesson was in the works, in which the hierarchy would try to make the point to him in no uncertain terms.

The car dealer walked us out to our rental car. It would not start. It was late, about 11 PM by the time we'd finished our discussion. Along the lines of our debate, he said he could make it start with magic, and it would be of benefit to us. I know such things can be done, because I've seen it, and done it myself under certain circumstances. But this wasn't one of those circumstances.

"You're tired and need to get to your hotel," he said. "Now look, I can make it start, and it will just prove my point."

I believe he could have made it start under normal circumstances, but the hierarchy was actually preventing it and he couldn't override it. I knew the car was not starting for some reason other than mechanical. At the time, I thought it was just to show him he wasn't as powerful as he thought, take his ego down a notch, and perhaps give him a chance to learn a little more humility. But you never know. All I knew for sure, was that I sensed the powers of light were at work, and that the hierarchy didn't want it to start for some reason, and that was good enough for me.

"There are higher spiritual forces at work here, Ralph. I know you are capable of making it start, you don't have to prove anything to me. But I don't want you to make it start. I am capable of such things myself, and I'd just do it myself it I *knew for certain* it was right. But as I said earlier, I won't interfere with what I believe are higher consciousness forces of light, taking care of things."

He tried anyway. It didn't work. Finally, he gave up, and offered to lend me one of the other cars on his lot. It wouldn't start either. Then another. Then another. Then another. These were not "junkers" either, they were new and barely used BMW's, Jaguars, Mercedes, Porches, Corvettes, etc. - yet nothing would start.

Finally, after about 20 cars, he was getting a little jangled (because of the strangeness of this occurring after our conversation, and the ridiculous odds against none of his fine cars starting).

"I'm really sorry about this. I don't get it. I'll drive you to your hotel myself, and have your car ready and delivered to you first thing in the morning."

Interestingly enough, his car started. But then, halfway to the hotel, it died and would not re-start.

"This is ridiculous. It's _____ unbelievable," he said as he pounded his steering wheel in frustration.

"I'll go call my wife and have her pick us up. I'm really sorry about this Jon."

"No need to be sorry - it's out of your control. There's some reason for this."
He just looked at me with a frightened, perplexed stare, then walked off.

We were in a bad industrial area of the city, and he had to walk two blocks to reach a phone. A half hour later, his wife arrived, and again we were off to the hotel.

When we got near the hotel, we were stopped at a roadblock. There were ambulances, paramedics, police, and flashing lights everywhere.

"What's going on???" We asked the police officer at the roadblock.

"There's been a chemical spill of some kind. We're getting everyone out."

Ralph argued with the police in his typical NY style, "But these people have a hotel at _____. And they've got to get there."

The officer responded politely, even though Ralph's comment was rude and stupid, "That's right near the center of the spill. I'm afraid you're going to have to find another hotel because I can't let you in there."

It was a seriously toxic chemical that was dumped by a tanker truck that was in an accident with another semi. They had evacuated and hospitalized people in and around the area of the hotel. Had the cars started, and had his car not broken down, we would have been in the midst of it right when it happened. The next day, all his cars started easily.

Who do *you* think it would be smarter to defer to regarding the actions and events in your life, your selfish separate self, or someone or something like a guardian angel - someone with far greater insight, who has greater wisdom, and the best intentions for everyone in mind? I can't tell you how many other examples I've seen of the hierarchy to the rescue. And some of those times I had to look very foolish. It was always worth it, whether I knew the outcome or not.

A Few Last Words

Here are a few things I want to stress: the sub-conscious is also programmed through strong desires and fears. And remember, whatever one holds as an ideal effects the programming (also see chapter on Ideals). Be aware of all these ways your programming can be altered, and be very discriminating as to what you allow to enter, and what you allow to remain. But most importantly, one more time - you must really *want* to change.

Chapter Seventeen

Goals, Ideals, Self-discipline, Consistency/Perseverance

Everyone knows what a goal is. It's when you get a hockey puck past a goalie. But there are other kinds of goals too - even more important. Field goals, etc..

But other than that, people set goals of all kinds to achieve specific results. But many people set goals they fail to meet. Why? The teachings address different reasons and cures for this problem, including the areas of consciously developing self-discipline, and dealing with subconscious programming.

Developing Self-Discipline

During my first year at the monastery, I was having a hard time keeping up with my schedule, and getting my personal meditation schedule done consistently everyday. I was also having trouble concentrating during meditations.

My work load was intense. Between working in the kitchen, studies, courses, sessions with Zain, meditations and technique practices, and music practice/retraining, I was stretched very thin. Hairline thin. I was only getting about 3 hours sleep - every few days. I thought I'd reached a breaking point. So I sought out Zain for advice. He was eating at the time, and had to stop in order to help me.

"I know you think you are under severe hardship, and in part you are. You are in a period of learning self-discipline. And without it, NO ONE becomes anything of worth. Even in the worldly occupations. Those who are wealthy, who did not inherit their wealth, do you think they have not gone through hardships to learn self-discipline?"

"I don't know."

"Many of the most respected, most influential, most powerful, and most money making of the worldly professions, have such rigorous periods of training. Doctors, Lawyers, Wall Street execs, Record or Movie execs, business execs - any big profession has its big dues to pay first - and its hard times to endure. And the military - whether you are an 18 year old buck private, or you are in officer's school being groomed for the Admiralty, you have *severe* periods of discipline, *severe* hardships during training, and worse. But it too eventually pays off for those who choose that life (if they make it through it alive, or without dropping out or being kicked out)."

"I see your point. In fact, I hadn't thought about it, but I'd personally heard of the hardships of intern doctors from a friend. Interns are kind of like 'elders' I guess. They're no longer students really, but not full doctors either. And they have to pull hours like mine, with similar lack of sleep. But *they* are having to make life and death decisions at the same time."

"And those of any path in life, who go through their periods of hardships, and learn self-discipline, usually have their respective 'pay offs', when they finally become 'Adepts' in their profession. Just like the doctors, and such, do they not?"

"That's true."

And my chosen path was no different. Well, actually it was very different. I was training to become enlightened, to become a sort of saint. Someone to serve God, and the people of the world. Expecting it to be easy would be naive. But the "pay off" of enlightenment, Universal harmony, and peace of mind, was also the biggest pay off of them all. Even though it would still be the hardest work.

My talk with Zain definitely helped. But still, "knowing" all that, didn't really make it that much easier for me while I was going through my own hard times of training. It just gave me more conviction. But sometimes actions do more for you than words.

One time I slept through a very important morning group meditation and meeting that was on my schedule. I was lucky I wasn't in the army. If I were in the military, it would have been like missing revelry, calisthenics, and a first aid and war game briefing. If I were a med student, training for heart surgery, I just missed a class on resuscitation, and artery suturing. You get the picture. It was a bad move. But it was the last time I ever did that. I woke up in the cold pool. An unheated cold pool - in Tibet. An elders initiation in a way. Tough love. But I had chosen this path, and I had let myself fall asleep "on duty". And like I said, it did the trick.

While my training, and learning self-discipline was hard, I never regretted it. And it has come in very handy on many occasions. If fact, it still serves me to this day. Even this book would not have been completed otherwise, because I have been so ill during most of the past year. Deathly ill. I rarely have even been out of bed, yet for the most part, I work on it anyway, from waking, to sleep. No one without similar training and self-discipline could have accomplished it. But I must, and will, finish it. I'm not doing it for money. I have no need for that. I am not writing it for people's entertainment either. I am only doing it for those who find it helpful, or desperately need it.

Back on that particularly hard day for me though - the one in which I woke up in the pool, I started feeling a bit sorry for myself (getting negative), and my selfish separate self began to use my mind to sidetrack me. It wasn't bad, but it was performing the very early phase, subconscious, "tricks" - maneuvering for "building a case". A case for what? For eventually getting the heck away from all these things I was doing, and the people here - all the "stuff" that was threatening its power and control over me. At such an early stage, only a true teacher can perceive those kind of mind games.

As I walked around thinking heavy thoughts, I went by Zain, who noticed my "energy", and as fate would have it, he was trying to eat again.

"What's troubling you?" he said as if he didn't know.

"Nothing."

"Then I am a fool?"

"No. It's just the same thing we talked about. Self-discipline. And I'm having a hard time concentrating during my meditations, and getting them all done. I don't know if you noticed it, but I was asleep this morning during the meditations and meeting, and some of the elders threw me in the pool."

"Noticed it? Who do you think thought of the pool thing? I know how much you love freezing water first thing in the morning."

"Thanks."

"I do it every morning myself. It is very healthy. And very good for the self-discipline too. Did you know there are people who join clubs that go into the freezing water for fun?"

"I guess I'm an honorary member now."

He laughed. I was already feeling better, more positive, and more "on track" again.

"It was good for me. I admit it. I think it will definitely shift my self-discipline into high gear."

He tried to take a bite of his food while I was talking, but I apparently didn't talk long enough for him to get it down.

"This goes hand-in-hand with your meditation problems too. Self-discipline is directly related... (swallow) to concentration. If you have poor concentration, you will likely have poor self-discipline, and vice-versa. They are very much the same thing, only each affects a different 'time span'. Concentration involves using your will to hold your mind on whatever you choose, for a given period of time. Self-discipline involves using your will to hold your mind in a certain direction for a longer time span, and thus achieving a specific result. The result could be physical, mental, or spiritual. Could this wait till I'm done eating?"

"Of course Father, I didn't intend to..."

But he went on talking anyway.

"The most common factor here is *using your will* to direct the mind. Anything that strengthens the will, in either the area of concentration or self-discipline, will strengthen the ability in both areas. So you need to consider both."

"I can wait, really, there's no problem."

Concentration

"Oh, I was done anyway.

Some meditation techniques are specifically designed to develop concentration. Most people don't realize just how bad their concentration is until they start doing a meditation that involves concentration. They are shocked at how out of control their own mind is, how much mental garbage there is in there, and how much jabber is constantly going on. You just can't seem to stop the jabber, and once you've noticed it, it can really amaze you. I was confronted with this problem of concentration, and my mind wandering, way back when I was a young... Oh, what was I saying?"

He was joking, but I just decided to bow out and let him finish his meal.

Later that day, Mother Farida noticed me cursing beneath my breath when I was trying to meditate under an apple tree.

"You are upset about something?"

"Mother, I'm having a very hard time with my meditations. I just can't seem to concentrate and keep my mind on what I'm supposed to be thinking. It's very frustrating and I feel like I'll never get it."

"The separate self will rebel against the attempts to get control of the mind, and thus the 'monkey mind' can seem to get worse, even though all the more effort is put forth to develop concentration. So many students get disillusioned and frustrated, thinking they are not getting anywhere. But this is just a phase. If you simply stay consistent, and persevere in your meditations, you will develop concentration, you will achieve your goals. Don't let the separate self use the frustration trick to throw you off. That is what it is trying to do - and apparently succeeding right at this moment. Are you maintaining your meditation schedule, and staying consistent."

"Well, I miss some of my exercises."

"I thought so. You must stay committed. Do not let up."

"'Let up'? On my exercises?"

"Let up on everything you do to transcend your separate self. On the consistency of your self-discipline."

Strength of Will

"Consistency and perseverance are aspects of strength of will ('will power'), or self-discipline. Developing and strengthening these aspects of will, are something like safely developing a body. You must exercise on a regular schedule (applying and developing consistency). You must do it, even if it's hard because your undeveloped 'muscles' are weak and it becomes painful (applying and developing perseverance). But while you must exercise to your maximum limit, you must also not over-do it. Thus, while you should have an overall goal or 'ideal' of how you ultimately want your 'body' to be, you must focus on specific little goals, little muscle groups and training parameters, in order to achieve the ideal."

"So perhaps I am trying too hard, to do too much, or expect too much right away."

"Perhaps. That is for Zain to determine. But definitely, do not get frustrated. It just feeds the selfish separate self and slows your progress. Relax, be kind and gentle with yourself, and just be consistent. More than anything else, sheer consistency will let your separate self know you are not going to give up. If you let the self know it will not win, it will just give up in time, and you will gain control of your own mind."

Be Moderate In All Things

The Children teach that moderation, coupled with consistency and perseverance are the best way to insure that you will achieve your goals. Put simply, don't bite off more than you can chew (moderation - a smaller bite is easier to chew), but once you've chosen your bite, *make sure* you chew it properly, and *finish it* (consistency and perseverance).

Mother Farida went on. "Like I said, the separate self rebels at attempts to discipline it. If you are not moderate in your attempts at self-discipline, its rebellion is extremely strong, and you are more likely to fail. Every time you fail at self-discipline, the separate self grows stronger and your power of will grows weaker. When you moderately discipline your self, it is easier to discipline yourself because it is milder. And because it is easier it is generally more successful, and this allows your strength of will to grow consistently. Every time you moderately apply self-discipline, your strength of will gets more powerful. Fasting, which is used for both purification, and self-discipline, is like this. If you are using it for the development of self-discipline, you don't start with a 30 or 40 day fast, you start with a short fast - one day, or three days. You succeed in that, then the next time, your will is stronger. Then you can go 4 days, or 7. Then 10. If you were to start your first fast with two weeks, then fail, what have you done?"

"Weakened your will and given more power to the separate self."

"Precisely. Whatever you do to discipline yourself, should be with such moderation and total commitment. Approaching the development of self-discipline in this way will one day result in your powers of will being rock-hard. Then you can totally discipline the self in any way, at any time, with no problems."

Later in the day, Zain gave me a reading list regarding my questions.

Build Strength of Will Slowly
One Stone At A Time
If One Attempts to Lift A Stone Larger
Than One's Strength
It Can Crush You Under Its Weight

❖

The Drop of Water, Can Carve the Rock
The Glacier Can Carve The Mountain
Thusly do Consistency and Perseverance
Overcome All Obstacles

❖

In All things, Be Moderate.

❖

When The Two Minds Oppose Each Other
Neither's Goal is Achieved.
Want What You Want
And Tend to Both Branches and Roots.

❖

The Jellyfish that Drifts With the Tide
Is Wiser Than a Man With No Ideal.

I thought over Mother Farida's advice, and got what I could understand at the time out of the ancient texts. I was soon applying myself consistently. But after I started actually noticing an improvement in my concentration, the dark forces threw a new challenge at me. Bugs. Bugs came out of everywhere, every time I started meditating.

After this happened repeatedly, I went to Zain and told him about it.

"Ignore them," he said.

"Ignore them? But they fly around my head, up my nose, crawl on me, bite me!"

"Ignore them. They are nothing but a test. If you can transcend it, and continue with your exercise, they will go away. If you fight it, and let them bother you, they will continue forever."

It took a while. One time a whole swarm of tiny little bee like things actually found me in an inner music room, and started stinging me. This doesn't happen to everyone, so relax. Although a few of my students did have to endure the same thing with normally placid little crickets, that came out and bit them every time they started meditation. The only cure? Whether it is bugs, or any other distractions, just hold to your concentration consistently, and eventually the distractions will give up and never bother you again.

The Big Picture - Setting your Ideal

We have already covered this somewhat in another chapter, but it is a very important concept that is also pertinent here. An Ideal is the encapsulation of the end result of all your goals, of everything you ultimately want to be, and most importantly, *a way of being,* all wrapped up in one symbolic concept. If the greatest thing you can achieve is Universal Consciousness, then the greatest ideal would be one of the Universally Conscious beings. Since your ideal is a way for you to be, it can be set in one concept of being, such as that exemplified in the lives of any of the enlightened ones, past or present. Choose whatever you are most familiar or drawn to - Jesus, Buddha, Black Elk, or whomever. If you have a true teacher, that is the optimal choice.

We have already discussed how what you think and do, radically changes everything in your life. When you establish an ideal, and keep it in your conscious mind, it can have a powerful effect on your life. But this effect is only as strong as your application of the ideal in your life.

So consider who or what is the ULTIMATE you would have in your life, and in the lives of others. Once you determine your ideal, then close your eyes, meditate on it, contemplate it. *Feel, and completely visualize being* like your ideal, as if it were indeed real. This is one way to set your ideal.

Getting the Conscious and Subconscious in Sync

For anything to really be effective, including goal achievement, self-discipline, or ideals, the conscious and subconscious minds must work together. Many times a person makes major conscious mind decisions, but the programming of the subconscious mind is in conflict with those, and keeps working at counter-purposes to the conscious goal. Since so much of what we think and do comes from the subconscious, this can totally nullify your conscious desires, and in fact, make things happen that are opposite to what you want. Properly setting your ideal will have an effect on both the conscious and subconscious realms of your being.

For instance, a person may have decided they want a successful career, and they do all the right conscious things to make it happen. They get training, apply for work, etc.. But if the subconscious is programmed for failure, the person will do things that counteract, and defeat the conscious goal. They may be stupid little things, like the slip of a word at the wrong time, or being late for an appointment, or even little physical "screw-ups". It can defeat you in many ways.

Programming Your Ideal

To get your ideal programmed into the sub-conscious, use the tools of affirmation, complete visualization, meditation, and if available, the Atlantean vibrational sounds.

Once an ideal is fully programmed into the subconscious, the sub-conscious will work towards achieving it. This doesn't mean that you can sit back and let the sub-conscious do all the work for you. You must still consciously apply your ideal in all situations - concentration and self-discipline comes into play again.

When you have set your ideal, check up on yourself by keeping a list of your daily activities, and reviewing them daily to see how you are doing with living up to your ideal.

Summary

Remember, if you have no ideal, you are like a piece of driftwood being tossed about by the tides of external forces, or one of those toys that moves on the floor in a random direction until it runs into something, upon which it turns around and moves in another direction until it runs into something else, etc., etc..

If you have an ideal, but it's not in harmony with Universal will, then your life is but a temporary illusion, the rewards of which are empty and negative. Only an ideal that is in harmony with the eternal Universal flow brings lasting peace and fulfillment.

Whatever your ideal is, self-discipline, consistency, and perseverance are determining factors in whether the manifestation of your ideal is great, has little effect, or fails to manifest altogether. Look at those who have excelled in their chosen directions. How do they do it? They have very definite goals and they work at it consistently. Michiel's favorite quote from the *I Ching* was always "Perseverance furthers". If someone else can do it, so can you. And what better reason could you have to exercise strict self discipline and consistency, than for the goal of being a channel for the manifestation of the Universal Spirit?

Chapter Eighteen
Patience, Humility, Faith and Trust

Believe Not What You Read or Hear.
Have Faith Only When You Know.

❖

Experience Oneness With The Universal Spirit.
Only Then Will True Faith be Yours.

❖

Unselfish Love, Kindness, Harmlessness.
These Things You Can Believe In.

❖

Trust Only The Universal Spirit.
Know that All things Are
Right For Those Who Do the Will of God.

❖

Exercise The Qualities
Of Unselfish Love - Patience and Humility,
And The Virtues of Unselfish Love -
Kindness, Harmlessness, and Compassion.

Faith

"Father, when I was young, I was told that faith was one of the most important things to have, and that I should have faith. Faith in God. Even the texts say
something about Jesus saying if you had the faith of a mustard seed, you could
move mountains."

"Yes, but mustard seeds have a great deal of faith, and one should not seek to
compare oneself to the great mustard seed."

"I'm serious. Be serious for a moment will you?"

"Oh, yes, you are serious. I thought you were Peniel. OK."

"Then I was taught, 'Ask and you shall receive', but when I prayed, my prayers
weren't answered."

"You know the old punch line to that - you got answered, but the answer was
just no."

"Yeah, I was told that. But then why do they say you will receive? Then they
gave me answers like 'that only applies to certain things', or that I didn't have
enough faith. One time when I was in a great deal of pain, I just prayed for it to
go away, and it wouldn't. I started wondering what kind of God would not stop my
pain, and that led to me thinking about all the suffering in the world, and eventual-

ly, led to me becoming an atheist."

"But you aren't an atheist now. And do you have faith?"

"Faith in what? I know there is something, but I don't know what it is. I mean, I don't *really* know."

"You will someday soon Peniel. That's what you have been working for. It is a premise of the ancient teachings that faith should *not* be 'blind'. You were asked to have blind faith by those in your past. Your faith was based on believing in something you didn't know, so your faith was really nothing. We also teach that you should not have faith just because someone tells you that you should believe something, or 'programs' your mind to believe something. Also, just because something is written in a book, doesn't make it true or real, and this should not be the basis of faith either. Too many people think just because it is written, it is so."

"Including the ancient texts and teachings?"

"Definitely including them - they are but paper, leather, stone, words, ideas. And they are all for the interpretation by the limited intellectual brains of people in this limited physical life.

Instead, the Children promote direct *experience,* that will *result* in faith. To put it into one statement, "Experience Oneness/God first - *then* have faith. Then you will have true faith, naturally.""

"In that sense, when I think about it, I guess I do have faith that God exists. Because I have directly experienced, at least touched, the Universal Consciousness for a moment. So at least I know it exists, and still have faith that something exists that is far more immense...""

"As we said before, when you are out of the physical body, and away from its limitations of consciousness, you can have a greater understanding and knowledge of things than you can when your consciousness is locked into the physical. This doesn't mean you have to die. It can be experienced during deep meditation or an out-of-body experience. In such a high state of consciousness, you can experience Oneness. But when you 'come down' to your normal state of consciousness, you don't retain the direct knowledge or experience. Once you have 'touched' and experienced these higher levels of Universal Consciousness though, you can have a 'knowingness' of what you experienced. At that point, even though you no longer directly experience total Oneness with all, you *know* that such exists, and you know that there is more than you are aware of. This is when it is appropriate to have such 'faith'. That is what you have. But there is much more when you finally do have a death experience, and achieve enlightenment. Then you become part of it, and it stays with you. Once you know yourself that there is a 'God', and a saintly hierarchy, a force that flows and interweaves with all things, and can guide all things, and you are guided and part of it all - then you can have true 'total faith', even when you aren't directly in touch with knowing what is behind the scenes. You will be able to have faith that as long as you are surrendered to God, and the Universal Will and Flow, whatever happens will be right."

"I can't wait."

"Yes you can. But you don't have to. Yet you do."

"And the sound of one hand clapping?"

"Ask Uri, he only has one."

"I will tell him you said that, and ask to hear it."

"Enough of the Zen for now. Getting back to the point, until you have such

266

an experience, there is one other thing you can have faith in: Unselfish Love, and its virtues. You can have faith that caring, kindness, harmlessness, compassion, are good things. Even though without Universal Consciousness to guide your decisions, these virtues can lead you to make mistakes, they are still far better to have, than not."

Trust

The ancient teachings say that because of the darkness that pervades most everything and everyone here on the Earth plane, you should trust nothing and no one - only the Universal Spirit and those with Universal Consciousness. This is a paradox. Because if you are in the flow of Universal Will, and you understand the Universal Spirit, you know you can trust that whatever happens is perfect, in a certain way. Thus you *can* trust everything, and everyone, while trusting nothing and no one. Talk about Zen - Wheww!

Attributes of Unselfish Love

Patience and Humility are virtues, but applied to spiritual growth, they are more than that. They are "attitudes" of letting go, surrendering to the Universal flow. They are attributes of Unselfish Love.

Patience

Michiel had this to say about it:

"Patience is usually associated with waiting. But Patience as a spiritual attitude does not mean a state of standing still or passive waiting, but rather an ACTIVE waiting - waiting to see what will come while you are submitting to Universal Will. For submission to the Universal Will brings subsequent manifestation of the Universal Spirit. Heavenly bodies exemplify this kind of patience. So does nature."

From the *I Ching:* (hexagram 5 - Waiting)

"All beings have need of nourishment from above. But the gift of food comes in its own time, and for this one must wait. This hexagram shows the clouds in the heavens, giving rain to refresh all that grows and to provide mankind with food and drink. The rain will come of its own time. We cannot make it come; we have to wait for it. The idea of waiting is further suggested by the attributes of the two trigrams—strength within, danger in front. Strength in the face of danger does not plunge ahead, but bides its time, whereas weakness in the face of danger grows agitated and has not the patience to wait."

From *Stranger in a Strange Land:*
"Waiting is."
From the *Bible:*
"Be still, and know that I am God."

Michiel had more to say, which echoed my earlier problems with concentration during meditation.

"Patience is very pertinent to self-discipline and meditation. Almost always, a person who begins to meditate, will get frustrated. The separate self rebels against the attempt to transcend it, and it will shift the mind into high gear, jabbering away, and doing everything it can to distract the concentration. Furthermore, getting impatient with oneself, because of a failing of self-discipline of any kind, gives the separate self just what it wants. Such frustration is accompanied by *stopping* the

267

self-discipline, and *feeding* of negative thoughts. That's how the separate self succeeds in distracting you and getting you off course. These are tricks the self is using against you, pulling at you with, and they can only be overcome by having *the patience* to be consistent and persevering. Instead of wasting time and giving energy to the separate self by 'getting upset with yourself', simply start your meditation again, or start your self-discipline again. If you do this, you defeat its tricks, and eventually win. Such patience pays off."

From the *I Ching:* (hexagram 52 - Keeping Still - Mountain)
"...When a man has thus become calm, he may turn to the outside world. He no longer sees it in the struggle and tumult of individual beings, and therefore he has that true peace of mind which is needed for acting in harmony with them. Whoever acts from these deep levels makes no mistakes."

Selfishness has created all our problems. Everyone desperately cries out for happiness. Tolerance, humility, and patience are things that make for happiness, yet most people avoid them. And few are willing to pay the price for happiness - transcending the separate self by living a life of Unselfish Love.

It is simple cause and effect: the seed sown must one day be reaped. We disappointed others in the past. When we find ourselves being disappointed, we can learn patience.

Patience gives us all of time and space to understand things.

When we use our free will and mind to walk a path of spiritual growth, our return to Oneness is accompanied by suffering. There is no way around it. We must endure this suffering, with patience, understanding, and humility - the more humble we are, the more quickly, and easily, we will finally return to Oneness.

Humility

Humility is the opposite of being egotistical, or self-centered. It is the way of true Love, being receptive to God, surrendering to the Universal Spirit, the Universal Will, flowing, and being in harmony with the Universe. Humility is the most endearing and beautiful quality. **But it is the most important quality you could ever have as a student, or a true teacher serving God.**

In one of my early courses with elder Raga, he tried to tell me something that I needed to hear very badly, but I didn't have ears to hear yet.

"To a person who lacks humility, 'appearing' to 'be right' is more important than actually '*being* right' (which might require admitting making a mistake in order to correct oneself so they can actually '*be* right'). A person who is humble, doesn't 'personally' or 'selfishly' care if they are right or wrong, they are just concerned with being right for the sake of helping others, thus they are more often right than wrong, and will more quickly correct any mistakes if they find they are wrong. They also seek perfection in the service of God, and welcome the criticism of others, so that they may correct mistakes they have missed.

Having the 'attention' of others, is also important to those who lack humility. Ego-ism, self-centeredness, pride (in the sense of being 'personally' proud), and its close relative, vanity, are the opposite qualities of humility. The egotistical and self-centered person wants to control everything 'his or her way', and sees his or her self as the most important thing there is - and the thing which all other things, and all other beings, revolve around. The prideful person wants credit for their accomplishments. The humble person attributes all of their successes, capabilities, and accomplishments, to simple facts of reality, or God working through them, rather than to their own prideful abilities."

Then he looked directly at a new female novice, who was "fixing" her hair while he spoke, and said,

"The person who gives importance to physical appearances also doesn't understand the beauty of humility."

Michiel was quite fond of this saying:

"Rather than the egotistical attitude of the separate self, which is one of being a great mountain, humility is having an attitude of being a receptive little valley. Nature wears down the great mountain, and fills the valley with rich topsoil, lakes, and abundance. Thus, a person who is truly humble, and in need, cannot be passed by, and is made great by God."

Zain's favorite reference to the subject was: "Nature abhors a vacuum."

My old Zen archery teacher's favorite saying was "A cup must be empty, before it can be filled. A humble person who is not full of their own self-centered thoughts and information, is able to be filled with wisdom from the Universal Spirit."

A person with a humble attitude, learns very quickly, adapts to situations easily and quickly, "flows" with whatever changes are presented to them by life or people, and can communicate and relate to others better than anyone else. Why? Simply because they "get out of their own way". They get their "self" out of the way of dealing with the rest of the world and reality. Thus, their separateness doesn't wall off their openness to others, or anything in life, nature, or the Universe. Rather than putting time and energy into "themselves", or defending themselves or their ideas, they keep an open mind and consider the input of others. They also don't wall off their own Unselfish Love and compassion for others.

Often, students, like animals, will seek to establish a "pecking order" amongst other students. Everyone wants to consider themselves more evolved, or "higher", than the other. Generally, the ones that are most concerned with this, are the least humble, and thus the least evolved. Jesus emphasized this at the last supper. Remember the earlier story? It was a custom to wash the dust off a guest's feet, but the apostles were all too "important" to lower themselves to wash the others' feet. So Jesus did it, shocking them, and driving home the important point of humility, reminding them that, "The greatest among you would be the servant to all."

In the end, those who make it their priority to be "number one" will be the last, and those who's priority is to be humble, will be number one (and not care whether or not they are number one).

Humility Goes to the Movies

Movies are such a powerful form of entertainment. Combining the elements of storytelling, acting, and music, can touch and inspire people like nothing else. Below are some wonderful spiritual movies I would recommend for inspiration and understanding. If you can't find them locally, you can rent through the mail, or buy them (you may want to do that so you can see them more than once, or show them to friends/family). Here are two companies that have most of these movies for rent and sale: Best Video - 1-800-RAREVID (website is www.bestvideo.com); Video Vault - 1-800-VAULT66 (www.videovault.com).

"Groundhog Day" (Bill Murray. Excellent parable for reincarnation and learning to give and care about others);

"Kung Fu"; The *original,* old TV series and pilot movie (not the new series "Kung Fu, the legend continues"). Lots of examples of humility in general, and the humble attitude a student monk must have to learn and grow. Lots of good spiritual lessons between a few "kung fu" fighting scenes;

"Lost Horizon" (The story of a place called Shangri-La. There is an old black and white version directed by Frank Capra ['It's a Wonderful Life'] starring Ronald Coleman, or a newer color version staring Peter Finch, Michael York, Liv Ulman [it's a musical also, with a Burt Bacharach soundtrack and score.] Both versions are based on the James Hilton novel, which "mysteriously" somewhat depicts our "Shargung-La" monastery and community);

"Brother Sun, Sister Moon", which I would like to talk about here. "Brother Sun, Sister Moon" was beautifully filmed by the famous Italian director Franco Zefferelli ("Romeo and Juliet"), and has a soundtrack by Donovan. It is the story of St. Francis of Assisi. It contains many examples of humility, but the scene where Clare expresses her realization of humility to Francis, is one of the nicest examples.

Francis has long ago left behind the "normal" world, and lives a simple life as a beggar monk, serving God and attending the poor and infirm, outside the city. Even though Clare is an exceptional person, and even prior to Francisco's (St. Francis) changes, she cared for the lepers who were exiled from the town, she has not *dedicated* her *life* to serving others, or to God. And while there was an obvious bond and attraction between Clare and Francis, and an appreciation of his changes and work, she nevertheless remained with her wealthy family in the city. One day, she comes running through the fields, happily calling for Francis. When she finds him, she asks to be taken into his order, and essentially declares "I don't want to be loved anymore, I want to love. I don't want to be *understood* any longer - I want to *understand"*. This moment in the movie is an incredibly touching, and beautiful expression of humility.

Unfortunately, the enlightenment of St. Francis is one of those one in a billion events, and since he had no tradition to properly prepare or train him for it, and no true teacher, it left him confused, and with many problems. Yet he was "looked after to a great extent, and his enlightenment, his great love, and broader perspective on life was undeniable, and a beautiful sight to behold.

"Strange Cargo" (Clark Gable); A hardened, cynical criminal, condemned to years in an old French "swamp island" type prison, suddenly encounters a new prisoner - a mysterious, kind, Christ-like prisoner. He then escapes with other convicts, and the Christ-like prisoner, and comes to a personal crossroad in his path. He faces his karma, and at the most critical moments in his life, he ultimately chooses to lend his will to the "good" part of himself. In doing so, he ultimately finds peace and the Love of a good woman.

"Meet John Doe" (Gary Cooper); Wonderful story about two things - the importance that the "average person on the street" can have - the "John and Jane Does" of the world. And how simple kindness, humility, and caring, could make this world a virtual paradise. Also illustrates how the selfish, powerful, "dark ones" of this world, do everything they can to prevent this. Very inspiring.

"Beyond Tomorrow"; Three loveable old men die in a plane crash, but remain on the Earth plane as ghosts to watch over and help a good hearted young couple, one of which is facing the dangers of getting sucked into a selfish, superficial, materialistic existence. Excellent parable of self-sacrifice, and love.

"Dr. Strange" (TV movie); Not made all that well, or totally true to the incredible metaphysical stories it was based on, but still, a great story of Good against Evil, humility, and how many things that are unseen by most, do really go on in the world.

"Circle of Iron"; Basically a martial arts movie, with many Zen , humility, and other lessons.

"Star Wars"; A classic parable of good vs. evil, and the "great fight" between them on many different levels.

"Brother Orchid"; Cute, wonderful movie with Edward G. Robinson as a "tough guy" gangster who goes to Europe trying to buy "class". When he returns, his former second in command (Bogart), tries to kill him. Left for dead, monks from a local monastery who raise flowers, help him recover. At first he just figures it's a good hide out, and approaches being a monk and working in the gardens with the same scheming selfish attitude that got him to the top of the gangster ladder. He eventually changes, and discovers "real class" there.

"You Can't Take it With You"; A Frank Capra film. Heart warming story about a zany, but extraordinarily kind and open minded family, who are thrown together with a powerful socialite family, through the proposed marriage of their children. The results are both hilarious, and fascinating.

"Resurrection"; Ellen Bernstein. Great movie about a woman who has a near death experience that changes her life in many ways - and more than once.

"The Ten Commandments"; Yul Brenner, Charlton Heston. This classic depicts the story of Moses. Even if you've already seen it, next time watch it with an eye towards ego/humility.

"Jesus Christ Superstar"; A musical that may be a bit hokey and dated, but it's one of the best depictions of Jesus that we've seen. In order to really get the feeling for it, you have to listen to the lyrics of the songs. If you do that, you'll get a new insight into the being known as Jesus, and his experiences, along with some really good lessons.

"Joseph"; This movie beautifully illustrates the value of compassion and forgiveness. Joseph is put through many tests and trials and through his kindness, honesty and devotion to God, he overcomes them all. He had 12 brothers (like the twelve apostles), and in the end, he helped them in spite of their treachery towards him. His forgiveness and great love transformed this situation into one of love and unity.

"And the Rains Came"; This takes place in India in the early 1900's. Merna Loy plays a disatisfied, rich and superficial woman who is visiting there. Tyrone powers plays a kind doctor. A huge rainstorm hits, and major floods wash over the land, killing many people. The special effects are quite good considering it's an old film. Next, a plague hits them, and even more people are dieing. One of the nicest things about this film is seeing Merna Loy evolve and become a caring person. She begins taking care of the sick and dies herself.

Great "Soulmate" movies.

Since we're on the subject of movies, we may as well mention a few exceptional "soulmate" spiritually romantic movies:

"Peter Ibitson"; Gary Cooper. After being separated from his soulmate as a child,

Peter "accidentally" finds her as an adult. He unjustly ends up imprisoned for life, yet their mutual dreams bring them together every night, until they finally join together forever.

"Portrait of Jenny"; A supposedly true story, surrounding a painting bought by the filmmaker. A tale of a ghostly girl with a beautiful spirit, who appears at different ages as she grows up, crossing over different time zones to be with her soulmate. Her soulmate was a starving artist, whose only remarkable painting was his portrait of "Jenny".

"Somewhere In Time"; Christopher Reeves. Jane Seymour. Wonderful story, in which he realizes his soulmate lived in an overlapping, earlier time period, in which he had already hypnotized himself to travel back in time to be with her. And so he does it again. Paradoxical, very romantic.

Sticks and Stones

The opposite side of the coin to the "I'll scratch your back if you'll scratch mine", kind of "love" that most people have, is the "I won't scratch your back if you don't scratch mine" polarity. People sometimes refuse to love or care about someone who doesn't love or care about them. Even people who have spiritually grown significantly, and are generally more loving, compassionate, and caring to most people, can "shut down" if someone dislikes them, or they even just *think* that someone doesn't care about them as much as they want them to, or expect them to. This is a sad and serious predicament, because most people *don't love* or care about others. So you'll have to scratch almost everyone you meet off your "who to care about" list. And if *they* never find anyone to care about them, how will they ever start caring about others? I had one elder student, who was very aware and very compassionate ordinarily. But if someone didn't like her, disliked her, or disappointed her as far as their caring, she would stop loving, stop caring about that person. Her excuse was that she didn't want to be anyone's "doormat". I guess only "doormats" Unselfishly Love. And only those who love others more than themselves will be One with the Universal Spirit. Then I will be a doormat.

Other people stop loving, just because they are personally "hurt" that the other person isn't loving as much as they could be, or aren't giving them love at all.

I'm not talking about letting someone do something destructive to you or anyone else. I'm just talking about words here, or ego insulting actions, or lack of love and caring from someone else, not physical harm. Sticks and stones can break your bones, and you should do something about them if possible, but words, words can never hurt the real you.

Someone can only injure your ego, your selfish separate self, not the real you. And if you are truly humble, there is no target for the arrows being slung by someone else's separate self. If you can be offended, how can you help someone else? People you want to help will sometimes deliberately try to offend you, just to defend their separate self. But when you are Unselfishly Loving, it doesn't matter what someone thinks about you, or says about you. You see them as an upset child who needs love. You realize that the reason they are striking out at you, is because they have problems that need healing and transcending - problems that need your love and help.

Sure it hurts, and it can make you sad when someone you love doesn't love you. But not loving them isn't going to help you, or them. Whereas continuing to love them, even through your own pain, just might.

My Piece of Humble Pie

You cannot really learn unless you're humble. Period. You cannot grow unless you are humble. Period. To be humiliated, which is often looked at as a "bad" thing, is a great goodness. Being appreciated, given attention to, glorified, praised - those are harmful to humility. Humiliation could be the greatest gift someone could give to you. To be willing to be a fool, and to really see and admit mistakes, and short-comings, is what makes true greatness in anything.

Like I mentioned earlier, when I was young, and first discovered and went to the monastery, I was thrilled. But I was a very egotistical young man. My separate self was proud and strong. I thought I was great. I was sorely lacking in humility. And I didn't think there was really very much anyone else could teach me. This was all "secretly" of course, inside me, semi-subconsciously.

As it is in many spiritual orders, it is tradition to take or be given a new name when one starts their new monastic life. I had been bugging Zain for a name for quite some time, and he seemed to avoid it. But finally he gave it to me. He recognized my monstrous ego, and gave me an appropriate name. No, it wasn't Godzilla or Frankenstein. It was the name of a character from history. It was a very famous ruler, and depending on how you looked at it, a great and powerful leader. But this character was someone whose ego was so great, that he thumbed his nose at God. I didn't know that at the time. Zain told me to go to the library and look the person up, and that there were many rulers of the same name. He said that because they all had the same name (and he wouldn't tell me which one I had been), I would have to figure out for myself, which one of them I was. Of course, I chose the one who sounded the greatest. But Zain was trying to tell me something about myself when he gave me that name. His intent wasn't for me to go on an "ego trip" about having been this "great ruler" in a past life, it was for me to realize my ego, and the type of ego I had. But he knew there was no point in pointing it out to me then - I wouldn't have listened. So I took it to be a "great" name, such was my ego.

My first year at the monastery presented many challenges to my ego - daily. Soon, the pressure on my separate self "ego" was seemingly "unbearable". Everyone always seemed to be "in my face", pointing out my faults, and showing me ways to improve (how dare they). From a humble point of view, this is food for the famished, but from a selfish state of mind, it's like being force fed the kinds of food you hate. For someone who has an attitude that they don't really want to see any truth about themselves, it is a horrible nightmare. It means they don't really want to change also. As a consequence, I focused only on the "insult" of being corrected, and the humiliation and "destruction of self-esteem" that came from being told I was always "falling short". I was focusing on the ego irritation rather than my spiritual growth. I began to consciously and subconsciously do things to create problems, ultimately resulting in my being asked to leave by a counsel of the Inner Circle. I put up an appropriate argument, but really hoped to leave deep inside. My selfish separate self - my ego - had had enough, and I was letting it gain back lost ground.

Upon my arrival back in my "old life", I found it to be a breeze. Unbeknownst to me, even the little bit of "forced" ego transcension I had gone through, made the previous "big" problems of my life seem insignificant. Life was easier without some of my baggage. But slowly, I became snared in the web of my own selfishness again. It had only been six months, but like a cancer that wasn't completely eradicated, my ego grew back, the resultant problems in my life grew back, and the disease of my separate self overtook me. My life fell apart. My girlfriend left me. I wasn't even a legal adult yet, but it seemed like my life was over, disintegrating and miserable. It was all worse than ever. I became deathly ill, and on my death bed, I "accidentally" discovered what my name really meant. I saw the historical character I was named after, being played in a movie on TV as I laid in bed with a fever. It was God revealing it to me. What a monumental egoed out jerk the guy was. The realization of my grand egotism hit me like a ton of bricks. I finally saw myself, and all its bullglory. I called a Native American healer I knew, who helped me with my illness. I rapidly recovered, and returned to my teacher. I couldn't communicate with Zain as well as I would have liked, I was still a puppy, and my newfound humility, and new respect for him, made it difficult to express myself well at the time. But I told him something like, I had realized that if I could only be as great as his little finger, I would be greater than my entire being, and I would be able to accomplish much more (I told you it wasn't a very good expression). Regardless of the lousy analogy, he understood my humility, took me back, and I began my *real* growth - and it happened fast. This time, I *wanted* to change, I *wanted* to give, and I *welcomed* any chance to see myself so I could get better - thus, this time it was very easy in comparison.

One day, I was sitting in meditation, in a room adjacent to where Zain was eating and speaking to a small group of his elder monk students. I was already feeling elated in my meditation. My new found humility had transformed something inside me, and all of a sudden, my Kundalini shot up my spine and filled me with the light and of God. While this was happening to me, Zain got up from his meal, came up to me, touched the energy coming out of the top of my head, and gave me a new name. "He will be called Peni-el. He is now my eldest."

I didn't bother asking at the time what it meant - I was too high from being full of bliss and spiritual energy to care. In fact, I never asked, it just came to me one day.

Ironically, I later found out that the bigger the ego, the more powerfully one can manifest the Universal Spirit, once that ego becomes a *servant* of the Universal Spirit. How appropriate.

Now, do you want to have a hard time, and protect your ego so others will *think* you're right all the time? Or do you want to have an easy time, and be humble and *become truly right* all the time? Do you want others to *think* you're great, or do you want to *be* great? You're free to choose, and you will live with the consequences of any choice you make.

Chapter Nineteen

The Children of the Law of One
Basic Meta-Physics of Science-Magic

I need to warn you that this chapter is a bit more intellectual than the others. So other than the segment about crystals, unless you are a die-hard metaphysics enthusiast, you may want to skip this chapter. But before you decide to do that, I'd like to say that the segment about "the oldest known name of God", and that name's metaphysical significance is (to me at least), one of the most important and profound spiritual concepts I have ever found, and played an important role in changing my life.

Before I get into everything else in this chapter, I want to say something about metaphysics. Many people think that metaphysics supercedes the laws of physics, but the teachings say that this is not the case. True metaphysics should just expand on the true laws of physics. Over the years, physicists have *often* discovered that some of what they thought were "final" facts, or immutable laws of physics, weren't so immutable after all, and thus not really laws. And in the future more "laws" may be broken. But there *are* certain immutable true laws of physics. They are the ones that are aspects of Universal Law, and as such, will always remain the same. These are the laws that any other law, metaphysical principle, or concept, must be in harmony with, and be measured against. Thus if a person wants to learn and understand true metaphysics, there is no better place to start than by studying and understanding the great laws of the Universe. Here are quotes from some of the ancient texts that discuss the basic concepts involved:

All Is Vibration
All Vibration Follows Universal Law
All Gives All Receives
All Loves

All Vibration
Seeks its own Level
To find any Level
Set forth the Vibration
By Law you Will Go there
By Law it Will come.

❖

Always is there a Greater Vibration
Always is there a Lesser Vibration

275

❖

In Harmony With Universal Law
All Vibration moves as One Flow
Interrupt the Flow only to Find
In This Natural Order thus does it Go
In Forever Passing Through, Divided in Two
Receptivity be the Way of Emptiness
The One calls to Come and Fill
Giving be the Way of Abundance
The One Flows forth to Fill

Always then the Way of the Flow
Dependence on That Which is Above
The Object of Dependence
To that Which is Below
Two will Repel
Two will Attract
Two will Together, Interact
Look then to Four
For All that Need Be
For All Creation
Vibration Be
One.
Two.
One and Two.
Three.
One and Two
Beget Four
Thus Opens the Infinite Door

❖

Yod He Vau He
Pronounce it Right
To Open The Gates of Heaven
And Live in the Light

❖

Build Ye Life As The
Pyr-a-mid
Four Corners Converge Above
With Fire in the Middle
The Fire of Love
Life, Mind, Truth, Love
Spirit

❖

Energy Great
Does Course Through This Earth
Collect and Direct, if it Be Your Will
With the Shape of The Temple,
Pure Stones and Gold Laden Box.
Or With The Mind, Focused and Pure
Lowered in Vibration
To Ten in Meditation

❖

Vibration Does Flow
In Body and Soul.
High and Low, In All Flesh is Written
Tune may you to the Right Vibrations
Colors and Sounds, That Change What We Know
Use Them May You
to Heal, Sow, and Grow

❖

Power Great
Above and Below
Key Are Vibrations, Secret but to Few
Find them You Will
By Measure and Trial
And Use of the Word
That Rules All Creation

❖

Describe A Rainbow
To a Blind Man Will You?
Open Your Eyes.

❖

Senses Five
Does Man Perceive.
The Focus on Self
Restricts All That Is.
Limited in Scope
The Ocean not Seen.
A Drop of Rain
He Believes Is His World.
So as He Believes
So He Shall Be.

So Let it Be Written

❖

Everything Orbits Something

❖

All Matter Is As The Universe,
Stars, Planets, Time and Space.

In Search of Real Metaphysics

When I was a young teenager, I was fascinated with metaphysics, and in particular, concepts about astral travel, unknown energy, and color/sound healing. I read everything I could find, and much of it was exciting, and mentally stimulating. But I soon came to realize that not one of the books gave any *real* facts about color or sound or their "workings" in theory. Sure, some gave information, but it made no real sense when you looked into it objectively and thoroughly. It was just metaphysical mumbo-jumbo. You might read something like, "Purple is the color of Aquarius, Thursdays, and blah blah blah, and is associated with the note low C. Purple can be used to heal the gall stones and blah blah blah". But how did purple *do* that, why, and what source was this information from? Could it be proven? And I was a musician, yet I couldn't understand what the heck "low C" was. Other mentions in the book indicated that they were not using the system of sharps and flats in the chromatic musical scale, so it couldn't mean C flat. And there was already a mention of "regular C". In all the books I read, I couldn't find ONE thing that a real metaphysician, a scientist, or would-be scientist, could actually experiment with or use. I was *so* happy to find that the Children had teachings that actually gave me the physics involved with these sciences, and facts that made sense. With this information, I was able to discover many things like the *real* colors associated with *real* musical notes. I could demonstrate it mathematically and prove it, and I could make a device that combined the two. This was real metaphysics at last.

Crystals

Many people have heard about quartz crystals. And most people sense that there is something very special about them. Friends and books may have made references to "crystal energy", and healing with them (or related crystals), and talked about how "cosmic" they are. I'd heard all that too, but it was almost always too vague and unsubstantiated for me. I wanted to know more - and I wanted facts. Here are some of those facts - the "real" metaphysical scoop on crystals.

Crystals are amazing energy transmutators - they can take electricity and change it to physical vibration. They can also do the opposite - take vibration, and change it to electricity.

Because of the transmutating property of crystals, they have been used by most people on a daily basis for quite some time, and many people aren't even aware of it. In fact, for many years crystals were vital to the workings of radio and TV. The crystals transform the vibrations of electricity, changing them to the very rapid, and specific, vibrations of radio/TV waves. Those waves travel through the air to wherever we are, and then crystals change them back to electricity, allowing us to hear or see something that is going on in a far away place. Each receiving crystal is "tuned" to a specific frequency of vibration, which matches a transmitting crystal. By changing your receiving crystal, you "change channels". This is the same for radio, TV, walkie-talkies, CB, Ham, whatever. Before the advent of synthesized tuners, you had to have a different crystal for every different channel (frequency) you wanted to use.

Some of you know how all cigarette lighters used to have a "flint and wheel" (stone age stuff) that made sparks that ignited either lighter fluid, or butane. Many modern lighters have switched to a different system - crystal technology. Instead of spinning a wheel with your thumb to make a spark, you just push down a button or plunger, and it makes a "click", and lights. Those lighters use a tiny piece of crystal, that creates an electrical spark - with no batteries or anything. They take advantage of a property of crystals they call "piezo-electric". It's amazing how they work. When you press down on the lighter's button, it "cocks" a piece of plastic or metal, and when you hear the click, you are hearing the sound of the crystal being struck by that plastic or metal piece snapping down on it. When the crystal is struck, this creates a vibration pressure on the crystal, causing it to give off a spark of electricity, igniting the butane.

You may know that almost every watch, and many clocks these days have "quartz movements". The quartz crystals in these are used to do the opposite of the quartz in the lighters. It's the same stuff, it's still quartz crystal, but they use it a different way. In this case, instead of using a vibration (strike) to make electricity, they use electricity (a battery) to make the crystal vibrate. The constant vibration of the quartz, due to applying electricity to it, is the basis for measuring off the seconds minutes and hours. Because the quartz vibrates in a consistent manner, they can count how many times it vibrates per whatever time period, and calculate that to keep time.

All of that is pretty amazing really, but crystals can do much more.

In Atlantis, the Sons of Belial used lasers and geothermal type approaches to create energy to feed their power hungry energy demands. As was mentioned earlier, their power plants were instrumental in the terrible destructive Earth changes that destroyed Atlantis. But the Children were more power conservative - it's not that they had to "do without", but they found that the vast amounts of power that exists in the Earth's bio-field, was plenty for all their needs. So they used crystals not only for healing, but for powering their buildings and their vehicles. The last of the Children's greatest power plants was the "Great Pyramid" in Egypt. (The Great Pyramid was also used for Initiation - more about that in the chapter on the death experience).

Vishnu, who was an expert on both ancient technology and the present state of the world's technology, explained more to me about the power of the Great Pyramid in Egypt.

"You have probably heard many things about the bible's legendary 'Ark of the Covenant'. If you know about electronic components, (which I did since I was a 5 year old little genius electronics freak) and you read even the worldly bible's description of the Ark, (which I hadn't) you will realize that this was a giant electric 'capacitor'. A capacitor is a device, usually found in an electronic circuit, that stores up electricity to a certain level, then releases it in a burst. This is why the Ark had the reputation that if you touched it or got too close to it you would get zapped by a lightning bolt from God. The size of the Ark as a capacitor, held a charge big enough to make a bolt that would easily kill anyone who got near it - and would kill many people."

"When I was a child I opened the back of our TV. There was a label on one area that said 'Warning! High Voltage! Do not Touch!' To me it was an invitation. So what did I do? I touched it, and I got a shock that sent me flying across the room and slammed into a wall! I later found out it was a capacitor. And it was only about the size of a salt shaker. So I can imagine what a huge thing like the Ark would put out - they probably should have called it the 'Arc' instead - you know, like an electric arc?"

"Yes... anyway... only David, in his humility, was able to touch the Ark without being killed."

"Why?"

"Because of his advanced spiritual development, his energy centers, his chakras, were prepared to deal with such power, and the frequency of the electricity. And of course, with the guidance of the hierarchy, and his destiny, the raw power was transformed and channeled in such a way that it only made for a Kundalini experience, a communing with God, and instead of being killed, he came out of it wiser and more powerful."

"But you said the Ark was a power device in Egypt in the Great Pyramid, why did David have it and what was he doing with it?"

"It was once the power storage device inside the Great Pyramid, yes. And I will get to that in a moment. But first understand what we started to discuss.

The Pyramid had a layered capstone of copper and custom created quartz crystal from Atlantis. The Pyramid would collect energy from the Earth's bio-field, and focus it in the Ark. The Ark would release regular bursts of a specific frequency of electrical energy that would be transmuted and transmitted from the crystal capstone. All the Children's buildings and vehicles had receiver crystals tuned to the Pyramid, and would pick up and change the energy back into usable power. We are still using this here today.

Now as for your question about how David came into possession of it. Read the texts to get the entire story. But basically, during what they called the Exodus - when Moses freed the Jews in Egypt, the Jews went on a sort of freedom celebration rampage as they left, and took all kinds of Egyptian treasures, taking everything they could on their way out of town. This, which has been omitted greatly in the world's modern bible, was one of the primary things which incited the Pharaoh to pursue them. And one of the things they took from Egypt, from the Great Pyramid, was..."

"The Ark!"

"Yes. Then of course, over time, knowledge of its original use was lost, they did not understand its power, and attributed it to a power of God, which was quite logical to them. It would strike people down who got near or touched it, and this was easily interpreted by some that it must be some sort of temple God lived in, and only the holiest of people were allowed to get so close to God. And in it, they eventually put the pieces of the commandments Moses brought them, that he smashed in his righteous indignation and despair over their unconsciousness and selfishness."

"Where is it now?"

"We have a version of one the capacitors here as you know, but the one from the Great Pyramid, is located in a small church in Ethiopia."

"A small church in Ethiopia??"

280

"Yes, I know it sounds odd, but there is a good reason. It was brought there by a small contingent of Jewish priests because they held it in very high regard as a holy religious item, and were concerned about it being desecrated or destroyed during an impending invasion."

"But why Ethiopia?"

"It is a long story, but basically it is because of bonds that had been formed there by the coming together of Solomon, and the 'queen of Sheba', who was the ruler of what is now called Ethiopia. Just read about it in the texts when you have time."

Healing with Crystals and Vibration

All things vibrate, and have different vibratory characteristics. Did you know that body parts, including cells, and organs, have "vibrational signatures"? There are "healthy" vibrational signatures as well as diseased vibrational signatures. Understanding these scientifically, and having the advanced technology to alter our bodies' vibrational signatures, allows us to heal many ailments. In Atlantis, crystal technology was used for this. But the amount of knowledge and experimentation involved in cataloging all the different vibrational and electrical parameters of every detailed part of a human body is immense - it staggers the imagination. Not to mention the technology involved in creating the right crystals, and methods of applying them. The technology needed to properly use such knowledge is also incredibly advanced. But it was done in Atlantis, and the technology and knowledge was brought to Egypt, and then some of it to Tibet. It has been recently rediscovered by modern scientists, which we will get to in a moment.

Atlanteans used very sophisticated crystal technology to heal, and many people internally "remember" or intuitively sense that this kind of healing did, and does, exist. So they try to use quartz crystals this way, or go to healers who use crystals. But such crystals are wild cards, they are all formed differently, and perform differently, and most who use them are deluding themselves because they don't know what frequencies they are actually dealing with, or how to properly apply them even if they had the right crystals for the task. Atlanteans had an entire science devoted to the understanding of the body's vibrations. And they had real scientific technology for using crystals to manipulate vibrations very specifically - Atlanteans didn't just pick up a crystal at the local bookstore and try to start healing with it. Whether it was to be used for healing, or powering a house, Atlantean technology gave them access to many different specifically designed crystals, each designed to specific parameters according to their scientific knowledge of making each one a specific tool for a specific vibratory function. There were thousands of specifically tuned crystals available for healing alone. Using a quartz crystal without the extensive knowledge involved in using it properly, is not only likely to be useless, but it can be harmful under certain circumstances. In other instances, the placebo effect can induce healing though.

For those who want to use crystal vibration healing techniques, there are viable alternatives from modern scientific research. There are a couple of amazing devices that are close to the old Atlantean technology, but it took resources like government laboratories and scientists to develop them. They are called the Electro-Acuscope, and the Electro-Myopulse, manufactured by a company called Electro-Medical, in Fountain Valley, California. While the devices use the same principles involved with Atlantean crystal healing (neutralizing disease frequency vibrations and transmitting healthy frequency vibrations), they use a somewhat different method of creating the body frequency vibrations (vibrational synthesis). While not as sophisticated or powerful as the Atlantean technology, these amazing devices not only heal, but give the body and mind a "tune up" so it can function at its maximum potential. We studied and tested these machines extensively and objectively for about 10 years. It is our opinion that if every doctor used one, hospitals would have about 90% less patients. And while the devices remain relatively unknown, even suppressed, they are used by Super Bowl winning football teams, PGA pro golfers, Olympic athletes, Walter Reed Hospital in Washington D.C. (where the top U.S. government politicians and military leaders go), and the Pope.

So if you're serious about vibrational healing these days, the company can give you a referral to a doctor, physical therapist, or chiropractor who has one, or you can buy your own if you have the money.

The Vibratory Nature of the Universe

Everything in the Universe is vibrating. Even light is vibrating (different frequencies of vibration give us the different colors, just like different frequencies of vibration give us the different notes in an octave of sound).

The so-called 5 physical senses, touch, smell, hearing, taste, and sight, are all biological "sensors" that, for the most part, detect vibration in different ways. While smell doesn't directly sense a vibration, it is directly sensing physical objects in the air, that have different vibrational parameters. Each sense perceives vibrations within specific, limited frequency bands. For example, through the sense of hearing, most people perceive vibrational frequencies in the 20 to 20,000 cycle per second range - we call that "sound". The eyes pick up much faster vibrations that we call light.

But these 5 biological sensors we use, only pick up a *very, very small* part of the infinite vibrational frequency spectrum. There are other frequency bands that the 5 senses cannot perceive, which puts a BIG hole in our information about what is REALLY there. And for most people, this very limited data from the 5 sensors *is the only thing that allows them to be in touch with the world around them.* We are, for the most part, virtually blind in this Universe.

Humans have built machines that pick up *some* of the vibrations we can't get with our 5 senses. These machines translate what they pick up into the range that we can get with one of our senses. For instance, our eyes don't pick up on x-rays - they only see the slower vibrating visible light range. So we made x-ray machines that take pictures to show us the result of using the x-rays, on a film that we can see with visible light. Can you imagine being able to see such things as x-rays and gamma rays all the time? Radio waves are also in a vibrational frequency band that is not within the range of any of our senses. The circuitry in a radio or TV changes these vibrations to frequencies of vibration our senses of sight and hearing can perceive. There are many other things that we do not normally perceive. But all of these things, and much, much more, are available for us to perceive when we transcend the limits of our separate self.

Illusions

Because of my early fascination with such things, I spent a great deal of time with Vishnu, "bugging" him with all the unanswered questions from my early fascination with metaphysics and science.

"I always hear references to life being an illusion, or what we are perceiving is actually an illusion. Does that have to do with our limited senses?"

"Life being an illusion is more a question I think I'll let you save for Zain, but I can answer you about sensory perception illusion.

In part, because of the limitations of our senses, much of what we perceive is an illusion. A table, for instance is not what it seems to us."

"In moments of higher consciousness, I have seen what looks like a crawling or vibration in wood or stone, is that what you mean?"

"It is part of what I mean. You may be seeing the life of the molecules of the object, or the auric vibrations. But I would need to know more specifics of your perceptions - which we'll discuss later perhaps.

To give you an easier-to-understand example of obvious illusions, consider the modern invention of television, and the 'picture' you see on it. The 'pictures' we see are not pictures at all, but many individual lines of parts of the picture, flashing at us one at a time. They start at the top or bottom of the screen, and go to the other end. But these lines appear faster than our human perception can process, so we don't see them as individual lines being 'flashed' one at a time. Instead, the many lines seem to be there all the time, making whole pictures. Movies are similar. As many as 30 *still pictures* are being flashed in one second. We see it as a seamless presentation, and have the illusion that the people and things on the screen are moving, but they aren't. Certain animals with better perceptions just see the lines on a TV, or the still pictures flashing during a movie.

That is just ONE of many examples. But there are even more far reaching illusions about life and the world around us. Even the TV *set* is not really what it seems to us.

The True Reality Beyond our Perceptions

Even the most 'solid' physical objects are but atoms (and the parts/energy they are composed of) vibrating at various rates, in various arrangements. These vibratory rates and arrangements of atoms are perceived by us, through one or more of the very limited 5 senses of an Earthly human body. We then process this sensory information, and in our limited consciousness, 'perceive' these atom groups as the 'things' that make up the world we live in, the *things* that are all around us - TV's, cars, carpets, skin, air, - you name it. What we think all these *things* are, is the result of the warped assumptions our brain makes - the assumption being based on the very limited data we get from our senses, about a certain arrangement and frequency of vibration of atoms. And atoms are just a building block of the same One thing - the 'stuff' of the Universe. Thus, everything we think we see, is really just an illusion - not its true form - just a 'conceptual form' created by our brain. We put together an 'image' or 'idea' of what we think we're perceiving, by virtue of our programming, expectations, experiences, etc., manipulating the bits of information we get from our highly limited senses. When you see the movement or vibration in a solid object, like you were just talking about, whatever it is you are seeing, is because your consciousness is expanding beyond its limitations, and you are glimpsing a bit more of reality."

"So our consciousness and our limited senses really create a perceptual handicap."

"It's even worse than that Peniel. We are already starting with the great handicap of perceiving such a small part of the world around us. Then to make matters worse, we process that information through the 'filters' of our emotions and pre-conceptions. This all leaves us with a very inaccurate illusion of reality.

And just a little change in the frequency of the vibration of atoms (how fast or slow they vibrate) in a molecule (group of atoms), can completely change our perception of what it is. For example, we know the slower vibrating molecules of H2O as ice, a solid; as the frequency of vibration increases, we know them as water, a liquid; faster still, as steam; faster yet, as Hydrogen and Oxygen gas. Then where?"

"I don't know."

"As vibrational frequency increases, a more etheric quality develops. Something may even seem to vanish (like steam), but *nothing* is ever lost in the Universe, it just changes form. Sometimes the apparent form is changed by atoms joining groups (molecules), or what I like to call 'atomic cults' [Author's note: no relation to "poison gas cults"]. But regardless of how they are arranged, or how they appear, the true reality of it all is that it's always the same One energy vibrating at different frequencies."

Orbital Life - The Relationship Pattern of the Universe

We discuss some aspects of solar system relationships in the chapter on soulmates. And while some of the material below is somewhat repeated, this was a continuation of the above conversation with Vishnu, and it is pertinent in this chapter, in its metaphysical sense.

"Looking to outer space you find countless stars, 'Suns' like the star of this solar system, with planets of their own in orbit. Constantly moving, vibrating, they follow the same Universal Laws of All, as does the atom, the micro-cosmic solar system.

The Universal Orbital Pattern which is also the basis of Solar Systems & Atoms.

Indeed, ANYWHERE we look in life, be it outer space, or inner space, EVERYTHING is either atoms or solar systems. They are like octaves of the same thing: micro/macro cosms. There is nothing else. What is a building? A tree? They, and anything else that *seems* to be something else, are but an assembly of atoms/solar systems.

I can't emphasize the significance of this enough. It is one of the most important facts there is, and understanding its full meaning is one of the great keys to understanding the Universe, and our lives."

"What are these other great keys?"

"The next great key can also be seen with atoms and solar systems. It is their *orbital pattern*, their *orbital relationship*. It is **the one primary pattern** that exists in the Universe. It pervades everything, and all else is built upon it. Peniel, it is what our human male/female relationships are based on. It is what makes soulmates, soulmates."

"But aren't orbits separate things amongst separate solar systems or atoms? How could it be what everything in the Universe is built upon? And how could it be what human relationships are based on?"

"Look into space at night. Each shining "star" you see is either a 'Sun' - an

284

object radiating light, that is surrounded by and orbited by planets, or a planet, giving off light reflected from the light of a star. Study what scientists have discovered about the 'solid' objects that surround us - water, trees, buildings, stones, earth, plants, human bodies - they are all made of atoms. And what are atoms? Microscopic 'stars' being orbited by planets, but very tiny, and very, very rapidly - they are an octave of the stars and our own solar system. Read the ancient texts. We have had this knowledge long before the ignorant masses 'discovered' that the Earth wasn't flat. Before they 'discovered' that the Earth wasn't the center of the Universe. Before they discovered that the Earth revolved around the Sun, rather than what they previously thought - that the Sun revolved around the Earth. Before they 'discovered' atoms. Soon they will 'discover' more, and more.

Consider: what if everything is orbiting something else? What if when you get smaller than atoms, and bigger than solar systems, the same, or similar, circular orbital pattern is found? It does - in some way or another, even though they haven't 'discovered it yet' [Author's note: much of this has recently been discovered by modern science]. What if it goes on infinitely like a never ending spiral? It must. It is the pattern of creation, of the Universal Spirit.

If you contemplate it for a while, the 'pattern' of an atom or solar system is, in a sense, *the only reality*. It is the primary form of life in the Universe. This pattern is the *basis* of the building blocks of *our* illusions. And what is *it* comprised of? This amazing, all pervasive pattern consists of 'individual' parts functioning as One. This Oneness is achieved by virtue of the nature of the polarities of the individual parts - plus/minus, male/female. Electrons of an atom are like the planets of a solar system. They are oppositely charged (the opposite 'sex') to the nucleus of an atom, and they are attracted to each other - just as the planets and 'Sun' of a solar system are. The polarized parts flow together in a particular 'way' that is dictated by Universal Law. The pattern is orbital because of the nature of polarized relationships in space. There is always a center, a central sphere that gives, that flows out energy, and 'attracts' - and that central object is surrounded by objects that are attracted to, and attach themselves to, the center object. In the case of a solar system, the Sun is the center that all the planets revolve around. In the case of an atom, the nucleus is the center that all the electrons revolve around. They are the same thing. The outer objects' (electrons or planets) momentum, their 'speed' as they travel through space, becomes a circular movement once they are attracted to and attached to their central object (the Sun, a Star, or a Nucleus). That movement is cyclic - in other words, it keeps orbiting around and around at a certain speed, repeating its cycle in a given period of time, thus a vibrational occurrence is created of 'cycles per... something' (second, day, year, whatever). In the case of the Earth orbiting the Sun, it is 1 cycle per year. In the case of other planets it is faster or slower. In the case of atoms, it is very, very fast - and different for each atom.

Taking this a step further, what if everything is orbiting something, which is also orbiting something else? Then all of them function as ONE. And a complex vibrational pattern exists. They each link up with all other objects, becoming a part of *their* flow and one with *them*. In the entirety of the Universe, All things are interconnected as One in this way. And the *basis of all this is the Universal pattern* we see exemplified so perfectly in the atom or star systems. It follows and reflects Universal Law perfectly. This pattern flows in perfect harmony with Universal order."

"I am beginning to understand. But I still don't understand the 'relationship' it has to human relationships."

"What if this form, this pattern, represents the relationships of beings? What if each atom is a conscious being composed of soulmate beings? What if each solar system is a conscious being composed of soulmate beings (each planet and 'Sun' is a being, in and of itself, that make One being together)? What if every being plays two roles, like both parent and child at the same time - surrendering to something, and directing something? What if every 'star' is both in an outflowing, 'positive polarity', 'directing' position to its planets, but also is like a 'planet' to something else that *it* orbits? What if the planets are taking a receptive, 'negative polarity', surrendering posture, to a 'sun', but are functioning like a 'sun' to something else that orbits it, or is affected by it? According to the teachings of the Children, and my personal realizations, all of the above is true."

Many, many things can be learned and understood by contemplating the above concept. Contemplation of this pattern has guided the understanding of masters, in all matters of Universal and Earthly life, and thus can also provide the contemplative seeker with profound answers.

Truly understanding the meaning of this pattern, and applying it to human life, can provide the deepest understanding of the nature of men and women, and male/female relationships. It is the perfect pattern of the harmonious interaction of polar opposites. Thus, with contemplation, it can show us the way to have perfect relationships, helping us achieve perfectly harmonious interaction with our own soulmates, and other humans.

Beyond the 5 Senses

Earlier we said that *for most people,* the 5 senses are the only thing that allows them to be in touch with the world around them. A person who is Universally Conscious, has transcended the separate self and perceives things with more than the 5 senses, and experiences them directly, without the "filters". But you don't have to achieve Universal Consciousness to start perceiving more - anyone can achieve greater perception if they work on it.

When we expand our consciousness, we can access other means to perceive spectrums of vibration, normally beyond human reach. We can sense these other spectrums (or planes) if we transcend the physical limits, and "tune-in" to them. This takes place when there is an activating of an evolutionary spiritual energy phenomenon called the "kundalini". The kundalini lies dormant, inside us all. When the kundalini becomes active, it traverses the spine, energizing nerve centers (called plexus) and endocrine glands that are normally dormant, or just performing on a "lower" vibratory level, maintaining normal physical body functions. The activation of the kundalini causes the subsequent activation, or "awakening" of seven centers along the spine, called "chakras" in some spiritual traditions. They are like new, previously unused senses in a way. Each of the chakras allows receiving and transmitting on different planes of vibration. For instance, probably the most famous of the chakras is the pituitary, or "3rd Eye". When this is opened it gives one what has been called "second sight". This new perceptional capability will vary depending on the degree of opening. A medium level opening will give one the ability to see the energy fields that surround all things. Much more can be perceived when it is fully open, and functioning in coordination with the other chakras. When the chakras are properly opened, you essentially *exist* on these different planes also. Here's a not very good allegorical example: you could think of it kind of like this. You have 7 television sets, each with a different "show" that is a different version of the same show about your life and the world around you, playing on them. One is black and white, one is color, one lets you see "previews" of the future of upcoming shows", one lets you see everything like an x-ray machine. One lets you see the atoms in everything. One lets you see your life like a "picture in a picture" TV showing 2 different channels, with the big picture being the entire Universe, and the little one in the corner being what's going on in your life at the time, etc., etc.. But rather than being just a "show" for you to watch, they allow you to become part of the show, and live in, and interact with the show. And the kundalini is the power supply that initially turns these TV's on - TV's you have never even seen before, or knew existed.

(Caution: if the kundalini rises and opens chakras without proper preparation, guidance, or control, it is something like being a radio that has no tuner, no means of selecting and maintaining the desired frequency; this opens one up to receive any vibration erratically. Some cases of insanity and "possession" are results of this occurrence. We caution you to not use any technique that forces kundalini, unless you are under the guidance of a true teacher). We deal more with kundalini and related subjects in part two of this book.

Spiritual Stimulation of the 5 Senses

Vishnu continued imparting his wisdom:

"Some physical vibrations that can be picked up by our 5 senses, have 'harmonics' (parallel vibrations of a higher frequency) and forms that correspond with higher 'spiritual' vibrations. When we pick up these vibrations, the harmonics and forms stimulate a 'like response' within the person receiving them. This can be experienced through any of the senses. Using sound for an example again, it would be like hearing beautiful music that takes you to levels of spiritual elation, rapture, giving you feelings of peace, and Unity with the Universe. When this happens, all that is actually taking place physically is that an array of vibrations within a certain frequency band is being received by you (hearing the music)."

"So why do you get those effects, those emotions and feelings from the music?"

"I was just getting to that. Because the vibrational form, movement, and harmonics resound within you, and allow you to tune-in to the 'source' of which they correspond. That 'source' is what the composer was 'connected to', or feeling, when the music was composed. The sense of smell is not as simple. But here are just a few examples of the ways harmonious Universal vibrations manifest to various senses:

To vision - a mandala; spiritually elating dance movements; elating colors and art; the beauty of nature - like a sunset.

To touch - the feeling of the Universal life energy/prana/chi/ki, flowing through your body; a loving touch.

To hearing - spiritually elating music or sounds; the sounds of nature.

To smell - the fragrance of a flower or pure incense. Frankincense, myrrh, lavender, and others, in their pure state, are excellent for meditation and creating a spiritual vibration in the environment. The effect of odors on a physical body is unequaled. It is very powerful. They can even stimulate past life memories. The sense of smell is the *only* one of the senses directly connected to the brain, and the outside physical world. Smells come from physical particles in the air, that directly contact parts of the brain, which is accessed through your nose. Smells actually directly activate emotion centers in the brain, and thus, those emotions can trigger childhood memories, or even past life memories. Odors can thus be healing, or create problems. Keep in mind that an odor that is beneficial to one person may not be for another. Try various types; you'll know which are for you. The combination of Frankincense and myrrh, or the combination of Lavender buds and Orris root powder, are the most powerful for stimulating past life emotions, and thus memories - because these were used in our ancient temples and healing centers."

Music

"Music is a powerful force spanning the Infinite to the finite. As with other vibrations, it can be harmonious, healing, spiritually stimulating, or, inharmonious, degenerating, stimulating the self, instigating self-indulgence.

Music has no language barriers, and is as close to a language of the Universal Spirit that you will find.

Even the planets make music. They all make vibrations that can be sensed as sound in the right state of consciousness, with the right chakras active. And when you hear the solar system as a whole, the planets weave ever changing chords as they travel about in their orbits, getting closer and further away from other planets."

You may have heard of tests done in which "classical" music was played to one test group of plants, and "rock" music was played to another. The plants that were played the classics flourished and grew towards the source of the sound, while the plants that were played the rock music withered away from the sound source and died. That doesn't mean that all rock music is detrimental, or that all classical music is beneficial. While looking in to the specifics of this experiment I found several things that would greatly effect the outcome. One, it wasn't a double-blind study, and the prejudices of the scientists (toward classical and against rock) could have greatly influenced the plants (remember the "smart" rats experiment?). Also, I found that the classics played were of the more refined and melodic classical composers, while the rock music played was some of the most discordant (from negative, degenerative, selfish-oriented composers). There is some very spiritually oriented rock music around if you look for it. All styles of music have the polarities of positive and negative, it's up to you to choose.

While we are touching upon the subject of music I will mention something about playing a musical instrument (including the voice). Spontaneous composition or playing can be done as a meditation. Letting go and letting the Universal Spirit flow through you, play through you, is a very beautiful, ecstatic experience. Those of you who may have experienced this with music know what I mean. But it is that way with everything when you transcend the separate self and do things in the spirit of Unselfish Love. In letting go and letting the Universal Spirit flow through you, everything becomes a meditation. That is the art of dying, always giving-up (giving upwards to the Universal Spirit). For the one who lives such a Universal lifestyle, ALL is a musical instrument as you play with vibrations throughout the Infinite vibrational spectrum. Come play the song of Love, the song of life, the music of the spheres.

The Name of God that is the Formula for Creation

As I studied various ancient texts in the library, I found it amazing that there were so many different names for God. Not gods. But different names for the "One God", even within the same religion sometimes. For instance, Elohim, Jehova, the God of Abraham, etc.. As Gabriel was putting away some scrolls behind the table I was studying at, I asked about this.

"Why are there so many names for the Universal Spirit?"

"Ah, it is a question. Sometimes it is because of different cultures or languages, sometimes it is because of translations from one culture or language to another, sometimes it is translations within one culture, sometimes it is for control and confusion - to change the truth or meaning of God."

"What is the most ancient name for the Universal Spirit? Great trivia question, isn't it?"

"Trivia?"

"Yes, like a game show or something?"

"Game show?"

Gabriel was an elder Adept monk, who had been there a long time, not to mention that he *was* also a librarian after all. I may as well been asking him about Disco music. So I dropped it, and went back to the original question.

"The most ancient name for the Universal Spirit, is Yod He Vau He. But this ancient name is far more than just what another religion calls their version of the concept of God, or even a name. In fact, it was not meant to really be just a 'name' at all. It is from before our time of human manifestation on Earth. It is the physical word equivalent of a vibrational, or thought form. It is an actual representation of the Universal Law that governs the 'primary pattern' [discussed earlier]. The name itself, is the key to creation, and the representation of the Universal Law of polarities, and the replication/reproduction of all vibration. And remember, EVERYTHING is vibration. Contained in this one name for the One, is the actual formula for creation, and the manifestation of all life within the One. Thus this name of God, is probably the single most significant metaphysical concept there is."

"It sounds pretty deep and heavy."

"No. It is the simplest thing in the Universe, just the hardest to really understand by the un-initiated, and unenlightened."

"There's no way *I'll* be able to get it then."

"Not at all. 'The name' is represented by four letters of what is now called the Hebrew alphabet, which have numerical, as well as symbolic, meanings."

"Oh, that is very clear now...", I said respectfully but with playful sarcasm. "So *what is the name already!?*"

"*I told you,* Yod-He-Vau-He (YHVH) [allegedly Pronounced Yohd-Hay-Vah-Hay]."

"Right, I'm sorry, I got off on the letters and numerology thing."

"You asked about why different names for God within the same religion. This is one that was changed through time, translation, and misinterpretation, to many variations of the original, including, within several religions. Consider the similarities: Yahweh, Ya-Ho-Wah-Ho (YHWH), Ya-Ho-Wa, and Je-Ho-Vah, to name a few (Jehovah and Yahweh stuck pretty well). YHVH is also sometimes referred to as "the tetragrammaton" in magic and metaphysic circles. The first part, which was the positive polarity or "father" part of the name of God, was Yod, yes? See the similarity there even - Yod, God, Yod, God - not too hard to change through time and even pronunciation."

"Yes, someone with a lisp or speech impediment could have started a whole new name of God to fight over."

"Ah... yes, I suppose that could be.

The ancient teachings say that 'He who can pronounce this name properly opens the gates of heaven'. This saying is vastly misunderstood. But even now, in some major religions it is forbidden to even attempt to pronounce YHVH."

"Why?"

"In the early days of 'religion', certain 'priests' or high priests in power positions, who wanted more power, didn't want the common people to know this great key. They wanted people to need to go to the priests and turn to the religion for their understanding of God and spiritual matters."

"Hey - how else are you going to make a buck and control everyone???"

"Exactly. This gave them great power and control, so they hid the name, changed the name, or made it forbidden to say by anyone other than the 'high holy people'."

I later asked Zain more about it, and he not only explained the details of the name, but taught me how to chant it as a meditation. It created major changes in my consciousness.

"The symbolism and structure of Yod-He-Vau-He is simple, yet deeply profound. And when its few simple elements combine, they give birth to the entire complexity of life. In part, YHVH represents that perfect simple pattern we spoke of earlier - the atom or solar system. It also speaks of human procreation, and stellar/planetary procreation. The first part, "Yod", represents the positive (+), "Sun", "light", "the Father" principles. The first "He" represents the "negative", *not in the sense of "bad" or "evil"*, but in the sense of (-), negative polarity, *pure* darkness like that of the void of space, the receptive, the Mother principles. "Vau" is the meeting of Yod and He; the place of interplay, intercourse, and combining of the first two principles. It is its own principle, and the place of conception of, and the birth of, the second "He" (again, pronounced "hay"). The second "He" is the offspring of Yod and He, the result of their interaction, their subsequent creation. The second "He" has the same attributes as its Father, the Yod, in that it actually IS a Yod in its own macro or microcosmic realm. The second "He" is on a vibrational plane an octave apart. The second "He" begins the cycle (Yod-He-Vau-He) again, but AS THE YOD in micro-cosm or macro-cosm, and its polarity is reversed from its "father" YOD. Interestingly, the "father" principle, Yod, was distorted through translation over time from "Yod" into "God", which is also often given a "father" principle connotation."

This took me some time and deep contemplation to grasp the entirety of, and the great significance of it. But I eventually did. In fact, it ultimately led to a great deal of scientific research I conducted, applying the name to light, sound, and music. I have included some other profound aspects, and an attempt at giving you examples that may help certain of you understand it better. Understanding vibration and music can make it easier.

The cycle of YHVH creation continues as an Infinite spiral. It can best be understood intuitively, but maybe these illustrations will help a bit.

```
YOD
  HE
  VAU
    HE/YOD.......octave
(Infinite        HE
vibrational      VAU
spiral)            HE/YOD.......octave
                 HE
                 VAU
                   HE/YOD......octave
```

YHVH makes a spiral (similar to DNA double helix don't you think?), each Yod in the same place on a circle of the spiral, but just above, or just below - on its own circle. These are "octaves" of vibration, and can represent a micro or macro-cosm world of existence.

To further help understand the way YHVH works, consider the vibrational realm of sound, and facts relating to music.

A common frequency of the musical note of "A" that is universally used to tune instruments, is 440 cycles per second (also called 440 hertz [hz]). But there are an infinite number of "octaves" of "A", above and below 440hz. For instance, the next octave of "A" above that is exactly double, exactly times 2 - i.e., 880 cycles per second, whereas the octave of "A" below that is 220 cycles per second, exactly half, exactly divided by 2. Note that the next higher note of "A" is exactly double, and the next higher one from that is exactly double, etc., and that vibrational doubling will go on infinitely, even after it goes beyond the realm of sound. Likewise, the next lower note of "A" is exactly half the frequency, etc., etc.,

"A" x 2 = "A" x 2 = "A" x 2 = "A" x 2 = "A"   (etc., continuing infinitely)
55hz   110hz   220hz   440hz   880hz (etc., continuing infinitely)
octave   octave   octave   octave   octave

The "A" represents YOD; the multiplication by 2, represents the HE, and its intercourse (VAU) with the YOD; the next octave is the second HE, which is the off-spring or creation of the YOD and HE's intercourse (VAU).

Below is another way of looking at it. In this example, the YOD and the first HE are of equal value (hz), and the combining or intercourse of the two (VAU) is represented by the equals sign (=). The numbers shown below the YHVH's are the cycles per second of octaves of "A".

YOD + HE = HE/YOD + HE = HE/YOD + HE = HE/YOD
110 + 110 =   220 + 220 =   440 + 440 =   880
          (again, this continues infinitely up and infinitely down)

Don't be frustrated if you don't understand it easily or even for quite a while. I didn't. Then one day it just hit me and all fell into place.

Yod-He-Vau-He represents many things in One. It is comprised of a numerological sequence that represents all things in the first four numbers. Einstein said we never need to count more than four to understand all things. He understood YHVH. Here are the One, Two, Three. Four. Such as: the Infinite ONE; TWO:

the dichotomy, polarities positive and negative, Yin and Yang; THREE: the three-fold nature of spiritual, mental, and physical; the Christian Trinity of Father, Son, and Holy Spirit; etc.. FOUR: the rebirth, the offspring, the cross, crucifixion and the transition to a new plane. Thus YHVH is both the formula of the "primary pattern" - and the formula for the procreation of the primary pattern.

YHVH's most important representation is: the means of transition and mani-festation of creation infinitely throughout ALL. As we have partially shown, this may be seen through studying the Law as it is reflected in music. In one octave of vibration is a Universe! Every octave is a duplicate of another except that it is of a higher or lower frequency. The note "A" is an "A" whether it is played in the high-est octave of an instrument range, or the lowest. As the frequency of vibration increases, and goes beyond the range of hearing, it eventually comes within the range of sight. But the same law that dictates the repeating notes of various octaves holds true. Colors are like the notes in the octave of vision. Each color has a "note" - each color is a note, each note is a color. This principle allows you to find any note, in the "octave" of any vibrational frequency band. For instance, you can take the frequency of 440 for the note "A", and keep doubling it to find the higher octaves. You can keep doubling it past the frequency band of sound, and on into the frequency band of light. You can then match your figures against the known frequencies for colors of light, and precisely determine the color of each note! Who could have imagined you could do such a scientific thing using the oldest name of God?

If one truly understands YHVH, one understands the Law governing all vibra-tion, and all creation.

Misery Loves Company - but so Does God.

Raises in consciousness, sometimes happen in what seems to be giant leaps, even though it may just be the result of a long "build-up" towards some specific real-ization. One of my "leaps", came when I was lying down outside, looking up into space. It was during a meditation exercise, called the "planetary polarity attune-ment" technique (outlined in part two of this book). As I was lying there, I really felt connected to the Earth. I felt my body held by gravity, as one with the Earth, and began feeling the entire Earth spinning (as it actually does), and both the Earth and my body, simultaneously flying through space, orbiting the Sun. Something "clicked" in a big way. And it just all came together, I was actually experiencing and realizing these things that had previously just been intellectual concepts to me. It was a combination of finally "realizing" that primary "orbital pattern of the Universe" concept, and YHVH, which is essentially the same thing. The Sun was a Yod (and a He to something else). I was a Yod (and a He to something else). It was incredible. And the difference between intellectually understanding all we've covered in this chapter, and realizing it, was like night and day. It was one of my major changes, my major "little enlightenments" towards total enlightenment. We'll discuss my next "biggy" "little enlightenment", in the next chapter.

Chapter Twenty
Men, Women, and Soulmates

Gosh, talk about your complicated issues. What could be more complicated, and be such a prime focus of our lives than relationships? And I thought metaphysics was complicated! But actually, once you understand a little of the basics of life, relationships aren't really that complicated at all.

Missing Pieces

I had been very lonely since I was a young boy, both in the sense of the world as a whole, and in the sense of missing a mate. Of course, I didn't know anything about the concept of soulmates, I just knew I missed "someone" that wasn't there, who was kind, thought like me, and was supposed to be living with me. Again, I wasn't an average child by any means. How about a 5 year old romantic? I made a tape collage of love songs that I fell asleep to every night, as I snuggled my teddybear (and when I got too old for the teddybear, a pillow).

I did learn about the concept of soulmates eventually. And while I had a girlfriend before I left for the monastery, it wasn't that "perfect dream relationship" I had always longed for or read about.

As you may remember early in the book, I mentioned that I mistook Anastasia's kindness, attention, and love, for "that she had a thing for me". And even if I hadn't, I would have had a "thing for her". Well, I had that crush for a while, until I found out she wasn't interested in me in "that way", and then I went back to looking, longing, and being lonely.

And Time Marches On

A couple of years later, even after returning to the monastery with my new humility, I was still alone. And my true learning was really just beginning. I had been back about a year. I was well over my early infatuation with Anastasia. But I was still really wishing I had a woman in my life. But I was unattractive. Not physically, mind you. But unattractive in a "real sense". I was unattractive on the inside. I didn't even have *myself* together - so I certainly wasn't able to be together with someone else in a relationship that would be positive, and helpful to the woman. I wasn't serving God, or Unselfishly Loving, so I really didn't radiate any love or charisma. Boring. I, like most men, was a "wanter" rather than a "giver". I was inwardly wimpy - weak. Most women want a man that is inwardly strong, and not "needy" of them. That goes even more so for higher consciousness women. And even *higher* consciousness women *also* want one who is at least dedicated to God and achieving enlightenment, if not already enlightened. But that didn't stop me from wanting one anyway.

One day I asked Zain, if he knew where my soulmate was, or how I could find her, and if I would ever find her. His answer was, as expected, an enlightening ego blow.

"Your questions are irrelevant." he said.

"Why?" I asked befuddledly.

"Because, what you imagine a soulmate to be, and what you think a soulmate relationship is, and would be like, is not accurate."

"You mean you can't have an idyllic relationship with anyone?"

"No. **You** can't have such a relationship. The kind you imagine in your mind at this time. It cannot exist for you *at this time in your life and consciousness.*"

He said, "Until the Universal Spirit reigns on the throne of your will, such a relationship would be one of major conflict, not bliss.

You are not 'right' within yourself, you are not right with your relationship with God, and any soulmate relationship you might have now, is doomed to failure, even if [as I naively anticipated and hoped], *your* soulmate has an 'angelic' demeanor as you imagine."

He smiled like a cat that swallowed a canary, and said, "Don't get me wrong, a soulmate relationship at the state of consciousness you are in *now,* could be *good* for you - but only in the sense that it could intensify your stress, and thus might speed you on your path".

I managed a "squirmy" nod and an insincere smile, acknowledging his amusing comment.

"Why?" I said.

"Because she would make your life miserable and you would fight all the time." [later in this chapter I explain why that is so].

The bottom line was, he strongly advised against anyone, including "the center of the world" (me of course), making an effort to find a soulmate. Which he was about to explain.

Next, he gave me a concerned stare, "The hierarchy knows what is best - if you need a burr under your robe, karma will find a soulmate for you at this time in your consciousness. But it is most sublime when the coming together of soulmates is the outcome of spiritual development, and they are of higher consciousness."

He told me I needed to let go of my desire for, and attachment to, women for now.

"You should concentrate on finding God first. Then you should always first and foremost be *God's* soulmate, God's helpmate - totally 'in love with' and devoted to, the Universal Spirit."

"Then," he said, "and only then - after you have become attached to the Universal One, and found inner and outer harmony, will those who should be with you in Oneness with Spirit, be with you in the beautiful harmony you are imagining."

I understood. But I hadn't "realized" it yet. Or understood how very important it was. It was going to be my next "biggy" - jump in consciousness - the hard way.

Shortly after that conversation, a new female novice, arrived at the monastery. As soon as I saw her, I was "in love" - meaning I developed a very serious selfish "crush". Her name was Venus (of course, she had to be named Venus), and she looked like an angel (which shouldn't have mattered to me, but it did). It was terrible - I had never been more infatuated in my young life. But she showed no interest in me. So I went to Zain, and asked if he could help me with my problem. Specifically, I asked if there was any way he could "pull some strings and set me up" with her. First, he gave me a long list of texts to look up in the library. Then he said, "No problem, leave it all to me." I was elated - but as it turned out, my crush was to end up crushing my selfish separate self. And it was one of the most painful experiences in my growth.

As The Sun and The Planets,
Are We In True Form.
Lovers One, Yet Seeming Apart.
Elements of One Flow When In Our Right Way,
Separate and Opposite, When Lost Is The Way.
One Being With Multiple Parts,
Before Time On Earth.
Male and Females,
Lost on the Earth.

Outer Parts Lost First
Then To the Core
Reverse it We Must, In Reverse Order

The Female Elements of Each Soul-ar System,
Orbiting Like Planets on
The Outer Reaches of Us,
Were the First to Enter
The New Space of Earth.
Tempted and Allured, they Separated From
The Male Elements, and Reversed Polarity.
Becoming Like Male Elements,
Out of Balance.
The Male Elements Were the Next Exposed,
And Reversing Polarity,
They Became As Female Elements.
The Former Male elements
Now Reversed In Polarity,
Turned From The One,
And Towards The Former Female Elements.
Now All Had Reversed Roles,
And Lost Their Place With the One.
All Were Out of Universal Harmony and Flow,
Planets No Longer Attracted to Suns
By Their Gravity,
And No Longer Orbiting The Suns.
Now Suns Chase The Planets
And Chaos Reigns In The World of Humans.
Now For the Return
The Order of The Fall Must Be Reversed

You Who Would Find Your Soulmates

Men, Seek Not Women
Seek God First
Then Accept The Women Who Come to You
With Unselfish Love

Women, Attempt Not, to Change a Man
Seek God First
And Find a Man Who
Is One With the One
A Man Who Sought God First

So, after reading the teachings and having them go in one ear and out the other, I went to find out what strings had been pulled to get me together with Venus. This is what that clever devil, Zain, did to "help" me get Venus. He pulled some strings all right. He set me up all right. But he knew what would happen also. What he did was to arrange things so Venus and I had to share the same living quarters. He even asked her to do things for me - things she may have done out of love if she loved me, like give me massages, make dinners, etc. She agreed to do this, taking it as a test, and as part of her learning giving, and self-discipline. She did it, but she didn't like it. It's not that she hated it, she was a good person, and a giving person, but she didn't *like* it, or enjoy it like when you do something for a mate you care for. It drove me nuts! Her mat was right next to mine. She slept right next to me every night, but she didn't have any interest in me as a man.

Then to make matters worse, she ended up being attracted to my best friend there, Ulysses, a fellow monk who was also a musician. He was someone I played with during practice every day, spent leisure time with, and enjoyed a great rapport with. Everyday, Venus would come and fondly watch Ulysses, while we played our music, and practiced. And I could tell he liked her also. She even proposed to him, asking to become his mate. She wanted to move out of my quarters, and in with him. And I knew that. But Zain asked her to wait, because I wasn't "well done" enough yet. He was driving me nuts. She was driving me nuts. It was driving me nuts. Actually, the truth was, it was only me driving me nuts, but I didn't see it that way at the time.

Finally, one day I couldn't take it anymore. It was too much to bear. I grabbed a parka, walked out the back gate, and began wandering the mountains in extreme emotional distress. I wandered for days. It was hard and painful, and it was all I could do. Then finally on the fourth day, it hit me. I had to give up women. Essentially, I had to "marry" God. I had to pull myself together and focus only on God - become devoted to God, and serving God. As soon as I truly realized this, and I did it inside, it all fell into place. So many things changed in my mind, my thoughts and emotions. And as I would soon find out, in my life.

One of the major changes brought about by this realization, was that, all of a sudden, I finally understood women. I never understood them before! As with most men, they were like aliens to me previously - like that "Women are from Neptune, and Men are from Uranus" type stuff. The way they thought and behaved really made absolutely no sense to me before. Now I know that there is no way women can be really understood or appreciated by any man, until the man becomes enlightened or at least partially enlightened. Sure, therapists can help you put band-aids on things, or just "accept" your mate. And relationship seminars can teach you to fake caring about each other, and how to go through the motions, but only *real* unselfish caring makes the *real* difference. And a woman who is really unselfishly loved, can blossom like fields of flowers in a spring rain.

I realized what a woman's place was (it was in the home where they belong - [joke] sorry, I just couldn't resist that joke). I realized women's place in the grand scheme of things, and the beauty of the "receptive principle" which they manifested. They weren't for being *taken* from, they were for giving to - not in the giving to their selfish separate self, or spoiling someone, but in the same sense that the Sun gives to the planets, and they create life. Like the Mother Earth, every thing that the Sun gives to her, she takes in, and gives birth to new creation. If you give a woman even just a little real Love, if she is also a caring woman, she takes what you give, adds herself to it, multiplies it, and gives even more. You get so much back in return for so little, it's phenomenal.

Previously, I had never been treated very well by women, to say the least. At best, I was ignored. For the first time, I really knew why. And also for the first time, I could love them without "wanting" them, or being "needy" and "longing for them".

I had now turned towards God for my nourishing rather than women, and I turned to God to serve, rather than women (in the sense of constantly trying to please a woman because you want something from them or you don't want them to be "negative, or in a bad mood" with you).

I made it back to the monastery that evening, and entered the residential area through the side kitchen door. There were over 50 people in there preparing food for evening meals, including women. All the women turned and looked at me as I came in, all with a big kind smile on their faces.

I had let go of Venus, during those 4 days in the mountains, and she happily got together with her true love. But within a week, I had 5 proposals. All of a sudden, I was attractive. And it was all just a simple change that seemed so hard before. All I had to do was Unselfishly Love, instead of want.

But none of the 5 women that wanted to be with me then, were my soulmates, and I still hoped for someone that would really be a part of me, a help-mate that served the Universal Spirit along with me.

I went to Zain to ask his guidance, and he told me I should accept and love whomever comes to me for love and caring, and especially not reject anyone just because I didn't think they were my soulmate. That's the beginning of another quandary, and a long story for another time.

Then he started to tell me about the disintegration of male/female soulmate relationships in Atlantis. One of these stories sounded remarkably like the bible story of Adam and Eve - and as I soon found out, with good reason. He told me to read some of the biblical scrolls, about "Adam and Eve", then talk to him about it.

And I Didn't Even Need a Library Card

Like I said earlier, when I first arrived at the monastery In Tibet, I was delighted to find that it had an extensive library which included many ancient writings. This was "library heaven" for a young man who, as a teenager, read every book about metaphysics, spirituality, and religion, that he could get his hands on. And

I'd heard about the Vatican library, and the Dead Sea Scrolls, but both were off limits to the public. Here I was able to read original manuscripts of the writings that eventually became the bible, along with the sacred texts of many other religions. These old biblical writings were relatively *new* manuscripts compared to many there. But right now I was focused on the biblical scrolls (particularly ones dealing with Adam and Eve).

Some of these biblical manuscripts were much like the famous Dead Sea Scrolls. But the translations of the Dead Sea Scrolls have been hampered, and some authors have written out and out fake alleged translations of them. Also, unlike the Dead Sea Scrolls which were sold here and there and spread all over the place, our biblical scrolls were complete, properly preserved and intact. And we had them in both the original languages and hand, and all had been unbiasedly translated into several languages. There was far more in them, than in the modern bible, including such seemingly less significant scrolls detailing things like Jesus' dietary teachings! I really had to keep focused on what I was doing. But as I read them, old memories that I found disturbing came back to me.

"Father?" I said. "As I was reading the old biblical scrolls, it reminded me of my youth. I read the bible earlier in my life, quite thoroughly, and I found it to not only be confusing, but conflicting with its own teachings."

"Yes."

"Well, why would that be, if the writings were true, valid, and important - I mean, why do we consider it something to study and learn from, other than to understand the beliefs of others better?"

"First, what *we* have is complete, and unadulterated. Which you will understand the great significance of when you have read even more of them. And secondly, you must understand that much of it was not literal - it was written symbolically, and as allegory, in order to convey basic spiritual ideals and principles, in a palatable form for the masses."

"I understand that, but still, much doesn't make sense. I rejected it myself years ago."

"You rejected a very different thing, that you did not have the keys nor wisdom to understand. But still, it had truth in it, did it not? Don't reject the ancient scrolls because of that son, learn to understand it."

"How?"

"For the seeker of the deepest level of truth within, it includes a 'code' consisting of all kinds of symbology, including numerology. Since you have read it, I'm sure you noticed that certain numbers seem to appear repeatedly throughout the stories. Things like 'It rained for 40 days', or 'He wandered through the desert for 40 days', etc., etc.. 3's and 7's are also extensively used."

"Yes, I have, and it did seem rather odd that there were so many repeated numbers and patterns, but I didn't even really think about it at the time."

"That was the idea. You weren't supposed to think about it, they didn't want you to."

"What do you mean?"

"The original bible manuscripts included a numerological reference called the Kaballa, or Quaballah. And other sections that tied logical explanations to what appeared to be contradictions, after these sections were removed or modified. These sections of the bible gave the perceptive seeker the keys to unlock the manuscript's secrets, so they could be understood on deeper levels, and multiple levels. Even to use just the numerology as an example, if you understood that the number 4 or 40, numerologically represents a total transformation - a crucifixion - a death and rebirth of some sort, a given story may mean something much different, or much deeper to you. Or that 3 represents a 'whole' or 'a body', it adds new meaning to the stories, yes? The modern bible is missing its keys. It has been for many decades. You can check with Gabriel, but I believe the Kaballa alone was deliberately 'deleted' around the third century A.D.."

"Why?"

"The usual, power, control of the masses, or someone wanting some kind of personal gain. Yet at our library here, it has remained intact in its original form. As you know, much of it is written in the grand master's own hand."

"So it's all an issue of breaking this numerical code?"

"No, I didn't just say numerical code. There is a symbolic code also. You cannot take things so literally, you must open up your mind to the Universal symbology of things. And some of it is simply literal."

Thus the Atlantean Children's interpretation and understanding of the meaning of the bible's stories, may be, usually are, very different than anyone else's.

Adam and Eve - as Soulmates

"Can you give me some examples right now Father?"

"I can give you an example that goes to the very core of what you have been going through lately, how would that be?"

"Great!"

"Consider, for instance, the bible story of Adam and Eve. Here we have a story of the origins of human life on Earth, the story of the 'original' soulmates, and 'original' sin. The bible gives a version that can be taken literally or symbolically. The Atlantean version of creation, is similar, but they did not code the true meanings.

What do these stories offer us? Understanding of what happened to us and our soulmates. It can help us answer questions like you asked me, 'Where is my soulmate?', and, 'Why are they not with us right now?'. The fact is, something is obviously wrong, and we need some answers so we can set it right.

In order to understand who our soulmates may or may not be, and how to find them, we first need to understand what a soulmate is, and why we now find ourselves separate from our soulmates. The story of Adam and Eve, when looked at in a certain light, can help us understand this."

"How? It hasn't helped me."

"Be patient."

"I'm sorry Father. Please go on."

"The typical interpretation of the bible story of Adam and Eve is what, Peniel?"

"Well, basically it's that Adam was the first human created by God, and then Eve was created from him, because he was lonely."

"Yes, yes. What else?"

"They lived in paradise and needed nothing. God said they could eat anything, except the fruit from one particular tree in the Garden."

"What tree?"

"The tree of the knowledge of good and evil."

"Good. Sounds like a strange tree to have fruit you can eat from, don't you think?" I nodded. He looked at me eagerly and said, "Then what?"

"Then Eve was tempted by a serpent, telling her that if they ate the forbidden fruit, they would be as powerful as God. She subsequently tempted Adam with it. They ate the fruit, hid from God, and were kicked out of paradise."

"OK. Good enough. The newer ancient teachings say this story was a parable loosely based on the ancient Atlantean teachings, about the first Atlantean soulmate group to lose Universal consciousness. The ancient texts basically say that they lost their Universal consciousness because of selfishness that led to separating from the One. The Atlantean texts don't conflict with the bible story, but it does add details and shed new light on it. The later teachings further say that the story was written to allegorically represent *all of us* who fell out of oneness with the Universal Spirit, not *just* one couple."

"Not just Adam and Eve?"

"Yes and no. If you remember your history, which I know you do, you'll remember that the ancient Atlantean historical records say that we all started as spiritual beings, that were not male or female. We were 'both', in that we had both male and female 'parts' inside ourselves. At some point, we came upon the Earth, and beheld the wonders of its physical plane. To exist on this plane though, we had to change from our 'angelic' spiritual form, into a denser, physical form - in other words we needed physical bodies to fully interact with the physical plane. In the process of making this change, we discovered that we divided into male and female parts, and subsequently, male and female bodies. Enter the concept of Adam and Eve. Unfortunately, along with this change, came 'self' consciousness, and worse, 'self'- ishness. This is what led to our separation from the Universal Spirit - i.e., what the bible calls eating of the forbidden fruit. This was not real fruit, not a real tree - the knowledge of good and evil meant the duality of the physical plane, rather than Oneness. And the biblical 'original sin', was the selfish separation from God, which brought us into this duality - the action of eating the forbidden fruit, and karmic results - becoming entangled with, caught in, and 'cursed with' the plane of duality - the physical plane on Earth - the plane of 'the knowledge of good and evil'."

"Then the 'hiding from God' was actually the separation, and 'cut off' from Universal consciousness we created ourselves."

"Good."

"And the being 'kicked out of Eden' was our own subsequent pursuit of self-ishness."

"Very good."

"But what about the separation of soulmates. What then happens to Adam and Eve to part them?"

"There are several different teachings that involve the story of our manifestation on earth, and the separation of soulmates. And of course various comparisons can be drawn between all these Atlantean teachings, and the bible's story of Adam and Eve. One of the most important things that we need to understand, is that losing touch with our 'soulmates', or finding them, is not really the primary problem. It is our separation from God, and our selfishness, that *caused* the subsequent separation with our soulmates. And dealing with those primary problems must be our primary focus, or we cannot have a good soulmate relationship, or a coming back together in Oneness with each other, or God. To those ends, we should examine the comparison of the Atlantean teachings, with the bible story. But keep in mind there were two waves of manifestation, and parts apply to both, while other parts only apply to one or the other."

He then went on to discuss these teachings. In the comparisons below, the Atlantean teachings will appear in regular type. The associated bible story will be in bold type.

1) We had all the wonder and beauty of the entire Universe, which we lived in and enjoyed, after creation. **[Adam and Eve lived in the bible's "Garden of Eden"].**

2) We could wander and enjoy the entire Universe, with no cares, as long as we remained One with it all, in our Angelic state. **[And we see in the bible story that as long as "Adam and Eve" remained open, receptive, humble and obedient to the will of the Universal Spirit (God), all was in perfect balance, and peace, harmony, and happiness prevailed.]**

3) But we had free will. In coming upon the wonders of the unique experience of the Earth, we found that we enjoyed the sensations of delving into the polarized material plane. But to do this, we had to lower our vibration, and partake of the separateness of manifesting into physical existence. We were faced with an option to either just appreciate it, but not get "attached" to it, or get fully involved, and enmeshed in it. In contemplating their free will choices, and realizing we could do other than God's will, we exercised this right selfishly. This resulted in separation from the One, and the creation of a world full of selfish people. **[Adam and Eve chose to eat the fruit from the tree of the knowledge of good and evil (dichotomy, duality, material manifestation). And in so using their will to go against the will of God, they separated themselves from God (the One). The original "sin", selfishness, was committed, and by the Universal Law of cause and effect, separation from God ensued (this was the "casting out" from Eden/Paradise). Thusly no longer one with God, or in harmony with Universal Will, they accumulated negative karma from selfish behavior, that resulted from their separate self consciousness, which created a life of suffering and darkness.]**

Losing Touch

"So as usual, it all comes back to selfishness, and this led to the separation from God, and the whole mess."

"But becoming separated from God was just the beginning. The teachings clearly indicate that the reason why we are not together with our soulmates, is because we separated from them via selfishness. It is the end result in a chain of events. It started with 'self' consciousness, which led to the developing of selfishness and separation from the Universal Spirit. Then it went further, and our selfishness led to our ultimate aloneness."

No Blame

"But what about how this has all come to be blamed on 'Eve', or the feminine aspect. It seems that 'Adam' was as much at fault, if not more so."

"Very insightful. I'm proud of you. 'Eve' has been blamed for the 'fall', and for all the problems humankind has had since, along with the tempting serpent.

This is partly due to the way some religions have presented the story of Adam and Eve, and the way various social orders choose to see it. This created a scourge on women throughout the ages. But women should not be singled out for blame. Like you said, even in the orthodox biblical way of interpreting the story, it never would have been such a problem if 'Adam' had not partaken of this 'fruit', regardless of whether Eve did or not. But did Adam have any more of a chance to resist temptation than Eve? Yes and no. It's not nearly as simple as it all seems."

"What do you mean? It doesn't seem all that simple to me, as it is."

Father laughed, and smiled at me like a parent who was lovingly amused at the innocent ignorant remarks of his 5 year old child.

"I mean that a realization of the nature of our true beings totally changes the perceptual meaning of the story. The better you understand what was said earlier, (that our true form is both male and female soulmates who are really just aspects of a singular being), the better will your perception reveal to you the truth in the story.

Again, our angelic nature was a sexual-polarity integrated being - both male and female elements within *one* "angel". That's why angels are sometimes perceived as sexless or neutral sexually - it's not because they are sexless, but because they are balanced, they contain both sexes in one being, in harmony, see?"

"I'm stunned. What a realization. I'd never even considered it in quite that way before."

"But those elements weren't even considered 'male and female' as they would be now, until way after our degeneration."

"Now you're losing me again - I'm afraid I'm having a hard time getting a good grip on that Father."

"To grasp the polarities of our human condition is difficult without Universal consciousness. Let me think.... Perhaps the best way we can understand it with our limited brains, and limited viewpoint, is to try and understand it using several scientific analogies from the ancient teachings."

"Oh good, my limited brain should have a much easier time with 'scientific analogies' from the ancient teachings."

"It won't be that difficult. I am actually trying to make it simpler for you to understand, so don't block up your brain with fears of complications that don't exist."

"I'm sorry again Father. Maybe I should just keep my mouth shut."

"Sure. I'm certain that will be simple for you. I'd like to see you accomplish that for a day sometime."

"I can, I just... Oh. Sorry. *Please* go on. I'll try not to interrupt you."

"Never try anything. Either do or don't do."

I put my hand over my mouth.

[Before we go on with Zain's examples, let me interject this little pre-concept. Now, keep in mind that the terms "positive" and "negative" which are used in the examples you're about to read, are meant in the sense of the nature of polar opposites, such as those found with electrical charges and the ends of a battery. He isn't using the terms to mean "good" or "bad", as in "having a positive or negative attitude". While we do use the terms in that way elsewhere in the book, it is an entirely different meaning than what are used in the following examples.]

Still with my hand over my mouth, I nodded to Father to indicate I would be quiet and let him continue his discussion. He raised an eyebrow over the ridiculousness of me putting my hand over my mouth, and then he went on.

"First, let's draw a comparison between electricity, and the male/female polarities within us. People often think of electricity as positive and negative charges. But actually, it is just one energy, and it flows through something as 'one electrical flow', moving in one direction in a circle; it is only when you divide this flow by *severing* this flow, this circuit, *separating* the oneness of the flow somewhere, that you get the polarities - the polar opposite terminals of + and - . When severed, it is called 'positive' on the side where electrons would be outflowing, and 'negative' on the other side where there is a receptive, or 'vacuum' condition (an absence of electrons, and a condition of 'wanting' to accept electrons). When the circuit is intact, the flow is one circle, moving from the direction of what would be the positive terminal *if* it were cut, to the direction of what would be the negative terminal *if* it were cut."

"But what does that have to do with soulmates Fa... Sorry."

"OK. Let's try something else. Perhaps one of the best ways to understand our natures, is by contemplating stars and atoms, and understanding them better.

Look around you, *everything* you see is an 'illusion' of sorts, created by atoms grouped together in certain ways, and vibrating at different speeds. Look outside the planet, and you find vast infinite space, sprinkled with stars and planets. Stars and planets are virtually the same as atoms, but on a different scale. **Atoms and star systems are all there really is in the entire Universe.** And if we observe them, we find they both act in virtually the same manner - they have the same 'pattern' of existence. It is a pure pattern of a radiating energy, receiving energy, male/female attraction, attachment and dependence. And every element of a star system or atom, plays all these various roles. It is a 'pattern' of a 'way of life' that fits into everything else in the Universe harmoniously. Both follow some perfect marching orders that the Universe has come up with for life in harmony with all other life. Both function on positive and negative polarities attracting and engaging with each other. Male and female elements in a perfect perpetual dance. In that sense, it could be said that the entire Universal order is based on 'sex'.

The Universal Orbital Pattern which is also the basis of Solar Systems & Atoms.

The workings of the atom, and of solar systems *are just like our essential beingness-* our true nature. It is what we really are. Our true natures can thus be likened to the elements of an atom - electrons which are negatively charged ([-] receptive/female principal) are attracted to, and in the orbit of, the nucleus which has positive charge ([+] outflowing/male principal) of an atom. It is the same with the planet or planets (female) that are in orbit of a star (male) in One solar system. It is not by accident that we call the planet we live on 'mother' Earth. If the Earth is the 'mother' of life here, who is the 'father'? The Sun. Life would not exist without the interaction, the intercourse of the energies of either.

A solar system is not *really* a bunch of planets and a star, it is *one whole being.* The male and female elements (stars/planets) are soulmates within this one being."

"But they don't have relationships like soulmates, like humans."

"Don't they? Even though you don't *see* the Sun and planets 'touching' each other, they are indeed 'touching' and in constant contact with each other. There is also constant, interplay or intercourse of many energies. You just don't perceive it with your limited senses, although human scientists can pick up some of them with their scientific sensors. Yet they generally ignore things that aren't 'physical'."

"What energies?"

"Take 'gravity' for just one thing. Ask a scientist why the planets are orbiting the Sun. Gravity. But just what is gravity? What does that really mean? Scientists don't *really* understand what gravity is. Could it actually involve outflowing love and attraction?"

"Are you saying that's what it is?"

"Just think about it, and go put your hand over your mouth again. At least you *look* like you're listening better that way."

Give and Take

In my much earlier days at the monastery, I asked some other fundamental questions, and Zain explained the infinite link of all things in the Universe, and the concepts of equality and superiority.

"Father, I know I am young, but I have studied and traveled a great deal. In many, many cultures, and religions, men dominate."

"Do they now. My, you must have studied and traveled a great deal," he said in a pleasantly sarcastic way. My ego wasn't really "getting it" at the time of course. So I just went on.

"All these men and women, are taught by their culture or religion, that the men are superior to women. And in most cultures there are classes, and some serve and some rule. But here, at the monastery, it seems mixed. I see both, yet there is an equality also. There is no feeling of superiority or self-centeredness in the Adept true teachers, yet they are served."

"You cannot compare the inequity and barbaric mindset of such cultures and religions, to what we are, do, and manifest here. That is why it is confusing to you.

It is simply Universal order. Nothing more. Everything is both 'guider' to something and 'guided' by something, subordinate to something, and superior to something, there is always someone better than you, and lesser than you. Including with me. This is how the Universe 'runs', how all things link via their polarity. It is just polarity, not superiority or inferiority. Each individual's duty, is to find what they are attracted to, supposed to surrender to and be subordinate to. That's what each of us are personally responsible for, not for getting someone to be subordinate to us. Then once we find our proper place, our proper subordination in the great scheme of things, then whatever is meant to do that with us, in the infinite link of the Universe, will do it - of its own accord. I am subordinate ultimately only to the Universal Spirit. In my place and relationships here at the monastery, I am subordinate to Michiel, but that, is superceded by my subordination to the Universal Spirit. You chose to be subordinate to me as a student, but someday, you will only be subordinate to, and serving God. As the grand master said, 'He who would be the greatest, would be the servant to all'. I am not served or treated with respect because I desire to be. I just am. I just serve. I just focus on my surrender and humility to God. And in the security and fulfillment of that relationship, I have all I need, and I am free to love and give to all of you. If you wish to learn humility, and take such a stance with me, you need to have an attitude of respect and humility. But only because that's what you want from me, and thus need to do. But that is your prerogative, and you make it your place if you choose to, I don't make it your place."

"I understand. That makes sense."

"Good. Then see if this makes even more sense to you. The stars, planets, electrons, nuclei, men and women, all contain both the female and male elements, and should play both roles, in the proper order. A planet plays an outflowing (male) role to its moons, which are attracted to, and one with, the planet. A star, such as our Sun, plays an outflowing (male) role to the planets in this solar system, which in their attraction to the Sun, become one with the Sun, and receptive to its energy. But a star (such as our Sun) is *also* attracted to, one with, and receptive (female principal) to, something *else* (such as the 'black hole' at the center of our Milky Way galaxy, which our Sun orbits). So it plays both roles. That is the way of things in the Universe - all things. Only humans resist it and go against this flow. They all want to be God only, the center only, served only. And none want to be humble and serve, and give."

"Some do."

"Yes. All too few."

"So it has to do with attraction?"

"That is just one way you can look at these Universal 'give and take' links. There is certainly the 'attracted to' viewpoint - i.e., the moon is attracted to and orbits the planets, the planets are attracted to and orbit the stars, the stars are attracted to and orbit galactic centers, galactic centers are attracted to...

But again, there is the flip side. You can also see it from the "outflowing" viewpoint rather than the "attracted to" viewpoint - the planets flow energy to the moons, the Suns flow energy to the planets, the black holes flow energy to the Suns (contrary to what many scientists think), and something is flowing energy to the black hole, and something is flowing energy to that, and that, etc."

"And people?"

"On the human level, the polarities we split into, i.e., men and women, reflect these principals in different ways when we are separated in consciousness, and on the Earth plane. Men and women, once One, are very different when separated into their polarities, and the lower the person's consciousness, the greater the difference will be, and the greater the lack of harmony.

Again, each one of us has within us both the male and female, both the receptive and the outflowing qualities. Totally equal, yet in different positions. We all are supposed to be receptive to something, and outflowing to something else."

"But men and women are so different, and some tend to be dominating and some submissive, and in all cases, it always seems to turn into a nightmare and a big mess. What are we supposed to be in this state?"

"It's not a question of what we are supposed to be, so much as what happened to us, and what we are, what we have become, and what we will make of things. Yes, the differences can vary widely. But there are certain qualities that are generally associated with men and women, *as generalities only*. A few of the qualities that are associated with the female, negatively charged, receptive side, are: emotional sensitivity, passivity, mutability, adaptability, and being more intuitively oriented than logically based. Qualities that generally are contributed to the male/outflowing side, are: emotional insensitivity/suppression, aggressiveness, being dominating, being more fixed, and logically oriented rather than intuitively based."

"So we are stuck with these limited ranges, as long as we are male and female?"

"No. As males and females grow in consciousness, they thus get closer to becoming One again, and all the stereotypical male/female qualities begin to merge until you are a complete balanced being. Thus, a higher consciousness male will have more emotional sensitivity, intuitive ability, etc., and a higher consciousness female will also have more dynamic capabilities, and logic, etc.."

"Wow. Thank you Father. That last statement really made things click."

"I'm glad you have 'clicked' son."

Back to the Fall

Later that year, after I digested some of the earlier concepts, and had some realizations, we had another discussion about the whole Adam and Eve, soulmate split concept.

"Father, I understand much of what we previously discussed about the 'Adam and Eve' 'fall' allegory now, in a new light. But would you explain more about the idea of 'Eve' being the first to be 'tempted'?"

"When we are functioning as whole angelic beings, the one being's female *elements* are on the perimeter, our 'outside' so to speak, and the male elements on the 'inside', just like planets are on the 'outside', or perimeter areas of a solar system, or electrons outside the nucleus of an atom. That's why 'Eve' went first, so to speak. Let's use the solar system as an example again. Because the female element is on the 'outside', it is the first to make contact with other things outside the system. For example, our solar system travels through space as 'one whole thing', one being, which it is. Now, if it were to come upon a 'solar system eating monster' - who would get eaten first? The planet that was the farthest out from the center, the planet that was on the 'outside' most periphery. And these are 'female' elements of the 'one solar system being'. Thus, when we came upon the trap of the material plane, the outermost parts of our being, the female elements of our one angelic whole being, were *affected first,* and were the first to separate off from us as a whole (the 'Eve' principal). Then later, the center, or the male element of our being, got exposed to, and also drawn into, separation. (Adam seemingly 'following' Eve's lead). But remember, we were one being. It was us as a whole angelic being who 'fell' into separation - not women only. It is not women that caused men to fall, it was just the first *element of us* to experience the temptations of the new plane, and the first part of us to separate and become lost."

Adam, the First to Return

"So the female element broke away first. Does that mean that they must also be the first to return to the male element in order for the reuniting of soulmates to take place?"

"Not at all Peniel, as you learned long ago, the ancient manuscripts reveal that the 'Adam' referred to in the bible, was actually an Atlantean. And not just any Atlantean. This was the same entity who, in one of his later Atlantean incarnations, was master Thoth, the grand master of the Children of the Law of One. This was also the same entity who was later known as many others, including Jesus. The meaning of this is staggering. Not only was he the first human male being of the second wave, to separate from the Universal Spirit, he was also the first to return to Oneness. And because he was the first to return to Oneness, he was of the highest consciousness. This also made him the best guide to others trying to achieve what he had already achieved. That's why he is considered our grand master. It's not just some title or position he was appointed to. And because consciousness continues to grow and expand, and he was the first to return to Universal consciousness, he is always a step ahead of the rest of us, and thus *always* of the highest consciousness. He was thus the guide of the Children, their spiritual leader, if you will, from even before the days of Atlantis, then on, throughout many of his incarnations, and beyond. We continue to walk in his footsteps when we leave this plane."

"That is incredible. But it doesn't quite answer my question."

"Let me finish. You have the idea backwards. If the female element must rejoin the male first, and the female has achieved higher consciousness or enlightenment (which they would need to if they were seeking to rejoin with their soulmate) - what would they be rejoining to? A normal selfish man? How could that work? It's the opposite, and that is why I was telling you about master Thoth. When he returned to Oneness, he rejoined his connection, his link to God. And in doing so, and becoming thus enlightened, he made it possible for his higher consciousness female soul-mates to join him in this return also. Otherwise, if he was still separate, still lost, still selfish, they would have had to bypass him if they chose to return to Oneness. This is a very important point, and how he made it possible is where the story of Adam and Eve intersects with, and becomes quite relevant to, 'The Spiritual Path'."

"How's that??"

"Remember that Eve, because of the receptive and 'outer' nature of the female element within us, was the first element to separate from Oneness and fall into darkness. The Adam element followed, and getting 'kicked out of paradise' was not far behind. This was, in a sense, the creation of the first 'Path'. It was the path taken by *leaving* Oneness. From then on, a way back to Oneness with The Universal Spirit has existed and been awaiting our recognition and return - the path of Unselfish Love."

In the Right Order, Polarities Vanish to become One Flow

As was said earlier, everything in the entire Universe orbits something else. Electrons orbit nuclei, Moons orbit the planets, planets orbit the stars, stars orbit black holes, black holes orbit.... This process, just as in an atom, requires polarity; requires having opposite sexes; requires the receptive qualities and outflowing qualities; and this is where male and female come in. But in order for everything to function as One harmonious thing, it also requires all the polarities to be in the right order. This is because the "flow" of the circle of Universal energy moves in only one direction. Zain explained it to me using the idea of the Star Exercise, which is very much like a basic electric circuit.

"The Star Exercise reflects this great principle, this great Universal pattern. What is it we do when we do the Star Exercise alone Peniel?"

"We take in Universal Life Energy, through our breathing, and through our left hand, which we visualize as receptive."

"Receptive - like the female principle, yes?"

"Yes."

"Go on."

"Then the energy passes through us, and we send it out through the right hand."

"Again, we control the flow of this energy with our visualization - so we visualize it going out the right hand, and the energy follows our thought, yes? But when done with a circle of people, linking together by holding hands, the energy flows in a circle, going in a direction dictated by the fact that the left hand is receptive, and the right hand is outflowing. If one person is not receptive on the left, the flow stops for all. But when everyone is submissive and receptive in their proper place, and outflowing in their proper place, all becomes one, is one, there is no inequality, no beginning or end of the flow in the circle. It no longer *comes* from the positive pole and *goes* to the negative pole, it is always just *flowing* - it just is. As in consciousness (and life) there is always someone 'below' you and someone 'above' you. But it doesn't matter, the chain is One, the flow is One, and when you 'plug into it', all are simply The One. This is the way of the Universe, and the way of soulmates who have achieved the consciousness."

Putting the Batteries in the Wrong Way

"So the fall was like letting go of each others' hands, turning around in different directions towards each other, wandering off, etc.?"

"Very much so, when we manifested on Earth, and eventually separated into male and female parts, selfishness set in. The great circle was broken. And it was as you just said. All this jumbled up our "polarities" badly, and our ability to be receptive in our proper place, and outflowing in our proper place. Just as if some were trying to do the Star exercise facing one direction, and some were trying to do it facing the other direction, and none were making the great circle - it's a big polarity mess."

"So Father, is this polarity mix up and separation also why men 'chase' after women, instead of 'chasing' God as they should be?"

"Yes. When we (our soulmate group) were just one being, our polarities were in order, and harmony reigned within us, and with our connection to God. But our male and female parts, reversed polarity when we separated from the One. That's because our separation was the result of turning away from being receptive (-) (female principal) to the Universal Spirit and submissive to Universal Will. We turned away 180 degrees - totally opposite of the way we need to be, for us to be in our proper order. Then the male and female parts separated within each of the beings that had separated from the One. The female and male elements also essentially became turned 180 degrees from each other, in order for separation to occur. You can see this in magnets. If you turn them one way, they attract and join together physically, and with their energy fields, but if you turn them 180 degrees in the other direction, they repel and separate. So what male and female elements are truly supposed to be in the spiritual or angelic state, got scrambled in the human state, and the normal polarities of male and female sort of reversed. You can't be truly in either the receptive (female), or outflowing (male) polarity, if you are cut-off from the Universal flow. Both men and women are lost if they are not One with the Universal Spirit. Thus, men are insecure and confused about what they are supposed to really be, they are confused about both their masculine, and their feminine (receptive) side. Many 'block' their feminine side, by generating hostile thoughts about homosexuality. But their feminine side doesn't really have to do with homosexuality, it has to do with internal balance and being receptive to God. Their receptive side is the very thing that gives them the ability to be 'attached' to, to be a 'wife' to, the Universal Spirit, which then allows them to be a true 'father' and giver to everyone else. In our lost, and selfish, state of present existence, men desire to attach themselves to women rather than to the Universal Spirit. And in the women's confused and lost state, many women try to get men to be attached to them, and get men to do what they want them to, rather than urging the man to seek the Universal Spirit, and follow Universal Will. Then when women finally get men attached to them, and get men to do what they want, what do they do?"

"They don't like the men anymore because they are weak!"

"Yes, they get 'repulsed'! They end up having no respect for the men they can control, even after they tried so hard to control them. They ultimately feel that the men they control are somewhat loathsome and repellent. And then they begin to 'nag', or be what they call 'a bitch' to the men, etc.. Of course they do. This is only natural. She is virtually driven by nature to nag a weak man. The man is selfish, needy of her. The woman senses the man is all wrong. This is how it goes when men are not right with themselves and the Universal Spirit."

"But they still do it, they still have relationships."

"Sure, but like what? Many women have decided that men are either 'little boys' that want a woman to be like a mother to them, or they have decided that men are brutal and abusive, or just jerks. And it's all true depending on the course the man has taken. Some women have given up on finding a decent man. Some 'settle' for a man because they think they can find no one any better, or no one perfect. Some have turned to their own sex. But what most women think men are is not what they really are - at least it's not what they are meant to be. An average 'normal' man is polarity reversed - they 'suck' energy rather than giving it. A 'real' man is One with the Universal Spirit, and radiates - and while they still have the masculine qualities, they have a very different nature than what most women have come to expect. A real man - a 'spiritual' man, is in control of his self, and his strength is not 'macho force', but rather it is the strength of the Universal Spirit that permeates him and flows through him from deep inside. He does not dominate women and his environment by force, and selfishness. He radiates the light of God within him, and that automatically influences his environment with the strongest force there is - Unselfish Love."

"Are you saying it's all men's fault?"

"No. Why do you have to go to such extreme polarities? It either has to be mens fault or womens fault to you?"

"No, Father, it's just I guess I don't have a full understanding yet, and the last things you said, led me to believe that men were at fault."

"The things I said did not 'lead' you to believe that, you lead yourself to believe that."

"That's true, I'm sorry." I did an affirmation to myself, "I am always humble."

"Men certainly need to 'get it together', get back to God first, but women aren't totally blameless here. If a woman really wants to change, and find the right kind of man, there are men out there who are One with the Universal Spirit, or at least dedicated to achieving that. Granted, there are very few. But a higher consciousness woman who asks the Universal Spirit for guidance in this, will find what they are looking for. But many women would rather attach themselves to a man who isn't attached to the Universal Spirit, because the *woman* doesn't want to be receptive to the Universal Spirit *either. Because she is selfish, and wants to remain that way.* And they know they have to go through the same changes as the male, which means the death of the selfish separate self. A woman who wants an Unselfishly Loving man, must eventually become Unselfishly Loving also. And just as with men, not that many women are willing to do what is necessary to achieve that either.

As you know, many men chase after women. And many women like and support that behavior (and they are just as much to blame for all the problems as long as they take such an attitude).

So we live in a world full of polarity mixed-up, selfish men and women. Of course, it all makes for one big mess! It cannot work - this is all out of polar balance, and causes all kinds of relationship problems. Can you imagine the chaos in the Universe if the stars and planets behaved this way? Can you imagine what would happen if the planets tried to 'lure' the Sun, and the Sun broke out of its orbit and began chasing after planets? It would cause a chain reaction of disaster and chaos all over the Universe. The polarities must take their proper places, or discord will never end."

Problems with Partners of Different Consciousness Levels

"But with such fragmentation, how can anyone ever hope to find their soulmates, and return to harmony with them, since they are all likely to be at different levels of consciousness?"

"You have two different questions there. Sometimes people will be already living with their soulmates (usually unknowingly), and it is the worst relationship they ever had. This is due to a couple of things. For one, they have strong internal bonds and 'Karmic' ties, that draw them together. But remember, these people who were once a harmonious soulmate group, separated from God, and then from each other, in selfishness. They thus had strongly opposing feelings and attitudes, and thus took opposing directions in life. So when soulmates get back together because of Karma, rather than because they have both evolved and become more loving, higher consciousness beings, the sparks of conflict can really fly. But even though this is often an intense and very upsetting type of relationship, it can sometimes be a good scenario for growth. Such a relationship is full of turmoil, as each person is forced to constantly battle with each other's, and their own egos and selfishness. The growth can come from transcending the turmoil, facing yourself honestly, and using 'the mirror' your partner 'shoves in your face', as a guide for changing yourself. But often such undeveloped soulmates can't take the heat of the relationship, and will break up with worse Karma between them than they had before.

If partners who find themselves in a soulmate relationship are at *similar* levels of consciousness, but not really the same level, they can either grow together or keep each other down. But if one partner is of a higher state, or growing faster, they may need to separate if the other partner refuses to catch up or keep pace.

Unfortunately, in most relationships, soulmate or not, one partner will advance on their spiritual path, beyond the other partner. It is very, very rare that two people move at the same pace in the same direction, even those who have shared spiritual paths. This leaves the other bewildered, and usually hostile, and can often result in harmful attempts to manipulate the higher consciousness partner, and 'keep them down' spiritually.

Often, because of the natural receptivity and sensitivity of the female principle, female soulmates learn their karmic lessons sooner than their male counterpart. They also find it easier to be humble and receptive with a true teacher, than does a male principle. There are exceptions of course, but there are many women on spiritual paths that have no spiritual equal, or spiritual better, male counterpart in their life. Sometimes it's just because they don't really want that, and all the real final changes it would entail for them, but other times, it's just that there isn't anyone around. This presents a great problem because of the following prerequisite of the path: just as 'Eve' left and 'Adam' followed, to get back, Adam must return first, then Eve will have the opportunity to go with him also. Fortunately, Universal Law provides a solution in such cases. If Adam does not return first, Eve can find *another* 'Adam' if she wishes to. Unfortunately for the men, the burden is on the men to surrender to the Universal Spirit first, before their soulmates, or they leave no viable alternative to their female counterparts. This is not as bad as it may sound though, for at those levels of consciousness, we achieve the primary perfect male and female archetype again, and it is *just as totally satisfying and comfortable for the female to be with the new soulmate,* as the old - as long as the old soulmate has not achieved enlightenment, and is being rejected."

"So can higher consciousness women help the man they are with, raise their consciousness so they can be with them in harmony?"

"Many women attempt to change and improve their men. I have never seen it work, nor do I know anyone who has. For whatever reason, it seems that men must either learn from the school of hard knocks, or a true teacher. It is part of their false male ego. They refuse to truly grow or accept their female soulmates as their teacher, let alone equal. It could be that a woman might just happen to start 'teaching' a man at the same time he has actually decided to change on his own, and it might work out. Or they think they are teaching one, but it ultimately breaks down, or it is false teaching. But from everything I've seen and know of, they cannot truly *make* a man 'seek the light' or serve the Universal Will, and attempting to do so, even if temporary results seem to have been achieved, will only fail, and impair the woman's own development. But like I said, it is very fortunate for the female that she can find a new soulmate, that is just as fulfilling, just as real, as the original, should the original fail to achieve their enlightenment."

Real Romance - Reuniting with your Soulmate

"So Father, bottom line. As far as soulmates go, we are all just up a creek without a paddle for the most part?"

"Not at all. But for soulmates to *harmoniously* reunite, it requires *both* the male and female elements to *truly* 'want God' so to speak - to be receptive to the Universal Spirit and Universal Will.

The male soulmate must be the first to change his polarity, and become receptive to the Universal. It's like he needs to traditionally 'marry' - love, serve, and obey, etc., but it is the Universal Spirit he must do this with, and have nothing else more dominant in his life. A man who has done this can remain One with the Universal Will and consciousness, regardless of whether his soulmates are with him. This allows him to be able to wait for his soulmate to appear in his life. And when she shows up (or is already in his life), if she is of lower consciousness, he can patiently wait, or help her to 'catch up' to him, while *he* still remains in the

Universal flow, and thus her negativity or lower consciousness, cannot throw him off. It also allows him to become the soulmate of a woman who has no hope of retrieving her original soulmate - either because he has gone on to higher planes already, or because her original soulmate is of lower consciousness.

If a woman has realized she must return to the Universal Spirit, and her soulmate has not, she may 'jump' soul-groups and find another male who she has an affinity with, and who is appropriately spiritually oriented. This new male will become her new soulmate. While this may seem disappointing, it is not really, and is far better than the alternative. The new soulmate is just as valid as the original, and there is just as much love.

It can also be possible that a soulmate has evolved more rapidly, and already left the Earth plane. In the case of a *man* who's soulmate has already gone on, it is too late, but, as mentioned above, another woman who is without her original soulmate may 'jump' to another enlightened man, and become his soulmate. This is not allowed to be an enlightened man's choice though (nor would he want it to be if he were enlightened), for it is only the female who is allowed to 'choose' who to attach to - when polarities are functioning in their proper order, in harmony with Universal flow. Just as the planets choose what Sun they will orbit. Also, in the case of a woman who's original soulmate has already gone on, she can choose a new soulmate. But in both cases, a man or woman may rejoin their original soulmates after leaving the Earth plane, although it is unlikely to happen, because usually by that time, it isn't desired anymore because they are just as harmonious and 'happy' with their new soulmate situation."

"The right kind of soulmate rejoining is something I have dreamed of since I was a child Father. And while I have finally let go of my desires, and am totally focused on serving the Universal Spirit, it still seems like a wondrous thing."

"Peniel, it will come to you. I have seen it. And you are right, when soulmates join *in higher consciousness,* it is a time to rejoice. It is also a beautiful thing to behold, for it changes and expands the nature of their whole beingness together, like two or more caterpillars going into a cocoon, and emerging as One incredible butterfly. The male and female elements combine all their individual gifts and traits. But as in procreation, the sum of this union is greater than just the total of the two. Much more is created from the interplay of their combined energies. Thus, aspects of a 'new being' are created. The soulmate elements function together as one - a psychically bonded team working toward the same goal.

One final thing to think about - we can have more than one original soulmate. Contemplate it. Think about why. I am through for now. I have other work I must attend to."

"Thank you Father."

Chapter Twenty-one
Earth Changes and You

Man Will Battle Man
Some for Freedom
Some for Power
Some for Hate
Some for Food

A day will Come
That need not Be
That may not Be
But if Great Be the Battles
Great Mushrooms Will there Be
That Burn, then Freeze
Destroying All that I See
Or those that are not Free

New People Will Come From Far Away Stars
Some Ones of the Light,
Some Sons of the Dark and Cold
A Hand May the Ones Offer
Or Watch in Sorrow Only
Remains to See
As Free Will Changes the Things That Will Be
Earth there Will be, but Man May there Not

Know that it is Written
What Ever Events Free Will
Will Cause to Be
When All is Over
Those Who Chose the Light
Will Be Free From the Darkness of Night

But Remains to See
If They Will Live Amongst the Stars
Or Live Amongst the Earth

As Was In The Dark Times Of Atlantis

The time Will come Again.
Those Of the Darkness
Those Who Would Enslave
Those who Thirst for Power
Will Grow in Power
Controlling Communication, and Education
For All to Believe Their Ways Are Good
Their True Ways they Will Not Show
They Come instead As Great Men
Solving problems
Created Themselves, both False and Real
To Convince All the People
That Changes Must There BE
Then will they Come To Our Aid
With Concepts Good
World Peace and Harmony
But the Truth Hidden is
Slavery They Sell
Which Many will Buy
Their Choice Bringing Hell

As the Dark Ones Take Control
Nature Spins Out of Control
The Universal Spirit, acting Through Nature
Becomes The Redeemer
Of Those Who Reject The Dark Powers

The Selfish Evil Ways of Man
The Dark Ones and Their Pawns
In Ignoring the Universal Laws
That Guide Nature And the Stars
Will Cause Such Great Imbalance
That Stars Will Fall from the Sky
The Sky Will Burn, Scorching The Evil
Turn Dark and Cold, Freezing the Evil
The Earth Will Shake, Leveling the Evil
The Oceans Will Convulse,
To Drown the Evil
The Earth Will Open, Swallowing the Evil
Spewing Molten Rock to Bury the Evil
The Earth Will Tip, The Mighty Oceans Will Spill
To Wash the Evil Away
Great Mountains Will Sink
Ocean Land Will Rise on High

One of the things I came across in the great library, that were heaviest to my heart (at the time), were the predictions of Earth Changes. From the ancient Atlantean you've just read, to the predictions of simple tribal wise men from diverse cultures all over the world. It seems that there is unprecedented agreement. But free will is a modifier of the great Earth changes, and people's choices can make worse, or make better what will come to pass. But no doubt, if you aren't afraid to open your eyes, you can already see irreversible damage to the Earth that must follow the laws of Cause and Effect. Yet there is more to this than meets the eye - our own personal free will choices will be the determining factor in our own realities of the kind of future world we will each live in.

Ecology Isn't Just About the Earth

Many people misunderstand the need for ecological balance. From anti-environmentalists you hear things like "Forget the owls, save the humans!" This kind of thinking comes from the blindness of selfish separate selves. Such people are so deeply enmeshed in their selfish selves, that they don't see many important things, including things that they think are separate, yet directly impact themselves. They don't see the big picture - that they, we, all creatures, all things, are part of the great Oneness of the Universe. They obviously also don't understand that since we are all part of and One with the Universe, that we are the Universe. And thus all life, all creation, is "us" too, and just as important and critical to the entire balance of things in the Universe, and in this case, nature. But contrary to the appearances of their "pseudo-compassionate" statements in support of "humans first", they don't care about other humans either. As Universal Law would have it, their selfish ignorance renders them so short-sighted that they don't even realize this simple equation: if the owls are going, so are *they* - ultimately. Funny thing is, environmentalism really is a matter of saving the humans too, even more so. Humans are more fragile than many other species.

I have absolutely no doubt that the Earth *is* going to *change* - and quite dramatically. Other than my personal experiences and observations, there is the unprecedented, almost ridiculous quantity of predictions from unrelated cultures the world over throughout history, that *all* point approximately to this time period. To anyone with an open mind and the courage to face their fears, and to many scientists trying to be objective, something is very, very "off" in nature. It is so obvious. And many scientists are trying to warn humanity. But to me, my many personal experiences are the most profound. In my last days before leaving the monastery, I had five days of visions myself. In later days, I have spent time in Universities, studying people who were having visions, including famous musicians who were having visions of the future, and writing about them in their songs.

The ironic thing is, regardless of what humankind has done, or does, to the environment, the Earth is going to live on - the Earth will be OK. What is really in doubt is whether or not it will continue to support *human* life, or many of the other fragile forms of life that exist right now. True environmentalism is not about saving the Earth, it is only about saving life as we know it, and human life is just one of the species of "life as we know it", on this one planet alone. I'm not sure what the current figures are on species extinction. I think I heard a figure of about 180 species a day becoming extinct. Even if it's only 1 species a week, it means something is very wrong, and that life as we know it is losing its support network. Recent scientific reports talk about birds, reptiles, and fish being born all over the world, without a given "sex" - they will not be able to reproduce. Other studies show a radical decline in human sperm levels. Sure, you can do something about somethings, but many people need to open their eyes first, and some need to open their eyes to the fact that some things can be changed, and some have simply gone beyond the Cause and Effect point of no return. Those who "can't see it", are simply too afraid to face it - they are cowards.

All Signs Point in the Same Direction

The ancient Atlantean texts, have their own predictions about what will occur regarding Earth changes in the next few years. There are also predictions about socioeconomic changes. As I mentioned earlier, they were the 'heaviest', most frightening things I ever read *at the time*. Later, I came to realize the benefit, the need. And now, I welcome some of the cleansing Earth changes, while I am still heavy of heart about the suffering they will bring.

Here are some of my earlier discussions with Zain.

"Before I came to the monastery, I read things about what they call coming 'Earth changes'. Are there going to be changes on the Earth? And if so, what kind of changes - what will they be?"

"It is written. In fact, it is written and it is written and it is written. But first, before I tell you any more, keep in mind what you have learned about free will, and karma. Some changes are destined because they are past the karmic 'point of no return', they are simply ripples in the pond of the Universal Law of Cause and Effect. But others can still be modified with free will, within certain parameters.

Coincidentally (if you still believe in 'coincidence' by now), our library is full of ancient prophecies from dozens of unrelated cultures all around the world. Many of these cultures didn't even know of the existence of the other cultures. Yet they have similar prophecy, they virtually all point to such major changes in the Earth around the end of this very century, or just shortly after, and many predict the same things. How can this be that they all agree when they knew not of each other. Only one answer - Inner Being, Inner voice."

"What are the most common prophecies between these cultures?"

"One of the common threads running through most ancient prophecies, is the prediction that Earth changes will eliminate about two-thirds of the human population on Earth, leaving one third, who are purified by the experience (although they will need true teachers at that point). But things have changed since these prophecies were made, and while they may still hold true, there are a few 'free will forks in the road' that could alter the course of the future in ways which could eliminate *all* life on Earth, or at least all human life."

"ALL life - that's, that's..."

"That's hard to comprehend or accept, or bear. I know. But regardless of the *extent* of which life will be eliminated, the fact is, there will be a great loss of life, both amongst the many life forms, and the human. It will be bad enough, regardless of the extent. It will be painful to those of us with true compassion. As if it were not painful enough, and bad enough already.

There will be greater earthquakes than ever "recorded" or known by modern humans, volcanoes, land masses sinking and rising, the Earth will turn on its own axis, there will be waves from the oceans miles tall, numerous new plagues (and the return of old ones), and such human violence - all these things each taking their share of the various life forms. Possible occurrences (extra things not necessarily pre-destined) are asteroid or comet collisions, or near misses that still cause great devastation because of their effects. Nuclear war, and biological/chemical warfare are recent developments that bring the new possibilities, even those beyond the ancient predictions. Know this - humankind has never developed a weapon they have not used.

But the worst thing Peniel, is that before the great Earth changes occur, we are most likely going to see political changes that will establish a tyrannical world elite. Who will these be? It will be comprised of the reincarnations of the old, but now secret, brotherhood of the Belialians. This will be so powerful that only the Universal Spirit, through the forces of nature, will be able to destroy it. And the things the Belialians will do will be so terrible, that most people will eventually welcome the mass destruction nature delivers, as redemption."

I was quaking in my robes. Since the days I first laid eyes on him, everything I had ever heard from this man's mouth, was always absolutely true. And worse, I felt it inside also. And the evidence in the library, at least evidence of predictions, were also overwhelming.

"So we're pretty much all going to die, or most of us, and it will be like a living hell, all in my lifetime?"

"We are all going to die anyway, are we not Peniel? Even if none of this comes to pass? So relax, you are going to die anyway. But I am not telling you about these changes to inspire fear. When fear dictates our thoughts and actions, it is usually harmful [more about this on the chapter on the death experience]. These changes are simply things that are going to occur, whether we like it or not, whether we believe it or not. But like a harsh winter, it can devastate those not prepared for it, but if you *know* winter is coming, and will be harsh, you simply ready yourself. And if you can help your neighbors, that is the greater good. One who has transcended the selfish separate self doesn't experience fear, per se. In time you will understand. What was once a feeling that caused the self to react *irrationally,* becomes a mere warning mechanism that helps you choose *rational* action. Fear transmutes into an awareness of potentials of harm or problems, which alerts you to be wary, and to take appropriate action."

Atlantis Revisited

"I understand. It's just that what you are talking about is more than just a bad 'winter' coming up."

"Of course. But I thought it was a good allegory of sorts didn't you? Are you saying I give bad allegories? Wait till you are a teacher and you try it - it's harder than you think. You'd probably come up with something about having to use an outhouse being like the inevitable tide of events!"

He was trying to lighten the mood a bit by joking around with me. But then he continued with the seriousness of the subject, and reminded me of the cycles of history.

"As in Atlantis, we are again in the beginning of a period of radical changes for the Earth and its inhabitants, physically, mentally, and spiritually (the entire threefold nature). Humanity's selfishness has taken its toll and is starting to come back in full fury. With the damage that has been done already, there is no preventing the great Earth changes within the next decade. Given a sufficient raise in consciousness, those things that are not past the 'karmic point of no return' could be altered by free will, however, many are past the point of no return. Ask your-self if the first drops of rain from this great storm of purification, have not already begun to fall.

There are many things today that are similar to conditions in Atlantis before the great Earth changes that destroyed it - including the political powers. The forces of darkness - the Sons of Belial, have grown very powerful, and seek to enslave the world, at any cost. Many people who are not directly Sons of Belial, are pawns - by virtue of their own selfishness they 'unconsciously' follow the conscious evil ones. This is no excuse however, because they chose their 'unconsciousness'. They are but selfish cowards who have willingly participated in the evil that will bring their own destruction. The brave people of this world open their eyes to what is hap-pening, and refuse to be pawns. Even many of the brave ones are not aligned with the light yet, but at least they have resisted the darkness. These people can save themselves. After they suffer the horrors of what is about to befall the people of the Earth, they will have been purified enough - involuntarily as it may be - and this purification will awaken them to the Spirit within, and return them to serving Universal Will."

"Then at least some good will come of this."

Cosmic Maid Service or Judgment Days

"Oh, more than *some* good Peniel. The coming Earth changes are not 'bad' things, in and of themselves. They are necessary now. Necessary for a clean up of both the Earth, and of humans.

As all of these changes come to pass, we are given the opportunity for tran-scension into a new world of Unselfish Love and harmony. Some will approach the sufferings of this purification with patience, understanding, and Unselfish Love. Others will react with selfishness, negativity, and resistance. Universal Law dictates that each individual, through their attitudes and resultant actions, create, and mod-ify, their own experiences. Those who Love Unselfishly, will ultimately experience the 'heaven' of that attitude, while those who are negative, will ultimately experi-ence the 'hell' brought by that."

"So it will be like Atlantis all over again?"

More Final Than Atlantis

"There are some distinct differences between the Earth changes of Atlantis' day, and what is going to take place now. First, we cannot escape them as the Children did when they fled Atlantis. But also, there are various possibilities for intervention during these great Earth changes. It may be that we will even have some outside help. Many things are not determined fully. Free will choices are still dominant, particularly in whether or not there will be nuclear annihilation, which would create a much bigger mess if it is more than a very limited warring or act of violence."

"So is there anything we can do about any of it?"

"Yes and no. We can't stop the purification - it is badly needed anyway and we shouldn't *want* to stop it. We shouldn't see it as a 'bad' thing."

"But can we do anything about it for ourselves, to survive it?"

"What for? That is the most important question. Do you want to survive to save your selfish separate self, or to help be here to truly free others and point them to the way back to Oneness, and free them from their selfish separate selves?

But to answer your question directly, yes, and *know - know to make Inner preparations.* There are some physical preparations one could make, and perhaps that will be done by you or others. I will not be involved because I will be gone by then. But think! Think! What good are physical preparations if you don't make the spiritual ones - what's the point? Raise your consciousness first, then help others do the same if you wish to. There is nothing more to say!"

"I have heard people discuss possible 'safe' areas - places of refuge during the coming changes. I know of many areas that will be more or less free from earthquakes, etc., more or less safe - barring nuclear war and the like. But I tell them what my teacher told me, and his told him, and the ancient teachings told us all. Make your spiritual changes your priority first. *Raise your consciousness* **first.** After you have done that, if you still want to pursue safer physical areas, then look for areas where people who have higher consciousness are living. That doesn't mean where the people with the greatest knowledge are, but rather, where those with the greatest kindness and harmlessness are. The greater the consciousness concentrated in a certain area, the greater the chance of being safe. Even on a one-to-one basis, the ground could be falling out from under your neighbors' feet, while under your feet, the ground is lifting you above a flood or tidal wave. *Raise your consciousness first, and then it won't even matter what happens to you!* And like he said, we're all going to die someday anyway. And regardless of how, do you want to be prepared to go on, or be stuck with karma that forces you back to a life on the Earth, over and over again - a life of pain and pleasure, or just possibly just pain, on an Earth that is very different than what you know now?

For one thing, at this time, because of free will factors, we still don't know if the Earth of the immediate future will even be inhabitable. But regardless of whether it is or not, the main thing *you* can do is to become a truly good person, an Unselfishly Loving person. If there is to be any intervention (the flow, God/hierarchical help, extra-terrestrial or whatever), the humans who have changed to a new vibration, a harmless, caring, Unselfishly Loving vibration, are the people who will be 'safe' - one way or another. If the Earth becomes uninhabitable, or there is not intervention, those who have transcended this plane by becoming Unselfishly Loving, can just go on to a higher plane. And if *you* were a "higher being" from outside this plane, intervening and saving people, who would you choose to save? The selfish who live out of harmony with the Universe and Nature? Or the Unselfishly Loving, who live in harmony with the rest of the Universe?"

"The Unselfish ones who are harmless, and helpful to all life in the Universe."

"Exactly."

"But many people think they will be saved from the tribulations."

"Indeed. What a surprise they have in store if they don't change. There are *many* people out there, who are under the delusion that they are *going to be* saved from facing the trials that are coming up for us all. And they think that they don't need to do anything - except perhaps, talk about it, or 'believe' in this or that. Some think Jesus will save them, without them becoming really good people, just because they believe in Jesus. Some think aliens will save them, some think they'll go to 'the 4th dimension'. The biggest "hole" I see with these hopeful, 'wishful thinking" scenarios, is the lack of personal responsibility that they allow for. Some believe that ONLY whatever they think, or believe, or 'accept', will totally create their reality. So they think that if they don't 'give energy to' Earth changes or the coming chaos and destructions, they will not be subject to them, because they did not create them for themselves - so they won't have to experience them. But they take this precept to the extreme - and this precept is only half of a paradox - only partially true. When you meet one of those Peniel, or when you write in the future, tell those who believe that way, that if you *really* don't believe you can be harmed, by Earth changes, or anything else that you don't 'allow in your consciousness' or 'draw to yourselves', here is a simple test of how well it works, or how up to the challenge you are. Try this why don't you - believe you can't have a car accident, (otherwise you'll 'attract one to yourself' if you believe you can have car accidents), then once you get that in your head, I dare you to try driving through red lights all the time. (I'm not really recommending or inciting people to do this - I'm trying to make a point with a very real scenario). The fact is, if you drive through intersections against red lights constantly, you ARE going to suffer the consequences - whether you BELIEVE someone will save you from an accident or not. Don't believe me? See what happens if you are foolish enough to try it. And why wouldn't you try it - because you know there is *likely* to be a car coming through the other way - even if you've never seen it, even if you can't see it. The changes that have happened to the Earth, and are coming back to us from what has been done, is just as certain as traffic coming the other way. We are talking about reality here. And Universal Reality. Our species has been running the red lights of nature. They have run the big red lights and broken Universal Law. You personally have probably done so also, unless you are already enlightened. Most of the people of the world have run the big red lights. And there simply is NO way of escaping the consequences of breaking Universal Law. Unlike on Earth, with man-made laws, there is ultimate justice in this Universe. That is Karma."

Interestingly enough, when Zain came to the United States in his later years, he would drive in city traffic, as fast as a car would go, through red lights and all, and never had an accident, or even a ticket. Zain however, truly understood Universal Law, was One with the Universal Spirit, and thus he was just part of the Universal flow - for real. He didn't just profess or lightly believe in some philosophy or spiritual principle. He had 'become'.

"Father, why do so many people believe they will be saved from all these things at the last minute."

"Despite a lack of logic regarding there being any substance to the various fantastic theories of unearned salvation, and a preponderance of evidence that we are facing REAL ecological and socio-political disaster, the illogical salvation theories are what many people desperately *want* to hear and believe - so they believe. They buy into this mental/emotional panacea, this religious 'fire insurance'."

"Why? Why do they close their eyes when opening them is their best chance to get through whatever happens?"

"Simple. Fear and laziness. The selfish separate self doesn't want to die and let the Inner Being take its place on the throne, nor does it want to face its Karma, or the reality of the Karma created by what has been done to the entire Earth. So they exhibit the 'Ostrich Syndrome' - they hide their heads and think they're safe. They do this because they're so full of fear that they don't think objectively or logically, thus they are more than happy to accept these unfounded theories of 'Salvation without need for personal purification, enlightenment, or responsibility'. Just think for a moment, why would we deserve such unjustified salvation? Do you really believe the Universe works that way? Do you not think there are Universal Laws that govern the functioning of all things? Do you think you can break those laws and nothing will happen? What alien or higher being, who really is a higher being, is going to save parasites that are so destructive, so disharmonious to nature and Universal flow?"

"Parasites?"

"That's what ALL unenlightened humans are - destructive, inharmonious parasites. Or like a virus, or bacterial infection in the body of the Earth. *So what* if the destructive parasites are ordinary, relatively nice people with 'good' *beliefs,* even the metaphysical beliefs or religious beliefs such as many religions have? Do you know what the Universe's response to that is? 'SO WHAT.' If there *is* going to be ANY outside help, from the predicted return of the Christ, to the space brothers, to whatever, the logic is that they are only going to save those who are TRULY *different* than the rest - truly worthy of saving. Meditation is not going to do it for you. And just having a lot of metaphysical knowledge, or religious beliefs, certainly doesn't make you worth saving. Neither does being a *relatively* good person. If that's what you think, you'll have a BIG and unnecessary shock when the changes come to your door, and you stare death in the face, only to realize you *aren't* ready, when you could've been!"

He was getting very intense, and a crowd of other students had gathered around by this time. He looked around at them all, and pointed. But he was also pointing and speaking to all humanity.

"How many of you can say you are truly giving, that you care about others MORE THAN YOURSELF, that you love Unselfishly all the time, and that you have truly and completely transcended your selfish separate self and your physical body and mind? Not many. And if you haven't CHANGED in that way, you'd better get busy, and you'd better make it your TOP priority. Drop everything else you are doing in your life AND GET BUSY with what is really important and eternal - before it's too late. Be brave, and take a completely honest look within yourself. Are you truly good enough to live in a perfect paradisiacal world? Look for, and *see* the things about you that still need perfecting. Be glad when you find the imperfections! It means you've seen them early enough to do something about them! Face the things you have been avoiding. Do the things that inside you know you must do. Change for the better, so that you CAN save yourself, so you CAN be saved, so you CAN go on to a wonderful place - whether it be on a physical plane or a spiritual one. And if you think you have truly changed and transcended yourself, consider this: those who achieve the death of the selfish separate self, and thusly attain enlightenment/Universal Consciousness, either leave this plane, or stay to be a true teacher, and help others achieve the same. When you meet those who only have knowledge, and only tell of wisdoms and truths by moving their lips, and talking about it, or worse, telling people they don't need to do anything but 'think positive' or 'believe in Jesus', or just *believe* in anyone or anything, you tell them this: You will not be saved, nor can you be helping other people be saved - i.e., helping them become truly loving and enlightened, while just disseminating theories of *'Don't worry; Just go with the flow and don't bust your buns changing to be an Unselfishly Loving person; Just have positive thoughts and faith and you'll be taken to paradise in the 'rapture', or the '4th dimension', or to a 'wonderful new planet you can trash again'; or, 'Don't worry, the space brothers will fix all the toxic waste and neutralize the bombs.'* Surprise, surprise! You must act. You must change. YOU MUST LIVE AS THE GRAND MASTER TAUGHT US THROUGH HIS EXAMPLES ON EARTH!"

All of us were so moved, and stunned, that we were silent for at least five minutes.

Years later, a musician named Neil Young wrote a post apocalypse song called "After the Gold Rush" (referring to the 'gold rush' of a nuke explosion, not the romantic gold mining days of the old west). It was based on visions. Here are excerpts from some of the lyrics: "I was lying in a burned out basement, with the full moon in my eyes"; "I was thinkin' about what a friend had said - I was hopin' it was a lie."; "There were children cryin', and colors flyin' all around the chosen ones." "All in a dream, the loading had begun. Flyin' mother nature's silver seed, to a new home in the Sun." Are you one of the silver seed? Or will you be watching the deserving "chosen ones", the silver seeds, leave you behind as you recite your beliefs, clutch whatever the holy book of your religion is, or your book about the Pleiades, while you wonder why you aren't going too?

Along the same subject, one day I had asked Zain about all the references I'd read about God's "chosen people". This is what he had to say:

"The ancient teachings say the 'chosen ones' are not 'chosen' because of genetics, their heritage, beliefs, being God's favorite brats, or through knowledge - they are the ones who have MADE themselves 'chosen' - *vibrationally changed* by their own HARD WORK and SELF-SACRIFICE. Thus, if there is intervention in the hard times, or last days of life as we know it now on Earth, the true 'chosen' will be *recognized* by their enlightened, selflessly loving *vibrational signature*. And if there is no intervention, the "chosen" (those who chose to change for real), will still have vibrationally mandated their rise to a higher plane of existence, when the time comes to leave here - BECAUSE they are the ones who have gone through the fires of purification in order to become totally harmless and giving. You had better GET REAL. You had better WAKE UP. You had better dispel your self-centeredness."

"I'm working on it. Like I said before, I read about Earth changes even before coming to the monastery. And sometimes I would talk to my friends about it, because I could feel what was coming. But they said to me 'How can you live in such fear?'. What can you say to someone who looks at you that way?"

"I say, who is it that is living in fear, the one who is able to see and deal with the obvious realities, or the one who blocks them out, and doesn't want to see it - thus doesn't. Those who cannot see the writing on the wall, are the ones living in fear. We who have accepted death, have accepted life. And we thus have nothing to fear. Who is more afraid, and wiser, the Ostrich who sticks his head in a hole in the ground to avoid the predator about to eat him? Or is the squirrel who stores his nuts for the winter, knowing he may need them because of the dire conditions to come?

And also tell them this: whether the Earth of the future is habitable or not, you should be prepared to leave this plane, leave your body. Even if there are *no* Earth changes, *someday you **will** die anyway,* and to do it 'right', you should have experienced 'death' (transcended yourself) beforehand. And to live right, to attain Universal Consciousness, to become a fully Unselfishly Loving being, you must also have experienced death beforehand." [Again, the last chapter in part one of this book discusses the death experience].

Lots of Water, but Few Cups

The 'heaviest' teachings were yet to come. They were something I was yet to learn about, that hadn't even crossed my Ostrich mind. I guess I had a "safety net", even in my own relatively open minded beliefs. What was the "safety net"? Since I believed in reincarnation, and knew we kept getting chances to "get it right", at least there was that. But then Zain told me about the ancient Atlantean teachings regarding the next historical cycle.

"The primary difference between the time of Atlantis and now is that THOSE WHO ARE NOT FREE FROM THEIR KARMA, FREE FROM THE NEED TO REINCARNATE, WILL HAVE NO BODIES TO RETURN TO AFTER THE CHANGES."

That was a shocker. It took me a few minutes to assimilate and grasp all that it meant. Zain could see this, and just waited until I recovered, then he went on.

"Many people will die as a result of these forthcoming Earth changes, leaving far fewer human inhabitants on Earth afterwards. There is even the possibility of total extinction of human life on Earth. But let's say there are still humans living on Earth, which is likely. These people will have gone through major changes, physically, mentally, and spiritually. These will be the seeds of a new human race. Their consciousness will be of Oneness with the Universal Spirit. This will be a great new age. But think about your lessons regarding Universal Law. The Universal Law that dictates that vibration will seek its own level, will make a sort of 'Natural Selection' of who will be able to reincarnate. You know the teachings on conception of a child, and consciousness. Thus, those who do not free themselves from selfishness, would not be of the consciousness that would allow them to incarnate in the offspring of the new higher consciousness inhabitants of the new Earth - not for a very long time at least."

"What about materialization rather than birth."

"What about it? We were able to do that when we first came to this plane because our consciousness and nature was so much of the spiritual plane. And certainly anyone with such consciousness can do that. But what are we talking about here? The selfish, material bound masses of the Earth plane? Who of them will be capable of materialization?"

"So what will happen to those that don't make it?"

"Since the Earth will not be an option for them, and since they are still bound to the selfish separate self, and the material plane, something else must happen to them, because nothing is ever truly destroyed or lost in this Universe. Things only change form. So what will happen to them? The ancient teachings say they will incarnate within the bowels of Saturn, and live in a lava like state for millions of years, awaiting the right conditions for them to be able to return to the Earth, to try and get it right."

I was stunned. Speechless.

The New Age

And what of a new age on Earth? The possibility exists. But it is important to keep in mind that we are spiritual beings. That is our true state, our real state. We are not this physical baggage, this animal we inhabit while on Earth. We fell here. But we do not really belong here. The Earth is not our home. So if you really achieve the kind of spiritual enlightenment that would entitle you to be a citizen of such a glorious new age in which everyone has Christ consciousness, and then you are give the choice to either stay here, or return to angelic bodies and travel the Universe in bliss, in "heaven", what would you choose? It wouldn't really matter, but most people do enjoy traveling if they can afford it and don't have insecurity issues. But RIGHT NOW, there are only two valid reasons for being here, other than for a visit. Again, we fell from our spiritual state here, and took on this physical state as an aspect of our separation from the One, making the physical form part of our separate self. So first, we need to be here until we break free of our bonds to the Earth and our selfish separate selves. So the first valid reason to be here is because we must while we work towards attaining enlightenment and Oneness again. Then, once that is attained, we are free to go, but the compassion that brought us to our rebirth in Oneness, also makes us want to stay to help others who are still slaves to their selves, and bound to the Earth. Thus, staying to help others is the only other valid reason for living on Earth at this time.

Help Wanted

What is needed most today? First, that people be warned that they will be dealing with the repercussions of their actions, and that humans as a whole will also be dealing with grand repercussions on an Earth-wide scale. What is of primary importance is that you are doing one of two things - helping to awaken others to the Spirit within them and without them, or developing that awareness yourself (you cannot give that which you don't have).

The Greatest Service you Can Do
For the Universal Spirit, is To Serve Others.

The Greatest Service to Others, Is
Awakening them to the Universal Consciousness
That Lies Within them,
And helping them Free themselves
From their Selfish Separate Self.

Thus, we first need to prepare ourselves so that we may be an instrument in helping our brothers and sisters prepare. What is meant by prepare? To become One with the Universal Spirit; To be One spiritually, mentally, and physically. We must be transcendent of selfishness, regardless of what takes place around us.

Many are making the move "back to the land" towards self-sufficiency in order to better prepare for the coming changes and to live in harmony with nature. This is wise if it is in harmony with Universal flow rather than spurred on by selfish motivation. Although living in harmony with nature, with the land and elements, is a normal inclination when the physical is more in tune with Spirit, ultimately, you must be where you are needed most for the Universal Work, not where *you want* to be, or where it is most natural to be. For some it may be in the countryside, for some in the city, for some a foreign country. What are your *motives* for being where you are? What are you doing?
FIRST YOU HAVE TO DO IT YOURSELF OR YOU WON'T HAVE THE ABILITY TO REALLY HELP OTHERS. PEOPLE SHOULD PRACTICE WHAT THEY PREACH, AND TEACH BY EXAMPLE.

324

Chapter Twenty-two

The Death Experience

As Fallen Fruit, Yields the Seeds of New Life
The Self Must Yield to The Universal Spirit.

❖

One Must Experience Death To Be Re-Born

❖

Birth And Death Are But Cycles
Of One Continuous Life.

❖

If You Take All My Possessions,
My Body, My Mind, My Loved Ones,
Then, What Would I have Left?
My True Self, The One, The ALL.
And What Would You have?
Nothing.

❖

Nothing Can Harm Me

❖

I Live In My Center
Surrounded by My Life
I Die, I Live,
Through the Ages
Above All Strife.

❖

Feel, Do Not Fear
Be Wary, Do Not Fear

Fear Attracts What You Fear
Fear Invites Injury and Attack

Fear Avoids Right Action
Fear Lives in The Dark

Nothing Can Hurt The True Self

❖

Being the Wise Man, or the Fool,
Fighting Dragons, or Surrendering to Roaches,
Matters Not,
To the Fearless One Who has Faced Death
And Lives in the Service of God.

❖

Walk With Death By Your Side
Behold The Wonders
And New Life Will Be Yours.

One day I had the first of what would be many extraordinary meditations. It was a deeper and more profound meditation than I had ever had. While my eyes were closed, I began seeing a circular aura of dim light, with a dark hole in the center. It looked sort of like a glowing purple "donut shaped" cloud surrounded by a dark void. In the days previous to that first time, I would occasionally start seeing it again. Sometimes this light would do different things. It would come and go altogether, or might get brighter for a while, vibrate, and sometimes I would seem to get closer to it, and further away from it. It felt good. It felt great. And I'd heard things about seeing a light during meditation, but I wasn't sure if this met the descriptions, or was really the light I had been hearing about. So I went and found Zain to ask him about it. He was picking fruit at the time in one of the domes. I described it to him and then asked, "Is this 'the light' I keep hearing about?"

"Depends. 'Seeing the light' can be figurative for enlightenment or realization. But as you grow, new senses activate also. It is one of the lights you may experience. By your description of it, you are seeing your upper chakra, and one of the passageways out of your body. Everyone perceives this a little differently, and some never see it at all."

"It feels so good when I see it."

"That's because you are growing, you are getting closer to experiencing the Universal Spirit directly. You are getting a 'taste', a glimpse of what will soon be much more."

"Why am I just getting a glimpse?"

"Because you are not letting go all the way yet. One can attain glimpses of Universal Consciousness in several ways, including meditation. But these are temporary visions of what you can achieve. They are good to have, because it gives you a 'taste' of the wonders that await you, and can thus motivate you on your path. But you cannot attain permanent Universal Consciousness, without first having a *conscious* death experience. You cannot be fully Unselfishly Loving, if you have not had a death experience. Oddly enough, you cannot really live until you've died."

Before we go on, let me make something very clear. I'm not talking about "real", physical death here - just the "essence" or "experience" of it. More like the "near death" experiences you hear about in the news, where someone gets a severe

326

injury and temporarily die, and what they experience prior to coming back changes their life forever. But a spiritual death experience brought on by meditation, and spiritual techniques, is even more profound, and accomplished without having to physically get near death to experience it.

When you physically die, you always have a death experience. But you don't always need to physically die, to have a death *experience*. A death experience may, or may not be, accompanied by physical death, as in the 'near death' experiences discussed above. But for our purposes in this chapter, we are just talking about the *experience* of death, not physical death - except for my own personal experience which I will tell you about later. Continuing with Zain's answer to me...

"Once one consciously experiences death, it totally changes their life forevermore - for several reasons. For one, the selfish separate self 'dies' - and this breaks the hold it has had on us. The Inner Self, the part of you that is the Universal Spirit, can never end, never die, never be hurt, never be destroyed. Thus the Inner Being takes its proper place on the throne of our life, and the separate self stops struggling for control."

"So the separate self is forever dead and gone within us, and we no longer have selfishness."

"Basically, but not quite. The separate self's death is really only a temporary experience. And only the self's *separate consciousness* experiences this death. But to the separate self, the experience seems total, eternal and final. And in fact, it *is* the final demise of the strange independent life that took control of us, became a selfish monster, and had us believing that *we* were really *it*."

"So it comes back on you to torment you again?"

"While separate self consciousness only dies temporarily during a conscious death experience - it dies long enough for you to fully experience Oneness with the Universal Spirit, and attain Universal Consciousness. When you come out the other side of the death experience, the separate self is re-set, re-placed, re-born, but *under the influence of the Universal Spirit* - in the service of Universal Will. [Author's note: It's kind of like unplugging a digital clock - the memory, the time that was set, ceases to exist, but the *clock* still exists, and when you plug it back in, you can set a new time.] Think of it like one of these robot things that are on TV and movies throughout the world these days. One that has been running on a rampage of its own selfish survival programming. If they manage to 'unplug it', it 'dies' - but then you can reprogram it when you fix it, so when you plug it back in, it comes back to life, to do your bidding, instead of its own. You have been living with such a robot your whole life - your separate self. So you see, the separate self actually remains, but once it 'dies', it ceases to exist as the 'king', 'queen', or 'commanding general' of your life that it was, and it takes its proper place as the instrument, the servant, of the Universal Spirit."

"Can I accelerate or cultivate this experience so it happens sooner - I want to get on with it as fast as possible!?"

"You have been cultivating it daily, with your meditations, with facing your ego, and with disciplining yourself to transcend your selfishness. But the biggest thing that is hampering you now, is your fear of death."

"I'm not afraid to die."

"Yes you are."

"No I'm not."

"Then we have nothing to discuss."

"I'm sorry. I should say, I don't think I'm afraid, I don't feel like I'm afraid."

"Let's see. If you really want to accelerate it , you can begin to bring it on faster - your vision in your meditations is a doorway. When you see that hole in the center of the light. Move towards it, move into it. Eventually, you will enter a void, and then see another light, a greater light than you can imagine. Move towards that. Go into it. Then we will talk more."

I started working on this immediately. But the harder I tried, the more the violet light donut retreated from me. Eventually I learned I could not make it come, I could only get it to come, by allowing it to. It was passive control, not active, that this thing responded to.

Finally, one day I did it, I entered the hole. All of a sudden I was thrust beyond my control, through it, and into nothingness. I felt like I was nothing. I panicked, and I was swept back to where I began - back into my body, with a jolt. I now realized I was afraid.

I found Zain again, and told him my story. He didn't have to say "I told you so", we just both knew, and knew that I'd learned one more time, a lesson in humility, and respect.

Don't Fear the Reaper

"You began, just began, to experience death. It is your self only, who is afraid. It is your spirit that urges you on and loves the feeling.

While everyone fears death, this fear is unfounded. *The fear of death is created and fostered by the separate self,* as a means of keeping its control and its selfish, separate 'life'.

But you must go through it eventually. If you don't do it now, you will experience it anyway, because it is your destiny as a previous Adept of our order. Especially in your case, being one of the old ones, the ancient Initiates, it may be even more intense. But you must experience it, because it will be the thing that finally changes you in many, and very real ways."

"How will it change me?"

"One of the things about the conscious death experience that permanently changes us, is when we *real-ize* that our *true consciousness,* what we really are, *doesn't end with death.* When we thusly experience that our true consciousness not only remains, but also has eternal life, we lose the terrible fear of death from that moment on. During the death experience, our true self also bathes in the light and Oneness of the Universal Spirit. From then on, *we* know what really awaits us when we die. Then we have the attitude of 'So why be afraid of it?' that stays with us. We know we don't need to be anymore. And if you have positively changed your life, and become Unselfishly Loving, the plane of light and love that awaits, is beautiful beyond description, beyond words."

"And if not?"

"As the teachings point out, the death experience also leaves *you* knowing that nothing can hurt you anymore, and you become fearless."

"And so you do stupid things that might get you killed?"

"Perhaps, but more likely, smarter things that will make your life even safer, but more importantly, more worthwhile, and take the monkey off your back that you didn't even realize you were living with *every* moment until now.

It's hard for one who has not experienced death, to imagine how much of a hold fear, fear of death, has on us - and how much it affects the way we live our lives. It affects all our feelings, all our decisions, all our actions. It's there with us all the time. Once free from fear, life is lived with great feeling, great zest, great lightness, and great freedom. When you are free from fear, actions are no longer controlled by what we are afraid of, they are controlled by the real you, and based on what is right."

"But shouldn't we be afraid of certain things, or we will be open to, or even cause, bad things to happen to us and be harmed?"

"Fear can and does have a purpose, but only in its proper place, only when it is not really 'fear' anymore. It should become a warning mechanism only. For instance, when you are driving a vehicle, and you see the gauge that says your engine is boiling over, do you scream in pain because of the hot water coming out of the engine, or take action to remedy it? If we say that our life is like a car on a highway, and you see a truck crossing the line up ahead and veering toward you, you can take calm, logical, sensible action to avoid an accident, if you aren't in the grip of fear? However, if you are in the grip of fear, your action will be from panic, and you are far more likely to do something stupid that will actually cause an accident. Fear attracts what it fears. If you put a 6" wide plank down on the ground, and asked people to walk across it, they would do it every time without falling off. But put that same plank across a small pool of water with air bubbles, and tell people that the pool is filled with boiling water, their fear will actually *cause* them to lose their balance some of the time. So to the contrary of your question and 'fears' about not having fear, the truth is quite the opposite - fear can bring you harm, and fearlessness can save you. Fear is the way the uninitiated live their lives. Not the initiated, not the enlightened being who is One with the Universal Spirit.

"I'm still afraid of doing it."

"No you're not."

"Yes I am."

"Haven't we had this conversation before?"

"Well... sort of."

"Why be afraid of death Peniel?! It will happen anyway. Along with transcending our fear of death and realizing that death is but a doorway, comes the *realization* that your present lifetime, your present body, *will* die, it *will* end. And this awareness stays with you every moment you live. Once you experience it, you don't fear it anymore mind you, you are just constantly aware of it."

"I know I'm going to die someday."

"Sure, everyone *says* they *know* they're going to die - but no one *really* thinks they will. They do quite the contrary - they constantly block it out. When you really 'get' that you *are going to die,* it changes you - this gives you a feeling of cherishing every moment, every flower, every person. And it doesn't go away like it would if you just had a near car accident or such. It *permanently* changes you. You no longer take anything or anyone *for granted.* Each moment is new and full, and you walk with death at your side, touching your shoulder, constantly reminding you to live life to the fullest, appreciate it to the fullest, and live the righteous life of a servant to the Universal Spirit."

The Creation of the Death Experience

"If I avoid this, you say I will still have it via destiny? Does this happen to all students?"

"Each is different. Some who aren't destined, do avoid it."

"How do others have a death experience? In fact, how will it be if I don't voluntarily do this in my meditation now?"

"How does one have a death experience? Well, with some people, like you, like I said, it is unavoidable - it happens to them. Situations bring it about. Sometimes the conscious death experience happens in tandem with a physical death experience. Those who have had near death experiences that weren't under the influence of drugs, anesthetics, etc., are lucky indeed.

But generally, the conscious death experience is the end result of long efforts at spiritual growth. Meditation, self-discipline, working with a true teacher, 'ego-busting', all put pressure on the separate self and 'corners' it. The pain of all that, along with losing attachments, of seeing the darkness in the world, all build up, and at some point you just can't take it anymore. This has been called the 'Dark night of the Soul'. This is the point when a person will either 'flip out' - or flip 'in', according to their free will choice. The self will tell you to run, at any cost, run! It urges you to get away from the source of the pressure. If you do so at such an advanced stage, you can go insane. But if you hang on, if you endure the suffering with patience, understanding, and love, you will have a conscious death experience, and break through to the other side. When I experienced this, it was like I was totally engulfed in darkness and depression, and all there was other than that, was this thin light thread of my personal teacher's love for me. I hung on to that thread with all the strength I could muster - I just blindly held on. And soon, I faced my dweller (see below), and passed on to a new consciousness. This must happen to you, because you died enlightened, time after time. And you chose to come back and do it again. It was your choice."

Ancient History

"What have I done about it before?"

"Different things. But long ago, it was more ritualized. In the old days, a student that was close to having the death experience, was given a push - thrown into the deep water, so to speak. For instance, during the days of our time in Atlantis this was done, and during our work in Egypt, the Great Pyramid was used for such Initiation. The student would be given an 'elixir' that stimulated the imagination. Then, they would begin to be treated as if they had actually died. They were placed in a sarcophagus, a death ceremony was performed, the rites of death were gone through, and the sarcophagus was taken to what is now called the King's Chamber in the Pyramid. There, the combination of the student's training, the elixir, the death rituals that were being done to the student, the energy of the Pyramid, and the hierarchical guides that would come, would all combine and precipitate the death experience. The student would transcend their dweller, and be met by the hierarchical guides, who would share their journey of initiation into Universal Consciousness. The next day, the student that walked in was no more, and an Initiate walked out."

"But this doesn't happen anymore?"

"The hierarchical guides still come when it is your time. But it is just left to the flow to determine the means, and time."

"And the 'dweller', you have told me of this before, and I have seen it in my meditations. Quite a bit to look forward to."

"There really is Peniel - in a wonderful and very positive sense. Just let go and transcend your fear."

"Can you tell me more of the dweller since it appears we are about to have a date and a meaningful relationship?"

The Dweller on the Threshold

"The 'Dweller on the Threshold' is several things. In Biblical allegory, it is the angel that was placed at the gates of Eden to keep Adam and Eve from returning. It is the most horrible demon you could possibly imagine. It is nothing but your own separate self.

Before you can have a conscious death experience, you must first really see the thing that you have created, that is about to die. It is a terrible selfish monster. And if you fear it, you will recoil. If you give it life, you will not be able to pass. Only by feeling Unselfish Love, even when confronted by this monster, will you be able to pass."

"And what awaits me when I pass?"

Beyond the Threshold

"Once you pass your dweller, you will enter a void. A place of nothingness and darkness. Somewhere in that void, you will find a light. Always look towards the center of the light, and use your will to move towards it, and into it. Do not get distracted by anything that may happen around you - even if phantoms grab at you. Just concentrate on the light. When you move into the light, when you are engulfed in the light, you will be free, be One with the Universal Spirit. At this point, you will be given a choice to stay on the Earth plane and help others, or to go on and remain in paradise. The choice is yours, and there is no blame to going on. That is the final bottom line."

I never did voluntarily go through my death experience in meditation. Actually, before I even really got a chance, I became very ill. I developed a serious infection, and I began a 30 day fast on juices, and herbs. At the end of that time, I was still very ill, and Zain recommended a water fast. I fasted for 40 days on water. During the last 5 days, I had 3 death experiences, both physical and spiritual. During the final one, I met my guides, and I was given a tour of all things. All things on the Earth, all life, the entire Universe. I then, under their guidance, totally repro-grammed my brain. I had 5 days of visions of the future, then I began my journey as an Initiated monk, and each moment has been a miracle of life ever since.

Things to Do Today (Before I Physically Die)

Until you have a death experience, there is a special "death awareness" tech-nique you can develop that can have a profoundly beneficial effect on your life - even before you have a death experience.

Everyone should CONSTANTLY be reminding themselves that they could physically die *at any time*. Remember, you are in fact *going to die someday*. One of these days you **will be** *just a few minutes from death*. Seriously think about that. Contemplate it for awhile. And in thinking about it, think about *how* you are *leaving* things, and how you are using your life *right now*. Here are *some* exam-ples:

1) If you were going to die in five minutes, is the way you have left things with the people in your life, how you want to leave them?

2) Are the last things you said, what you want to have left said?

3) Have you left anything *unsaid* that you would have wanted to say before

you're gone for good?

4) With the perspective of knowing that you are going to die at any minute, how important to you is that issue of _____ that *really irritated* you (about living with so and so, or what so and so does, or the things you don't like about how or where you must live, etc., etc.,).

5) Is the terrible argument you had about_____really important?

6) Have you done what you wanted to, or needed to do, with your life?

7) What is the legacy you are leaving? Are your last actions the actions you would want to be your last?

Walking With Death by Your Side

Here's a method you can use to remind yourself of death. Personalize it, and keep it with you. Live your life consciously aware that death is always standing by your side, only an arm's length away. Then you will live accordingly. You won't live in fear - quite the opposite. It frees you to live life fully. I highly recommend everyone contemplate their death - and it shouldn't just be something you remind yourself of daily, it should be constant, or at least as frequent as you can make it. It really helps keep things in perspective, and changes the way you live. When you are always aware you might be dead any second, you really live. Awareness of death, begets real life.

PART TWO

DATE:	1	2	3	4	5	6	7	8	9	10	11	12	13	14	15	16	17	18	19	20	21	22	23	24	25	26	27	28	29	30	31
MORNING																															
Write Dreams																															
Cold Shower																															
Yoga & Star Exercise																															
Pineal Wave																															
Grand Circulation Breath																															
Sacred Breath																															
Affirmations																															
AFTERNOON																															
Planetary Polarity																															
Meditation Walk																															
Color Visualize/Chakra																															
Sounds/Affirmation Tape																															
EVENING																															
Mirror Exercise/Chanting																															
Conscious Breath																															
Counting Breath																															
Unselfish Love Contmpl.																															
Daily Review/Dreams																															
Affirmations																															

Part Two

Our Meditations, Exercises, Techniques, & Dietary Considerations

Introduction to the Meditations

Before I begin giving instructions for various meditations, energy techniques and techniques for growth, here is an introduction as was given to me by Raga in my first courses on the subjects.

"For most people, the Soul, or Inner Being, is but a 'prisoner' of the separate self, locked in the body and forced to go along for the ride. As has been said, the true you, the Inner Being, needs to make the transition from servant of the selfish separate self, to its master (if freedom, peace and harmony are to be found). The meditations and techniques you are about to learn, are tools to help you achieve this, but they will only work properly in the right hands, with the right attitude, and with the right help."

The following meditations were created by the Atlantean Children of the Law of One before our written history, to help maintain spiritual awareness. They can also help you develop into a powerful tool for the Universal Spirit. They are presented here to *help* you change, to find your natural balance, to be the director of the body-mind-self, to be spiritually, mentally & physically powerful, and to fulfill your maximum potential - all for the manifestation of the Inner Being, in the service of God, under the direction of, and within the flow of, Universal Will.

As was said in part one of the book, meditations are not the magic key to enlightenment. You also need humility, Unselfish Love, and a true teacher, to shift control of your life from your selfish separate self, to your Inner Being. If you don't have these things, meditations are not going to do nearly as much for you as they could. In fact, they can even be detrimental in the sense that they can help your selfish separate self be more successful at *its* pursuits. But assuming you are traveling a properly balanced spiritual path, meditations *can* help you, and are an *important* part of the path.

The Children's Meditation Training Program

The following meditations can be arranged as a training program, which is how they have always been initially taught by the Children, and how we are presenting them for you here. Printed on an adjacent page, you will find a meditation chart checklist. It is designed to cover a month at a time. Photocopy it and use it without fail if you want to insure consistency and self-discipline. Using the chart is a vital key to not letting your separate self side-track you from being unwaveringly consistent in doing the training (which is important). If you want the meditations to be really effective, you must spend enough time doing each one. Try different lengths, and feel the differences. How long you do each meditation is up to you, and your schedule, although the full program will take you 3 to 6 hours a day to do traditionally, and most effectively. Of course, if you don't have time, you can shorten them or cut what you wish. But first ask yourself what it's worth to you, and examine what you are doing with the rest of your time, and what that's worth.

We hear many people complain that they can't possibly spend that much time doing it. They say they have jobs, and/or families, and they have to make a living and survive in the world, unlike having the "luxury" of being in a monastery like I did. So let's look at the realities of that.

I can't speak for all monasteries, but I don't know of any "free ride" or "easy living" ones that just let you sit on your butt all day and meditate once in a while. In ours, I worked the equivalent of *two* full-time "outside world", "real world", "real life" type of jobs, PLUS did all the meds, yoga, group meds, courses, and spent time reading. I got very little sleep, and at that, it wasn't daily sleep. But that's how important to me it was. I would have done the same in the outside world. Now if it's not as much of a priority in your life, or you really can't make the time, that's fine. Just be honest about it, and don't envy others for having or making the time. But most people just don't prioritize and realize how much they could do if they really, really want to, and what they could skip in their normal routines.

If you truly absolutely don't have the time to do the full schedule as presented here, that's OK. But have a constructive, positive attitude towards it, and create an alternative schedule. ANY amount of meditation is better than none. Even if it's only one a day for five minutes - it's better than nothing, and it is doing something. And maybe there are ways to make extra time that you haven't thought about yet.

First and most obvious is, do you really need as much sleep as you take? Then think about other fruitless time you might be spending that might be able to go. The average person could do the entire schedule just by cutting out TV alone. If you really put your mind to it, you'll come up with your own ideas for how to re-arrange what you spend your time on, and how to save time on what you *must* do. Here are a list of just a few areas you might be able to streamline or eliminate to make time for higher priorities (obviously they don't apply to everyone): **TV; Movies; Eating Out; Sports; Commuting**/having someone else drive instead of you, so you could spend that time meditating. Arranging different situations to minimize commuting time. Carpooling; **"Hanging** out"/or "shooting the breeze" chatting with people in person, on the phone, or email; **Meals** - can they be more simple for less cooking/cleaning time? Can someone else prepare your meals so you have more time to meditate? Could you do more "crock pot" meals of soups/rice, or make large bags of pre-made salads, etc.?; **Parties; Reading** books that are not helping improve your life or otherwise necessary; **Shopping** - like carpools, shopping can sometimes be shared/turns taken. Many cities even have on-line internet shopping and delivery available now; **Entertainment; Going** to the bathroom - do a quick med while sitting on the pot!

Then if that isn't enough, just customize a med schedule, and do what you can. But once you decide what you can do, and make a schedule, consistency is vital.

Meditation is just one of many tools.

Back to my very early course with Raga:

"Of course, this training does not make for the great spiritual transition in itself, it is but one outgrowth of a change made through using your free will to harmonize & align with Universal Will. A more important factor in making this transition is having a true teacher. That's because you can directly experience Unselfish Love & the Universal Spirit through an enlightened being. Through a true teacher you can clearly see yourself, expose your illusions, and through humility and Unselfish Love, transcend your selfish separate self. Meditations & exercises "tune-up" your vehicle, so to speak, allowing the Universal Spirit to use you to your maximum capacities. But Love, Humility, and Service are what will give your Inner Being the controls of this powerful vehicle you are creating.

You must be consistent in doing the exercises you will be learning, in order for them to really work. If you stick with your schedule 'whole heartedly', along with transcending your selfish separate self with the help of your teacher, you will change, you will grow, you will ultimately achieve enlightenment. The exercises themselves will also help you transcend your separate self by means of the self discipline it takes to do them properly & consistently, and through the transcendental effects of them. But, if you are not doing the exercises consistently, with full commitment, then you are still slave to your selfish separate self, and have not really surrendered to the flow of the One. For that reason alone the full transition would not take place. It's all interconnected. So make God, service to God, and the attainment of Universal Consciousness the priority in your life. Use your charts without fail, and even more importantly, humbly use your teacher without fail.

You will not need to do all of these exercises for the rest of your life. But you should do them sincerely, as perfectly as possible, and without missing even one, for at least 21 weeks. Every person is different, and some meditations work far better than others, for each individual. But sometimes the separate self will fool you into thinking you don't like a meditation, or it doesn't work well for you, when in fact it may be the very one that would ultimately work best for you. After you have completed 21 weeks perfectly, then you will better know the best ones for you, and can discuss tailoring a special meditation group for yourself with your teacher."

"You said they take hours. Should we do them all at the same time, or just whenever we have time?"

When to Meditate

"Neither. When people meditate, they experience greater balance, peace, and 'centeredness'. This helps them stay out of the 'illusions' that hectic day to day life gets them to 'buy into' believing is real. But some of these effects from the meditations are temporary, and sort of 'wear off' as the day 'wears on'. For this reason, the Children have found it very important that meditations be done not all at once daily, but at least broken into three times a day. Thus your meditation training schedule is broken up into morning, afternoon, and evening meditations, and should be done in the following order:

Morning meditations are: Writing dream log; Dip in the cold pool [or cold shower as a modern equivalent]; Yoga; Star Exercise; Pineal Wave; Grand Circulation of Breath; Sacred Breath; Affirmations; Setting your 'Kind for a Day' goal.

Afternoon meditations are: Planetary Polarity Attunement; Meditation Walk; Color Visualization/Chakra exercise; Atlantean Vibrational Mind Integration Sounds.

Evening meditations are: Mirror exercise/chanting; Conscious Breath;

Counting Breath; Contemplation of Unselfish Love; Daily activities review, reviewing dreams; Evening affirmations.

Although they are not included in the training schedule, if possible, you should allot some time each day for: Reading spiritually inspiring writings (re-reading this book fulfills that); Listening to or playing spiritually uplifting, positive music; Doing group breathing, chanting, or energy flow exercises. These activities are optional and thus were not included on your printed schedule. If you intend to do them however, write them in on your printed schedule. You should also include the personal things you have received from your teacher on your schedule.

Finally, before you do each exercise, always bring your ideal to mind, visualize yourself surrounded by white light, and ask the guidance and protection of the Universal Spirit."

[It should be mentioned here that most of the above chapter applies only to those who choose this path at all; it does not apply to those of other paths (however, similar development must take place at some time if an entity is to evolve, regardless of the particular path).]

Using the Vibrational Sounds CD or Cassette

We discussed this powerful tool earlier in this book (in part one). This chapter will cover the specific instructions on how to use it.

Ancient Hi-Tech

Ancient hi-tech. No, it's not an oxymoron. As hard as it may seem to fathom, the audio-vibrations on the Atlantean Vibrational Sounds recording were originally developed long before the days of Moses, even longer before Edison conceived the idea of a recording device. Yet, they are the most advanced consciousness altering tool modern science can offer. More importantly, they are the single most effective way to achieve sub-conscious programming changes. Modern technological breakthroughs and years of research have allowed the techniques to be re-created.

You can order it with just the vibrational sounds, or with affirmations and induction as detailed below, already recorded for you by an elder. There are now 7 different versions available to assist you with different things. The one described word for word later, is Vol. 1, for Spiritual Development/Growth. Other versions are: Vol. 2 - Healing affirmations/visualization; Vol. 3 - Habit Changing/Developing Healthy Habits; Vol. 4 - Male Virility; Vol. 5 - Stress Management; Vol. 6 - Sounds Only (no affirmations); Vol. 7 - Ancient Chinese Healing Visualization. See the back of the book for order info.

Making a second tape for Re-programming Affirmations

If you order just the vibrational sounds recording, the sounds on the tape will take you into a deep altered state, where you can access your subconscious mind easily. Thus, if you give yourself re-programming affirmations, they will take hold more effectively, and have deep roots. But the sounds will take you so deep, that it is very likely that you will not be consciously thinking about giving yourself affirmations. *Thus, you will need to make a second tape, that you will listen to at the same time as the Vibrational Sounds.* This second recording, which we will call your "voice" or "affirmations" tape, will have your own voice on it, giving yourself the affirmations you want, to make the changes you want.

Making Affirmations for Your Specific Needs

If you have not ordered the recording with the affirmations, below, I have given general affirmations that are used by the Children of the Law of One. This is so you can record them yourself if you wish. I assume you will record them with a cassette tape or micro cassette tape deck. Also, if you are doing it yourself anyway, you may also want to add some special affirmations that address specific needs you have, or particular changes you want to make.

Here are some very important tips and instructions to get the most out of your tape. First, your affirmations should be phrased positively rather than negatively. For instance, if you had a problem with anger, and you wanted to stop being so angry, you should not say "I am not angry" or "I will not be angry anymore". Instead, you would say something like, "I am always peaceful, calm, and clearheaded". Also, avoid the "will" concepts, like "I *will* be peaceful". That places *when* you will be peaceful sometime in an undetermined future (which may never happen). Always use "I am". Also, while the above affirmation example is fine for someone who wants to be a total pacifist, it would not be fine for someone who does not. For instance, if you want to defend yourself, or someone else, if attacked, that affirmation would work towards preventing it. You would want to add something, making it like this: "I am always peaceful and calm, unless I am attacked". But then again, there are also times when most people might need to be aggressive, even though you're not being attacked per se. Like during an argument. If you want to be able to still have fire during a verbal confrontation, the affirmation needs to be more elaborate and precise still, like this: "I am always peaceful and calm, unless I am attacked, or I need to be aggressive during a confrontation". Better, you see. But still, what if you want to remain peaceful and calm during an attack? Well, if you have come to the conclusion that it is better to follow the Universal Spirit's Will than your separate self's, then your goal should be to always do the Will of the Universal Spirit. If you do, then there is a catch all affirmation addition that should be worked into most of your personally created affirmations. Using the above example, it would go like this: "I am always peaceful and calm, as long as it is within the Will of the Universal Spirit. When it is within the Will of the Universal Spirit, I am strong, powerful & forceful". If it makes you uncomfortable, or you wish to replace the words "the Universal Spirit" in any of the affirmations, with the word God, or your preferred name of your deity, by all means feel free to do so. But whatever you call your God, always use the "Will of God" phrase to be safe. As you can see, formulating affirmations is very touchy. You must always keep in mind that your sub-conscious mind is like a computer. It will take things literally according to its understanding. And there is an old computer programmer's saying regarding what you program a computer with: "Garbage in, garbage out". Read the chapter on formulating affirmations before you make any.

Adding Visualizations to your Affirmations Tape

On the same tape that you will be recording your affirmations on, you will also record guided visualizations, and what are considered "classic" self-hypnosis "induction" techniques. These will all work towards making the effects of the vibrational sounds even more effective. The exact wording of this visualization & induction are given at the end of this chapter, in italics.

Universal Re-programming Affirmations

There are some affirmations that the Children have every student use. I have included most of them below, and you may use them if you wish. If you choose to use these, or do your own, they should be read after the guided visualization and "induction" commands on your voice affirmations tape. I have included them along with the visualization and induction commands, in the proper order. If you don't want to use one, or any of them, just cross them out. Also, if you wish to add your own personal affirmations, you can do them after the Universal ones. While you are recording your tape, begin reading your personal affirmations when you see the following sentence:

[READ YOUR AFFIRMATIONS HERE]

After reading your affirmations, you may begin reading the remaining part of the induction.

Recording and Listening to Both your Tapes

If you are taking the route of making your own, rather than ordering one with the induction, visualizations, and affirmations already on it, in order to do this technique, you will need two tape players (or one CD player for the sounds, and one tape player for your voice recording). That's because you will need to listen to the vibrational sounds recording, and your affirmations tape at the same time. The sounds tape must be played back in stereo, because some of its effects have to do with sending different frequencies of sound vibrations into each ear separately. But your affirmations tape can be played on either a stereo unit, or the little mono cassette recorders like students use to record a lecture. When you are doing it that way, you will place the mono deck near your head, and put stereo headphones on for the sounds tape. Then you start both tapes at the same time. If you have two stereo players, like two "walkman" type units that require headphones or "boom box" type portable stereos, you can buy the "in the ear" type of stereo headphones from Radio Shack or Walmart, etc., then use them for one of the decks, while you use the regular type "over the ear" stereo headphones for the other.

To record your affirmations voice tape you will need something other than a walkman (unless it's a recording walkman). Again, the "student" type, or a home stereo cassette deck/boom box with a microphone input will due. If you want real good quality, book time at a recording studio. You can also have a recording studio "mix" the Atlantean sounds, and your voice tape, onto one single stereo tape, making using it easier to use.

It's important that you don't have noises while your recording your tape. A baby crying, a voice, a TV, or a phone ringing may not seem like much. But when you listen to the tape, noises like that can disturb your induction into the deep state you want to be in for the tape to be effective. Also, rather than speaking loudly, speak gently, and relatively close to the microphone (about 6 inches is generally good). Remember, you are trying to guide yourself into a very relaxed, deep state of consciousness. Also, if you turn your head just a bit, you won't get those "pops" that can happen from your breath directly hitting the microphone as you speak. And if you make a mistake, just go back and start again. Some mistakes are not really noticeable, but others again, can jar your consciousness out of the deeper state.

Of course, if you order the sounds with the affirmations/visualizations already on it, all you will need is one CD player or stereo tape player, and stereo headphones.

The Vibrational Sounds are about 28 minutes long. Time the recording of your affirmations tape to match that. The final phrase on your affirmations tape is "Wide Awake", and that should come at 28 minutes from when you started recording your tape. This doesn't really need to be exact, but the closer the better. Use a timer if you have one, a clock if you don't. In order to get the "Wide awake" command to end up at 28 minutes, you may need to read a little faster, or a little slower, or leave pauses between various parts of the affirmations or induction, in order to time everything to end up the right length. The easiest way to match it all up is to read your script slowly through, up until the end of the affirmations, then wait until a little past 27 minutes, and start reading the rest.

The Script for your Affirmations Tape

See and feel yourself surrounded with white light. Relax, Relax, Relax. See and feel yourself surrounded with white light.

You can leave a modified state and return to your normal alert and awake state of mind at any time by thinking the words "wide awake".

Your body is totally relaxing from your toes to the top of your head. Feel the bottoms of your feet relaxing now. Your toes are relaxing. Now the tops of your feet are relaxing. Now your ankles are relaxing. You are becoming more and more relaxed. Now your calves are relaxing. And on up to your knees. Feel your knees relaxing now. Now your thighs are relaxing. Feel them relax. Let them go. Now the relaxation is moving into the hips. Feel your hips relaxing. Now your groin area is relaxing. Now the tummy area is relaxing also. Feel your butt relaxing now. Now every part of your body from your waist down to your toes is totally relaxed. Feel it relaxed now. Relax, Relax, Relax. Now the relaxing feeling is moving up from your waist, up from your stomach and into your chest. Feel your chest relaxing now. Feel your breasts relaxing now. Now your back is relaxing - first your lower back is relaxing, now your middle back is relaxing, and finally your upper back is relaxing and the relaxation is merging with your chest and stomach areas. Your entire torso is relaxed now. Now feel your hands relax. And your wrists. Now your forearms are relaxing. Now the upper arms. Now on up to your shoulders, your shoulders are relaxing now. Now your neck is relaxing. Now your entire body from the neck down is totally relaxed. Now your scalp is relaxing. Feel it relax now. Now your forehead and eyes are relaxing. All the eye muscles are totally relaxing. Now your nose, and now your mouth is relaxing. Your entire face is relaxing - feel it. Now your entire body is relaxed, but it is even relaxing a bit more now - feel it. Relax, Relax, Relax.

You are becoming more and more relaxed with every breath you take.

Now you are going to count backwards from 10 to 1. When you hear the number one, you will be in a very deep, transcendent modified state of consciousness, totally relaxed and one with the Universal Spirit.

As you count backwards, completely visualize yourself stepping down a stairway.
Ten, deeper, deeper deeper, down, down, down;
Nine, deeper, deeper deeper, down, down, down;
Eight, deeper, deeper deeper, down, down, down;
Seven, deeper, deeper deeper, down, down, down;
Six, deeper, deeper deeper, down, down, down;
Five, deeper, deeper deeper, down, down, down;
Four, deeper, deeper deeper, down, down, down;
Three, deeper, deeper deeper, down, down, down;
Two, deeper, deeper deeper, down, down, down;
one. You are now in a very deep, transcendent altered state of consciousness.

Relax relax relax. You are going to count down a second time and when you hear the number one you'll be in an even deeper modified state of consciousness.
Ten, deeper, deeper deeper, down, down, down;
Nine, deeper, deeper deeper, down, down, down;
Eight, deeper, deeper deeper, down, down, down;

Seven, deeper, deeper deeper, down, down, down;
Six, deeper, deeper deeper, down, down, down;
Five, deeper, deeper deeper, down, down, down;
Four, deeper, deeper deeper, down, down, down;
Three, deeper, deeper deeper, down, down, down;
Two, deeper, deeper deeper, down, down, down;
one. You are now in a very deep, transcendent altered state of consciousness. You are one with Universal Life energy, it is flowing through you now, you feel it.

You are about to board a beautiful new silver train. While you walk up the boarding ramp, which is protected from the weather by a blue awning, rain begins to fall around you. You enjoy the wonderful scent of the rain, & the fresh air as you walk towards the train. Once inside the train, the temperature is perfect. You look around, and notice the hidden lighting is soft, and the interior is very attractive, and comfortable-looking. You walk over to your seat, which is a large recliner with a great window view. As you sit in your chair, you sink down into its soft cozy embrace. It holds your body perfectly, which lets you completely relax as you lay in it. There are empty chairs all around you, and all of a sudden, you see people you know & like boarding the train, and as you warmly great each other, they take seats in the chairs all around you. Someone you particularly care for, sits in the empty chair next to you. Think of that person now. You look at each other, and if you feel like it, you hold hands as the doors close and the train slowly begins to move. The slight motion as it glides along is very soothing & relaxing. You are full of feelings of serenity, peace, and love. Out of the window, you see a full moon and stars shimmering brightly against the velvet midnight blue of the night sky. The sky turns a heavenly purple blue, as the sun begins to rise from behind the distant mountains. There are brilliant golden- orange and red rays of sunshine reaching up across the sky-illuminating the puffy white clouds. There are vast meadows of lovely flowers dancing in the moist green grass. They are all different shapes and sizes, and every color of the rainbow. Beyond the grassy meadows are rolling hills with huge old trees, and beyond those, you see majestic blue mountains. The highest peaks are covered with snow. Four white birds fly along with the train just outside your window. Three of them turn off towards the mountains, while the fourth climbs higher into the sky. You sense that there are angelic beings watching over you, and accompanying you on your journey. You realize they are always there around you, invisibly protecting and caring for you, both night and day. You feel the warm morning sun shining on your skin. It all feels just perfect. You completely relax and enjoy this. Relax, Relax, Relax.

Now mentally check out your body for any tension spots that may remain, if you find any, release them and feel all tension draining out of your body into the earth. Relax, Relax, Relax.

You are an instrument of the Universal Spirit's Will, and this makes you very happy and secure. You do the Universal Spirit's Will. It flows in you and through you. (Your Will be done God, in me and through me. I am a blessing to everyone.)

Every day you are more and more self-disciplined. You are self-disciplined.

Self-discipline comes easily for you.

Your memory is becoming perfect.

You have excellent concentration. You are easily able to hold your attention on anything you need or want to. Your mind is clear and focused. Your mind focuses easily and intently on any task you have before you. You are thorough, efficient and speedy in doing your tasks.

Even when you are concentrating and focusing on something, you are still aware of what is going on around you.

Your body produces and utilizes whatever substances are necessary for optimum spiritual, emotional and physical health. You desire the foods and supplements that will provide your body with what it needs to produce whatever substances are necessary for optimum spiritual, emotional and physical health. You want and desire only the foods and products that are healthy for you. See and feel yourself full of energy, feeling healthy and vital. Your immune system is super strong, and can fight and kill any invaders.

You want people to bring things up to you so you can become more positive, selflessly loving, and effective as an instrument of the Universal Spirit's Will. You welcome people bringing things up to you that you can improve about yourself, or do better next time. You don't care about whether or not you are thought of as being right by other people. It doesn't matter what people think of you, it only matters that you are doing the Universal Spirit's Will with Unselfish love. You want to do things positively & properly, in order to help others. Everything you do is done well, positively, and right, because you are humble and letting the Universal Spirit do things through you. You surrender to the Universal Spirit, and let the Universal Spirit flow through you, thus you can do anything. Through you, the Universal Spirit can accomplish anything it needs to do.

You are always aware of your environment and what's going on around you. You are always aware of the presence and activities of other people around you.

You are humble and selflessly loving. In any situation, you are flexible and flowing if you need to be and it is within the Will of the Universal Spirit.

You have a deep inner calm and inner peace. You are courageous and face everything with the security of knowing you are One with the Universal Spirit, and doing the Universal Spirit's Will. You know that nothing can hurt the real you, the spirit you, the part of you that is the Universal Spirit, and thus you are fully secure in any situation, and can positively and powerfully deal with any situation. Feel yourself feeling this deep security, peace, and power, now.

You have the confidence of knowing that you are doing the Universal Spirit's Will, and that the Universal Spirit is working through you. This gives you a feeling of total confidence. Feel this selfless confidence now.

You have a dynamic and magnetic personality. You are in control of any situation that it is in the Will of the Universal Spirit for you to control. You are receptive to the Universal Spirit, the saints, the Universal Spirit's Angels and true messengers of the Universal Spirit. You are positive to, and the master of, all things that it is the Will of the Universal Spirit for you to be master of.

You are considerate and sensitive to the feelings and needs of others. You have deep spiritual love and concern for everyone everywhere. You are unselfishly giving when it is within the Universal Spirit's Will and this unselfish giving makes you feel good and fills you with a deep inner peace and security.

See and feel your entire being filling with unselfish love energy. Waves of compassion are flowing into you filling you with caring and compassion for all beings everywhere.

You are compassionate and selflessly loving. This brings you total inner peace. You know you are a good and caring person, and this gives you total peace within yourself.

See and feel yourself being compassionate - it's very powerful, very intense. See and feel unselfish Love energy flowing in you and through you, filling you with peace and contentment. Feel these feelings of peace, contentment and calm within your being now.

Your inner and outer strength is growing rapidly, thus your ability to serve the Universal Spirit grows and grows. You are a blessing to all who come into contact with you, as you manifest the Universal Spirit's love and energy in their life. It feels so wonderful to feel this infinite unselfish Love! With every breath you take, with every moment that passes, all the power of the Universal Spirit's Love flows into you, through you, and around you. You are surrendered to the Universal Spirit and the Universal Spirit's Will now. You are out of the way now and the Universal Spirit has taken over. You are feeling relaxed, happy and carefree because you know that whatever the Universal Spirit needs to do through you, will be done. And since you are letting go and letting the Universal Spirit take over in your life, everywhere you are is where the Universal Spirit needs you to be, so that you can be an instrument of his actions everywhere you are, in any situation. You feel the wonderful lightness and relief of surrendering fully and joyously to the Universal Spirit's Will. You are filled with the peace, strength and joy that doing the Universal Spirit's Will brings. It's exhilarating and rejuvenating. You feel a tremendous weight has been lifted off of you as the Will of the Universal Spirit becomes your will- they are one! Your vitality is renewed and strengthened as Unselfish Love washes over you and through you. You care about everyone who comes into contact with you, and you are kind when it is in the Universal Spirit's Will.

Your desire to Unselfishly Love and do the Universal Spirit's Will is powerful, constant and passionate. You have a deep unswerving conviction to be a perfect servant and instrument of the Universal Spirit, and this powerful feeling lives within you every second of every day! It gives you profound stability and you are deeply devoted and committed to this ideal. See and feel yourself being this way now. See and feel the positive strength rising up in you. It is powerful. The positive force of the Universal Spirit and unselfish love are so powerful within you that you easily overcome any hurdle, and obstacles become stepping stones. In service to the Universal Spirit's Will, you have tremendous courage and will power. You are fearless and joyful. Serving the Universal Spirit makes you feel wonderful, happy and secure. You happily do whatever tasks the Universal Spirit needs you to do, and you welcome the tasks you are given by the Universal Spirit.

When you need to transcend upsetting emotions or emotional turmoil, you still feel people and events, but you feel them from a calm, peaceful, and secure place. You can still fight, confront, be powerful, strong, active, and aggressive if necessary and within the Will of the Universal Spirit - yet you remain emotionally protected - centered in your calm, clear, peaceful place, regardless of the intensity of what is all around you. This gives you stability, calm and peace while you are totally aware of the situations and feelings around you, and allows you to react and do whatever is necessary to deal with the situations and people around you.

When you need to transcend your body, you float above it, secure and protected in a sphere of white light that permeates your entire being. You are protected from pain and harm in this light, and you feel love, peace, calm, and security. You can still act, react, and do whatever you need to do from this state.

You hear what others have to say clearly. You comprehend and understand the meaning other people are trying to communicate to you.

You communicate with others clearly, accurately, succinctly, and fully. You are aware of whether or not others have understood your communication.

I am always conscious and careful about everything I think, feel, say and do.

You are whatever you need to be, and do whatever is needed to do the Universal Spirit's Will in any given situation at any time. Thus, when necessary, you are patient and tolerant of the behavior and shortcomings of other people, if that is what the Universal Spirit needs you to be. And when necessary you are aggressive or intense, if that is what the Universal Spirit needs you to be. Also, when necessary, you are an invincible fighter, if that is what the Universal Spirit needs you to be.

When it is within the Will of the Universal Spirit, you can wait with calm peace of mind and patience.

You are one with Universal Life Energy, it is flowing through you now, you feel it.

You are one with the Universal Spirit, and you are always conscious of that fact.

[READ YOUR AFFIRMATIONS HERE]

You remember everything you have experienced during the use of this tape. Every time you use this tape, it will be even more effective and you will experience greater levels of desirable modified states of consciousness. Anytime you want to return to this deep, relaxing, transcendent altered state, all you need to do is think about it, and return to this state in your mind, or say to yourself the words "relax, relax, relax". Anytime you say or think the words "relax, relax, relax" to yourself, or a very close friend or loved one says "relax, relax, relax" to you, you will immediately return to the deepest, most relaxing, most transcendent altered state you have ever experienced. And in that state, you will be able to direct your mind and body to do whatever you want them to.

In a moment you will gradually return to waking consciousness. But first, see and feel a healing white light energy flooding your body, flowing through you, healing and rejuvenating you. As I count from 1 to 5, you will gradually *return to waking consciousness, and when I reach the number 5 you will be fully awake, totally rejuvenated, alert, vital, virile, clear headed, completely refreshed, calm, and feeling good. 1 feel your blood circulating through your body. 2. 3, begin to stretch now. 4, at the next count you'll be wide awake and feeling good. 5 wide awake, wide awake.*

The Star Exercise

(The Star Exercise can generate tremendous amounts of Universal Life Energy, or "Chi"/"Ki". If you choose to do this exercise, you do so at your own risk, and we take no responsibility for what may happen to you. I have done it for many years, and I have never known anyone hurt by it, but it is powerful. Like a circuit breaker that trips and shuts off the power when more energy than the circuits can handle attempts to pass, sometimes if your body is not yet strong enough to handle the energy flowing through it when you do the star exercise, it will knock you down. If it happens, don't worry about it, you'll get stronger. But when doing this exercise, make sure that the area around you is free from anything that could damage your body if it were to fall. Do not do this exercise if you are subject to epileptic seizures.)

The Star Exercise is much more than a yoga exercise, yet the Children also considered it to be the ultimate yoga exercise. Some feel it is the only yoga exercise a person needs to do. In any case, it is an incredibly powerful means of stimulating the Kundalini, and storing, generating, and transmitting, Universal Life Energy (this energy has many names: prana, bio-cosmic energy, ki, etc.). When you do the Star Exercise, it not only permeates your own body with energy, but it flows in and out of you, allowing you to use it to give energy to others, to heal, and to flow energy with a group of people.

Universal Life Energy is very high frequency, etheric, having some attributes that could be described as spiritual and physical, yet the energy can be affected & directed by the mind and emotions. Universal Life Energy permeates everything. It can be seen as an "aura", or projected energy beams. It can be photographed by means of "Kirilian" electrophotography. In all your yoga exercises, and meditations, you should be conscious of, and working with, this energy. Its supply is limitless, only your separate self can inhibit it.

When you do the Star Exercise, it is best to remove shoes and socks if possible. To do the Star Exercise, stand with your feet about a yard apart, arms straight out to your side like this:

Turn your left palm up, right palm down. Begin breathing intensely, and deeply. Sometimes you may want to do this breathing rapidly, as hard as you can.

Other times you may want to do it slowly, yet still deeply and intensely. The purpose of this breathing is to draw Universal Life Energy from the air into your Solar Plexus Chakra (One of the functions of the Solar Plexus Chakra is to store up a charge of this energy, kind of like a Life Energy battery). It is not so different from rubbing a balloon to make static electricity.

While you see & feel the energy entering your Solar Plexus and building there, also see & feel the energy distribute from your Solar Plexus, throughout your whole being. At the same time, visualize the energy flowing into your left hand, through you, and out of your right hand. Continue doing this. Depending on the circumstances, it may take anywhere from a few breaths, to 144, to get the desired energy effect from the Star Exercise (which is a feeling of transcension and well being, and a "rush" of energy that you can feel and sometimes see). However, you won't experience this intense energy rush until after you finish your breathing and go on to the next step. Next, inhale, hold the breath, and while you continue the visualization, silently say to yourself this affirmation: "I am one with Universal Life Energy, it is flowing through me now, I feel it." At this point, if you have done it correctly, you should start feeling the energy rush. Only hold your breath and enjoy the energy for as long as is comfortable to you. Exhale, continue the visualization and affirmation.

If you wish, the energy pouring out of your right hand can be given to someone or something. We also use it as a healing light. This is the same energy that's associated with pyramid phenomenon (the word pyramid means "fire in the middle").

Some people will tell you that the rush you get is from getting too much oxygen via hyperventilation. But ask yourself, if that is so, why doesn't a person breathing pure oxygen get the same effect? And how does it sometimes work with as little as one breath?

As I said earlier, the Star Exercise is great to do with others. The first time I did it was in a circle with a hundred people. The amount of energy that spun around and around through us in that circle was phenomenal. It was like a whirlwind of cosmic energy. It was the first time my "third eye" chakra opened up, and I saw the life energy that vibrates within and around all things. As you read earlier, when I told my teacher about this experience, he strongly admonished me to ignore the phenomenon.

If done with just one other person, it can be done in two ways: 1) Stand facing each other and grasp each other's hands (making a mini-circle for the energy). 2) Stand side-by-side, and join just the hands that are between you, leaving one person's hand open and up for receiving energy from the heavens, and the other person's hand open and downward for sending the energy to the Earth. It looks something like this:

If doing it with a group of people, form a circle with all joining hands. Besides the same visualizations you do when you are doing it alone, also visualize the energy going around the entire circle, and gaining strength as it gets a boost from each

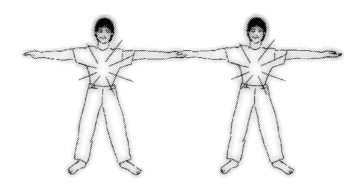

person in the circle. It has been my experience that no one should be left outside the circle when you do this, due to the tremendous power that "flies off" the circle.

The Pineal Wave

The pineal wave is a technique that dates way back to the *earliest* days of the Children of the Law of One. In fact, it dates back to a time before we even had fully physical, or male/female bodies. Its purpose is to empower and cleanse our soul in the very center of the Earth. It also provides rejuvenation and attunement with the energies of the Earth.

Stand erect, feet together. Visualize your pineal gland (which is located approximately between the ears, and behind the eyes in the center of the head). This is the place of the seventh chakra, and is called the "seat of the soul". It is the home of the "spark of life" - the spiritual part of us that gives our bodies life. Visualize your pineal as a ball of white light energy. Inhale, maintaining the visualization, then exhale *sharply,* shooting the ball of light down through your body, deep into the very center point of the Earth. The center of the Earth is beyond molten lava, it is like an inner Sun, it is a significant energy center. After "shooting" your "ball of light" down into the Earth, allow it a second or two to reach the Earth's center, then begin to inhale again slowly, feeling the energy come up from the Earth, then up into your body, and back to the pineal. Repeat at least three times.

Planetary Polarity Attunement

The purpose of this ancient Atlantean exercise is to align us with the energy field of the Earth, thus putting us in tune with the Earth and all its energies. It is said that one of the effects of this is tremendous rejuvenation, physical regeneration, and long life.

Get a compass and find the exact direction of north/south. Lie down flat on your back with your body aligned north/south, your head pointing towards the south. Relax your body. Watch your body breathe. Feel yourself dissolve into oneness with whatever you're laying on (you are not supposed to really believe this is happening, just imagine feeling the sensations). Extend this feeling to whatever is below that until you feel you are part of, and one with, the ground, the Earth itself. Imagine the immensity of the planet Earth, and visualize it suspended in space, slowly spinning around on its axis. Feel it spinning, and your body laying there is moving with it. Feel your body moving with it. Next feel the lower part of your body, which is facing north, becoming energized (kind of like the magnetized end of a compass needle that aligns with the Earth's magnetic field). Begin feeling your chakras becoming energized as if you were doing the color-chakra exercise, but don't go past the heart chakra, remain with the lower chakras for now. After five minutes, reverse your position so your head is pointing north and your feet south. Follow the same procedure as just given except this time start visualizing the upper part of your body being energized; begin with the heart chakra and go up to the crown chakra. Continue for five minutes. As with the other meditations, if you can, do them for a longer period of time.

Mirror Exercise-Chanting

As we said elsewhere, the Children of the Law of One were the most knowledgeable in the advanced Atlantean vibrational sciences. "Modern" science has just begun to consider things like the physical health effects of electromagnetic fields from power lines, computers, TV's, etc.. And they have only recently discovered that the body has bio-electric and energy fields, and even the brain gives off electricity in the form of brainwaves.

We have always known that people are always transmitting various energies, and always receptive to various energies.

One of the mechanisms of energy transfer, is through the eyes. The left eye is receptive to vibration, the right eye transmits. Doing the following meditation regularly will, over time, train you to be in the habit of looking into a person's left eye (which to you will be on your right). This will allow you to instantly "plug in" to their vibration, transmit yours, and avoid being unduly affected or influenced by energy coming through their eyes into yours.

The mirror exercise develops: Concentration; Self-discipline; Your abilities to "read" higher frequency vibrations/"auras"; Your visual communication abilities; Your abilities to influence others via energies transmitted through the eyes; Your abilities to defend against others influencing you through the eyes; Awareness of previous incarnations of yourself and others; Your circumvent force (the area of vibrational influence that surrounds you like a giant aura).

This exercise should be done in a darkened room, using a candle or two in front of the mirror you're using. The mirror need not be large; as long as you can see your eyes it's fine, although it's more desirable to see your entire face. The mirror should be placed one to two feet from your face.

If you can, burn a little pure (crystal, gum, or powder) incense before starting the exercise (Frankincense & Myrrh are strongly recommended if possible).

You may either sit on the floor or in a chair, whichever is most comfortable for you; the important thing is to keep your spine straight & erect.

To begin the exercise, look into the eye of your reflection that is on your right side (this would actually be your right eye) and start chanting a mantra. Refrain from blinking if you can, especially when you are seeing phenomenon or other faces (it can jolt you out of the altered state that is allowing you to see these things). Continue doing the exercise for at least ten minutes. A half-hour will generally yield more results.

Selecting a Mantra

Select a mantra (word or words used for chanting) that you feel drawn to. "Om" and "Yod-He-Vau-He" are both excellent mantras. A mantra helps develop concentration, and can effect you in many ways through the vibration of sounding the words. It can stimulate upper chakras, stimulate your attunement to the "sound current" of the Universe and thus Universal Consciousness, and invoke the energy of all the chanting that has been done throughout time, by those who have used that same chant. But it is also important that you understand the meaning of the mantra you choose, and it is best if it represents a profound idea or ideal. We have already described the meaning of Yod-He-Vau-He in the chapter on vibration.

You may experience a great deal of phenomenon doing this exercise, i.e., seeing all kinds of faces from past lives, "auras" etc. Whatever you experience, stay focused on what you are doing, don't allow anything to lure your attention away. You may come to experience what some call "The Dweller on the Threshold", the hideous devil that is nothing but your selfish separate self, your fears, desires, etc., (discussed in the chapter on the death experience). If you do, let me remind you that the Dweller is also "The Angel guarding the Gates of Eden", and the only way you can pass, is through love, Unselfish Love. Look that beast right in the eye and love it. In this way you can transcend self and return to Paradise, Oneness with the Universal Spirit.

Breathing

The ancient teachings of Atlantis describe the breath as a bridge between the sub-conscious and conscious minds. Think about it for a moment - breathing is both a sub-conscious process (i.e., your body keeps breathing automatically whether you think about breathing or not), and a conscious process (i.e., you can take it out of "automatic" mode, and consciously control it - breathe fast, slow, deeply, shallow, hold your breath, etc.). Your other organs are mostly under sub-conscious control. For instance, an average person can't consciously digest their food or control their heartbeat. But even *these* things can be *consciously* manipulated once you master consciously accessing the sub-conscious. Breathing is one of the methods that can be used to bridge the entire conscious/sub-conscious gap and re-integrate your being.

There are many different ways to approach this through the breath. You can control it, meditate on it, leave it alone and watch it, concentrate on it, and coordinate other mental or physical functions with it.

The breath is also our link to the etheric. We are given life, and given breath. The Universal Spirit breathes each breath into us. When we cease breathing, our body ceases to live. Breath links us to everyone else. Think of all the billions of molecules in each breath of air we breathe in and out. How many have been breathed by others? There is a chance that one of those molecules was breathed by President Clinton, Lincoln, Alexander the Great, Genghis Khan, Jesus, Benjamin Franklin, and ....

Conscious Breath

One way to acquire sub-conscious control and conscious integration, is to really become *aware* of your breathing, without controlling it. If you allow your sub-conscious mind to control your breathing for you, but at the same time become *conscious* of the breathing *without* trying to control it *consciously,* you can achieve an integration of sub-conscious and conscious aspects. This gives you a key to all sub-conscious and conscious activities. And through the passive concentration necessary to bridge these aspects, the conscious mind becomes still, quiet, free from the constant internal noise and reaction to external stimuli which prevent/block the reflection of Universal Consciousness.

Sit with your spine erect, and begin to "watch" your body breathe; just be aware of your breathing. That's all there is to it. At first, until your concentration develops, your mind will wander all over the place. As soon as you realize that your mind has wandered, bring it right back to watching your breath, don't waste energy reprimanding yourself for not maintaining concentration, that just gives more energy to the selfish separate self (and that's what it wants—to keep you from getting control). Frustration is the ally of the separate self. ***Bringing yourself back*** *to the object of concentration immediately upon recognizing that you've wandered off, applies to all concentration/meditation techniques.*

The Sacred Breath

The Sacred Breath was the most guarded meditation secret of the Children of the Law of One. It was never taught, or written down. In fact, a teacher did not even reveal it to a student, until the student developed a basic awareness of it, and then asked about it. Nevertheless, some other traditions have picked it up over time, via keen observation. Let me explain.

The Sacred Breath is a "staple" meditation of a true teacher. It becomes so natural, so much of a second nature, that they just do it automatically from time to time, without even thinking about it. When a teacher is doing this meditation, it doesn't "show" very much. There is a little breathing that can be mistaken as a sigh, and a subtle shift in energy. It takes keen awareness and observation for an elder student to perceive that their teacher is doing "something". But nevertheless, this meditation was only passed on when the student noticed "something", and asked their teacher what they were doing. Then the student was ready to learn the Sacred Breath. But as I mentioned in part one, it is time for these things to now be revealed openly.

The Sacred Breath involves several aspects of meditation: Active, conscious breath control; The "little death" of lingering during the period after exhalation, and prior to inhalation; The taking in of Universal Life Energy through the breath into the Solar Plexus; And concentration.

Start by inhaling, then exhaling deeply and completely (like a deep sigh). Now here's where it's tricky: You want to begin inhaling, but so subtly, slowly and minutely that you can't even tell you are inhaling - but you want to make sure you are inhaling. I guess you could say that is the paradox or Zen quality to this meditation. You don't want to think of your subtle inhalation, as an inhalation. You want to completely visualize that you are just inhaling the prana, the Universal Life Energy, right into your solar plexus.

Now, when you start to feel that you need to take a breath, go ahead and take one - then again, exhale fully and deeply as if you were sighing. Repeat this for as long as you have time for. You can also do this throughout your day anytime you think about it, in order to bring your consciousness back to **true** reality (to break the illusion of the day to day reality most people think is *more* real).

Grand Circulation of Breath

The Grand Circulation of Breath is a multi-purpose meditation. Besides creating all the usual benefits of meditation, it also stimulates and rejuvenates the whole being, and helps bring balance and health to the body. The Grand Circulation develops: Concentration; Body integration; Awareness of Universal Life Energy or Ki; Awareness of the "energy body" and its interrelation with the physical body. It also aids in transcension of the physical plane, and balances & increases the flow of Universal Life Energy through the body via main "circuits" (called meridians). And here's an interesting side-effect: some people with colds or allergies have experienced unclogging of the nasal passages when they did the Grand Circulation.

The exercise may be done lying down, or sitting with your spine straight. If you have difficulty with falling asleep or "spacing out" (wandering thoughts), you should do it sitting up.

This meditation involves circulating energy around the governing meridians of the torso, in coordination with your breathing. You will begin by visualizing energy coming up from the base of your spine, continuing up the spine area, over the top of the head, down the middle of the face, down the front of the chest to the groin, then back up from the base of the spine. Also, as I just mentioned, you will be visualizing this energy movement in coordination with your breathing. Basically, you will inhale during the visualization of the energy rising up the back, and you will exhale during the visualization of the energy going down your front. It's important to also develop an "overview visualization" of the "whole" circulation of this energy, seeing it as one flowing circular band, even though you are concentrating on moving the energy "one section at a time". It is also important not to stop moving the energy as you traverse the sections - keep it flowing, moving along its path.

Begin to inhale slowly, visualizing your breath as an energy at the base of the spine. As you inhale, see your "breath energy" slowly moving up *the spine area* - passing over the small of the back; passing over the middle point of the back, passing over the area of your spine between the shoulder blades (still inhaling slowly); moving up the back of your neck; up the back of the skull to the forehead; down the center of the face to the upper lip (this completes the inhale/first part of the flow). Starting with the lower lip, you begin your exhale; continue on down a path centered along the front side of the body, passing over the chest area, the abdomen, the area in front of the spleen chakra (a couple of inches below the navel), back to the starting point at the base of the spine. Do not pause your energy visualization when you get to the end of your exhale at the base of the spine. Continue the visualization, as you begin to inhale and repeat the same cycle just as before. Repeat for as long as you have time for. A half-hour is good.

Until you become familiar with coordinating your visualization with your breathing as we just described, you may have a little difficulty visualizing the entire flow cycle within one breath. Just stick with it, it won't take you very long to master it. Some people experience running out of breath before the end of a visualization cycle. If you have this problem, you are inhaling/exhaling too slowly. Speed up your visualization to make it match a comfortable period of inhaling/exhaling. Just make sure that you are consciously controlling your breath, not just letting your body breathe normally.

Counting Breath

Concentration is a prerequisite to true meditation and an invaluable aid in anything you do. The development of concentration is a primary purpose of the counting breath exercise, although as with all the other techniques given here, it has integrative effects on the entire being.

This breathing exercise can be done with passive or active breathing - you can either just let your body breathe normally, or take conscious control of your breathing. Do it both ways for a while, and you'll discover which is best for you.

Sit with your spine straight. As you inhale, count to yourself silently, "one"; as you exhale, again count "one". As you inhale again, count "two"; exhale, count "two". Continue like this until you get to "ten", then start the cycle over again with one. Your objective is to be able to do five sets of one through ten without your mind wandering. When you can do that, your concentration is well developed. Don't expect to be able to do it right away, it takes time, it takes practice, but like everything else, the more you practice the better you get. Remember, when you find that you have drifted off somewhere, immediately go back to counting your breath without wasting concentration. If you will just be persevering/consistent with your exercises, you will get results, but be patient. Waiting IS!

Contemplation & Visualization of Unselfish Love

[Note: The following exercise requires understanding of the difference between "love", and "Unselfish Love". Reading part one of this book first, is recommended. Do this exercise when you are not tired.]

Step One

Part of this exercise involves feeling Unselfish Love for someone you don't like. Some of the people you don't like may deserve your feelings, they may be bad, or have done terrible things. This exercise is not intended to help you accept or "be alright with" the negative personality, lifestyle, or actions that some beings have created for themselves. Or to get you in the mental disposition to allow them back into your life. It is to get you to let go of them in an Unselfishly Loving manner, and also get you to relate to the essential being, the spiritual spark inside them, and still love & care for that. We can, and should have *compassion* for the spirits of those whose choices have led them into patterns of destruction and suffering. If we don't, we are having a spiritual crisis ourselves. But we don't want to personally accept those choices as "alright".

To begin this visualization meditation, ask yourself the following questions - and answer them: "What is Unselfish Love?"; "What does it mean to be Unselfishly Loving?"; "Am I always Loving Unselfishly?" (and if the answer to that is no, think about the most recent situations in which you haven't loved Unselfishly, and go on to the next question); "Why did I not Love Unselfishly in that situation?"s Once you have thought about it, let go of the thought about why you didn't Love Unselfishly. Why? The reason why you did not Love Unselfishly is not as important as making sure you *will* Love Unselfishly from now on. Now, again think about the situation in which you were not Unselfishly Loving. Completely visualize it again in your mind, only this time, visualize yourself being Unselfishly Loving, and visualize the results of that.

Finally, ask yourself "What should I be doing to express/manifest Unselfish Love all the time?". Ask the Universal Spirit, the One, "What would you have me do?". And do an affirmation like, "I am Unselfishly Loving".

Step Two

Start by "calling up" the feeling and concept of Unselfish Love. Do this by visualizing someone you have the most Unselfish Love for. It could be a child, parent, great friend, dog, relative, etc.. But if you have a teacher or a "personified ideal", who Unselfishly Loves you also, that is who you should start with. Feel the Unselfish Love. Feel their Unselfish Love for you, and/or your Unselfish Love for them. While you are holding on to that feeling, think of someone you like but haven't really felt Unselfish Love for. Feel Unselfish Love for the essence of that person - their spirit. Now think of someone you don't like. Feel Unselfish Love for their spirit also. If they have done something hurtful, or harmful, that is inexcusable to you, be sure you only extend your feeling to their essence, their spirit, their Inner Being. Then expand your love to embrace everyone and everything you can conceive of.

Kind for a Day

This simple little exercise also develops Unselfish Love, by directly accessing it through one of its attributes - kindness. Every morning, choose one person in your life, who you will put out an *extra* effort to be thoughtful of, humble with, and kind towards. All through the day, stop and consider their feelings, their needs, what it's like to walk in their shoes. And treat them special. Maybe get them some tea, or give them a massage, or make them a special meal, or a gift from your heart. The next morning, choose a different person.

(Meditation Walk

The meditation walk is a method that synchronizes your breathing with the number of steps you take while walking. Begin walking. Step, step, step, step.... Once you have set the pace (up to you), begin breathing in coordination with your walking. For instance, you could inhale during two of your steps, hold your breath for the third, exhale for the next two steps, leave your breath exhaled for the next step, then repeat immediately (inhale for two steps, etc.). Or you could inhale for four steps, hold for two, exhale for four, hold exhale for two, etc. Create a pattern that is most comfortable for you. If you wish you may even eliminate the "holding breath" part of the meditation, which would make it go something like this: Inhale (however many steps you choose), exhale (same number of steps as inhale), etc. You can use any number of steps you choose as long as the inhale and exhale number of steps are equal. Experiment and see what works best for you.

Although it is particularly beneficial to walk outdoors, you can even do this exercise walking back and forth, "pacing", indoors in a small area. Try to do this exercise everyday at the same time.

You can do the meditation walk for as long as you wish, but it should be done for *at least* five minutes.

If you are doing this properly you will find that you are more aware/conscious of your environment. This is because the meditation brings you greater integration/Oneness within yourself, and without (your environment).

Remember, if you find yourself walking in front of a moving truck or such, you aren't doing it right. Start again after you get out of the hospital. (for those of you who are too serious minded, I should explain. That statement is meant to be humorous).

Kundalini

When a being truly becomes devoted to serving the Universal Spirit, surrenders to Universal Will, and develops Unselfish Love and Harmlessness, many things change within them. The changes are physical, mental, and spiritual. One of the most profound forces involved in these changes, is the Kundalini.

Kundalini comes as an activation of energy along the spine. Some people have described it as a fiery breath that roars up your spine. It has also been interpreted as a goddess, or the serpentine fire that lives at the base of the spine, and from time to time, comes to life and rises all the way to the top of the head, bringing enlightenment. As the Kundalini force passes through the body's endocrine glands and their corresponding nerve centers, there is a stimulation and "awakening" of the seven centers or "chakras", that are associated with these glands and nerve groups. This brings new awareness and activity in areas of the vibrational spectrum that were previously self-blocked from the person's experience. And that gives a person powerful new abilities, and great responsibility.

When the Kundalini rises, it can be painful, although the state of spiritual elation tends to nullify any pain. It is usually afterwards that you can have a very sore back for days. And if the body is not pure enough, and has not been prepared for this powerful evolutionary energy, it can cause a great deal of distress, and illness, as the body rushes to "catch up", to purify itself enough, and to develop "nerve circuits" that are strong enough to handle new energies. All this can be made easier, and even brought on by, purification and attunement of the physical body, in coordination with the mind and spirit. Meditations, yoga, diet, etc., can all help make the changes brought about by the Kundalini, as smooth & easy as possible.

Before we go on about that, I must give you a stern warning. As we said earlier in the book, the abilities obtained from this should coincide with, or be the result of, self-transcendence, and active Unselfish Love. Kundalini should come naturally, as you evolve into a better, more kind and giving person. It is like a kiss that the Universal Spirit gives you when you are thinking or doing something right. It may come when you have a spiritual realization, especially during meditation. However, through doing certain exercises, such as Kundalini yoga for one, you may also activate the Kundalini, but this is FORCING it. Such exercises are good IF they are under the guidance of a True Teacher and correspond with the entity's spiritual growth, but can be very dangerous and detrimental in other circumstances (see chapter on VIBRATION in Part One). Would you let a baby play with wires from an electrical outlet? Of course not. Yet that electrical energy can be very constructive if channeled in the proper manner by one who has PREPARED to utilize it FIRST. It's the same with the power of the Kundalini. For this reason we only give the most powerful techniques that pertain to unlocking such power, to those who have demonstrated their harmlessness and Unselfish Love. There are books and teachers that will give such to anyone, but please, heed my warning.

There are other means of forcing the Kundalini also, including drugs and scientific devices. And there are teachers who give "Shakti" to their students to stimulate this, but as at least one teacher I know of has learned, obtaining temporary "enlightenment" by Kundalini raised by Shakti, or any other means, does nothing to make for a better person. In fact, it usually strengthens the selfish separate self, and makes for a "spiritual ego". To use an example, let's say there is a path that winds up the mountain of consciousness; the top of the mountain is Universal Consciousness, Oneness with the Universal Spirit. Inducing or forcing enlightenment through external means is like temporarily airlifting a person to the top of the mountain. Sure, they experience Universal Consciousness, but it's only temporary, they have not climbed there themselves, and they do not belong there. They must come back down, and it's quite a fall. Sometimes an experience such as that can be helpful - if it is only done one time for purposes of instilling inspiration and knowing what wondrous things await you when you finally achieve Universal Consciousness the right way. But when someone has such an experience, and then "comes back down", there are two alternate paths a person can choose. 1) A person can pick themselves up and begin walking their spiritual path to the top, step by step; or 2) They can (as most do) take the attitude of "I know what it's like now. I've made it. I don't need to walk the long hard way". Then the person usually tries to keep getting there with a "short cut", and becomes hardened in separate self consciousness. Then they only get further and further from their true spiritual path, and from the mountain top. Don't fool yourself, there are no short cuts.

Physical Aids to Spiritual Consciousness

The physical body can be a window of sorts to your entire being. Everything is interconnected, all One, and when you apply things such as herbs, yoga, diet, etc., on the physical plane, you affect your mental, emotional, and spiritual aspects as well.

When you apply mental thoughts that involve spiritual energies to things like yoga, and what you eat, it aids the spiritual effects of the physical applications, making these things even more powerful.

Yoga

Yoga is a very old discipline that tones your body, while freeing up, and flowing Universal Life Energy, and sometimes facilitating the activation of Kundalini (discussed later). It also can incorporate, and provide the benefits of, meditation. Originally developed by the Children, yoga has taken many different forms over the centuries. Thus, there are now many different "types" of yoga. One of the most popular, and well known, is Hatha yoga, which involves moving and stretching your body in various ways.

Physically doing yoga exercises without the interplay/integration of the mental and spiritual, would be like going through the motions of playing a musical instrument without actually playing anything. It will still have some effect, but nothing compared to when you combine the exercises with the application of will and visu-

359

alization.

The body is a precision instrument, through which the essential you expresses itself in the physical plane. It's a vehicle that can be a well maintained, finely tuned instrument, or neglected and out-of-tune. The more aware you become that your natural function is to manifest the Universal Spirit, the more aware you become of the body's need for purification, balance, and attunement with Universal Forces. The more spiritually "tuned-up" a body is, the better it can perform as a vehicle for the Universal Spirit.

It's impractical to teach yoga in this book, but instructional and workout videos of our techniques have been made if you are interested in learning (see back of book). It is being called "Tibetan Yoga" since most people wouldn't relate to "Children of the Law of One Yoga". But it is the system we've used for thousands of years. Some techniques are similar to other styles, but some you will find nowhere else - like our acupuncture meridian balancing energy techniques. It's easy to learn, and the workout flow takes only 20 minutes. Scientific tests have verified the great power of the meridian balancing techniques, and they can be done anytime you need them, in just a few minutes.

[P.S. - It's best to do Yoga naked if possible. Clothing, especially footwear or socks, restrict/disrupt some of the body's energy flows.]

Tai Chi

Tai Chi is considered by some to be similar to yoga. It both is and isn't. Tai Chi, and its various counterparts, are "newer" than some of the yogas, and were originally developed by high consciousness monks as "inner forms" of the different fighting styles or "Kung Fu's". These inner forms were used to develop such things as inner strength, Universal Life Energy (or Ki/Chi) power, accuracy, and concentration. But while Tai Chi was developed to be an integral part of a fighting system , it is even more than that. Tai Chi, like yoga, is a form of meditation and flowing life energy. It has become its own entity, which is a beneficial and beautiful system of spiritual development and health maintenance. It takes far more time to learn than yoga however, and many years to master.

Elixirs

Elixirs are plants, elements, or mixtures, consumed to gain spiritual development or power. They have been used since the days of Atlantis. The Children once used them to help the most advanced students induce the death experience. Even back then, they were to be used once only in an entire lifetime, either to induce the death experience, or get a glimpse of the "top of the mountain" to establish the reality of the goal. Native Americans, and shamans the world over however, have repeatedly used plants like Peyote to expand their spiritual awareness, gain insight and knowledge, to facilitate healing, and perform spiritual rituals. Elixirs can help, but only under special circumstances and with close guidance. Properly used, they can give a spiritual push, or a glimpse of enlightenment, etc., but if the experience gives false confidence, false pride, a spiritual ego will result that will impede any true spiritual development. And some will want to keep taking the elixir to reach the heights of the Universal Spirit, rather than climbing their own path. The use of elixirs without guidance, can also lead to astral problems - "aura holes", the attachment of disincarnate being and "things", and even possession. Since many elixirs are now illegal in most countries, and the dangers outweigh the potential benefits, we no longer use them, and we recommend avoiding them.

Diet

When you eat, you should be feeding your spiritual body with energy as well as your physical body. You should also choose a diet that is right for you. Every body is different, and every diet needs to be adjusted for a given body. Similarly, you can not single out a diet for the body without considering it's mental and spiritual implications. You are a whole being, a spiritual, mental, and physical Universe in itself, and must regard all things in the realization of such if you are to evolve.

Charging Your Food

At this point of leaving our section on yoga and beginning our section on diet, I would like to recommend a practice that crosses over and includes both subjects.

If you took an energy photograph (like Kirilian photography) of just picked food, you would find that it loses it's life energy about twenty to thirty minutes after it's picked (depending on the type of food) and loses it's slower frequency energies and many of its physical attributes (vitamins, etc..) in about the same amount of time after it is cut. "Charging" your food with Universal Life Energy before you eat, restores the food's lost energy, and then some (depending on you). To charge your food before eating, place your hands at the sides of your bowl or dish, as near the food as possible. Then visualize the energy flowing through you, into the food, making the food radiant with light. It is essentially like doing a mini Star Exercise, and giving the energy to your food. This can be done mentally without the hands, but it is best that you learn to walk before attempting to run, so it's best to do it with the hands at first, and at least until it's mentally automatic. Seeing teachers of the Children of the Law of One (and some of their offshoots) do this over their food, became the source of many religions "saying grace" before meals.

A healthy diet

Much could be written on the subject of diet for health and healing (and much has!) but rather than do that here, I will refer you to Paavo Airola's book How to Get Well which reflects much of the Children's dietary recommendations, and the Edgar Cayce readings on diet. In reading the Cayce material, keep in mind the time in which it was written (in respect to the evolution of the mass consciousness of that time, and the condition of food then as compared to now [no chemicals, hormones, antibiotics, radioactivity, etc.]), and that *each* reading was given *specifically* for *the individual the reading was being done for only.* Some generalities can be made, but be cautious. Every body is different, and has different needs.

We've examined new books that give diets based on blood type. It sounded like there could be some validity to it, and some people say they feel good on it. But after reviewing the diets, and not finding *any* scientific basis or research to explain them, we feel they are contrived and cannot recommend it.

For now we can follow basic nutritional "rules of thumb" that are in harmony with the laws we can observe in the workings of nature, but there are as many "perfect" diets as there are individual bodies. What may be beneficial to some may be of no value, or even *detrimental,* to others.

How to find Your Special Perfect Diet

In order to find the perfect "fine-tuned" diet for *your* body, you must first approach the body with the right attitude, and a true understanding of what it is. Rather than thinking of your body as *you,* always keep in mind that it is just a vehicle. A vehicle that the real you "rides" in, lives in, and uses. But even more importantly, keep in mind that it is a vehicle *for the Universal Spirit,* a tool that the Universal Spirit uses if you allow it. It is no less than the "temple" of the living God. When you embrace that attitude towards your body, and use your free will to eat accordingly, you will know what to eat for maximum health, and be able to choose a perfect diet for your body at any given time.

Beware of rationalizing to yourself - "convincing" yourself that your body "needs" a certain food, when it is really your *desire* for it in disguise. When your diet is dictated by the desires of the selfish separate self, your body suffers many nutritional imbalances and harm. When the desires of self are in control, you have a "pleasure seeking machine" to contend with - and the more it gets, the more it wants. It remembers pleasures and constantly seeks "encores" in an insatiable cycle that results in deterioration of the whole being. In part, this is the effect of wasting vital life energies, eating un-natural foods, and eating what is desired rather than what is needed. For those who are overweight or have certain health problems related to carbohydrates, we have seen people who've had remarkable results using the Atkins diet, or similar low-carb diets.

You are what you eat and what you think, both physically and mentally. The body is built, and is constantly rebuilding itself, solely from the materials you provide it with. Also, the mind is behind all this construction, it is the builder. Without the proper attitude, a pure diet is worthless, like having all the lumber to build a house but not having anyone to put it all together properly. But the lumber is important also. Both factors must come together properly. Cells regenerate at such a rate that every seven years the cells in your body are replaced! What are they being replaced with? [Interesting note about seven year cycles: Psychologists say that everyone goes through a personality change every seven years. There is also a spiritual transformation that takes place in seven year cycles. Coincidence?]

Live Long and Prosper

Earlier in the book, when we were talking about the age of the monastery's head Adept monk, Michiel, we briefly mentioned modern scientific research that verifies the human ability for an incredibly long lifespan. Dr. Josef P. Hrachovec of the University of Southern California Gerontology center has been studying the aging process for years. He has concluded that the body has a potential of living a century or longer, and through proper diet, exercise, and emotional control, a life span could be "stretched like a rubber band". Some of the Children's old records indicate it was not uncommon to live to be 800, 900, even a thousand years old in the past - and with a high quality of life. This is attributed to the higher mineral & nutritional quality of food in the past, the lack of pollution & toxins, the diet, the use of mind, and daily rejuvenation of life energies. But in certain conditions, some of these things can still be duplicated. On my way to the monastery, I met a strong healthy young man of 140, with bright red hair and sparkling clear blue eyes. He stopped once every hour of his life, and meditated for 10 minutes. But his *mother* was still taking good care of him also, so who knows!

Basic Dietary Considerations

Here are some of the dietary "rules of thumb" we spoke of earlier:

1   Eat foods that are as pure as possible in as natural a state as possible (mostly raw) (organic).

2   Balance your intake of acid and alkaline forming foods to 80%

alkaline to 20% acid.

3   Don't mix fruits and vegetables.

4   Don't mix sweets and starches.

5   Minimize how many different foods you eat at one meal (try to keep it   to three)

6   Eat foods grown as locally as possible.

7   Eat only when you are really hungry.

8   Chew very well.

9   Drink *pure* water.

10 Relax. Don't eat when you're tense or upset.

11 Eat about two-thirds of what would normally make you full. An excess of nutritional elements in the system becomes toxic.

Vegetarianism

The question: Vegetarian, to be or not to be? The answer to that is really quite complex. There are spiritual considerations as well as health considerations - pro and con. The Children's teachings promote vegetarianism, but there are exceptions.

Protein

Many western countries and their medical establishments are "high protein brainwashed". They have been taught to believe that protein is more important than it is, and that you must eat meat to get it. Most people can get the protein they need from a proper vegetarian diet, although some cannot.

How much protein and what kind of protein (animal, vegetable, dairy, etc.) does a person need? It varies greatly depending on the individual. Genetics plays a big role in this. Remember, the following are generalizations and there are exceptions: If your ancestors were mainly meat eaters, you will have a predisposition to meat, and probably need more protein. If your ancestors didn't eat dairy, you are likely to have a low tolerance for dairy, and it will tend to clog you up with mucous and make you prone to colds and flu. If they ate a lot of dairy, such as in some Scandinavian countries, you will be more inclined to digest, and ingest the nutrition from dairy products.

Then there is the food supply issue. Animals raised for food eat far more food than they become. It is simply bad logistics for the world food supply.

On the other side of the issue, some people don't do well with strict vegetarian diets. Their body just can't adapt. Their bodies don't absorb the nutrition (including vitamins) from vegetables and fruits as well as they do from meat. But if that person will be as strict a vegetarian as they can healthfully be, then their children and grandchildren will be able to be more strict, or full vegetarians. The Children teach people to **be as much of a vegetarian as you can be without causing health problems that will interfere with being a vehicle for the will of the Universal Spirit.** Almost everyone can at least cut out red meat, although some people need to supplement their diet with yeast or some other form of B12 (the only other dietary source being red meat).

Vegetarianism, Consciousness, and Spirituality

Some people are vegetarians because of their religion. They just believe it is more spiritual, or gives you a higher consciousness, even without really knowing the reason why. They just take it on faith.

Does diet affect your consciousness? Certain foods do. But it is not a necessary prerequisite to enlightenment, nor a way of attaining enlightenment or higher consciousness. It's actually the other way around. A person usually improves their diet as a *result of* a raise in consciousness. But I have seen many vegetarians that were just as selfish and harmful as any meat eater, or worse. And I have seen meat eaters that are higher in consciousness than vegetarians. I know some enlightened people who consume alcohol, although they don't consume it for purposes of a selfish "get off" as most people do. Would Jesus eat a hamburger? Probably not. But if he did, would his consciousness be one iota higher or lower because of it? Absolutely not. Did not eating hamburger make Jesus or Buddha what they were? No. So it's best not to get fooled by "trappings" of spirituality, but rather stick to the tangible issues like kindness, harmlessness, and giving. With that in mind, I will say that Children of the Law of One teachings state that alcohol, tobacco, chocolate, sugar, and spinach, in that order (alcohol being the strongest) all inhibit the spiritual functioning of the chakras, including inhibiting your "Inner Voice" and intuition, and red meat can inhibit upper chakra functions. The effects of spinach and chocolate are relatively minor. Spinach has nutritional value, but you can almost get the same things from other dark green leafies like kale and chard - in any case, it's not such a big deal if you eat it. The same with chocolate, although rather than nutritional value, it isn't good for your body and is one of the great self get offs. But again, it's not such a big deal. Alcohol on the other hand, has severe effects, radically supressing the spiritual nature, and letting the dark side, the selfish side, blossom - thus it should *never* be consumed by anyone who is not enlightened.

Obviously, compassion for animals is a reason to avoid meat. What kind of consciousness doesn't care about killing and harming animals? Going to the market and buying packaged meats makes it easy not to think about the process involved in getting it there. But how would you feel about personally killing an animal eye to eye? If you have a pet, how would you feel about killing and/or eating it? What makes your pet so different from the other animals? Maybe just that you're familiar with it? So it's all right to kill things you don't know personally? I had a friend who grew up on a farm and had a pet cow. She said the cow was very aware and interacted with her very much like any other pet would. Then her family slaughtered it and it broke her heart.

There are variations in the consciousness of animals, and if you are sensitive to that, it is worse to eat a more aware animal than a less aware animal. That goes for plants too, because plants also have consciousness, and can suffer when you kill them. Getting back to animals as an example, when you look in the eye of a chicken or a fish, there is not a lot going on there. There is "someone at home" in there, but just barely. But when you look into the eye of a whale, or a dog, there is very much an aware, thinking, feeling, creature in there. This awareness is less for a cow or deer, but still far more than that of a chicken. My teacher had a rule of thumb generalization for what to eat, "If it can run from you, don't eat it." But that rule can still overridden depending on your body's need while you are on the path, or functioning as a servant for the One. Many of us are genetically oriented to animal protiens unfortunately. But like I said, even vegetables are alive, and have consciousness. Scientific tests have proven this. Plants are even quite psychic. One experiment indicated that a house plant experienced some kind of arousal when animals or other plants were killed in another room, or when its "owner" was in distress many miles away. And a vegetarian kills plants. So what are we to do?

Ideally, in a more pure human physical state, the ultimate diet would be fruitarian. You don't kill fruit - it is being produced by the plant as a sacrificial offering in order to further it's reproduction (it's a tasty treat that a bird or some other animal eats, who then passes the seeds through their digestive system - thus "planting" the seeds with "fertilizer". I have known some people who tried to be fruitarians, but their bodies were not genetically adapted to it, and every one of them got sick and had to quit the diet. There may be some people out there who can do it though.

The Bottom Line

Basically eating is an issue of survival, and health. Most people must kill something on this Earth, in order to stay living on the Earth themselves. That's disgusting, but true and inescapable for most. Can you justify that? Most people obviously do. But most people have no more of a good reason to live than the things they are killing, yet they do it anyway, and justify it. It comes down to why you are here. As I mentioned in part one, the teachings say, and it is my belief, that we don't really belong here. We are not supposed to be bound to this physical plane. And there are only two reasons that justify being here: 1) Working on yourself so you can get free from it and/or help others; and 2) Being here to help free others (after achieving #1). If you are doing one of these two things, then eat what you will to further your consciousness, stay alive, and strong. And if you must kill an animal or a plant because your body needs it (not because your self desires the food), thank them from your Inner Being when you kill them and eat them - thank them and honor them for sacrificing themselves to help you help the Universal Spirit to do Its Will through your vehicle, and eat with no guilt.

Food Pollution

Animals raised for slaughter are injected with hormones and antibiotics. Milk becomes more polluted every day, not only from the hormones and anti-biotics given to the cows, but also from sanitizer detergents, PCB's radiation, herbicides, and others. Chickens are sometimes fed arsenic to increase their appetites so they'll eat more and gain weight. Laying chickens are given anti-biotics, tranquilizers, rephthalic acid, and yellow dye (to make their sickly egg yolks look normal) just to name a few. You get all these goodies in their eggs (along with some PCB). Fish are often treated with anti-biotics and subjected to the countless forms of poisonous water pollution that are destroying the oceans (including radioactive waste). Of course, animal products aren't the only things that are adulterated. Vegetables and fruits have become dangerously polluted too. You have to scrutinize *everything* you use, consume, or live around.

Most fruits and vegetables are grown with, and sprayed with poisons. Some people buy organic produce from natural food stores but unfortunately, many things sold as organic are not. Ask for proof from your store. Find out where they get their food and trace it back to the source if you can. You will get resistance, but how important is it to you? If enough people start asking for proof, eventually the stores will have to produce it as standard procedure. Also, if you decide to go organic, be thorough, go all the way. Consider the toxins you get from inorganic foods or products as if they were bullets fired at your body's cells. If you get shot, you get shot. Even just one bullet (one inorganic substance you use or consume) can have very detrimental effects. If you go through the trouble of eating organic produce, shouldn't you purify other areas of assimilation? What's in your water? Organic vegetable oils? Vinegar? Herbs? Nuts? Natural soaps? Do you use deodorants? Detergents? Fabric softener? Hydrogenated or "fractionated" oils that are in many packaged "health foods", are more detrimental to health than "junk food". There are hundreds of things to consider, and they will all be revealed to you if you are open, willing to change, *and not resisting giving up things you like, and doing or using things you don't like.* This all comes to one who obtains that consciousness, that selfless attitude of the body being one with, and a vehicle for, Spirit.

Fasting

Diet is but part of the cycle of assimilation and elimination that we must consider as a whole in order to achieve purity. We have just discussed diet and it's implications, but if your body is full of stored up toxins from past dietary habits, a pure diet won't be sufficient to attain a pure, balanced state. To expect a pure diet to do that would be like expecting a clogged drain to unclog itself just because you stopped putting the things in it that clogged it up in the first place. That's where fasting comes in. Fasting facilitates the elimination of stored up toxins. The ancient dietary teachings of Jesus, indicate that we should fast seven days for every year we have eaten impure foods (that doesn't mean you have to do the fasting all in one period). Normally, the body's eliminative and digestive organs accumulate & eliminate. They are busy breaking down the food you eat, providing the body with nutrition, storing fat, eliminating food by-products and toxins, etc.. But when you start a fast, the body's eliminative and digestive organs don't have new food to work with, so they turn to all the stored toxins, diseased cells, tumors, etc., and begin to break up and expel them.

Fasting is not only beneficial to the physical body, but to the mental and spiritual aspects of your being also. More than diet, fasting can be a very spiritual experience that raises your consciousness. An extended fast has tremendous value in developing discipline, transcendence of the physical plane, and strength of will.

The Spiritually enlightening effects of fasting have been documented throughout time. Especially effective in this way is the forty day water fast - this can be accompanied by vivid spiritual visions and revelations. I strongly recommend against doing this without proper supervision and guidance however.

Juice fasts are the way to go for healthy cleansing of the body and a good dose of spiritual boosting too. But even that should be done with guidance. And don't jump right into an extended fast however, start with a four day juice fast and work your way up from there. The selfish separate self rebels at attempts to fast, but if you can get past the third day, you've usually gotten past the point of your greatest weakness and self's greatest temptations. That doesn't mean that the temptations will stop, they may even get stronger and more vivid, but if you've past the three day mark you've demonstrated and developed enough strength to transcend the selfish self's urges, and that strength grows as you continue to transcend.

Rather than going into all the specifics of juice fasting, I again refer you to Paavo Airola's book How to Get Well; He covers it all and there is no need to repeat here what has been said so well.

Cold Shower

A cold shower benefits the whole being. It has rejuvenating, healing, and stimulating effects with the entire body, including: the organs, circulatory system, nervous systems, glandular system (including endocrine glands associated with the Chakras), muscles, etc. It aids the digestive and assimilative processes. It actually increases the blood count. A cold shower taken daily, builds resistance to disease and infections. Mentally, a cold shower increases alertness. A cold shower also increases the flow of Universal life energy/prana/chi/ki throughout the body, whereas a hot shower tends to drain or have a resistive effect on these energies. And as an added bonus, the cold shower is a great means of transcending the selfish separate self, especially for those who don't "like" cold water.

You may start your shower with warm water if you like, you can even alternate hot-cold, hot-cold, just as long as you end with the cold.

Finally, always remember that a cold shower is not hard to come by in the shadows of the Himalayas.

Color Visualization– Chakra Exercise

Each chakra corresponds to its like vibration in the color spectrum. "Color therapy" can be used to stimulate the chakras via physical projection of color and light. But more importantly, we can use the power of visualization to stimulate the various chakras. Physically, the areas of the chakras are associated with complex nerve bundles or plexus', and the location of special endocrine glands.

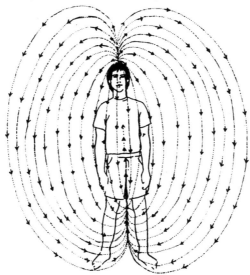

First we have the root chakra, the area below the gonads; its color is red. Next is the second chakra, located behind the area about two inches below the navel (towards the spine); its color is orange. The third chakra is the Solar Plexus; located behind the area below the cartilage of the breast bone (but in front of the spine); its color is golden yellow. Next we have the fourth or heart chakra (you can guess its location); its color is green. Then we have the fifth chakra, sometimes called the thyroid or throat chakra; its color is blue. Centered at the pituitary gland located behind the middle of the forehead, is the sixth chakra, also called the third eye or ajna; its color is purple. Finally we come to the crown chakra or "thousand petaled lotus". Sometimes called the Seat of the Soul, it centers at the pineal gland in the middle of the head; its color is violet-white.

From the poles of the root chakra and the crown chakra, energy flows and surrounds you in a form akin to a magnetic field.

Sit with your spine erect. Visualize colored light energy at each chakra starting with the root chakra and flowing upwards in the order as was just given in the previous paragraph. Dwell on each chakra for at least one breath cycle (inhale and exhale), longer if you can visualize the colors better. When you are done with the crown chakra, begin again at the root chakra. Keep repeating this for twenty minutes or as long as you have time for.

Dreams

In the state of rest (sleep) the body receives maintenance from certain mental and spiritual functions. Our awareness turns from the external environments to the internal (sub-conscious), and we may become aware of the spiritual influences through the internal (dreams) just as we are conscious of the external in it's "waking" state.

Many dreams are opportunities, lessons, and experiences that are presented by your Inner Being. These are often of the nature of a "preview" of experiences to be dealt with, or of presently existing circumstances that should be seen as lessons and a means of growth. These dreams are important, and should be dealt with accordingly. However, not all dreams are of that type.

Some dreams can be of a psychic or precognitive vision, out-of-body experience, intuitive problem solving, etc..

Physical illness or disturbances, or mental disturbances in either the conscious or sub-conscious realms, can affect or even create and dominate dream experiences. These are the only dreams that should be ignored.

Due to lack of coordination with the threefold nature that most people have, many people are not aware of their dream experiences, thus the great benefits from them are lost. We can turn this around however, and use our dreams to help us. How?

Integrating our fragmented consciousness, and getting full benefits from dreams can be facilitated in several ways:

1- Extending the waking consciousness into the dream. This is accomplished through becoming aware that you are active and functional in a dream *while* dreaming. You may use a key symbol to trigger recognition of awareness within a dream. For example, Don Juan told Carlos Castaneda to look at his hands in a dream. Doing this triggered *conscious* dreaming. A light would be an excellent choice for a symbol if you use one, as you will see if you contemplate it.

2- Extending a dream into waking consciousness. This method (which also aids in the development of the first method) is done by recording your dreams every morning. Keep a pen and notebook near your bed, and as soon as you begin to leave your dream state and enter the "waking" state, write down whatever you can remember of the dream, even if it is only a fragment, a word, or a feeling. Don't wait until you're awake - *do it when you first notice you are leaving the dream state.* The more you do this, the easier it will become to remember your dreams, and remember them fully. Before you know it you will be filling pages at a time.

3- Daily reviewing of your dreams. Dream symbology varies among individuals. The best way to understand the meaning of your dreams is to take in the whole picture intuitively. Don't rack your mind trying to figure out details and such. The meaning of your dreams will become more clear to you as you study them. With time, experience, and openness, what you need to know will be revealed to you.

4- The following affirmation aids all the previously mentioned methods; "I remember my dreams and am conscious of them while dreaming." This should be repeated silently to yourself as you are going to sleep.

Remember to keep in mind all the different causes that can manifest in a dream other than a lesson or psychic experience so you won't be trying to read-in something profound when it is nothing but an upset stomach predominating the experience!

Reviewing the Day's Activities

Write down what your day's activities actually were. Do this every night. Do not read this record until a month has passed from the time you wrote it. After a month has passed, compare your past activities and experiences with your current ones. Get out the paper you wrote your ideal on and compare it with these to see how you are doing with living up to your ideal. Also look at your dream log, and see if there is any relationship to your past dreams, and your present life.

Close your eyes, go back and view the experiences you had during the day. Do you find any negative experiences? Did you become negative, upset, about something? Make any mistakes?

Go back again to the beginning of the day and re-experience it, but this time change it around. See negative experiences as occurring positively. See things you negatively reacted to, as lessons, and see yourself reacting in a positive, constructive manner instead. Where you made mistakes, see yourself making the proper decisions. Follow your new positive experiences and decisions through to their results.

The mind creates. Through doing this exercise you will begin to break out of negative patterns and create new patterns that are in harmony with Universal Will.

A Bid for Cooperation

There are many spiritual groups (and individuals) who, although they are on different paths, are on essentially the same path, climbing the mountain of the One. As they get closer to the top of the mountain where all are One and there are no separations, they realize more of their Oneness with the others on various paths. If our similarities are kindness and compassion, then our differences in insignificant beliefs and dogma should not separate us. All spiritual movements who believe that goodness and caring are the most important spiritual attributes, should bond together under the banner of kindness and giving. At least network. Now is the time for us to communicate, to establish bonds of giving, to begin to work as ONE spiritual movement rather than thousands of little moves.

Quite some time ago, the Ananda Cooperative Village had a forest fire on their land. It was good to see that many people, groups, and organizations, offered them assistance. That was just a little example of what we can accomplish through giving with Unselfish Love.

Many people didn't know of the incident at Ananda until after the crisis was over. There was some word of mouth communication about it, and there was mention of the occurrence in a few alternative publications, but because of the time involved in publishing, it was a while before the spiritual community at large was informed. We should have a rapid and effective means of communication between all cooperating groups, and a system of mutual assistance established. Possibly "HAM" radio could serve as a communication link. Any ideas? This will become more important as we go through the great changes that are at our door. But now is the time to act, not later.

If your religion/group does not think that your way is the only way, and what you have just read makes sense to you, please contact us. In the future physical communication may not be as easy as it is today.

It is partly true that those who are meant to be together, will be. But shouldn't we all be together, so together that we're ONE?

A Final Word

This book is full of information that takes time and repeated exposure to really assimilate. Consistent review of the ancient, and not so ancient teachings, even though you think you know it, can keep giving you a greater understanding of the nature of Oneness and Unselfish Love. It can also give you greater insight into who you really are, and what you are doing with your life, and help you grow. If that's what you're interested in, you might want to begin reading the book again (even if you have already done so many times), and read a little of it every day, until you are One with the knowledge, and you *know* for certain that you are not getting *anything* out of it anymore. I can't stress highly enough how important this is, and how much you'll miss if you only read it once.

More about us & our projects:

The Golden Rule & Its Significance

"The Golden Rule" is a term commonly used for the principle of Unselfishly Loving others. It is sometimes quoted as "Do unto others as you would have them do unto you", or "Love thy Neighbor as thy self". The common present translation of the Bible quotes Jesus as saying: *"I give you a new commandment, to love each other as I have loved you."* While this is clearly the ultimate commandment Christians are supposed to live by, the same principle is also a belief of other spiritual paths (and all basically "good" people, religious or not). While people often disagree on religion & politics, most everyone can agree on the "goodness" and "rightness" of living by the Golden Rule, regardless of culture or religious belief. Thus it's an ideal in which all kind hearted people can join together towards the common goal of manifesting Unselfish Love and its virtues, in tangible ways. Ironically, while the Golden Rule is possibly the most vital positive, constructive principle in the world, in both a spiritual and practical sense, it's often not given the importance it's due, or it's misunderstood, forgotten, ignored, or given up on. It's time to change that.

The Golden Rule Organization (GRO)

GRO is the umbrella name for multiple projects undertaken by our monks, priests, ministers, GRO's friends, supporters, and members.

Instead of promoting a religious dogma, we promote *and practice* the simple, universal, Golden Rule of Unselfish Love (and its virtues, such as compassion & harmlessness). That doesn't mean all those involved are "perfect", "saints", or unselfishly loving all the time - but they are at least sincerely "working on it". All people who live by the Golden Rule, are embraced as kindred spirits, regardless of other beliefs. We encourage the transcension of selfishness, and direct experience of God. We practice & teach methods of attaining those goals, including scientifically proven meditation techniques.

Whirled Peas in Love

A word about world peace - some very caring, good people, promote it. But world peace can be attained without citizens or rulers who are Unselfishly Loving, kind, caring, harmless, or even just basically good - in fact, you can have world peace under a horrible dictatorship. But if you have "world Unselfish Love", you have a wonderful world, AND world peace. Thus, rather than *focusing* on peace, we promote the Golden Rule, knowing world peace would be a natural outcome - along with many other wonderful things for the people of the world. GRO is here to remind everyone of the GR's true importance, meaning & practicality, and facilitate ways to awaken it within, and manifest it in the world. It's all about how you can change your life, and the world, one-by-one, starting with yourself.

Projects, Planned Projects & "Wishlist"

1) Continued production of books, GRO workbooks, CD's and cassettes.

2) A place for visitors, seminars, temporary studies, or trying a monastic lifestyle.

3) A referral service to help people find GR "pen-pals", a GR oriented church, GR club, or GR study group near them.

4) Maintaining a website, updates, and publishing the free on-line newsletter.

5) Back to the Basics Classes and Communities. Spiritually/philosophically based on Unselfish Love and Oneness with God, the focus will be on living with kindness, caring, giving, sharing, and harmlessness. Those committed to living by the Golden Rule can live, learn, and practice things like organic gardening, hydroponics, "putting up" food, herbology, alternative medicine/healing, woodworking, and other sustainable self-sufficiency skills. Of course, your spirit/soul is the only thing that really "survives" forever, and thus should be everyone's first priority. But if your goal is to be Unselfishly Loving and help others, learning old fashioned living skills and how to live in harmony with nature, can also be helpful.

6) Creating a spiritual resort.

7) Organizing and facilitating the Golden Rule Fellowship or Church project, including training.

8) A new monastery!

9) A food growing project that would use new energy and vibrational technology, coupled with the latest greenhouse technology, to create a new agricultural model for poor farmers world-wide. It will also demonstrate methods of growing that work regardless of environment or electricity availability. We already have a plan for this, and it is well underway. The success of this would make farming profitable again for small families, and hopefully also help feed the world.

In the next section we will discuss our projects involving seminars, programs, and what you can do for spiritual growth at home, with like-minded friends or family, or local churches.

A Golden Rule Fellowship, Church or Club

One goal we have is for everyone to be able to have places of spiritual practice and fellowship for those of like mind. Again, because this is based on the simple, yet profound premise of the Golden Rule, its precepts and teachings don't conflict with most any other religion's beliefs. We believe in actively supporting the Universal Spirit/God/"The forces of Light" with "good" thoughts, words, and deeds, in order to *displace* the dark forces of the world. We teach those principles, and ways to achieve enlightenment & returning to Oneness with God/Spirit, via developing unselfish love. Contact us if you'd like to become a member, network, or find a fellowship near you (or start one). But there are also other alternatives that may even be better at this point.

We aren't suggesting anyone leave their present religion. In fact, if you already have a house of worship, you may be able to get permission from them to start a "Golden Rule Club" or study group. But many people have contacted us hoping that we have a monastery, study group, meeting place or "church" near them, so they can work with, or meet with others of like-mind and share experiences and inspiration. We are working on building and maintaining a database of houses of worship that support the non-dogmatic fellowship of members who just want to simply focus on living by the Golden Rule, and a database of independent non-denominational GR study groups and clubs. Check our website or contact us if you would like a referral. Our new *Golden Rule Workbook* is a step-by-step guide for applying the Golden Rule in your life for spiritual development. It includes methods for applying it alone, with strangers, family, friends, or starting local GR workgroups. It even has guidelines for creating "mini-monastery" situations with roommates.

Our Seminars, Monk Retreats, &
"𝕸onk for a 𝕸onth" Programs

As mentioned in the book, we are also working on alternatives to traditional monasticism. One idea, is a "growth intensive" concept, where people can experience being a "monk for a month". Other ideas are also being considered, and will change with the times. Write to us, or check our website for updates.

We Could Use Your Help

How You Can Help

We have never charged for spiritual counselling (which we donate much time to). Yet if we are to be here for others, we need the financial means to survive. We also need to earn our own money to support our own projects. We gratefully accept gifts, but we also work for what we earn and totally support ourselves. But earning money must allow us time for both helping others, and doing our own spiritual work on ourselves. A mail order business of products that aid the body/mind/spirit, is perfect for us (if it does well). It at least allows some of us to still remain isolated & cloistered while working, and meditate, teach, and learn, throughout the workday/night.

If people buy products and gifts from us that they would normally buy anyway, they get the goods they want, and we earn our own support at the same time! If there are any products you would like to see us carry, that we don't already have, please let us know.

There are also other ways you can help us grow, and help yourself and others - like doing GR clubs, study groups, book promotion, etc.. If you're interested, please read the section about it later in the book.

Other ways to help GRO grow
Book distribution problems

Our book is supposedly carried by major chains & distributors, but there are strange problems. People often tell us they have tried hard to find the book, but are told by stores that they're backordered, out of stock, or don't carry it. Yet distributors insist the stores have them and there's no problem, no backorders. We are told that it would be a best seller if this "availability issue" didn't exist.

We now carry the book ourselves. This not only insures availability, but we also get more $ that way.

How you can help promote the book:

1) If a major book chain store told you they are out of stock or backordered, ask for the manager. Write down the specific store, location, **manager and employee name**, and send it on to us. Also let them know you were told their stores stock this book, which you and friends want, and they're losing sales.

2) If you want to do even more, sit down with the phonebook, and call all the bookstores in your area that aren't a long distance call. Ask them if they carry it, and if they have it in stock, and if they don't, ask them if they would start carrying it. Then if you want to do even more to help, call the *headquarters* of the chains and ask *them* to carry it in all their stores.

3) It would be a big help to contact as much media as you can to help get the word out. - radio shows, newspapers and newsletters, magazines - anyone you think might be interested in this type of book, the vibrational sounds, or interviewing the author. Just contact whomever you think appropriate, and request it! Contact us for a list of some magazines and radio shows if you like.

4.) You can let independent bookstores know that they can buy direct from us.

We recently received a bad book review from *Venture Inward,* the magazine of the A.R.E. (the organization started by Edgar Cayce). It was clear to us that the "review" had a deliberate agenda of sabotaging the book, and was not in the least a "legitimate" review. If you like, you can read a copy and make up your own mind, then send your comments to the ARE if you feel like it. We think they should print a retraction, and a real and honest review. While you're at it, put in a good word with the A.R.E. bookstore, and their on-line bookstore. You can call the A.R.E. toll free, or at (1-757-428-3588).

Tools For
Spiritual Development

We carry all kinds of interesting, spiritual, and practical things, including: energy wheels, great music CD's (including the music of Jon Peniel), alarm clocks that lull you to sleep and wake you up using affirmations in your own voice, hi-tech hormones that scientific studies have shown to restore aspects of youth and vitality, our own special "Chateau Maya" coffee, our own Shargung-la herbal tea blends mixed by our monks, the purest incense, lapis pendants and more. Please let us know if there is something you think we should be carrying or offering. You can find the products listed on our website, or contact us for a catalog.

VIBRATIONAL
SOUNDS
WITH SPECIAL
AFFIRMATIONS

Atlantean Vibrational Sounds
Recording CD's or tapes:

Vol. 1- Spiritual Development/Growth
Vol. 2 - Healing affirmations/visualization
Vol. 3 -Habit Changing/Developing Healthy Habits

Vol. 4 -Male Virility
Vol. 5 -Stress Management
Vol. 6 -Sounds Only (no affirmations)
Vol. 7 -Ancient Chinese Healing Visualization (given to us by a Dr. of Psychology who trained with Dr. Carl Simonton MD, the famous cancer therapist who uses psychology and visualization techniques for therapy).

All versions are $17.95 each. Please specify volume number, and if you want it on CD or tape when you order. Recordings are not to be used when operating motor vehicles, or equipment.

NEW BOOKS FROM US
The Golden Rule Workbook

By Jon Peniel. Not everyone can or wants to drop everything and join a monastery or community, so we have created a guide for those of you who want to work on spiritual growth at your own speed, wherever you are in the world, with or without a teacher. While this is "new ground", it is our hope that *The Golden Rule Workbook* can help you grow spiritually, wherever you are, and in whatever circumstances you find yourself in. The idea is to help you apply the principle of the Golden Rule in your daily life, and with like-minded friends, family, or even strangers who are also trying to spiritually grow (and are willing to work with you). It covers various possible living scenarios, including just living at home with family, doing a "study group" or church associated club, roommate situations, and actually creating an intentional roommate situation as a "semi-mini-monastery". $17.95 + s&h.

Announcing our new "Little Book":
Little Messages of Guidance
from Angels & Saints

*This is a handy pocketbook of excerpts from the translated ancient teachings (that look like this,) which are at the beginnings of each chapter of **this** book ("The Children of the Law of One and the Lost Teachings of Atlantis"). It's great for quick inspiration. Keep it on a table, desk, or in your pocket or purse, and whenever you have a question, or want a little guidance, just open it randomly to any page and see if God has a "little message" for you.*

MORE HI-TECH TOOLS

The Nova Dreamer- If you need help with "conscious dreaming" (also called "lucid dreaming") this hi-tech tool can help. It is a sleep mask blindfold that actually "senses" when you start dreaming, and then briefly flashes built in lights to gently "signal you" to be aware that you are now dreaming (so you can become "conscious" in your dream). But it's more than just the hi-tech mask. It's a complete kit for getting started with lucid dreaming. Includes Sleep Mask, "A Course in Lucid Dreaming" and Nightlight. $275 + s&h

"DREAM FRIENDLY" ALARM CLOCKS!
Remember your dreams with the Zen Alarm Clock
When the clock's alarm is triggered, the chime bar strikes just once, making a beautiful pleasant tone. 3 1/2 minutes later, it strikes again.   Strikes become more frequent over 10 minutes...eventually striking every 4 seconds until shut off. During this progressive awakening you can work on dreams and affirmations in the alpha -theta state. You can time and guide meditations, and it's also a gentle way to start or end meetings on time. $99 + s&h

THE MOTIVAIDER HELPS YOU TO BE WHO YOU WANT TO BE
This is an invaluable aid to changing yourself through changing thought patterns, doing affirmations throughout the day, and reminding yourself of your goals & ideals.   Caught up in the pressures of the everyday world, it's easy to fall into old habits, and forget about changing or making new habits. The MotivAider is designed to help you remember the things you want to do, at whatever intervals you choose. Set it to remind you as often as every minute, or as seldom as every twenty-four hours. Its silent vibration will remind you of your intentions - often when you need it most. Remember to breathe deeply, adjust your posture, smile, show appreciation, or open your heart! Developed by a clinical psychologist, it helps you change your thought patterns to let go of destructive habits, learn positive new habits, attain goals, reinforce intentions and promote well-being. Strongly and highly recommended by Jon Peniel. $69.95 + s&h

ENERGY SPINNERS: Now you really CAN move things with your mind. Here's an amazing little device that's sensitive to life

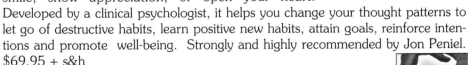

energy. Just put your hands near it, and THINK about the energy from your hands spinning it's aluminum propeller! Prove to yourself, or others, that unseen energies exist. Develop healing, concentration, and visualization skills. Only $19.95 with special experiments from Jon Peniel. Great gift too. Really Works! We promise! Item #0022 $19.95 + s&h

Try a Shargung-la Tea!

Himalayan Meditation Blend Tea

This isn't a dessert tea, it's a serious herbal mixture blended by us. A special mix of Gotu Kola and Kava Kava, we use this tea prior to meditation, to help with opening spiritual centers, enhancing psychic awareness, and deep relaxation. Item #2004 $5.99 + s&h

"Music that Feels Good"

From the late '60's to the mid '70's, part of Jon's work was accomplished through the music business. He worked behind the scenes playing on, arranging, and helping create and inspire much of the "positive" popular hits of that era. Jon always gave what he worked on a beautiful and spiritual touch to inspire the public through sound, melody and spiritually oriented/positive lyrics. When the mainstream music industry and radio started getting "darker" in the mid 70's, he abandoned it, and we started our own small independent small record label of positive, uplifting music. Most of our albums are Jon's compositions and performances, and other albums he either produced, composed, arranged, performed on, or all the above. All albums are available on CD or tape. Described below are just 3 titles, but our full line contains over 20 titles of "Music that *Feels* Good".

GRO Music Sampler - this is a full length CD with single song selections from most of our albums. It gives the listener a chance to get the feel of each individual CD, while enjoying a diverse album that stands on its own. It's kind of like having a radio station of exclusively GRO music. Songs are announced so you can write down your favorites. Special discount offer for the sampler CD only - $9.95 + s&h

Dreamweavers - Created by Jon for children, this album has 2 beautifully soundtracked children's stories read by "Starry Eyes, the Fairy Godmother". Each story is a half-hour long, and has special sounds that calm, relax, and help children drift off to dreamland. The subtle heartbeat sound in the background mimics a mother's heart, and works on newborns and children of all ages (adults love it too). The stories teach positive lessons in a fun format. We've also had positive feedback from those who are homebound, hospitalized, institutionalized, imprisoned, and for those dealing with childhood abuse syndrome. But first and foremost, children love these, and you'll never have to fight to get them to bed/nap again! $17.95 + s&h

"**Transformation**" by J. Peniel, is an album of original "new age" style compositions. Songs like "Deep Space", and "Whale Love" will move you emotionally and "take you away from it all". Great for meditation, massage, creating a soothing spiritual atmosphere, etc.. $17.95 + s&h

The Yoga of the Children of the Law of One

Vol. 1 - Tibetan Yoga Instructional Video. Feel great everyday with these uplifting, revitalizing, energizing techniques. Easy to learn, step-by-step instruction for doing the yoga flow we have done for thousands of years. Includes our ancient acupuncture meridian balancing techniques that get your body's energy systems flowing and in balance in just minutes - with only a few waves of your hands. Filmed on the beaches of Maui. $19.95 + s&h

Vol. 2 - Tibetan Yoga Flow 20 Minute Workout Video. Once you have learned the techniques, you can do the 20 minute yoga workout along with your "video partner", while simultaneously enjoying some of our beautiful music. Filmed at the hauntingly beautiful "Garden of the Gods" in Colorado. $19.95 + s&h

ORDERING INFORMATION:

Our website is www.atlantis.to (note: that's ".to", not ".com")
email: kind@atlantis.to

Mailing Address: Windsor-Hill, 2431 Main St, #C-410, Alamosa, CO 81101

See all our products on the web, or call for a free catalog.
We now have secure on-line ordering available too.

Order line: 1-800-845-7991. Outside the US, call 954-563-1987
When the order line is busy, you will get a voice mail recording, so please leave your name, number and the best time to reach you since they will gladly return your call.

Contacting Us

You are also welcome to request more info or contact us for:

Becoming involved with any of the projects of the Golden Rule Organization (people who want to be kind, harmless, help each other, including networking, joining or creating a Golden Rule study group or fellowship, the "Back to the Basics" project, seminars, "Monk for a Month" programs, etc.);

Potential "householder" or community projects;

Helping out in some way;

Getting on our mailing list for energy products, upcoming books, tapes, music, training seminars, visits, etc.

Email

The quickest way to contact us is via email and you can do this even if you don't have a computer: Contacting us is easiest via email. If you have a desire to write and don't have a computer, there are internet services available in most areas of the country. They are sometimes referred to as an 'internet cafe', but are found in the yellow page listings of the phone book under internet services. You can also use computers and email in most public libraries. Free email service that you can use from anywhere (such as a library), is available from www.hotmail.com, and many others. You may Email us at: kind@atlantis.to (please note: that's ".to", not ".com") Don't forget to include a return email address, and perhaps also a regular mail address. Please keep in mind we are very backed up on our correspondence, including emails, mail, and phone.

Mail

Mailing Address: GRO c/o Windsor Hill, 2431 Main St, #C-410, Alamosa, CO 81101
(Note: Mail is forwarded to us and may take a week or two extra *after* reaching the above mailing address, and then who knows how long to get to and read.)

(When you write or email, please specify exactly what you are writing for - it saves us time - thanks. Also, if you are sending regular old mail, please allow a good amount of time for a response, because it often takes quite awhile to get the mail, and respond to it. If you feel like telling us about yourself, please do!)

Donations or Gifts

We do not have non-profit status, so donations or gifts are not tax deductable. If you wish to make us a gift of money or whatever, please include a note letting us know if you intend us to use it for anything we wish or a specific purpose (like The Farm Project, Book printing or promotion, etc.). Certain things, like the farm project, need checks made out specifically to it. Such things can be arranged by phone.

Phone

You can call the order line and ask them to give us a message, but because of our meditations and monastic lifestyle, we don't take calls. But if you need to speak with a monk via phone, just buy a pre-paid calling card (either from our mail-order biz, or elsewhere), then email or call the order line to set an appointment. Give your pre-paid calling card info, your phone number, and various dates/times that would work for you. We'll set an appointment, and call you back.